Comparative Stylistics of **Welsh** and **English**

Arddulleg y Gymraeg

KEVIN J. ROTTET AND **STEVE MORRIS**

UNIVERSITY OF WALES PRESS
CARDIFF

www.uwp.co.uk

British Library Cataloguing-in-Publication Data
A catalogue record for this book is available from the British Library.

ISBN: 978-1-78683-254-2 (hardback)
            978-1-78683-255-9 (paperback)
e-ISBN: 978-1-78683-256-6

The University of Wales Press acknowledges the financial support of Swansea University and Indiana University.

Typeset by Marie Doherty
Printed by CPI Antony Rowe, Melksham

Contents

Rhagair / Preface v

Acknowledgements xiii

1 Comparative Stylistics and Translation Techniques 1

2 Nouns and Pronouns 29

3 Prepositions 65

4 Welsh possessive constructions 121

5 Issues in the Verb Phrase: Tense/Mood/Aspect and Modality 157

6 Phrasal Verbs 219

7 *Cael* and *Get* 273

8 Adjectives and Adverbs 297

9 Lexical Issues: Word formation and collocations 337

10 Welsh Verbless Clauses and Verb-noun Clauses 437

11 Information structure: Topic and focus 473

Bibliography 501

Index of Terms 509

Index of Words and Expressions
Welsh 517
English 523

Daeth y syniad ar gyfer y llyfr hwn yn wreiddiol mewn cwrs a ddysgwyd gan Kevin Rottet ym Mhrifysgol Indiana ar arddulleg gymharol y Ffrangeg a'r Saesneg. Ysbrydolwyd cynnwys y cwrs gan lyfr arloesol Vinay a Darbelnet, *Comparative Stylistics of French and English*. Techneg y cwrs oedd cymharu strwythur y ddwy iaith trwy gorpws o gyfieithiadau a fedrai ddatgelu nodweddion sy'n debyg neu'n wahanol – nodweddion y byddai dosbarthiadau iaith traddodiadol yn eu crybwyll yn unig neu yn eu hanwybyddu'n gyfan gwbl. Gwnaeth y dechneg hon gryn argraff, ac yr oedd y syniad o ymestyn y math yma o gymharu i'r Gymraeg a'r Saesneg yn eithaf naturiol. Roedd Kevin Rottet a Steve Morris wedi cyfarfod flynyddoedd ynghynt mewn cwrs Cymraeg dwys yng Ngogledd America dan nawdd *Cymdeithas Madog* (y Sefydliad Astudiaethau Cymreig yng Ngogledd America), a pheth digon naturiol oedd i'r bartneriaeth gydweithredol bresennol ddilyn yn sgil hynny.

Beth yw ystyr *arddulleg* i ni yma? Fel yng ngwaith clasurol Vinay a Darbelnet, cyfeiria'r term at nodweddion ieithyddol sydd ar gael fel opsiynau, nodweddion y gall yr ysgrifennwr neu'r cyfieithydd ddewis o'u plith â rhyddid. Gwahaniaethir rhwng *cyfyngiadau* neu *ataliadau*, y nodweddion hynny mewn iaith nad oes dewis yn perthyn iddynt, ac *opsiynau*, y nodweddion hynny y mae modd eu dethol (neu beidio) gan ddibynnu ar yr hyn sydd orau gan yr ysgrifennwr, cywair y testun ac ati. Fel unrhyw iaith fyw, yn ddigon amlwg, mae'r Gymraeg wedi wynebu cryn newid yn ystod y canrifoedd diwethaf; ond yn achos y Gymraeg, yn sicr, mae cyflymdra'r newidiadau hyn wedi cynyddu yn ystod yr ugeinfed a'r unfed ganrif ar hugain wrth i niferoedd cynyddol o siaradwyr Cymraeg ddatblygu eu meistrolaeth o'r Saesneg a byw mwy o'u bywydau trwy gyfrwng y ddwy iaith. Nid yw'n syndod darganfod mewn sefyllfa o'r fath, felly, fod adnoddau arddulliadol yr iaith leiafrifol yn wynebu llawer o heriau dros amser. Un o amcanion y llyfr hwn yw 'dal' llawer o'r amrywiaeth arddulliadol yma tra bo'r iaith yn parhau'n gynhyrchiol ac yn egnïol. Mae'r llyfr yma'n ddisgrifiadol o fwriad, yn hytrach na bod yn argymhellol; hynny yw, ceisiwn osod patrymau a welir yng nghorpws y testunau, a threfnu eu bod ar gael i ysgrifenwyr a chyfieithwyr Cymraeg a all eu haddasu neu beidio fel y gwelant yn dda a chan ddibynnu ar anghenion eu testunau.

Seilir y dadansoddi cymharol o'r Gymraeg a'r Saesneg a geir yn y llyfr hwn ar gorpws o gyfieithiadau sy'n cynnwys ychydig dros ddeg ar hugain o nofelau a hunangofiannau. Cyhoeddwyd tri ar ddeg o'r gweithiau yn Saesneg, gyda'r cyfieithiadau Cymraeg yn eu dilyn.[1] O fynd i'r cyfeiriad arall, mae'r corpws yn cynnwys pedwar gwaith ar bymtheg yn y Gymraeg sydd â chyfieithiadau Saesneg wedi'u cyhoeddi. Yn ogystal â'r gweithiau hyn, defnyddiwyd dau waith ar hugain yn y Gymraeg heb gyfieithiadau, er mwyn rhoi enghreifftiau ychwanegol o strwythurau. Cynhyrchwyd yr holl gyfieithiadau yn yr ugeinfed neu'r unfed ganrif ar hugain – mae hynny'n wir am y rhan fwyaf o'r fersiynau gwreiddiol, gyda rhai eithriadau, fel gwaith Lewis Carroll o'r 1860au, Daniel Owen o'r bedwaredd ganrif ar bymtheg, ac un stori fer gan Syr Arthur Conan Doyle. Yr ydym wedi dewis cyfieithiadau sy'n cynnwys testunau o arddulliau eithaf llenyddol (fel *Monica* gan Saunders Lewis) i arddull lawer mwy sgyrsiol a chyfoes (fel *Caersaint* gan Angharad Price, neu nofelau *Lladd Duw* a *Crawia* Dewi Prysor). Mae'r nofelau yn cynnwys rhai storïau i blant, fel gwaith Roald Dahl neu lyfr cyntaf cyfres Harri Potter, nofelau ditectif (gan gynnwys gwaith gan P. D. James ac Ian Rankin), a ffuglen glasurol Gymraeg gan Islwyn Ffowc Elis, T. Rowland Hughes a Kate Roberts. Mae'r hunangofiannau'n cynnwys rhai Hugh Evans, W. J. Gruffydd, Meic Stevens, D. J. Williams, Iorwerth Peate a Dr J. Lloyd Williams. Mae rhai o'r testunau'n cynnwys naws ranbarthol yn fwriadol, fel hunangofiant dwy-ran Meic Stevens yn iaith y de, neu nofel glasurol Caradog Pritchard *Un Nos Ola Leuad* gyda'i thafodiaith ogleddol gref. Pan fo modd, rhoddir enghreifftiau o'r strwythurau a drafodir o fwy nag un testun, gan mai'r hyn sydd o ddiddordeb yw cyfoeth yr opsiynau arddulliadol sydd ar gael i ysgrifenwyr a chyfieithwyr Cymraeg yn hytrach na hynodweddau arddulliadol yr ysgrifennwr unigol.

Bwriedir y llyfr hwn ar gyfer tri math o ddarllenydd:

1. myfyrwyr ar fodiwlau cyfieithu, neu ysgolheigion annibynnol sy'n gweithio ar gyfieithu, rhwng y Saesneg a'r Gymraeg;
2. myfyrwyr sy'n astudio'r Gymraeg ar lefelau uwch;
3. ieithyddion neu fyfyrwyr ieithyddiaeth sydd â diddordeb yn strwythur yr iaith Gymraeg.

Er bod eraill wedi ysgrifennu am gyfieithu rhwng y Gymraeg a'r Saesneg, mae'r dull a ddefnyddir yn y llyfr hwn – sef astudio patrymau sy'n codi o gorpws o gyfieithiadau fel dull o daflu goleuni ar strwythur y ddwy iaith ac ar fethodoleg cyfieithu – yn newydd yng nghyd-destun y Gymraeg.

Mae'r ddau awdur yn dod â'u harbenigeddau penodol i'r dasg. Un o brif feysydd arbenigedd Kevin J. Rottet yw cyswllt ieithoedd gyda diddordeb

---

[1] Mewn un achos, sef *Alice's Adventures in Wonderland*, ceir dau gyfieithiad gwahanol o'r un gwaith, a gyhoeddwyd nifer o flynyddoedd ar wahân.

penodol yn effeithiau strwythurol ieithoedd mewn cysylltiad â'i gilydd. O ganlyniad, ef yw prif awdur penodau 1, 4–7 a 10–11, sy'n ymdrin yn bennaf â materion strwythurol ar lefel yr ymadrodd (y bennod ar Gystrawennau Meddiannol y Gymraeg) neu'r frawddeg neu ddisgwrs (y bennod ar Adeiledd Gwybodaeth). Mae gan Steve Morris yrfa hir mewn addysgu'r Gymraeg fel ail iaith i oedolion, ac mae wedi gweithio'n helaeth ar eirfa'r Gymraeg. Mae'n gyd-ymchwilydd ar brosiect *CorCenCC – Corpws Cenedlaethol Cymraeg Cyfoes*, ac ef yw prif awdur penodau 2, 3, 8 a 9 (gan gynnwys y penodau ar Enwau a Rhagenwau, ac Ansoddeiriau ac Adferfau).

Hoffem ddiolch i Sefydliad Astudiaethau Uwch (IAS) Prifysgol Indiana a Phrifysgol Abertawe am eu cefnogaeth ariannol i'r prosiect hwn – heb hynny, ni fyddai wedi ei wireddu. Hefyd, hoffem ddiolch i Christopher Robbins, yr oedd ei bedair semestr yn astudio'r Gymraeg ym Mhrifysgol Indiana wedi ei wneud yn arbennig o gymwys i fwrw golwg myfyriwr sy'n astudio'r Gymraeg dros ddrafftiau rhai o'r penodau a chynnig adborth, ynghyd â'r grwpiau gwahanol o fyfyrwyr a ymrestrodd ar gwrs Kevin ar arddulleg gymharol y Ffrangeg a'r Saesneg ym Mhrifysgol Indiana. Yr oedd eu diddordeb byw wedi sicrhau bod perthnasedd y pwnc i ieithoedd eraill fel y Gymraeg yn fwy amlwg byth. Ar ben hynny, yr ydym yn ddiolchgar dros ben i Llion Wigley a holl staff Gwasg Prifysgol Cymru am eu harweiniad, eu cyngor a'u cefnogaeth.

Kevin J. Rottet, Prifysgol Indiana
Steve Morris, Prifysgol Abertawe

The idea for this book was born in a course taught by Kevin Rottet at Indiana University on the comparative stylistics of French and English. The content of the course was inspired by Vinay and Darbelnet's classic text of the same name. Impressed at how the technique of comparing the structure of two languages via a translation corpus was able to reveal similarities and differences that were only hinted at or were even entirely absent in traditional language classes, the idea of extending this sort of comparison to Welsh and English was quite natural. Kevin Rottet and Steve Morris had met many years earlier during an intensive Welsh course in North America sponsored by the organisation *Cymdeithas Madog* (The Welsh Studies Institute in North America), and so the collaborative partnership followed naturally.

What do we mean here by *stylistics*? As in Vinay and Darbelnet's classic work, the term refers to linguistic features of a language that are available as options, features among which the writer or translator can freely choose. A distinction is made between *constraints* or *servitudes*, those features of a language which involve no choice, and *options*, those features which one can select, or not, depending on the preferences of the writer, the register of the text, etc. Manifestly, the Welsh language has been undergoing considerable changes in recent centuries, as do all living languages, but in the case of Welsh the rate of these changes has almost certainly increased in the twentieth and twenty-first centuries as increasing numbers of Welsh speakers have ever higher competence in English and live more of their lives through the medium of both languages. It is hardly surprising to discover than in such a setting, the stylistic resources of the minoritised language face many challenges over time. One of the purposes of this book is, then, to capture much of this stylistic variety while it is still productive and vibrant. The book is intentionally descriptive rather than prescriptive. That is, we seek to lay out patterns that are observed in the corpus of texts and make them available to Welsh writers and translators, who can then adopt them or not, as they see fit and depending on the needs of their texts.

The comparative analysis of Welsh and English found in this book is based on a translation corpus consisting of just over thirty novels and auto-biographies. Thirteen of the works were first published in English with later Welsh translations.[2] Going in the other direction, the corpus includes nineteen Welsh works with published English translations. In addition to these works, another twenty-two works in Welsh with no published translation were drawn on to provide additional examples of structures. All of the translations were made in the twentieth or twenty-first century, which is also true of most of

---

[2] In one case, that of *Alice's Adventures in Wonderland*, there are two different translations of the same work published many years apart.

the originals with a few exceptions such as Lewis Carroll's works from the 1860s, Daniel Owen's from the late nineteenth century, and one short story by Sir Arthur Conan Doyle. We have selected the translations to include texts ranging from a fairly literary style (such as found in Saunders Lewis's *Monica*) to a much more colloquial and modern style (such as that of Angharad Price's *Caersaint* or the novels of Dewi Prysor such as *Lladd Duw* and *Crawia*). The novels include some children's stories such as the works of Roald Dahl or the first book in the Harry Potter series, detective novels including works by P. D. James and Ian Rankin, and classic works of Welsh fiction by Islwyn Ffowc Elis, T. Rowland Hughes and Kate Roberts. The autobiographies include those of Hugh Evans, W. J. Gruffydd, Meic Stevens, D. J. Williams, Iorwerth Peate, and Dr J. Lloyd Williams. A few of the texts are deliberately regional in character, such as Meic Stevens's two-part autobiography written in south Walian, or Caradog Prichard's classic novel *Un Nos Ola Leuad*, penned in a very strong north Walian dialect. When possible, the structures discussed in the book are exemplified from more than one text, since the interest here is not so much in the stylistic idiosyncrasies of the individual writer as in the wealth of stylistic options that multiple Welsh writers and translators have at their disposal.

This book is intended for three types of reader:

1. students in translation modules or independent scholars working on translating between English and Welsh;
2. students studying Welsh at higher levels;
3. linguists or students of linguistics who are interested in the structure of the Welsh language.

While others have written about translation between Welsh and English, the approach adopted in this book, that of studying patterns that emerge from a translation corpus as a way to shed light both on the structure of the two languages and on the methodology of translation, is new in the context of Welsh.

The two collaborators each bring their particular specialties to the task. One of Kevin Rottet's main areas of expertise is language contact, with a particular interest in the structural effects of languages in contact. Consequently, he is the primary author of Chapters 1, 4–7, and 10–11 dealing largely with structural issues at the level of the phrase (such as Chapter 4 on Welsh Possessive Constructions) or of the sentence or discourse (such as Chapter 11 on Information Structure). Steve Morris has made a long career in teaching Welsh as a second language to adults and has worked extensively on the vocabulary of Welsh. He is a co-investigator on the *Corpws Cenedlaethol Cymraeg Cyfoes (CorCenCC)* project. As such, he is the primary author of

Chapters 2, 3 and 8, 9 including the chapters on Nouns and Pronouns, and Adjectives and Adverbs.

We would like to thank both the Institute for Advanced Studies (IAS) at Indiana University and Swansea University for their financial support of this project, without which it would not have been possible. We also thank Christopher Robbins, whose four semesters studying Welsh at Indiana University uniquely qualified him to bring the eye of a student of Welsh to the drafts of some of the chapters to offer feedback, and the various cohorts of students enrolled in Kevin's course on the comparative stylistics of French and English at Indiana University whose keen interest in the topic made its relevance for other languages such as Welsh all the more apparent. In addition, we are very grateful to Llion Wigley and all the staff at the University of Wales Press for their guidance, advice and support.

Kevin J. Rottet, Indiana University
Steve Morris, Swansea University / Prifysgol Abertawe

Acknowledgements

The University of Wales Press gratefully acknowledges permissions granted for material from the following works:

Gwasg Gomer
Roberts, Selyf. 1984. *Trwy'r drych a'r hyn a welodd Alys yno.*
Jones, Meinir Pierce. 1981. *Llinyn Rhy Dynn.*
Rowlands, John. 1980. *Chwerw'n troi'n chwarae.*
Elis, Islwyn Ffowc. 1990 [1953]. *Cysgod y Cryman.*
    English translation
    Stephens, Meic. 1998. *Shadow of the Sickle.*
Elis, Islwyn Ffowc. 1956. *Yn ôl i Leifior.*
    English translation
    Stephens, Meic. 1999. *Return to Lleifior.*
Elis, Islwyn Ffowc. 1955. *Ffenestri tua'r Gwyll.*
Griffith, W. J. 1958. *Storïau'r Henllys Fawr.*
Gruffydd, W. J. 1942. *Hen Atgofion.*
    English translation
    Lloyd, D. Myrddin. 1976. *The Years of the Locust.*
Gwanas, Bethan. 2003. *Gwrach y Gwyllt.*
Hughes, T. Rowland. 1979 [1946]. *Chwalfa.*
    English translation
    Ruck, Richard. 1954. *Out of their Night.*
Hughes, T. Rowland. 1947. *Y Cychwyn.*
    English translation
    Ruck, Richard. 1969. *The Beginning.*
Hughes, T. Rowland. 1943. *O law i law.*
Lewis, Saunders. 1930. *Monica.*
Lisa, Mari. 1990. *Ar Gortyn Brau.*
Martell, Owen. 2000. *Cadw dy ffydd, brawd.*
Rees, Edward. 1968. *T. Rowland Hughes.*
Roberts, Eigra Lewis. 2003. *Rhannu'r tŷ.*
Roberts, Eigra Lewis. 1980. *Mis o Fehefin.*
Roberts, Kate. 2001 [1936]. *Traed mewn Cyffion.*
Williams, D. J. 1959. *Yn chwech ar hugain oed.*
Williams, D. J. 1953. *Hen Dŷ Ffarm.*

Y Lolfa
Jones, Eurwyn Pierce. 2014. *Y Cylch Brith*.
Lewis, Caryl. 2003. *Dal hi!*
Owen, Llwyd. 2006. *Ffydd Gobatih Cariad*.
Owen, Llwyd. 2010. *Faith, Hope, Charity*.
Prichard, Caradog. 2012 [1961]. *Un Nos Ola Leuad*.
Price, Angharad. 2010. *Caersaint*.
Prysor, Dewi. 2012. *Lladd Duw*.
Prysor, Dewi. 2008. *Crawia*.
Stevens, Meic. 2009. *Y Crwydryn a mi*.
Stevens, Meic. 2004. *Solva Blues*.
Stevens, Meic. 2003. *Hunangofiant y Brawd Houdini*.

Gwasg Gee
Peate, Iorwerth. 1976. *Rhwng Dau Fyd: Darn o Hunangofiant*.
Roberts, Kate. 1959. *Te yn y Grug*.
Roberts, Kate. 1956. *Y Byw sy'n cysgu*.
Roberts, Selyf. 1965. *Wythnos o Hydref*.

Seren Books
James, Siân. 2006. *The Awakening*.
Jones, John Idris. 2002. *Feet in Chains*.
Roberts, Elisabeth. 1991. *Pestilence*.
Stephens, Meic. 1997. *Monica*.

Gwasg Carreg Gwalch
Griffith, Ieuan. 1991. *Seidr chwerw*.
Roberts, Wiliam Owen. 1987. *Y Pla*.
Roberts, Wyn G. 1989. *Bai ar Gam*.

David Higham Associates
Dahl, Roald. 1988. *Matilda*.
Dahl, Roald. 1964. *Charlie and the Chocolate Factory*.

Soho Press and Vanessa Holt Ltd.
Lovesey, Peter. 2003. *Rough Cider*.

Rily Publications
Meek, Elin. 2008. *Matilda*.
Meek, Elin. 2002. *Charlie a'r Ffatri Siocled*.

The Blair Partnership
Rowling, J. K. 1997. *Harry Potter and the Philosopher's Stone* © J. K. Rowling 1997.

Green Heaton Agency and Scribner
James, P. D. 1972. *An Unsuitable Job for a Woman* © The Copyright Estate of the Late P. D. James; reproduced by permission of Green and Heaton Ltd and Scribner, a division of Simon & Schuster Ltd; all rights reserved.

Hodder and Stoughton
Gill, B. M. 1981. *Victims* © 1981 B. M. Gill; reproduced by permission of Hodder and Stoughton Ltd.

St Martin's Press & Macmillan
Ross, Jonathan. 1989. *A Time for Dying* © 1998 Jonathan Ross; reprinted by permission of Tor/Forge Books; all rights reserved.

Canongate Books Ltd
Mitchell, Philip. 1995. *One Moonlit Night* © 1961 Mari Prichard; English translation © 1995 Philip Mitchell.

1

Comparative Stylistics and Translation Techniques

Comparative stylistics is a technique for closely comparing the stylistic resources of two languages to observe how each deploys its linguistic devices in ways that reflect its own characteristic idiom and expressive spirit.

The primary methodology involved in comparative stylistics is the study of texts and their translations. Two French academics, Jean-Paul Vinay and Jean Darbelnet, pioneered this methodology in their classic work entitled *Stylistique comparée du français et de l'anglais: Méthode de traduction* (first edition 1958, publ. by Marcel Didier, Paris), a foundational text in translation studies. The technique of juxtaposing examples of linguistic patterns in one language with phrasings considered equivalent in the other has been shown to reveal facts about the basic structure and subtler stylistic preferences of the languages which are not otherwise apparent even to fluent speakers. This technique, working from the top down (the 'top' being the finished text), is completely different from the approach of traditional language classes which start from the bottom up (beginning with how the most basic ideas are conveyed in the foreign language).

Vinay and Darbelnet's study was based on French and English, which were (and of course still are) spoken by millions of people, many of whom are monolingual in their respective languages. Thus, these languages serve for many as the sole vehicle of long and complex cultural traditions. Interestingly, Vinay and Darbelnet expressed doubts (p. 233 fn. 7) about whether the methodology they developed would be fruitful for studying the languages of a bilingual community, noting that prolonged bilingualism leads to a fusion of cultures and, ultimately, of metalanguages (meaning, here, cognitive representations of the world in linguistic terms). Although they undoubtedly did not intend it as a challenge, this claim felt like one, and the case of Wales appeared to be a fertile testing ground for examining it. And while it is doubtless true that Welsh and English 'metalanguages' are not as different today as they once were, we find that there is nonetheless a characteristic stylistic idiom in much contemporary Welsh writing which differs in significant ways from that found in English. Given the increasing importance of translation and translation studies in contemporary Wales, the timing is appropriate for a study that sheds light on some of the ways the structures and stylistic patterns of English and Welsh traditionally differ from each other, in order to make the Welsh patterns available to the student, writer, translator or linguist for whom the English-like patterns may be the ones that come most readily to mind.

Vinay and Darbelnet's classic work was both a comparative stylistics of French and English, and also a more general methodology for translation. Indeed, given that the primary lens through which the language comparisons are observed is that furnished by texts and their translations, the methods in the toolkit of the translator are necessarily of key interest. We turn now to a brief discussion of some of these tools.

1.1 Basic notions of translation

Some of the basic ideas of translation will be discussed under the following five headings: (1) Source Language and Target Language; (2) Constraints versus Options; (3) Translation Units; (4) Overtranslation; (5) Registers and Situational Variation.

1.1.1 Source Language and Target Language
When a text was originally written in Welsh and later translated into English, Welsh is said to be the *source language*, and English the *target language*. This study also draws examples from texts with the opposite arrangement, that is English as source language (SL) and Welsh as target language (TL). Indeed, it is important that works going in both directions be examined since the comparison may reveal differences of technique. One way to verify that a particular linguistic correspondence really holds true of a pair of languages is to verify whether it is found when translating in both directions.

Throughout this work, quoted examples will be given in columns side by side; the source language will systematically be on the left and the target language on the right. In most cases, a word or phrase which is of particular interest to the discussion is in bold print. Other kinds of highlighting, especially any occurrence of italics, were already present in the published texts being quoted unless otherwise noted.

1.1.2 Constraints versus Options
Not all of the differences between two languages are the focus of a study of comparative stylistics. It is important to distinguish between *constraints* and

options. Constraints (or *servitudes*) are places where the language user has no choice but to use a given form. Consider the following example from the novel *Harry Potter and the Philosopher's Stone* and its Welsh translation:

Ron picked up a green bean, looked at it carefully, and bit into a corner. [STONE 129]

Cododd Ron ffeuen werdd, edrych arni'n ofalus ac yna brathu cornel. [MAEN 81]

There are many grammatical differences between English and Welsh that can be seen in this one brief example, but most of them involve matters imposed by the grammars of the two languages. For instance, the Welsh equivalent of *green bean* is *ffeuen werdd*. That *ffeuen* 'bean' is a feminine noun is a constraint, a fact of Welsh grammar that the translator has no control over. Similarly, the form and position of the adjective *werdd* 'green' are not freely chosen: adjectives must come after the noun they modify in Welsh, not before it as in English, and when an adjective modifies a feminine singular noun (like *ffeuen* 'bean') it must undergo soft mutation (thus, *gwyrdd* 'green' appears as *werdd* in this example).[1] These facts about the placement and form of the adjective are constraints imposed by Welsh grammar that the proficient user of Welsh has no choice but to follow. Constraints like these are of key interest in a traditional language class but are not the major focus in a study of comparative stylistics.

Options, on the other hand, are places where a writer (or translator) has more than one possibility from which to choose. Options constitute the primary focus of a study of stylistics. Consider the following example:

Harry sat up and gasped; the glass front of the boa constrictor's tank had vanished. [STONE 35]

Cododd Harri ar ei eistedd. Syrthiodd ei geg ar agor. Roedd y gwydr ar flaen tanc y neidr wasgu wedi diflannu'n llwyr. . . [MAEN 22]

To express 'sat up', the translator could have chosen *eisteddodd i fyny* (literally 'sat up'), a frequent and unsurprising wording in modern Welsh. But in this case the translator opted for a different formulation, *cododd ar ei eistedd* (literally 'rose on his sitting'). While the literal rendering of English phrasal verbs such as *to sit up* in Welsh using VERB + PARTICLE is generally possible in

---

[1] In addition, *gwyrdd* 'green' is one of a fairly small number of high frequency adjectives which have feminine singulars showing an internal vowel change, in this case <y> → <e>.

informal registers,[2] other possibilities exist and are preferred in more formal styles. In addition, in the phrase *cododd ar ei eistedd* we see an example of a much larger phenomenon in Welsh idiom, namely a construction involving a possessive where none occurs in English. In fact, numerous verbs of bodily posture show the same competition between an older, more traditional Welsh formulation using a possessive idiom, and a newer, English-style verb + particle construction; for instance 'to turn around' can be *troi rownd / troi o gwmpas* (lit. 'turn around') or *troi yn ei unfan* (lit. 'to turn in his spot'); 'to stand up' can be *sefyll i fyny* (lit. 'stand up') or *codi ar ei draed* (lit. 'rise on his feet'). It happens that such possessive patterns are found throughout idiomatic Welsh. When seen in this light, the example *codi ar ei eistedd* ceases to be an isolated, one-off lexical example and becomes illustrative of something larger that permeates much Welsh stylistic idiom. Once this fact is recognised, it becomes possible to treat such patterns together as we do in the present volume.[3]

As Vinay and Darbelnet (1995: 16) put it, 'grammar is the domain of servitudes whereas options belong to the domain of stylistics.' Nevertheless, the distinction is sometimes clearer in theory than in practice, and it is not always possible to draw a rigid distinction between them, as we will see in various places in the chapters that follow.

1.1.3.i Translation Units

One of the most basic tools in the translator's toolkit is the proper identification of the *translation unit* (TU). The term TU refers to each of the minimal chunks of an utterance (or of a text) for which a translation can appropriately be sought. A translation unit may be as small as a word, but it may also be a phrase, a collocation, or a group of words that function together and that must be handled together. An equivalent should be sought for the TU rather than for the individual elements that make it up. The main kinds of units are simple units, collocations, and formulae.

1.3.i Simple units

In the most straightforward case, each word in the source language equates to a single word in the target language. In the following example, the Welsh original and the English translation have the same number of words (with the one exception that the particle *i mewn* corresponds to 'in' in English); the Welsh words of the example can easily be matched up with the English words of the translation once basic word order differences are taken into account:

---

[2] The topic of phrasal verbs is explored in depth in Chapter 4.
[3] Possessive idioms in Welsh are discussed in Chapter 4.

Daeth	Mrs Jones	i mewn	i	nôl	rhai	o'r	llestri. [BYW 13]
came	Mrs Jones	in		to fetch	some	of the	dishes

'Mrs Jones came in to fetch some of the dishes.' [AWAKENING 13]

But cases like the above are not particularly common. It is more frequent that the number of words in the source and target language texts is not the same, and so the words do not match up in such a transparent way. Some TUs are simplex lexical items (normally, single words) in one language whose equivalents are two or more words in the other:

Un tro, yn ddiweddarach, ro'n i'n rhoi glo ar y tân a sylwes i ddim bod tair **cath fach** Siamaidd yn cysgu yn y bwced lo. . . [HUNAN 124]

Another time, I was putting coal on the fire and I failed to notice three Siamese **kittens** sleeping in the hod on top of the coal. [SOLVA 124]

Gwnâi hi ei rownd **ar gefn** beic 'da buddeie bach yn hongian o'r cyrn. [HUNAN 75]

She used to do her round **on** a bicycle with small churns hanging from the handlebars. [SOLVA 75]

And do you think your father really meant her to **own** the house forever? [MAT 204]

Ac ydych chi'n meddwl bod eich tad wir yn bwriadu iddi **fod yn berchen** y tŷ am byth? [MAT 198]

Alternatively, the TU may consist of multiple words in both languages, but the words may not mean the same thing individually:

Hen ddyn bach cryno, yn gwisgo ffunen sidan ddu a het *Jim Crow*; yn eistedd yn **y Sêt Fawr** am ei fod yn drwm ei glyw; [HENAT 31]

. . .a small, compact, old man, wearing a black silk cravat and a 'Jim Crow' hat; sitting in the **elders' pew** because he was hard of hearing; [LOCUST 33]

The examples above reveal the following correspondences:

cath fach	('small cat')	::	kitten
ar gefn	('on the back of')	::	on (with certain means of transportation)
bod yn berchen	('be the owner of')	::	to own
y sêt fawr	('the big seat')	::	deacon's bench, elders' pew (in a chapel)

The translator must recognise that these Welsh phrases are each a single translation unit and not the accidental juxtaposition of two different units. For instance, the usual translation of *cath fach*, in most contexts, is 'kitten' and not 'small cat'.

1.1.3.ii Collocations

Collocations are among the most customary phrasings of a language, occupying an intermediate place between word combinations which are completely free (*buy a shirt, eat an apple*), and idioms where none of the lexical items is freely chosen (*kick the bucket* 'to die', *compare apples and oranges* 'to compare unlike things'). Typical examples of collocations are sequences consisting of two lexemes, such as *heavy smoker, badly mistaken*, or *sit an exam*, in which one of the lexemes (called the **base**) is chosen freely by the speaker based on what she wants to talk about, but the other (called the **collocate**) is not. Possible collocates are predetermined by the conventions of the language; they are more or less arbitrary and unpredictable. In the collocation *sit an exam*, for instance, once a speaker has freely selected the term *exam* because she wants to talk about an upcoming test, the choice of verb that goes with it is actually quite limited; *take an exam* or *sit an exam* come to the mind of the (British) English speaker as customary phrasings or as the 'right' way to put it. Foreigners learning English, although they might well understand the collocation *sit an exam* when it is encountered in context, could not predict in advance that *sit* will be used this way in English. For instance, in Welsh the traditional equivalent is *sefyll arholiad* (literally 'stand an exam'), and in French it is *passer un examen* (literally 'pass an exam').

Consider the following examples of collocations from the translation corpus:[4]

'You would be a lot better off, Miss Honey,' she said, "if you gave up your job and **drew unemployment money**." [MAT 204]

'Fe fyddech chi'n llawer gwell eich byd, Miss Honey,' meddai, 'petaech chi'n rhoi'r gorau i'ch swydd ac yn **codi arian diweithdra**.' [MAT 198]

Hen ddyn bach cryno, yn gwisgo ffunen sidan ddu a het *Jim Crow*; yn eistedd yn y Sêt Fawr am ei fod **yn drwm ei glyw**; [HENAT 31]

. . .a small, compact, old man, wearing a black silk cravat and a 'Jim Crow' hat; sitting in the elders' pew because he was **hard of hearing**; [LOCUST 33]

---

[4] In some cases we draw examples from a Welsh text that does not have a published English translation. This is the case, for instance, with *Yn chwech ar hugain oed*, the second volume of D. J. Williams's autobiography. In such cases we provide our own English translation in italics and, of course, no bibliographic code or page number is given.

Daethom ein dau yn **ffrindiau mawr** heb yn wybod i ni, rywsut. [CHWECH 164]

*We two became **good friends** (or **great friends**), somehow without our knowing it.*

In these examples we see several instances of collocations which must be recognised and handled as such, rather than being translated word-for-word. Thus, the usual verb in Welsh to talk about 'collecting' money in various contexts, including receiving a pay cheque or a pension or even taking out a loan, is the verb *codi* (literally 'to raise'); *yn drwm ei glyw* (lit. 'heavy his hearing') is equivalent to the English expression *hard of hearing*, and 'good friends' are just as likely to be called *ffrindiau mawr* as *ffrindiau da*.[5]

1.1.3.iii Formulaic language

The category formulaic language refers to conventionalised chunks of language whose form rarely varies from one occasion of use to the next. Some of these are routine phrases used in particular social contexts ('It's nice to meet you.' 'Thank you very much.' 'I'm sorry to hear that.' 'How are you?' 'I beg your pardon.'):

'**I do beg your pardon**. I will not trespass further on your time.' [THIEF 8]

'**Mae'n ddrwg gen i**. Wna i mo'ch poeni chi ymhellach.' [LLEIDR 16]

Another group includes idioms, phrases whose conventional meaning is not inferrable from the literal meanings of the individual words that make them up. Idioms have a meaning that must simply be learned. They are said to be *non-compositional* since their meaning is not built up by adding together the meanings of their individual pieces, and as a result, a translation must be sought for the idiom as a whole.

Yr oedd Wil, bellach, yn mynd '**fel cath i gythraul**', a rhyw ferch fach y rhoddasai reid iddi yn sgrechian 'Help' nerth ei phen. [O LAW 61]

Will was now going **hell-for-leather**, with a little girl to whom he had given a ride screeching 'Help!' at the top of her voice. [FROM 41]

In this case, *fel cath i gythraul* (lit. 'like a cat to the devil') is a unit that has no direct English equivalent, though similar idioms are possible such as 'hell-for-leather' or 'like a bat out of hell'.

---

[5] Collocations are explored further in Chapter 9.

1.1.3 Overtranslation
Overtranslation generally results when a translator fails to recognise a multi-word sequence as a single translation unit, treating it instead as a series of independent units, and translating each separately. For instance, to render *ar gefn beic* literally as 'on the back of a bike' or *cath fach* as 'small cat' would be examples of *overtranslation*.

1.1.4 Registers and Situational Variation[6]
The Welsh language is characterised by an extremely broad range of registers depending on such factors as the level of formality, the medium of communication (writing versus speech), the age of the participants in the interaction and how well they know each other, and the setting (public or private, the chapel, the stadium or the pub, etc.). The same message can generally be communicated in more than one way in Welsh, with a number of linguistic variables coming into play including not only pronunciation but also lexical and even grammatical choices. To take a simple example, the future tense notion "I will not sing' can be expressed in any of the following ways ranging from the most formal and literary at the top, to the most colloquial and regionally marked at the bottom:

> Ni chanaf.
> Ni chanaf i ddim.
> Chanaf i ddim.
> Chana' i ddim.
> Gana i ddim.
> Gana i'm.

There are multiple variables at play here, including:

- verbal negation (preverbal *ni*, circumverbal *ni ... ddim*, or postverbal *ddim* alone);
- whether the negated verb undergoes aspirate mutation or soft mutation;
- whether subject pronouns can be left out;
- pronunciation (whether to pronounce or omit final <f>, whether to pronounce *ddim* fully or contract it to *'m*).

Literary texts, such as the bulk of those making up the corpus used in this study, often include a fair amount of variation along these lines, typically

[6] Previous works exploring register in Welsh include the following: Ball (1988), Davis (2016), Fife (1986), Jones (1993), Prys (2016), and Willis (2014, 2016).

using a more formal or literary style for the narrator's voice, and much more informal language in character dialogue. But there is also significant variation and change across the twentieth century, with significant changes in Welsh grammar and vocabulary at all levels due in no small part to the increasingly strong pressure of English on the Welsh language.

In broad terms, a translator strives to maintain the register of the source text in the translation. The target text should have more or less the same level of formality as the source text, but it is rarely the case that specific linguistic variables that serve to mark register have direct equivalents in both languages. For instance, mutation choices can play a role in marking register in Welsh—selecting the soft mutation instead of the aspirate mutation in negative contexts generally indicates a more informal register – but mutation is not a category of English grammar. Such cases of mismatch are quite common, meaning that the translator must find features of register variation in the target language that achieve the same purpose as those in the source text. As a translation technique this is called *compensation*.

Consider the following example from the first volume of D. J. Williams's autobiography, *Hen Dŷ Ffarm* and its translation:

Hwyrach mai help, ar y cyfan, ac nid rhwystr i sgrifennu'n wrthrychol am fy nhadcu yw'r ffaith nad wyf yn cofio dim amdano'n bersonol, er i'm llygaid, yn ddiau, syllu'n syn arno, lawer tro. Ond y mae gennyf lun ohono a dynnwyd yn 1868, ac yntau'n drigain oed y flwyddyn honno. [HDF 65]	It may be, on the whole, a help rather than a hindrance to me in writing objectively of my grandfather that I do not personally remember him, although doubtless my eyes looked upon him many times. But I have a photograph of him that was taken in 1868, when he was sixty years old. [OFH 78]

The Welsh original contains numerous features of formal and literary style:

- lexical choices such as *hwyrach* 'perhaps' and *yn ddiau* 'doubtless'
- the subordination structures *nad wyf yn cofio* 'that I do not remember' and *er i'm llygaid . . . syllu* 'although my eyes . . . looked'
- the absence of pronouns to reinforce inflected prepositions with *arno* 'on him' (for *arno fe*), and *gennyf* 'with me' (for *gen i*)
- the presence of grammatical particles usually omitted in informal registers such as *Ond y mae gennyf lun ohono a dynnwyd yn 1868. . .*
- the impersonal verb form *dynnwyd* 'was taken'
- infixed pronouns such as *i'm llygaid* 'to my eyes' (for *i fy llygaid*)

- the absolute clause (*ac yntau'n drigain oed*, lit. 'and he thirty [years of] age')
- the inflected demonstrative in *y flwyddyn honno* 'that year' (for informal *y flwyddyn 'na*)

The English translation contains far fewer overt linguistic cues of register; for instance, the last sentence of the passage ('But I have a photograph of him that was taken in 1868, when he was sixty years old.') contains no particular indication of register save, perhaps, the full form *photograph* instead of the abbreviated *photo*, whereas the corresponding Welsh sentence has at least six relevant features that mark the sentence as belonging to a formal register. But in English too, the presence of just a few formal features, and the complete absence of informal features, suffices to identify the register of the text. Among the few specifically formal features we see in this English translation are lexical choices (*hindrance, doubtless* and *look upon*) and the absence of contraction (*that I do not* for *that I don't*).

Clearly, most of the features of formal register in the Welsh text have no exact English counterpart. The translator's task is simply to render the meaning of the text in English, and to do so using enough features of formal English to convey the same literary flavour as the Welsh original.

Passages written in dialect do not necessarily show compensation, and indeed, selecting a regional English dialect as a translation of a regional Welsh one, or vice versa, would rarely be an appropriate strategy, unless the setting of the novel is recast from the Welsh countryside to the English one, for instance. At most, the translation of a passage in dialect may be expected to be informal in character. Two examples follow below:

'Hi!' meddai Dafydd, yn ei ddull nodweddiadol, wrth rywun gerllaw, 'dyna beth od, 'n awr. Fe wedodd y cwrw bŵer o bethe rhyfedd wrthw i, o bryd i' gilydd. Ond wedodd e ariod wrthw i, chwaith, 'mod i'n berchen stad Rhydodyn'. [HDF 60]

'Hee,' said Dafydd in his characteristic way. "Now, that's funny. The beer has told me many strange things from time to time, but it has never told me that I'm the owner of Rhydodyn estate.' [OFH 71]

'Yeh'll do summat useful or yeh'll get out.' [STONE 311]

'Gwna rywbeth defnyddiol neu gwadna hi.' [MAEN 198]

In these fairly typical examples, the dialect present in the source language is not reflected in the target language.

However, in rare cases, the use of dialect may be an essential part of the story. In the Welsh novel *William Jones* by T. Rowland Hughes, the title character moves from north Wales to the south. Several scenes are constructed around the difficulty he has understanding the local dialect:

'Shwmâi?' meddai un.	"Ow are you?' one of them greeted him.
'Go lew, wir, diolch.'	'Pretty well, indeed, thanks.'
'O, Northman, ifa?'	'Oh, Northman, is it?'
'Ia, o Lan-y-Graig . . .	'Aye, from Lan-y-Graig . . .
Sir Gaernarfon.'	Caernarvonshire.'
'Shwd ma' petha'n mynd yn y chwareli 'na nawr?'	"Ow're things lookin' up in those quarries now?'
'Y?'	'Uh?'
'Shwd ma' petha'n mynd yn y chwareli lan 'na?'	"Ow're things goin' in the quarries up there?'
'O, go lew, wir.'	'Oh, pretty well, indeed.
'Gwd, w. Mae'n dwym 'eddi.'	'Good, mun. 'S warm today.'
'Y?'	'Uh?'
'Hoil twym?'	"Ot sun?'
'Ydi wir.' [WILLIAM 102]	'Yes, indeed.' [WILLIAM 80]

Given the role that inter-dialect difficulty plays in this story, the translator had little choice but to use non-standard English features to convey the flavour of this scene, but he also included a footnote to the reader (p. 80) explaining that 'the point of this dialogue, which cannot be conveyed adequately in a translation into another language, is to bring out the difference between the colloquial idiom of North and South Wales.'

1.2 A Methodology for Translation

With this understanding of the basic concepts of translation, we turn now to a typology of the different translation strategies as identified by Vinay and Darbelnet: 1. Borrowing 2. Calquing 3. Literal Translation 4. Transposition 5. Modulation 6. Equivalence 7. Adaptation. Each of their seven strategies will be discussed in turn with examples showing its application to English and Welsh.

1.2.1 Borrowing
Sometimes a translator may opt to maintain words or phrases from the source text intact, without translating them. This is often the case with proper names, or terms of address that function as proper names. The Welsh novel *Y Byw sy'n Cysgu* has two published translations which differ in their handling of kinship

terms used as terms of third-person reference or terms of direct address. *The Living Sleep* regularly translates these terms into English whereas *The Awakening* leaves the Welsh terms untranslated:

'Ia, ond 'd oeddach chim ddim yn poeni fel yna, wedi i **taid a nain** farw.' [BYW 93]

'But you didn't suffer like this when **grandad and grandma** died.' [LIVING 77]

'Yes, but you weren't as sad as when **Taid and Nain** died.' [AWAKENING 90]

Maintaining Welsh terms of address such as *Taid* and *Nain* functions as a reminder to the reader that this is a Welsh story, set in Welsh-speaking Wales. Keeping expletives in the original language can serve a similar purpose:

'**Diawch**, mi wnei di longwr, fachgan. Gwnei, **'nen' Duwc.'** [CHWAL 117]

'**Diawch**, you'll make a seaman, lad. Yes, **'nen' Duwc.'** [OUT 123]

Foreign words, that is, words borrowed from a third language, quite often French, may simply be kept intact too, especially when they are in principle equally foreign to both languages, but they may also be translated. In the next two examples, both from the same work (Jonathan Ross's detective novel *A Time to Kill*), the French phrase *amour propre* and the Italian phrase *sotto voce* were both italicised in the English original, thus marked as foreignisms. The Welsh translator kept the French phrase intact, including the italics, but translated the Italian phrase into Welsh as *yn ddistaw bach* ('very quietly'):

'You think you owe it to your ***amour propre***, David,' Rogers corrected him. [TIME 99]

'Rwyt tithau'n meddwl fod arnat ti rywbeth i dy ***amour propre***, Dafydd,' cywirodd Rogers ef. [AMSER 157]

The note could have been written in an attempt to pull the plug on the nasty suspicions of the police; to perhaps suggest ***sotto voce*** that we might chuck in our hand at trying to find her. [TIME 96]

Ella fod y nodyn wedi'i sgwennu mewn ymgais i ddileu amheuon yr heddlu; i awgrymu ella, **yn ddistaw bach**, y gallan ni roi'r gorau i geisio dod o hyd iddi. [AMSER 153]

Sometimes a foreign-origin word or phrase occupies an uncertain area between clearcut cases of consciously foreign terms, and integrated borrowings that are simply part of the borrowing language's vocabulary. The three French-origin terms *baccarat*, *chaise longue*, and *panache* occur in the same detective novel in English without any signal of their foreign origin. The Welsh translator has kept all three French terms, but put them in italics:

. . . at the dealer's end of what Rogers could identify as a **baccarat** table. [TIME 27]	. . . dros ben y deliwr ar fwrdd yr adwaenai Rogers fel bwrdd ***baccarat***. [AMSER 41]
. . . a small reception desk on which lay a leather book and a telephone, and a visitor's gilt **chaise longue**. [TIME 28]	. . . desg groeso fechan ac arni lyfr lledr, teliffon a ***chaise longue*** lliw aur a neilltuwyd ar gyfer ymwelwyr. [AMSER 43]
. . . he approached Lingard who, at close quarters, now showed rough edges and a lessening of his normal **panache**. [TIME 45]	. . . nesaodd at Lingard a oedd, o graffu arno yn fanylach, yn dangos arwyddion blerwch a'i ***banache*** arferol dan gwmwl. [AMSER 71]

It is noteworthy that *panache* has undergone the soft mutation triggered by the third person singular masculine possessive, but otherwise retains its French (and English) spelling. This is probably because any respelling (as *banash* or even *banas*) would undermine the readers' ability to identify the word. Similarly, the decision whether to apply a mutation or not for words like *panache* whose status as Welsh words is marginal is an option.

The decision about whether to flag foreign-origin words or phrases that are maintained in the translation often reflects whether the word can easily be construed as a nonce Welsh word or not. In the world of drug abuse, the English words *addicts* and *fix* are both kept in the text *A Time to Kill*. Neither poses any particular problem for Welsh pronunciation or grammar (there is considerable precedent for using an <-s> plural on borrowed nouns of English origin and even on some native Welsh words, e.g. *pregethwrs*, an informal variant of *pregethwyr* 'preachers'), so a simple Welshification of the spellings (as *adicts* and *ffics* respectively) enables the translator to keep the English words and dispense with italics:

. . . desperately sick **addicts** . . . and if availability in particular was held back from anyone who couldn't pay for a **fix**. . . [TIME 108]	. . . **adicts** sâl ofnadwy . . . ac os oedd o'n dal y cocên yn ôl rhag ryw foi oedd yn methu talu am **ffics**. . . [AMSER 172]

On the other hand, the two examples below maintain the English spellings of *pervert* and *Caesarian*, and in fact flag both words with italics. This is probably because of the difficulty of construing these straightforwardly as Welsh words: if *pervert* were a normal Welsh word it would be expected to undergo soft mutation in this context (as *panache* did above), and any Welsh respelling of *Caesarian* would be likely to render the word difficult to recognise:

If anyone were a psychosexual **pervert** it was Louis himself. [VICT 127]	Os oedd rhywun yn **pervert** seicorywiol, yna Celt ei hun oedd hwnnw. [LLINYN 142]
A child by **Caesarian** section, McKendrick had said, was perfectly feasible. [VICT 10]	Roedd Harris wedi dweud y byddai'n gwbl bosibl iddi gario plentyn a'i eni trwy lawdriniaeth **Caesarian**. [LLINYN 8]

In the case of *pervert*, a Welsh rendering occurs elsewhere in the same novel:

What was it the police had said about Sally Gray's murderer? A sexual **pervert**. [VICT 27]	Beth oedd yr heddlu wedi'i ddweud ynglŷn â llofrudd Llinos Rees? **Dyn gwyrdroëdig** yn rhywiol. [LLINYN 29]

This shows that the earlier decision to maintain the English word *pervert* was not motivated by a lack of an appropriate Welsh equivalent. Rather, the choice of whether to maintain the English word or find a Welsh equivalent is an option available to the translator and can be deployed for special effect.

1.2.2 Calquing

A calque is a literal translation that maintains the word order or other aspects of the grammatical structure of the source language, without making the changes that would be necessary for the target language's grammar. There are certainly calques based on English models in contemporary Welsh, though it is unusual to find cases where a published translation introduces a calque not already used by Welsh speakers. Attested examples in Welsh include both instances of word formation (*lawrlwytho* is a calque of 'download', i.e. *lawr* 'down' + *llwytho* 'to load') and grammatical patterns (the causative pattern *cael ei wallt wedi ei liwio* 'to get his hair dyed' is considered a calque, as opposed to other more traditional formulations such as *cael lliwio ei wallt*).

From the literary corpus, a good example of a calque is the *tea-party* of *Alice in Wonderland*, which becomes *te-parti* in Selyf Roberts's translations: *te-parti* is a calque on the English *tea-party*. This is clear in that the order of the two elements is that of English, not Welsh. In Welsh one would expect *parti te*, the same order seen in *seibiant coffi* 'coffee break', for instance, where the modifier (*te*) follows the word it modifies, unlike English where it precedes. But Selyf Roberts was not innovating by using this calque in his translation of *Alice*. The calque already existed, being first attested in 1886 (according to the Geiriadur Prifysgol Cymru).

Indeed, a literary translation may certainly use calques once they exist and are an established part of the language, but a careful translator would be very unlikely to introduce calques into the language for the first time as part of a translation.

1.2.3 Literal Translation

Here, literal translation refers to cases where a translator renders the original directly and straightforwardly, but with all of the necessary grammatical adaptations made so that the translation perfectly obeys the grammatical norms of the target language. The following are some fairly typical examples:

Daeth Mrs Jones i mewn i nôl rhai o'r llestri. [BYW 13]	Mrs Jones came in to fetch some of the dishes. [AWAKENING 13]
He got out of the car to consult the other driver. [UNSUIT 156]	Aeth allan o'r car i ymgynghori â'r gyrrwr arall . . . [GORTYN 200]
Harry's last month with the Dursleys wasn't fun. [STONE 110]	Doedd mis olaf Harri gyda'r Dursleys ddim yn hwyl. [MAEN 68]

In these cases all of the constraints of Welsh grammar are obeyed, and there are few or no real options (other than, to a limited extent, lexical choices). Unlike the case of the calque, there is nothing about such literal translations that reveals that the chunk in question is in fact a translation.

1.2.4 Transposition

Transposition refers to a common translation technique in which one part of speech or word class is replaced with another without changing the meaning of the message. Probably the most common type of transposition involves a noun in one language that is recast as a verb in the other. Quite often, it is an English noun that is translated as a verb in Welsh, as below where we see that *some overtime* has become *gweithio'n hwyr* ('to work late') and *serious head injuries* become *anafu'u pennau'n ddifrifol* ('to injure their heads seriously'):

Well, Carol was in for a disappointment unless she was planning **some overtime**. [CIDER 7]	Wel, ei siomi gâi Bronwen, oni bai ei bod hi'n bwriadu **gweithio'n hwyr.** [SEIDR 12]
There had been a motorway pile-up and two of the patients had **serious head injuries**. [VICT 101]	Roedd yna ddamwain car erchyll wedi digwydd a dau o'r teithwyr wedi **anafu'u pennau'n ddifrifol.** [LLINYN 114]

A second common transposition has an adjective recast as a noun, or vice versa:

A heno, yr oedd y plasty bach hynafol **yn dangnefedd i gyd**, a choch y gorllewin yn ei res ffenestri Sioraidd. [CRYMAN 12]	This evening, the ancient little grange looked **so peaceful**, with the red glow from the western sky reflected in its row of Georgian windows. [SICKLE 8]
. . . o flaen y tân coed **gwresog** ar lawr yr aelwyd. [HDF 177]	. . . in **the warmth** of the wood fire. [OFH 223]
'. . . being so many different sizes in a day is **very confusing**.' [ALICE 49]	'. . . ac y mae newid taldra gynifer o weithiau mewn un diwrnod **yn ddryswch mawr**.' [ALYS II 43]
There should be more **honesty** between them. [VICT 27]	Fe ddylen nhw fod yn fwy **onest** gyda'i gilydd. [LLINYN 29]

While many examples of transposition represent options, the first one above, *yn dangnefedd i gyd* – an example of the construction *yn* NOUN *i gyd* where the noun can vary – represents a constraint in English. English does not readily permit nouns in this pattern (*The little grange was all peace* is hardly viable English),[7] although some nouns are possible such as 'smiles' in a sentence like *She was all smiles*.

A third common transposition has an adjective transposed as an adverb, or vice-versa:

---

[7] The asterisk is used here and elsewhere to mark ungrammaticality, i.e. forms that are generally unattested in fluent speech or forms that are anomalous.

Gwnaeth **de brysiog aflêr** iddi ei hun . . . [MONICA 50] [lit. 'She made herself a hurried, messy tea.']

She made herself some **tea, hurriedly and messily** . . . [MONICA 50]

Gwelais hi droeon yn taflu **golwg annwyl a hiraethus** arnynt pan âi am rawiad o lo neu rywbeth i'r cwt . . . [O LAW 198] [lit. 'a loving and longing look']

Many a time I saw her **look lovingly and longingly** at them [*my father's tools*] when she went into the shed for a shovelful of coal or something . . . [FROM 163]

Some transpositions entail others in their wake, in a kind of chain reaction. The example just shown from the Welsh novel *O law i law* has the noun phrase *golwg annwyl a hiraethus* (lit. 'a loving and longing look') recast as the verb phrase '(to) look lovingly and longingly'. That is, where the source language had a noun modified by adjectives, the target language has a verb modified by adverbs. Cases like this are said to involve a *double transposition*. Or consider the following, in which *smocio'n hamddenol* becomes 'having a leisurely smoke':

Ond ar ôl gorffen priddo tatws neu doi'r dâs, yr oedd pleser i Ifan o gael rhoi ei bwys ar ben y wal a **smocio'n hamddenol** ac edmygu gwaith ei ddwylo . . . [TRAED 90]

But after earthing-up the potatoes or thatching the haystack, it was a great pleasure for Ifan to lean against the wall **having a leisurely smoke** while admiring the work of his hands . . . [FEET 75]

Here, the Welsh verb *smocio* has become the noun *a smoke*, and the adverb *yn hamddenol* has become the adjective *leisurely*.

Some constructions result more or less automatically in a double transposition. For instance, in Welsh, numerous expressions of emotion consist of an existential subject with the verb *bod* 'to be', plus a noun of emotion naming the abstraction whose existence is predicated, and a prepositional phrase (or inflected preposition) identifying the human experiencer. In the following example, the inflected preposition and its object (*arnoch chi* 'on you') become the subject (*you*) in English, while the Welsh noun of emotion (*hiraeth*) becomes an adjective (*homesick*):

Ella **bydd arnoch chi hiraeth** wedi mynd i Lundain. [TE 57]

Perhaps **you'll be homesick** in London. [TEA 54]

Frequently, the transposed elements appear to switch places with each other in translation. Vinay and Darbelnet refer to such cases using the French term *chassé-croisé.*[8] Consider *Roedd ofn y lle arni hi* (lit. 'was fear [of] the place on her') which becomes 'She was afraid of the place.' The human experiencer (the object of the preposition in Welsh) becomes the grammatical subject, and the noun of emotion becomes the verb:

Roedd **ofn** y lle arni **hi**

She was **afraid** of the place

This pattern (which is further discussed in Chapters 2 and 3) is often found with expressions of shame, fear, sorrow/regret, surprise, and longing, among others:

She was a bit frightened of this place now. [MAT 186]	**Roedd ychydig o ofn y lle arni** nawr. [MAT 180]
Mae'n syn gennyf feddwl, ac y mae cywilydd arnaf gofio mor hy oeddwn gyda hi. Ni phetruswn wenieithio iddi. [RHYS 231]	**I am surprised** to think, and ashamed to remember, how free I made with her. I flattered her in the most shameless way. [RHYS 221]
I'm sorry I had to bother you. [TIME 122]	**Ddrwg gen i** i mi orfod tarfu arnach chi. [AMSER 195]

Some transpositions result from a lexical gap in the target language. For instance, there is no easy Welsh equivalent for the English adjective *embarrassing*. The loanword *embaras* functions as a noun with no derived adjective, so a common solution for saying that something 'is embarrassing' is to use the phrase *codi embaras ar (rywun)*, literally 'to raise embarrassment on (someone)', in which the lexical gap is handled by a transposition:

He sensed her embarrassment. Death, he thought, was **embarrassing**. [VICT 28]	Gallai o synhwyro'i dryswch a'i hanniddigrwydd. Mae marwolaeth yn codi **embaras** ar bobol, meddyliodd. [LLINYN 32] [lit. 'Death raises embarrassment on people, he thought.']

---

[8] Originally referring to country dance moves in which partners end up exchanging places with each other, the term *chassé-croisé* is also used by extension to refer to 'actions or situations in which persons or things cross each other or change positions backwards and forwards' (OED, entry *chassé-croisé*).

There are numerous Welsh idioms with *codi* 'to raise' which similarly refer to creating emotional states in someone (e.g. *codi ofn ar* 'to frighten'), so *codi embaras ar* is very much in the spirit of idiomatic Welsh.

1.2.5 Modulation

The category *modulation* refers to translations which represent a change of point of view or a different way of conceptualising the event. Sometimes this involves describing the same scene by focusing on a different aspect or detail of it. In *Through the Looking Glass*, describing the Red Queen as half a head taller than Alice gives way to describing her as *drwyn a thalcen yn dalach* (literally 'a nose and a forehead taller'):

[W]hen Alice first found her in the ashes, she had been only three inches high – and here she was, **half a head taller** than Alice herself! [THRO 143]	[P]an gafodd Alys hyd iddi yn y lludw 'd oedd hi'n ddim mwy na thair modfedd o uchder, a dyma hi'n awr, **drwyn a thalcen yn dalach** nag Alys ei hun! [TRWY 29]

A translation by modulation like the above is generally motivated by a desire to find a more usual or conventional phrasing in the TL than a direct translation would give.

Sometimes modulation offers a way to handle plays on words or puns. Since puns depend on accidental homophony – two unrelated words happen to sound alike – it is unlikely that the same homophony would exist in both the SL and the TL. The translator can sometimes find a suitable homophony involving a different aspect of the situation – in other words, by appealing to a modulation. Lewis Carroll made much use of puns in *Through the Looking Glass*. The example below draws on the homophony of English *bough* meaning 'branch' and the first syllable of *bow-wow*, the onomatopoeia used to imitate the barking of a dog. The Welsh word *cainc* 'bough, branch' would not lend itself to rendering the English play on words directly, so in this case the translator looked to a different part of the tree, the *bôn* 'stem, trunk' and created a pun with the playing of a trombone (*trombôn*):

'There's the tree in the middle,' said the Rose: 'what else is it good for?' 'But what could it do, if any danger came?' Alice asked. 'It says **"Bough-wough!"'** cried a Daisy: 'that's why its branches are called **boughs!**' [THRO]	'Mae'r goeden yn y canol,' ebe'r Rhosyn. 'i beth arall y mae hi'n dda?' 'Ond beth allai hi ei wneud pe deuai rhyw berygl?' gofynnodd Alys. 'Mi fedr chwythu'i **drombôn,**' ebe'r Rhosyn. 'Mae ganddi hi **fôn,** wyddoch,' meddai'r llygad y Dydd,

'ac mae ganddi gainc neu ddwy!'
[TRWY 26–7]

Similarly, *rattle* (a kind of toy for infants) and *rattlesnake* (a creature that children find scary) become *tegan* ('toy') and *bwgan* ('bogeyman, ghost'):

'It's only a **rattle**,' Alice said, after a careful examination of the little white thing. 'Not a **rattle***snake*, you know,' she added hastily, thinking that he was frightened: 'only an old rattle – quite old and broken.' [THRO 168]

'**Tegan**, dyna'i gyd,' meddai Alys ar ôl gwneud ymchwiliad manwl o'r peth bach gwyn. 'Nid **bwgan**, wyddoch,' ychwanegodd ar frys, gan feddwl ei fod wedi dychryn. 'Dim ond hen degan – hen un, ac wedi torri.' [TRWY 56]

Several kinds of modulation are particularly common. One involves figurative language. Sometimes a figure of speech works in both languages and the translator may then choose to render it directly. The following quote contains two examples, neither of which is a conventionalised figure in either language, but as creative metaphors they work in both:

Yr oedd **fel crempog fawr a lot o dyllau ynddi a chyllell ddur las** rhyngddi a Sir Fôn. [TE 10]

Her eyes ranged over the snow, far over the snow that lay **like a crumpet, pitted with holes**, and between her and Anglesey, **the steel-blue knife-blade** of the Straits. [TEA 14]

Figurative language is not always created anew by the writer but is often conventionalised, in which case a figure in the SL text may be replaced by an equivalent conventionalised figure in the TL which serves roughly the same purpose but may not literally mean the same thing. The Welsh expression *cadw llygad barcud ar* literally means 'to keep the eye of a kite on' someone or something. This is a totally different image than the English notion of keeping someone or something 'on a [fairly] short leash', which takes us to the realm not of birds but of dogs, though both expressions refer to maintaining tight surveillance. Similarly, when a situation turns disastrous, in English one can say that 'the balloon went up' whereas in Welsh, things 'went pigs' feet' (*mynd yn draed moch*). And lastly, driving *fel cath i gythrel* ('like a cat to the devil') is a different mental image than driving 'like the wind', though both amount to 'very fast':

... so it's likely that Stephanakis **kept** her supplies of it **on a fairly short leash**. [TIME 113]

... felly mae'n debyg fod Stephanakis **yn cadw llygad barcud ar** ei chyflenwad hi. [AMSER 113]

I'd say she's either heavily tied up in the knocking off of Stephanakis, or she knew enough about it not to have waited around **when the balloon went up**. [TIME 96]

Yn fy marn i, naill ai mae hi'n gysylltiedig go iawn efo lladd Stephanakis, neu mae hi'n gwybod digon amdano fo i beidio ag aros yno **ar ôl i bethau fynd yn draed moch**. [AMSER 152]

Helion ni'n pac yn gloi, tyrru i gar Austin estate Gary, a gyrru **fel cath i gythrel** am Solfach. [HUNAN 231]

We packed up quickly, piled into Gary's Austin estate car and drove **like the wind** to Solva. [SOLVA 231]

A figurative expression may be introduced in the target language formulation where the source language was not figurative:[9]

... and **narrowly** escaped a capital sentence. As it was he suffered a long term of imprisonment ... [BAND 212]

O drwch blewyn llwyddodd i osgoi'r gosb eithaf, ond bu'n rhaid iddo ddioddef cyfnod hir yn y carchar ... [CYLCH 18] [lit. 'by a hair's breadth']

Both Miss Stoner and I gazed at him **in astonishment**. [BAND 230]

Syllodd Miss Stoner a minnau arno **â'n llygaid fel lleuadau llawn**. [CYLCH 45] [lit. 'with our eyes like full moons']

The lie – **like something they could pick up and examine** – lay between them. [VICT 115]

Gorweddai'r celwydd rhyngddynt – **fel blaidd yn cysgu**. [LLINYN 128] [lit. 'like a wolf sleeping']

Rebus knew from her voice, from its slurred growliness, that she would be **fast asleep** by the time he reached the kitchen. [KNOTS 81]

Gwyddai oddi wrth ei llais, oddi wrth y ffordd roedd hi'n llusgo siarad, y byddai'**n cysgu fel twrch** erbyn iddo gyrraedd y gegin. [CHWERW 70] [lit. 'sleeping like a boar']

---

[9] Among our examples it is more often the case that the Welsh translators introduced figurative language not present in the English source text than the reverse, but a large quantitative study would be needed to verify whether this pattern holds true in general.

Dunster had to sell everything at a loss **and was ruined**. [CASE 35]	A hynny'n golygu bod Doran yn gorfod gwerthu popeth ar golled **ac mi aeth yr hwch drwy'r siop**. [BAI 37] [lit. 'and the sow went through the shop.']

It is not always the case that only one translation strategy applies at a time. The following examples show not only the introduction of figurative language, but also the transposition of English past participles being used adjectivally, as Welsh prepositional phrases:

It was wrapped in thick brown paper and **scrawled** across it was To Harry, From Hagrid. [STONE 248]	Roedd wedi ei lapio mewn papur llwyd trwchus, ac **mewn ysgrifen traed brain** ar ei draws roedd i Harri, oddi wrth Hagrid. [MAEN 157–8] [lit. 'in crow's feet script']
Harry, Malfoy and Fang stood **transfixed**. [STONE 319]	Safodd Harri, Mallwyd a Ffang **fel delwau**, fel petaent wedi eu parlysu. [MAEN 203] [lit. 'like idols]
'By the light of the corridor lamp I saw my sister appear at the opening, her face **blanched with terror**, her hands groping for help, her whole figure swaying to and fro like that of a drunkard.' [BAND 216]	'Yng ngoleuni'r lamp olew yn y coridor, gwelwn fy chwaer yn dod i'r golwg ger y drws, ei hwyneb **yn wyn fel y galchen** mewn braw, ei dwylo'n ymbalfalu am gymorth, ei chorff i gyd yn siglo o un ochr i'r llall fel meddwyn.' [CYLCH 24] [lit. 'white as chalk']

Figurative speech may also be omitted in a translation, which can become more strictly literal. For instance, silence falling *fel cadach* ('like a cloth') becomes a straightforward statement about characters falling silent:

Disgynnodd distawrwydd **fel cadach** ar y cwmni. [LLEIFIOR 28]	The young women fell silent. [RETURN 22]

The examples considered so far involve similes or metaphors, kinds of figurative language based on a comparison of one thing with a completely different thing. The comparison can be explicit (using *like/as* in English and *fel* in Welsh) or implicit. Metonymy is a different kind of figure of speech based not on comparison but on contiguity – a thing is named for a related or associated thing. In the following example, a simile (*siarad fel melin* 'to speak like a mill'), is translated with a metonymy in which the body part responsible for speech, the tongue, is used as a reference to the abundant speech itself:

Byddai'n ddigon distaw pan fyddai ei gŵr yn y cylch, ond **siaradai fel melin** wedi iddo fyned i'w wely. [HENAT 145]	She had little to say when her husband was there, but **her tongue was loosened** after he had gone to bed. [LOCUST 124]

Like metaphors, metonymies do not necessarily have conventionalised translation equivalents in both languages. Probably because metonymies are not necessarily recognised as figurative language by the layperson as readily as are metaphors, they are often translated with less figurative renderings:

Mi **gei stumog** yng ngwynt y mynydd, ac mi wneith les iti. [TE 36] [lit. 'you'll get a stomach']	The mountain air **will make you hungry** and it will do you good. [TEA 36]
'I ladd gafodd o, yntê?' 'Ia, **ar ganiad** ryw noson.' [TRAED 21] [lit. 'at the ringing']	"He was killed, wasn't he?" "Yes, **when he was leaving work** one night." [FEET 18]

In the first example, *mi gei stumog* (lit. 'you'll get a stomach') means 'you'll get hungry'; a reference to the physical condition of hunger is transferred by metonymy to the part of the body associated with hunger. In the second example, *ar ganiad* (lit. 'at the ringing') means 'when the workday was over'; the sounding of the hooter used to mark the end of the workshift becomes a name for the event that it marks.

The next two examples go in the opposite direction, from English as source language to Welsh as target, but similarly show suppression of a metonymy. In the first example below, a *fractured skull* becomes a way to refer to 'a person with a fractured skull', as though the person were reduced to just this one characteristic, admittedly the most relevant fact about the person at the time. And in the second example, the English expression '*the sun is over the yardarm*' is a nautical idiom meaning that it is now late enough in the day to stop work and begin drinking. This is a metonymy in that, in the original context, the position of the sun in the sky betokens an event that begins when the sun is in that position, a transfer of meaning by association. Not having this same idiom available in Welsh, the translator refers directly to the taverns being open, with no figure of speech:

It'd be nice to think we had **another fractured skull** staggering around waiting to be handcuffed, wouldn't it? [TIME 86]

Basa'n braf meddwl fod gynnon ni **ddyn arall â phenglog friw** yn crwydro hyd y lle 'ma'n disgwyl cyffion? [TIME 137]

I understand that the **sun's probably over the yardarm** by now and I'm going to have a drink. Will you join me? [TIME 102]

Dw i'n dallt **bod y tafarnau ar agor** erbyn hyn, a dw i am gael diod. Be amdanoch chi? [AMSER 163]

In all of the above cases the metonymy was not maintained in the translation; the translators opted in each case for a more literal rendering. But sometimes a successful translation is based on finding an equivalent that is motivated by metonymy. The Welsh verb of motion *ymlusgo* literally means 'drag itself'; it can often be rendered 'creep' or 'crawl', but the translator selected 'puff', a solid conventional choice to describe the laboured movement of a train:

Ymlusgodd y trên yn araf a swnllyd i fyny'r cwm. [WILLIAM 104]

The train **puffed** slowly and noisily up the valley. [WILLIAM 82]

'Puff' is technically a verb of sound, but here it functions as a verb of motion by being coupled with the expressed path ('up the valley'), whence the metonymy: the sound the train makes while moving along becomes a verb for the movement itself.

Another kind of modulation which is not about figurative language concerns grammatical changes that reconceive an event differently. One such pattern involves the idea that a notion is equivalent to the negation of its opposite; for instance, 'healthy' could be described as 'not sick', and 'not punctual' amounts to 'tardy'. The following examples illustrate modulation by negation of the opposite:

Ond **gwael** yw'r busnes y misoedd hyn . . . [MONICA 10]

But business **hasn't** been **at all good** these last few months . . . [MONICA 9]

Edrychodd hi'n ddryslyd arno: ond **doeth oedd peidio** â dadlau â chlaf. [CYCHWYN 33]

She looked at him in perplexity: but **it was unwise** to argue with a sick person. [BEGIN 32]

He was a **late riser** as a rule . . . [BAND 207]

Nid oedd yn un am **godi'n gynnar** fel arfer . . . [CYLCH 12]

Nid aeth oddi wrth benelin ei mam yr holl amser y bu'n gwneud y grempog. [TE 53]

She stayed at her mother's side all through the making of the pancakes. [TEA 50]

It had **not** been **unlike** looking into a dazzling light. [TIME 24]

Roedd o **fel** edrych ar olau llachar, llachar. [AMSER 37]

In these examples we see the following equations:

poor = not good;
it was wise not to = it was unwise to;
to rise late = not to rise early;
she didn't go = she stayed;
not unlike = like.

1.2.6 Equivalence

The category of *Equivalence* mostly includes fixed chunks of phraseological language such as proverbs, clichés and idioms. The translator's task in these cases is to look for an equivalent formula in the target language.

Tebyg at ei debyg. [TE 46] [lit. 'Like to its like.']

Birds of a feather. [TEA 44]

'Mi ddaeth adra' o'r chwaral ganol dydd fel 'tai o, ac nid chi, oedd yn ista'r arholiad. 'Sut mae o'n bwrw drwyddi, tybad?' medda' fo dro ar ôl tro amsar cinio, **ar biga'r drain**.' [CYCHWYN 200] [lit. 'on the pricks of the thorns.']

'He came home from the quarry midday as though he, and not you, was sitting the examination. He was **like a cat on hot bricks** at dinnertime and saying 'How is he getting on, I wonder?' over and over again. [BEGIN 201]

By her father's own account **they hadn't been on speaking terms** for God knows how long. [TIME 96]

Yn ôl ei thad, **doedd yna'r un gair o Gymraeg rhyngddyn nhw** erstalwm. [AMSER 152] [lit. 'There wasn't a word of Welsh between them.']

Sometimes the equivalence bears on a *metalinguistic* element; that is, sometimes an author makes overt reference to a linguistic form in the language (a suffix, a particular pronunciation, a dialect vocabulary word, etc.). Since these cases are unlikely to be directly transposable into the target language, the translator's task is generally to find an equivalent structure that is analogous.

The Welsh text *Chwalfa* here refers to a variety of disease names that all bear the Welsh suffix *–wst*: *gymalwst* 'gout; arthritis', *gewynwst*[10] 'rheumatism' and *anwydwst* 'influenza', and the writer makes direct reference to this suffix as a way of saying that these and any other diseases are included in his comment:

... y feddyginiaeth orau i'w chymryd pan ddywedai'i drwyn a'i wedd a'i dafod fod Bol-rwymedd arno, pelenni cryfhaol a oedd yn Wrthfustlaidd ac yn Droethbarol, beth bynnag a olygai hynny, a ffisig at y Gymalwst a'r Gewynwst a'r Anwydwst a phob **-wst** arall a oremesai'r corff dynol. [CHWAL 95]	... the best physic to take when his nose, complexion and tongue indicated Constipation, diuretic – whatever that meant – and antibilious tonic pills, medicine for influenza, arthritis, neuritis and every other **-itis** that ever plagued the human body. [OUT 99]

The translator was able to draw on the fact that English disease names often end in *-itis*, which can then be used as a metalinguistic equivalent in the translation.

1.2.7 Adaptation

In Vinay and Darlbelnet's classic work, the category of adaptation refers to instances in which the cultural situation referred to in the source language text does not exist in the target language culture. The translator's task becomes to find an equivalent cultural situation, the translation strategy called *adaptation*.

In the case of Welsh and English, the cultural worlds are not as different today as those of French and English in Vinay and Darbelnet's study. Examples of adaptation can be found, though: *y Tylwyth Teg*, the 'little people' or fairies of traditional Welsh folklore become simply 'fairies' in translation, and *lilliputian*, a literary reference to the tiny people of Lilliput in the English novel *Gulliver's Travels* becomes a reference to a *corrach* or 'elf':

Merch fechan eiddil yr olwg ond prydferth fel dol oedd hi, a'i llygaid glas, breuddwydiol, a'i chroen glân a chlir a'i gwallt melynwyn yn gwneud i rywun feddwl am **un o'r Tylwyth Teg.** [CHWAL 74]	Small and frail-looking, she was a girl with a doll-like beauty, her dreamy blue eyes, fair clear skin and pale golden hair reminding one of **a fairy.** [OUT 77]
... a **lilliputian** kitchen ... [TIME 22]	... cegin i **gorrach** ... [AMSER 34]

---

[10] Today spelled *gewynnwst*.

Proper names of societies, associations or even songs can be replaced by more meaningful analogous references from the target culture:

. . . the **Abbotsburn Businessmen's Fellowship** [TIME 74]	. . . y **Cymrodorion** [AMSER 188]
She came in for lunch without even noticing that I was there. This is pure **Mills & Boon**, but true. [CIDER 28]	Daeth i'r tŷ i gael ei chinio ac fe'm swynwyd ganddi cyn iddi hyd yn oed sylwi fy mod i yno. Gall hyn swnio fel un o nofelau **Cyfres y Fodrwy**, ond nid yw hynny'n ei wneud ronyn yn llai gwir. [SEIDR 39]
On the way he hummed repetitively to himself a few bars of *Happy Days are Here Again* . . . [TIME 60]	Ar y ffordd bu'n hymian drosodd a throsodd ychydig fariau o 'Moliannwn'. . . [AMSER 95]

Proper names of characters may be retained in a translation, but if the setting of the novel is transposed into the target culture's society, it may make more sense to replace typical and evocative character names by similarly typical names from the target culture. The English detective novel *Rough Cider* is recast from a story taking place in England to one taking place in Wales, and thus very English-sounding character names like Carol Dangerfield were replaced by typically Welsh names like Bronwen Pugh. And the villainous schoolboys evocatively named Crabbe and Goyle in *Harry Potter and the Philosopher's Stone* are renamed with references to villains from well-known Welsh folktales as Edeyrn and Efnisien:

I turned right about and went to see Carol Dangerfield, the department secretary. [CIDER 4]	Troais ar fy sawdl a mynd i weld **Bronwen Pugh**, ysgrifenyddes yr adran. [SEIDR 9]
Draco Malfoy and his friends **Crabbe and Goyle** sniggered behind their hands. [STONE 169]	Dechreuodd Dreigo Mallwyd a'i ffrindiau, **Edeyrn ac Efnisien**, biffian chwerthin y tu ôl i'w dwylo. [MAEN 107]

Sometimes it would not make sense to find a cultural equivalent from the target culture. The translation of the Welsh novel *Gwen Tomos* maintains Wales as the setting for the story, so Welsh cultural references are not inappropriate even in the English translation. However, at other times a cultural reference may be deemed too obscure to be meaningful to an English readership, and then the best solution may be briefly to explain the cultural reference, or simply to drop it altogether if the context doesn't require it:

Gallai ddarllen ychydig, neu yn hytrach wneud allan gerdd fasweddus debyg i'**r eiddo Dic Dywyll** a'i dosbarth – y rhai a fu yn boblogaidd un tro yng Nghymru – a gallai gyfrif pwysau mochyn. [GWEN 10]

He could read a little and he could understand **a** ballad of poor taste, the type that was popular in Wales at the time, and he could estimate the weight of a pig. [GWEN 17]

Here there is enough other information about the cultural reference in question – the ballads of poor taste that were popular in Wales at the time – so the specific example of the character named Dic Dywyll, whom English readers are unlikely to recognise, was simply dropped in the translation.

1.3 Summary

The seven translations strategies seen in the preceding discussion are listed in the following table with a representative example of each to serve as a reminder.

Strategy	Example	
	Source text	Translation
1. Borrowing	*wedi i taid a nain farw*	*when Taid and Nain died*
2. Calquing	*A Mad Tea-party.*	*Te-parti gwallgof.*
3. Literal translation	*Daeth Mrs Jones i mewn i nôl rhai o'r llestri.*	*Mrs Jones came in to fetch some of the dishes.*
4. Transposition	*o flaen y tân coed gwresog*	*in the warmth of the wood fire*
5. Modulation	*Mi gei stumog yng ngwynt y mynydd.*	*The mountain air will make you hungry.*
6. Equivalence	*Tebyg at ei debyg.*	*Birds of a feather.*
7. Adaptation	*the Abbotsburn Businessmen's Fellowship*	*y Cymrodorion*

The reader should keep these various strategies in mind in the following chapters, as they will be called upon in the discussion of different aspects of the structural comparison of Welsh and English.

2

Nouns and Pronouns

2.0 Nouns and Pronouns – Introduction

The principal emphasis of this chapter is to consider: (i) in section 2.1 how the function of the noun in both languages is different and (ii) in section 2.2 how pronouns may be used in contrasting ways e.g. how the English pronoun '*it*' might be conveyed in Welsh.

Apart from obvious differences such as gender and number, the chapter examines how nouns in Welsh can combine, for example, with the definite article in situations where this does not obtain in English or in order to introduce an epithet or an insult. Situations in which the Welsh noun may be used as the equivalent of an English adjective, adverb or verb are discussed. In many instances, Welsh favours a verb-noun over an English noun. Particular attention is given to cases where a noun combines with the preposition '*o*' and is followed by another noun functioning in a descriptive role or acting as a modifier.

Our second section here looks at pronouns and their functions, in particular where these are not similar in the two languages. The discussion of nonreferential feminines in Welsh is extensive not only because this can be a strategy for giving English '*it*' in Welsh but also because the pronoun '*hi*' is frequently combined with prepositions in a nonreferential way e.g. *mynd amdani, dal ati, dod trwyddi, bod wrthi* etc. This also provides the basis for a number of expressions e.g. *y gwir amdani*. Indefinite pronouns which give *-ever* forms in English are outlined as are the conjunctive pronouns which connect/contrast different pronominal elements and which are not uncommon in all registers of Welsh.

2.1 Nouns

2.1.a Gender and number
All nouns in Welsh possess a grammatical gender – masculine or feminine. This grammatical gender will occasionally correspond to a biological gender e.g.

dyn	[man]	>>	masculine noun
bachgen	[boy]	>>	masculine noun
ci	[dog]	>>	masculine noun

menyw	[woman]	>>	feminine noun
merch	[girl]	>>	feminine noun
gast	[bitch]	>>	feminine noun

However, we cannot depend on the biological = grammatical gender equivalence always being obvious e.g.

cath	[cat]	>>	feminine noun
plentyn	[child]	>>	masculine noun (even if the child is female)
arth[1]	[bear]	>>	feminine noun

In the case of inanimate nouns, the grammatical gender has to be learnt. There will often be useful clues given that singular, feminine nouns will take a soft mutation after the definite article, will require the feminine forms of certain numerals and will cause any subsequent adjectives to take a soft mutation.

As a result, the translator needs to remember that any associated pronouns may not be able to be rendered literally and may need to be changed to reflect the 'biological reality' of the target language. In our first example, Hagrid is talking about an owl which takes the third person singular masculine equivalent pronouns 'he/him' in English. However, owl is translated into Welsh by the feminine noun equivalent 'tylluan' and therefore, its associated pronouns are the singular feminine forms 'hi/ei + aspirate mutation:

Harry tried to wave the owl out of the way, but **it** snapped **its** beak fiercely at him and carried on savaging the coat.
'Hagrid!' said Harry loudly. 'There's an owl –'
'Pay **him**,' Hagrid grunted into the sofa.
'What?'

Ceisiodd Harri chwifio'r dylluan o'r ffordd, ond cleciodd **ei ph**ig yn ffyrnig arno gan ddal ati i dynnu'r gôt yn gareiau.
'Hagrid!' meddai Harri'n uchel. 'Mae 'na dylluan –'
'Tala **iddi**,' chwyrnodd Hagrid i mewn i'r soffa.
'Be?'

---

[1] GA actually stresses (NB f not m) after its entry for 'bear'. The story of 'Goldilocks and the Three Bears' is therefore 'Elen Benfelen a'r Tair Arth'. GA gives 'arth wryw' [arth = gwryw meaning 'male'] for a he-bear and 'arthes' for a she-bear (even though 'arth' is a feminine noun).

'**He** wants payin' for deliverin'
the paper. Look in the pockets.'
[STONE 77]

'Ma' **hi** isio'**i thâl** am ddanfon
y papur. Drycha yn y pocedi.'
[MAEN 48]

A further example from the same novel, refers to a dragon a noun whose
equivalent in Welsh – *draig* – is feminine and includes the same gender cross-
over in the associated pronouns between the two languages:

'I – I know I can't keep **him** forever,
but I can't jus' **dump him**. I can't.'
[STONE 293]

'Wn – wn i na cha' i **mo'i ch**adw **hi**
am byth, ond fedra'i ddim **ei gadael**
hi yn rwla-rwla. Fedra'i ddim.'
[MAEN 187]

2.1.b Mutation of proper nouns

The norm in Welsh is for proper nouns referring to Welsh place names (and
some foreign ones) to mutate. There is greater resistance to the mutation of
Welsh – and especially non-Welsh – personal names[2]. The examples below,
however, offer us examples of mutations (mainly, but not exclusively, the soft
mutation) in both formal and informal registers.

Meddyliodd am **Fyrddin** bach a'i
bib [. . .], ond er ei waethaf llithrai'i
feddwl a'i lygaid tua'r tryblith
niwlog a oedd yn y papur newydd.
[CYCHWYN 37]

He thought about **Myrddin** and his
flageolet [. . .] but despite himself
his mind and glance strayed to the
foggy blur in the paper. [BEGIN 36]

Daeth ysfa dros **Ddic Bugail** i
gydio yn ei barseli a'i gwadnu hi
am ei fywyd yn ôl i'r Gogledd.
[CHWAL 82]

An urge came over **Dick Shepherd**
to lay hold of his bundles and leg it
back North for dear life. [OUT 85]

Rai dyddiau cyn i **Fartha**
Ifans ddychwelyd o'r De . . .
[CHWAL 152]

Some days before **Martha Evans**
returned from South Wales . . .
[OUT 161]

. . . ac fe ddywedodd hynny wrth
y **Fargherita** benddu lygatddu . . .
[CRYMAN 43]

. . . and said as much to the black-
eyed, dark-haired **Margherita** . . .
[SICKLE 34]

[2] PWT (II.26–II.30) and DAT (127–34) discuss this in more depth. In their discus-
sions of the mutation of personal names, they both note the resistance to mutation in
informal registers and in non-Welsh personal names. Our examples, however, provide
evidence that this is not always the case.

... a chynghorodd fi yn ddilynol i beidio ag ymwneud ond cyn lleied ag a fedrwn â **Thwm**. [GWEN 28]

... She advised me to keep away from him [= **Twm**] as much as possible. [GWEN 34]

... ryw ambell frycheuyn o ffaeledd hyd yn oed **ym Mhegi**, ei merch. ... [HDF 173]

... a mote of a failing even in her daughter Pegi. ... [OFH 217]

2.1.c 'Yn' plus noun (yn NOUN)

This is discussed more fully in Section 10.2.1 of Chapter 10.

2.1.c.i 'Yn' plus noun being used adjectivally or adverbially

The use of predicative 'yn' with a noun offers an idiomatic and alternative method of rendering certain adjectival or adverbial phrases into Welsh. In these examples, Welsh has predicative 'yn' with a noun which corresponds to an equivalent adjectival phrase or descriptive element in English. All the examples apart from the last one arise from examples where an original Welsh text has been translated into English. Thus, these are examples of transposition, in this case translating nouns as adjectives, or vice versa. Note the tendency for the prepositional phrase '*i gyd*' to follow the noun. This strategy is one which readily lends itself to translation in the other direction when appropriate as evidenced by the final example.

Yna troes Monica ato a chododd ei chleddyf a thrywanodd ef rhwng ei ddwyfron oni syrthiodd **yn gelain** dros y dibyn i blith y dorf ... [MONICA 47]

Then Monica turned to him and, raising her sword, plunged it into his breast, so that he fell down **dead** [lit. as a corpse] and hurtled over the edge into the crowd below ... [MONICA 47]

A heno, yr oedd y plasty bach hynafol **yn dangnefedd i gyd**, a choch y gorllewin yn ei res ffenestri Sioraidd. [CRYMAN 12]

This evening, the ancient little grange looked **so peaceful** [lit. all peace] with the red glow from the western sky reflected in its row of Georgian windows. [SICKLE 8]

Sylwai pawb mor anniddig ydoedd, fel ci methedig yn ffroeni'r helfa ac **yn gynnwrf i gyd** ... [CYCHWYN 216]

All noticed how fretful he was, like a decrepit hound scenting its quarry and **all a quiver with eagerness** [lit. all excitement] ... [BEGIN 218]

Gangling and languid in his tallness, pale-skinned and feminine

Roedd **yn goesau a phennau gliniau i gyd** [lit. all legs and knees], in his features with a soft mouth and wide grey eyes . . . [TIME 78]

yn welw ei groen a merchetaidd ei wedd, gyda cheg feddal a llygaid llwyd llydain. [AMSER 123]

2.1.c.ii As an equivalent to 'like' or 'as' NOUN

This is implied in the examples above in 2.1.c.i and can be considered as a rather more formal option to the use of the preposition *'fel'* which often introduces comparisons.

Ni welodd mo'r wiwer **yn fellten goch** rhwng y brigau. [CRYMAN 31-32]

He didn't see the squirrel **like a red flash** between the branches. [SICKLE 24]

Aeth **yn dân gwyllt** trwy y lle. [CWM 60]

The story went through the district **like wildfire** . . . [GORSE 62]

. . . yn crwydro'r heolydd **yn ddynion i gyd** . . . [CYCHWYN 59]

. . . tramping the streets **like men grown** . . . [BEGIN 59]

2.1.c.iii The verb-noun 'BOD' + yn + NOUN corresponding to a semantically equivalent English verb

This is one particularly useful strategy for translating participles in English which can often be quite challenging. Corresponding adjectives are not always possible in these contexts and the use of 'bod' with predicative 'yn' and a noun can offer a semantically acceptable alternative. Our first examples focus on present participles.

Ym mhen isa'r dyffryn, tua Henberth, yr oedd niwlen wen, a honno'n drifftio i fyny'r llechweddau coediog, **yn fysedd ac yn fodiau i gyd**. [CRYMAN 18]

At the lower end of the Vale, towards Henberth, a white mist drifted up the wooded slopes, **poking into every nook and cranny** [lit. all fingers and thumbs]. [SICKLE 13]

Merch mewn mantell werdd, ei gwallt gwinau**'n gwmwl** am ei phen ac yn cyrlio i'w llygaid ac yn sgleinio gan y glaw. [CRYMAN 70]

A girl in a green raincoat, her brown hair **framing** [lit. a cloud about] her head and curling into her eyes and shining in the rain. [SICKLE 57]

'Mae'r peth **yn gysgod** ar eich meddwl chi, ond ydi?' [CYCHWYN 228]

'The matter is **overshadowing** your mind, isn't it?' [BEGIN 230]

In a similar way, the past participle can also be conveyed:

Bu arfau fy nhad yn llond fy meddwl . . . Maent **yn bentwr taclus** yng nghongl y cwt . . . [O LAW 197]	My father's quarry tools have been uppermost in my mind . . . They have been in a corner of the shed, **neatly piled up** . . . [FROM 163]
. . . fe gawson hyd iddo fo'n y fan honno ar ei linia ar ochor y lôn wedi tynnu ei sgidia â'i draed o'**n swigod i gyd** . . . [NOS 32]	. . . they found him there on his knees, with his shoes off and his feet **all blistered** . . . [NIGHT 24]

In addition, it is also possible to convey the English verb using this construction with more idiomatic impact than would result from the use of a simple periphrastic verb construction as shown in our final examples:

Yr oedd wyneb glandeg Karl **yn rhychau** ar ei hyd ac ar ei draws . . . [CRYMAN 29]	Karl's handsome face **was furrowed** and his eyes showed pain. [SICKLE 22]
He did as she suggested and let her thighs **cushion** his head. [VICT 151]	Gorweddodd a'i chluniau'**n obennydd** dan ei ben. [LLINYN 171]
. . . and both footmen, Alice noticed, had powdered hair <u>that curled all over their heads</u>. [ALICE 58]	. . . a sylwodd Alys fod gan y ddau fwtler wallt wedi'i bowdro, **yn gyrliau i gyd**. [ALYS II 54]

This construction lends itself particularly well in instances where a past participle in English is the semantical equivalent of '*covered in*' or '*bedecked in*'. Our final example here suggests that more contemporary writers in Welsh are adapting this to other semantical fields (in this case, a clothing trade name which is sufficient to convey what the character is wearing. Note how the English translation expands on this.)

'. . . and he would give these vagabonds leave to encamp on the few acres of **bramble-covered** land which represent the family estate . . .' [BAND 213]	'. . . ac mi fydd yn rhoi rhwydd hynt i'r rapsgaliwns hynny wersylla ar yr ychydig erwau o dir garw, a'r rheini'**n drwch o fieri**, sy'n weddill o ystâd y teulu . . .' [CYLCH 19–20]
Wedi bod yn lladd rhai o'r gwartheg ar y tircyfri oedd y taeogion, ac roeddynt oll **yn waed drostynt**. [PLA 111]	The serfs were slaughtering cattle on the bondlands, and they were **covered in blood**. [PEST 83]

... ac mae llawr y cyntedd **yn fôr o bapurach,** rhubanau a phentyrrau bach personol o anrhegion. [FFYDD 269]

The floor is **covered in paper** and ribbon and personal piles of presents. [FAITH 186]

Prin deirblwydd oed, a'i fochau'**n gymysgedd amryliw o laid a jam.** [CRYMAN 33]

He was scarcely three years old, his cheeks **smeared with dirt and jam.** [SICKLE 25]

... yn gwisgo siwt *Levi* las wedi colli'i lliw ... a bŵts cowboi sodle uchel, ac yn cario câs gitâr tolciog **yn sticeri awyren drosti.** [HUNAN 140]

... dressed in a faded blue Levi suit ... high-heeled western boots and carrying a battered guitar case **covered in airline stickers.** [SOLVA 140]

... cerdda Wil i mewn i ganol yr olygfa **yn Pringle i gyd** gan siarad ar ei ffôn symudol ... [FFYDD 55]

... I watch Will walk into view, **wearing a bright Pringle sweater** and holding his mobile to his ear. [FAITH 43]

The next example illustrates how this predicate noun construction can even correspond to a whole relative clause in English:

[A] byddai Pegi a finnau, **yn blant bach,** o dan ei gerydd am rywbeth neu'i gilydd, cyn amled â neb. [HDF 144]

[A]nd Pegi and I, **who were small children at the time,** were often rebuked by him for something or other. [OFH 179]

2.1.c.iv 'Yn' plus noun(s) to explain or restate an earlier noun

This device is useful for expanding on the meaning of a primary noun i.e. the noun which is the main focus of the sentence. In the first example, this has not been carried over fully into the English translation and is summarised in the expression '... *everything in its wake.*' The predicative '*yn*' is normally repeated after every noun when it is used in this way although our final example is one where this does not occur.

Tywalltodd y tân o Cathay i Persia, fforest o dân yn llosgi bob dim o'i flaen, **yn fynyddoedd, yn ddinasoedd, yn bobloedd, yn ddynion, yn ferched, yn blant.** Nid arbedwyd neb. **Yn hen nac yn ifanc.** [PLA 114]

... which hurled mighty hailstones and bolts of fire which struck from Persia to Cathay, a wild forest of fire, burning **everything in its wake** [lit. mountains, cities, people, men, women, children], sparing **neither young nor old.** [PEST 86]

Scarlet, green and gold, they all went into the mill together to produce high-quality cider . . . [CIDER 32]

Byddai'r cyfan ohonynt, **yn goch, yn wyrdd ac yn felyn,** yn mynd drwy'r felin gyda'i gilydd a chynhyrchu digon o seidr o'r radd flaenaf . . . [SEIDR 46]

. . . ym Mlaen Llechau yr ochr arall i'r cwm o Ferndale y ganed ac y maged y plant i gyd, mi gredaf – **yn bump o fechgyn** iach a chryfion . . . [CHWECH 109]

. . . *all the children were born and bred in Blaen Llechau at the other end of the valley to Ferndale – five healthy and strong boys . . .*

Yr oedd tyrfa fawr, **yn wŷr a gwragedd a phlant,** tu allan i'r Neuadd a chadwai rhyw ddwsin o blismyn olwg warcheidiol arnynt. [CHWAL 33]

Outside the Hall about a dozen constables were keeping a watchful eye on a large crowd **of men, women and children.** [OUT 33]

2.1.d. Uses of articles and demonstratives

2.1.d.i Family relationships with the definite article[3]

Prefixed personal pronouns denoting possession used to refer to family relationships are often replaced by the definite article in Welsh, especially in more informal registers. This is more common where the relationship is one with which the listener is already familiar and there is not need to specify what it is.

Mae**'r mab yng nghyfraith** yn gwerthu ceffyla. [PLA 71]

My son-in-law's a horse-dealer. [PEST 54]

'Does dim llawer er pan ges i de efo Mr a Mrs Morris **a'r ferch**.' [CYCHWYN 217]

'I had tea with the Morrises **and their daughter** not very long ago.' [BEGIN 219]

---

[3] A similar use of the definite article for parts of the body should also be noted as in the two examples below:

'Yr ydw' i'n poeni am **y llygaid 'ma**. Mi ddaeth Dafydd â'r 'Llusern' imi gynna', ond 'fedra' i ddim gwneud rhych na rhawn o'r print.' [CYCHWYN 38]

'I am worried about **these eyes of mine**. Dafydd brought the 'Lantern' to me just now, but I can't make out the print at all.' [BEGIN 37]

Dechreuai'i bregeth bob amser yn dawel. [. . .] Cyn hir **codai'r llais**, âi afon redegog yn rhaeadr . . . [CYCHWYN 47]

He invariably began his sermon quietly. [. . .] Ere long **his voice rose** sharply, the rolling river of words became a waterfall . . . [BEGIN 46]

A dim ond weithiau y mae'**r gŵr** yn gweithio. [TRAED 187]

My husband only works sometimes. [FEET 154]

2.1.d.ii Epithets/insults in Welsh using the definite article

Welsh does not employ the pronoun '*you*' before these as is usual in English. The definite article is almost always used here in Welsh and this is occasionally followed by the preposition '*i*' (also '*â*') which can be conjugated to refer back to the recipient of the insult as is the case in the first example below. Our final example illustrates how some translators have used the literal translation of the definite article back into English as a device for emphasising the Welshness of a particular context.

Y bwystfil blêr i ti . . .
[CRYMAN 79]

You blundering oaf . . .
[SICKLE 64]

'Oh, **you wicked wicked little thing!**' cried Alice, catching up the kitten, and giving it a little kiss to make it understand that it was in disgrace. [THRO 128]

'O, **yr hen gath fach ddrwg!**' gwaeddodd Alys gan godi'r gath fach a rhoi cusan iddi ddeall ei bod dan gerydd. [TRWY 13]

'**Liar,**' she said, laughing white teeth and pink tongue. [TIME 106]

'**Y celwyddgi,**' meddai, gan chwerthin eto gyda'i dannedd gwynion a'i thafod pinc. [AMSER 169]

'I'll give you pigtails, **you little rat!**' [MAT 114]

'Fe gei di blethau, **y llygoden fach â ti!**' [MAT 108]

'Wel, **y diawl bach,**' meddai rhyw fachgen o'r tu ôl. 'Y nhwrn i oedd hwnna.' [TRAED 35]

'Well, **the little devil,**' said a boy from behind, 'that was my turn.' [FEET 31–2]

2.1.d.iii Epithets of trade or profession: metonomy of place for the person

Metonomy is common in Welsh with reference to a place with which a person is closely associated. Names (in particular surnames) in Welsh are frequently linked to places or professions which allow someone to be differentiated from others sharing the same surname (or even a common given name). For example, two different people sharing the surname *Jones*, one of whom works as a butcher and the other a taxi driver, might be referred to, respectively, as *Jones y cig / Jones bwtsiwr* [= *Jones the meat / Jones butcher*] or *Jones y gyrrwr / Jones tacsi* [= *Jones the driver / Jones taxi*]. The first example below is one where the translator into Welsh has employed metonomy to refer to the daughter of a publican.

. . . the publican's daughter, Sally Shoesmith. [CIDER 32]	Sally Shoesmith, **merch y dafarn leol** . . . [SEIDR 46]
Câi ei dial ar honno hefyd am ei gwneud hi'n gyff gwawd i bawb wrth i **Jones Plismon** ei thywys i ben draw'r ciw. [RHANNU 178]	*She would get revenge on that one too for making her the laughing stock of everyone when **Jones the policeman** led her to the end of the queue.*
Yna, â'r gynulleidfa ar ei heistedd, cenid un o donau hwyliog y plant o Raglen y Gymanfa, a **Dafydd Ifans y Siop**, y codwr canu, yn arwain. [CHWECH 77]	*Then, with the audience seated, one of the children's cheery tunes from the Cymanfa programme was sung with **Dafydd Ifans the Shop**, leading the singing.*

2.1.d.iv Noun with demonstrative 'cw [= acw] not rendered in English (or equivalent to first person plural pronoun)
The demonstrative '*acw*' (frequently shortened to *'cw* in speech) is semantically connected with nouns or situations/locations which are at some distance from the speaker. It is not always possible to render this in English, especially when it is encountered in informal registers where it has a vague sense of '*over there*' which either doesn't need to be matched in English or cannot be mirrored by an equivalent expression. We give several examples where it corresponds to '*our (place of residence)*'. It should also be noted that it can be used to refer to one's home when the speaker alludes to it in another location usually with an implicit understanding that the listener knows where that location is.

'Deuddeg o'n i'n cychwyn **o'r Borth 'cw**, ond yr oedd gin i fwstás a locsyn pan ddois yn f' ôl.' [CHWAL 110]	'Twelve I was when I started from Porth, but I had a moustache and whiskers when I got back.' [OUT 116]
'They were living together in the apartment,' he told them. [TIME 53]	'Roedden nhw'n byw efo'i gilydd **yn y fflat 'cw**,' dywedodd wrthynt. [AMSER 83–4]
'Gadewch i mi siarad efo fo, Mr Morris. Mi a'i â fo **acw** i swpar heno.' [CYCHWYN 127–8]	'Let me speak with him, Mr Morris. I will take him to supper **at my house** tonight.' [BEGIN 128]

'Diawcs, mae gan **Dafydd** 'cw feddwl ohono 'i hun y dyddia' yma, fachgan,' meddai Dic . . . [CHWAL 138]

'Diawcs, **our Dafydd** thinks himself somebody these days, lad,' Dick remarked . . . [OUT 138]

'Pam na ddowch chi **acw?**'

'Why don't you come **home** with me?'

'**Acw?**'

'**Home** –'

'Mae'r mab yng nghyfraith yn gwerthu ceffyla. Dwi'n siŵr y basa fo'n fodlon eich helpu chi.' [PLA 71]

'My son-in-law's a horse-dealer. I'm sure he could help you.' [PEST 54]

2.1.e. Nouns in apposition with the preposition 'o': NOUN o NOUN (occasionally ADJECTIVE o NOUN)

This is a productive construction in Welsh where one of the nouns is the 'main noun' and the other fulfils a descriptive or modifying function. In our discussion of these nouns, we have divided our examples into semantically similar groupings where either the first or the second noun is in apposition to another noun. It is also possible for the first noun to be replaced by an adjective or by a demonstrative. The use of an adjective + 'o' + noun is more prevalent in informal registers.

The first noun relates to immensity or size

Yr oedd y siopwr – mi gwelaf o y munud hwn – yn **glamp o ddyn tal** . . . [GWEN 20]

The shopkeeper, whom I can see this very moment, **a big, tall man** . . . [GWEN 26]

The description of '*a big, tall man*' could also be given by mirroring the English with a noun and two adjectives – in this case, '*dyn mawr, tal*'. The NOUN + o + NOUN modifier offers a stylistic alternative to simply following the same pattern.

The Fish-Footman began by producing from under his arm a **great letter** . . . [ALICE 59]

Dechreuodd y Bwtler-Bysgodyn trwy gymryd o dan ei gesail **glamp o lythyr** . . . [ALYS II 54]

Cawr o ddyn gwladaidd, afrosgo, oedd y **priodfab o hwsmon**, yn araf a chynnil ei eiriau, a dwfn iawn ei lais. [CYCHWYN 138]

The bridegroom, a farm-bailiff by calling, was a **huge, clumsy yokel**, deep-voiced and sparing of words. [BEGIN 138]

... a hefyd **cloben o gath ddu
anferth** a orweddai ar y gadair . . .
[GWEN 29]

... a **large black cat** which lay asleep
on a chair. [GWEN 34]

The first noun is an expletive[4]

'Mae Dan bach 'di ca'l **cythral o
gollad** . . ' [RHANNU 214]

'*Good old Dan has had a **helluva
loss** . . .'*

Other combinations here include:

uffern o, coblyn o, andros o, diawl o

They all share a similar function of strengthening the sense of the main noun
they are modifying within an informal register or dialogue.

The first element is a demonstrative (the neutral 'hyn' or 'hynny')

This is an alternative to the more usual noun + gender specific demonstrative.
Its use tends to be more within formal contexts however some combinations
have become commonly used expressions e.g. '*yn hyn o beth*' (= in this
respect, in this matter) and '*ar hyn o bryd*' (at this moment). The use of the
plural '*hynny*' is less common and can be used in the formula '*hynny + o +
NOUN + a + VERB*' to convey a limited amount of the noun in question.

Nid oedd **hyn o argraff** yn gywir . . .
[DYDD 93]

***This impression** wasn't correct . . .*

Cyn gorffen **hyn o bennod** . . .
[WILLAT 125]

*Before finishing **this chapter** . . .*

Y noson honno, noson glir,
serennog, swatiodd y pump ohonynt
o amgylch tân bychan. Doedd
hynny o wres a ddeuai ohono'n
ddim. [PLA 200]

*That night, a clear, starry night, the
five of them huddled around a small
fire. **The amount of heat** coming
from it was (almost) nothing.*

The second noun is an ethnicity

This is a useful alternative to using adjectives of ethnicity. Our first example
could have been rendered '*meddyg uchel Seisnig*' and '*gwas ffarm Almeinig*'

---

[4] See also section 9.6 on swearing/profanity in Chapter 9.

but the use of the noun is a stronger, less ambiguous marker of ethnicity and the NOUN + o + NOUN construction facilitates this.

Yr oeddent yn dystion o'r gymrodoriaeth sydyn a oedd wedi troi **meddyg uchel o Sais** a **gwas ffarm o Almaenwr** yn ddim ond dau filwr yn yr un uffern. [CRYMAN 51]

They were witnesses to the same comradeship which had reduced **an eminent English doctor** and a **German farmhand** to two soldiers sharing the same hell. [SICKLE 40]

Gan y bydd y **darllenydd o Gymro neu Gymraes** yn hen gyfarwydd eisoes â phrif ffrydiau llenyddiaeth Gymraeg . . . [BIRT 100]

*As the **Welsh** [implicitly Welsh-speaking – both masculine and feminine versions of the ethnicity noun 'Cymro/Cymraes' are used]* **reader** *will already be very familiar with the main streams of Welsh literature . . .*

Es i am ginio unwaith gyda **ffrind o Lydawr** . . . [CRWYD 14]

*I once went for dinner with a **Breton friend** . . .*

. . . fe'i dilynwyd gan Dr D. Dilwyn John, **mab di-Gymraeg i ffermwr o Gymro** ym Mro Morgannwg. [RHWNG 101–2]

. . . *he was followed by Dr D. Dilwyn John, **the non-Welsh-speaking son of a Welsh** [speaking] **farmer** from the Vale of Glamorgan.*

The second noun is a profession

. . . fe fenthyces i recordydd stereo chwarter trac Sony gan **ffrind o forwr**. . . [HUNAN 164]

. . . *I borrowed a Sony quarter-track stereo recorder from a **sailor friend** . . .* [SOLVA 164]

. . . byddai'n arfer mynd ar ddydd Sul i'r capel ac ymddiddan ar y ffordd â'i **gymdogion o ffermwyr** yn Llansadwrn. [BIRT 260]

. . . *he would usually go to chapel on Sundays and converse on the way with his **farmer neighbours** in Llansadwrn.*

Yn ddiweddarach, fe syrthies i mewn cariad â **merch o au-pair** o Odense yn Nenmarc . . . [HUNAN 117]

*I fell in love with a Danish **au-pair girl** from Odense . . .* [SOLVA 117]

Clywsai Dan si o lawer cyfeiriad i'w **gŵr o deiliwr** adael arian mawr a thai ar ei ôl; [CHWAL 171]

Dan had heard it rumoured in various quarters that **her husband, a tailor**, had left a large sum of money and considerable property; [OUT 180]

... gan orfod edmygu er hynny ogoniant y llais a'r llefaru ac angerdd ysgubol y **proffwyd o chwarelwr**. [CYCHWYN 47]	... while nonetheless constrained to admire the glorious voice and impassioned ardour of the **quarryman-prophet**. [BEGIN 46]
... trefnwyd i ffarwelio â'r hen flaenor ac â'r **llanc o bregethwr** yr un pryd ... [CYCHWYN 237]	... arrangements were made to say goodbye to the old deacon and the **budding preacher** at the same time. [BEGIN 239]

The second noun is a word for man/woman or boy/girl or husband/wife

Llygoden fach o ddynes yswil, nerfus ... [CHWAL 171]	A shy, nervous **little mouse of a girl** ... [OUT 180]
Swydd eglwysig, Seisnigaidd oedd, gwahanol a hollol groes i'r uchelgais i ddringo pulpud Moreia, **hen wlanen o ddyn** yn gwisgo coler-gron a het fflat a socasau ... [DYDD 115]	*It was an ecclesiastic, English job, different and the complete opposite of his ambition to go up into the pulpit at Moreia, **an old drip [of a man]** wearing a dog-collar and a flat hat and gaiters ...*
Grêt o ferch – pladres bryd golau, ond â chorff union gymesur. [HUNAN 117]	She was a **tremendous girl** – a huge blonde, but with a perfectly proportioned figure. [SOLVA 117]
Ac fel y sylwai Owen ar **fechgyn eraill o 'rybelwyr'**, sylweddolai mor hynod ffodus ydoedd. [CYCHWYN 71]	And Owen, observing **other boys, rubble-shifters like himself**, realised how remarkably fortunate he was. [BEGIN 71]
Pwy yn ei iawn bwyll fyddai'n dewis ei glymu ei hun wrth ferch sbwnjer diog fel hwn a'i **hen slwt gegog o wraig**? [RHANNU 214]	*Who in his right mind would chose to tie himself to the daughter of a lazy old sponger like him and his **old mouthy slut of a wife**?*

The second noun is "peth" (= 'thing')

It is not always possible to find a direct translation equivalent for 'peth' in this construction. Occasionally, there is fairly direct equivalence e.g. 'da o beth' = 'a good thing' however this is not always the case and as our examples show, the translator may need to expand the construction in English to convey its meaning fully.

Yr oedd ganddi lais soprano peraidd ac yr oedd wedi arfer ei ddefnyddio bob Sul er pan oedd yn **ddim-o-beth**. [LLEIFIOR 27]

She had a fine soprano voice and she had used it every Sunday **since childhood**. [*Lit: since she was nothing of a thing*]. [RETURN 21]

'Whiw!' chwibanodd Wmffre, 'dene **felltith o beth**.' [GWEN 87]

'Whew! That's **bad luck**.' [*Lit: a curse of a thing*] [GWEN 76]

Ond y mae'n **helynt o beth** fod y gallu i ddarllen cerddoriaeth yn mynd yn brinnach, brinnach mewn gwlad mor gerddorol ei hanian. [WILLAT 46]

But it's a **troublesome thing** [*Lit: a trouble of a thing*] that the ability to read music is becoming rarer and rarer in a country with such a musical spirit.

Syn o beth oedd gweld y dieithriaid hyn a drigai yn y fwrdeisdref a'r castell yng Nghricieth. [PLA 180]

It was **an astonishing thing** [*Lit: an astonishment of a thing*] to see these strangers living in the borough and the castle in Cricieth.

Other examples

These illustrate that this construction can be applied to other contexts and that writers have adapted it to their own needs and styles. In this sense, it is as productive in formal contexts as those more informal ones discussed earlier in this section.

Mae hi'n ddel, ond bod ganddi wyneb fel plentyn wedi'i sbwylio, a **phwt o drwyn**. [MONICA 7]

She's pretty, but she has the face of a spoilt child, and a **snub nose**. [MONICA 5]

Roedd ei gusan yn brifo'i gwefusau, mor wahanol i'r **ieir bach yr ha' o gusanau** y bu Dan a hithau'n eu rhannu. [RHANNU 171]

His kiss hurt her lips, so different to the **butterfly kisses** [*Lit: butterflies of kisses*] that Dan and she had been sharing.

. . . nid oedd gennyf unrhyw amheuaeth bellach fy mod wedi glanio mewn **Sodom o le** a'm bod ar goll . . . [DYDD 14]

. . . *I had no doubt now that I had landed in a **Sodom of a place** and that I was lost. . .*

Ac er eu gwaethaf troai'r crintachrwydd yn wir edmygedd pan glywid, yn yr emyn olaf,

And despite themselves their grudging acknowledgement turned to genuine admiration when his

y **môr o lais** yn arwain y gân. [CYCHWYN 47]

voice, mighty as the sea [*Lit: the sea of a voice*] led the singing of the final hymn. [BEGIN 46–7]

Edinburgh was a schizophrenic city, **the place of Jekyll & Hyde** sure enough, the city of Deacon Brodie ... [...] He hunted in **the hard-man's drinking dens**, in the housing estates ... [KNOTS 220]

Dinas sgitsoffrenig oedd hi, ia, **Jekyll a Hyde o ddinas** yn bendant iawn, dinas Deacon Brodie ... [...] Bu'n hela ym mhob **ffau llewod o dafarn** [*Lit: every lions den of a pub*] y gwyddai amdani ... [CHWERW 187]

NOUN + o + ADJECTIVE / ADJECTIVE + o + NOUN[5]

The examples of NOUN + o + ADJECTIVE are normally comparative ones, preceded by '*fel*'. The adjective in the ADJECTIVE + o + NOUN construction is almost always a modifier of the second noun.

'Yr ydw i wedi bod **fel llygoden o ddistaw**,' ebe hi. [SELYF 118]

'*I have been as quiet as a mouse*,' she said. [*Lit: like a mouse of quiet*].

Agorodd y drws **fel malwoden o ara'** ... [AMSER 252]

... he unlocked the door at **a deliberate snail's pace** ... [TIME 158] [*Lit: like a snail of slow*]

Nid oeddwn i **yn fawr o werth** fel bargeiniwr ... [CHWECH 182]

I wasn't of much use [*Lit: great of value/worth*] *as a negotiator* ...

Ond **bychan o beth** ydoedd hyn; [WILLAT 66]

But that was a small matter.

2.1.f. Verb-noun used or translated as a noun
By its very definition, the Welsh verb-noun can be used either as a verb (in a periphrastic construction) or as a noun. Indeed, it is often more appropriate – stylistically – to use a verb-noun where English has a noun, in particular more abstract nouns. Verb-nouns treated as full nouns routinely get assigned the masculine gender:

y caru / y gweithio / y torri i mewn ...   *NB gafael >> mynd i'r afael*

---

[5] See also Chapter 8 sections 8.1.5.i and 8.1.5.ii.

They can also be modified by adjectives (*y canu hyfryd*), demonstratives (*y canu hwn*) etc.

Bob gyda'r nos a phrynhawn Sadwrn clywid eco ei gŷn a'i forthwyl dros yr ardal, ac yna glec sydyn **y saethu**. [TRAED 27]

Every evening and Saturday afternoon the sound of his hammer and chisel was heard throughout the district, followed by the sharp crack of **the explosion**. [FEET 24]

Ac yn awr fe'i daliwyd gan afiechyd cyn i'r tŷ fod yn barod, canlyniad y **gweithio caled**. [TRAED 27]

And now illness had overtaken him before the house was ready, the result of **the hard work**. [FEET 24]

Yno cawsant bwyllgor dwys ynghylch llenni i'r ffenestri, matiau i'r lloriau, llathau i'r grisiau, silffoedd a bachau a phethau tebyg, a phennwyd dydd **y symud**. [CHWAL 148]

There they debated earnestly about such matters as curtains for the windows, floor-mats, stair rods, hooks and shelves, and decided upon a date for **the move**. [OUT 156]

Quite often, the English equivalent is a gerund, thus an English verbal noun which is itself quite like the Welsh verb-noun.

[D]on't be thinking she wasn't involved in **chummy's drug trafficking**. [TIME 96]

[P]aid â dechra meddwl nad oedd ganddi hi ddim i'w wneud efo'**r delio cyffuriau**. [AMSER 153]

Rhan o swyn **y caru hwn** ydoedd ei ddirgelwch honedig i'r cariadon. [HDF 110]

A part of the charm of **this courting** was its pretence of being a secret between the two lovers. [OFH 135]

Ond yn ôl at Jaci Penrhiw, ynteu, wedi'**r crwydro maith hwn** ar ôl ei achau ef a'i briod. [HDF 64]

But to return to Jaci Penrhiw after **this long wandering** on the trail of his lineage and of his wife's. [OFH 76]

Nid oedd **y troi cefn a'r gadael** yn ddim o'i gymharu â bwriad yr adar duon o fradychu eu cydweithwyr, yma ar eu tomen eu hunain. [RHANNU 119]

This turning one's back and leaving were nothing compared to the strike breakers' intention to betray their fellow workers, here on their own ground.

2.2 Pronouns

2.2.a "It" ("What") = y peth

This section and 2.b. examine ways in which the English gender-neutral pronoun '*it*' (of which there is no equivalent in Welsh) may be conveyed. The definite article '*y*' and the noun '*peth*' (= *thing*) will occasionally be used in Welsh where the pronoun '*it*' is more likely in English. This holds true particularly when it is used in place of the pronoun '*yr hyn*' (or informally '*beth*') at the beginning of a relative clause which is the complement of a copular sentence. When '*y peth*' is used with a neutral pronoun meaning, it may also correspond to English '*something*' or '*nothing*' if the accompanying verb is negative.

Rogers moved to join her, conceding a sort of defeat, though not feeling unduly cast down **about it**[6].
[TIME 102]

Symudodd Rogers i ymuno â hi, gan gyfaddef rywfodd ei fod wedi ei drechu, ac na theimlai'n arbennig o flin **ynglŷn â'r peth**. [AMSER 163]

Y peth a'i gwylltiai oedd fod y peth wedi mynd ymlaen mor hir . . .
[TRAED 58]

What made her angry was that **it** had gone on for such a long time . . .
[FEET 51]

I was only wondering why you didn't **report it** to us at the time . . .
[TIME 15]

Dim ond meddwl roeddwn i, tybed pam nad oeddach chi 'di **reportio'r peth** i ni bryd hynny . . .
[AMSER 23]

Y peth a bwysai fwyaf ar feddwl Ifan oedd sut yr âi i dŷ ei fam i nôl Sioned. [TRAED 58]

What weighed heaviest on his mind was how he was going to go to his mother's house to fetch Sioned.
[FEET 51]

Peth ar ei ben ei hun yw stryd mewn maestref o'r dosbarth canol.
[MONICA 38]

Now a road in a middle-class suburb is **something unique**.
[MONICA 37]

. . . then she would find it difficult to refer to a man she had been living with and about whom she must presume **I knew nothing**.
[TIME 90]

. . . yna mi fyddai hi'n ei chael hi'n anodd cyfeirio at ddyn yr oedd hi wedi bod yn byw efo fo, a hithau'n cymryd yn ganiataol **na wyddwn i ddim am y peth**. [AMSER 143]

---

[6] Compare this to the use of '*amdani*' in section 2.2.b of this chapter.

2.2.b. Nonreferential feminines[7]

When a verb is followed by a preposition and is either nonreferential or connected with an '*it*' pronoun, this almost always corresponds to the feminine third person singular in Welsh. Given that combinations with different prepositions in this context occur fairly commonly in Welsh and can be either as the object of a verb or as its subject, we have divided our discussion below accordingly. Examples are also given of the use of the nonreferential feminine directly with a verb (both as object and as subject). The actual pronoun '*hi*' is not always used, especially in more formal contexts, however any preposition will still be in the third person singular feminine conjugation or when the direct object of a verb, the initial '*ei*' remains together with the associated aspirate mutation.

In general, pronouns (words like *he, she, it, him, her*) refer back to some noun that has recently occurred in the discourse, and whose referent is recoverable (identifiable) by speakers or listeners. For instance, in the exchange: *What do you think of my new shirt? I don't think **it** matches those trousers*, the pronoun '*it*' refers back to the noun '*shirt*', which is the most recent appropriate referent for it. This is the most usual way of using pronouns. Occasionally, however, some languages use pronouns in nonreferential ways, i.e. in uses in which there is no referent for the pronoun at all: its use in such cases is simply idiomatic and must be learned as such. In English, the pronoun '*it*' is used nonreferentially, for instance in weather expressions (*it is raining / it was really windy*) and in impersonal expressions (*it is important to learn verbs*). It can also occur in some idioms as a dummy direct object ('*dummy*' being another term for '*nonreferential*'), such as *to beat it / to suck it up / to cop it*. In Welsh, which has no exact equivalent for '*it*', the pronoun which is used nonreferentially in numerous idioms is '*hi*', literally '*she*'.

2.2.b.i Object

(1) Amdani:

(i) *Nothing for it/ Nothing to be done . . . but . . .*

However, there was the hill full in sight, so **there was little to be done** but start again. [THRO 139]	Fodd bynnag, dyna lle'r oedd y bryn yn y golwg, a **'doedd dim amdani** ond ail-gychwyn. [TRWY 26]
Nid oedd dim amdani, wedyn, ond i'r ecseisman fynd yno i weld â'i lygaid ei hun. [HDF 137]	**There was then nothing for the exciseman to do** but go and see for himself. [OFH 172]

---

[7] PWT (4.131) calls this the '*hi* gwag' or 'empty *hi*' i.e. when it refers to a general rather than a specific state.

(ii) The expression *'y gwir amdani'* corresponding to *'the (plain) truth is'* / *'the fact is'*

'[D]yma'r wagan fwya cythreulig yn holl greadigaeth Duw; dyna ydi'r **gwir plaen amdani** . . . [HEN ATGOFION 126]

'[T]his is the most fiendish waggon in the whole of God's creation; that's **the plain truth** . . . [LOCUST 109]

Y gwir amdani oedd bod Trev yn ddylanwad anwaraidd ac yn godwr twrw. [HUNAN 110]

The truth was that Trev was an unruly influence, a shit stirrer to put it bluntly. . . [SOLVA 110]

Y gwir amdani oedd nad trio neidio'r ceunant yr oedd, ond fe'i hyrddiwyd bron trosodd gan y twr bechgyn cryf . . . [TRAED 33]

The fact was that he hadn't wished to jump the gully, but he had been almost flung over by the crowd of hefty lads . . . [FEET 30]

(iii) *Verb + am + nonreferential feminine*

'Tyd 'laen. Mi w't ti'n **gofyn amdani** tro 'ma.' [RHANNU 190]

'Come on. You're **asking for it** this time.'

(2) Arni:

(i) *Dechrau arni = To get going, begin doing something*

Pan oedd Begw yn meddwl pa bryd y caent ddechrau ar eu te, dyma Winni yn **dechrau arni** wedyn. [TE 41]

Just as Begw was thinking of starting with her tea, Winni **began talking** again. [TEA 40]

'[. . .] [D]oeddan ni brin wedi **dechra arni** bora 'ma nad oedd rhyw grwydryn . . . yn trwyna yn ein petha ni . .' [PLA 158]

'[. . .] [W]e'd only just got going this morning when some tramp . . . starting sticking his nose in our business . . .'

Ar ôl cael tamaid o swper, gwthiwyd y bwrdd yn ôl a gwneud cylch o gwmpas y tân, a gwyddai Begw y byddai Dafydd Siôn yn **dechrau arni**. [TE 28–9]

After supper the table was pushed back so that we all sat in a half-circle round the fire. Begw knew that Dafydd Siôn would **get going** any moment now. [TEA 29]

(ii) *Cael hwyl arni = To be enjoying it / getting into it*

These were local townspeople putting on a show. **Not badly. In fact, rather well.** [VICT 97]

Criw o'r dre yn creu dipyn o ddifyrrwch oedd y rhain, ac yn **cael hwyl eithaf arni** hefyd. [LLINYN 109]

(3) Ati:

Dal ati = To keep at it / keep doing something[8]

Yn fy nyddiau coleg diweddarach ni fyddwn yn methu yr un arholiad. Rhyw grafu trwyddi yn nes i'r gwaelod nag i'r top a wnawn yn ddieithriad; ond yn **dal ati** o hyd fel y crwban hwnnw. [CHWECH 243]	*In my later college days I wouldn't miss any exams. Without exception, I would scrape by nearer the bottom than the top; but I would still **keep going** like that old tortoise.*

Keep playing. [STONE 246]   **Dal ati i chwarae.** [MAEN 219]

(4) Iddi:

(i) *Bwrw iddi = To get on with, immerse/throw oneself fully in something*

O'r dechrau cyntaf wedi i 'nhadcu symud i Benrhiw ymddengys iddo **fwrw iddi**'n ddyfal ac egniol 'yn cloddio a bwrw tail' . . . [HDF 75]	When my grandfather came to Penrhiw he **threw himself into it** from the start, energetically and persistently 'digging and dunging' . . . [OFH 90]
Roedd pethe fel hyn yn digwydd i bawb; roedd rhaid i bobol jyst **bwrw iddi** a gobeithio'r gore. [HUNAN 13]	Such things were happening to just about everyone, and people had **to get on with** their lives and hope for the best. [SOLVA 13]

(ii) In the expression *Rhoi'r gorau iddi = To give something up, quit doing something*

'Only it got so cold, and it snowed so, they had to **leave off**.' [THRO 128]	'Ond fe drodd mor oer, a bwrw eira gymaint fel y bu rhaid iddyn nhw **roi'r gorau iddi**.' [TRWY 14]

(5) Trwyddi:

(i) *Bwrw trwyddi = To manage, cope* (lit.: to hit through it)

Yr oedd Ifan yn falch bod ei wraig yn **bwrw drwyddi** mor huawdl . . . [TRAED 63]	Ifan was pleased that his wife was **dealing with the situation** so capably . . . [FEET 55]

---

[8] In the imperative '*daliwch ati*' the meaning is '*keep at it / keep going / persevere*'.

(ii) *Dod trwyddi* = *To come through [it], cope*

If her mother had anything to do with it, she would **cope** admirably . . . [KNOTS 82]	Os byddai a wnelo 'i mam rywbeth â hynny, **fe ddeuai drwyddi**'n iawn . . . [CHWERW 70]

(iii) *Torri trwyddi* = *To cut to the chase, get to the point*

A chofiaf amdano byth, wedi hir betruso, ryw noswaith ar dop North Street ar ein ffordd adref o'r gwaith gyda'n gilydd . . . yn **torri trwyddi** o'r diwedd ac yn gofyn yn syth i fi: 'A fyddi di'n *bartner* i fi, 'te?' [CHWECH 108]	*And I always remember him, after a long hesitation, one night at the top of North Street on our way home from work together . . .* **getting to the point** *at last and asking me directly: 'Will you be my partner then?'*

(6) With a compound preposition:

Ar ôl with the sense of being delayed, behind, late.

They were, after all, over an hour **late**. [CIDER 33]	Wedi'r cwbl, roeddent dros awr **ar ei hôl hi**'n cyrraedd. [SEIDR 47]

'Two days **wrong**!' sighed the Hatter. [ALICE 70]	'Dau ddiwrnod **ar 'i hôl hi**!' ebe'r Hetiwr gydag ochenaid. [ALYS II 41]

(7) With (transitive) verbs: As the 'dummy' object in numerous informal expressions all meaning more or less '*to leave*' (cf. the similar '*to beat it*' in English).

Well inni'**i throi hi** . . . [PLA 86]	We'd better **get a move on** . . . [PEST 67]
Wedi i'r ddau y tu allan hen gyrraedd pen eu tennyn ac yn awyddus i'**w heglu hi** . . . [PLA 88]	The other two were frantic with impatience, longing to **get out** . . . [PEST 69]
A dyma ni i gyd yn **ei chychwyn hi** am Weun . . . [NOS 45]	So we **set off** for the Waun . . . [NIGHT 36]
'Cerwch i nôl eich gitâr. Fydd yn rhaid i ni '**i siapo hi** – maen nhw'n disgwyl amdanoch chi yn y Sherman.' [HUNAN 274]	'Get your guitar. We'll have **to go** now [lit. get a move on / shape up]. They're waiting for you in the Sherman.' [SOLVA 274]

Rhuthrodd y mab ar ôl ci Iorwerth
Gam ond fe wyddai'r ci'n amgenach
ac **fe'i miglodd hi** tua'r stesion . . .
[WILLAT 97]

*The son rushed after Iorwerth Gam's
dog but the dog knew differently and
bolted off towards the station . . .*

Daeth ysfa tros Ddic Bugail i
gydio yn ei barseli a**'i gwadnu
hi** am ei fywyd yn ôl i'r Gogledd.
[CHWAL 82]

An urge came over Dick Shepherd
to lay hold of his bundles and **leg it**
back North for dear life. [OUT 85]

(8) With the verb 'cael':

(i) To find (experience) something + adjective

Lingard, wondering if Deborah
had given the daft bugger a cocaine
Mickey Finn and **finding it difficult**
to keep a straight face, said . . .
[TIME 82]

Gan ddyfalu tybed a oedd
Debbie wedi rhoi Mickey Finn
llawn cocên i'r diawl bach gwirion,
a**'i chael hi'n anodd** iawn cadw
wyneb syth, meddai Lingard . . .
[AMSER 130]

She said that **they found it difficult**
to understand with the proprietor
interpreting . . . [TIME 46]

Dywedodd hithau eu bod nhw'n
ei chael hi'n anodd deall gan fod
y perchennog yn cyfieithu . . .
[AMSER 72-3]

Yn y dechrau roedd y chwarelwyr
llechi . . . yn **ei chael hi'n ddrwg**
dan law'r perchennog, yr Arglwydd
Penrhyn. [CRWYD 128]

*In the beginning the slate
quarrymen . . . **had a hard time** [lit.
found it bad] under the owner, Lord
Penrhyn.*

(ii) To be 'in for it', to 'cop' it

Fi fydd yn **'i chael hi** gan 'Mam pan
awn ni adra'. [CHWAL 16]

It's I who **will cop it** from Mam
when we get home. [OUT 16]

(9) Others:

(i) Gwneud = To make (it) + adjective

Ond yn gymysg â hyn oll yr oedd
rhyw bengamrwydd pinwyngar a**'i
gwnâi hi'n** fynych **yn anodd iawn**
byw gydag ef. [HDF 143]

But mixed with this there was that
opinionated wrongheadedness that
sometimes **made it a very hard
thing** [lit. made it very difficult] to
live with him. [OFH 179]

(ii) Cychwyn = To make / start / head (off) for

Felly fe rois i draed dani a'**i** **chychwyn hi** am ddiogelwch cymharol canol y ddinas. [HUNAN 81]	So I quickened my pace and **headed** for the comparative safety of the city centre. [SOLVA 81]

(iii) Mentro (ar) = To venture (something) / Give (something) a go

... os yw pawb arall yn bwyta'r pethau gwaharddedig hyn i fi – a byw, pan na allwn innau **ei mentro hi**? [CHWECH 39]	*... if everyone else is eating these things which are forbidden to me – and living, why can't I **give it a go** too?*
Even so, it was wise to broach the possibility before Saturday. I **took the opportunity** the next evening. [CIDER 32]	... tybiwn y byddai'n ddoeth imi grybwyll y posibilrwydd cyn dydd Sadwrn. **Mentrais arni** y noson ganlynol. [SEIDR 46]

(iv) Bod wrthi = To be at it, to be doing it

Yn un ar bymtheg oed gallai John gnoi dybaco a smocio pib fel petai wedi **bod wrthi** o'r crud ... [CHWECH 79]	*At sixteen years of age John could chew tobacco and smoke a pipe as if he had **been doing it** / **at it** since he was born ...*

(v) Various other examples of the nonreferential feminine as the object of a verb:

Oherwydd pa frenin y goedwig, mewn difri, a chanddo ddim parch i'w stumog a'**i gwelai hi**'n werth estyn ei bawen am ryw lipryn llwyd fel hwn ... [CHWECH 111]	*But what king of the forest, in all seriousness, with any respect for his stomach, would **consider it** [Lit: see it] worthwhile to stretch out his paw for a pale weakling like that ...*
Roedd y newyddion fod Godfrey yn dal yn fyw ac yn iach ac, yn bwysicach, yn **ei lordio hi** o gwmpas yr ardal, wedi ysgwyd Jojo fwy nag y disgwyliai. [LLADD 184]	*The news that Godfrey was still alive and well and, more importantly, **lording it** about the area, had shaken Jojo more than he expected.*
Byddai wedi **ei gadael hi** ar hynny am y tro, ond teimlodd ei waed yn berwi pan ddwedodd Edward ... [RHANNU 106]	*'He would have **left it** at that for the time being, but he felt his blood boiling inside him when Edward said ...'*

Sut wyt ti'n **ei mwynhau hi?** [CRYMAN 83]	How are you **enjoying it?** [SICKLE 68]
O, do, a bu ond y dim iddo **roi** **ei droed ynddi** drwy gyfaddef ar funud gwan ei fod yn gweld ei cholli. [RHANNU 102]	*Oh, yes, and he nearly **put his foot in** **it** by confessing that he missed her.*

2.2.b.ii Subject

The following example shows that where a masculine pronoun might be expected to correspond to English '*it*', Welsh again shows preference for the feminine '*hi*' as a subject pronoun as well as an object pronoun:

'What day of the month **is it?**' [ALICE 70]	'Pa ddiwrnod o'r mis **yw hi?**' [ALYS II 68]

There is no gender association between the '*it*' (= '*hi*') and the nouns '*diwrnod / day*' or '*mis / month*' both of which are masculine. Almost without exception, the feminine third person singular '*hi*' will be used to render '*it*' in these contexts as further illustrated by our next examples:

If you're going to ask me **how long** **it took** him to die, I'm saying it depends. [TIME 19]	Os wyt ti ar fin gofyn i mi **faint o** **amser gymerodd hi** iddo fo farw, wel mi ddeudwn i fod hynny'n dibynnu. [AMSER 29]
It was quite clear to them that they were at this moment standing in the presence of a master. [MAT 108]	**Roedd hi'n hollol amlwg iddyn** **nhw** eu bod nhw'n sefyll yng ngŵydd meistr yr eilad honno. [MAT 102]
It was *her* turn now to become a heroine if only she could come up with a brilliant plot. [MAT 136]	**Ei thro *hi* oedd hi bellach** i fod yn arwres, petai hi ond yn gallu meddwl am gynllwyn gwych. [MAT 130]
. . . **a hithau'n amser te** . . . [HDF 115]	. . . **and as it was tea-time too** . . . [OFH 141]
Os mentrai fy mam, yn gwrtais ac yn bwyllog, awgrymu **ei bod hi'n** **bryd bwyd**, a bod eisiau'r ford . . . [HDF 156]	If my mother ventured courteously and circumspectly to hint **that it** **was meal-time** and she wanted the table . . . [OFH 196]

Cyn hir roedden nhw am y gorau yn codi ffrae â mi, wedyn **roedd hi** fel petaen nhw wedi cymryd yn eu pennau mai Sais o'n i a **dyma hi'n dechrau** mynd yn flêr. [CRWYD 47]

*Soon they were doing their best to start an argument with me, then **it was** as if they had got into their heads that I was English and **it started** [Lit: **here it is starting**] to get messy.*

Pawb drosto'i hun **ydy hi**'n y pen draw. [PLA 256]

It's everybody for himself in the end.

Finally, we have two examples of the masculine '*ef/fe*' (= *he*) or NW '*fo/o*' where the nonreferential '*hi*' might hitherto have been expected. We can state that in general, this occurs in informal, spoken registers and may be a way of avoiding possible ambiguity of meaning when the main focus of the utterance is connected with a feminine '*hi*' expression.

This was where **it** had happened; this was where her job really began. [UNSUIT 42]

Dyma lle y digwyddodd **o**; dyma lle'r oedd ei gwaith hi'n dechrau go iawn. [GORTYN 54]

'Mae gynno'ni Aelwyd yma. Rhaid ichi ddwad, Mrs Rushmere. Fydda' **fo** ddim yn edrych yn rhyfedd i wraig *specialist* ddod i Aelwyd yr Urdd, na fydda'?' [LLEIFIOR 28–9]

'We have a branch of the Welsh League of Youth here. You must come, Mrs Rushmere. **It** wouldn't look odd if a consultant's wife came to our meetings, would it?' [RETURN 22]

2.2.c. Pronouns preceded by the definite article (reduplicated pronouns)

This occurs invariably when there is an element of emphasis on the reduplicated pronoun. The use of the definite article with the pronoun is not a compulsory element of the emphasisation of it (as demonstrated by our final example below) however it is fairly common practice, especially in spoken Welsh[9].

'**Y fi**?' meddai hi, 'beth wna i mewn lle felly, a finna'n dallt dim gair o Saesneg?' [TRAED 69]

'**Me**?' she said. 'What would I be doing in a place like that, not understanding a word of English?' [FEET 61]

---

[9] Historically, these are related to the *myfi, tydi, hyhi* etc. forms. These forms have now been replaced to a very large degree by the definite article + pronoun forms in all registers.

'You *are* Mrs Stephanakis, aren't you?'

'Chi[10] ydi Mrs Stephanakis, yntê?'

'**I was**,' she said calmly, 'and trying to get his name out of my life.' [TIME 102]

'**Y fi** oedd hi,' meddai'n dawel, 'a dw i'n trio anghofio i mi ddwyn yr enw erioed.' [AMSER 162]

... he realised that his necessarily short-term physical needs ... were not to be placated by **her**. [TIME 85]

Sylweddolodd nad **y hi** oedd yr un i fodloni ei anghenion corfforol ... [AMSER 135]

'Mae pawb yn poeni gormod yn 'u cylch nhw o lawer. **Y nhw** sydd wedi dewis 'u byw, ac mae pawb wedi anghofio erbyn hyn mor gwta y buo hi efo'r arian rheini.' [TRAED 139]

'Everybody is worrying far too much about them. **They** have chosen the way they want to live, and everybody has forgotten how selfish she was with that money.' [FEET 123]

2.2.d. Resumptive pronouns

It is normal in Welsh to employ a resumptive pronoun in a relative clause when reference is made (in the following examples with a preposition) to the antecedent in the main clause. To end either of the examples below simply with the preposition '*with*' and no accompanying pronoun would not conform to the stylistic and grammatical norms of the language.

'Ydi o'n un cas, neu'n anodd byw **efo fo**?' [TRAED 76]

'Is he bad-tempered, or difficult to live **with**?' [FEET 67]

... hyd y deallais, 'r oedd 'nhadcu yn ddyn digon **caredig a hawddgar i weithio gydag e**. [HDF 67]

I understand that my grandfather was **kind and pleasant to work with**. [OFH 80]

2.2.e. Indefinite pronouns (-EVER forms in English)

(i) Ever

Welsh differentiates '*ever/never*' according to the tense used. '*Byth*' is used with the present, future, imperfect and conditional tenses and '*erioed*' with the past, perfect and pluperfect. The last two examples below suggest that occasionally, '*byth*' or '*erioed*' may be stylistically inappropriate (especially in the '*ever since*' combination).

---

[10] Given that there is also emphasis on '*you*' in this first sentence, the translator could also have chosen to include the definite article here > '*Y chi ydi Mrs Stephanakis . . .*'.

'Fuoch chi 'rioed yn Sir Fôn?' meddai Winni, gan edrych tuag at yr ynys honno. [TE 39]

'Have you ever been to Anglesey?' Winni asked, looking across towards the island. [TEA 38]

... she walked sadly down the middle, wondering how she was ever to get out again. [ALICE 22]

... cerddodd Alys i lawr y canol, gan feddwl sut fyth yr âi allan eto. [ALYS I 14][11]

How could they ever make up for this? [STONE 303]

Sut medren nhw byth wneud iawn am hyn? [MAEN 193]

Cedwais ef hyd heddiw oblegid dyma'r prawf fy mod i'n ddieuog gerbron Hannah. [MONICA 33]

I've kept it ever since because it's proof that I'm not guilty as regards Hannah. [MONICA 32]

'Fyddwch chi'n breuddwydio weithiau?' [TE 41]

'Do you ever dream?' [TEA 40]

'*Ever*' may also modify an interrogative. However, whereas '*ever*' may occur independently (as in our examples above), the Welsh equivalent '*bynnag*' which is used with interrogatives can never be used on its own without an accompanying interrogative. In more formal usage, the interrogative (apart from '*pwy*' = '*who*') is preceded by the further modifier '*pa*'. This is often omitted in neutral and informal registers.

(ii) Whatever

[Pa] beth bynnag with a noun replacing '*beth*' when necessary. In dialogue or informally, the distantly related[12] '*ta beth*' may be preferred. The examples preceded by '*gan*' below are also connected to the '*ta beth*' construction.

As a doorkeeper, or whatever he was supposed to be, he made a sham of the enamelled security badge pinned to his straining dinner jacket. [TIME 28]

Fel porthor, neu beth bynnag ydoedd, dygai anghlod ar y bathodyn diogelwch enamel a biniwyd ar ei siaced ddu, a oedd yn rhy fach iddo. [AMSER 43]

... Sleath hesitated only momentarily before climbing down the slope of the grass bank to the

... oedodd Saunders am ennyd cyn dringo i lawr y llethr glaswelltog tua'r llwybr a mynd yn ei flaen yn

---

[11] Although ALYS II 11 has: ... *cerddodd yn drist i lawr y canol gan feddwl* **sut yn y byd yr âi allan** *eto*.

[12] See PWT 4.127 [a] for further explanation of the etymology of '*ta beth/ta pwy/ta faint*' etc.

towpath and continuing his slow
walk to **whatever** he was seeking.
[TIME 77]

'**Whatever your reasons** may
be, you are perfectly correct'
[BAND 210]

... 'y codi o flaen y cŵn deillion'
fel y dywedid (**gan nad beth** yw
tarddiad y fath ymadrodd) ...
[HDF 85]

Roedd crochan anferth o bwnsh, a
phobol yn ei lanw â **ta beth** oedden
nhw wedi dod 'da nhw; [HUNAN 92]

llesmeiriol i gyfeiriad **beth bynnag**
yr oedd yn chwilio amdano.
[AMSER 122]

'**Pa ddulliau bynnag** a
ddefnyddiwch i resymu, rydych
chi'n berffaith gywir' [CYLCH 15]

... and of getting up 'before the
blind dogs,' as they used to say,
whatever might be the origin of the
saying ... [OFH 104]

There was a huge cauldron of punch,
which people kept topping up with
whatever they'd bought. [SOLVA 92]

(iii) Whenever
[Pa] bryd bynnag although it should be remembered that it may also be rendered simply by use of the conjunction '*pan*' (= '*when*') to convey a more
defined time than '*pryd bynnag*'.

... and it seemed to be a regular rule
that, **whenever** a horse stumbled,
the rider fell off immediately.
[THRO 195–6]

Pan oedd ganddi bres poced, pleser
cyntaf Monica oedd mynd i dŷ
bwyta. [MONICA 13]

Ac ymddengys ei bod yn rheol
gyffredinol **pryd bynnag** y baglai
march cwympai'r marchog oddi
arno ar unwaith. [TRWY 86]

Whenever she had money to spend, it
was Monica's favourite treat to spend
it in a tea-room. [MONICA 12]

(iv) Wherever
[Pa] le bynnag or again, more usually (and less formally) *lle bynnag*. Again,
the '*gan nad*' expression is also documented.

They'd only need the dates, the name
of the hotel or **wherever** the client
had booked into ... and they're in
business. [TIME 68–9]

Cododd yno res o feudai helaeth a
dwy bing (bin) rhyngddynt, a'u toi â
hen lechi bach, brau y cyfnod, **gan**

Dim ond y dyddiad, enw'r gwesty
neu **lle bynnag** roedd y cwsmer
wedi bwcio ... a dyna nhw ar ben eu
ffordd. [AMSER 108]

He built a row of two outhouses
with two walks between them, all
roofed with crumbly old slates of

nad o ble y ceid hwy. [HDF 75]

that period, **wherever** they may have been obtained. [OFH 91]

(v) Whoever
This is the only *–ever* expression which is never introduced by the modifier *'pa'*. *'Pwy bynnag'* (or informally *'ta pwy'*) is therefore the most usual translation here. We note *'pwy fynno'* (= *whosoever may wish*) below as one possible alternative.

'Pwy sy'n mynd i dalu?'
'Gaiff **pwy fynno** wneud.'
[TRAED 96]

'Who's going to pay?'
'**Whoever** wants to.' [FEET 86]

(vi) However
[Pa] fodd bynnag is used both as modifier with, for example, an adjective > *however hard one tries. . .* and also as a neutral expression on its own. In this case, another option can be *'sut bynnag'* although it is not possible to use *'sut bynnag'* as a modifying expression in the formal register.

However, the egg only got larger and larger. [THRO 183]

Sut bynnag, y cwbl a wnaeth yr wy oedd mynd yn fwy ac yn fwy . . . [TRWY 72]

However, there was the hill full in sight, so there was nothing to be done but start again. [THRO 139]

Fodd bynnag, dyna lle'r oedd y bryn yn y golwg yn glir, a 'doedd dim amdani ond ail-gychwyn. [TRWY 26]

2.2.f. Welsh dative of reference left untranslated in English
This occurs in the second person singular/plural only and is more associated with spoken registers. It is often difficult to find an exact equivalence in English and as our examples show, it may be omitted entirely without changing the meaning of the text. Combinations with this construction tend to occur with (i) *dyna/dyma* (= *there is/here is*) (ii) *yn wir* (= *indeed*) / *yn siŵr* (= *sure, definite*) / *yn sicr* (= *sure, certainly*) and (iii) simply the preposition *'i'* and the pronoun *'ti/chi'*. There is an element of emphasis or highlighting the point being made by the speaker here and referring it directly to the listener.

'Rydw i'n licio bod yn y tŷ,' meddai Owen, 'ond am yr ardal, **dyma iti** bictiwr o anobaith.' [TRAED 141]

'I like being in the house,' said Owen, 'but as for the district, here's a picture of hopelessness.' [FEET 125]

And **certainly** the glass *was* beginning to melt away, just like a bright silvery mist. [THRO 131]	. . . ac **yn wir ichi** roedd y gwydr *yn* dechrau toddi, yn union fel rhyw darth ariannaid disglair. [TRWY 18]
Hi piau nhw, **yn siŵr i ti**. [MONICA 7]	They're hers, I'd wager. [MONICA 6]
Mae honno'n hen gân gin Winni, mae hi bownd o gyrraedd adra cyn nos **iti**. [TE 45]	That's an old story of hers, she's bound to go home before dark. [TEA 43]

2.2.g. Conjunctive pronouns in Welsh

The conjunctive pronouns are usually used to connect (and sometimes contrast) two different pronominal elements:

She drank from her glass again and **he** looked at his wristwatch. [TIME 110]	Yfodd eto o'r gwydr ac edrychodd **yntau** ar ei wats. [AMSER 175]

In this example, **she** did one thing and **he** did another, both at the same time. A further consideration here is that the pronoun **she** is implicit (yet unstated) in the Welsh because of the context and from what has been understood prior to the example above. The use of **yntau** contrasts with what **she** did while drawing attention to what **he** did.

Stylistically, the use of conjunctive pronouns can be a versatile way of expressing nuances of meaning and we will consider these in greater depth in this section.

(i) Dyma / dyna + conjunctive pronoun

The example includes the contrastive element normally associated with the conjunctive pronouns but the pronoun is also preceded by the demonstrative '*dyma*' (= *here is/are*). This can be a useful link (normally not translated) as it operates as a verbal link for the contrastive element[13].

Huw aeth gyntaf i smalio cuddiad tu ôl i'r wal, ac wedyn **dyma finna**'n gneud run fath . . . [NOS 8]	It was Huw who went first to hide behind the wall and then **I** did the same . . . [NIGHT 2]

---

[13] PWT 2.43 refers to '*dyma/dyna*' as defective verbs.

(ii) Additionality (also, too – negative either)
Here the element of reinforcement will often correspond to an extra phrase in English with a sense of additionality, commonly *'too / as well / also'*. This may even be further reinforced in Welsh by adding *'hefyd'* (= *too, also*) to the conjunctive pronoun.

'Y fi?' meddai hi, 'beth wna i mewn lle felly, a finna'n dallt dim gair o Saesneg?'
'Mae mam Gwen yn dwad,' meddai Owen.
'A fedar **hitha** ddim gair o Saesneg,' meddai'r tad. [TRAED 69]

'Me?' she said. 'What would I be doing in a place like that, not understanding a word of English?'
'Gwen's mother is coming,' said Owen.
'And **she** can't speak a word of English, **either**,' said the father. [FEET 61]

Sylwodd Vera fod llygaid Marged yn gwenu, a **gwenodd hithau**. [LLEIFIOR 56]

Vera noticed that Marged's eyes were smiling and **she too smiled**. [RETURN 46]

Why wouldn't they believe **I** was involved **as well**? [TIME 105]

Mi allsan gredu fod gen **innau** law yn y peth **hefyd**. [AMSER 167]

(iii) Contrast of two referents with a change of subjects
We have seen that conjunctive pronouns in Welsh are used primarily to contrast two referents. However in the examples below, there is a switching of subjects and the pronouns are used with both of the referents and not just the one being contrasted.

The call had left him vaguely irritated with what had sounded to be a bossy and hard-nosed female – though one with a sense of humour – and, not least, because **she** must have **in her turn** thought **him** a pompous and uptight bugger. [TIME 94]

Roedd ei llais caled wedi ei adael yn flin braidd er fod ganddi ddogn go dda o hiwmor a hwyrach ei bod **hithau, yn ei thro**, wedi meddwl ei fod **yntau hefyd** yn hen ddiawl hunangyfiawn, sychlyd. [AMSER 149]

Edrychodd Sioned ar Bertie, ac **yntau arni hithau**. [TRAED 113]

Sioned looked at Bertie and **he at her**. [FEET 100]

(iv) Reinforcing a noun: NOUN + Conjunctive pronoun
These are examples of nouns (very often a proper noun) being reinforced by the use of an additional conjunctive pronoun. Once again, it will be seen that

these remain either unstranslated or convey the additionality element – *and X as well / ac X yntau / hithau.*

Aethai **Bet hithau** i weini, ac yr oedd Ifan a Jane yn hollol ar eu pennau eu hunain erbyn hyn. [TRAED 145]

Bet [lit. she also] had gone into service so that Ifan and Jane were by this time completely on their own. [FEET 129]

Mae **Charles Edwards yntau**'n hoff iawn o'r ddelwedd o'r Cymry yn alltudion . . . [BIRT 102]

*Charles Edwards is **also** very fond of the image of the Welsh as exiles . . .*

It didn't cross my mind that he was married, let alone a father, and I'm sure **Barbara** didn't suspect it either. [CIDER 34]

Chroesodd y syniad y gallai Duke fod yn briod, heb sôn am fod yn dad, mo fy meddwl i, ac rwy'n sicr nad oedd **Barbara hithau** wedi amau hynny chwaith. [SEIDR 48]

Daeth y Norddmyn o Norwy dan ddyfod heibio i Ynysoedd Orch a Shetland a chyrraedd Iwerddon [. . .] Ar eu hôl daeth y **Daniaid hwythau** gan ymosod ar draethau dwyrain Prydain . . . [PEATCYM 47]

*The Northmen from Norway came passing by the Orkney and Shetland isles and reaching Ireland [. . .] After them came the **Danes** [lit. them as well] attacking the beaches of east Britain.*

(v) Reinforcing a possessor
Here, the possessive pronoun is reinforced by the addition of a conjunctive pronoun. This is especially true when there is a contrastive element in the phrase.

Waeth iti daflu **fy newydd innau** i mewn yr un pryd. [TRAED 60]

You might as well throw in **my news** at the same time. [FEET 52]

Yr oedd ei dad yn siarad â'**i chwaer yntau** yn ymyl un o'r ffenestri. [LLEIFIOR 14]

His father was chatting with **his sister** near one of the windows. [RETURN 9]

(vi) Absolute clauses (See Section 10.3, Chapter 10)

2.2.h. Eiddo
'*Eiddo*' is a noun meaning '*property / possessions*'. It can be used with the preposition '*i*' to express that something belongs to someone:

Mae'r cyfan yn eiddo iddi hi – Everything belongs to her

By extension, it can also convey the possessive pronoun:

Mae'r cyfan yn eiddo iddi hi – Everything is hers

Rhyw ddiwrnod caent orffen talu hwnnw, a byddai'r tyddyn **yn eiddo iddynt**. [TRAED 24]	One day they would repay it all and the property would be **theirs**. [FEET 21]
His movements were unhurried and economical . . . [CIDER 33]	Roedd pob symudiad **o'i eiddo** [*Lit: every movement of his belonging*] 'n bwyllog a diwastraff . . . [SEIDR 48]
Erbyn iddynt gyrraedd y dorlan bella fe ddaeth buwch arall **o'u eiddo** o'r niwl yn croch frefu, a chi yn dal yn sownd yn ei chynffon. [PLA 169]	*By the time they reached the furthest bank another of **their** cows came out of the mist loudly mooing with a dog still fast at its tail.*

2.2.i. Generic human referent ('dyn' etc.)
There is no direct Welsh equivalent to the English indefinite pronoun '*one*'. The options for conveying this in Welsh are outlined below:

(i) dyn [always indefinite – never 'y dyn']
Literally '*man*' although it is used to cover all genders as a generic, indefinite pronoun and as seen in our second example, any associated possessives are also masculine.

. . . y cwestiwn a ddaw i **ddyn**, yn naturiol, yw . . . [HDF 56]	. . . **one** naturally asks whether . . . [OFH 66]
Why couldn't **one** have total control of **one's** mind? [VICT 100]	Pam na allai **dyn** reoli **ei** feddwl yn gyfan gwbl ac yn effeithiol? [LLINYN 113]

(ii) y sawl
'*Those*' and therefore always giving a plural, collective sense.

If **you** give alms **you** might have a deep psychological reason for giving them, or **you** might be purely good . . . [VICT 20]	Mae gan **y sawl** sy'n rhoi elusen neu gynhorthwy gymhelliad seicolegol dwfn dros wneud hynny, meddyliodd. Un ai hynny neu **'i fod** o'n naturiol dda drwyddo draw . . . [LLINYN 22]

(iii) ti / chi / X

The use of either of these mirrors the contemporary English tendency to use the pronoun '*you*' more frequently as a generic human referent. The Welsh writer has the option to use the second person singular (familiar) '*ti*' as well as the plural (formal) '*chi*' here – this will depend on the listener. The English '*you*' is sometimes omitted entirely or rendered by an impersonal construction as in examples two and three below.

When **you** learnt to live with paralysis – or tried to – **you** learnt to live in this sort of untidiness too. [VICT 21]

Pan ydach **chi**'n dygymod, neu'n ceisio dygymod â pharlys, buan iawn rydach **chi**'n dysgu byw efo blerwch . . . [LLINYN 22]

There was a light drizzle on the wind, and **you could feel** the chill of an October evening. [CIDER 7]

Roedd ychydig o law mân a ias noson hydref yn y gwynt . . . [SEIDR 12] [*In this example, the sense of 'you could feel' has been omitted*]

You can hear the same sort of thing if **you** walk through a riding-stable when the horses are being fed. [MAT 142]

Mae'r un math o sŵn **i'w glywed** [lit.: to be heard] wrth gerdded drwy stablau marchogaeth pan fydd y ceffylau'n cael eu bwydo. [MAT 135]

(iv) rhywun

Another Welsh indefinite that can be used is '*rhywun*' [= *someone*].

Merch fechan eiddil yr olwg ond prydferth fel dol oedd hi . . . yn gwneud i **rywun** feddwl am un o'r Tylwyth Teg. [CHWAL 39]

Small and frail-looking, she was a girl with a doll-like beauty . . . reminding **one** of a fairy. [OUT 77]

What sort of conversation did **you** strike up with a stranger? [VICT 86]

Am be mae **rhywun** yn dechrau sgwrsio efo rhywun diarth? [lit. About what does someone start conversing with someone strange?] [LLINYN 98]

Apparently people in public life are subjected to more of that kind of thing than **most of us hear about**. [CIDER 8]

Mae'n debyg fod pobl sy'n byw bywyd cyhoeddus yn cael mwy o brofiadau o'r fath nag y **byddai rhywun yn tybio**. [SEIDR 13]

2.2.j. Conclusions

Given that Welsh does not possess the pronoun 'it', rendering this pronoun in the language may present challenges to the translator. Conversely, knowing when it is appropriate to use 'it' when translating from Welsh into English can also occasionally exercise the mind. We have seen that any ambiguity is less when we have an object consisting of a preposition plus the singular third person 'hi'. However, out of context, this is not so apparent in cases where the pronoun is the subject – for example, we need a context to tell us whether '*faint o amser gymerodd hi?*' is best rendered by '*how long did she take*' or '*how long did it take*'. Similarly, as seen in our final section, the fact that Welsh does not possess a generic human referent such as the English '*one*' demands a variety of different strategies from the translator. Finally, in the case of the Welsh conjunctive pronouns, there can be a degree of nuance of meaning associated with these which may require additional elements so that they may be conveyed accurately in English.

3

Prepositions

3.0 Introduction

Locating the precise preposition needed for a particular phrase or expression and aligning these between two languages can often present particular challenges for translators. In some cases, there will be equivalence between both e.g.

> *Rhoi'r llyfr <u>ar</u> y bwrdd*   –   *To put the book <u>on</u> the table*

In many cases, however, this will not follow:

> *Codi'r llyfr*   –   *To pick <u>up</u> the book*
> *Codi'r llyfr <u>oddi ar</u> y bwrdd*   –   *To pick the book up <u>from</u> the table*
> *Edrych <u>ar</u> y llyfr*   –   *To look <u>at</u> the book*

The prepositional mismatch between Welsh and English provides the focus of the first section of this chapter. We consider various Welsh prepositions and how they may be rendered in English. It is not our intention to provide the reader with exhaustive lists of how prepositions operate distinctly in the two languages. We do, however, draw attention to a number of the main mismatches and how these have been accommodated by translators in their work.

We have given over a complete section to discuss the various ways in which the preposition '*ar*' may be used in Welsh. Its semantic connections to certain emotions and conditions are discussed as these are common and require different translation strategies compared to their English equivalents. In 3.2i.e we draw attention to some common noun/verb-noun combinations followed by '*ar*' and others which are preceded by '*ar*'. Given that many verbs are also followed by '*ar*' (where there is either a mismatch or no equivalence in English), sections 3.2ii and 3.2iii discuss some of the more common of these.

The use of certain prepositions as heads of clauses is the subject of 3.3. The appropriate prepositions are treated under separate headings and include:

'*Gan*' clauses
'*Dan*' clauses (including how both these can be used to convey the English present participle)
'*Trwy/Drwy*' clauses
'*Wrth*' clauses
'*Am*' clauses
'*O*' clauses

The idea of *chassé-croisé* introduced in Chapter 1 is expanded in section 3.4 in particular in the context of verbs of emotion (fear, sorrow, regret etc), liking and disliking, need, doubt, remembering, debt and others. Our final section deals with preposition stranding in informal varieties of Welsh.

3.1.i Preposition mismatch between Welsh and English

The focus in this section is when a mismatch occurs between the generally accepted meaning of a preposition in either language e.g. Welsh '*i*' usually corresponds to English '*to*' > '*rhowch y llyfr i'r athro*' = '*give the book **to the** teacher*'. However, there may be occasions when this accepted equivalence does not offer a clear match e.g. '*mab **i** athro yw Dafydd*' = '*Dafydd is the son **of** a teacher*'. It is not possible to give comprehensive examples of every time this semantic mismatch occurs between both languages, however, we will look at most of the main prepositions in Welsh where this may happen and give some examples of each one.

â [*with – in an instrumental sense*[1]]

Er bod fy nghlust yn llosgi, prin y gallwn beidio â chwerthin am **y tro a wnaethai â mi**, ond cymerwn arnaf fy mod yn digio yn dost wrtho. [GWEN 19]

Although my ear was burning I could not help laughing at **the trick he had played on me**, but I pretended that I was annoyed. [GWEN 25–6]

A sôn am giperiaid, tua'r adeg hon gwelais **dro doniol yn cael ei chwarae ag un ohonynt**. [WILLAT 183–4]

And talking about gamekeepers, it was about that time that I saw a funny trick being played on one of them.

[1] We have used *Y Geiriadur Mawr* to give the principal, commonly accepted meanings of the prepositions in this section.

am [*about, at, around*]

Ron had started telling people off
for **laughing at** Quirrell's stutter.
[STONE 283]

... roedd Ron wedi dechrau dweud
y drefn wrth bobl am **chwerthin
am ben**[2] atal dweud Quirrél.
[MAEN 181]

Olreit ta, meddwn i, a **rhoid fy
nghap am**[3] **fy mhen** ac allan â fi.
[NOS 64]

Alright then, I said, and **I put my
cap on** and out I went. [NIGHT 52]

'Felly'n wir. A minne wedi 'magu **am
y Berwyn â chi**[4], yn ochrau'r Bala.'
[LLEIFIOR 29]

'Indeed now! I was brought up **on
the Berwyns**, quite close to Bala.'
[RETURN 23]

In the distance, **on the far bank**, a
man strolled. [VICT 151]

Cerddai dyn **am yr afon â nhw**.
[LLINYN 170]

ar [*on* – see also section 3.2]

Bodlonodd pob un o'r bechgyn
ond tri (a minnau'n un), ar
ddysgu ar y cof[5] lyfryn tenau coch
– *Curtis's Outlines of History*. . .
[WILLAT 88]

*All of the boys but three (of whom
I was one) were satisfied with
memorising a thin red book –
Curtis's Outlines of History*. . .

Y mae un olygfa arall a Nwncwl
Jâms yn ffigur canolog ynddi wedi
aros yn fyw iawn **ar fy nghof**.
[HDF 159]

One more scene in which Uncle
Jâms is the central figure remains
vivid **in my memory**. [OFH 199]

Gwyddai ar ei gof lawer o hen
gerddi gwerin, ac yn arbennig
ganeuon Siaci Pen Bryn
(Cerngoch). . . [CHWECH 164]

*He knew many old folk songs by
memory and especially the songs of
Siaci Pen Bryn (Cerngoch)*. . .

---

[2] Although '*at*' is a common meaning of the preposition '*am*', with the verb '*chwerthin*'
[*to laugh*] it is almost invariably followed by the noun '*pen*' [*head*] with a literal meaning of '*laughing at the head (of)*'
[3] Literally '*put my cap around my head*'.
[4] Am X â chi = on the other side of X to you / across the X from you.
[5] Literally '*learning on the memory*'. The next two examples demonstrate further uses
of '*ar*' with the noun '*cof*' [= *memory*]

Roedd mynd mawr <u>ar</u> y gitâr[6], ac roedd cannoedd o entrepreneurs yn neidio ar y drol. [HUNAN 58]

The guitar was getting big and lots of entrepreneurs were jumping on the bandwagon. [SOLVA 58]

Casnewydd, Caerdydd, newid trên, wedyn **milltir <u>ar</u> filltir** o lesni caeau a choed a pherthi. [CHWAL 79]

They passed through Newport and came to Cardiff, where they changed trains; after that the journey lay through **mile <u>after</u> mile** of green fields, woodland and hedgerows. [OUT 82]

Cafodd **cannoedd <u>ar</u> filoedd** o bobol eu gadael yn sownd ar yr ynys drwy'r nos. [HUNAN 194]

Hundreds <u>of</u> thousands were left stranded on the island all night. [SOLVA 194]

Un diwrnod sylwais ar ddau o'r bechgyn a'u pennau ynghyd **fel pe baent <u>ar</u> ryw ddrwg.** [WILLAT 117]

*One day I noticed two boys with their heads together **as if they were <u>up to</u> some mischief.***

. . . wedi colli pob **llywodraeth <u>arno</u>'i hun.** . . [WILLAT 168]

*. . . having lost **all control <u>of</u> himself** . . .*

. . . i fynd **<u>ar</u> ofyn Sid Gronow,** y dyn pysgod lleol, am bàs – gan taw fe oedd un o'r ychydig bobol yn y pentre oedd yn gyrru fan. [HUNAN 8]

. . . **to beg a lift <u>from</u> Sid Gronow,** the fishmonger and one of the few people in the village who drove a car. [SOLVA 8]

'Ac os oes yna rywbeth alla i 'i neud, peidiwch â phetruso **dod <u>ar</u> fy ngofyn i.'** [RHANNU 298]

*'And if there's anything I can do, don't hesitate to **come and ask me.'***

Chwifiodd y goruchwyliwr ei law **arnynt** cyn iddynt fynd o'r golwg. . . [CHWAL 16]

The manager waved <u>to them</u> before they were out of sight. . . [OUT 15]

ar ôl [*after*]

This can sometimes be used to convey '*as a result of*' or '*left / bequeathed by*'. In the second example, the translator has approximated this to the English noun '*cast-off*'.

---

[6] Literally '*there was a big go on the guitar*' i.e. the guitar was very popular. There are many such idiomatic uses of the preposition '*ar*' in Welsh which don't find direct, literal equiavalents in English. For more detailed discussion, see section 3.2.

Roedd Mam a Dada'n amyneddgar iawn 'da fi, ac roedd rhyche ar fy mysedd **ar ôl** y tanne dur, ac ro'n nhw'n nafu ac, ambell waith, yn gwaedu. [HUNAN 61]

Mam and Dad were very patient with me, and soon my fingers became grooved **by the steel strings** and would hurt and sometimes bleed. [SOLVA 61]

Daethpwyd o hyd i ddwy hen gôt, un **ar ôl** Williams Jenkins a'r llall **ar ôl** Gwilym . . . [CHWAL 83]

Two ancient coats, **cast-offs** of William Jenkins and Gwilym, were unearthed . . . [OUT 86]

at [*to > motion towards*]
This preposition often involves a sense of motion towards an object or subject. As the examples show, this may often find a more meaningful equivalent in English by the use of a different, more semantically appropriate preposition. It may also approximate the English '*for*' with the sense of '*for the purpose of*'.

. . . eu **cariad at** y cwmwd bach, shiprys hwnnw, Cwm Wern . . . [HDF 170]

. . . their **love for** that little barley-and-oats commote Cwm Wern . . . [OFH 213]

. . . fe ofynnon nhw i fi a licen i **fynd i fyw atyn**[7] **nhw** . . . [HUNAN 127]

. . . they asked me if I'd like **to move in with them** . . . [SOLVA 126]

Wel, dyna saith mlynedd o **baratoad at fod yn athrawon ysgolion** wedi eu cwblhau [WILLAT 89]

*Well, there's seven years of **preparing to be school teachers** completed.*

'Os wt ti isio cwffas, dewisa di rywun **at dy faint**, 'nei di?' [CHWAL 153]

'If you want to fight, choose someone **your own size**, will you?' [OUT 162]

Corn tun, hir, main, a hollol ddiarddurn, ydoedd hwn, yn **tynnu at** bum troedfedd o hyd, wedi ei **lunio at y gwaith**, mae'n amlwg . . . [HDF 135]

It was a long, slender completely plain tin horn **about** five feet in length, **made to serve the purpose** evidently . . . [OFH 169]

dan [*under*]
'*Dan*' at the beginning of a clause is discussed in section 3.3ii. The following example is where it is combined with an illness to describe a health condition.

[7] '*At*' will usually be used with people however the more usual '*i*' [= *to*] is seen with places cf. '*Ar ôl i ni adael Penybont a **mynd i D**ŷ'r Ysgol i fyw* . . . [WILLAT 208] = '*After we left Penybont and went to the Schoolhouse to live* . . .'

"Dydi hi ddim yn gryf, fel y gwyddoch chi, ac mae hi **dan annwyd trwm** yr wythnos yma. . .' [CHWAL 144]

'She is not strong, as you know, and **she has got a heavy cold** this week . . .' [OUT 152]

dros/tros [*over*]
By extension, '*dros*' has come to mean '*for > on behalf of*' as well as '*for > reason why*'. The conjugated forms of '*dros*' can be useful to give the English '*covered (in) something*'.

Roedd o'n **esgus <u>dros</u> beidio â chydyfed** â dyn y rhoddai gyffion amdano ryw ddydd. [AMSER 49]

. . . but a civilised **excuse <u>for</u> not drinking** with a character he expected one day to put handcuffs on. [TIME 32]

Wedi bod yn lladd rhai o'r gwartheg ar y tircyfri oedd y taeogion, ac roeddent oll **yn waed <u>drostynt</u>**. [PLA 111]

The serfs were slaughtering cattle on the bondlands, and they were **covered in blood**. [PEST 83]

. . . ac ar y parcdir goed derw preiffion â'u dail yn drymion **<u>drostynt</u>**. [CRYMAN 14]

. . . and some fine oak trees in **full** leaf. [lit. leaves heavy over them] [SICKLE 9]

drwy/trwy [*through*]
Conjugated forms of '*drwy*' in combination with verb-nouns are employed to strengthen the meaning of the action described e.g. the addition of '*drwyddo*' [= through him] in this example is rendered in English by the addition of the adjective '*violently*':

Roedd y gŵr ag un llygad yn **crynu drwyddo**. [PLA 105]

The one-eyed man . . . .. **shaking violently**. [PEST 79]

A similar function can be observed in these further examples the final one illustrating similar usage with a noun:

He remembered the night they had spent together, and **<u>shuddered</u>**. [KNOTS 90]

Cofiodd y noson a dreuliasant efo'i gilydd, ac **aeth cryndod <u>drwyddo</u>**. [CHWERW 78]

She's **<u>pretty</u> upset** herself . . . [CIDER 106]

Roedd hithau **wedi cynhyrfu <u>drwyddi</u>** . . . [SEIDR 143]

The old man **perked up** and said his was a pint of Usher's . . . [CIDER 88]	Siriolodd yr hen ŵr **drwyddo** a dweud mai peint arall o seidr gymerai o. [SEIDR 120]
Llonnodd **drwyddo** wrth gymryd y llyfr oddi ar y silff. [CHWAL 174]	He thrilled **with delight** as he took the volume from the shelf. [OUT 183]
. . . gwelent fod y lle'n **ferw drwyddo**. [CHWAL 26]	. . . they saw that the whole place was **seething with excitement**. [OUT 27]

Again as a conjugated preposition, '*drwy*' may express the entirety or wholeness of the noun or verb-noun which it qualifies.

Ac er iddyn nhw chwilio a chwalu'r dref **drwyddi** roedd y gath wedi mynd ar goll . . . [PLA 125]	*And even though they searched and searched **throughout the whole** town, the cat had got lost . . .*
. . . recordiwyd yr **albwm drwyddo** mewn deuddydd. [HUNAN 259]	*. . . the **whole** album was recorded in two days.* [SOLVA 259]
Darllenodd **y bennod drwyddi** i'm gwraig a minnau . . . [RHWNG 99]	*[He/she] read the **whole** chapter to my wife and me . . .*
We got **very warm**. [VICT 80]	Mi gynheson ni **drwyddan**. [LLINYN 90]

er [*since, for > although*]
A common collocate for '*er*' is '*mawr*' [= *big, large, great*] which often occurs with '*syndod*' [= *surprise*] or '*siom*' [= *disappointment*] although these are not exclusive.

. . . diolchodd i Sandra am ei help ac **er mawr syndod iddi** gwthiodd bapur chwegain i'w llaw. [SELYF 60]	*. . . [he] thanked Sandra for her help and **to** her great surprise pressed a ten shilling note into her hand.*
'Ond **er fy siom**, yr hyn a ddeudodd oedd, 'Wel a deud y gwir, chlywais i neb gwerth gwrando arno ond Dan bach ni!'	*'But **to** my disappointment, what she said was, 'Well, to be honest, I didn't hear anyone worth listening to apart from our Dan!'*
. . . they were, in his experience, either too pretty for masculine comfort, or too bloody clever **for their own good**. [TIME 68]	. . . yn ei brofiad ef, roeddent naill ai mor ddel nes gwneud i ddynion eraill deimlo'n anghyfforddus, neu'n rhy glyfar o'r hanner **er eu lles eu hunain**. [AMSER 106–7]

Bodlonai'r rhain yn eithaf cysurus ar roi cinio rheng go dda ar ben tymor, a chael gan eu deiliaid, **er eu mawr golled**, yn fynych, gydymgeisio mewn magu ffesants a phetris iddynt hwy. [HDF 81]	Without any uneasiness at all, the others satisfied their sense of obligation by providing a good rent dinner on quarter-day and by getting their tenants, often **at a great loss to themselves**, to compete with each other in breeding pheasants and partridges for them. [OFH 98–9]

It is worth noting the combinations:

er gwybodaeth   –   *for information*
er enghraifft   –   *for example [e.e. = e.g.]*

gan [*by*]	>	**bod gan [NW]** / **gyda [SW]** [*to have i.e. possess*]
gyda [*with, i.e. together with*]	>	**efo [NW]**

'Sut mae Mrs Thomas **efo chi?**' gofynnodd Edward Vaughan. [LLEIFIOR 82]	'How's Mrs Thomas[8]?' [RETURN 69]
Ac mae'r lle'n lân ac yn deidi **gyda hi**, a'r gwelye'n gysurus. [LLEIFIOR 57]	And **she keeps** this place clean and tidy, and the beds comfortable. [RETURN 47]
Mae Trem-y-Gorwel 'ma'n ddigon taclus **gennoch chi** rwan. Rhaid inni gofio bod genno'ni le arall i edrych ar ei ôl hefyd, yn rhaid? [FFENEST 37]	*'You have Trem-y-Gorwel looking quite tidy now. We need to remember that we have another place to look after as well, don't we?'*
Yn llawer rhy fuan gennyf fi daeth dydd y gystadleuaeth, a'r côr a'i gefnogwyr yn cerdded gwaith ugain munud i stesion Bangor. [WILLAT 149]	*The day of the competition came **far too soon for me/for my liking** and the choir and its supporters were walking for twenty minutes to Bangor station.*

[8] The translator has omitted '*efo chi*' [= *with you*] as there is no need (and not an easy way) to convey it in English. Literally the example here is '*How is Mrs Thomas with you?*' This use is more prevalent in informal registers. In the second example, the same translator has turned a similar '*gyda hi*' [= *with her*] into '*she keeps*' in English maintaining the semantic connection with '*gyda hi*'.

i [*to, for*][9]
'*i*' may correspond to English '*of, from*' when used in expressions of extremities of distance.

Yn un pen i'r babell safai Charlie heddychlon ... [CHWECH 229]	*At one end of the tent stood the peaceful Charlie ...*
Bu tawelwch am ennyd a gallent glywed lleisiau'r taeogion yn y pellter **yr ochr bella i'r eglwys**. [PLA 235]	*There was a short spell of silence and they could hear the voices of the bondsmen at the far end of the church.*

In the context of a relation, relationship or friend belonging to someone, Welsh prefers the use of '*i*' to English '*of*'.

Tua'r un pryd, etifeddodd Letitia rai cannoedd **ar ôl hen ewythr iddi**, ac aeth yn ddynes fawreddog. [CHWAL 100]	About this time, Letitia was left some hundreds of pounds **by an old uncle** [lit. after an old uncle to her (=of hers)] and she blossomed out into a lady of substance. [OUT 104]
Sally wasn't **a neighbour of theirs**. [VICT 85]	Doedd Llinos ddim yn **gymydog iddyn nhw**. [LLINYN 96]
Cecil Humphreys, **mab i fasnachwr llwyddiannus** yn y dref. [CHWAL 174]	Cecil Humphreys, **the son of a prosperous tradesman** in the town. [OUT 184]

o [*of, from*][10]
Where English uses '*for*' in expressions relating to size or age, as in the examples below, the corresponding preposition in Welsh can be '*o*' (although '*i*' and sometimes '*am*' would also be possible here).

Roedd hi'n gallu codi twrw i ryfeddi **o grotes bum troedfedd** a sgidie seis tri am ei thraed! [HUNAN 263]	Tessa could make a lot of noise **for a five foot nothing chick** wearing size three shoes! [SOLVA 263]

[9] See also in Chapter 2 (2.f.) *Welsh dative of reference left untranslated in English* and Chapter 10, Section 2e on *verbless relative clauses for* **ac iddo / ac iddi / ac iddynt etc.*
[10] See also in Chapter 2 (1.e) *Nouns in apposition with the preposition 'o'.*

For a heavyweight he'd moved fast to get there before me. [CIDER 126]	**O ddyn o'i faint**, mae'n rhaid ei fod wedi symud yn eithriadol o gyflym i gyrraedd yno o fy mlaen. [SEIDR 168]
Hogyn mawr **o'i oed**. [CYCHWYN 15]	A big lad **for his age**. [BEGIN 13]

Other examples are idiomatic or established use following specific adjectives e.g. '*balch* **o**' [= *glad* **to**].

Yr oedd Owen **o'i ben a'i ysgwyddau'n dalach** nag ef, ac ymsythodd i'w wneud ei hun yn dalach fyth. [CYCHWYN 15]	Owen, **a head and shoulders taller** than he, straightened up to make himself taller yet. [BEGIN 13]
Yr oedd Elin yn **falch iawn o'u** **gweled** . . . [TRAED 81]	But Elin was **very glad to see** **them** . . . [FEET 71]

The particular use (in the literary register) of the preposition '*o*' with a verb-noun to express its subject within a preposition led sub-clause should be noted.

I hyn, mewn rhan, yr wyf i ddiolch **am fedru ohonof** ymgynnal dan dreialon go chwerw drwy oes braidd yn hir. [WILLAT 15]	*It is for this, partly, which I am* grateful **that I have been able** *to* *maintain myself during quite bitter* *trials and tribulations throughout a* *rather long life.*
Pan ganem y darn, âi popeth ymlaen yn hollol hwylus, **nes cyrraedd** **ohonom** y rhan fwyaf cynhyrfus. [WILLAT 51]	*When we sang the piece, everything* *went ahead quite fine,* **until we** **reached** *the most exciting part.*

An especially versatile and useful combination of '*o*' with the noun '*rhan*' [= *part*] includes meanings such as '*regards / regarding, concerning, from the perspective of* etc. In addition, when combined with an appropriate infixed pronoun e.g. '*m* [first person singular] >> *o'm rhan (i)* there is an equivalent to the longer English expression '*as far as I'm concerned / for my part*'.

Bûm i, wedi dyfod dipyn yn hŷn yn *saethwr* mawr; ond, erbyn hyn, da gennyf ddweud, i'm dwylo i fod yn bur lân **o ran gwaed**. [HDF 121]	When I became a man I was a great shooter, but to-day, I am glad to say, my hands are fairly clean **as regards** **blood**. [OFH 150]

Dr Grimesby Roylott's chamber was larger than that of his stepdaughter, but was plainly furnished. [BAND 229]	Er bod siambr Dr Grimesby Roylott yn fwy nag un ei lysferch, **o ran**[11] dodrefn roedd yr un mor blaen. [CYLCH 43]
'I deducted a ventilator.'	'. . . Fe ddeuthum i'r casgliad fod yn rhaid bod yno awyrydd o ryw fath neu'i gilydd.'
'But what harm can there be in that?'	'Ond pa niwed yn y byd allai fod yn hynny?'
'Well, there is at least a curious coincidence of dates.' [BAND 233]	'Wel, o leiaf, mae yna gyd-ddigwyddiad rhyfedd **o ran y dyddiadau**[12].' [CYLCH 49]
I can't think there could be any doubt about his identity when he was found dead by a neighbour who knew him **by sight**. [TIME 104–5]	Fedra i ddim meddwl fod 'na unrhyw amheuaeth ac yntau wedi cael 'i ddarganfod yn farw gan gymydog oedd yn 'i nabod o'n iawn **o ran ei weld**. [AMSER 167]

oddi [always combines with another preposition]
'*Oddi*' is the first element in a number of possible prepositional combinations. Its exact meaning (often referring to location) will depend on the preposition with which it combines e.g.

> *oddi wrth*   >>>   *from (somebody i.e. a letter from the bank manager) in opposition to the pronoun 'at'*

'Taw â chlegar,' **oddi wrth** ei thad. Clegar – clegar – hen air hyll. [TE 9]	'Stop that yowling!' cried her father [*Lit: from her father*] Yowling . . . an ugly word . . . [TEA 13]
Ond os dilewyrch fy maboed yn yr ysgol, cefais fywyd brenhinaidd pan oeddwn yn rhydd **oddi wrthi**. [HENAT 105]	But if my boyhood days were grey and drab in school, I had a glorious time out **of it**. [*Lit: when I was free from it.*] [LOCUST 92]

[11] This is an example where an adverb plus participle in English may successfully be conveyed using the '*o ran*' link. The more literal meaning here would be: '*Although Dr Grimesby's chamber was larger than that of his stepdaughter, as far as furniture was concerned it was just as plain.*'
[12] It would not be possible to render '*a curious coincidence of dates*' with *'cyd-ddigwyddiad rhyfedd o ddyddiadau*'. However, the '*o ran*' link makes an acceptable connection between '*coincidence*' and '*dates*'.

Among the shoal of papers left on his blotting pad was a sealed envelope **from** the Administrative Chief Superintendent. [TIME 58]

Ymhlith yr anialwch o bapurau a adawyd ar ei ddesg roedd amlen dan sêl **oddi wrth** brif Uwch Arolygydd yr Adran Weinyddol. [AMSER 91]

Ymhen ychydig ddyddiau fe ddaeth llythyr **oddi wrtho**, llythyr byr, swta ei frawddegau, na ddangosai ddim o'i wir deimlad. [TRAED 129]

Within a few days a letter arrived **from him**, brief and brusque in style, revealing nothing of his true feelings. [FEET 114]

oddi ar   >>>   *off, up from (movement upwards – informally, by extension, 'since' with time)*

She'd driven **off** a straight stretch of highway into a tree. [CIDER 19]

Roedd hi wedi gyrru **oddi ar** y ffordd a mynd ar ei phen i goeden. [SEIDR 27]

... it seemed to be a regular rule that, whenever a horse stumbled, the rider fell **off** instantly. [THRO 195–6]

Ac ymddengys ei bod yn rheol gyffredinol pryd bynnag y baglai march cwympai'r marchog **oddi arno** ar unwaith. [TRWY 86]

I don't know why, but villains take a special dislike to being robbed themselves. [TIME 24]

Wn i ddim pam chwaith, ond mae lladron wastad yn gwrthwynebu'n chwyrn pan fydd pobl eraill yn dwyn **oddi arnyn** [Lit: steal *off/from them*] nhw. [AMSER 37]

Ni welais yr un o'r ddau, drwy wybod i mi, byth **oddi ar** hynny. [CHWECH 137]

*I've never seen either of the two, as far as I know, ever **since** then.*

oddi am(gylch)   >>>   *around – again location*

Tynnodd ei ddwylo **oddi am** yr onnen a rhedeg draw at y nant. [CRYMAN 228]

He removed his hands **from around** the trunk of the ash and ran over to the stream. [SICKLE 188]

... a chyn i mi allu tynnu'r cadach **oddi am** fy llygaid ... [GWEN 18]

.. before I could pull the handkerchief **from** [Lit: *from around*] my eyes ... [GWEN 25]

oddi mewn (i)   >>>   within (something)

After the rumbustiousness of the storm, the fire ensemble and the drinking song – which calmed **him** – the love duet needled the calm away. [VICT 97]	Ar ôl cythrwfl y storm, yr ensemble tân a'r gân yfed – a oedd wedi tawelu'r cynnwrf **oddi mewn iddo** [*Lit: calmed the excitement **within him***] – drylliodd deuawd y cariadon ei hunanfeddiant. [LLINYN 109]

These combinations may also be used adverbially.

'I wish they'd get the trial done,' she thought, 'and hand **round** the refreshments!' [ALICE 103]	'Buasai'n dda gennyf pe gorffennent y treial,' meddyliai, 'a dyfod â'r bwyd **oddi amgylch**.' [ALYS 62]

rhag [*before, from* – however, the meaning will depend on the verb or other part of speech with which it is associated]
Examples with verbs include:

Achub / arbed rhag	>>>	To save from
Atal / rhwystro rhag	>>>	To prevent from
Cadw rhag	>>>	To keep from
Cuddio rhag	>>>	To hide from
Dianc rhag	>>>	To escape from
Gwahardd rhag	>>>	To forbid from
Gwylio rhag	>>>	To look/watch out for
Rhybuddio rhag	>>>	To warn against

Expressions with '*rhag*' include:

Rhag blaen	>>>	At once
Rhag ofn	>>>	In case
Rhag [eich] cywilydd	>>>	For shame [Shame on you]
Rhag llaw	>>>	Before hand

wrth [*by, near*]
The association with this preposition is with closeness to a location. By extension, as in our first example, it can include an additional '*by way of*' sense i.e. *She is a lawyer by (way of) her profession.* It may also reinforce the sense of closeness together in the combination '*wrth ei gilydd*' where no direct equivalent is found in English.

Teilwr ydoedd **wrth** ei alwedigaeth, a
William Williams **wrth** ei enw i'r ychydig
a'i gwyddai ... [CHWECH 138]

*He was a tailor **by** profession and
William Williams **by** name to the few
who knew it ...*

Dywedodd y gallai doctor ennill
ei filoedd, ond na allai athro ysgol,
National neu *British*, wneud hynny
na chadw enaid a chorff **wrth ei
gilydd.** [WILLAT 9]

*He said that a doctor could earn
thousands but a school teacher
National or British couldn't do so or
keep body and soul **together.***

yn [*in*]
'*Yn*' – in contrast with '*mewn*' which also means '*in*' – is always used with
definite nouns. However, it may occur in expressions (as in the first example)
or as a link between two indefinite nouns which form expressions (examples
two and three). It will be noted that there is a consequent mismatch between
its usual meaning and its meaning within these expressions.

Yn un peth yr oedd Edith a fi ymhell
o fod yn perthyn i'r un donfedd
naturiol... [CHWECH 136]

***For one thing** Edith and I were far
from belonging to the same natural
wavelength ...*

... **ochr yn ochr** â ... [TROW 153]

*... side **by** side with ...*

Doedd wybod beth a ddeuai **wyneb
yn wyneb** â dyn pe gwneid hynny.
[PLA 60]

You never knew what might be
lurking among the trees. [*Lit: There
was no knowing what might come
face to face with someone if that was
done*] [PEST 46]

3.1.ii Dative shift
There are many verbs which can take a direct object and indirect object at the
same time. In this pattern, in English, the direct object occurs first (shown
in single underline below), followed by the indirect object (shown in double
underline). The indirect object is preceded by a preposition ('to' or 'for'):

I baked a cake for John.
I told the good news to my sister.
I gave flowers to my mother.
John brought some chocolates to his father.

In English, many of these verbs allow an alternation (called 'dative shift' by
linguists: the term 'dative' refers to indirect objects) in which the indirect

object can be stripped of its preposition and moved up to occupy the position of the first object:

I baked John a cake.
I told my sister the good news.
I gave my mother flowers.
John brought his father some chocolates.

Welsh does not allow the dative-shift alternation, so whenever a verb has two objects, one of them must be preceded by a preposition. The following examples illustrate the correspondence in which an English sentence with dative shift has been rendered in Welsh with a preposition (variously *i*, *wrth*, *am*, etc. depending on the verb) preceding its indirect object:

Bant â fi lan yr heol dan ddawnso i **ddweud y newydd da wrth Byron.** [HUNAN 60]

I danced off up the road **to tell Byron the good news.** [SOLVA 60]

Lingard, wondering if Deborah had **given the daft bugger a cocaine Mickey Finn** . . . [TIME 82]

Gan ddyfalu tybed a oedd Debbie wedi **rhoi Mickey Finn llawn cocên i'r diawl bach gwirion** . . .[AMSER 130]

I'd bought her a dress. My sort, not hers. I doubt if she would have worn it. [VICT 39]

Ro'n i wedi **prynu ffrog iddi.** Fy math i o ffrog, nid 'i math hi. Mae'n gwestiwn gen i fydda hi wedi'i gwisgo hi. [LLINYN 44]

3.2 Uses of the preposition 'AR'

The preposition '*ar*' [= *on*] is – semantically and syntactically – a particularly versatile one in Welsh and for this reason merits a section of this chapter to itself. It is used (often in combination with nouns) to convey a number of different emotional states (which may be expressed in English by a particular verb) and also follows many verbs to give specific meanings.

3.2i Emotions and other conditions
3.2i.a Maladies / disease / health conditions
The two most frequent prepositions in this context are '*gan/gyda*' and '*ar*'. It is customary to state that any health conditions which are tangible e.g. back pain, headache, upset stomach take the preposition '*gan/gyda*' whereas any which one is unable to touch directly take the preposition '*ar*'.

Roedd **peritonitis** <u>arni hi</u> a chafodd lawdriniaeth ar unweth. [HUNAN 250]	**She had peritonitis** and was operated on immediately. [SOLVA 251]
Roedd **atal dweud amlwg <u>ar</u>** Victor ... [HUNAN 100]	Victor who had **a pronounced stutter** [*Lit: There was an obvious stutter <u>on</u> Victor*] ... [SOLVA 97]
... you **make one quite giddy.** [ALICE 66]	... rydych chi'n **codi pendro <u>arna'</u> <u>i</u>.** [*Lit: You raise a giddiness <u>on</u> me.*] [ALYS 64]

It is not possible to physically touch peritonitis, a stutter or a sense of giddiness and Welsh prefers the combination of a noun or a verb-noun connected to the object by the preposition '*ar*'. The first example below illustrates the difference in the use of '*gan/gyda*' and '*ar*' here. A headache can be touched but the *need* for an aspirin is an intangible condition as are amnesia and stress:

He **had a headache** and **needed an Aspirin.** [VICT 119]	Roedd **ganddo gur pen** ac roedd **arno angen aspirin.** [LLINYN 132]
Teimlai'n bur heini, a thybiai mai'r **amnesia ydoedd yr unig ddrwg <u>arno</u>** o ganlyniad i'r ddamwain. [SELYF 72]	*He felt very fit and wondered that the* **amnesia was the only thing wrong with him** *as a result of the accident.*
Ni allai osgoi bod **straen <u>arno</u>** ... [SELYF 72]	*He couldn't avoid being* **under stress** [lit. ... that there was stress <u>on</u> him].

3.2i.b Positions of authority
To be in a position of authority regarding someone else can be expressed by use of the preposition '*ar*' as in the example below.[13]

... mae Miss Trunchball yn **Brifathrawes <u>arnoch</u> chi.** [MAT 63]	... your Headmistress is Miss Trunchball. [MAT 69]

It would be possible to say "... *eich Prifathrawes yw Miss Trunchball*" but the '*ar*' construction emphasises the authority element here. Similar relationships are highlighted with '*athro*' [= *teacher*], '*rheolwr*' [= *manager*] and '*gweinidog*' [= *minister*] in the next examples:

---

[13] See also the discussion on the identificational sentence in Chapter 11, section 11.1.3.

... dyn [...] na ddylasai erioed fod yn **athro ar** blant. [CHWECH 63]

... *a man who should never have been a **school teacher**. [Lit: a teacher on children]*

... aeth Charlie ati i sôn am yr holl glybie yfed yno, a'r ffortiwn ro'n i'n mynd i'w gwneud **'da fe yn rheolwr arna i!** [HUNAN 148]

Charlie told me about all the drinking clubs in Manchester and about the fortune I was going to make **with him as my manager!** *[Lit: ... with him a manager on me]* [SOLVA 148]

Ym Mhenuel, y capel Methodus yr own i'n aelod, a'r Parch. Benjamin Watkins **yn weinidog arno** ... [CHWECH 141]

In Penuel, the Methodist chapel of which I was a member and where the Rev Benjamin Watkins was minister [Lit: ... a minister on it]

The connection with authority extends to related concepts such as *duty [= dyletswydd ar]* or *maintaining order [cadw / rhoi trefn ar]*.

3.2i.c Further conditions / states of life / moods
These are quite varied but many relate to degrees of difficulty or ease and consequently with adjectives expressing badness >> worse or goodness >> better.

'**Mae** hi'n **braf arnoch chi**, Gwen, yn cael hogiau ifanc i'ch helpu *a* rhoi fferins i chi.' [TRAED 69]

'**You are lucky** [lit. It is fine on you], Gwen, to have boys to help you and give you sweets.' [FEET 61]

... gallasai fod yn llawer iawn **gwaeth arnaf** ... [HENAT 111]

... indeed I could have been far **worse off** [lit. it could have been much worse on me] [LOCUST 96]

Eto i gyd yr wyf yn credu y buasai'n **well ar gyflwr meddyliol** yr ardal pe baent yn gwybod mwy am Ned Cando ... [HENAT 127]

Yet I believe it would be **better for the mental state** of the place if they knew more about Ned Cando ... [LOCUST 110]

Amser pryderus oedd hwn arnom, ond heliodd Twm ni i'w rwyd yn lled ddidrafferth. [GWEN 42]

We went through an agonising **time**[14], but Twm got us safely into his net without much trouble. [GWEN 45]

[14] Lit. *This was a worrying time on us.* Here the translator has chosen to change this into a personalised past tense in English which succeeds in capturing the full meaning of the original text.

... byddai'n **ddrwg iawn arnoch chwi** a'ch swydd pe bai gorfod i chwi ymddangos o flaen yr ustusiaid. [WILLAT 202]

*... it would be **very bad for you** and your position if you had to appear before the magistrates.*

Things couldn't have looked **worse for him**. [CIDER 49]

Edrychai'n gwbl anobeithiol **arno**.[15]

Indeed, this can be taken to the extreme to give the sense that all is completely lost or finished. The use of the verb '*canu + ar*' is an idiomatic way of expressing that all is at an end.

Ped aethai'r tân fymryn yn nes yn ôl, dyna **ddiwedd arnom**. [CHWECH 185]

*If the fire had gone slightly closer back, it would have been **the end of us**.*

Ond roedd hi wedi **canu arno**. [PLA 93]

He had **had it**. [lit. It had sung on him]. [PEST 72]

By extension, and with the expression '*Beth sy'n bod ar / What's the matter with*' in mind, an '*ar*' combination can be used to convey a sense of something not being as it should be or the possibility of change.

'Maen nhw'n deud mai bachgen direidus ydi Twm, ond er na dda gen i mo'i fam o, weles i ddim llawer **o'i le ar y** bachgen . . .' [GWEN 28]

'They say that Twm is a mischievous boy, but I've never found much **wrong with him**, though I don't like his mother.' [GWEN 33]

Y mae'n **newid go fawr arnaf** erbyn hyn. [HENAT 9]

Things are **very different indeed for me** now. [LOCUST 15]

The use of '*ar*' to convey moods and states of life is quite versatile in Welsh and is not necessarily confined to any particular set of combinations. The following vary from desire to enjoyment to depression.

He didn't **feel much like singing**. [STONE 338]

Doedd fawr o **awydd canu arno**. [lit. There was not much desire of singing on him.] [MAEN 215]

---

[15] It is also possible to combine *edrych* with *ar* with the sense of *to look at*. However, the verb coupled with the degree of badness (or hopelessness) and followed by the preposition '*ar*' combine to describe how bad things look for the subject rather than the way in which he might be looking at anyone/anything else.

... gwaeddais am help, a syrthiais dan ddynodiau'r lladron gwaedlyd, ac **aeth yn nos arnaf** a chollais fy ymwybyddiaeth. [GWEN 286]

... I called for help. At that point I collapsed under their brutal attack and **I lost consciousness.** [*Lit: and it went into night on me and I lost consciousness.*] [GWEN 203]

Cydiodd Dan eto yn y cyfieithiad o waith Goethe, ond nid oedd **hwyl darllen arno.** [CHWAL 172]

Dan took up the translation again, but was in no **mood for reading.** [lit. there was not a mood of reading on him.] [OUT 181]

She had been reading Wilde's *The Birthday of the Infanta* and **found it singularly depressing.** [VICT 129]

The Birthday of the Infanta, Oscar Wilde roedd hi'n ei ddarllen, a **chodai'r felan arni.** [lit. ... and it raised the blues on her.] [LLINYN 144]

3.2i.d Smells and tastes

The idea that an object has a smell or a taste may be conveyed by an '*ar*' construction i.e. there is a smell/taste <u>on</u> something/someone.

Roedd y mariwana hwn yn frown ei liw 'da lot o hade a brige mân ynddo fe. Roedd **gwynt egr iawn arno fe** ... [HUNAN 103-4]

This marijuana was brown in colour with lots of seeds and twigs. **It had a pungent smell** and was exceedingly strong. [SOLVA 104]

She had told him sleepily that **he smelt of grass** ... [VICT 125]

Roedd hi wedi dweud wrtho'n gysglyd fod **aroglau gwelltglas arno fo** ... [LLINYN 140]

'Dydi'r dail ddim i fod i gael 'u taflu i ffwrdd. Maen' nhw i fod yn y boilar am ddyddia' nes **bydd rhyw flas ar y te** ... [CHWAL 115]

[The little monkey] was throwing tea leaves away every day. They ought to be in the boiler for days until there is **some taste on the tea** ... [OUT 121]

He couldn't swallow without water and they were distinctly **unpleasant** to chew. [VICT 119]

Allai o mo'u llyncu heb ddiod o ddŵr ac roedd **blas rhy ddrwg arnyn nhw** i'w cnoi... [lit. there was too bad a taste on them to be chewed] [LLINYN 132]

3.2i.e Noun/Verb-noun + 'ar' / 'ar' + noun/verb-noun
Many combinations of nouns or verb-nouns with 'ar' are well known and well
established, for example:

angen	– need >> something is necessary, needed
chwant	– desire >> combined with 'bwyd' [= food] to convey 'hunger'
cywilydd	– shame >> ashamed
dyled	– debt >> also without this noun but with a specific sum to translate 'to owe' [Mae arno fe £5 i mi – He owes me £5]
eisiau	– lack, need, want >> wanted, needed, lacking
golwg	– look, appearance >> looking like, appearing like
ofn	– fear >> afraid, frightened (of)
syched	– dryness >> thirst, thirsty

These all follow the pattern 'bod' + Noun/Verb-noun + 'ar' + object. The following illustrate further usage of this combination. The combination 'mynd
yn + Noun + ar + object' should be noted as an equivalent of 'to make a +
Noun + of something'.

You're mad. [MAT 202]	Mae **colled arnoch chi**. [MAT 196]
I don't **blame you**. [CIDER 117]	Wela i ddim **bai arnat ti**. [SEIDR 157]
Methodd Ceridwen â thosturio wrtho. Hwyrach am y byddai'n **wastraff ar** dosturi. [FFENEST 22]	*Ceridwen couldn't pity him. Perhaps because it would be a **waste of** pity.*
Fel arfer, **aeth yn draed moch arno ef** a'r dynion dan ei ofal . . . [HENAT 96]	As usual, **he** and the men under his command **made a proper mess of things** . . . [LOCUST 85]

'Ar' may also combine with other nouns / verb-nouns to create particular
expressions:

ar + agor	>	ar agor	=	open
ar + cael	>	ar gael	=	available
ar + cau	>	ar gau	=	closed, shut
ar + cof	>	ar gof	=	memorised, in the memory
ar + coll	>	ar goll	=	lost, missing
ar + gwaith	>	ar waith	=	working, in operation
ar + unwaith	>	ar unwaith	=	immediately, at once
ar + verb-noun			=	about to + verb-noun

Other less common examples follow. It should be noted that there may be a prepositional mismatch between Welsh and English, an example of which can be observed in the combination with '*winc*' below:

A cheisiodd Robert Gruffydd eto daflu **winc** anferth **ar** ei wraig. [WJ, Hughes 52]	*And Robert Gruffydd tried again to give a huge **wink** __to__ his wife.*
Yr oedd yn beth diarth iddo ddod fel hyn **ar ganol tymor**, heb fod achos. [CRYMAN 246]	It was unusual for him to arrive like this **in** mid-term, without good cause. [SICKLE 204]
Rydan ni **ar ffo** fel pawb arall. [PLA 96]	We are **fleeing** the city [lit. on flee], like everyone else. [PEST 74]
Aeth holl ffrindiau da'r wythnosau cynt **ar chwâl** a theimlodd eto gyffro curiad calon. [RHANNU 246]	*All the good friends of the past weeks were **scattered/broken up** and she once again felt the excitement of a heartbeat.*

3.2i.f Time
An option with expressions of time, especially when there is an element of barely arriving or accomplishing an act by the hour/date specified, is to connect the subject through the use of '*ar*'.

'**We** are **only just in time** to prevent some subtle and horrible crime.' [BAND 233]	'. . . Ac os felly, **cael a chael** fydd hi **arnom** i rwystro trosedd gyfrwys ac ofnadwy.' [CYLCH 50]
He had come home **very late**. [VICT 10]	Roedd hi'n **hwyr iawn, iawn arno**'n cyrraedd adre. [LLINYN 9]
Roedd hi'n **hwyr y noson honno arni**'n agor y parsel y bu'n ei warchod mor ofalus yr holl ffordd i'r Castell. [RHANNU 120]	*It was **late that night** that __she__ opened the parcel she had been protecting so carefully all the way to the Castle.*

3.2i.g Weather
'*Ar*' can be used with the noun '*tywydd*' [= *weather*] where '*in/during*' would be appropriate in English.

Meddyliai sut hwyl a gâi, tybed, **ar dywydd mwll** fel hyn. [TRAED 146]	She wondered how he was getting on **in** such sultry weather as this. [FEET 129]

Ar dywydd garw esgusodid y plant gan y prifathro caredig am fod yn ddiweddar yn cyrraedd yr ysgol ambell dro. [HDF 146]

In rough weather our kind headmaster excused those children who came to school late. [OFH 182-3]

Yr oedd yn rhaid i'r gwas a'r gweithiwr aros allan bron **ar bob tywydd**, glaw a hindda, a dyfod adre gyda'r nos yn wlyb at y croen. [CWM 39]

The servant and farm worker had to be out **in every type of weather,** foul or fair, and they often came home at night wet to the skin. [GORSE 42]

3.2ii 'Ar' after verbs that regularly take an oblique object

Our intention is to consider in this section many of the verbs which connect to their object with the preposition 'ar'. In this sense, the use of 'ar' to connect to a noun or a noun phrase which is the object of the verb is a constraint rather than an option. These may be described as verbs which 'take' or are normally 'followed by' the preposition 'ar'. In section 3.2iii, it will be seen that 'ar' can also occur after other verbs in an optional or conative construction.

Here we list some of the verbs, give their meanings and one example of each in context together with any further notes. Any equivalent English preposition is underlined although there is not a corresponding preposition in every case. The verb, its preposition and corresponding oblique object are shown in bold.

achwyn ar

to complain about

Ni allai Nwncwl Jâms, felly, **achwyn ar ei lwc**, yn enwedig o gofio ei gyfraniad gweddol ysgafn ef at gyllid y teulu . . . [HDF 149]

Uncle Jâms then could not **complain about his luck,** especially in view of his somewhat slight contribution to the family income . . . [OFH 186]

aflonyddu ar

to disturb

Os nad oedd arian i'w cael am weinyddu'r ddwy swydd cawn fraint a werthfawrogwn yn fwy hyd yn oed nag arian – cael defnyddio'r meicrosgop bryd y mynnwn heb neb i **aflonyddu arnaf**. [WILLAT 33]

*If there was no money available to administer the two posts, I would receive an honour which I would appreciate much more than money – being allowed to use the microscope whenever I wanted without anyone **disturbing me.***

alaru _ar_

Yr ydw' i wedi **'laru _ar_ fod adra'n**
segur. [CHWAL 114]

to be fed up <u>with/of</u>

And I am **fed up with being at
home** doing nothing. [OUT 120]

amharu _ar_

'Yr ydw' i'n gobeithio nad ydyw'r
gwlybaniaeth a'r oerni a'r arogl
afiach wedi **amharu _ar_ iechyd Kate.'**
[CHWAL 144]

to harm, interfere <u>with</u>, impair

'I hope the wet and cold and
unhealthy smell have not **done
harm to Kate's health.'** [OUT 152]

blino _ar_[16]

O'r diwedd **blinodd** arweinwyr y
Dosbarth **_ar_ y dwndwr**; galwyd
cyfarfod o'r holl aelodau . . .
[WILLAT 30]

to tire / grow weary <u>of</u>

_At last the directors of the class **grew
weary <u>of</u> the din**; a meeting was
called of all of the members . . ._

bodloni _ar_

Bodlonodd pob un o'r bechgyn
ond tri (a minnau'n un), **_ar_ ddysgu
ar y cof** lyfryn tenau coch . . .
[WILLAT 88]

to be satisfied <u>with</u>

_All of the boys but three (of whom
I was one) **were satisfied <u>with</u>
memorising** a thin red book . . ._

craffu _ar_

Holmes walked slowly up and down
the ill-trimmed lawn, and **examined
with deep attention the outsides of
the windows.** [BAND 226]

to scrutinise, examine, look <u>at</u> closely

Cerddodd Holmes yn araf i fyny
ac i lawr y lawnt, a edrychai fel pe
bai wedi ei rhwygo yn hytrach na'i
thorri, gan **graffu _ar_ saernïaeth
allanol y ffenestri.** [CYLCH 39]

chwibanu _ar_

Clywsant y plisman ar y chwith
yn **chwibanu**'n isel **_ar_ y llall.**
[CHWAL 113]

to whistle <u>at / to</u>

They heard the constable on the
left **give a low whistle <u>to</u> the other.**
[OUT 119]

---

[16] Similarly '_danto <u>ar</u>_' in more informal registers.

cymryd _ar_

'You must confine yourself in your room, **on pretence of a headache**, when your stepfather comes back.' [BAND 231]

to pretend [lit. 'to take _on_']

'Pan ddaw eich llystad yn ei ôl o Lundain, rhaid i chi encilio i'ch ystafell ar unwaith, gan **gymryd arnoch fod gennych ben tost**.' [CYLCH 46]

edrych _ar_

. . . a sêt fawr fechan . . . lle na allai y rhai a eisteddai ynddi **edrych ar** y pregethwr heb gael _stiff neck_ . . .[GWEN 60–1]

to look _at_

. . . a narrow big pew, whose occupants suffered the discomfort of a stiff neck through **gazing at** the preacher. [GWEN 58]

effeithio _ar_

Yr oedd Wil James y tu hwnt i **effeithio arno** gan yr atgof. [CRYMAN 170]

to affect

Wil James, of course, was beyond **being troubled** [lit. affected _on him_] by the memory . . . [SICKLE 141]

[17]galw X _ar_ / enwi _ar_ / rhoi enw _ar_

Then she said **to call her Debbie.** [TIME 81]

Gwyddai Nwncwl y ffordd i'w gwneud yn ynfyd grac, bob amser, drwy **alw'r enw hwn _arni_.** [HDF 154]

'Fo ddechreuodd, Elen Ifans. **Galw enwa _ar_ 'nhad**.' [RHANNU 137]

to call someone or something X

Bryd hynny ddeudodd hi wrtha i am **alw Debbie _arni_.** [AMSER 129]

My uncle knew how to make her hopping mad at any moment by **calling her this name.** [OFH 192]

'It was him who started it, Elen Ifans. **_Calling my father_ names**.'

erfyn _ar_

Am y rheswm hwn **erfyniais _arnynt_** wneud a allent i sicrhau etholiad Savage. [WILLAT 31]

to implore

For that reason I **implored them** to do what they could to ensure Savage's election.

---

[17] It should be noted that this is different from '_galw ar_' which is used for '_to call upon_' >>> _galw _ar_ rywun _i_ wneud rhywbeth_ – to call _on_ someone _to_ do something.

[18]*gweiddi* <u>ar</u>

to shout <u>at</u>

Roedden nhw'n **gweiddi <u>ar</u> ei gilydd** ac yn cadw sŵn wrth ddathlu dyfodiad mis Mai a'r haf. [PLA 234]

*They were **shouting <u>at</u> each other** and making a racket celebrating the arrival of the month of May and the summer.*

gwenu <u>ar</u>

to smile / grin <u>at</u>

'Ia,' meddai Owen gan roi tro ar ei ben a **gwenu'n** hynod gyfeillgar **<u>ar</u> bartner ei dad** . . . [CYCHWYN 19]

'Yes,' replied Owen, turning his head with a most friendly **smile <u>at</u> his father's partner** . . . [BEGIN 17]

manteisio <u>ar</u>

to take advantage <u>of</u>

Melltithiodd ei hun am nad oedd wedi **manteisio <u>ar</u> y cyfle** i olchi'i hun yn dawel yn yr Arno pan gafodd gyfle. [PLA 82]

He cursed himself for having **missed the chance** [lit. for not having **taken advantage <u>of</u> the chance**] of washing himself off in the Arno. [PEST 65]

manylu <u>ar</u>

to go into detail <u>about</u>

Manylais <u>ar</u> hyn oblegid yr effaith ryfedd a gafodd ei agwedd ar y bechgyn. [WILLAT 34]

*I **have gone into detail <u>about</u> this** because of the strange effect that his attitude had on the boys.*

mennu <u>ar</u>

to affect

Y gwir amdani oedd fod Ashcroft yn ferch salw, wrthun, ond doedd hynny ddim i'w weld yn ffrwyno nac yn **mennu** dim **<u>arni</u>** . . . [HUNAN 87]

To be blunt, Ashcroft was a plain ugly, obnoxious Jane, but that did not seem to inhibit or to **deter her**. [SOLVA 87]

rhagori <u>ar</u>

to excel <u>at</u>, to do better than, surpass

Ddiwedd Mawrth aeth tri ohonom i'r Penrhyn Hall i gyngerdd pwysig a gynhelid gan adrannau'r Côr Mawr a fwriadai gystadlu yn y Plas Grisial, a cheisio **rhagori <u>ar</u> orchest Côr Caradog**. [WILLAT 35]

*At the end of March, three of us went to the Penrhyn Hall to an important concert which was held by sections of the Great Choir who intended competing at the Crystal Palace to try and **surpass the achievement of Côr Caradog**.*

---

[18] Also '*bloeddio <u>ar</u>*'.

syllu ar

Both Miss Stoner and I **gazed at him** in astonishment. [BAND 230]

to stare / gaze at

Syllodd Miss Stoner a minnau **arno** â'n llygaid fel lleuadau llawn. [CYLCH 45]

sylwi ar

Holmes drew one of the chairs into a corner and sat silent, while his eyes travelled round and round and up and down, **taking in every detail** of the apartment. [BAND 227]

to notice, take in

Tynnodd Holmes un o'r cadeiriau gwiail i'r gornel wag ac eistedd yno'n dawel, tra symudai ei lygaid i fyny ac i lawr o amgylch y lle, gan **sylwi ar bob manylyn** yn yr ystafell. [CYLCH 41]

tarfu ar

'It is probable that he will be away all day, and that there would be nothing to **disturb you**.' [BAND 219–20]

to disturb, bother

'Mae'n debygol y bydd oddi cartref drwy'r dydd, ac na fyddai dim byd i **darfu arnoch**.' [CYLCH 29]

torri ar

The Hatter was the first to **break up the silence**. [ALICE 50]

to interrupt, break up

Yr Hetiwr oedd y cyntaf i **dorri ar y tawelwch**. [ALYS II 68]

troi ar

He knew there were times when he **disgusted her**. [VICT 69]

to disgust, make one feel sick

Roedd o'n gwybod ei fod o'n **troi arni**, ambell dro. [LLINYN 78]

3.2iii 'Ar' after verbs that normally take a direct object (conative construction)

This section deals with normally transitive verbs in Welsh which may be used with 'ar' in the presence of a degree modifier (e.g. *tipyn, fawr, mymryn* etc.). Let us consider the following example:

... ni fyddai raid iddynt ond **canmol tipyn ar ei ferch**, ac yn y funud talai yr hen ŵr am y *shot*. [GWEN 10]

... they had only to **say something good about Gwen** and he would immediately buy them a drink. [GWEN 18]

The verb here is '*canmol*' [= *to praise*]. The use of '*ar*' after '*canmol*' is not constrained and it is normal for it to be followed directly by its object as in:

... pob un yn **canmol ei wraig**. [W], ... *everyone praising his wife.*
Hughes 23]

The difference between the two is the inclusion of the degree modifier '*tipyn*' in the first examples. To say *canmol ei ferch tipyn or *canmol tipyn ei ferch would not make sense grammatically. The presence of the degree modifier therefore requires the addition of '*ar*' in our first example but is not necessary at all (and indeed would be incorrect) in our second example. Similarly:

The inconvenient thing about Mrs Lockwood was her voice, which was so soft that I had to ask her to repeat almost everything. Even then **she didn't raise it a semitone**. [CIDER 27]	Siaradai mor dawel nes bod yn rhaid imi ofyn iddi ailadrodd popeth bron. Hyd yn oed wedyn, **ni chodai'r mymryn lleiaf <u>ar</u> ei llais**. [SEIDR 38]

Here the Welsh translation conveys the sense of '*not raising one's voice by a semitone*' through the use of a degree modifier after the verb '*codi*' [= *to raise*] so that the Welsh literally states '... *she didn't raise her voice by the smallest jot...*' with '*mymryn lleiaf*' [= *smallest jot*] coming between the verb '*codi*' and the object '*ei llais*'. Once again, the link is made in Welsh with the preposition '*ar*' although as the example below illustrates, without the degree modifier, the object of '*codi*' will just follow the verb with no prepositional link:

Heb **godi ei llais**, atebodd Alice yn bwyllog... [SEIDR 137]	*Without **raising her voice**, Alice answered prudently...*

Further examples of the Welsh 'conative construction'[19] using '*ar*' when a degree modifier (underlined) is present follow. These are not the only verbs

---

[19] A 'conative construction' in English would be one describing an attempt at an action rather than directly executing the action itself. The following would be an example of a conative in English where Welsh has a direct object:

Duke leaned against a tree, **whittling at a piece of dead wood** he'd found. [CIDER 35]	Pwysai Duke yn erbyn un o'r coed yn **naddu darn o bren** y daeth o hyd iddo ar y llawr. [SEIDR 50]

'*Whittling <u>at</u>*' a piece of wood rather then directly '*whittling*' it is the conative element here.

in Welsh where this is possible and as in the previous examples, all can be used directly with an object, without a degree modifier and therefore without the need for the 'ar' link.

adnabod   *to know, get to know, recognise*

Ni ddeuthum i nabod fawr arno, er   **I did not get to know him at all**
fy mod i'n dair ar ddeg oed adeg ei   **well**, although I was thirteen years
farw. [HDF 165]   old when he died. [OFH 207]

agor   *to open*

He **opened** the bedroom window **a**   **Agorodd fymryn ar** y ffenest.
little ... [CHWAL 194]   [LLINYN 174]

blino[20]   *to tire, bother*

Wedi cyrraedd i'w lawn dwf yr oedd   *Having reached his full extent, he*
yn balff o fachgen hardd, llydan o   *was a hunk of a good-looking boy,*
asgwrn, ac yn gydnerth drosto, yn   *wide-shouldered and strapping all*
rhyw bump ac wyth o daldra, braidd   *over, about five foot eight tall, slightly*
yn fyr efallai at safon arferol yr heddlu,   *short perhaps for the normal police*
a **blinai hynny beth arno** ar un   *standard, and that **used to bother***
cyfnod, mi gredaf. [CHWECH 281]   ***him a bit** at one time, I think.*

camdrin   *to misuse, mistreat, abuse*

... ac er iddo **gamdrin llawer ar**   *... and even though he used to*
ei gorff drwy ddiota ac ymladd   ***abuse his body a lot** by drinking*
a phethau tebyg yn ei ddyddiau   *and fighting and similar things in his*
cynharach ... [CHWECH 120]   *younger days ....*

ceryddu   *to admonish, berate*

'R oedd hi'n rhy fwyn ei natur i   *She was too gentle of nature to **berate***
geryddu rhyw lawer arnom mewn   ***us very much** in any way.*
unrhyw ffordd. [CHWECH 38]

---

[20] 'Blino *ar*' appears also in section 2ii. However, these are quite different. 'Blino *ar*' is 'to tire *of*' where the use of 'ar' is constrained. 'Blino' meaning 'to tire' as a transitive verb [i.e. *The work tires Siân* v *Siân is tired of the work*] only requires the 'ar' link when the degree modifier 'p/beth' is added as in the example here.

condemnio

Bu amser pan oedd ei enw ar enau pawb yn y pentref, ac ni byddai hyd yn oed y duwolion yn **condemnio llawer arno.** [HENAT 127]

to condemn

There was a time when his name was on everyone's lips in the village, and even the pious were **not too hard on him** [lit. did not condemn too much on him.] [LOCUST 110]

cynhyrfu

. . . a chanodd y plant yn dda er bod yr *Inspector* gyda'i fawredd tra-awdurdodol wedi **cynhyrfu peth arnynt.** [WILLAT 210]

to excite

. . . *and the children sang well even though the Inspector with his overly authoritative greatness had **excited them a bit.***

deall

Dysgid plant Cymreig mewn iaith estron nad oeddym yn **deall ond ychydig iawn arni** . . . [HENAT 100]

to understand

Welsh children were taught through a foreign language of which we **understood very little** . . . [LOCUST 88]

digio

Yr oedd Mr Hughes yn ffitio i'r dim i'r troad arbennig a oedd yn hiwmor fy mam, a châi hi chwerthin yn garedig am ben ei fân wendidau heb **ddigio dim arno.** [HENAT 104]

to annoy

Mr Hughes answered well to my mother's special turn of humour, and she was permitted to laugh, not unkindly, at his little failings without **giving the slightest offence.** [LOCUST 91]

disgyblu

'Roeddwn i'n credu 'mod i wedi **disgyblu digon ar eich meddwl** *bourgeois* chi i wneud ichi ddeall beth ydw i'n ceisio'i ddweud rŵan. [CRYMAN 166]

to discipline

I thought **I'd disciplined your bourgeois mind enough** to make you understand what I'm trying to say. [SICKLE 137]

dychryn

Beth, tybed, a wnâi Florence? A oeddynt wedi **dychryn digon arni**

to terrify, frighten

*What, I wondered, would Florence do? Had they **terrified her enough*** i beri iddi gadw'n ddistaw am yr arian? [SELYF 204]

to make her keep silent about the money.

dysgu

to learn

Fel yr wyf yn myned yn hŷn, yr wyf yn **dysgu** <u>mwy a mwy</u> **ar** y wers hon . . . [HENAT 35]

I learn this lesson **more and more** as I get older . . . [LOCUST 36]

egluro

to explain

Could you try to **explain that a little bit.** [MAT 73]

Allet ti geisio **egluro** <u>ryw ychydig</u> **ar hynny?** [MAT 67]

gweld

to see

After lunch, **I didn't see much of Barbara.** [CIDER 35]

Ar ôl cinio, **welais i** <u>fawr</u> **ar**²¹ **Barbara.** [SEIDR 50]

helpu

to help

'Ia, ond 'yn bod ni'n meddwl y basat ti'n licio **helpu** tipyn **ar** dy dad a dy fam.' [TRAED 107]

'Yes, but we thought you might like to **help** your mother and father a bit.' [FEET 95]

lleihau

to lessen, decrease

The fact that he'd killed a man didn't **take anything from his kindness** to me. [CIDER 67]

Doedd y ffaith ei fod yn llofrudd yn **lleihau** <u>dim</u> **ar ei garedigrwydd.** [SEIDR 94]

llonni

to cheer (up)

Wel, mae digon o le iddi hi, Martha bach, gwaetha'r modd, ac mi fasa' hi'n **llonni** <u>tipyn</u> **ar yr aelwyd,** on' fasa? [CHWAL 226]

Well, there's plenty of place for her, Martha bach, more's the pity, and she would **cheer up the home** <u>a bit,</u> wouldn't she? [OUT 239]

---

²¹ In contemporary Welsh, probably through interference from English, the preposition 'o' might also occur with 'gweld'.

magu

to rear

Un chwaer a oedd gan fy nhad, Marged, ac yr oedd yn hoff iawn ohoni gan mai hi a **fagodd lawer arno** pan yn blentyn. [HENAT 34]

My father had one sister, Margaret, of whom he was very fond, for she had had **a major share in rearing him.** [LOCUST 35]

meistroli

to master

He was visibly affected by what he'd been saying. [CIDER 108]

Ar ôl iddo **feistroli tipyn ar ei deimladau** [lit. after he had mastered a bit on his feelings] ... [SEIDR 146]

newid

to change

... **ni newidiais ddim ar** fy mholisi addysgol. [WILLAT 240]

I did not change my educational policy at all.

poeni

to worry, bother

The fact that he might be igniting a potential time-bomb **didn't worry him.** [VICT 178–9]

Doedd y ffaith y gallai fod yn cynnau fflam a ffrwydrai'n dân difaol **yn poeni dim ar** Ellis. [LLINYN 203]

sirioli

to cheer, enliven

On the walk back across the field Harry tried to **liven things up** by unfastening Barbara's headscarf and passing it to Duke. [CIDER 43]

Wrth i ni gerdded yn ôl ar draws y cae, ceisiodd Harry **sirioli tipyn ar bethau** drwy gipio sgarff Barbara oddi ar ei phen a'i roi i Duke. [SEIDR 62]

symud

to move

Estynnodd Llew ei law i **symud tipyn ar y bleind**, a ffrydiodd golau i'r ystafell. [CHWAL 59]

Llew stretched out his hand and **moved the blind slightly.** Light streamed into the room. [OUT 61]

tacluso

to tidy

I limped around the kitchen, **tidying up** ... [CIDER 62]

Herciais o gwmpas y gegin i **dacluso ychydig ar y lle.** [SEIDR 89] *tawelu*

to quieten, appease

There wasn't anything I could usefully do except try to **appease Bernard**. [CIDER 169–70]

Yr unig beth y gallwn i obeithio ei wneud oedd ceisio **tawelu rhyw gymaint ar Bernard**. [SEIDR 222]

temtio

to tempt

Buasai i un arall o'r teulu ennill ysgoloriaeth yn **ormod o demtio ar Ragluniaeth**. [TRAED 110]

For one more member of the family to win a scholarship would be to **tempt Providence too much**. [FEET 97]

torri

to cut

He had even **had his hair cut a little**. [VICT 95]

Cawsai **dorri dipyn ar ei wallt** cyn dod, hyd yn oed. [LLINYN 107]

ysgafnhau

to lighten

Dechreuodd y pethau hyn newid y ffordd o weithio ac **ysgafnhau llawer ar dreth y corff**. [HDF 93]

Such inventions as these began to change the whole mode of work, **lightening the tax on the body**. [OFH 114]

ystwytho

to make flexible

Cure you? Well, no, love – it will just **ease your joints a little**. [VICT 83]

Na, chaiff o ddim gwared ohono fo ond mi **ystwythith rywfaint ar y cymala** i chi, cariad. [LLINYN 94]

3.3 Prepositions as heads of clauses

The focus in this section is on the different ways that prepositions in particular may introduce clauses or work with verb-nouns in particular to form participles in Welsh. Each preposition is dealt with separately below with a fuller exploration of how and why these operate.

3.3i 'GAN' Clauses
3.3i.a Coordination
In these examples, '*gan*' is followed by a verb-noun which links an action co-occurring or coordinated with the action in the main clause. In every case, English prefers the conjunction '*and*'.

Cododd Alis ar ei heistedd eilwaith **gan syllu** ar y cwmni dros y ffordd. [MONICA 7]

Alice sat up again **and peered out** at the people across the road. [MONICA 6]

Ron strode off down a row of books **and started** pulling them off the shelves at random. [STONE 245]

Brasgamodd Ron i lawr rhes o lyfrau **gan ddechrau** eu tynnu oddi ar y silffoedd rywsut rywsut. [MAEN 156]

... she was hard at work on the white kitten, which was lying quite still **and trying** to purr. [THRO 127]

... roedd hi'n brysur ar y gath fach wen, a honno'n gorwedd yn berffaith lonydd **gan geisio** grwnan. [TRWY 13]

It may occasionally be preferable to employ a noun in English here:

Bu agos i Owen dagu **gan chwerthin.** [TRAED 79]

Owen nearly choked **with laughter.** [FEET 70]

3.3i.b Present participle

The equivalent to the English present participle is formed in Welsh by the use of a preposition (in these examples '*gan*' – see below for others) with a verb-noun. '*Gan*' is preferred when the action linked is similar to that described in 3.3i (a) above. It can occur at the beginning of a sentence as well as in the middle but will refer to an action which precedes the action in the main clause (even though they both co-occur at some stage)[22].

'Very strange!' muttered Holmes, **pulling** at the rope. [BAND 228]

'Rhyfedd iawn, yn wir!' **gan dynnu**'r rhaff unwaith eto. [CYLCH 42]

Here, the *pulling at the rope* had already begun before Holmes muttered what he did. However, the two actions also happen at the same time. This can be observed in our other examples:

'Fuoch chi 'rioed yn Sir Fôn?' meddai Winni, **gan edrych** tuag at yr ynys honno. [TE 39]

'Have you ever been to Anglesey?' Winni asked, **looking** across towards the island. [TEA 38]

Leaving his car in the almost deserted Lysle Street, he walked

Gan adael ei gar yn Stryd Gefn, a oedd erbyn hyn bron iawn â bod

---

[22] PWT 484 notes that in the written language the use of '*gan*' in this way is often marked by a comma before the preposition.

through a narrow passage leading from it into an open car park. [TIME 27]

yn wag, cerddodd ar hyd lôn gul a arweiniai o'r stryd at faes parcio agored. [AMSER 42]

... she walked sadly down the middle, **wondering** how she was ever to get out again. [ALICE 22]

... cerddodd yn drist i lawr y canol **gan feddwl** sut yn y byd yr âi allan eto. [ALYS II 11]

3.3i.c Since / because

In this context, '*gan*' is invariably followed by the verb-noun '*bod*' or an adverbial clause in an appropriate inflected verb form (*gan ei bod / gan y byddai / gan nad oes / gan y gallwn* etc.). When introducing an adverbial clause with emphasis, '*gan*' combines with '*mai*'.

Finally, **as nobody seemed about to explain** anything, he said 'I'm sorry...' [STONE 60]

O'r diwedd, **gan fod neb fel petaen nhw am egluro** dim byd, meddai, 'Mae'n ddrwg gen i...' [MAEN 38]

Then came the horses. **Having four feet**, these managed rather better than the foot-soldiers... [THRO 195–6]

Yna daeth y meirch. **Gan fod ganddynt bedwar carn** llwyddodd y rhain ychydig yn well na'r gwŷr troed... [TRWY 86]

Cawsant ganiatâd i fynd yn bennoeth **gan mai** i'r mynydd **yr aent**... [TEA 37]

They were allowed to go without hats, **as they were going** to the mountain... [TEA 37]

3.3ii 'DAN' Clauses

These are very similar to those with '*gan*' above however without the suggestion of action preceding the main clause. As the action expressed begins at the same time as the main clause, therefore, these are often (although not exclusively as illustrated by the final set of examples) associated with verbs of motion such as:

mynd / dod

to go / to come

Daeth rhyw fyddigions drwy'r drws **dan** hanner baglu, a'u dillad nhw'n edrych fel rhywbeth ar gyfer yr opera neu'r Savoy Hotel. [HUNAN 133]

Some society toffs **staggered** [lit. came <u>under</u> half staggering] through the door, dressed for the opera or the Savoy Hotel. [SOLVA 133]

... a **daeth** Eric, y plentyn, i lawr o'r llofft **dan grio**. [TRAED 131]

Eric, the child, **came** downstairs, **crying**... [FEET 117]

But Mike Teavee was already off and **running**. [CHARLIE 125]

Ond roedd Mike Teavee wedi **mynd dan redeg** yn barod. [SIOCLED 163]

Taflodd Owen yr arian ar y bwrdd mewn tymer, a chafodd glustan gan ei fam. Torrodd yntau allan i feichio crio, a **than grio yr aeth** i'w wely. [TRAED 37]

Owen flung the pennies on the table in a fit of temper, and his mother boxed his ears. He burst into tears and, **sobbing, went** to bed. [FEET 34]

rhedeg

to run

Mi gollodd ei phen yn lân wedyn a **rhedeg dan sgrechian** at y cymdogion. [AMSER 65]

She really panicked then and **ran yelling** blue murder to her next door neighbours . . . [TIME 41]

eistedd

to sit

Deuai Ifan yno, ac **eisteddai** wrth y tân yn y gegin **dan synfyfyrio**. [TRAED 97]

Ifan would come there and **sit** by the kitchen fire, **lost in thought**. [FEET 34]

other verbs of motion

. . . **cerddent** bob yn ddau neu dri **dan** ysmygu a sgwrsio am waith eu hysgolion; [WILLAT 158]

. . . *they **would walk** in twos or threes **smoking and chatting** about the work of their schools . . .*

Yn fuan, dyma Tegwyn Huws . . .. yn **llamu** at y meicroffôn **dan weiddi** . . . [HUNAN 249]

Suddenly, Tegwyn Huws . . . **leaped** to the microphone **shouting** . . . [SOLVA 249–50]

Yr heddlu enillodd, a dyma Merêd a'r criw'n **cael eu hel** o swyddfa'r slobs **dan** regi'n groch . . . [HUNAN 224]

The police won and Merêd and crew were **ejected** from the cop shop **swearing loudly** . . . [SOLVA 224]

Heidiodd fflyd o wylanod tua'r llong **dan** grawcian yn swnllyd. [PLA 52]

. . . and seagulls **swooped** around the ship **with their shrill cries**. [PEST 40]

with a directional particle (implying a verb of motion such as 'mynd')

Over she **toppled**, into the hole head first, **screeching** like a parrot. [CHARLIE 110]

Lawr â hi [lit. Down with her] i'r twll, â'i phen gyntaf, **dan sgrechian** fel parot. [SIOCLED 145]

Bant â fi lan yr heol **dan** **ddawnsio** i ddweud y newydd da wrth Byron. [HUNAN 60]	**I danced off** [lit. Off with me . . . dancing] up the road to tell Byron the good news. [SOLVA 60]

The final examples are of '*dan*' clauses without verbs of motion but where the action again is concurrent[23].

Ond mewn munud, **gafaelodd** ynof a'm cusanu **dan lefain**, Monica, O Monica. [MONICA 34]	But in an instant he **grabbed** me and kissed me, **all the while crying**, 'Monica, Oh, Monica.' [MONICA 33]
'Dwi 'di chwythu dy ben di?' **gofynnodd** Jojo **dan wenu**. [LLADD 165]	*'Have I blown your head?'* **asked** Jojo *smiling*.
. . . yn y chwarel, pan gâi gerrig da a'r rhai hynny'n hollti fel aur, ac yntau'n **chwipio gwaith** trwy ei ddwylo **dan ganu** . . . [TRAED 90]	So it was in the quarry when he had good stones which split cleanly and easily; **he would sing** as the **work skimmed** through his hands . . . [FEET 81]
He took two tablets out of their wrapping and ate them slowly, **grimacing** at their after-taste. [VICT 119]	**Estynnodd** ddwy dabled a'u cnoi'n araf, **dan dynnu stumiau**'r un pryd. [LLINYN 132]

3.3iii 'TRWY/DRWY' Clauses
In more informal registers, '*trwy/drwy*' may introduce clauses which explain or give a reason (similar to '*gan*' under 3.3i.c).

Y peth a'i gwylltiai oedd fod y peth wedi mynd ymlaen mor hir, **drwy fod gan Sioned le i ddisgyn** yn nhŷ ei nain. [TRAED 58	What made her angry was that it had gone on for such a long time, **since Sioned had had a bolt-hole** in the form of her grandmother's house. [FEET 51]

[23] See also Ifans (2006: 364) who notes that '*dan*' is used if the verb-noun refers to a condition.

Otherwise, 'trwy/drwy' connects with clauses discussing the means by which
an action was achieved or carried out often corresponding to English 'by'
(= by means of). The expression 'drwy wybod i mi' is heard with the meaning
of 'as far as I know'.

Dywedai greddf Jane wrthi fod y
nain yn dial arni hi **drwy swcro a
chymryd part** Sioned. [TRAED 52]

Jane's intuition told her that the
grandmother was getting her own
back **by assisting and encouraging**
Sioned. [FEET 46]

... he decided to work off his
remaining stiffness **by walking back
to his office** ... [TIME 85]

Penderfynodd hefyd gael gwared ar
y stiffrwydd a oedd yn dal i'w blagio
trwy gerdded yn ôl i'w swyddfa ...
[AMSER 135]

Ni welais yr un o'r ddau, **drwy
wybod i mi,** byth oddi ar hynny.
[CHWECH 137]

*As far as I know, I never saw either
of them ever again.*

3.3iv 'WRTH' Clauses

'Wrth' is used in adverbial clauses to give the meaning of 'while / when / as'
an action takes place or 'for the duration' of an action.

... and she tried to curtsey **as she
spoke** – fancy *curtseying* as you're
falling through the air! [ALICE 21]

A cheisiodd wneud cyrtsi **wrth ofyn**
– meddyliwch am wneud *cyrtsi* a
chithau'n syrthio trwy'r awyr! [ALYS
II 10]

A lady ... who had been sitting in
the window, rose **as we entered.**
[BAND 208]

Wrth inni fynd i mewn, fe gododd
merch fonheddig o'i sedd yn y
ffenestr. [CYLCH 13]

When Rogers made no reply
– ... – Stuchley peered at him ...
[TIME 92]

Wrth i Rogers beidio ag ateb
– ... – craffodd Stuchley arno ...
[AMSER 146]

Lluchiai'r llestri, a gwnâi sŵn
anferth **wrth hwylio ei brecwast ei
hun.** [TRAED 54]

She rattled the dishes and made a
clatter **as she prepared her own
breakfast.** [FEET 48]

3.3v 'AM' Clauses

'Am' like 'gan' and 'trwy' can introduce clauses relating to the reason for
something happening or causal clauses. It also occurs after the verb-noun
'bod' and is followed by another verb-noun in the following contexts:

3.3v.a *Near future >> about to / going to*

Finally, as nobody seemed **about to explain anything**, he said 'I'm sorry. . ..' [STONE 60]

O'r diwedd, gan fod neb fel petaen nhw **am egluro dim byd**, meddai 'Mae'n ddrwg gen i . . .' [MAEN 38]

'I met her just now going to her mother's and she told me to tell you not to expect her. **She will have supper** with mother.' [FEET 42]

'Mi gwelis i hi rŵan yn mynd acw at Mam, ac mi ddeudodd wrtha i am ddeud wrthoch chi am beidio â'i disgwyl hi. **Mae hi am gymryd swper** efo Mam.' [TRAED 47]

3.3v.b *Desire/ wanting >> an alternative to 'eisiau'*

'**Dwyt ti ddim am roi'r arian** i dy fam?' [TRAED 37]

'**Don't you want to give the money** to your mother?' [FEET 34]

. . . 'and now you're going to tell me the how of it. **I want everything**; how it started, what you've done and what you've made out of it.' [TIME 79–80]

. . . 'a rŵan rwyt ti'n mynd i ddeud wrtha i sut ddaru ti wneud hynny. **Dw i am glywed popeth** [lit. I want to hear everything], sut ddaru o ddechrau, be wyt ti 'di 'neud a be wyt ti 'di gael am 'i 'neud o.' [AMSER 126]

3.3v.c *Intention*

For a few minutes all went on well, and she was just saying '**I really shall do it this time** –' [THRO 139]

Am rai munudau aeth pethau ymlaen yn iawn, a hithau'n dweud '**Rydw i am ei gwneud hi'r tro hwn** –' [TRWY 25]

I understand that the sun's probably over the yardarm by now and **I'm going to have a drink**. Will you join me? [TIME 102]

Dw i'n dallt bod y tafarnau ar agor erbyn hyn, a **dw i am gael diod**. Be amdanoch chi? [AMSER 163]

3.3vi 'O' Clauses

Clauses linked with the preposition '*o*' relate to the reason why, as a result of whatever reason an action has occurred and by extension '*given that*', '*in view of*'. A common collocation is with the verb-noun '*edrych*' >>> '*o edrych yn ôl*' = *looking back, in retrospect*.

In glancing over my notes of the seventy odd cases in which I have during the last eight years studied the methods of my friend Sherlock Holmes . . . [BAND 207]

And I think that, **given some openess** about who you passed your information to, you could well be sleeping in your own bed tonight. [TIME 79]

Knowing your daughter – as I do not – have you any idea of why she should go away like this? [TIME 90]

O ddysgu'r adnodau, bob yn un, ond yn gyson fel y gwnaem ni, nid oedd y gwaith yn anodd. [HDF 101]

Ac **o sôn am garwriaethau Nwncl Jâms** clywais 'mam yn adrodd am un tro go smala yn digwydd iddo. [HDF 112]

Thinking back . . . [CIDER 27]

O fwrw golwg dros fy nodiadau ar y deg a thrigain o achosion dros yr wyth mlynedd diwethaf sy'n cofnodi dulliau gwaith fy nghyfaill Sherlock Holmes . . . [CYLCH 11]

A dw i'n meddwl, **o gael peth gonestrwydd** ynglŷn ag i bwy ddaru ti roi'r wybodaeth y cait ti gysgu'n dy wely dy hun heno 'ma. [AMSER 124–5]

O 'nabod eich merch – a thydw i ddim – oes gynnoch chi unrhyw syniad pam y byddai hi'n mynd i ffwrdd fel hyn? [AMSER 142]

Learning these verses one by one, as we used to do, the work was not difficult. [OFH 124]

And **speaking of Uncle Jâm's courtships**, I heard my mother related an amusing thing that happened to him. [OFH 137]

O edrych yn ôl . . . [SEIDR 38]

3.4 Chassé-croisé

Chassé-croisé[24] is used to describe a double transposition when translating between two languages. Many of these in the context of English–Welsh / Welsh–English will require a preposition-linked expression in Welsh and these are the primary focus for our discussion here.

. . . I seem to have **frightened her off**. [CIDER 6]

. . . mae'n amlwg fy mod i wedi **codi dychryn arni**. [SEIDR 11]

English has a verb *frightened* followed by an adverb *off*. In Welsh, this is not possible and it is translated by a verb-noun *codi* plus a noun *dychryn* and linked to the personal object (*her*) by the third person singular (feminine)

[24] See also Chapter 1 for more discussion on *chassé-croisé*.

conjugation of the preposition *ar* > *arni*. The literal meaning in Welsh here is *to raise fright on her*.

O, **mae'n ddrwg gennyf** eich brifo, Mrs Maciwan . . . [MONICA 41]	Oh, **I'm sorry** if I offend you, Mrs MacEwan . . . [MONICA 40–1]

Here, Welsh follows a pattern using the third person singular form of the verb-noun *bod* >> *mae* with an adjective *drwg* and the first person singular conjugated form of the preposition *gan*. English translates this with the first person singular of the verb *to be* >> *I am* with the adjective *sorry*. Again, in Welsh it would not be possible to express this in the same way. The literal meaning in Welsh in this example is *it is bad with me*.

Not all of our examples will include a preposition in Welsh – for example, *regret* can be expressed by *maen edifar gen i* with its literal meaning of *it is regretful with me* or by using the verb-noun *edifarhau* (often shortened to *difaru*). In this section, we consider *chassé-croisé* from a semantic point of view, starting with how different emotional states may be expressed in both languages.

3.4i Emotion: fear
Welsh uses the verb-noun *bod* in its third person singular form with the noun *ofn* (= *fear*) and then the preposition *ar*[25] linked to the subject. Therefore, *I am afraid* becomes *There is fear on me*. The idea of *fear* as a participle e.g. *a man fearing death* would be linked with the preposition *â/ag* >>> *dyn ag ofn marw arno* (lit. a man with a fear of death on him).

She was a bit frightened of this place now. [MAT 186]	Roedd ychydig o ofn y lle arni nawr. [MAT 180]
Yn union fel heno y teimlai pan fyddai wedi bod allan yn caru, fel **plentyn ag arno ofn** cael drwg gan ei fam. [TRAED 60]	It was exactly like this when he had been out courting, like a **child dreading** a scolding from his mother. [FEET 53]
Yr oedd ganddo fwy o ofn ei fam na'i dad, a pheth oedd i'w wneud? [CWM 192]	. . . **he was far more frightened of his mother than his father**. What was to be done? [GORSE 185]
It was calculated to embarrass and **alarm Barbara** in front of everyone. [CIDER 43]	Ei fwriad oedd **codi braw ar Barbara** a'i bychanu yng ngŵydd pawb. [SEIDR 61]

[25] This may come before or after the noun i.e. *mae ofn arno* or *mae arno ofn*.

However, our final example here shows that it is sometimes possible to express the subject with the form of *bod* employed rather than with the personalised *ar* (although it is likely that the additional *ar* in the example following the verb-noun *edrych* would make the possible construction **roedd ofn edrych ar hogyn arna i* slightly clumsy although not grammatically impossible).

'Fuo' neb mwy *strict* na fo 'rioed. **'Roeddwn i ofn edrach ar hogyn** pan fyddai o gwmpas . . .' [O LAW 149]	'There was never a more strict one than he is. **I was fightened to look at a boy** when he was about . . .' [FROM 118–19]

3.4ii Emotion: sorrow, regret

The expression *mae'n edifar gen i* is discussed above and would be viewed as belonging to more formal registers of Welsh, with the verb-noun *edifarhau / difaru* being preferred elsewhere. Sorrow in an apologetic sense is introduced by the phrase *mae'n ddrwg gen i* (or in SW *mae'n flin gen i / gyda fi*). This is sometimes shortened to simply *drwg gen i*. In the final example *to feel sorry for himself* has been translated as *teimlo'n ddigalon* – the verb-noun *teimlo* (= *to feel*) with the adjective *digalon* (= *low, depressed*). The reflexive element here makes the *drwg gen i* construction impossible and the more literal *drwg drosto ei hun* could be perceived as being more in the spirit of the equivalent English expression.

Erbyn hyn, **yr oedd yn edifar ganddo** anwybyddu cymaint o agweddau ar fywyd coleg. [TRAED 143]	But now **he regretted** not having shared in so many of the College activities. [FEET 124]
A finnau, wrth ail-feddwl ac ail-droi'r pethau ddwed'soch chi yn 'y meddwl yn nyfnder nos, yn dyfalu beth fydde wedi digwydd pe bawn i wedi derbyn eich cariad chi, ac yn **'difaru?** [FFENEST 31]	*And me, when thinking and turning over the things you said in my mind in the depth of the night, guessing what would have happened if I had accepted your love, and **regretted it?***
I'm sorry I had to bother you. [TIME 122]	**Ddrwg gen i** i mi orfod tarfu arnoch chi. [AMSER 195]
He didn't **feel sorry for himself** at all; this would probably be the best Christmas he'd ever had. [STONE 241]	**Ni theimlai'n ddigalon** o gwbl; mae'n debyg mai hwn fyddai'r Nadolig gorau erioed iddo. [MAEN 154]

3.4iii Emotion: shame

A similar expression using **bod** in the third person singular >>> **mae** with a noun **cywilydd** (= *shame*) and a personalised preposition **gan**[26] is employed in Welsh for the English **to be ashamed**. As in 3.4i, the sense of '*causing shame*' or '*making someone ashamed*' is conveyed with the verb-noun **codi**. We include one example of the adjective '*cywilyddus*' (= *shameful*) used in place of '*cywilydd*' although this is not common in modern Welsh.

Ond **roedd ganddo gywilydd** cyfaddef nad oedd digon o arian ganddo i dalu am y fordaith. [PLA 71]	Salah **was ashamed** to admit that his store of money didn't run to paying for the passage. [PEST 54]
'And all about a rattle!' said Alice, still hoping **to make them a** *little* **ashamed** of fighting for such a trifle. [THRO 171]	'A'r cwbl o achos rhyw degan,' meddai Alys, yn dal i obeithio **codi cywilydd arnynt** am ymladd dros beth mor ddibwys. [TRWY 59]
. . . **a chywilydd gennyf** ddweud na phlannwyd brigyn yn ôl yno byth wedyn gan na mab na ŵyr i 'nhadcu. [HDF 81]	**I am ashamed** to say that not a twig was ever planted back, either by son or grandson of my father. [OFH 98]
Yr oedd y wraig gyda'i diffyg dygiad yn atgas ganddi, ac eto yn wyneb yr ing sydyn hwn **yr oedd yn gywilyddus ganddi** beidio ag ateb yn garedig. [MONICA 10]	She disliked this uncouth woman, and yet, confronted with this sudden outburst, **she was shamed** into making a kind response. [MONICA 8]

3.4iv Emotion: homesickness, longing, yearning

Here again the same pattern as in i–iii above is followed in Welsh with the noun **hiraeth**, notoriously difficult to translate exactly into English but usually associated with a sense of *longing* or *missing home*.[27]

Ella **bydd arnoch chi hiraeth** wedi mynd i Lundain. [TE 57]	Perhaps **you'll be homesick** in London. [TEA 54]

---

[26] Again, this may come after or before the noun i.e. *mae cywilydd gen i* or *mae gen i gywilydd*. It is possible to use the preposition '*ar*' in this context too *mae cywilydd arna i*.

[27] One of the closest words in meaning to '*hiraeth*' is the Portuguese '*saudade*'.

3.4.v Emotion: surprise

The possibilities here are more numerous and revolve around the two key words (i) *syn* = *surprised* and (ii) *rhyfedd* = *strange*.

(i) *Syn*

Syn – although an adjective – may be used in a similar way to i–iv. *Bod yn syn gan* equates literally to *to be surprised with/by* when its equivalent in English is actually *to be surprised* with the preposition *gan* linking with the appropriate subject to express the English subject pronoun.

Mae'n syn gennyf feddwl, ac y mae cywilydd arnaf gofio mor hy oeddwn i gyda hi. [RHYS 231]	**I am surprised** to think, and ashamed to remember, how free I made with her. [RHYS 221]
Nid oedd yn syn gan yr un o'r ddau glywed . . . [TRAED 108]	**Neither of the parents was surprised** to hear this . . . [FEET 95]

Syn can also link directly with the verb-noun *bod* as can the verb *synnu* >>> *bod wedi'i synnu*.

Ro'n i braidd yn syn; ro'n nhw'n dwgyd yr holl bethe da yn y pantri, ac wedi gwagio'r ffrij hyd yn oed. [HUNAN 93]	**I was a bit taken aback**; they were stealing all the goodies. [SOLVA 93]
Actually, **he was surprised at** his own inspired guess that Webber might be involved . . . [TIME 94–5]	Fodd bynnag, **roedd wedi'i synnu gan** ei ysbrydoliaeth yn dyfalu bod gan Llywelyn ran yn yr achos . . . [AMSER 150]

The combination *syn o beth* should be noted in the sense of *it was a surprising thing to. . .*

Syn o beth oedd gweld y dieithriaid hyn a drigai yn y fwrdeisdref a'r castell yng Nghricieth. [PLA 180]	*It was a surprising thing to see these strangers who lived in the borough and the castle in Cricieth.*

Using the verb *synnu* (= *to be surprised*) is however a useful alternative to the lesser used *bod yn syn gan* pattern. The first person singular forms *rwy'n synnu at* (= *I'm surprised at*) and *synnwn i / ddim* (= *I would be surprised / wouldn't be surprised*) are particularly useful.

I'm surprised it didn't take the whole of the top of your head off! [MAT 64]	**Dw i'n synnu** na thynnodd e gorun dy ben di i ffwrdd! [MAT 58]
A **'synnwn i ddim** nad y clyfrwch hwn y tu hwnt i glyfrwch cynol a wnaeth frad Vic yn y pen draw; [HDF 137]	And **I should not be surprised** if it were this super-canine cleverness that betrayed Vic in the end . . . [OFH 171]
Synnwn i damed nad o'n nhw'n fy ngalw i'r hen rech sobor 'na yn stafell chwech neu beth bynnag. [CRWYD 101]	*I wouldn't be the least surprised* if *they called me that old sober fart over there in room six or whatever.*
'**Rydw i'n synnu**'ch clywed chi'n deud hynna, Daniel.' [RHANNU 187]	*'I am surprised* to hear you say that, Daniel.'
A dyna Robert Hughes, Uwchlaw'r Ffynnon, a'r oriel ddarluniau a baentiodd ef ei hun. Gwelais hi a **synnais** o wybod na chafodd y gŵr addysg yn y gelfyddyd. [WILLAT 227]	*And there was Robert Hughes, Uwchlaw'r Ffynnon, and the gallery of pictures he had painted himself. I saw it and* ***was surprised*** *to know that the man never had any education in art.*

The noun **syndod** (= *surprise*) is employed in combinations such as *er mawr syndod* (= *to great surprise*) or *mewn syndod* (= *in surprise*) as well as occasionally in a verbless phrase.

. . . diolchodd i Sandra am ei help ac **er mawr syndod iddi** gwthiodd bapur chwegain i'w llaw. [SELYF 60]	*. . . he thanked Sandra for her help and* ***to her great surprise*** *pressed a ten shilling note into her hand.*
Alice looked around her **in great surprise**. [THRO 147]	Edrychodd Alys o'i chwmpas **mewn syndod**. [TRWY 33]
Ond **syndod** mor ffurfiol a diddiddordeb ydoedd y darlithiau a gaem. [WILLAT 87]	*But it was* ***surprising / a surprise*** *how formal and uninteresting the lectures we had were.*

(ii) *Rhyfedd*

The adjective **rhyfedd** follows the verb-noun **bod**, again in a singular third person form in the appropriate tense and followed by the preposition **gan**.

This can appear without **bod** and **gan** as a verbless clause[28] as in the first examples below where the negative element **dim** lends a '*no wonder / no surprise*' meaning.

Cywilyddiodd Cannwyll wrth y fath fochyndra. **Doedd ryfedd** fod y byd yn mynd â'i ben iddo. [PLA 163]

Candle was ashamed at such foulness. **No wonder** *that the world was imploding.*

Doedd ryfedd yn y byd gen i [HUNAN 207]

This **didn't surprise** me [SOLVA 207]

'**Mi fasa'n rhyfedd iawn gin** 'i dad o feddwl 'i fod o'n deud pethau'r un fath.' [TRAED 14]

'His father would have been surprised to hear Ifan say such a thing.' [FEET 12]

Accepting that no person in his or her right mind would choose to walk the canal bank for pleasure, **he was not surprised** that he and Sleath were virtually the only two persons left in their world. [TIME 77–8]

Gan dderbyn na fyddai neb call am gerdded ar hyd glannau'r gamlas er mwyn pleser, **doedd dim rhyfedd** mai Saunders ac ef oedd yr unig ddau oedd yno. [AMSER 122–3]

The use of the associated verb **rhyfeddu *[at]*** should also be noted when there is an element of surprise and marvel/wonder.

Rhyfeddwn, yn fynych, **at** gof y plant y bûm i'n athro arnynt drwy'r blynyddoedd wedi gadael coleg. [HDF 101]

I often marvelled at the memory of children in my classes throughout the years after leaving college. [OFH 123]

3.4vi Liking / disliking

The verb-noun **hoffi** corresponds with the English *to like* and when negated, with the English *to dislike*. However, Welsh possesses other constructions to convey the idea of *liking/disliking* which can be expanded to express the wider idea of being *glad* or *displeased*. An appropriate third person singular form of the verb-noun **bod** plus either a *liking* adjective – **da** (= *good*) – or a *disliking* adjective – **cas** (= *nasty, odious*) – finally connected to the subject by the preposition **gan**.

>>> *Mae'n dda gennyf eich gweld* – *I'm happy to see you*
Mae'n gas ganddi fwyta uwd – *She hates eating porridge*

---

[28] See also Chapter 10 *Welsh verbless clauses*.

Both of these could also be rendered with an adjective such as *balch* (= *glad*) or a verb *casáu* (= *to hate*):

>>>   *Rwy'n falch o'ch gweld chi*
        Mae hi'n casáu bwyta uwd

Liking:

The '*mae'n dda gennyf*' construction can occur without the initial form of *bod* > '*da gennyf eich gweld*'. Note the example where the noun '*calon*' follows '*da*' as an intensifier. The negative may be formed by replacing the form of *bod* with the negative particle *ni(d) / na(d)*.

Cerddodd tua'i lety yn nannedd gwynt oer ac **yr oedd yn dda ganddo gyrraedd** ei ystafell. [CHWAL 170]	He walked back to his lodgings in the teeth of a biting wind and **was glad to get to** his room. [OUT 179]
Bûm i, wedi dyfod dipyn yn hŷn yn *saethwr* mawr; ond, erbyn hyn, **da gennyf ddweud**, i'm dwylo i fod yn bur lân o ran gwaed. [HDF 121]	When I became a man I was a great shooter, but by to-day, **I am glad to say**, my hands are fairly clean as regards blood. [OFH 150]
Yr oedd yn dda ganddo weled y diwedd. [TRAED 78]	**He was glad** when it was all over. [lit. It was good with him to see the end] [FEET 69]
Rhyw un hanner tudalen o lythyr a gefais oddi wrtho erioed. **Byddai'n dda calon gennyf ddod o hyd i** honno heddiw. [CHWECH 164]	*I only ever received about half a page of a letter from him. I would be really glad to find* that today.
Ond gwn fod yno, yn fy amser i, gôr aelwyd o bedwar llais yn canu mewn eisteddfod, weithiau – er **nad da gan fy nhad** o gwbl, oedd cystadlu. [HDF 179]	But I know that there was in my time a home choir of four voices that sometimes sang in eisteddfodau, although **my father did not care for** competing. [OFH 225]

By extension, the comparative degree of the adjective *da >> gwell* can be used in the same construction to express preference.

Ar un wedd **yr oedd yn well ganddo Geini** na neb yn y byd, ond ei wraig a'i blant . . . [TRAED 62]	There was a sense in which **he preferred Geini** to anybody except his wife and children . . . [FEET 55]

Pan ddaw llong i mewn i harbwr **gwell gan y capten gael** yr un clochydd bob tro i gywiro'r cwmpodau . . . [MONICA 10]	Whenever a ship comes into harbour **the captain always prefers** to have the same craftsman reset the compasses . . . [MONICA 9]

By changing the preposition following **gwell** to '**i**', the meaning is altered to an advisory one i.e. *it would be better (for one) to do X rather than Y*. Following this construction with a negative as in *it would be better for one not to do something* is rendered by using the verb-noun **peidio** with the preposition **â**.

'Yes, I think **we had better do** as you suggest.' [BAND 225]	'Ie'n wir, **well i ni dderbyn** eich awgrym.' [CYLCH 37]
Meddyliodd Elin Gruffydd y **byddai'n well iddi dorri ar ei thraws** yn y fan yma. [TE 56]	Begw's mother thought that **the time had come to interrupt**. [lit. that it would be better for her to interrupt her] [TEA 53]
'[A]nd *she* can watch us – only **you'd better not come** *very close*,' he added. [THRO 171]	'[A] mi fedr *hi* ein gwylio. Ond **well ichi beidio â dod** yn rhy agos,' ychwanegodd. [TRWY 58]

Disliking:

The discussion above can be mirrored in the context of *disliking* using an adjective such as **cas** (= *nasty, odious*) or other semantically similar ones. An alternative is to negate the '*da gennyf*' construction to create the opposite meaning.

Cas gennyf, yn grwt, **ydoedd** dweud fy adnod ar goedd yn y capel . . . [HDF 101]	As a boy **I hated saying** my verse publicly in chapel. [OFH 123]
He detested this bringer of doom and disaster role he had so often to play . . . [TIME 51]	**Yr oedd yn wrthun ganddo**'r rhan [lit. It was repugnant with him] honno o'i waith, bod yn gennad arswyd a gwae . . . [AMSER 80]
Erchyll ganddo'r syniad y gwelid ef ar y bws chwech bob dydd trwy weddill ei oes. [MONICA 52]	**He was horrified at the thought** [lit. Horrific with him the idea that. . .] of being seen on the six o'clock bus every day for the rest of his life. [MONICA 52]

Wel, mi wyddost **nad dda geni mo'r bobol** ... [GWEN 155]	Well, you know, **I detest** those people ... [GWEN 127]

The mirroring with the '*da gennyf*' construction does not extend to the comparative degree of the semantically opposite '*drwg*' (= *bad, evil*) >> **gwaeth**. However, this merits particular attention as it combines with the preposition '*i*' to translate the expression in English '*might as well do something*' >>> '*[g]waeth i chi wneud rhywbeth*'.

Waeth iti daflu fy newydd innau i mewn yr un pryd. [TRAED 60]	**You might as well throw** in my news at the same time. [FEET 52]
Of course, they want to hear the details; **they may as well hear them.** [UNSUIT 10]	Eisiau clywed y manylion maen nhw. **Waeth imi ddweud wrthyn nhw ddim**[29].
'I think **I may as well go in** at once.' And in she went. [ALICE 76]	'**Waeth imi fynd i mewn** ar unwaith.' Ac i mewn â hi. [ALYS II 75]

This construction can be further expanded by the addition of the preposition **heb** followed by a verb-noun >>> *waeth i chi heb siarad*. The implication is that one *might as well not speak*, i.e. there is no point in speaking, it wouldn't serve a purpose to speak.

'Well, **it's no use *your* talking about waking him**,' said Tweedledum ... [THRO 167]	'Well, **waeth i *chi* heb siarad ynghylch ei ddeffro**,' ebe Twidldwm ... [TRWY 55]
Maen' nhw'n dweud na all neb gadw cyfrinach oddi wrth ferch, a **waeth i minnau heb dreio.** [SELYF 97]	*They say that no-one can keep a secret from a girl, and **there's no point in me trying**.*

When combined with the preposition *gan*, there is an idea of indifference. This usage is mainly confined to informal registers.

'**I don't care about the colour**,' the Tiger-Lily remarked ... [THRO 141]	'**Waeth gen i am y lliw**,' meddai Lili'r Teigr ... [TRWY 26]
'**I don't give a tinker's toot** what your mummy thinks!' [MAT 114]	'**Waeth gen i** beth mae dy fam yn ei feddwl!' [MAT 108]

[29] Note the use of '*[dd]dim*' as a tag for this construction in more informal registers of Welsh.

It is appropriate also to consider the use of the adjective *gwiw* (= *fitting, suitable, appropriate*) again as a predicate to the subject (similar to *waeth i* above). *Gwiw* (or *wiw* / *fiw* in more informal registers) can be negated – indeed is most often encountered in its negative form – (again, like *waeth*) by the particle *ni* in formal registers which causes a soft mutation. More informally, the mutation remains but the negative particle is omitted or replaced by *does* before the adjective. *Gwiw* is connected to its subject by the preposition *i* and is translated as an act one would not *dare* commit or an act which would not be *suitable/fitting* sometimes corresponding to English *woe betide*.

Does wiw i Gruffydd Davies besychu ne' dishan pan fydd hi'n cysgu . . . [CHWAL 226]	Griffith Davies **dare not** cough or sneeze when she is sleeping . . . [OUT 238]
Ond **doedd fiw i chi fynd** yn rhy agos . . . dyna 'nghamgymeriad i mae arna i ofn. [PLA 132]	But **you couldn't risk** getting too close. That was the mistake I made. [PEST 92]
Gwlithodd llygaid Idris wrth syllu arno: cofiai mai felly bob nos am fisoedd lawer y cysgasai ei fachgen yntau, Gruff, ac **nad oedd wiw ei roi yn ei wely** heb ei beiriant pren. [CHWAL 137]	As Idris gazed down at him his eyes dimmed as he recalled that this was how his own boy, Griff, had for many months gone to sleep, and **woe betide if he were put to bed** without his wooden engine. [OUT 144]

3.4vii Need

Two nouns *angen* (= *need*) or *eisiau* (= *want*) are commonly employed in Welsh to translate English *need*. This is, however, a further example of *chassécroisé* where English has the subject plus a simple verb >>> *Siân needs / she needs* but Welsh has the appropriate third person singular form of the verb-noun *bod* with the noun (*angen* or *eisiau*) and the preposition *ar* linking to the subject >>> *mae angen / eisiau ar Siân / arni hi*. The object (if there is one) comes after *angen / eisiau* >>> *Siân needs money* > *Mae angen/eisiau arian ar Siân*[30].

---

[30] It should, however, be noted that there is a tendency to use these as verb-nouns as well more closely mirroring the English. This is particularly true with *eisiau* with the meaning of *to want*, e.g.

'Well, of course, that was the headmaster, quite different. **You need rest**.' [STONE 374]	'Wrth gwrs, fo ydi'r Prifathro, mae hynny'n wahanol. **Rwyt ti angen gorffwys**.' [MAEN 239]

Cychwynnodd yr adloniant yn ara gydag ychydig o gantorion lleol **ag angen gwersi canu'n amlwg arnyn nhw**, heb sôn am ysbrydoliaeth, yn plycio gitare rhad yn dila. [HUNAN 184]

The entertainment started slowly, as a few local singers who were obviously **in need of music lessons** and inspiration feebly strummed cheap guitars. [SOLVA 184]

'Madam,' he growled, 'I'm a police officer **needing an interview** with Mrs Stephanakis, so please don't play games with me.' [TIME 93]

'Madam,' ysgyrnygodd, 'un o swyddogion yr heddlu ydw i ac **mae arna i eisio**[31] **siarad** â Mrs Stephanakis, felly byddwch cystal â rhoi'r gorau i chwarae gemau efo fi.' [AMSER 148]

... teimlem ein tri **fod mawr angen mwy o raen a rhwbio ar y canu** ... [WILLAT 35]

... we three felt that the **singing needed** much more polishing and refining [lit. there was a great **need** of more polishing and refining **on the singing**].

An alternative construction is to use the noun **rhaid** (= *necessity*), however the subject prepositional link here is **i** not **gan** with the object following the preposition e.g. *I need to go* >> *(Mae) rhaid imi fynd*. Semantically, **rhaid** carries a greater element of *need* with *compulsion/necessity* than either **angen** or **eisiau**. The negated **ni raid** in the final example is associated with formal registers only (*does dim rhaid* being more usual in informal registers).

Yn awr, Alis, **rhaid iti orwedd yn ôl** a cheisio cysgu. [MONICA 7]

Now Alice, **you must lie down** and try to sleep. [MONICA 6]

Ond cofio'r nifer o ddynion culion, dialgar oedd yn llenwi pulpudau'r Llannau, **ni raid i neb synnu.** [CWM 189]

But **it is not surprising** [lit. There is no need for anyone to be surprised] when one remembers how many bigoted and intolerant men were to be found amongst the Welsh incumbents in those days.

... she remained a wife **needing to be informed** officially and in good time about her husband's death. [TIME 93]

... **byddai'n rhaid iddi gael gwybod** yn swyddogol am farwolaeth ei gŵr. [AMSER 147]

[31] '*Eisio*' is an informal variation of the standard '*eisiau*'.

3.4viii Emotion: doubt / suspicion[32]

The verb '*amau*' corresponds to the English '*to doubt*' although Welsh often prefers the adjective '*amheus*' (*doubtful*) after a third person singular form of '*bod*' and reconnected to the subject by the preposition '*gan*':

> *mae'n amheus gen i* >>> lit. *it is doubtful by me* >>> I doubt

Our examples illustrate that some authors prefer the use of the nouns '*cwestiwn*' (*question*) or '*amheuaeth*' (*doubt*) which may also be connected through the preposition '*gan*' to the subject:

I suspected the bastard was pushing it behind my back, probably in the club as well. [TIME 121]	**Ro'n i'n amau** fod y bastard yn gwerthu'r stwff y tu ôl i 'nghefn i, ac yn y clwb 'na hefyd mae'n debyg. [AMSER 193]
A dyna'r tro cyntaf i mi ddechrau **amau** a oedd pawb yn dweud y gwir, bob amser. [HDF 123]	That was the first time I began **to doubt** whether everybody invariably told the truth. [OFH 152]
... and **suspecting** that his normally stone-cold sober chief had had a drink or two ... [TIME 73]	**Amheuai** fod ei fòs – a oedd, fel arfer, mor sobr â sant – wedi cael diod neu ddau. [AMSER 115]
I doubt whether the Lockwoods had ever heard of the occasion. [CIDER 43]	**Mae'n amheus gen i** a oedd teulu'r fferm, mwy na finnau, wedi clywed am y dathliad arbennig hwnnw. [SEIDR 62]
It was doubtful that Sickert had understood the implication in Rogers's words ... [TIME 124]	**Roedd hi'n amheus** a oedd Sycharth wedi deall yr awgrym yng ngeiriau Rogers ... [AMSER 197]
I'd bought her a dress. My sort, not hers. **I doubt**[33] if she would have worn it. [VICT 39]	Ro'n i wedi prynu ffrog iddi. Fy math i o ffrog, nid 'i math hi. **Mae'n gwestiwn gen i** fydda hi wedi'i gwisgo hi. [LLINYN 44]

[32] See also Chapter 9, 3 '*to wonder*'.
[33] The English use of '*if*' in place of '*whether*' to introduce an indirect question can sometimes influence usage in Welsh but in general the use of the particle '*a*' is still favoured in formal registers even if it is omitted as in this example (although the soft mutation which follows it remains at the beginning of '*fydda hi*').

I saw marks on Barbara's throat that I now know to be love bites . . . [CIDER 36]	Sylwais ar farciau cochion ar wddf Barbara ac, erbyn heddiw, **does gen i ddim amheuaeth** [lit. I have no doubt that] nad olion cusanu oeddan nhw . . . [SEIDR 52]

Another useful expression in this context is:

Does dim dwywaith [am]	*There is no doubt [about]*

It can be thought of more literally as *there are no two ways about it* given that *dwywaith = twice*. The conjugated preposition *amdani* can round off the phrase when the meaning is more impersonal. By extension, the implicit lack of doubt here can make this an equally useful way of implying *certainty* too.

I can't think **there could be any doubt** about his identity when he was found dead by a neighbour who knew him by sight. [TIME 104–5]	Fedra i ddim meddwl **fod 'na unrhyw amheuaeth** ac yntau wedi cael 'i ddarganfod yn farw gan gymydog oedd yn 'i nabod o'n iawn o ran ei weld. [AMSER 167]
It is certain, therefore, that my sister was quite alone when she met her end. [BAND 217]	**Does dim dwywaith** felly nad oedd fy chwaer ar ei phen ei hun pan fu farw. [CYLCH 26]
Nid oes dwywaith nad Ysgol Lenyddol Montréal . . . oedd y mudiad llenyddol cyntaf ac ymwybodol o wir bwys yn hanes Canada Ffrengig. [BIRT 30]	*There's no doubt that the Montréal Literary School . . . was the first, conscious literary movement of real importance in the history of French Canada.*

3.4ix Remembering

'*Cofio*'[34] is the verb-noun which usually corresponds to English '*to remember*'. There is also the construction [*mae*] *cof gan + subject* [*+ preposition 'am*'] >>>

---

[34] '*Cofio*' when the meaning '*to remember about something*' is implicit, is followed by the preposition '*am*' which does not always require translation in English, e.g.:

Cofiai am fore Llun yn niwedd Gorffennaf a'r ysgol newydd dorri ac yntau'n fawr ei siom am na châi fynd i'r chwarel. [CYCHWYN 11]	**He remembered** [*in other words, it was something about which he remembered*] a Monday morning at the end of July when the school had just broken up, and his bitter disappointment at not being allowed to start work in the quarry. [BEGIN 9]

mae cof gen i am yr hen ddyddiau meaning *I remember the old days* which could also be expressed *rwyf yn cofio'r hen ddyddiau.* The difference is similar to that between English '*I remember*' and '*I have a memory of.*' It is possible to modify the noun '*cof*' (but not the verb-noun '*cofio*') with the adjective '*brith*' [= *speckled*] which precedes the noun and gives a sense of a *vague* memory rather than a *clear* memory of something.

I remember the engine was running because I saw lots of exhaust smoke, so she'd probably been brought in it. [TIME 109]	**Dw i'n cofio** fod yr injan yn rhedeg oherwydd mi welais i lot o fwg egsôst, felly mae'n debyg 'i bod hi 'di cael 'i chludo ynddo fo. [AMSER 174]
Cofiaf yn dda amdanaf yn eistedd yn yr haul ar Gors Cefn Cyrnig ar fore Sadwrn mwyn yr haf . . . [HENAT 176]	**How well I remember** sitting in the sun on Cefn Cyrnig heath one calm Saturday morning in summer . . . [LOCUST 150]
Cof melys gennyf amdano yn fy anfon yn Chwefror 1894 i Gaernarfon i'r Ysgol Ganolraddol gyntaf yng Nghymru . . . [HENAT 19]	**I have a happy memory of his** taking me in February 1894 to Caernarfon to the first Intermediate School in Wales . . . [LOCUST 23]
. . . **mae rhyw frith go'** 'da fi o ddihuno yn nhŷ Anti Marrianne . . . [HUNAN 19]	**I can vaguely remember** being woken up in Auntie Marrianne's house . . . [SOLVA 19]

3.4x Debt

This has been discussed in 3.2i.e above. The sense of debt is connected with the preposition '*ar*' – money owed, debt or a duty is '*on*' someone in Welsh. As in previous examples in this section, a noun such as '*dyled / dyletswydd*' [= '*debt/duty*'] or a sum of money follows the third person singular of '*bod*' and the preposition '*ar*' connects to the subject. However, in this instance of '*debt*'-related phrases, it is common for the '*ar + subject*' to come before the noun and in particular before a sum of money owing and when this occurs, the noun will take a soft mutation.

Mae **ar bobl fel Bob Dylan ddyled fawr** i'r traddodiad canu gwerin . . . [HUNAN 56]	People like **Bob Dylan owe everything** to the folk music tradition . . . [SOLVA 56]

In humanity **I felt bound** to supply her with some sort of account. [CIDER 24]	Ac i fod yn deg â hi, teimlwn **ei bod yn**[35] **ddyletswydd arnaf** i adrodd fy stori wrthi. [SEIDR 34]
Ni fedrasant dalu dim o'r **arian oedd ar eu tyddyn.** [TRAED 88]	They were unable to repay any of the **money they owed on the house.** [FEET 74]

3.4xi Other

This final section includes various other examples of the '*bod*' (3rd person singular) + adjective + preposition '*gan*' conjugated according to the subject, construction. The final one illustrates how the English '*to find something + adjective*' can sometimes be translated with this kind of construction too.

'... ond **mae'n siŵr gin i** y rhydd hi rywfaint o'r arian i'w thad a'i mam.' [TRAED 102]	'... but **I'm sure** she'll give some of it to her own father and mother.' [FEET 91]
Mae'n sicr gennyf fod y peth yn fwriadol, ac eto ni welaf amcan y peth ... [TROW 152]	*I am certain that this was intentional, and yet I don't see its purpose* ...
Ni fu cofio ffigurau erioed yn **drafferth gennyf** ... [HDF 102]	**I have never had any trouble** in memorizing figures ... [OFH 124]
... **anodd gennyf feddwl** am neb tebyg iddi ymhlith merched heddiw. [HENAT 13]	**I find it hard to think** of anyone like her among the women of today. [LOCUST 17]

3.5 Preposition stranding

We refer here to the practice increasingly encountered in very informal registers of spoken Welsh of ending a statement with an unconjugated preposition when a conjugated preposition should normally occur. This is probably best explained as interference from spoken English where this is much more common.

---

[35] The predicate '*yn*' is used here but it would also be possible to say: '... *teimlwn fod dyletswydd arnaf*...', the difference being that the former (i) literally means '*I felt that it was a duty on me*...' and the latter (ii) '*I felt there was a duty on me*'. The corresponding sub-clauses would have been: (i) *Mae hi'n ddyletswydd arnaf* and (ii) *Mae dyletswydd arnaf.*

'Aye, ma popeth yn OK, Mam. Dim byd i **fecso am.** [FFYDD 177]

'Aye, everything's OK, Mam. Nothing **to worry about**, honest.' [FAITH 124]

'Pwy ffwc ti'n **siarad efo**, ffatso?!' medda Ceri. [LLADD 147]

'*Who the fuck are you **talking to**, fatso?!' said Ceri.*

The informality of the examples is evident both from the vocabulary and code-switching in the first one. In a more formal register and in standard usage, one would expect:

>>>   *dim byd i fecso **amdano**.*
>>>   *pwy wyt ti'n siarad **efo fo/hi?***

3.6 Conclusions

The decision as to which preposition should be used (if at all) to correspond between Welsh and English is a fundamental one which demands our attention. One instance of this (discussed in 3.1.ii) relates to the concept of '*ysgrifennu / writing*'. It is possible in English to *write a letter to someone* or to *write someone a letter*. In Welsh on the other hand, the latter example is not possible at all. The prepositional equivalent of English *write to* is always required. In addition, Welsh differentiates between *writing to a person* and *writing to a place*. The former is *ysgrifennu at* and the latter *ysgrifennu i*. This is just one example of many where there is a mismatch between the two languages. We have seen also that prepositions in Welsh perform wider roles than they may do in English, as in those which are used as heads of clauses or to convey the English present participle. The particularly versatile preposition '*ar*' has been discussed in detail in particular its association with emotions, conditions, moods and senses. Consideration of stranding, albeit in informal registers, is necessary to reflect the realities of contemporary usage which will be encountered in dialogues in particular and as a stylistic marker of some current speech patterns. It is beyond the scope of one single chapter to cover all the possible verb + preposition combinations in either language. Our main aim here has been to draw attention to the ways in which prepositions are used, as well as their respective functions, in Welsh and in English.

4

Welsh possessive constructions

4.0 Introduction

For speakers of other languages, idiomatic Welsh appears to be filled with possessives, many of which come as a surprise because no possessive would be possible in the English equivalent. Possessive patterns are very common in idiomatic Welsh. If Siôn sits up in bed, he may be said to *codi ar ei eistedd* (literally 'rise on his sitting'), and when crouching he is *yn ei gwrcwd* ('in his crouching'). On Susan's twentieth birthday she will *troi ei hugain oed* (literally 'turn her twenty [years] of age') and she will, one hopes, live to be *dros ei phedwar-ugain* ('over her eighty'). When drunk, Dafydd is *yn ei ddiod* ('in his drink'), when weeping he is *yn ei ddagrau* ('in his tears'), and when in a bad mood, he is *yn ddrwg ei hwyl* ('bad his spirits'). Perhaps he was injured in an accident—in Welsh, then, he 'got his injuring' (*Cafodd ef ei anafu*), or maybe he was bitten by a dog, in which case he 'got his biting' (*Cafodd ef ei frathu*). Either way, he is *yn waeth ei le* ('worse his place') than before. His friends will try to cheer him up, but everyone knows that he is *yn anodd ei blesio* ('difficult his pleasing').

In isolation, any of these formulations might seem like a one-off example, but collectively they illustrate something larger that permeates much Welsh stylistic idiom. These varied uses of possessives range from constraints to options. Even though the constraints are, by definition, places where one has no choice but to use the possessive in Welsh (at least in certain registers), such instances greatly increase the frequency of possessive constructions in Welsh where none occur in English, thus contributing to the overall 'feel' of the language in which idiomatic uses of possessives play an unmistakable role. The uses which represent constraints include compound prepositions, direct objects of verb-nouns, the *cael* passive, and 'bod' complement clauses. After briefly reviewing these obligatory contexts, the various stylistic patterns which are options will be examined.

We begin a quick survey of the more or less obligatory contexts and then proceed into the optional categories, without trying to draw too a rigid line between the two.

4.1 Compound prepositions and directional adverbial particles[1]

A number of compound prepositions in Welsh have a complex internal structure consisting of a short preposition and a noun. These function together as a compound preposition, such as *yn ymyl* 'beside, next to', *ar gyfer* 'for', and *yn erbyn* 'against'. Of interest here is that, when the complement of such a preposition is a personal pronoun, this takes the form of a possessive in Welsh (though not in English).[2] Thus, we get paradigms like the following:[3]

ar	fy nghyfer	'for me'		yn	fy erbyn	'against me'
ar	dy gyfer	'for you'		yn	dy erbyn	'against you'
ar	ei gyfer	'for him'		yn	ei erbyn	'against him'
ar	ei chyfer	'for her'		yn	ei herbyn	'against her'
ar	ein cyfer	'for us'		yn	ein herbyn	'against us'
ar	eich cyfer	'for you'		yn	eich erbyn	'against you'
ar	eu cyfer	'for them'		yn	eu herbyn	'against them'

Other Welsh prepositions that behave like this include *o amgylch* 'around', *o gwmpas* 'around', *o flaen* / *ymlaen* (yn + blaen) 'before, in front of', *gerbron* (ger + bron) 'before, in the presence of', *ynghylch* (yn + cylch) 'about, concerning', *er mwyn* 'for the sake of', *ar ôl* 'after, behind', and *uwchben* (uwch + pen) 'above, over'. The second word in each expression is a noun, even though it is not always possible to provide convenient English nouns as glosses for these. A handful of examples showing how compound prepositions work in context is given below:[4]

[1]   PWT 5.15–5.21 / THO 214, 217, 368
[2]   English has a small number of prepositions which can occur in a pattern very similar to the Welsh one. For instance, *for the sake of* takes the personal forms *for my sake*, *for your sake*, *for his sake*, *for her sake*, etc. and *in the midst of* has the shapes *in our midst*, *in your midst*, *in their midst*. But such prepositions are infrequent in English and may have an archaic flavour, whereas they are quite common in Welsh.
[3]   Possessive noun phrases vary in whether the possessor is repeated after the noun: *eich llyfr* or *eich llyfr chi* 'your book'. The same kind of variation is found in compound prepositions, thus *ar eich cyfer* or *ar eich cyfer chi* 'for you'.
[4]   At this point it would be useful to note that Standard Welsh does not allow preposition stranding, or leaving a preposition at the end of its clause with no complement (see Chapter 3), whereas such a pattern is quite common in English in all but the most formal registers:

Nid oedd dim i fyw **er ei fwyn** . . .   There was nothing to live **for** . . .
[LLEIFIOR 159]   [RETURN 137]

Standard Welsh requires the internal possessives in these cases. The standard language also excludes patterns like **yn erbyn hi* ('against her') or **ynghylch ef* ('about it'). Preposition stranding has entered informal Welsh via contact with English, but it is generally avoided by those wishing to find a more authentic or traditional Welsh style.

Yr oedd yn bwriadu'i darllen
drwyddi yn y tair wythnos
gwyliau Nadolig a oedd **o'i flaen**.
[CRYMAN 164]

He was intending to read the whole
lot during the three weeks of the
Christmas vacation that now lay
before him. [SICKLE 136]

Cododd yntau ar ei eistedd. Yr oedd y
wlad yn braf **o'i gwmpas**. [TRAED 44]

He sat up. The countryside was
lovely **around him**. [FEET 36]

Pan gaeodd Robert Pugh y drws **ar
ei ôl** ... [CRYMAN 218]

When Robert Pugh closed the door
behind him ... [SICKLE 180]

Teimlodd benglin rhywun yng
nghanol ei gefn, a chododd ei olwg i
weld Wil Parri'n gwyro'n filain **uwch
ei ben**. [CHWAL 155]

Looking up, he saw Will Parry
bending menacingly **over him**.
[OUT 164]

Yn f'ymdrechion, tebyg i mi dynnu
sylw gŵr ieuanc a safai **yn f'ymyl** ...
[CYMER 54]

*In my efforts, I must have drawn the
attention of a young man standing
beside me* ...

... the more they strained **against
it**, the tighter and faster the plant
wound **around them**. [STONE 345]

... mwyaf yn y byd roedden
nhw'n tynnu **yn ei erbyn**, tynnaf
a chyflymaf yn y byd roedd y
planhigyn yn ei lapio'i hun **o'u
hamgylch**. [MAEN 220]

An additional complication occurs with some of these complex prepositions: when the possessive is plural, the noun in a few cases may be made
plural to agree with it. This is obligatory with *uwchben* 'above', in which the
noun *pen* 'head' takes the plural form *pennau*. Thus, 'above them' is *uwch eu
pennau* and not **uwch eu pen*:

Roedd dwy odyn galch segur hefyd,
ac, **uwch eu penne nhw**, siop y gof,
Johnny Jenkins, oedd ar ei anterth
bryd hynny. [HUNAN 35]

Above two disused lime-kilns stood
Johnny Jenkins's blacksmith shop,
which was going full swing then.
[SOLVA 35]

On the other hand, with *ôl* (plural *olau*) and *blaen* (plural *blaenau*[5]) this kind
of plural agreement is optional. Thus, 'after us' can be rendered as *ar ein hôl*
or as *ar ein holau*, with no apparent difference in meaning. Similarly, 'before
you (pl.)' / 'in front of you (pl.)' can be either *o'ch blaen* or *o'ch blaenau*. This
variation is seen in the following pairs of examples:

---

[5] PWT [5.18ch] considers this usage as more typical of north Walian dialects.

Daeth y Norddmyn o Norwy dan ddyfod heibio i Ynysoedd Orch a Shetland a chyrraedd Iwerddon [. . .] **Ar eu hôl** daeth y Daniaid . . . [PEATCYM 47]

The Norsemen came from Norway coming past the Orkney and Shetland Islands and reaching Ireland [. . .] After them came the Danes . . .

Ond **mynd ar eu hola nhw** wnes i . . . [NOS 33]

But I **followed them** . . . [NIGHT 25]

[D]aeth ofn i'm calon wrth imi sylwi ar lwybr troellog y Neidr yn hongian ar serthni'r mynydd **o'n blaen**. [O LAW 201]

[M]y heart sank as I looked at the 'Snake', the winding path that clung to the steep mountain-slope **in front of us**. [FROM 165]

A moment later we were out on the dark road, a chill wind blowing in our faces, and one yellow light twinkling **in front of us** through the gloom to guide us on to our sombre errand. [BAND 234]

Eiliad yn ddiweddarach roeddem allan ar y ffordd dywyll, a gwynt oerllyd yn chwythu yn ein hwynebau, ac un golau melynwyn yn pefrio draw **o'n blaenau** drwy'r gwyll, i'n tywys ar ein neges brudd. [CYLCH 51]

Harry thought that none of the lessons he'd had so far had given him as much to think **about** as tea with Hagrid. [STONE 176]

. . . meddyliodd Harri nad oedd yr un o'r gwersi a gawsai hyd yn hyn wedi rhoi cymaint iddo feddwl **yn ei gylch** ag a wnaeth y te gyda Hagrid. [MAEN 109–10]

Most of the other nouns involved in compound prepositions (such as *cwmpas*, *amgylch*, *cyfer*, *cylch*) are never made plural. For instance, 'about them, concerning them' is *yn eu cylch* and not **yn eu cylchoedd*:

'Mae pawb yn poeni gormod **yn 'u cylch nhw** o lawer. Y nhw sydd wedi dewis 'u byw, ac mae pawb wedi anghofio erbyn hyn mor gwta y buo hi efo'r arian rheini.' [TRAED 139]

'Everybody is worrying far too much **about them**. They have chosen the way they want to live, and everybody has forgotten how selfish she was with that money.' [FEET 123]

. . . disgyblion ieuainc newydd agor eu llygaid ar y byd rhyfedd **o'u cwmpas**. [WILLAT 41]

. . . *young pupils who have just opened their eyes to the amazing world around them.*

. . . the more they strained against it, the tighter and faster the plant wound **around them**. [STONE 345]

. . . mwyaf yn y byd roedden nhw'n tynnu yn ei erbyn, tynnaf a chyflymaf yn y byd roedd y

planhigyn yn ei lapio'i hun **o'u
hamgylch**. [MAEN 220]

The set of compound prepositions overlaps with the directional particles used to construct phrasal verbs. (Phrasal verbs are examined in detail
in Chapter 6). The four elements *yn ôl* 'back', *ymlaen* 'on, forward, along', *o
gwmpas* 'around' and *o amgylch* 'around' can be treated either as invariable
adverbs, with no complement, or as compound prepositions, with an internal
possessive complement. The two patterns are illustrated below with the verb
dod yn ôl 'to come back', with the invariable particle in the lefthand column,
and the variable pattern with internal possessor on the right:

Rwy'n dod **yn ôl**.	Rwy'n dod **yn f'ôl**.	'I come back.'
Rwyt ti'n dod **yn ôl**.	Rwyt ti'n dod **yn d'ôl**.	'You come back'
Mae e'n dod **yn ôl**.	Mae e'n dod **yn ei ôl**.	'He comes back.'
Mae hi'n dod **yn ôl**.	Mae hi'n dod **yn ei hôl**.	'She comes back.'
Rydyn ni'n dod **yn ôl**.	Rydyn ni'n dod **yn ein hôl** (holau).	'We come back.'
Rydych chi'n dod **yn ôl**.	Rydych chi'n dod **yn eich ôl** (olau).	'You come back.'
Maen nhw'n dod **yn ôl**.	Maen nhw'n dod **yn eu hôl** (holau).	'They come back.'

Both of these patterns occur in Welsh literature. The following two examples
show the invariable pattern:

. . . a ninnau'n *bona-fide travellers* ar
feirch dwy-olwyn llwyd, yn **dod yn
ôl** o siwrnai bell. [HDF 169]

. . . and we were bona-fide travellers
on our grey bicycles **returning** from
a far journey. [OFH 212]

Ymhen tua dwyawr **daeth Twm
yn ôl**, ac aroglau siop chips arno.
[TRAED 84]

In about two hours, **Twm came
back**, bringing with him the aroma
of the chip-shop. [FEET 70]

The seven personal permutations (including both 3sg masculine and feminine
variants) are shown in the following examples:

'Deuddag o'n i'n cychwyn o'r Borth
'cw, ond yr oedd gin i fwstás a locsyn
pan ddois **yn f'ôl**.' [CHWAL 110]

'Twelve I was when I started from
Porth, but I had a moustache
and whiskers when I got **back**.'
[OUT 116]

Dos **yn d'ôl** i gysgu. [CHWAL 59]

*Go **back** to sleep.* (Go to sleep again. [OUT 61])

'You must confine yourself in your room, on pretence of a headache, when your stepfather comes **back**.' [BAND 231]

'Pan ddaw eich llystad **yn ei ôl** o Lundain, rhaid i chi encilio i'ch ystafell ar unwaith, gan gymryd arnoch fod gennych ben tost.' [CYLCH 46]

I didn't get any further before Alice reappeared. [CIDER 115]

Cyn i mi hel rhagor o feddyliau, daeth Alice **yn ei hôl**. [SEIDR 154]

Aethon ni **yn ein holau** i Rennes, wedi cael llond ein boliau, a chael ein talu ar ben hynny. [CRWYD 48]

*We went **back** to Rennes, having gotten our bellies full and having been paid on top of that.*

'Well i chi fynd **yn 'ych ôl** rŵan, rhag ofn i rywun 'yn gweld ni.' [TRAED 73]

'It would be better for you to go **back** now, in case someone see us.' [FEET 65]

They'll be along with the screens and floods as soon as they've bunged them **back** in the cells. [TIME 10]

Byddan nhw yma efo'r sgriniau a'r llifoleuadau cyn gynted ag y byddan nhw wedi 'u gwthio nhw **yn eu holau** i'r celloedd. [AMSER 13]

The same is true of *ymlaen, o gwmpas* and *o amgylch*, all of which may occur with an internal possessive or without one. This is illustrated below with examples of *edrych o gwmpas* 'to look around' and *mynd ymlaen* 'to go on, go ahead, continue':

It was the White Rabbit, trotting slowly back again, and looking anxiously **about** as it went, as if it had lost something; [ALICE 40]

Y Gwningen Wen oedd yno, yn dod yn ôl ar drot araf gan edrych **o'i chwmpas** fel pe bai wedi colli rhywbeth ... [ALYS 33]

'Oh gosh,' Matilda said, sitting up and looking **around**. [MAT 214]

'O'r annwyl,' meddai Matilda, gan eistedd i fyny ac edrych **o gwmpas**. [MAT 208]

'I'm very brave, generally,' he **went on** in a low voice: 'only to-day I happen to have a headache.' [THRO 170]

'Rwy'n ddewr iawn fel rheol,' **aeth ymlaen** yn isel ei lais, 'ond mae'n digwydd fod gen' i gur yn fy mhen heddiw.' [TRWY 58]

'Car number two,' the father **went on**, 'cost [. . .]' [MAT 51]

'Fe gostiodd car rhif dau,' **aeth** y tad **yn ei flaen** [. . .] [MAT 44]

There is no identifiable difference in meaning between the invariable formulations and the variable ones with internal possessor. We are thus dealing here with a stylistic option rather than a constraint.

4.2 Object pronouns

A well-known aspect of Welsh grammar which represents a clear constraint in the standard language is the fact that the direct objects of verb-nouns function syntactically (in certain ways) like possessives, for instance in taking possessive personal pronouns where English has object pronouns. The following examples show the various permutations with the verb-noun *gweld* 'to see'. The possessives cause the same mutations of the verb-noun as they do for a possessed noun:

'Dydach chi ddim yn **fy ngweld i** wedi aros ddigon hir?' [TRAED 59]

'Don't you think I have waited long enough?' [FEET 49]

Dy weld di'n sâl yn dy wely a'th wynab a'th ddwylo di mor wyn â'r gobennydd . . . [CYCHWYN 236]

Seeing you ill in bed and your face and hands as white as the pillow . . . [BEGIN 238]

I've certainly not **seen him** since . . . [TIME 110]

[D]w i'n bendant heb **ei weld o** ers hynny . . . [AMSER 175]

A pan fydda Nain yn ffwndro mi fydda'n mynd allan o tŷ'n slei bach heb i neb **ei gweld hi** . . . [NOS 104–5]

And when Gran was confused, she used to sneak out of the house without anyone **seeing her** . . . [NIGHT 88]

'Well i chi fynd yn 'ych ôl rŵan, rhag ofn i rywun **'yn gweld ni.**' [TRAED 73]

'It would be better for you to go back now, in case someone **sees.**' [FEET 65]

'Oddi yno wedyn deuthum yma i Lundain y bore 'ma, efo'r bwriad penodol o'**ch gweld chi**, syr, a gofyn am eich cyngor.' [CYLCH 28]

'. . . from whence I have come on this morning, with the one object of **seeing you** and asking your advice.' [BAND 219]

Dda gen i mo'**u gweld nhw** o gwmpas y pentra. [RHANNU 130]

*I don't like **seeing them** around the village.*

This use of possessives as direct objects becomes optional at a certain level of very informal, generally spoken Welsh where instead of *Dw i eisiau dy weld di* 'I want to see you' one may encounter *Dw i eisiau gweld ti* (see Davies 2016,

Willis 2016). The latter pattern is generally absent from all written styles except those attempting to represent very informal speech, such as dialogue in a novel.

4.3 The *cael* passive

The non-literary passive used in most contemporary Welsh consists of the appropriate form of the verb *cael* followed by a verb-noun with its object expressed as a possessive. This construction bears some resemblance to the preceding one, but in the passive, the repetition of the possessive object after the verb-noun is blocked (thus, 'Mair got hurt' is *Cafodd Mair ei brifo* but not **Cafodd Mair ei brifo hi*), whereas with verb-nouns generally, the repetition of the possessive object is not only possible but very frequent (*Bydda i'n ei gweld hi* 'I will see her'). The following examples are illustrative of the *cael* passive:

Peiriannau'n refio, rhegfeydd, olwynion certi'n clecian mynd a thyrfe a dyrnodie llwythi trymion yn **cael eu lluchio o gwmpas** fel sachedie o blu. [HUNAN 133]

Engines revved, curses flowed, cart-wheels rattled and heavy loads crashed and thudded as they **were thrown around** like sacks of feathers . . . [SOLVA 133]

Cafodd ei brifo gan yr ateb olaf. [TE 42]

That last remark had hurt her feelings. [TEA 41]

From **being** one of the most popular and **admired** people at the school, Harry **was** suddenly the most **hated**. [STONE 304]

Yn lle bod yn un o'r bobl fwyaf poblogaidd, yn **un a gâi ei edmygu'n fawr**, bellach **roedd yn cael ei gasáu** yn fwy na neb yn yr ysgol. [MAEN 194]

Alice got behind a tree, for fear of **being run over**, and watched them go by. [THRO 195]

Aeth Alys y tu ôl i goeden rhag ofn **cael ei sathru**, a'u gwylio'n mynd heibio. [TRWY 86]

With *wedi* tenses it is possible to omit *cael*. For instance, in the first example below, *ei fod o wedi cael ei dwyllo* '(that) he'd been conned' can become *ei fod o wedi'i dwyllo*. The same pattern is found with *newydd* for the recent past:[6]

---

[6] The same pattern (*wedi* + POSSESSIVE + VERB-NOUN) can function as the equivalent of an English past participle being used adjectivally (note that translating English past participles is discussed at length in Chapter 7):

Mae hi'n ddel, ond bod ganddi wyneb fel plentyn **wedi'i sbwylio**, a phwt o drwyn. [MONICA 7]

She's pretty, but she has the face of a **spoilt** child, and a snub nose. [MONICA 5]

Sypyn ydoedd mewn papur llwyd, ac **wedi'i lapio**'n daclus. [RHYS 152]

It was a small brown-paper bundle, neatly **packaged**. [RHYS 148]

Roedden nhw'n byw mewn tŷ newydd cysurus ar stad **newydd ei chodi** yn arwain oddi ar gomin yr Eglwys Newydd . . . [HUNAN 77]	They lived in a comfortable new house on a **recently built** estate off Whitchurch Common . . . [SOLVA 77]
. . . when he realised **he'd been conned.** [TIME 97]	. . . pan ddaru o sylweddoli **'i fod o wedi'i dwyllo.** [AMSER 154]
. . . the bolt was significantly oxidised, suggesting that **it had been generally unused** for some years . . . [TIME 95]	Roedd y follt wedi'i hocsideiddio'n sylweddol, gan awgrymu **nad oedd wedi'i defnyddio** ers rhai blynyddoedd . . . [AMSER 150]

Verb-nouns with passive interpretation also occur in a small number of prepositional constructions. The translations here are varied and context-dependent. The most common pattern is that seen in the first group of examples below, where, for instance, *roedd e i'w weld* means literally 'it was to its seeing': that is, 'it was to be seen'. More idiomatically in English, this could be rendered as 'it could be seen' or even 'it was visible'. Similarly, *roedd e i'w glywed* 'it was to its hearing' means 'it was to be heard', or idiomatically 'it could be heard' or even 'it was audible'. Sometimes the translations do not specify the sense of sight or hearing and just use the verb 'seem':

Doedd menywod lleol bron byth **i'w gweld** mewn tafarne y dyddie hynny. [HUNAN 66]	Local women **were hardly ever seen** in pubs in those days . . . [SOLVA 66]
. . . y **mae** ôl llafur yr hen ŵr a'i gynlluniau **i'w gweld** yno, o hyd, mewn llawer man. [HDF 99]	the marks of the old man's labour and planning **are still to be seen** there in many places. [OFH 121]
Roedd arfordir Dyfnaint **i'w weld** yn y pellter niwlog ar draws Môr Hafren . . . [HUNAN 80]	Across the Bristol Channel, in the misty distance, the Devon coast **seemed** quite close . . . [SOLVA 80]
Wedyn, fe glywes i sŵn chwerthin islaw – **roedd e i'w glywed** o'r tu fas. [HUNAN 210]	Then I heard someone laughing below; it **seemed** to be coming from outside. [SOLVA 210]

Other verbs can similarly occur after the preposition *i*, thus a price that 'was to its expecting' is one that was '(to be) expected', and coming here 'to my insulting' is coming 'to be insulted':

Petai'r fargen a'r cerrig yn dda, pris isel **oedd i'w ddisgwyl**, ond gan eu bod fel arall . . . [TRAED 88]

If the place allotted to them to work was a good one and the rock easy to handle they could expect a low price [lit. a low price **was to be expected**] . . . [FEET 79]

'Mr Griffiths, 'dydw i ddim wedi dwad yma **i f'insyltio**.' [LLEIFIOR 50]

'Mr Griffiths, I haven't come here **to be insulted**.' [RETURN 41]

Other prepositions can occur in this construction as well. *Heb* 'without' gives a negative passive. For instance, a drink that was 'without its touching' is an untouched drink:

She looked at his **untouched** whisky on the counter and frowned. [TIME 104]

Edrychodd ar ei wisgi ar y cownter, **a oedd heb ei gyffwrdd**, a gwgodd. [AMSER 166]

Canodd ddwywaith **heb ei hateb**. [MONICA 44]

She rang twice **without getting any response**. [MONICA 43]

Actually, he was surprised at his own inspired guess that Webber might be involved for, so far as he remembered, he **had never been suspected or convicted** of breaking offences. [TIME 94-5]

Fodd bynnag, roedd wedi'i synnu gan ei ysbrydoliaeth yn dyfalu bod gan Llywelyn ran yn yr achos, a hwnnw **heb ei amau na'i ddedfrydu erioed** o droseddau'n ymwneud â thorri i mewn. [AMSER 150]

The preposition *o* + possessive + verb-noun can give the sense 'from / by / through being VERBed' so *o'i adael*, 'literally 'from its leaving', means 'from [or though, or by] being left'. Note the lexicalised expression *o'i gymharu â* 'in comparison with, compared to' (lit. 'from its comparing with'), and its feminine and plural permutations *o'i chymharu, o'u cymharu â*:

Weithiau, byddai'r powdwr yn yr ergyd, **o'i adael yn rhy hir yn y faril**, yn lleithio, ac yn gwrthod tanio pan ddylai. [HDF 129]

Sometimes the powder in the charge would have got damp **through being left in too long** and would not fire. [OFH 161]

Nid oedd y troi cefn a'r gadael yn ddim **o'i gymharu** â bwriad yr adar duon o fradychu eu cydweithwyr, yma ar eu tomen eu hunain. [RHANNU 119]

*This turning one's back and leaving was nothing **compared** to the strike breakers' intention to betray their fellow workers, here on their own ground.*

Its spiny wings were huge **compared** to its skinny **jet** body . . . [STONE 292]	**O'u cymharu** â'i chorff tenau, gloywddu roedd ei hadenydd pigog yn anferth. [MAEN 186]

A possessive also functions as a direct object pronoun in the construction illustrated by 'John is easy to please', which comes out as 'John is easy his pleasing' (*Mae Siôn yn hawdd ei blesio*). Adjectives frequently found in this construction in the corpus include *anodd* 'difficult', *hawdd* 'easy', *gwerth* 'worth' and *amhosib(l)* 'impossible':

Pobl od oedd y Cymry, **anodd eu deall** ac **anos eu caru.** [CRYMAN 42]	The Welsh were an odd people, **hard to understand** and even **harder to love.** [SICKLE 33]
'Rwy'n barod i gyfaddef heno, er mor **anodd 'y mhlesio** ydw i, 'mod i'n fodlon ar y gwaith. . .' [LLEIFIOR 179)	'I'm willing to admit this evening that, however **hard I am to please,** I'm satisfied with the work . . .' [RETURN 154–5]
. . . y gymdeithas ym mro fy mebyd lle'r oedd pawb yn nabod ei gilydd, ac yn gwybod popeth **gwerth ei wybod** am ei gilydd . . . [CHWECH 56]	. . . *the society in the area where I grew up where everyone knew each other, and knew everything **worth** knowing about each other* . . .
Mae llwyau sir Gaernarfon, er enghraifft, yn **hawdd eu hadnabod** fel rheol oherwydd eu bod o gynllun arbennig . . . [PEATCYM 83]	*Lovespoons from Caernarfonshire, for example, are **easy to recognise** as a rule because they are of a special design.*
'. . . the folks would fly at his approach, for he is a man of immense strength, and absolutely **uncontrollable** in his anger.' [BAND 212–13]	'. . . byddai'r trigolion yn ffoi wrth ei weld yn agosáu, oherwydd mae'n ŵr aruthrol o gryf, ac yn un **amhosib ei drin** yn ei dymer.' [CYLCH 19]
This association was **worth cultivating.** [VICT 85]	Roedd y berthynas yma'n **werth ei meithrin.** [LLINYN 96]

4.4. 'Bod' complement clauses[7]

Verbs of perception (*I **heard** that John was ill*), of mental activity (*I **think** that it will rain*), and of discourse (*I **stated** that I was leaving*) are often followed by

---

[7] PWT – Y Cymal Enwol 6.92 / THO – The Noun Clause 353

a complement clause which in English begins with the conjunction *that*. (This conjunction can be deleted in less formal styles). The equivalent Welsh construction is very different, taking the form of a *bod*-clause (often called a 'noun clause') in which the grammatical subject of the lower clause is expressed with a possessive accompanying the verb-noun *bod*. The seven permutations of this form are illustrated in the following examples:

Dim ond imi ddeud wrtho fo **fy mod i** am fynd i'r Sowth i helpu Kate, mi ga 'i fenthyg dwybunt neu dair gynno fo ar unwaith. [CHWAL 145]

I have only to tell him [**that**] **I** want to go to the South to help Kate and I shall have a loan of two or three pounds from him at once. [OUT 153]

I heard the Queen say only yesterday [**that**] **you** deserved to be beheaded. [ALICE 77]

Mi glywais i'r Frenhines yn dweud ddoe ddiwethaf **dy fod di**'n haeddu cael torri dy ben i ffwrdd! [ALYS II 76]

He must have been covered in blood. [lit. . . . **that he is** blood over him] [CIDER 75]

Mae'n rhaid **ei fod o**'n waed drosto. [SEIDR 103]

Dwedon nhw wrtha i'n ddiweddarach **ei bod hi** wedi cael trawiad anferth ar ei chalon ac wedi marw yn y fan a'r lle. [HUNAN 97]

I was told later **that she'd had** a massive heart attack and had died instantaneously. [SOLVA 97]

'Do you think [**that**] **we** might have been lovers in a different life?' [TIME 110]

'Ydach chi'n meddwl ei bod hi'n bosib **ein bod ni** wedi bod yn gariadon mewn bywyd arall?' [AMSER 176]

'Thank goodness [**that**] **you** found me!' [STONE 194]

'Diolch byth **eich bod chi** wedi cael hyd imi!' [MAEN 123]

It was quite clear to them **that they were** at this moment standing in the presence of a master. [MAT 108]

Roedd hi'n hollol amlwg iddyn nhw **eu bod nhw**'n sefyll yng ngŵydd meistr yr eiliad honno. [MAT 102]

The *bod*-clauses illustrated above are interpreted as either present tense or imperfect, depending on context. In other words, the *bod*-clause in these cases is technically ambiguous as to tense, receiving its temporal interpretation from context:

He said accusingly, 'You weren't actually going to jump in that bilge at all, were you.' '**I'm afraid I was,**' Sleath answered in a soft and gentle voice . . . [TIME 78]

Dywedodd yn gyhuddgar, 'Doeddat ti ddim o ddifri'n bwriadu neidio i mewn i'r lobscws yna, oeddat ti?' '**Mae arna i ofn fy mod i,**' meddai Saunders mewn llais araf, tyner. [AMSER 124]

'What did Miss Trunchbull call *your father* when they were around the house at home?' '**I'm sure she called him Magnus,**' Miss Honey said. 'That was his first name.' [MAT 208-9]

'Beth oedd Miss Trunchbull yn galw *eich tad* pan oedden nhw o gwmpas y tŷ gartref?' '**Dw i'n siŵr ei bod hi'n ei alw e'n Magnus,**' meddai Miss Honey. 'Dyna oedd ei enw cyntaf.' [MAT 203]

Out of context, *Mae arna i ofn fy mod i* could mean either 'I'm afraid I am' or 'I'm afraid I was'. But in the dialogue in which this sentence occurs in *A Time to Kill*, the context makes clear that, while the 'being afraid' is present tense (*Mae arna i ofn*), the complement clause is imperfect ('[that] I was [going to jump]').

The *bod*-clauses are a constraint of Welsh grammar, since it is not possible to construct complement clauses with verbs like *dweud* 'to say' and *clywed* 'to hear' without them. We note that it is only when the complement clause expresses the present or the imperfect that the verb is reduced to the verb-noun *bod*. When the complement clause is in the conditional or the future it is unreduced:

'. . . and all I can hope for now is **that he'll resist** being arrested . . .' [TIME 99]

'. . . dw i ond yn gobeithio rŵan **y bydd o'n osgoi** cael ei arestio . . .' [AMSER 157]

Ar ôl cael tamaid o swper, gwthiwyd y bwrdd yn ôl a gwneud cylch o gwmpas y tân, a gwyddai **Begw y byddai Dafydd Siôn yn <u>dechrau arni</u>**. [TE 28-9]

After supper the table was pushed back so that we all sat in a half-circle round the fire. Begw knew **that Dafydd Siôn would <u>get going</u>** any moment now. [TEA 29]

4.5 Interim summary: constraint versus option with idiomatic possessives

Most of the contexts we have discussed so far are fairly well covered in Welsh grammars, whereas those to which we turn now generally go unmentioned.

This is partly because most of them can be considered stylistic options – this, coupled with the fact that it is generally possible to express the same meaning differently, often with a single-word equivalent. These contexts fall in three broad categories: 1. the use of possessives with phrases describing positions of the body, 2. in phrases used as modifiers of various kinds, and 3. the use of possessives with numbers.

4.6 Possessive phrases describing positions of the body

A large number of prepositional phrases involving a possessive are used in Welsh, generally as verbal complements, to describe positions or movements of the body. Quite a number of these have English phrasal verbs as their usual translation equivalent:

aros	ar ei draed	to stay up (at night)	('to stay on his feet')
aros	ar ei eistedd	to stay seated	('to stay on his sitting')
bod	yn ei blyg	to be bent over	('to be in his fold')
bod	yn ei ddyblau	to be doubled over	('to be in his doubles')
codi	ar ei draed	to get up, get to one's feet	('to rise on his feet')
codi	ar ei eistedd	to sit up	('to rise on his sitting')
codi	i'w sefyll	to get up, stand up	('to rise to his standing')
gorwedd	ar ei hyd	to lie down, stretch out	('to lie at his length')
mynd	ar ei bedwar	to get down on all fours	('to go on his four')
mynd	ar ei gwrcwd	to crouch down	('to go on his crouching')
mynd	i'w gwman	to crouch down	('to go to his crouching')
neidio	ar ei draed	to jump up	('to jump on his feet')
sefyll	ar ei draed	to stand up	('to stand on his feet')
sefyll	yn ei gwrcwd	to crouch down	('to stand in his crouching')
sefyll	yn ei unfan	to stand still	('to stand in his place')
troi	yn ei unfan	to turn around	('to turn in his place')

Most likely due to English influence, many of these Welsh idioms are now in competition with literal translations of the English phrasal verbs, e.g. *eistedd i fyny* 'to sit up' competes with *codi ar ei eistedd* (lit. 'to rise in one's sitting'). These possessive constructions can thus be considered options, at least in contemporary Welsh for speakers or writers for whom the English-inspired patterns are viable possibilities (for an extensive discussion of phrasal verbs, see Chapter 6).

The following table is organised alphabetically by the noun which occurs in the possessive prepositional phrases. The examples illustrate a wide variety of uses of this pattern and frequent English translation equivalents:

cefn	He stumbled **backward** and knocked over his lamp, which went out at once. [STONE 256]	Baglodd **wysg ei gefn** a tharo'i lamp drosodd. Diffoddodd honno ar unwaith. [MAEN 162]
	... trawodd Harri ef â holl nerth y fraich glwyfedig, a syrthiodd y llanc **ar wastad ei gefn**. [GWEN 88]	Harry struck him with his damaged right arm such a blow that he fell **on his back**. [GWEN 77]
crwmach	... sêt fawr fechan – gan faint y gwrthddywediad – lle na allai y rhai a eisteddai ynddi edrych ar y pregethwr heb gael *stiff neck*, ac felly aethant i'r arferiad o wrando **yn eu crwmach**, ac aeth rhai ohonynt yn naturiol gefngrwn. [GWEN 60–1]	... a narrow big pew, whose occupants suffered the discomfort of a stiff neck through gazing at the preacher. To over-come this **they slouched in their seats**, and as a result became permanently round shouldered. [GWEN 58]
cwman	'Ie, ond Wil,' cwynodd Terence, gan **droi yn ei gwman** ac ymbalfalu am ddau ysgub arall i'r bwch nesaf... [CRYMAN 103]	'Yes, but Will,' complained Terence, **crouching down** and groping for another two sheaves for the next stook... [SICKLE 84]
	With Rogers watching, **Hagbourne crouched** and fitted one of the keys in the lock of the box, then lifted its lid. [TIME 24]	**Aeth Howells i'w gwman** a gosod un o'r allweddi yn nhwll clo y bocs wrth i Rogers ei wylio, yna cododd y caead. [AMSER 36]
cwrcwd	Reaching Snape, **she crouched down**... [STONE 236]	Wedi cyrraedd Sneip, **aeth ar ei chwrcwd**... [MAEN 150]
	Munud wedyn fe **safodd yn ei gwrcwd** ar ben y mur. [MONICA 32]	A moment later **he was crouching** on top of the wall. [MONICA 30]

cwrcwd (contd.)	Wedyn dyma fi'n **codi ar fy nghwrcwyd**. Oeddwn i wedi dysgu sglefrio i lawr Rallt erstalwm pan fydda hi wedi rhewi. [NOS 105]	After that, I **got down into a crouch**. I'd learned how to slide down the hill ages ago when it had frozen before. [NIGHT 89]
dwbl / dyblau	Neville was **bent double**, wheezing and spluttering. [STONE 196]	Roedd Nefydd **yn ei ddau ddwbl**, yn tagu ac yn rhochian. [MAEN 125]
	He had a tall red night-cap on, with a tassel, and he was lying **crumpled up** into a sort of untidy heap, and snoring loudly. [THRO 166]	Roedd ganddo gap nos uchel am ei ben, gyda thasel, a gorweddai **yn ei ddyblau** yn dwmpath aflêr yn chwyrnu'n drwm. [TRWY 54]
	Pan ddihunes i y bore wedyn yng ngwely George V, roedd Tessa **yn ei dyble** gan boen yn ei bola. [HUNAN 250]	When I woke up in the morning in George V's bed, Tessa was **convulsed** by pain in her abdomen. [SOLVA 250]
eistedd	She **sat up** in bed and looked down at her large full breasts. [VICT 48]	**Cododd ar ei heistedd** yn y gwely ac edrych ar ei bronnau mawr llawn. [LLINYN 54]
gorwedd	... meddyliai rhai ohonynt mai cellwair yr oeddwn i'r tro hwn wedyn pan ddywedwn wrthynt yn fy ing **ar fy ngorwedd** y fan honno fy mod i wedi torri fy nghoes ... [CHWECH 65]	*Some of them thought that I was joking as I told them,* **lying there** *in my agony, that I had broken my leg.*
hanner	Yn y cyfamser aeth John, mab yr Eos, **at ei hanner** i'r llyn, a *gaff* ganddo; [WILLAT 201]	*Meanwhile, John, the Nightingale's son, went into the lake* **up to his waist** *with a gaff;*
hyd	There were four of them, **stretched out** on the warm-smelling grass. [UNSUIT 60]	Roedd yno bedwar i gyd, yn **gorwedd ar eu hyd** ar y gwelltglas cynnes. [GORTYN 76]

hyd (contd.)	Yr oedd Paul **ar ei hyd** mewn cadair freichiau yn darllen yr *Observer*. [LLEIFIOR 31]	Paul was **lolling** in an armchair with a copy of *The Observer*. [RETURN 24]
ochr(au)	Yna o dipyn i beth culhaodd y coridor ac fe fu'n rhaid iddyn nhw gerdded **wysg eu hochrau** i fyny'r grisiau llithrig. [PLA 205]	*Then in a short while the corridor narrowed and they had to walk* **sideways** *up the slippery steps.*
pedwar	– he hit the field **on all fours** – [STONE 237]	trawodd y cae **ar ei bedwar** – [MAEN 150]
	Ond edrychodd Chwilen arni'n awr **yn cropian o gwmpas ar ei phedwar** yn chwilio'n ddyfal am rywbeth. [PLA 119]	Chwilen Bwm watched her as she **crawled round** the floor, searching for something. [PEST 61–2]
plyg	Weithiau, pan welwn fy nhad **yn ei blyg** uwch ei lyfr a'i bapurau-siwrin a'i gyfrifon, sylweddolwn fod ganddo lawer ar ei feddwl; [DYDD 65]	*Sometimes, when I saw my father* **bent** *over his book and his insurance papers and his accounts, I realised he had a lot on his mind;*
sefyll	'I don't take a bath,' Miss Honey said. 'I wash **standing up**.' [MAT 189]	'Dw i ddim yn cael bath,' meddai Miss Honey. 'Dw i'n ymolchi **yn fy sefyll**.' [MAT 182]
	Cododd Karl **i'w sefyll** ac edrych arni. [LLEIFIOR 33]	**Karl got up** and looked at her. [RETURN 26]
	... dim ond y muriau mawreddog yn edrych i lawr arnaf **ar eu sefyll** mor llonydd â mynachod; a'r nos yn afon ddu, ddofn yn llifo'n araf heibio; [DYDD 85]	*... only the majestic walls looking down at me,* **standing** *as still as monks. The night is like a deep black river flowing slowly by;*
traed	Everyone fell over laughing except Hermione, who **leapt up** and performed the countercurse. [STONE 270]	Dechreuodd pawb ond Hermione rowlio chwerthin. **Neidiodd hi ar ei thraed** ar unwaith a gwneud gwrth-felltith. [MAEN 171]

traed (contd.)	A'i Fam o'n cadw gola lamp ac **aros ar ei thraed** trwy'r nos yn disgwyl amdano fo. [NOS 42]	And his Mam keeping the lamp lit and **staying up all night** waiting for him. [NIGHT 33]
	Codai'n foreach, **eisteddai**'n hwyr **ar ei draed** yn darllen. [CRYMAN 98]	He got up earlier, and **sat up** late reading. [SICKLE 81]
	Cododd Abel ar ei draed; . . . [RHYS 174]	**Abel got upon his feet.** [RHYS 167]
	He **stood up** as George Webber was shown in and indicated a chair. [VICT 79]	**Safodd ar ei draed** pan ddaeth Alun Hardwick i mewn a gofyn iddo eistedd. [LLINYN 89]
unfan	Cordelia reckoned that she must have **waited there immobile** in the shadows for nearly half an hour . . . [UNSUIT 135]	. . . barnodd Cordelia'i bod hi wedi bod yn **sefyll yn ei hunfan** yn y cysgodion am ryw hanner awr . . . [GORTYN 171]
	Cododd fy ngolygon ato, ac roeddwn ar fin agor fy ngheg pan **drodd yntau yn ei unfan** a dechrau craffu o gwmpas yr ystafell. [CAER 224]	*'I looked up at him, and I was about to open my mouth when he **turned around on the spot** and began staring around the room.'*
	'Ron i fel iâr yn pigo **yn 'i hunfan.** [CHWAL 170]	I was like a hen pecking **in just the same place.** [OUT 178-9]
	'Roedd ei chôt-fawr yn gadach amdani ar ôl **eistedd yn ei hunfan** drwy'r nos . . . [DYDD 12]	*Her overcoat was like a dishrag on her after **sitting in the same spot** all night long . . .*
wyneb	Unweth, es i dros y cyrn i bwll anferth yn llaca i gyd **ar wastad fy ngwyneb.** [HUNAN 189]	Once I went over the handlebars, **flat on my face** in a huge muddy puddle. [SOLVA 189-90]

A few phrases of this type have lent themselves to very idiomatic developments. *Ar ei ben*, literally 'on his head', has come to have several unpredictable meanings:

immediately, instantly	Gallwn eu clywed nhw lawr llawr yn chwerthin ac yn tynnu coes, yn bur feddw, ac yna rhaid 'mod i wedi syrthio i gysgu **ar fy mhen.** [HUNAN 186]	I could hear them below, laughing and joking and pretty drunk. I must have fallen asleep **instantly.** [SOLVA 186]
precisely, exactly	. . . **quite precisely** eleven-fifteen. [VICT 120]	. . . chwarter awr wedi un ar ddeg **ar 'i ben** [LLINYN 133]
	. . . at eight-thirty **exactly** . . . [TIME 13]	. . . am hanner awr wedi wyth **ar ei ben** . . . [AMSER 19]
headfirst[8]	Wyt ti'n gwybod dy fod ti'n mynd i uffarn **ar dy ben,** i ganol tân a brwmstan ac i ddamnedigaeth am dragwyddoldeb a thragwyddoldeb? [NOS 43]	Do you know you're going to Hell, **headfirst** into the middle of the fire and brimstone, to damnation for all eternity? [NIGHT 34]
	She'd driven off a straight stretch of highway **into a tree.** [CIDER 19]	Roedd hi wedi gyrru oddi ar y ffordd a mynd **ar ei phen** i **goeden.** [SEIDR 27]
	Uncle Vernon nearly **crashed into the car in front.** [STONE 31]	Bron i Yncl Vernon **fynd ar ei ben i'r car o'u blaenau.** [MAEN 19]
	Ron went speeding in the direction that Harry was pointing, **crashed into the ceiling,** and nearly fell off his broom. [STONE 348]	Brysiodd Ron i'r cyfeiriad roedd Harri'n pwyntio iddo, ac **aeth ar ei ben i'r nenfwd.** Bu bron iddo syrthio oddi ar ei ysgub. [MAEN 222]

---

[8] The idiom *mynd ar ei ben (i)* is the usual translation equivalent for 'to crash (into) something'.

straight, direct	. . . a **straight** answer . . .	. . . atab **ar ei ben** . . .
	[STONE 316]	[MAEN 201]

Similarly, *hanner* 'half' when used with possessives has taken on idiomatic meanings, including *yn ei hanner* used to refer to folding something in two or cutting something in half:

Pan o'n i'n byw yn River Street, un o'm jobsys bach i oedd torri'r Radio Times **yn ei hanner** ar ôl tynnu'r stêpls . . . [HUNAN 57]	When we lived in River Street, one of my little tasks was to remove the staples from the *Radio Times*, cut it **in half** . . . [SOLVA 57]
There was a single iron bed with a hair mattress and on it a sleeping bag and a bolster **folded in two** to make a high pillow. [UNSUIT 44]	Roedd ynddi wely haearn sengl ac arno sach gysgu a bolster **wedi'i blygu yn ei hanner** i wneud gobennydd uchel. [GORTYN 57]

The idiom *ar ei hanner* 'on its half' refers to something that is half used or half consumed:

. . . ar ymyl y soser lwch, **sigaret wedi'i diffodd ar ei hanner.** [LLEIFIOR 135]	. . . near the ashtray, **a half-smoked cigarette** had been stubbed out. [RETURN 115]
He smiled companionably at a man who, though his **partly used cigar** was still smoking on its ashtray . . . [TIME 123]	Gwenodd yn gyfeillgar ar ddyn a oedd – serch fod ganddo **sigâr ar ei hanner** yn dal i fygu yn y blwch-llwch . . . [AMSER 195]
. . . **half a bar of chocolate** [VICT 87]	. . . **bar o siocled ar ei hanner** [LLINYN 99]
. . . a red toothbrush and **half-used tube of toothpaste** [UNSUIT 48]	Brws dannedd coch a **thiwb o bâst dannedd ar ei hanner** [GORTYN 61]

And finally, *ar hanner* plus a possessive and a verb-noun or a noun can specify a particular activity that is halfway to completion:

. . . tua'r caeau yr oeddynt **ar hanner eu haredig** . . . [PLA 174]	. . . *towards the **half-ploughed** fields* . . .
– a'r rhaser yn llaw fy nhadcu **ar hanner ei goruchwyliaeth.** [HDF 68]	. . . and in my grandfather's hand the razor resting **halfway through its operation.** [OFH 81]

... y lip yn y sgubor **ar hanner ei gwneud** gan fy nhadcu ... [HDF 175]

... the creel that my grandfather **hadn't finished** making in the barn ... [OFH 220]

'R oedd hi tua thri o'r gloch y bore hwn a dram o lo **ar hanner ei llanw** gennym ac eisiau ei chwpla cyn mynd allan. [CHWECH 184]

It was nearly three o'clock that morning and we had a half-filled dram of coal that we wanted to finish before leaving.

Sbonciodd y rhes moduron dros ddarn ffordd a oedd **ar hanner ei thrwsio** ... [CRYMAN 73]

The car rattled over a section of the road that was **under repair** ... [SICKLE 60]

... bachgen addawol iawn, **ar hanner ei yrfa.** [CHWECH 203]

... a very promising boy, halfway through his career.

4.7 Modifier phrases with internal possessives: States of mind or bodily conditions

The patterns PREPOSITION + POSSESSIVE + NOUN (e.g. *yn ei ddiod* 'tipsy, drunk') and ADJECTIVE + POSSESSIVE + NOUN (e.g. *absennol ei feddwl* 'absent-minded') are frequently used to create idiomatic modifying phrases which almost always describe a state of mind or a physical condition. In many cases, they can be translated as adjectives or adverbs in English, though the translation equivalents also include prepositional phrases and verbs. We illustrate both of these patterns below, starting with the PREPOSITION + POSSESSIVE + NOUN combinations.

Probably the most common kind of translation equivalent for this pattern is an English adjective, or occasionally an adverb:

Mi fasa lobscows yn well pryd i'r hogan yna, wir, a hitha' **ar 'i chythlwng** bob amsar. [TE 53]

Lobscouse would make a better meal for that girl, **half-starved** as she always is. [TEA 50]

... ferched y Red Cross yn bwydo ffoaduried **ar eu cythlwng.** [HUNAN 108]

... the Red Cross ladies feeding **starving** refugees. [SOLVA 108]

'Roedd hi **ar gefn 'i cheffyl** am rywbeth. [TRAED 137]

She was **uppity** about something. [FEET 121]

... y piler hyfryd 'na o diriondeb, symylrwydd, daioni, gwirionedd a

... that lovely pillar of humanity, simplicity, goodness, truth and

nerth nawr yn fenyw druenus, **yn ei dagre**. [HUNAN 67]

strength was now a pitiful, **weeping woman**. [SOLVA 67]

Roedd Wilbert **ar ben ei ddigon** o weld llwyddiant ei fenter gyntaf ym my roc a rôl . . . [HUNAN 248]

Wilbert was **overjoyed** at his first foray into the world of rock-'n'-roll . . . [SOLVA 248]

. . . medde Charlie **yn ei ddiod**. [HUNAN 150]

. . . said a **pissed-up** Charlie. [SOLVA 150]

Âi'r tad i bob ffair pa un bynnag a fyddai ganddo fusnes yno ai peidio, a deuai adref dipyn **yn ei ddiod**, ac felly y gwnâi'r mab ar ei ôl. [GWEN 8]

Father always went to market whether he had any business there or not and had always come home a little **tipsy**, and so did the son. [GWEN 16–17]

. . . edrychent fel gwenoliaid **ar eu hediad**. [TRAED 33]

. . . they looked like **flying** swallows. [FEET 30]

Afterwards he was sad for a little time, but then we went to the sea and he was **happy** again. [UNSUIT 81]

Daeth oddi yno'n ddigon digalon ond erbyn i ni gyrraedd glan y môr roedd o **yn ei hwyliau** unwaith eto. [GORTYN 101]

Disgusted that the Slytherins had lost, he was trying to get everyone laughing . . . [STONE 241]

Roedd **o'i go'n las** am fod Slafennog wedi colli, ac roedd wedi ceisio cael pawb i chwerthin . . . [MAEN 153]

O'i hanfodd, dwedodd y ferch wrtha i lle roedd Tessa. [HUNAN 264]

Reluctantly the girl told me where Tessa was. [SOLVA 264–5]

Prepositional phrases are another common solution in translation:

. . . yr oedd o ar y pryd dipyn **yn ei ddiod** . . . [GWEN 105]

. . . he was **under the influence of drink** . . . [GWEN 91]

Byddent yn llawer mwy **wrth eu bodd** yn treulio diwrnod cyfan i bilio brwynen nag wrth ymegnïo yn y gamp o gwympo derwen. [HDF 142]

They would be more **at their heart's content** in spending the whole day 'just peeling a rush' than in addressing their energy to the feat of felling an oak. [OFH 178]

. . . oni bai am ei achos buasai Twm a Bet **ar ben eu digon**. [TRAED 120]

. . . if it were not for the occasion, Twm and Bet would have been **beside themselves with excitement**. [FEET 106]

Harry caught a glimpse of her face – and was startled to see that she was **in tears**. [STONE 215]	Cafodd Harri gip ar ei hwyneb – a dychryn wrth weld ei bod **yn ei dagrau**. [MAEN 136]

In some instances, the translator's strategy is transposition, using a formulation in which an English verb or verb phrase conveys the bulk of the semantics:

'Eich taid yn pregethu? O, **yr on i wrth fy modd** yn gwrando arno fe.' [CYCHWYN 243]	'Your grandfather preaching? Oh, **I did enjoy** listening to him.' [BEGIN 245]
Buasai wrth ei bodd yn ei gweld yn fflamio – y ddol yn cael mynd i'r 'tân mawr' ac nid Begw – y hi a'i hen wyneb paent, hyll. [TE 9–10]	**She'd like** to see it burning, the doll in hell-fire instead of Begwn, the doll with her ugly painted face. [TEA 13]
Deallodd yntau o'i chanfod yn ysu'r cig **ei bod hi ar ei chythlwng** er y bore. [MONICA 56]	He realised as she devoured the meat **that she had eaten nothing** since morning. [MONICA 57]
Tan ei gofal y mae hi. [MONICA 7]	She's **expecting a child**. [MONICA 5]
She could manage simple tunes on the piano, and Sue, **when she could be bothered**, could accompany the violin with the more difficult pieces. [VICT 130]	Byddai Alyn yn canu'r ffidil ambell gyda'r nos ac un ai Tess neu Nia (oedd yn gyfeilyddes dda, **pan fyddai yn ei hwyliau**) yn canu'r piano iddo. [LLINYN 145]

A particularly interesting set of terms in Welsh are those which function as equivalents of the English phrases *well off* and *bad(ly) off*, and their comparatives *better off* / *worse off*. It turns out that there are numerous Welsh equivalents for these phrases. Some take the form PREPOSITION + POSSESSIVE + NOUN (e.g. *ar ei ennill, ar ei golled*):

Magent ddigon o foch i dalu'r llog a'r trethi, ac er i Jane Gruffydd gynnig y cynllun o gael tair ffreitiad o foch i ffwrdd mewn blwyddyn yn lle dwy [. . .] rywsut nid oedd fawr **ar ei hennill**. [TRAED 88]	They managed to raise enough pigs to pay the interest and the rates, but although Jane arranged to send six pigs a year to market instead of four [. . .] she was not much **better off**. [FEET 74]

Ac nid wyf yn credu i neb fod **ar ei golled** o estyn y rhyddid hwn iddynt. [HDF 128]	I don't think anyone was **the worse off** for extending him this privilege. [OFH 160]

Other equivalents take the form ADJECTIVE + POSSESSIVE + NOUN, where the noun may be *lle* 'place' or *byd* 'world':

Roedd rhieni'r ferch wahoddodd ni yn berchen ar haid o filgwn rasio, ac roedd y teulu'n eitha llwyddiannus ac **yn dda eu byd**. [HUNAN 91]	The parents of the girl who invited us owned a successful greyhound racing kennels and were **well off**. [SOLVA 91]
Mae dy fam **yn well 'i lle**, ne be ddaw o fy sort i? [GWEN 40]	Your mother's **better off where she is**, otherwise there's little hope for my sort. [GWEN 44]
He was **better off** in his flat, no matter how dark and barren it seemed, no matter how like a cell. [KNOTS 163]	Roedd **yn well ei le** yn ei fflat, waeth faint mor dywyll ac anial yr ymddangosai, waeth faint fel cell. [CHWERW 140]
'You would be a lot **better off**, Miss Honey,' she said, 'if you gave up your job and drew unemployment money.' [MAT 204]	'Fe fyddech chi'n llawer **gwell eich byd**, Miss Honey,' meddai, 'petaech chi'n rhoi'r gorau i'ch swydd ac yn codi arian diweithdra.' [MAT 198]
The Hatter was the only one who got any advantage from the change; and Alice was a good deal **worse off** than before, as the March Hare had just upset the milk-jug into his plate. [ALICE 74]	Yr Hetiwr oedd yr unig un a gafodd fantais o'r newid, ac yr oedd Alys yn **waeth ei lle** o lawer na chynt, achos roedd y Sgwarnog Fawrth newydd daflu'r siwg laeth am ben ei phlât. [ALYS II 73–4]

There are yet other equivalents for the *well off* family, such as the following:

. . . gallasai fod yn llawer iawn **gwaeth arnaf** . . . [HENAT 111]	. . . indeed I could have been far **worse off** [LOCUST 96]
'Wedi ca'l gormod o'u ffordd 'u hunan maen nhw. Mae hi'**n dda burion arnyn nhw** o gymharu â gweision ffermydd yn Sir Fôn'cw.' [RHANNU 170]	*'They've got too much of their own way. They're quite **well off** compared with farmhands over in Anglesey.'*

Byddaf yn gofyn cwestiynau bellach na fedrai fy meddwl fyth eu dyfeisio cyn hyn; ac er na fedraf ateb na darganfod ateb yn unman yn fynych i'm cwestiynau, nid oes un amheuaeth fy mod **yn elwach** am eu gofyn. [DYDD 88]	*I now ask questions that my mind could never have devised before; and although I frequently cannot answer my questions, there is no doubt that I am **better off** for asking them.*
Ond tybed nad oedden nhw i gyd yn **well allan** yn eu caethiwed nag y bydden nhw o gael eu traed yn rhydd? [MIS O FEHEFIN 174]	*But weren't they perhaps **better off** in their slavery than they would be if they were set free?*

The last pattern to be discussed, and one which is highly productive in contemporary Welsh, takes the form ADJECTIVE + POSSESSIVE + NOUN. In this complex pattern, the adjective modifies the noun that follows the possessive, whereas the entire phrase together modifies another noun, generally one referring to a person. For instance, in the phrase *uchel ei llais* below, rendered in the published translation as 'strident-voiced', the adjective *uchel* 'high' modifies the noun *llais*, whereas the entire phrase describes *Leusa Roberts ei fam* 'his mother Liza Roberts':

... Leusa Roberts ei fam, siriol, lawn bywyd, **uchel ei llais**; [CYCHWYN 124]	... his mother Liza Roberts, cheery, vivacious and **strident-voiced**; [BEGIN 124]

The great majority of attested examples of this pattern in our data describe people, including physical states of the body, aspects of the appearance and personality, and states of mind. The adjectives and nouns which can appear in this construction are virtually unlimited. For instance, with the noun *llais* 'voice', in addition to *uchel* as shown above, the attested adjectives entering into the construction include *isel* 'low', *dig* 'angry', *tawel* 'quiet', and *dwfn* 'deep':

... aeth ymlaen **yn isel ei lais**, 'ond mae'n digwydd fod gen' i gur yn fy mhen heddiw.' [TRWY 58]	... he went on **in a low voice**: 'only to-day I happen to have a headache.' [THRO 170]
Aeth Florence ar ei draws, braidd **yn ddig ei llais**. [SELYF 193]	*Florence interrupted him **with a rather angry voice**.*
Dyma 'na ddyn **tawel ei lais** 'da gwallt cyrliog ... [HUNAN 194]	... a **quietly spoken** man with curly hair ... [SOLVA 194]

Cawr o ddyn gwladaidd, afrosgo, oedd y priodfab o hwsmon, yn araf a chynnil ei eiriau, a **dwfn iawn ei lais.** [CYCHWYN 138]

The bridegroom, a farm-bailiff by calling, was a huge, clumsy yokel, **deep-voiced** and sparing of words. [BEGIN 138]

Other nouns as well reveal the great productivity of the pattern. The noun *meddwl* 'mind' occurs in this construction with many adjectives, including the following combinations:

tawel	ei feddwl	'calm'
clir	ei feddwl	'clear in his mind'
absennol	ei feddwl	'absent-minded'
gwael	ei feddwl	'mentally ill'
gwag	ei feddwl	'empty-headed, scatterbrained'
byw	ei feddwl	'quick-witted'
chwim	ei feddwl	'quick-witted'
cynhyrfus	ei feddwl	'agitated'

Some combinations enjoy a high degree of lexicalisation; in other words, they exist as more or less conventionalised ways of expressing a given notion. For instance, *yn drwm ei glyw* is the conventional way of expressing 'hard of hearing' in Welsh, just as *yn fyr ei wynt* is a common way to say 'out of breath', and *yn ddrwg ei hwyl* 'peevish(ly), in a bad mood':

clyw	Hen ddyn bach cryno, yn gwisgo ffunen sidan ddu a het *Jim Crow*; yn eistedd yn y Sêt Fawr am ei fod **yn drwm ei glyw;** [HENAT 31]	. . . a small, compact, old man, wearing a black silk cravat and a 'Jim Crow' hat; sitting in the elders' pew because he was **hard of hearing;** [LOCUST 33]
gwynt	He was **out of breath** after a brief jog across the car park . . . [KNOTS 114]	Roedd **yn fyr ei wynt** ar ôl loncian ar draws y maes parcio . . . [CHWERW 96]
hwyl	'We've heard,' said Hagrid **grumpily.** [STONE 316]	'Glywson ni,' meddai Hagrid **yn ddrwg ei hwyl.** [MAEN 201]

In other cases, the specific lexical items inserted in the construction are not lexicalised but are freely chosen. The following examples, *Americanaidd ei acen* 'with a Yankee accent' and *Ffrangeg ei hiaith* 'French-speaking', naturally illustrate only one kind of accent that a speaker could have or language that one can be a speaker of. Any ethnic term or language name could occur just as readily in this pattern:

acen	. . . presents from a Santa **with a Yankee accent** [CIDER 30]	. . . derbyn anrhegion gan Siôn Corn **Americanaidd ei acen** [SEIDR 43]
iaith	Poblogaeth gymharol wasgaredig a geid yno, **yn Ffrangeg eu hiaith**. [BIRT 25]	*There was a rather scattered **French-speaking** population there.*

Without attempting to sort them according to their level of fixedness, we illustrate below a number of attested combinations, sorted alphabetically by the noun which is internal to the construction.

anadl	'Daddy and mummy!' Matilda burst out, **gasping for breath**. [MAT 238]	'Dad a Mam!' ffrwydrodd Matilda, **yn fyr ei hanadl**. [MAT 231]
bywyd	tyfasant i gyd yn ddynion cyfrifol, goleuedig, **glân eu bywydau**, yn asgwrn cefn i'r gymdeithas y troent ynddi . . . [HDF 131]	All these boys . . . grew up to be responsible, enlightened, and **clean-living** men, the backbone of their society . . . [OFH 164]
cam	. . . y traed **araf eu cam** . . . [O LAW 206]	. . . the feet **that moved so slowly** . . . [FROM 170]
	Ar yr heol, cerddai'r Major yn sionc, union-gefn, a **chywir ei gam** – yn union fel pe bai bataliwn o filwyr yn ei ddilyn yn eu cotiau-cochion crand o hyd . . . [DYDD 50]	*On the road, the Major walked jauntily, with a straight back and **an unwavering step**, exactly as though there were a battalion of soldiers following him in their yet grand red coats . . .*
casineb	Roedd e **'n hollol agored ei gasineb** tuag at y Cymry . . . [HUNAN 222]	He was **quite open about his dislike** of the Welsh . . . [SOLVA 221–222]
ffwdan	Yr oedd Mr Jones, y Person, hefyd y pryd hwnnw **yn fawr ei ffwdan** yn rhannu rhoddion Nadolig i dlodion y gymdogaeth a arferai fynychu'r gwasanaeth yn yr Eglwys . . . [GWEN 21]	About this time Parson Jones was **busily engaged** sharing out the Christmas charities to the poor in the neighborhood and the recipients, as usual, were those connected with the church. [GWEN 27]

golwg	Heb anthropoleg, byddai archaeoleg yn ddall mewn un llygad ac **yn fyr iawn ei olwg** yn y llall. [PEATCYM 3]	*Without anthropology, archaeology would be blind in one eye and **very short-sighted** in the other.*
gwala	Yr oedd Gwdig, fel pob amser, yn hwyliog ac yn bryfoclyd ac **yn fwytawr iach ei wala**. [LLEIFIOR 157]	Goodwich, as always, was in high spirits and a tease, and **his appetite never seemed to pall**. [RETURN 135]
iechyd	Yr oedd **yn wael ei iechyd** ar y pryd. [CWM 183]	He was **in poor health** . . . [GORSE 176]
parch	. . . yr hen Gapten Prance, morwr **mawr ei barch** oedd yn byw yn Solfach ers talwm. [HUNAN 281]	. . . old captain Prance, a **well-respected** mariner who had lived in Solva some years ago. [SOLVA 281]
siom	Cofiai am fore Llun yn niwedd Gorffennaf a'r ysgol newydd dorri ac yntau'n **fawr ei siom** am na châi fynd i'r chwarel. [CYCHWYN 11]	He remembered a Monday morning at the end of July when the school had just broken up, and **his bitter disappointment** at not being allowed to start work in the quarry. [BEGIN 9]
tafod	. . . mewn sgwrs â Nanti Leisa **chwim ei thafod** a'r cwmni diddan eraill . . . [CHWECH 53]	*. . . in a conversation with the **sharp-tongued** Nanti Leisa and the other entertaining company . . .*
troed	Deuai i hela i'm cartref. Meddai wn a miliast ruddgoch **gyflym ei throed**. [CWM 187]	He used to shoot over the land of my old home, accompanied by a red greyhound bitch (***swift of foot***). [GORSE 179]
tymer	I've a **short-tempered** seventeen-stone wife . . . [TIME 106]	Mae gen i wraig sy'n ddwy stôn ar bymtheg ac **yn fyr ei thymer** . . . [AMSER 169]

In addition to its great productivity, another aspect of the construction is that it is possible and even common to conjoin multiple phrases:

. . . darn o ddyn **tywyll ei groen** a **du ei flewyn** . . . [CHWECH 165]

*. . . a bit of a man **with dark skin and black hair** . . .*

Dyn bychan, bychan oedd 'Y Manawyd', fel y gelwid ef yn aml, un o'r dynion lleiaf a welsoch chwi erioed, un **cyflym iawn ei lafar a'i gam.** [O LAW 72]

'The Awl', as he was generally called, was a tiny little man, one of the smallest you ever saw, very **quick of movement and of speech.** [FROM 51]

'R oedd fy nhad yn ŵr bach **glew a pharod ei law a'i galon** at ryw fân swyddi nas cyflawnid gan bawb . . . [CHWECH 39]

*My father was a small man **with a hand and a heart that were quick and ready** for small jobs that not everyone took on . . .*

Os atebir y cwestiwn yn gadarnhaol, rhaid ein bod ni, athrawon ifainc drigain mlynedd yn ôl, **yn wannach ein cyrff, yn waelach ein hiechyd, yn arafach ein deall,** ac **yn wacach ein meddyliau** na ieuenctid heddiw. [WILLAT 55–6]

*If the question is answered affirmatively, we young teachers, sixty years ago, must have been **weaker of body, poorer in health, slower in comprehension and more empty-headed** than youth today.*

. . . a Ianto, **hir ei ên, brychlyd ei wyneb,** a'i gap a chlustiau yr un ffunud â'i dad, ac yn llawn mor ddoniol, yn yr un dosbarth â mi. [HDF 146]

. . . and Ianto was in my class, **long-chinned** and **freckled** and wearing a cap with ear-flaps to it, the image of his father and equally humorous. [OFH 182]

In the last century, however, four successive heirs were **of a dissolute and wasteful disposition,** and the family ruin was eventually completed by a gambler, in the days of the Regency. [BAND 211]

Yn ystod y ganrif ddiwethaf, fodd bynnag, roedd pedair cenhedlaeth o etifeddion **yn afradlon a gwastraffus eu natur,** a dinistriwyd y teulu'n llwyr yn y diwedd gan gamblwr ffôl, yn nyddiau'r Rhaglywiaeth. [CYLCH 17]

No dwarf himself, he was six feet and a couple of inches of masculine robustness **with black hair, a flat stomach,** a full complement of teeth unstained by his pipe-smoking . . . [TIME 6]

Roedd ef ei hun yn bell o fod yn gorrach: chwe throedfedd a modfedd neu ddwy o gorff, **yn ddu ei wallt, yn wastad ei fol** a chanddo'i ddannedd ei hun, a'r rheini heb eu staenio gan y bib a smygai. [AMSER 6]

Although the pattern seems to lend itself best to describing people, it is possible to use it as well to describe inanimate objects. In the following examples, the pattern is used to describe books, a chapel, city streets, trees, the night, bread, and even marijuana:

Fe'i gwelwn yn awr, capel bychan parchus, yn adeilad heb chwaeth na chytbwysedd, **dynwarediad Fictoraidd ei ddodrefn a'i addurniadau**; [DYDD 86]

*I see it now, a small respectable chapel, a building without taste or balance, **with imitation Victorian furniture and decor;***

Cyrhaeddon ni tua phump o'r gloch y bore ynghanol berw a bwrlwm gylis cul a strydoedd **gwan eu gole** marchnad ffrwythe a llysie fwya Ewrop. [HUNAN 132]

We arrived at about 5 a.m. in the hustle and bustle of the narrow alleys and **dimly lit** streets of the biggest fruit and veg market in Europe. [SOLVA 132]

... y coed uchel o gwmpas **yn amryliw eu gwisg** ... [HDF 188]

... the tall trees around **variegated in colour** ... [OFH 236]

Yn y nos **brin ei sêr** ac **aml ei chymylau** ... [LLEIFIOR 111]

In the **starless, cloudy** night ... [RETURN 95]

Chwe darn tenau o fara **prin ei fenyn** ar blât ... [CRYMAN 79]

Six thin slices of **sparsely buttered** bread on a plate ... [SICKLE 64]

Roedd y mariwana hwn **yn frown ei liw** 'da lot o hade a brige mân ynddo fe. [HUNAN 103–4]

This marijuana was **brown in color** with lots of seeds and twigs. [SOLVA 104]

A camp bed, a small wooden shelf full of books, mostly **of a technical character**, an armchair beside the bed ... [BAND 229]

Gwely cynfas ysgafn, silff fechan yn llawn o lyfrau (y rhan fwyaf ohonynt yn rhai **technegol eu cynnwys**), cadair freichiau wrth erchwyn y gwely ... [CYLCH 43]

4.8 Object of a comparative

A Welsh construction allows the object of a comparative adjective to be expressed as a possessive:

'R oedd ef a'i bartner, Benni Bwlch y Mynydd, gŵr nad oedd **ei**

He and his partner, Benni Bwlch y Mynydd, **than whom there was**

wreiddiolach yn y wlad, un tro wedi cymryd contract gan ryw ffarmwr digon tyn am y geiniog, i godi clawdd. [HDF 145]

no one more original to be found in the country, had once taken a contract of some farmer who was tight enough in money matters, to make him a hedge-bank. [OFH 181]

'R oedd yn saethwr da, ac yr oedd yn ei feddiant y pryd hwnnw ddryll un faril, cyn iddo brynu **ei well**; [CHWECH 84]

*He was a good shooter, and at that time he had in his possession a single-barreled rifle, before he bought **a better one**;*

'R oeddwn innau, o'r ochr arall, wedi cael dwy flynedd a hanner o brofiad ar y glo yn Ferndale o dan fy hen bartner, Abram, nad oedd **ei lewach** fel gweithiwr yn y cymoedd . . . [CHWECH 173]

*I, on the other hand, had had two and a half years of experience in coal in Ferndale under my old partner, Abram, than whom there was was **no more valiant a worker** in the valleys.*

'Drama un act wirioneddol ddigrif, gyda chraffter a sylwadaeth yn sylfaen i'w hiwmor', ydoedd barn *Y Goleuad*; 'darn o fywyd gwerth ei bortreadu', meddai Dyfnallt yn *Y Tyst*; a 'nid wyf yn meddwl fod **ei doniolach** yn yr iaith', meddai Llew Owain yn *Y Genedl*. [TROW 87]

*'A really funny one-act play, with shrewdness and commentary as the basis for its humour', was the opinion of Y Goleuad; 'a piece of life worth portraying', said Dyfnallt in Y Tyst; and 'I don't think there is **anything funnier** in the language', said Llew Owain yn Y Genedl.*

Oni eill plant Cymru ddeall a gwerthfawrogi emynau'r cysegr, nad oes mo'u **cyfoethocach** mewn unrhyw iaith, yna, cânt golled anaele, ac ni wna dim a ddaw iddynt trwy'r Saesneg i fyny am y fath golled â honyna. [EI FFANFFER EI HUN 182]

*If the children of Wales cannot understand and appreciate sacred hymns, of which there are **none richer** in any language, then they will have an incurable loss, and nothing that comes to them through English will make up for that loss.*

No possessive is included in the English translation in this construction. Where the Welsh is literally 'there are none *their* richer' or 'there is nothing *its* funnier', the English equivalent could use a *than* clause ('none funnier *than this drama*', 'none richer *than these hymns*'), but more often this is left because it is clear from context ('there are none richer', '[I don't think] there is anything funnier').

4.9 Possessives with numbers

Possessives occur idiomatically with numbers in three kinds of contexts: enumerating people, giving ages, and giving heights or weights. For enumerating people (e.g. *you three / the three of you / all three of you*), the Welsh formula is PRONOUN + POSSESSIVE + NUMBER, where the pronoun may be a conjunctive pronoun drawn from the set *ninnau, chithau, hwythau* or just a simple pronoun from the set *ni, chi, nhw*. Thus, for example, 'the three of you' may be expressed as *chi'ch tri* (i.e. *chi eich tri*) or *chithau'ch tri* (i.e. *chithau eich tri*):

Cerwch **chitha eich tri** adra. [NOS 35]

You three go home. [NIGHT 27]

"roedd y lle'n rhy fychan i'n cadw **ni'n tri**.' [LLEIFIOR 50]

'the place was too small for **the three of us**.' [RETURN 41]

Y nhw'u dau oedd yno. [PLA 94]

Both of them were there. (It must be Ricardo and Marco . . . [PEST 73])

Hwy eu dau a gafodd y loes drymaf o'i chlywed. [TRAED 100]

They were the two most deeply hurt by the news. [FEET 89]

I'll be seeing you sometime, **you two**. [MAT 116]

Fe welaf i chi eto, **chi'ch dwy**. [MAT 110]

When the enumerated group of people functions as the grammatical subject of its clause, it is also possible to omit the initial pronoun and use only POSSESSIVE + NUMBER, e.g. *eich tri*:

'Ewch **eich dau**,' meddai Edward Vaughan. 'Mi arhosa' i gartre heno.' [LLEIFIOR 164]

'**Both of you** go,' said Edward Vaughan. 'I'll stay home this evening.' [RETURN 141]

Daethom **ein dau** yn ffrindiau mawr heb yn wybod i ni, rywsut. [CHWECH 164]

The two of us (= *both of us*) *became great friends without our knowing it, somehow.*

Hyd nes yr oeddwn i tua deg oed, rhyfel agored oedd hi yn y tŷ rhyngom, gan ein bod **ein dau** yn 'bobl anodd eu trin' a'n hewyllysiau mor anhyblyg â'i gilydd. [HENAT 13]

Until I was about ten years old it was open warfare between us at home, as **we** were **both** 'difficult', each one as strong-willed as the other. [LOCUST 18]

The above examples illustrate one of the usual ways of rendering 'both of (them, us, you)' in Welsh (namely, possessive + *dau / dwy*). The other way is **y ddau (y ddwy) ohonyn nhw (ohonoch chi, ohonon ni)**:

I hate **them both**. [STONE 243]

Gas gen i'**r ddau ohonyn nhw**. [MAEN 154]

'Bloody liars, **the pair of you**.' [CIDER 83]

'Celwyddgwn uffern ydy'**r ddau ohonoch chi!**' [SEIDR 114]

'Both' plus a plural noun (both boys, both girls etc.) is rendered with **y ddau / y ddwy NOUN**:

'It is evident, therefore, that if **both girls** had married, this beauty would have had a mere pittance...' [BAND 223]

'Mae'n amlwg felly, petai'**r ddwy ferch** wedi priodi, mai dim ond cyflog mwnci fyddai'r dihiryn hwn yn ei gael.' [CYLCH 35]

... and **both footmen**, Alice noticed, had powdered hair that curled all over their heads. [ALICE 58]

... a sylwodd Alyd fod gan **y ddau fwtler** wallt wedi'i bowdro, yn gyrliau i gyd. [ALYS II 54]

A variant of the possessive pattern shown above deploys the pronoun *ill* in more formal style. Thus, 'the two of them' / 'both of them' can also be found as *ill dau / ill dwy*:

Cyd-bererinion oeddent **ill dwy** a'r iau'n trymhau ar eu gwarrau. [HEN 21]

They [lit. 'the two of them'] were fellow wayfarers, and the yoke on their necks was getting heavier.[OLD 20]

Lastly, when rendering 'both X and Y' in Welsh, it is often the case that the word 'both' is not actually rendered at all. Notice the use of the conjunctive pronoun (here, *minnau*) when the second conjunct is a pronoun:

... pan fyddwch **chi a minnau** yn isel ein pennau. [GWEN 105]

... when **both of us** are dead and buried. [GWEN 91]

Both Matilda and Lavender were enthralled. [MAT 108]

Roedd **Matilda a Lavender** wedi'u swyno. [MAT 102]

Both Miss Stoner and I gazed at him in astonishment. [BAND 230]

Syllodd **Miss Stoner a minnau** arno â'n llygaid fel lleuadau llawn. [CYLCH 45]

Collective numbers (e.g. *cannoedd* 'hundreds', *miloedd* 'thousands') can also be accompanied by a possessive where none would be possible in English:

... pobol **yn eu cannoedd** yn marw o afiechydon, newyn, diffyg maeth ac yn y blaen. [CRWYD 128]

... *people* ***by the hundreds***, *dying of diseases, hunger, lack of food and so forth.*

'Mae o'n werth **ei filoedd**, 'dw i'n siŵr, ac yn un o *stockbrokers* blaenaf y deyrnas, 'ddyliwn i.' [SELYF 252]

*'He's worth **thousands**, I'm sure, and he's one of the most prominent stockbrokers of the kingdom, I should think.'*

4.10 Age, height, weight

Possessives are used with ages in particular constructions:[9]

To reach (twenty), turn (twenty), be going on (twenty)[10]

In Welsh these are rendered as *cyrraedd (ei ugain oed)*, *troi (ei ugain oed)*, and variously *tynnu at / tynnu am* or *gyrru at (ei ugain oed)*:

... ar ôl iddynt **gyrraedd eu pedair ar ddeg** ... [PEATCYM 65]

... *after they **reach the age of fourteen** ...*

[9] The reader should note a couple of contexts in which a possessive is not used with ages. To express 'to be (a certain age)', the construction *bod yn* + NUMBER *(oed)* is used:
Ro'n **i'n bedair ar ddeg oed** ac roedd bywyd yn dechre mynd yn ddifrifol. [HUNAN 57].
'I was **fourteen years old** and life was beginning to get serious.' [SOLVA 57]
The pattern *yn* + NUMBER *(oed)* also shows up with *penblwydd* 'birthday' unlike in English which generally uses an ordinal number:
On the following Saturday Mike celebrated **his fifth birthday**. [VICT 63]
Roedd hi'n **ben blwydd Dylan yn bump oed** y dydd Sadwrn wedyn ... [LLINYN 71]
Possessives do not occur either when the age is used more or less like an attributive adjective:
... ddwy hogan **wyth oed** ... [TE 37]
... two girls, only **eight years old** ... [TEA 37]
[10] Occasionally the definite article is used instead of a possessive in this construction:
... a **fifty-year-old** neurosurgeon [VICT 135]
... llawfeddyg wedi troi**'r hanner cant** [LLINYN 151]

... a minnau'n awr **wedi troi fy mhedair oed** ... [HDF 164]

*... and I now having **turned four years old**. (... when I was four years old ... [OFH 205])*

... y ddau'n **tynnu am eu deg a phedwar ugain** ... [LLEIFIOR 188]

... both of whom were **getting on for ninety** ... [RETURN 163]

Ac yntau'n **tynnu at ei ugain oed** ac Owen yn ddim ond deuddeg ... [CYCHWYN 72]

Dafydd, **nearing twenty** [...] Owen, who was only twelve years old. [BEGIN 73]

Yr oedd Sioned yn **gyrru ar ei dwy-ar-bymtheg oed**, ac mewn ysgol wnïo ym Mhont Garrog. [TRAED 47]

Sioned was **almost seventeen** and in a sewing school in Pont Garrog. [FEET 42]

To be over (twenty), nearly (twenty), under (twenty), between (twenty and thirty)

The usual Welsh constructions involve the prepositions *dros* or *ar draws (ei ugain oed)* 'over', *ar fin (ei ugain oed)* 'nearly', and *o dan (ei ugain oed)* 'under', *rhwng (ei ugain a'i ddeg ar hugain oed)* 'between':

Bu fy nain farw yn niwedd 1911 **dros ei phedwar ugain oed**; [HENAT 12]

My grandmother died towards the end of 1911 **aged over eighty**. [LOCUST 17]

Yng Nghwm Eithin, yn amser fy maboed, yr oedd hen ŵr **ar fin ei bedwar ugain** yn ffarmio ... [CWM 36]

In Cwm Eithin when I was a child there lived an old farmer who was **close on eighty**. [GORSE 38]

Nid oeddwn i ond crwt **o dan ei ugain oed** ar y pryd, a Harri, mae'n siwr, **dipyn dros ei drigain**. [CHWECH 147]

*I was only a lad **under twenty** at the time, and Harry, certainly, was a bit **over sixty**.*

... **rhwng fy un ar bymtheg a'm pedair ar bymtheg oed**. [CHWECH 101]

*(I was) **between sixteen and nineteen years old**.*

... a girl of, say, nineteen ... [CIDER 15]

... merch **ar draws ei hugain oed**. [SEIDR 22]

In Welsh, people are construed as the possessors not only of their ages but also of their physical dimensions:[11]

. . . **six foot two**, I would guess . . . [CIDER 29]	Roedd **yn rhai modfeddi dros ei ddwy lath**. [SEIDR 41]
Ef oedd y dyn mwyaf a'r cryfaf ohonynt oll, **dros ei chwe throedfedd** a'i ysgywddau llydain yn ysgwâr a'i ben cringoch yn uchel. [CYCHWYN 22]	He was the biggest and strongest of them all, **over six feet in height**, broad and square of shoulder and with ruddy head held high. [BEGIN 21]
. . . dyn anferth, **dros ei ddwylath** ac yn llydan fel talcen tŷ. [CRWYD 59]	. . . *an enormous man **over six foot tall** (= 2 yards) and broad as the side of a house.*

4.11 Conclusions

The topics covered in this chapter have in common the occurrence of possessives in a variety of idiomatic Welsh constructions where no possessive is used in English. The constructions surveyed run the gamut from constraints to options. Clear cases of constraints involve the use of possessives where English uses object pronouns (*Dw i eisiau ei gweld hi* 'I want to see her'), whereas the options include the use of possessives with ages (e.g. *troi ei ugain oed* 'to turn twenty'. Here it is an option because it is also possible to say *troi'r ugain oed*). Perhaps most interesting of all are the idiomatic modifier constructions (e.g. *yn ei ddiod* 'tipsy, drunk'; *absennol ei feddwl* 'absent-minded') which represent a frequent and striking feature of Welsh style.

---

[11] There are occasional exceptions:
   'R oedd yn balff o ddyn cadarn **tua phump a naw o daldra** . . . [CHWECH 120]
   He was a well-built man around five foot nine.

5

Issues in the Verb Phrase:
Tense/Mood/Aspect and Modality

5.0 Introduction

As is true in the lexicon, in the verb system as well there is no one-on-one equivalence between English forms and Welsh ones. Sometimes English has more forms available or makes more distinctions than Welsh does. For instance, English obligatorily distinguishes between present progressive (*What **is she doing** right now?* ***She is singing***) and present habitual (*What **does she do** on Sunday mornings?* ***She sings*** *in the choir*). Welsh does not routinely make this distinction, generally using the same form (*mae hi'n canu*) for both. English speakers are required by their grammar to express this distinction every time they put a verb in the present tense; Welsh speakers are not.[1]

At other times it is Welsh that offers more possibilities than does English. In the preterite English generally has a single form, e.g. *she sang*, whose only variant is the periphrastic *she did sing* found in emphatic forms (*She did sing, I tell you!*), as well as in questions (*did she sing?*) and in negatives (*she did not sing*). Compared with this mere binary choice, Welsh has *canodd hi, (gw)naeth hi ganu, ddaru hi ganu, bu iddi hi ganu,* and *bu(odd) hi'n canu*. We could even add *iddi hi ganu,* as found in certain subordinate clauses (*Mae e'n meddwl iddi hi ganu* 'He thinks she sang') or after prepositions (*erbyn iddi hi ganu* 'by the time she sang'). Among these forms we can identify some regional variation (the *ddaru* form is virtually limited to north Walian) and register variation (the *bu* forms are more likely in formal or literary styles). Probably few or no Welsh speakers use all of these forms actively, but most use some subset of

---

[1] Indeed, it is possible to add an element to insist on one reading or the other, as we will see in this chapter. For instance we will see that adding *arfer* insists on the habitual reading (*mae hi'n arfer canu*) while adding *wrthi* focuses on the progressive reading (*mae hi wrthi'n canu*). But the basic form (*mae hi'n canu*), the one that is encountered far and away the most frequently, is neutral to the distinction and is compatible with both readings.

them. These examples confirm that there is not a one-on-one correspondence between the forms available in the two languages; they are not isomorphic.[2]

The examples just seen lend themselves to some general comments and definitions pertaining to the verbal systems of the two languages by way of introduction of the present chapter. A basic distinction must be made between **synthetic forms**, like *she sings* and *canodd hi*, and **periphrastic (or analytic) forms** like *she is singing* and *mae hi'n canu, buodd hi'n canu*, etc. In a synthetic form, both the lexical meaning ('utter melodious sounds with the voice') and the grammatical meanings associated with tense, mood, aspect and person (e.g. preterite, third person singular) are encoded in the same verb form (*canodd*). In a periphrastic construction, the information of the verb is split over at least two elements: the grammatical meanings are expressed by a helping verb (or auxiliary), and the lexical meaning is expressed by an uninflected form such as a verb-noun or a participle. Thus, in *gwnaeth hi ganu*, it is the finite auxiliary *gwnaeth* which tells us that we have a verb in the preterite with a third person singular subject. But *gwnaeth* doesn't inform us at all about what it is that she did – that information is given by the nonfinite verb-noun, *canu (ganu)*. The Welsh verb system presents a great deal of variation in which synthetic forms (like *canodd hi*) compete with periphrastic forms (like *gwnaeth hi ganu*).

We will also use the terms tense, mood and aspect to refer to the different categories of verbal inflection. These are defined briefly in the following paragraphs.

Tense refers, strictly speaking, to the time of the event described by the verb. A distinction is made between *absolute tenses* (basically past, present and future), which situate events with respect to the moment of speaking, and *relative tenses* (anteriority, posteriority, simultaneity), which situate an event with respect to some other event mentioned in the discourse. For instance, given the sentence *She ate in the pub,* we understand that the pastness of the verb situates it before the moment of speaking: it is past with respect to the present moment. This is considered an expression of absolute tense. On the other hand, in the sentence *She had eaten in the pub before her brother arrived,* the eating event is represented as past with respect to another event (her brother's arrival) which is also in the past. The tense marked in a past-before-past (or past anterior, that is, pluperfect) context thus involves relative tense.

Mood refers to categories of verbal inflection which convey information about the speaker's subjective attitude to the event. For instance, in *I wonder*

---

[2] Due to intense language contact, the isomorphism of Welsh and English has certainly been increasing in recent times. Some examples of this will be mentioned in the course of the chapter.

if you would like some cake, the conditional *would like* conveys not merely present tense (for which *want* would suffice) but also politeness and non-assertiveness. Such a use of the conditional is thus an example of mood. Mood is part of a larger category called **modality**, which refers to all of the linguistic devices (including but not limited to verb inflections of mood) which allow a speaker to talk about hypothetical situations, potential or imagined situations, and so forth: in other words, situations other than those of the real world as it currently exists.

Aspect refers to categories of verbal meaning that deal with the internal structure of the event. For instance, in *She is singing a song,* we convey that the event is going on right now – thus we have progressive aspect (as well as present tense, in this case) – while in *She used to sing songs,* we discover that her singing took place on a regular, repeated basis – thus, habitual or imperfective aspect (and that it was in the past). The English preterite, *she sang a song,* conveys only that the event happened and is completed – this is called perfective aspect.

The remainder of this chapter will explore several issues in the verb phrase of Welsh and English, particularly as relevant for the translator. We will focus on the following six areas: (1) the present tense, (2) the preterite and the imperfect, (3) the use of perfect tenses, (4) the impersonal forms, (5) mood and modality (6) issues of subject-verb agreement.

5.1 The present tense

The present tense in Welsh is usually constructed periphrastically using BOD YN + verb-noun.[3] The same form in Welsh can have either a progressive or a habitual interpretation: for instance, *mae hi'n canu* can mean either 'she sings (on a regular basis)' or 'she is singing (right now)'. The present progressive reading and its English equivalent in *-ing* are shown in the following examples:

'Cerwch i nôl eich gitâr. Fydd yn rhaid i ni 'i siapo hi – **maen nhw'n disgwyl amdanoch chi** yn y Sherman.' [HUNAN 274]

'Get your guitar. We'll have to go now. **They're waiting for you** at the Sherman.' [SOLVA 274]

I'm trying to clarify something slightly contentious. [CIDER 132]

Rydw i'n ceisio gwneud synnwyr o rywbeth sy'n poeni tipyn arna i. [SEIDR 177]

---

[3] PWT 3.19 *Y presennol parhaol* 'the present continuous'.

You're mixin' him up with somebody else. [TIME 135]	**Rydach chi'n cymysgu** rhyngddo fo a rhywun arall. [AMSER 214]
'At any rate I'd better be getting out of the wood, for really **it's coming on** very dark. Do you think it's going to rain?' [THRO 168]	'Sut bynnag, well imi fynd allan o'r goedwig oherwydd, yn wir, **mae hi'n mynd** yn dywyll iawn. Ydych chi'n meddwl ei bod hi am law?' [TRWY 56]

The same form is also used for present habitual, where English uses the simple present (*she calls, he works*):

'Tada **mae hi'n galw** ei thad, a finna yn 'nhad,' meddai Begw. [TE 40]	'**She calls** her father "daddy",' said Begw, 'I don't . . . I call mine "father".' [TEA 39]
Mae'r mab yng nghyfraith **yn gwerthu** ceffyla [PLA 71]	My son-in-law's a horse-dealer. [PEST 54] [lit. **sells** horses]
A dim ond weithiau y **mae'r** gŵr **yn gweithio.** [TRAED 187]	My husband only **works** sometimes. [FEET 154]
Mae hi'n rhegi fel cath, cofiwch. [TE 50]	**She swears** likes a trooper, you know. [TEA 47]
She lets out two of her rooms to lady lodgers only; no feeding, only a little cleaning by a hired help . . . [lit. a woman **comes in** to clean] [TIME 65]	**Mae hi'n gosod** dwy o'i hystafelloedd, i ferched neis yn unig; dydi hi ddim yn eu bwydo nhw, **mae 'na ddynes yn dŵad i mewn** i 'neud ychydig o lanhau . . . [AMSER 102]

Most of the time, the context is sufficient to eliminate any ambiguity between the progressive and the habitual readings of a Welsh present, but once in awhile a speaker or writer may wish to insist on one or the other reading, usually for special emphasis. Several strategies are available.

The present habitual can be expressed by the synthetic present/future paradigm (the *byddaf* paradigm) of *bod*. Though usually thought of today as the future tense of *bod*, one of its functions is to express habitual events in the present tense:

'**Fyddwch chi'n breuddwydio** weithiau?'	'Do **you** ever **dream?**' she asked.
'**Bydda**' yn y nos,' meddai Begw. [TE 41]	'Yes, at night,' Begw replied. [TEA 40]

Gan amlaf y mae'n helpu yn y siop, ond **bydd yn teithio** weithiau. I'r llongau y mae'n gweithio fynychaf, yn trwsio clociau a chwmpodau [MONICA 10]

Usually he helps in the shop, but sometimes **he travels around**. He works mostly for the ships, repairing clocks and compasses. [MONICA 9]

Weithiau yn fy ngwely, pan **fyddaf yn methu cysgu, byddaf yn myned** yn fy meddwl dros y tai yn fy hen ardal . . . [HENAT 10]

Sometimes, in my bed when I **cannot sleep, I bring to mind** the homes of my native place . . . [LOCUST 15]

Yr oedd lleuad lawn yn yr awyr, mor felyn bron ag y **bydd** ym mis Medi. [TRAED 32]

There was a full moon in the sky, almost as yellow as a September one. [FEET 29] [lit. as it **is** in September]

'**I never ask** advice about growing,' Alice said indignantly. [THRO 186]

'**Fydda' i byth yn gofyn** cyngor ynghylch tyfu,' meddai Alys yn ddig. [TRWY 75]

Alternatively, the verb-noun *arfer* can be inserted into the periphrastic construction to insist on a habitual reading.[4] *Arfer* is followed directly by a verb-noun with no mutation:

"**Rydw i'n arfer cael** 'y nghyflwyno i ddieithriaid, wyddoch chi,' ebe Catrin eto. [FFENESTRI 107]

'*I am usually introduced* to strangers, you know,' said Catherine again.

May I ask something of you that **is perhaps not asked by a woman?** [TIME 36]

Ga i ofyn rhywbeth iti . . . rhywbeth **nad ydi dynes yn arfer 'i ofyn?** [AMSER 56]

Adding *wrthi* is a way of insisting on the progressive reading:

We are right in the middle of watching one of our favorite programs. [MAT 94]

Rydyn ni wrthi'n gwylio un o'n hoff raglenni. [MAT 88]

A ddaru o ddim gweiddi na dim byd, dim ond gweddïo, **pan oeddan nhw wrthi'n cnocio'r hoelion.** [NOS 61]

And he didn't scream or anything, he just prayed, **while they were busy knocking the nails in.** [NIGHT 49]

---

[4] There is a related noun *arfer* 'custom, habit' which occurs, for instance, in the expressions *yn ôl ei arfer* 'as was his custom', *fel arfer* 'usually; as usual', and *(mwy) nag arfer* '(more) than usual'. However, the *arfer* of interest here is the verb-noun, which is clear in that it can take the aspectual particles *yn, wedi* etc.

Thus far, we have seen the following possibilities in the present tense:

mae hi'n canu	'she sings (on a regular basis)'
	or 'she is singing (right now)'
bydd hi'n canu	'she sings (on a regular basis)'
mae hi'n arfer canu	'she sings (on a regular basis)'
mae hi wrthi'n canu	'she is singing (right now), she is busy singing'

To this set we must add one more form. The present tense is sometimes expressed synthetically, using the verbal paradigm usually called present/future in Welsh grammars. This is most common with certain stative verbs, including verbs of ability (*gallu*, *medru*), volition (*mynnu*), and perception (*clywed*, *gweld*), where it can be found in all styles, including colloquial styles such as the dialogue of a novel:

''**Welwch chi** gapal Siloam, Nyrs?' 'Gwela'. Ond 'does 'na neb ar y ffordd eto. Rhy gynnar o lawar.' [CYCHWYN 33]

'**Do you see** Siloam chapel, Nurse?' 'Yes. But there's nobody on the road yet. Too early by far.' [BEGIN 32]

Os na **fynni** di, nid oes raid iddi ddod. Mi **allaf** ddweud nad wyt ti'n ddigon iach. [MONICA 9]

If **you're not willing**, she doesn't have to. I **can** say you're not well enough. [MONICA 7]

Do you hear the snow against the window-panes, Kitty? [THRO 129]

Glywi di'r eira yn erbyn chwareli'r ffenestri, Citi? [TRWY 15]

Kitty, **can you** play chess? [THRO 130]

Citi, **fedri** di chwarae gwyddbwyll? [TRWY 16]

'He does not say so, but **I can** read it from his soothing answers and averted eyes.' [BAND 211]

'Nid yw'n datgan hynny'n agored, ond **gallaf** ei synhwyro yn ei eiriau sebonllyd a'r llygaid sy'n osgoi edrych i fyw fy rhai i.' [CYLCH 16]

In written and more formal or literary style, use of the synthetic present can go much further. Statements of general truth may be expressed with this form, a usage reminiscent of the language of proverbs and adages such as *Gwyn y gwêl y fran ei chyw* ('The crow sees her chick to be white'):

Pan **ddaw** llong i mewn i harbwr gwell gan y capten gael yr un

Whenever a ship **comes** into harbour the captain always prefers

clochydd bob tro i gywiro'r cwmpodau . . . [MONICA 10]	to have the same craftsman reset the compasses . . . [MONICA 9]
Trawai golau'r haul ar ei blew, a threiddiai drwyddynt at y croen a'i ddangos yn goch gwan, megis y **gwêl** dyn ei gnawd ei hun wrth ei ddal rhyngddo a'r golau. [TRAED 44]	The sunlight shone on her fur and penetrated to the skin which was a pale red, like a man's skin when held up to the light. [FEET 39] [lit. like a man **sees** his skin]
Rhyfedd fel y **gwna** distawrwydd i chwi sylwi ar bethau! [O LAW 206]	Strange, how silence **makes** one notice things! [FROM 170]
Saif Cwm Eithin yng nghanol mynyddoedd Cymru, o ddeg i bymtheng milltir a mwy o bob man. **Rhed** afon fechan, risialaidd, ar hyd ei waelod, a ffordd dyrpeg ar hyd ei glannau. [CWM 1]	Cwm Eithin is a Welsh mountain valley [lit. **stands** amidst the mountains of Wales], from ten to fifteen miles or more from anywhere. A small, clear stream waters [lit. **runs** along] the valley bottom and there is a turnpike road. [GORSE 1]

In autobiographical writing and first-person narration, the writer may use this form to describe his or her own psychological state or inner reflections:

. . . fel yr **ystyriaf** y ddau hyn, hyd heddiw, ymhlith fy nghyfeillion agosaf oll. [CHWECH 38]	. . . *as I* **consider** *these two, until today, among my closest friends.*
Cofiaf am un gweinidog yr amheuwn i yn fawr a fu ef yn blentyn erioed. [CWM 194–5]	**I remember** a minister concerning whom I was very doubtful whether he had ever been a child. [GORSE 188]
I **confess** that I felt easier in my mind when, after following Holmes's example and slipping off my shoes, I found myself inside the bedroom. [BAND 235]	**Cyffesaf** i mi deimlo'n esmwythach fy meddwl pan gefais fy hun y tu mewn i'r ystafell wely, ar ôl dilyn esiampl Holmes a thynnu fy esgidiau oddi ar fy nhraed. [CYLCH 52]

The style of D. J. Williams in *Hen Dŷ Ffarm*, the first volume of his autobiography, makes repeated use of the short inflected present to make introspective comments on the narrative:

Ond nid dyna'r fan yn hollol y **terfyna**'r gyfranc hon fel y clywais adrodd arni lawer tro. [HDF 93]	But the story, as I many times heard it, **does not end** here exactly. [OFH 113]
Am ryw reswm rhy ddyrys i geisio'i 'sbonio **saif** y trwmpedwr hwn yn fyw ryfeddol yn fy nhgof hyd heddiw . . . [HDF 95]	For some inexplicable reason the trumpeter **stands** in my memory till this day, extraordinarily vividly . . . [OFH 116]
Mewn hunan-ymholiad mor onest ag y **meiddiaf** ei gynnal arnaf fy hun **teimlaf** fy mod i'n ddiffygiol ddigon yn y tri. [HDF 100]	In as honest a self-examination as **I am able** to hold, **I find myself** only too deficient in the three. [OFH 122]

Even action verbs may be encountered in the short inflected present in first-person narrative style, a usage thought of as a 'dramatic' present.[5] The following example shows short forms (*cerddaf, anadlaf*) alternating with the more usual long or periphrastic forms (*dw i'n nodio*) in the same passage. It is noteworthy that the English short present, usually reserved for present habitual, can also be used in this narrative style, as seen in the translation:

Cerddaf adref fel Huggy Bear cloff gan anelu am y bath, am gawl ac am gwely [. . .] **Anadlaf** yn ddwfn cyn agor y drws [. . .] **Dw i'n nodio** 'mhen, tynnu'n sgidie . . . [FFYDD 63]	**I limp** towards home, dreaming of the bath, some hot soup and my warm bed [. . .] **I take** a deep breath before opening the door [. . .] **I nod** and take off my shoes . . . [FAITH 49–50]

Despite the proceeding examples where the short inflected form clearly has a present tense interpretation, most of the time it functions as a synthetic future tense in Modern Welsh:

Mi **gei** stumog yng ngwynt y mynydd, ac mi **wneith** les iti. [TE 36]	The mountain air **will make** you hungry and it **will do** you good. [TEA 36]
'Pryd **daw** 'Nhad adre?' 'Ddim am oriau, waeth iti heb na phoeni.' [TRAED 45]	'When **will** father **be** home?' 'Not for hours yet, you'll have to be patient.' [FEET 41]

---

[5]   PWT 3.22.2 *Y presennol dramatig*, 'the dramatic present'.

'Mi **siaradwn** ni am y peth 'fory, Mrs Morris,' meddai. 'Efalla' y **byddwn** ni'n dau yn gliriach ein meddwl wedi cysgu trosto fo.' [CHWAL 177]

'We **will talk** about the matter tomorrow, Mrs Morris,' he said. 'Perhaps we two **will be** clearer in our minds after sleeping over it.' [OUT 187]

How **shall I ever forget** that dreadful vigil? [BAND 235]

Anghofiaf i byth y wyliadwriaeth arswydus honno. [CYLCH 53]

Cure you? Well, no, love – it **will just ease** your joints a little. [VICT 83]

Na, chaiff o ddim gwared ohono fo ond mi **ystwythith** rywfaint ar y cymala i chi, cariad. [LLINYN 94]

The following example brings up an important difference between the two languages:

'Dibynnu sut y **licia i**'r eglwys yma. Mae hi'n bell, ond **os licia i hi**, waeth gin i am y pellter.' [TRAED 14]

'It depends on whether **I'll like** the Church here. It is far but **if I like it** [lit. if **I will like** it] I won't mind the distance.' [FEET 12]

In so-called open conditions, in English, the *if*-clause – unlike the result clause – is in the present tense even when it pertains to a future time. The future is unnatural in the English *if*-clause:

> If **I like** it, I won't mind the distance. (cf. *If I will like it . . .)[6]

In Welsh, on the other hand, both clauses in an open condition sentence are generally in the short future:[7]

'**If I eat** one of these cakes,' she thought, 'it's sure to make SOME change in my size' [ALICE 45]

'**Os bwyta'** i un o'r teisennau 'ma fe **fydd** yn siŵr o achosi *rhyw* newid yn fy maint' [ALIS II 40]

'**If he is violent**, we **shall take** you away to your aunt's at Harrow.' [BAND 225]

'**Os bydd e'n dreisgar**, yna fe **wnawn** ni eich symud i dŷ eich modryb yn Harrow.' [CYLCH 38]

---

[6] The asterisk is used here to mark ungrammaticality, i.e. forms that are generally unattested in fluent speech.

[7] Hypothetical sentences are explored more fully in section 5.5.1 of this chapter.

Mi **gaf** wylio drwy'r ffenestr os na **allaf** i gysgu, ac wedyn mi **anghofiaf** yr oriau. [MONICA 7]	**I'll be able** to look out of the window if I **can't** [lit. won't be able to] sleep, and then I **shan't notice** the hours passing. [MONICA 6]

The same idiomatic use of a present tense in English where a future is logically called for is found after the conjunction *when*; thus we get *when you are thirteen* rather than **when you **will be** thirteen*. In Welsh, on the other hand, the logical future tense is found after *pan*;

'**Mi gei fynd** i'r chwaral **pan fyddi di'n dair ar ddeg** a dim cynt.' [CYCHWYN 11]	'**You shall go** to the quarry **when you are** [lit. will be] **thirteen**, and not before.' [BEGIN 9]
Fi fydd yn 'i chael hi gan 'Mam **pan awn ni adra'.** [CHWAL 16]	It's *I* will cop it from Mom **when we get** [lit. will go] **home.** [OUT 16]
. . . mi ddaw Mr Ernest yn ddyn clyfar eto, teilwng o'i dad, ac yn fawr ei barch yn y gymdogaeth, **pan fyddwch chi a minnau yn isel ein pennau.** [GWEN 105]	. . . Mr Ernest will become a clever man worthy of you and respected by all the neighborhood **when both of us are** [lit. will be] **dead and buried.** [GWEN 91]

The future tense is often constructed periphrastically using *bod* as an auxiliary, e.g. *bydd hi'n cerdded* 'she will walk'. That is, the same form we saw earlier as a habitual present is also used as a periphrastic future. This form *may* correspond to a future progressive in English (e.g. 'you'll be enjoying yourself' in the first example below), but more often it is equivalent to the simple future.

'I suppose you think **you'll be enjoying yourself** with that oaf? Well, think again, boy –' [STONE 309]	'Mae'n debyg dy fod ti'n meddwl y **byddi di'n mwynhau dy hun** efo'r llabwst? Well iti ailfeddwl, hogyn –' [MAEN 197]
'[A]ll I can hope for now is that **he'll resist** being arrested. He really does owe me that.' [TIME 99]	'[D]w i ond yn gobeithio rŵan y **bydd o'n osgoi** cael ei arestio; mae arno fo hynny o leia i mi.' [AMSER 157]
'We **shall spend** the night in your room, and we shall investigate the cause of this noise which has disturbed you.' [BAND 231]	'Fe **fyddwn ni'n treulio**'r noson yn eich ystafell chi, fel y dywedais, ac yn ymchwilio i achos y sŵn yma sydd wedi bod yn tarfu arnoch ynghanol y nos.' [CYLCH 46]

A periphrastic future can also be constructed using *gwneud* as an auxiliary. Note that in this case, no *yn* is used before the verb-noun. This particle occurs only when *bod* is the auxiliary:

I wonder if **I shall fall** right *through* the earth! [ALICE, 21]	Tybed a **wnaf syrthio** *drwy'r* ddaear! [ALICE, 13]
'Os bydd e'n dreisgar, yna **fe wnawn ni eich symud** i dŷ eich modryb yn Harrow.' [CYLCH 38]	'If he is violent, we **shall take you away** to your aunt's at Harrow.' [BAND 225]
You **will keep looking** while I'm away, won't you? [STONE 246]	**Wnewch chi'ch dau ddal ati** i chwilio tra bydda i i ffwrdd, gwnewch? [MAEN 156]

5.2 The preterite and the imperfect[8]

One of the basic distinctions made in the Welsh verbal system is that between the preterite (*y gorffennol*) and the imperfect (*yr amherffaith* or *yr amhenodol*). The preterite focuses on past events that are completed and whose internal structure is of no immediate interest: these events are simply represented as complete, undivided wholes. Thus, if we say *She wrote a novel / Sgrifennodd hi nofel* in the preterite, it makes absolutely no difference whether she did this in a couple days or took four years to do it, whether other things were going on at the same time, etc. The preterite simply represents the event as completed in the past.[9]

Narratives often involve a succession of completed events that advance the plot in a novel, a very typical use of the preterite. The following two examples are illustrative:

Yna **troes** Monica ato a **chododd** ei chleddyf a **thrywanodd** ef rhwng ei ddwyfron oni **syrthiodd** yn gelain dros y dibyn i blith y dorf; a phan **syrthiodd** datguddiwyd ei wyneb,	Then Monica **turned** to him and, raising her sword, **plunged** it into his breast, so that he **fell down** dead and **hurtled** over the edge into the crowd below. As he **fell**, his face was

---

[8] Jones (2010) is a very useful analysis of tense and aspect focusing on informal Welsh, and Chapter 4 of that work insightfully examines some of the issues addressed in the present section.

[9] We come back to the preterite though in section 5.3 of this chapter dealing with the use of perfect tenses.

a **gwelodd** Monica mai Bob MacIwan ydoedd. [MONICA 47]	revealed, and Monica **saw** that it was Bob MacEwan. [MONICA 47]
Canodd gloch ar ei ddesg a **daeth** geneth ieuanc i mewn. **Gofynnodd** yntau iddi ddyfod â dwy gwpanaid o de i mewn heddiw yn lle un. Yna **estynnodd** blat a chacennau arno a'u rhoi ar y ddesg. [BYW 62]	He **rang** the bell on his desk and a young girl **came** in. He **asked** her to bring in two cups of tea that day, instead of one. Then he **reached** for a plate of cakes and **put** them on the table. [AWAKENING 62]

Unlike the preterite, the imperfect focuses on the durative or prolonged nature of the past event, seeing it in process rather than completed at the time in question. As such, one of its uses is to describe a scene in the past, to set the stage for a narrative that is about to begin. The collection of short stories by Kate Roberts called *Te yn y grug* opens with a passage containing five verbs in the imperfect which describe the scene that the reader is being invited to picture before the action of the story even begins:

Eisteddai Begw ar stôl o flaen y tân, a'i chefn, i'r neb a **edrychai** arno, yn dangos holl drychineb y bore. **Cyffyrddai** ymylon ei siôl tair onglog i'r llawr, a'r llawr yn llawn o byllau mân yn disgyn oddi wrth facsiau eira ag ôl pedolau clocsiau ynddynt. Heddiw, yn wahanol i arfer, yr **oedd** ei gwallt yn flêr, a **hongiai**'n gynhinion di-drefn ar ei hysgwydd. [TE 7]	Begw **sat** on a stool in front of the fire, with the morning's tragedy written on every line of her body [lit. and her back, for anyone who **looked** at it, showing . . .]. The fringe of her three-cornered shawl **touched** the floor, where the lumps of frozen snow brought in by clogs still bore the imprint of their irons as they melted into little pools. Today, for once in a way, her hair **was** untidy, [and it **hung**] all in tangles upon her shoulders: [TEA 11]

While the Welsh verb morphology distinguishes very clearly (and obligatorily) between the recounting of completed past events (*troes Monica*) and those that picture a past event in progress (*eisteddai Begw*), English morphology does not; we find simple pasts in both cases (*Monica turned, Begw sat*). The English translator could have opted for a past progressive in the latter case (*Begw was sitting*), but this is an option rather than a constraint, and its repeated use in a single passage may sound laborious and repetitive.

Beyond description in the past, as in the passage from *Te yn y grug*, the imperfect is also selected for actions repeated on a regular basis in the past (*past habitual*). In the English equivalents we find periphrases using *used to* and *would*, as well as simple past. These three forms are more or less interchangeable in such contexts in English; for instance, the example below 'the scholars *used to carry* their books' could just as easily have been '*would carry*' or even just '*carried*'. The English simple past (*carried, came, talked*) is ambiguous in its interpretation since it can correspond to a Welsh preterite or an imperfect, whereas *would* and *used to* are not ambiguous in this way. Sometimes the English translator opts for an even more explicit expression of habituality, such as "he was in the habit of talking" in the last example below.

Cof gennyf fy mod yn cysylltu rhyw ddirgelwch mawr ynglŷn â'r cwd gwyrdd yn yr hwn y **cariai** y bechgyn eu llyfrau i ysgol Mr Smith. [RHYS 34]

I remember associating some great mystery with the green bags in which the scholars **used to carry** their books. [RHYS 37]

Bob hydref **dôi**'r eogiaid i fyny i afonydd y blaenau 'i gladdu' neu i fwrw eu hwyau yn 'y cladd' a **wnâi** eu torrau drwy sigl-rwbio yn y graean ar waelod y pwll. [HDF 121]

Every autumn the salmon **came** up to the upper reaches of the rivers to bury – that is, to shed their eggs in the hollows they **made** with their bellies by rubbing to and fro in the gravel on the bottom of the pool. [OFH 150]

Bwytâi'r bechgyn ar eu traed heb dynnu eu cotiau er mwyn cael brysio allan drachefn. [TRAED 31]

The boys **would eat** standing up without taking their coats off so that they could hurry out again. [FEET 28]

Siaradai ag ef am oriau bob dydd, a **gwrandawai** yntau mewn doethineb mud. [CYCHWYN 113]

He **was in the habit of talking** to him daily for hours on end, while the dog **listened** in dumb sagacity. [BEGINNING 113]

The imperfect can mark an event that *was going on* (past progressive) when a punctual event (in the preterite) took place, intersecting it. In the examples below we see this juxtaposition:

Agorodd y drws, a **daeth** Mrs Evans i mewn gyda wagen de yn llawn o gwpanau a soseri a brechdanau a theisennau a choffi poeth. **Yr oedd pawb yn siarad** yn frwd, a **chlywai**

The door **opened** and in **came** Mrs Evans with a trolley laden with cups and saucers and sandwiches and cakes and hot coffee. Everyone **was talking** enthusiastically, and

Greta nerf rhyw hen gynddaredd llwythol yn throbio drwy'r ystafell wareiddiedig, werdd. [LLEIFIOR 71]

Greta **felt** the nerve of some tribal excitement throbbing through the room. [RETURN 59]

Gorweddai'r hen gi ar bentwr o ddillad ar aelwyd y gegin, ond ni **chymerodd** yr un sylw o Owen pan **wyrodd** ef uwch ei ben. [CYCHWYN 112]

The old dog **was lying** on a pile of garments in front of the kitchen fire, but **took** no notice whatever of Owen when he **bent** over him. [BEGINNING 112]

When his telephone bell **rang** again, he **was looking** through the window at a view of sunlit slate roofs ... [TIME 60]

Pan **ganodd** ei deliffôn drachefn, **roedd yn edrych** drwy'r ffenest ar doi llechi'n sgleinio yn yr haul ... [AMSER 94–5]

The imperfect is the usual choice for describing past states of mind and cognition such as *meddwl* 'think', *gwybod* 'know', *adnabod* 'know', *edrych ymlaen at* 'look forward to', *gresynu* 'regret', *credu* 'believe', *tybio* 'believe, opine' as well as stative verbs such as *byw* 'live' and numerous expressions with *bod* dealing with durative states like possessing, owning, needing, and wanting:[10]

Edrychai ymlaen at ei swper. **Gwyddai** y câi gig oer a thatws wedi eu twymo. [TRAED 168]

He **looked forward** to his supper for he **knew** there would be cold meat and warmed-up potatoes. [FEET 140]

Edmygai agwedd ddi-falio'r bechgyn eraill wrth gerdded i'r dref yn y bore. [TRAED 41]

He **admired** the nonchalant attitude of the other boys as they strolled to the town that morning. [FEET 37]

Yr oedd Gwen a'm mam yn gyfeillgar iawn, a **thybiwn** innau nad **oedd** gwell na phrydferthach geneth yn y byd crwn na Gwen ... [GWEN 37]

Gwen and my mother were great friends and I **believed** that there **was** no prettier or better girl in the whole wide world. [GWEN 42]

---

[10] However, this is not a hard and fast rule. 'To think', for instance, is not always cast as a description of a state of mind, but can also be presented as a reaction to something, suggesting that an idea came to someone suddenly. This represents the thought as an event rather than a description, and the preterite is then the usual choice. For instance:

Fe barhaodd y storm yn ei hanterth am ryw ddwy awr. Pan ostegodd, **meddyliais** efallai y cawn gyntun bach, ond ni ddeuai cwsg. [BRITH 152]

The storm continued at full strength for some two hours. When it slackened, I ***thought*** *perhaps I would take a nap, but sleep would not come.*

| I found out who **owned** it. [MAT 202] | Fe ddes i wybod pwy **oedd yn berchen** arno. [MAT 196] |

'I'll whisper it,' said the Messenger, putting his hands to his mouth in the shape of a trumpet and stooping so as to get close to the King's ear. Alice **was sorry** for this, as she **wanted** to hear the news too. [THRO 198]

'Fe'i sibrydaf ef,' ebe'r Negesydd gan roi ei ddwylo at ei geg yn ffurf trwmped a phlygu er mwyn mynd yn agos at glust y Brenin. **Gresynai** Alys am hyn oherwydd **roedd arni hithau eisiau** clywed y newyddion. [TRWY 89]

In the introduction to the chapter we mentioned that the Welsh verb system reveals extensive variation between synthetic and periphrastic forms. That is true of both the preterite and the imperfect. We turn now to a discussion of this variation in form.

In addition to the synthetic preterite (e.g. *canodd hi*), Welsh also makes use of periphrastic preterites using three different helping verbs (*gwneud, ddaru, bod*). The first is *gwneud*, which takes a verb-noun as its complement with no accompanying *yn*:

Mynd i'r gwely wnes i, ar ôl ffaelu dod i gysylltiad â'r meddyg. [HUNAN 270]

After failing to get in touch with the doctor **I just went to bed**. [SOLVA 270]

... where **we hired** a trap at the station inn, and drove for four or five miles through the lovely Surrey lanes. [BAND 224]

Yno, **fe wnaethom logi** trap o dafarn yr orsaf, a gyrru am bedair neu bum milltir ar hyd lonydd [*sic*] hyfryd Swydd Surrey. [CYLCH 35]

He **didn't** deliberately **knock** the tray of coffee out of Mary's hands as she came in with it. [VICT 82]

Wnaeth o ddim taro Eleri'n fwriadol pan ddaeth hi i'w gwfwr yn cario hambwrdd a choffi berwedig arno. [LLINYN 93]

The second auxiliary that can be used in the preterite, associated particularly with north Walian, is the invariant *ddaru*. This occurs in the construction DDARU + (I) + subject + verb-noun:[11]

[11] *Ddaru* is from *darfu* '(it) happened', preterite of *darfod*. The construction originally took the form *darfu i mi (fynd)* lit. 'it happened to me (to go)'. The preposition is generally no longer part of the construction, as seen in *ddaru hi* rather than *ddaru iddi* in the example above from *O law i law*, and the auxiliary *ddaru* is usually soft mutated. In some areas it is reduced to *aru* in speech.

Who did you pass on the road? [THRO 198]

Pwy ddaru chi basio ar y ffordd? [TRWY 89]

Ddaru mi ladd rhwfun? *no danger.* **Ddaru mi neyd cam** a rhwfun? Dydw i ddim yn gwbod. **Ddaru mi feddwi?** *never.* Does dim isio i *chap* neyd y pethe ene i gael ei adel. [RHYS 320]

Have I killed anybody? No danger. **Have I wronged** anybody? I don't know that I have. **Have I got drunk?** Never. But a chap needn't do any of those things to be left behind. [RHYS 316]

Methu'n lan â gwybod be' i'w roi yn anrheg priodas inni y maen nhw. 'Does ganddyn nhw ddim modd i brynu dim o werth. Mi **ddaru nhw benderfynu** gwerthu'r ddau fochyn, ond mae prisia moch yn gynddeiriog o isel 'rŵan. [OLAW 225]

Failed utterly to know what to give us for a wedding present, they have. And they have no means to buy anything of value. They **did decide** to kill the two pigs, but the prices for pigs are furiously low now. [FROM HAND 187]

Ddaru ti ddeud dy hun nad oedden nhw, yn ôl pob tebyg, yn bwriadu'i ladd o. [AMSER 67]

You said yourself that they probably hadn't intended killing him. [TIME 43]

Ddaru chi ddim rhoi'r arian iddi, ddaru chi, nhad? [GWEN 48]

You didn't give her the money, did you father?

Ddaru can also be used instead of an inflected form of *gwneud*, to stand in for a lexical verb that has already occurred, in lieu of repeating it:

Be maen nhw'n bwriadu 'i neud . . . taflu cerrig a mosod, fel **ddaru nhw** ar Richard Hughes a'r lleill adag y cloi allan? [RHANNU 130]

*What do they intend to do, throw stones and attack, as **they did** to Richard Hughes and the others at the time of the lock-out?*

'Mae hi'n rhegi fel cath, cofiwch. Mi **ddaru** ar y mynydd.' [TE 50]

'She swears like a trooper, you know. She **did** when we were on the mountain.' [TEA 47]

A detailed study of the use of *ddaru* goes beyond the scope of this chapter, but it is clear that one of the contexts in which *ddaru* nearly always occurs in the northern varieties that use it is the fronting construction associated with focus.[12]

---

[12] See also 11, 1.2 and 11, 1.5 for the use of *ddaru* in focus sentences.

Regardless of whether the focused constituent is a noun phrase or a verb phrase, a preterite verb nearly always appears with *ddaru* in this construction:

Eich gwraig chi ddaru achwyn
bod Mam yn hel streuon arni hi . . .
[NOS 69]

. . . it was your wife saying that
Mom was gossiping about her . . .
[NIGHT 56]

Yr unig beth ddaru diclo tipyn ar
fy ffansi i oedd yr Hen Grafwr yn
insistio am i ti bregethu o flaen y
seiat gael iddyn nhw weled ffasiwn
stwff sydd ynot ti . . . [RHYS 316]

The only thing that tickled my
fancy a bit was Old Scraper insisting
that you should be asked to preach
before Communion, so that they
might see the sort of stuff there was
in you . . . [RHYS 316]

Mynd yno yn rhy fuan ddaru 'mi,
a nhwtha wrthi'n byta; a mi ges i
darten gwsberis a'i byta ar y setl.
[OLAW 16]

I went there too soon, and they
were eating, and I was given a
plateful of gooseberry tart to eat on
the settle. [FROM HAND 18]

Ond **gwrthod 'madael â nhw ddaru
hi** hyd y diwadd. [OLAW 197]

But refuse to part with them she did,
up to the end. [FROM HAND 162]

The third periphrastic expression that can often be translated as an English preterite uses *bod*. This form (which PWT 3.27 calls *y gorffennol penodol* or 'the definite past') describes an action that (1) went on for some time but (2) came to an end in the past. In this way it can be contrasted both with the imperfect, which does not specify whether the past continuous event ever came to an end,[13] and with the simple preterite, whose internal structure is not represented. As such, this is a verb form that has no exact equivalent in English. The clearest examples are like the following, in which the duration of the event is stated overtly in a prepositional phrase headed by *am* / *for* followed by a period of time. These duration phrases are underlined in the examples below.

Bu'n gorwedd ac yn pesychu felly
am ryw bythefnos, a gwyddem, heb
i'r Doctor ddweud gair wrthym, fod
y diwedd yn agos. [OLAW 97]

For about a fortnight **he lay** there,
harried by fits of coughing, and we
knew without having to be told so
by the doctor that the end was near.
[FROM 72]

---

[13] A sentence like *Roedd e'n canu pan ddes i i mewn*, 'He was singing when I came in', leaves open the possibility that he is still singing now, whereas *bu(odd) e'n canu* does not.

Am wythnosau lawer, **bu'r celwydd yma yn corddi** yn ei meddwl. [BYW 36]

For many weeks **this lie had churned about** in her mind. [AWAKENING 36]

Ac felly y **buont yn yfed** te ac yn en mwynhau eu hunain am hir. [BYW 83]

And there **they stayed** for some time, **drinking** tea and enjoying themselves. [AWAKENING 81]

We note that the English translation equivalents do not always use the preterite; sometimes a perfect tense works better in English, making overt the implied anteriority of a past completed event. (As we will see in section 3 of this chapter, English is more concerned than Welsh about the explicit marking of anteriority). The second example from *Y Byw sy'n cysgu* above shows an interesting attempt to render the durativity more explicit in English: the Welsh *buont yn yfed* has been translated as 'they stayed [. . .] drinking', with introduction of the verb 'stayed'.

When the total duration is not made explicit, the endpoint of the prolonged event is either stated or strongly implied. It is overtly stated in the next two examples below, with temporal prepositional phrases using *hyd* 'until' or *cyn* 'before'.

Aberthodd swper er mwyn hynny, ac yn ei gwely **bu'n troi a throsi** ac yn ail-fyw'r noson hyd oriau mân y bore. [TRAED 50]

She had sacrificed supper for that, and in bed she **turned and tossed** until the small hours of the morning as she re-lived the events of the evening. [FEET 45]

Where **had she been working** before leaving home? [TIME 56]

Yn lle **fuodd hi'n gweithio** cyn iddi adael gartref? [AMSER 88]

The necessary endpoint may be inferrable from the larger context rather than stated in the local one. In the following example from the detective novel *A Time to Kill*, the character who is being said to have lied has just been a murder victim, thus bringing the lying to a sudden end. But whereas the English 'she lied to us' is ambiguous, compatible with a reading in which she lied on a single occasion, the Welsh *fuodd hi'n deud celwyddau* makes clear that the lying went on for a period of time (which the character's death brought to an end):

She **lied** to us, which was the worst thing, driving her mother to distraction and eventually to a near nervous breakdown. [TIME 54]

Fuodd hi'n deud celwyddau wrthon ni, a dyna'r peth gwaethaf – a gyrrodd ei mam yn orffwyll ac yn y pen draw, o'i cho' jest iawn. [AMSER 86]

There is also a literary *bod*-preterite that takes the form *bu i rywun wneud rhywbeth* which seems to be equivalent to the simple preterite. Note that *bu* in this construction is always in the third person singular:

Ni fu i'r pen-blaenor grybwyll y mater. [RHANNU 191]	*The head deacon **did not mention** the matter.*
'A series of disgraceful brawls took place, two of which **ended** in the police-court . . .' [BAND 212]	'Digwyddodd sawl cweryl cywilyddus, a **bu i ddau o'r achosion hynny arwain** at ymddangosiadau yn llysoedd yr heddlu . . .' [CYLCH 19]
'. . . I have heard of you from Mrs Farintosh, whom **you helped** in the hour of her sore need.' [BAND 210]	'. . . mi glywais i amdanoch chi gan Mrs Farintosh, **y bu i chi ei chynorthwyo** yn awr ei chyfyngder.' [CYLCH 15]

Like the preterite, the imperfect can be expressed either synthetically (*canai hi*[14]) or periphrastically (*roedd hi'n canu*[15], *byddai hi'n canu, roedd hi'n arfer canu, arferai hi ganu*). However, unlike the preterite which is still part of the contemporary spoken language, the synthetic imperfect is confined today to literary and formal registers. (The same synthetic verb form can be used in speech as a conditional, a point to which we return in section 5 of this chapter). Earlier in this section we illustrated the synthetic imperfect (*canai hi*) and the most common, canonical periphrastic form using the imperfect of *bod* + subject + *yn* + verb-noun (*roedd hi'n canu*). The following examples show the periphrastic construction using *byddai*; we note that the English equivalent is variously a simple past (*bumped*), or one of the two periphrases (*used to go, would drink*):[16]

Byddwn i'n mynd i dafarn yng Nghaerdydd o'r enw The New Ely	**I used to go** to a Cardiff pub called the New Ely where a crowd of Welsh

[14] PWT 3.32, *yr amhenodol syml* 'the simple imperfect'.
[15] PWT 3.29, *y gorffennol parhaol* 'the continuous imperfect'.
[16] The fact that the *byddai* periphrastic imperfect, and the English periphrasis with *would*, are very similar in construction and historical development – they both have uses not only as imperfect but also as conditional – means that speakers today may be inclined to think of them as direct translation equivalents, but the translation corpus reveals clearly that there is no one-on-one equivalence between Welsh forms and English ones, even here.

lle **bydde** twr o fyfyrwyr o Gymru**'n yfed**, yn cymdeithasu ac yn canu trwy'r nos. [HUNAN 198]

students **would drink**, socialise and sing all night. [SOLVA 198]

. . . he appeared not to be looking where he was going and occasionally **bumped** into people. [TIME 77]

Doedd o ddim fel pe bai'n edrych i ble'r oedd o'n mynd ac o bryd i'w gilydd **byddai'n cerdded i mewn** i rywun. [AMSER 121]

Byddai fy nhaid yn **siarad** wrthyf [. . .] fel pe bawn gyfoed ag ef . . . [HENAT 25]

Grandfather **would hold forth** to me [. . .] as if I were of his own age . . . [LOCUST 27]

Welsh also has a periphrastic imperfect making use of the verb-noun *arfer* ('to customarily do, do habitually'), introduced in section 5.1. The construction takes the form (BOD) YN ARFER + verb-noun, where *bod* is inflected in either the *imperfect* paradigm (*roedd hi'n arfer canu*) or the *byddai* paradigm (*byddai hi'n arfer canu*). The English translations of these may just use one of the renderings appropriate for past habitual verbs (*used to* seems particularly frequent here), or make use of an adverb such as *usually*, or occasionally the expression *to be in the habit of*:

Byddai hi'n arfer golchi pob gwydryn ar ôl ei ddefnyddio gan Paul a'i ffrindiau gwingar. [LLEIFIOR 136]

She **usually washed** glasses immediately after Paul and his bibulous friends had been using them. [RETURN 115]

. . . chief constables **were not in the habit of hanging around**. [VICT 29]

. . . ac **nad oedd prif gwnstabliaid yn arfer loetran o gwmpas y lle** ar ôl oriau gwaith. [LLINYN 32]

I used to work for him at the Barbizan. [TIME 105]

Ro'n i'n arfer gweithio iddo fo yn y Barbizan [AMSER 167]

It could have been his imagination, but he thought he read in the eyes studying him an almost predatory interest **not usually extended** to him by women [lit. that women **didn't usually show** him]; [TIME 102]

Efallai mai ef oedd yn dychmygu, ond credai iddo ddarllen yn y llygaid ryw olwg sglyfaethus **nad oedd gwragedd yn arfer ei dangos iddo** . . . [AMSER 162]

It is also possible to conjugate the Welsh verb *arfer* directly, without using *bod* at all:

Arferai 'mam fynd i'r berllan, weithiau ... [HDF 127]	**My mother used to go out** to the orchard ... [OFH 158]
Tanforwr oedd ei brawd, Walter, wrth ei alwedigaeth – ond **arferai ganu acordion** Soprani 'Hundred and twenty bass' roedd e wedi'i brynu'n yr Eidal ar un o'i grwydrade. [HOUDINI 7]	Her brother Walter, a submariner, **played** a Soprani Hundred and Twenty bass accordion, which he'd bought in Italy on his travels. [SOLVA 7]
Arferai nifer o'r dynion **fyned** i Sir Amwythig bob blwyddyn i'r cynhaeaf i fedi gwenith, a dychwelent gan ddywedyd eu bod yn cael eu gwala a'u gweddill o fara gwyn. [CWM 4]	Some of the men of the glen **went** to Shropshire every year to the wheat harvest, and on their return they would say they had had their fill of wheaten bread. [GORSE 5]

As in the present tense, where insertion of *wrthi* can be used to reinforce a progressive interpretation, this is true in the imperfect as well:

Yr **oedd wrthi'n sgwrio**'r trywsus melfaréd o'r dŵr cyntaf, a'r dŵr yn sucio allan ohono o flaen y brws yn llwyd ac yn dew. [TRAED 12]	She **was scrubbing** the corduroy trousers after the first washing; the water squeezed out was thick and grey. [FEET 11]
Rogers **was putting** the folder in his wallet when Hagbourne came into the room carrying what was manifestly a heavy green strongbox. [TIME 23]	**Roedd** Rogers **wrthi'n rhoi**'r pecyn yn ei waled pan ddaeth Howells yn ei ôl yn cario bocs cadw pres trwm, gwyrdd. [AMSER 36]

The last forms that the preterite and the imperfect can take in Welsh are the reduced clauses known as *bod*-clauses (which have either a present or an imperfect interpretation, depending on context), and the noun clauses with *i*, which have a preterite interpretation. These are covered in Chapters 3 and 4.

5.3 The use of perfect tenses

Perfect tenses (e.g. past perfect or pluperfect, present perfect, future perfect) are used to mark certain events as having been completed *prior* (or *anterior*) to other events. In this they represent departures from the strict chronological order of a narration. Events that advance the narrative in the order that they occurred are said to be *foregrounded*, whereas a departure from the main narrative sequence that makes reference to some earlier event is *backgrounded*.

In most Welsh styles today, perfect tenses are constructed periphrastically, using BOD WEDI + VERB-NOUN (literally 'to be after [doing something]'): *mae hi wedi canu*, 'she has sung', *roedd hi wedi mynd* 'she had gone', *bydd hi wedi dysgu* 'she will have learned', etc. Since this study is based on a written corpus in which the narration is almost always set in the past, the pluperfect will be seen much more often than the present perfect or the future perfect. In addition to the periphrastic pluperfect (e.g. *roedd hi wedi canu* 'she had sung'), a synthetic pluperfect is widely encountered in older styles and in literary Welsh: *canasai* 'she had sung', *aethai* 'she had gone', *dysgasai* 'she had learned'. Both periphrastic and synthetic pluperfects will be seen in the examples throughout this section.

The backgrounding of information that generally entails the use of perfect tenses is routinely encountered in several functions. It may occur in a main clause, when reference is made to a prior circumstance that serves as background to, or sets the stage for, some later event:

Taflasai Monica y drws yn agored ac arhosodd i'r cathod fynd i mewn yn gyntaf. [MONICA 37]

Monica **had flung** open the door and was waiting for the cats to go in first. [MONICA 36]

Trawsai hen gôt glytiog amdano, ac am ei ben gwisgai het galed felynwen a'i hymyl yn dechrau ffarwelio â'r gweddill ohoni. [CYCHWYN 21]

He **had donned** an old, patched coat and was wearing a whitish-yellow bowler, its brim beginning to part company with the rest of it. [BEGIN 20]

In this pattern, the event in question may not in fact be out of chronological order with respect to the surrounding events; the point of the perfect tense here is to background the event.

Pluperfects often occur in subordinate clauses that make reference to an earlier event, where they are often required because of *sequence of tense* rules in both English and Welsh grammar. First, a pluperfect is generally used in subordinate clauses introduced by verbs of saying, asking, stating, wondering, thinking, learning, and so on, when that introducing verb is itself in a past tense:

Erbyn cyrraedd Bangor y noson honno, cafodd **fod** Arthur, ei hen gyfaill yn yr ysgol, **wedi taflu** ei

When he arrived in Bangor that night, he learned that Arthur, his old school friend, **had given up**

waith ymchwil ac wedi ymuno.
[TRAED 161]

his research to join the forces.
[FEET 143]

She thought that in all her life she
had never seen soldiers so uncertain
on their feet: [THRO 195]

Tybiai **na welsai erioed** yn ei bywyd
filwyr mor simsan ar eu traed:
[TRWY 86]

... one of my second-year students
who**'d messed up** an essay ...
[CIDER 86]

... un o'm myfyrwyr ail flwyddyn a
oedd wedi gwneud tipyn o gawl o'i
draethawd. [SEIDR 117]

Secondly, some subordinate clauses give a reason for a current state of affairs
by pointing to something that happened earlier and which plays a causal role
in the later event, as revealed by the presence of a conjunction like *because* or
since. The causal clauses are shown in small caps:

Yr oedd Twm yn llon iawn, a daeth
ar ei union i ddiolch i'm mam, ond
ni wnaeth hi lawer o siapri ohono,
OBLEGID YR **OEDD WEDI ACHOSI**
LLAWER O BOEN DIACHOS IDDI ...
[GWEN 28]

Twm was delighted, and he
immediately came to thank my
mother, but she did not make
him very welcome BECAUSE HER
APPEARANCE IN COURT **HAD UPSET**
HER. [GWEN 34]

... ac yng ngolau cannwyll GAN
FOD YR OLEW WEDI GORFFEN
YN SIOPAU'R PENTREF ...
[CYCHWYN 188]

... and reading by candlelight
BECAUSE THE VILLAGE SHOPS
HAD RUN OUT OF PARAFFIN ...
[BEGIN 190]

He wore round glasses held together
with a lot of Scotch tape BECAUSE
OF ALL THE TIMES DUDLEY **HAD
PUNCHED** HIM ON THE NOSE.
[STONE 24]

Gwisgai sbectol gron a gâi ei dal
at ei gilydd gan lwmpyn o dâp
selo O GANLYNIAD I'R HOLL
DROEON **ROEDD DUDLEY WEDI
EI DDYRNU** AR EI DRWYN.
[MAEN 15]

Thirdly, relative clauses often refer back to an earlier event, serving as they do
to modify or give more information about an antecedent:

Er bod fy nghlust yn llosgi, prin y
gallwn beidio â chwerthin am y tro a
wnaethai â mi ... [GWEN 19]

Although my ear was burning
I could not help laughing at the
trick he **had played** on me ...
[GWEN 25–6]

Yr oedd y traffig yn ddi-dor, ac
yr oedd ei bum synnwyr ar eu
heithaf yn ei gadw rhag damwain
fel honno a **welsai** ar y groesffordd.
[CRYMAN 73]

There was no let-up in the traffic,
and his five senses were alert lest
he too have an accident like the
one **he'd just seen** at the junction.
[SICKLE 60]

Ond wedi cyrraedd y tŷ a chael
eistedd yn y gadair, dechreuodd
meddwl Begw weithio ar yr hyn a
glywsai ei mam yn ei ddweud am
fam Winni. [TE 46]

But when she got into the house
and sat down, Begw's mind began
to dwell on what she **had heard** her
mother say about Winni's mother.
[TEA 44]

And temporal conjunctions like English *since, for*, and *by*, and the usual Welsh
equivalents *ers* and *erbyn*, are generally accompanied by a clause in a perfect
tense, since they specifically refer to a state of affairs which began earlier than
the reference time of interest. These temporal phrases are shown in small caps
in the examples below:[17]

Hogan ifanc oeddwn i radag honno,
wsti. Ond **rydw i wedi clywad** lot
fawr o betha rhyfadd ERS YR ADAG
HONNO. [NOS 44]

I was a young girl at the time,
you know. But **I've heard** a great
many strange things SINCE THEN.
[NIGHT 35]

ER Y NOSWAITH FLAENOROL **aethai**
gagendor rhyngddynt. [BYW 29]

An abyss **had opened** between
them SINCE LAST NIGHT.
[AWAKENING 29]

Ymhen tipyn dechreuodd ei fenyn,
ei fara, ei gig moch a'i wyau orffen
cyn diwedd yr wythnos [...] Un
wythnos **darfuasai** ei fara, ei wyau
a'i gig moch ERBYN BORE IAU...
[TRAED 130]

After a while he began to run out of
bread, butter, bacon and eggs before
the end of the week [...] One week
he **had run out of** bread, eggs and
bacon BY THURSDAY MORNING...
[FEET 116]

Aethai Bet hithau i weini, ar yr oedd
Ifan a Jane yn hollol ar eu pennau eu
hunain ERBYN HYN. [TRAED 145]

Bet **had gone** into service so
that Ifan a Jane were BY THIS
TIME completely on their own.
[FEET 129]

[17] Usually the perfect tense is not in the *since*-clause, but in the accompanying clause,
though there is variation in this:
Faint oedd er pan **adawsai** Aber Heli,
hefyd? [CHWAL 109]

How long was it SINCE HE **HAD LEFT**
ABERHELI? [OUT 115]

When I told her that Miss Stuchley **had been missing** from her apartment SINCE LAST EVENING she immediately jumped in and said that she'd known she'd come to a bad end. [TIME 65]

Pan ddaru mi ddeud wrthi **fod** Miss Stuchley **'di bod ar goll** o'i fflat ERS NEITHIWR, neidiodd i'r fei ar unwaith a deud 'i bod hi'n gwybod na ddôi unrhyw dda iddi hi yn y diwedd. [AMSER 102]

... the bolt was significantly oxidised, suggesting that it **had been** generally unused FOR SOME YEARS ... [TIME 95]

Roedd y follt wedi'i hocsideiddio'n sylweddol, gan awgrymu nad **oedd** wedi'i defnyddio ERS RHAI BLYNYDDOEDD ... [AMSER 150]

The examples seen above show instances where Welsh and English converge in using a perfect tense. However, the use of perfect tenses (present perfect, pluperfect) is noticeably less frequent in traditional Welsh style than in English. For instance, while English is nearly categorical in using a perfect tense with temporal *since*, it is often preferable in Welsh to use a present tense for an action that started in the past and is still going on in the present:[18]

Rydw i newydd fod gydag Erika, **sydd yn byw** ERS DDOE yn ei fflat. [ERLID 91]

I have just been with Erika, who **has been living** in her flat SINCE YESTERDAY. [HAVEN 94]

Rydyn ni'n sefyll yma ERS 11.30 NEITHIWR yn yr unfan. [ERLID 109]

We **have been standing** here in the same place SINCE 11.30 LAST NIGHT. [HAVEN 113]

Yr oeddwn i'n meddwl y byd o Mr Jones; ef **oedd** fy arwr ER PAN OEDDWN YN HOGYN BACH. [O LAW 163]

I thought the world of Mr Jones; he **had been** my hero EVER SINCE I WAS A SMALL BOY. [FROM HAND 131]

The verb accompanying temporal *since* in Welsh may also be in the preterite. This is one clue that the Welsh preterite and the English preterite are not identical. Traditionally it was quite possible to use a Welsh preterite with the semantics of a perfect:

---

[18] The translator working from Welsh to English may even make the unusual choice to use the English present, undoubtedly to convey the flavour of the Welsh:

'**Mae**'r hen Rees yn 'i fedd ERS DEUGAIN MLYNADD BELLACH, Meri Ifans. Hen foi duwiol dros ben, ond un cas gynddeiriog yn y chwaral.' [O LAW 17]

'Old Rees **is** in his grave SINCE FORTY YEARS NOW, Mary Evans. Very pious old boy, but nasty, terribly nasty, in the quarry.' [FROM HAND 3]

Dim ond ERS TUA 25 MLYNEDD y
cafodd muriau'r dref eu dymchwel
[YR ERLID 45]

Only 25 years had passed SINCE
THE TOWN WALLS **HAD BEEN**
DEMOLISHED [HAVEN 48]

Bu arfau fy nhad yn llond fy
meddwl ER PAN AETH DAFYDD
OWEN ADREF. [O LAW 197]

My father's quarry tools **have been**
uppermost in my mind EVER SINCE
DAFYDD OWEN WENT HOME.
[FROM HAND 163]

Cedwais ef hyd heddiw oblegid
dyma'r prawf fy mod i'n ddieuog
gerbron Hannah. [MONICA 33]

I've kept it EVER SINCE because it's
proof that I'm not guilty as regards
Hannah. [MONICA 32]

Chwarddodd Monica, y chwerthin
peiriannol, uchel a **fabwysiadwyd**
ganddi ER EI PHRIODAS.
[MONICA 44]

Monica laughed, the shrill,
mechanical laugh she **had**
adopted SINCE HER MARRIAGE.
[MONICA 44]

In fact, in many places where English prefers or even requires a present perfect
or pluperfect, Welsh is content to use a preterite.[19] Going from English source
texts to Welsh translation, both the present perfects and pluperfects may be
replaced with Welsh preterites:

I've never **been** more ashamed of
Gryffindor students. [STONE 303]

Fu erioed gymaint o gywilydd
arnaf o ddisgyblion Llereurol.
[MAEN 193]

'. . . I have heard of you from
Mrs Farintosh, whom you helped
in the hour of her sore need.'
[BAND 210]

'. . . mi glywais i amdanoch chi
gan Mrs Farintosh, y bu i chi ei
chynorthwyo yn awr ei chyfyngder.'
[CYLCH 15]

---

[19] This is one of the ways that the expression of tense/mood/aspect in Welsh has been
changing. There are two translations of *Alice in Wonderland* made by the same author
several decades apart. The earlier translation (coded as ALYS I) is considerably more
literary and old-fashioned in its linguistic choices than the more recent translation
(ALYS II). One of the changes is in fact the occasional replacement of a preterite by
a present perfect:

I wonder how many miles I've fallen by
this time? [ALICE, 20]

Ysgwn i pa sawl milltir y **syrthiais** erbyn
hyn? [ALYS I 12]

Ysgŵn i pa sawl milltir **yr ydw i wedi**
cwympo erbyn hyn? [ALYS II 9]

She had wanted to go and sit at his table [. . .] He **had stopped** her. [VICT 135]

Roedd hi ar dân i fynd i eistedd wrth yr un bwrdd ag o [. . .] Fe **roddodd stop** arni, wrth gwrs. [LLINYN 152]

She was up on the chimney-piece while she said this, though she hardly knew how she **had got** there. [THRO 131]

Roedd hi i fyny ar y silff ben tân tra siaradai er mai prin y gwyddai sut yr **aeth** yno . . . [TRWY 18]

There were five photographs in the envelope he **had found** in the sideboard drawer. [TIME 27]

Roedd pum llun yn yr amserlen y **daeth** o hyd iddi yn nrôr y seidbord. [AMSER 41]

And in the other direction, Welsh preterites often become English perfects in translation. Again, the Welsh preterite can correspond to either a present perfect or a past perfect, depending on context:

Yr oedd Ifan yn falch bod ei wraig yn bwrw drwyddi mor huawdl, ac yn dangos y fath synnwyr wrth fynegi'r drwg a **achosodd** Sioned i'w modryb Geini. [TRAED 63]

Ifan was pleased that his wife was dealing with the situation so capably and showing such good sense by pointing out to Sioned the harm she **had done** to her Aunt Geini. [FEET 55]

Ni theimlais innau, erioed, unrhyw whithdod oherwydd y diffyg hwn yn fy ngolygon. [HDF 140]

I have never felt aware of any loss due to my defective eyesight. [OFH 175]

'Pryd y gwelis di Dewyth Edward ddwaetha?' **'Welis i byth mono fo** ar ôl iddo fod acw yn gofyn imi gadw i dŷ o.' [BYW 78–9]

'When did you last see Uncle Edward?' **'I haven't seen him** since he came over asking me to keep house for him.' [AWAKENING 77]

'Fuoch chi 'rioed yn Sir Fôn?' meddai Winni, gan edrych tuag at yr ynys honno. [TE 39]

'Have you ever been to Anglesey?' Winni asked, looking across towards the island. [TEA 38]

The following examples are especially striking; the time period being referred to is effectively the speaker's entire life up to the moment of speaking. To use a preterite in English, in such cases, would tend to imply that the speaker was reflecting back on a life that is now over ('In my life I didn't read many biographies [and alas, that won't change now]'), as opposed to the perfect which implies that the event is still open-ended ('In my life I haven't read many biographies [but that could change]'):

Unwaith yn fy oes y **ces i** ddim tebyg i'r Nymber Wan hwn . . . [HDF 169]	Only once since that day **have I tasted** anything like Number one . . . [OFH 212]
Yn ystod fy oes **darllenais** amryw gofiannau . . . [RHYS 3]	In my time **I have read** many biographies . . . [RHYS 9]
. . . y bywyd a **gerais** gymaint, mewn atgof, ar hyd fy oes . . . [HDF 131]	. . . the unspoiled rural life **I have loved** so much in reminiscence all through my life . . . [OFH 163]
. . . yr unig ddydd o orfoledd digymysg a **gefais** yn fy mywyd. [MONICA 35]	. . . the only day of pure triumph **I've had** in my whole life. [MONICA 33]

Clearly, the Welsh preterite can include the semantics of perfect aspect in its interpretation, whereas the semantics of the English preterite represent a sharp break with the present.[20]

We noted earlier that a pluperfect event is backgrounded with respect to the foregrounded events that serve to advance the plot. For instance, the following example from Saunders Lewis's *Monica* functions as a comment on the character's current psychological state by referring to her past attitude:

O leiaf ni **ofalodd** hi erioed am sibrwd pobl o'i chwmpas. [MONICA 41]	At least she **had never paid** very much attention to the whispering of others. [MONICA 41]

---

[20] It is not impossible to find instances where Welsh has a perfect tense and English does not, such as the following:

Aeth i chwilio am y llyfr mawr lle y **dysgasai yn araf** sut i sgrifennu'r symiau o arian a wariwyd ac a dderbyniwyd ganddo. [RHANDIR 101]	He went to look for the big book in which he **was slowly learning** how to write down correctly all the sums of money spent and received by him. [FAIR 99]
Rhoesai hwnnw'i lif heibio ac **aethai ati i hollti** dau neu dri o flociau yn goed tân. [CHWAL 202]	The latter had laid aside his saw and **was busily splitting up** logs into firewood. [OUT 214]

But in both of these cases the English translator has opted to see the events in question as still in progress (i.e. simultaneous) rather than completed anterior events as the Welsh text has it by using the pluperfect.

The pluperfect in the English translation makes this discursive function clear – the fact that she had not paid much attention in previous times explains her behaviour at this point in the story – whereas a preterite ('she never paid . . .') would more likely belong to the foreground, playing a role in advancing the narration. This is less obvious in Welsh, where a preterite may be used with either type of event.[21] Similarly, in the following examples from *Traed mewn Cyffion*, the English translator has preferred to construe the Welsh preterites as departures from strict chronology, rendering them as background to the main narration. The English text thus emphasises that the characters are reflecting on prior events. The Welsh text is not as concerned to distinguish between anteriority and the main timeline of the narration:

Methai Owen ddeall paham y **troes** Gwen ei phen i ffwrdd a pheidio â dyfod â'i mam ato (mae'n debyg mai ei mam oedd y ddynes gôt sîl). Ond bwriodd yn ei feddwl na **welodd** hi mohono. [TRAED 70]	Owen could not understand why Gwen **had averted** her eyes, and **had not introduced** her mother to him. (The woman in the sealskin coat was probably her mother). But he decided that she **had not seen** him. [FEET 62]
Yr oedd Ifan yn falch bod ei wraig yn bwrw drwyddi mor huawdl, ac yn dangos y fath synnwyr wrth fynegi'**r drwg a achosodd** Sioned i'w modryb Geini. [TRAED 63]	Ifan was pleased that his wife was dealing with the situation so capably and showing such good sense by pointing out to Sioned **the harm she had done** to her Aunt Geini. [FEET 55]

Indeed, in English usage it is not unusual to have an entire mini-episode narrated in the pluperfect as a piece of a larger text that uses the preterite. This happens when the mini-episode is retrospective with respect to the main story line. The following examples contain multiple consecutive pluperfects in English:

---

[21] That the Welsh preterite is compatible with the backgrounded reading is shown, for one thing, by the fact that *erioed* is used for 'never' with the preterite instead of *byth*. The difference between these two adverbs is precisely that *erioed* is used with perfect tenses and *byth* with progressive or imperfect tenses.

He **had fallen asleep** in one of the bedrooms, very late in the evening. Then a couple **had come in**, and they **had lifted** him into the bathroom, depositing him in the bath. There he **had slept** for two hours, maybe three. He **had awakened** with a terrific stiffness in his neck, back, and legs. He **had drunk** some coffee, but not enough, never enough. [KNOTS 87]

Roedd wedi syrthio i gysgu yn un o'r llofftydd, yn hwyr iawn yn y noson. Wedyn fe **ddaeth cwpl i mewn**, ei gario i'r bathrwm a'i osod yn y bàth. Fe **gysgodd** yn y fan honno am ddwyawr neu dair. **Deffrodd** gyda chric yn ei war, a'i gefn a'i goesau'n brifo'n arw. Fe **yfodd** dipyn o goffi, ond dim digon, byth dim digon. [CHWERW 74–5]

Her father **had never talked** about her mother's death and Cordelia **had avoided** questioning him, fearful of learning that her mother **had never held** her in her arms, **never regained** consciousness, **never perhaps even known** that she had a daughter. [UNSUIT 10][22]

Ni **soniodd** ei thad air wrthi am farwolaeth ei mam ac ni **holodd** hithau, rhag ofyn iddo ddweud wrthi na fu'i mam erioed yn ei magu, na **chafodd** gyfle ei daro llygaid ar ei merch newydd-anedig, na wyddai am ei bodolaeth hyd yn oed. [GORTYN 16]

Y dyddiau cyntaf hynny ni ddrwgdybiodd ef ymddygiad Monica. **Canmolodd** ei doethineb hi yn ymwrthod â chaledwaith, yn gorwedd ac yn segura. **Sylwodd** yn wir ei bod hi'n dawedog ac anghofleidgar, ond un oriog **fu** Monica erioed. [MONICA 56]

In those early days he had no misgivings about Monica's behaviour. He **had praised** her good sense in refusing to do any hard work, in lying down and taking things easy. He **had noticed**, indeed, that she **had been** taciturn and undemonstrative, but Monica **had always been** a moody one. [MONICA 56]

Having strings of consecutive perfects, especially periphrastic ones using *wedi*, is less likely in Welsh than in English. It seems more common in Welsh either to have only the first verb in the pluperfect and then continue the mini-episode in the preterite, as in the above example from *Knots and Crosses*, or to

---

[22] It is possible to omit the auxiliary from successive occurrences of a perfect tense in English, letting multiple past participles depend on a single occurrence of the auxiliary. In this example, *[had] never regained* and *[had] never perhaps even known* are pluperfects, 'inheriting' their auxiliary from *had avoided*.

simply use the preterite throughout the mini-episode, as seen in the passages from *An Unsuitable Job for a Woman* and *Monica*.[23]

There is an optional rhetorical use of the pluperfect in English narration which takes a brief episode and casts it retrospectively (i.e. in the pluperfect) even though it is not in fact out of chronological sequence in the narration:

'No!' Stuchley **had stopped** him, his eyebrows down over suddenly angry eyes, his voice choked. 'You're not suggesting she did it!' His wife **had put** her hand to her mouth, uttering a muffled gasp. [TIME 52]	'Na!' **Torrodd** Stuchley **ar ei draws**, ei aeliau i lawr dros lygaid a oedd, yn sydyn, yn gynddeiriog, a'i lais yn tagu. 'Dydach chi ddim yn awgrymu mai *hi* wnaeth!' **Gosododd** ei wraig ei llaw dros ei cheg, ac ebychu'n ddistaw. [AMSER 82]

This use of backgrounding seems to function as a device to take a character's point of view, as though the character were reflecting back on something that had just happened. This rhetorical use of the pluperfect is eliminated in the Welsh text, which renders these verbs using the preterite.

Perfect progressive tenses

Both Welsh and English can construct perfect progressive tenses, for instance *she had been living* and *roedd hi wedi bod yn byw*, which specify both perfect aspect and progressive aspect at once, thus combining into one form the simpler constructions *she had lived / roedd hi wedi byw* (perfect) and *she was living / roedd hi'n byw* (past progressive). Sometimes both the original and the translation make use of this complex pattern:

[23] More recent writing, however, may reveal a much greater isomorphism of the two languages than was formerly the case. The following example from a recent (2012) book shows a more or less one-on-one correspondence of verb forms:

Wn i ddim a yw'r Herr Reichsminister **wedi cael** gwybod trwy Herr Reidenreich fod y bwrdd eglwysig **wedi dod** â'm swydd i ben fel prif feddyg y Paul-Gerhardt-Stift ar 31.XII, er fy mod i **wedi gweithio** yno ers 28 mlynedd, **wedi bod** yn ymladd yn y ffrynt yn y rhyfel ac **wedi cael** fy nghlwyfo, am fod fy ngwraig, yr wyf yn briod â hi ers 1906, o dras anaraidd. [ERLID 78]	I don't know whether the Herr Reichsminister **has been told** through Herr Reideureich that the church board **has ended** my post as senior doctor at the Paul-Gerhardt-Stift on 31.XII, although I **had been working** there for 28 years, **had fought** at the front in the war and **had been injured**, because my wife, with whom I **have been married** since 1906, is of non-Aryan descent. [HAVEN 80]

... she would find it difficult to refer to a man she **had been living** with and about whom she must presume I knew nothing. [TIME 90]

... mi fyddai hi'n ei chael hi'n anodd cyfeirio at ddyn **yr oedd hi wedi bod yn byw** efo fo, a hithau'n cymryd yn ganiataol na wyddwn i ddim am y peth. [AMSER 143]

Yr oedd Huw Powys ers rhai misoedd **wedi bod yn ymlusgo** hyd lawr bob twll a chornel, ac wedi hynny wedi dechrau cropian yn beryglus eiddgar drwy ddrysau, dan ddodrefn ... [LLEIFIOR 204]

For a few months past Huw Powys **had been finding his way** into every nook in the house, then crawling boldly through doorways, under furniture ... [RETURN 176]

But the target language does not always follow the source text so closely. Thus, we find instances where the perfect progressive corresponds to a simpler tense, either progressive (*roedd hi'n ei ddarllen*) or perfect (*mae hi wedi dweud*):

'**Mae hi wedi dweud** ei helynt wrtha'i yn ei dagrau. Ond rhedeg i lawr arno ... naddo.' [LLEIFIOR 91]

'**She's been telling** me about all her troubles, and weeping. But running him down ... no, not really.' [RETURN 77]

She had been reading Wilde's *The Birthday of the Infanta* and found it singularly depressing. [VICT 129]

The Birthday of the Infanta, Oscar Wilde **roedd hi'n ei ddarllen**, a chodai'r felan arni. [LLINYN 144]

And we also find the introduction of a perfect progressive form in the target text where it was not present in the original:

'We shall spend the night in your room, and we shall investigate the cause of this noise **which has disturbed you.**' [BAND 231]

'Fe fyddwn ni'n treulio'r noson yn eich ystafell chi, fel y dywedais, ac yn ymchwilio i achos y sŵn yma **sydd wedi bod yn tarfu arnoch** ynghanol y nos.' [CYLCH 46] [lit. which has been disturbing you]

Cordelia reckoned that **she must have waited there** immobile in the shadows for nearly half an hour ... [UNSUIT 135]

... barnodd Cordelia'i **bod hi wedi bod yn sefyll yn ei hunfan** yn y cysgodion am ryw hanner awr ... [GORTYN 171] [lit. that she had been standing in place]

In most cases the choice to use a compound perfect progressive rather than one of the simpler forms focusing on just one of these aspects is a stylistic option, not a constraint.

5.4 The impersonal forms

The so-called impersonal (*amhersonol*) forms in Welsh are verb forms whose distinguishing feature is that they have no grammatical subject. Consequently, there is no subject-verb agreement. There is a single impersonal form for each of several tenses, as the following examples show for *darllen, gweld*, and *canu*:

-wyd   preterite, e.g. darllenwyd, gwelwyd, canwyd
-id   imperfect, e.g. darllenid, gwelid, cenid
-ir   present, e.g. darllenir, gwelir, cenir
-er   imperative, e.g. darllener, gweler, caner

The Welsh impersonal forms are often found as translation equivalents of the English passive voice: *gwelwyd fi* 'I was seen', *gwelid fi* 'I was (habitually) seen, I used to be seen', *gwelir fi* 'I am seen / I will be seen'. However, the impersonal forms are not technically passives, first, because in passives, the undergoer of the action is promoted to grammatical subject, as revealed by subject-verb agreement (compare *gwelir fi / I **am** seen, gwelir ti / you **are** seen, gwelir ef / he **is** seen, gwelir ni / we **are** seen*, etc.); secondly, both transitive and intransitive verbs can appear in the Welsh impersonal form (e.g. *dod* 'to come' has *daethpwyd, deuir*, etc.) whereas only transitive verbs have passives.[24] The impersonal form is somewhat like a French verb that takes the pronoun *on* as its subject (*Au Sénégal on parle français* 'In Senegal, they/people/one speak French') or a German one that takes *man* (*Im Senegal spricht man Französisch*), except that *on* and *man*, though generic, always imply human agency, whereas the Welsh impersonal forms do not necessarily imply a human agent:

She never finished the sentence, for at this moment **a heavy crash shook the forest** from end to end. [THRO 194]	Ni orffenodd y frawddeg oherwydd y funud honno **ysgydwyd** y goedwig o'r naill ben i'r llall **gan sŵn ofnadwy**. [TRWY 85]

The most frequently encountered examples in the translation corpus are like the following, in which the direct object of the Welsh impersonal verb

---

[24] The Welsh *cael* passive is discussed in Chapter 4.

appears as the grammatical subject of an agentless English passive. The impersonal verb clearly serves the same purpose as the agentless passive, that of identifying an action without focusing on who (or what) did it:

Bob gyda'r nos a phrynhawn Sadwrn **clywid eco ei gŷn a'i forthwyl** dros yr ardal, ac yna glec sydyn y saethu. [TRAED 27]

Every evening and Saturday afternoon **the sound of his hammer and chisel was heard** throughout the district, followed by the sharp crack of the explosion. [FEET 24]

Magwyd yno deuluoedd graenus; ac yn ôl yr hanes nid aeth neb o Benrhiw erioed heb fod yn well ei fyd . . . [HDF 64]

Families were brought up there obviously well, and the story is that no one ever left Penrhiw but in improved circumstances . . . [OFH 76]

His sandy hair had been closely shaved in a tonsure down to the greyish skin of his scalp . . . [TIME 47]

Eilliwyd ei wallt melyngoch yn agos at groen gwelw-lwyd ei ben . . . [AMSER 74]

Small doses of the powder were alleged to promote happiness . . . [TIME 64]

Honnwyd bod dosau bychain o'r cyffur yn esgor ar hapusrwydd . . . [AMSER 100]

. . . hyd y **gellir deall** pethau . . . [HDF 61]

. . . as far as these things **can be understood** now . . . [OFH 73]

When an agent is expressed, it may be introduced by the preposition *gan* in Welsh, and *by* in English:

Gwelodd fy nhadcu gwympo'r genhedlaeth gyntaf o'r coed a **blannwyd ganddo ef** yn ddyn ifanc, newydd briodi. [HDF 80]

My grandfather saw the felling of the first lot of trees **planted by him** as a newly married young man. [OFH 97]

Y Gwir amdani oedd nad trio neidio'r ceunant yr oedd, ond fe'i **hyrddiwyd bron trosodd gan y twr bechgyn cryf** a ddeuai ar ei ôl ag yntau'n fychan. [TRAED 33]

The fact was that he hadn't wished to jump the gully, but he **had been almost flung over by the crowd of hefty lads** coming behind him, and he such a small boy. [FEET 30]

Peth ar ei ben ei hun yw stryd mewn maestref o'r dosbarth canol. **Ffurfir** ei chymeriad a **rheolir** ei bywyd cymdeithasol yn llwyr **gan ferched.** [MONICA 38]

Now a road in a middle-class suburb is something unique. Its character **is formed** and its social life completely **run by women.** [MONICA 37]

But it is also common to translate a Welsh impersonal form that has an expressed agent by an English active verb. In this pattern, the human agent named in the Welsh *gan*-phrase becomes the grammatical subject in English:

Adroddwyd wrthyf amdano **gan gyfaill** o ardal arall a'i cofiai yn ei flynyddoedd olaf, yn dlawd ei amgylchiadau . . . [HDF 98]

A friend from another neighborhood who remembered him in his last years **told** me of him being in poor circumstances . . . [OFH 120]

Chwarddodd Monica, y chwerthin peiriannol, uchel a **fabwysiadwyd ganddi** er ei phriodas. [MONICA 44]

Monica laughed, the shrill, mechanical laugh **she had adopted** since her marriage. [MONICA 44]

As these examples suggest, sometimes the most natural choice in English is simply an active verb with an expressed human subject. In such cases, the choice to use an impersonal form in Welsh is striking, especially when the identity of the agent is obvious from context. For instance, when children are given big lumps of toffee to chew on, it is obviously the children that have trouble chewing them:

Ar ôl iddynt fynd i'w gwely dôi eu mam â joi o gyfleth a'i roi yn eu cegau [. . .] Os byddai'r joi'n fawr byddai hyn yn waith anodd, a **cheid trafferth** i'w throi yn eu genau. [TRAED 134]

After they had gone to bed, their mother would come and place a lump of toffee in their mouths [. . .] If it was a big lump, that was very difficult; **they had trouble** turning it in their mouths . . . [FEET 111]

Similarly, when decisions are made while Monica is alone sweeping out bedrooms, we can be sure that it was Monica who made them. And knowing the organisation of ship's crews is enough to be sure that the decision to anchor the ship somewhere was made by the captain. These logical agents are simply identified overtly as the grammatical subjects in the English translations:

Gwenodd yn ddiflas gan ystyried mai tra sgubai hi llofftydd y **ffurfiwyd pob penderfyniad** o dipyn bwys yn ei hanes. [MONICA 49]	She smiled wryly as the thought occurred to her that it was while sweeping out bedrooms **she had made every decision** of any consequence in her life. [MONICA. 49]
– fe **benderfynwyd** eu bod am angori llong nid nepell o'r lan . . . [PLA 62]	**The captain decided** to anchor a little way from the shore . . . [PEST 47]

Other examples confirm the preference in English for a human subject when one is available or inferrable from context, where Welsh is often happy to use an impersonal form:

Yr oedd Ann Ifans yn ddynes hynaws, ddigrif, a thra bu'r plant yn y capel **diddorwyd Jane ac Ifan gan ei harabedd.** [TRAED 36]	Ann Ifans was an easy-going, humorous woman, and while the children had been at the chapel **she had regaled Jane and Ifan** with her witty stories. [FEET 33]
To go with it, **he could fairly be described** as being unbeautiful . . . [TIME 28]	Ar yr un pryd, **medrid ei ddisgrifio'n ddigon teg** fel person diolwg; [AMSER 43]
Ymhen rhyw bythefnos daeth Sioned a Bertie i fyny o'r dref ar brynhawn Sul. **Cafwyd** te yn y gegin orau, ac yr oedd y llestri gorau allan. [TRAED 111]	After about a fortnight Sioned and Bertie came up from town on a Sunday afternoon. **They had** tea in the best kitchen, and the best crockery was on the table. [FEET 99]
Pan fyddai Ifan yn cyd-hela â rhywrai eraill, **fe'i ceid yn misio** mwy na hanner ei ergydion. [HDF 124]	When Ifan was out shooting with others **he would miss** more than half his shots. [OFH 154]

In cases like these, the choice to use an impersonal form in Welsh represents a stylistic variant characteristic of formal or literary writing style; it is not always possible to account for each individual choice of an impersonal form since its effect is rather to contribute to the overall impression of register created in the text. However, sometimes there are identifiable reasons for individual choices. The replacement of the English active verbs in the following examples from *Alice in Wonderland* with impersonal forms works quite well because the Welsh impersonal can be used in a formal command or a decree, and thus befits the speech and activity of the king:

'Give your evidence,' said the King; 'and don't be nervous, or **I'll have you executed** on the spot.' [ALICE 105]

Trôdd y Brenin at yr Hetiwr. 'Rhowch eich tystiolaeth, a pheidiwch â bod yn nerfus neu **fe'ch lleddir** yn y fan.' [ALYS I 64]

'I beg pardon, your Majesty,' he began, 'for bringing these in; but I hadn't quite finished my tea when **I was sent for**.' [ALICE 105]

'Maddeuwch imi, eich Mawrhydi,' dechreuodd, 'am ddyfod â'r rhain i mewn: ond nid oeddwn wedi gorffen fy nhe pan **anfonwyd amdanaf**.' [ALYS 64]

Similarly, information about where particular classes are held in a school lends itself to a kind of 'officialese' which the impersonal forms can suggest:

Potions lessons **took place** down in one of the dungeons. [STONE 169]

Cynhelid dosbarthiadau Drachtiau mewn dyfnjwn. [MAEN 107]

Sometimes the subject/agent is inanimate – 'a heavy crash' or 'a roaring fire', as in the examples below – in which case attributing agency to them as the English text does is almost an example of poetic license on the part of the writer. In such cases, the Welsh impersonal allows the inanimate referent to be demoted or made less prominent:

She never finished the sentence, for at this moment **a heavy crash shook the forest** from end to end. [THRO 194]

Ni orffenodd y frawddeg oherwydd y funud honno **ysgydwyd** y goedwig o'r naill ben i'r llall **gan sŵn ofnadwy**. [TRWY 85]

[T]here was a roaring fire there. **It filled the whole damp hut with flickering light** . . . [STONE 59–60]

[R]huai tân yno. **Llanwyd y cwt tamp cyfan gan olau'n fflachio** . . . [MAEN 37]

We mentioned that impersonal forms are also possible with intransitive verbs. By definition, a passive is not possible with an intransitive verb in English: *The boys were eating a chocolate cake* can become *A chocolate cake was being eaten by the boys*, but the intransitive *They were eating* has no passive equivalent, because there is nothing to become the grammatical subject of the passive verb. It is sometimes possible, however, to translate Welsh intransitive impersonals as passives by teasing them apart into a verb and an object: *trefnu* can be 'to plan' but it can also be 'to make arrangements', and *golchi* 'to wash' can also be 'to do the washing'. From these transitive phrasings it is possible to construct English passives:

... **trefnwyd** i ffarwelio â'r hen flaenor ac â'r llanc o bregethwr yr un pryd. [CYCHWYN 237]	... **arrangements were made** to say goodbye to the old deacon and the budding preacher at the same time. [BEGIN 239]
Daeth y sŵn troed ymlaen at y beudy, lle **golchid** yn yr haf ... [TRAED 146]	The footsteps approached the cowshed, where **the washing was done** in summer ... [FEET 130]

Another possible English equivalent is an existential form, introducing the action using the formula 'there was (a)':

Yfwyd i lwyddiant y dyfodol a disgleiriodd llygaid y cariadon tra cydgodent eu gwydrau. [MONICA 26]	**There was a toast** to future success and the lovers' eyes sparkled as they raised their glasses. [MONICA 24]
There was a loud crash behind them and Uncle Vernon came skidding into the room. [STONE 57]	**Clywyd trwst mawr** tu cefn iddyn nhw a sglefriodd Yncl Vernon i mewn i'r stafell. [MAEN 36]

Impersonal forms of *cael* are frequently translated with the existential construction:

... a **chafwyd** canu cynnes, a gafodd i raddau yr un effaith ar Nansi ag a gafodd canu'r delyn ar y gŵr afrywiog hwnnw gynt. Llareiddiodd gryn lawer ar ei hysbryd ... [GWEN 160]	... **there was** such warmth in the singing, that Nansi was noticeably affected. [GWEN 131]
A dyna'r holl fân streiciau a **gafwyd** yn ystod y blynyddoedd diwetha. [TRAED 124]	And then **there was** the rash of miner strikes which had broken out in the last few years. [FEET 109]
Cafwyd 'cynhebrwng mawr' wrth gwrs, ac yr oedd Allt Lwyd, lle trigai fy nain, yn ddu gan bobl y diwrnod hwnnw. [OLAW 33]	**There was**, of course, a public funeral and Allt Lwyd, where my grandmother lived, swarmed with people that day. [FROM 17]

The text below, containing four impersonal forms, is a description of a visit to the Statue of Liberty in New York. Though it has no published translation, this passage can serve well to summarise the patterns discussed in this section. The first two verbs, *eir* (from *mynd* 'go') and *cerddir* (from *cerdded* 'walk') are intransitive and therefore do not lend themselves to any kind of passive. The generic human subjects *one* and *you* are both possible here. For the third verb, *ceir*, we have opted for an existential translation using *there is*, though it would be possible to continue on using *one has* or *you have*. Finally, the fourth impersonal form, *awgrymir*, is a transitive verb, which therefore lends itself well to translation with an English passive.

Geill dwsin o bobl sefyll o fewn i'r ffagl sydd yn ei llaw! **Eir** i fyny ganllath yn y peiriant-codi – hyd at draed y ledi fawr. Yna, **cerddir** i fyny'r grisiau troelleg hyd at gorun ei phen. O'r fan honno, **ceir** golwg ardderchog ar borthladd New York gyda'r dociau di-rif a'r wlad tuhwnt. Rhyddid! Y fath feddyliau cymhleth a **awgrymir** gan y gair. [EI FFANFFER EI HUN 97]	*A dozen people can stand in the torch that is in her hand!* **You go** *up a hundred yards in the lift, to the great lady's feet. Then* **you walk** *up the winding stairs to the crown of her head. From that spot,* **there is** *a splendid view of New York harbour with the endless docks and the countryside beyond. Freedom! Such complicated ideas* **are suggested** *by the word.*

We close this section on impersonal verbs with several examples where a constraint is involved rather than merely a stylistic option. In Welsh, as in many languages, indirect objects and oblique objects cannot become the subject of a passive the way a direct object can. Thus, in the example below from *Harry Potter*, 'Potter's been sent a broomstick' cannot become **Cafodd Potter ei anfon ysgub*, where Potter, the logical indirect object, becomes the grammatical subject of *cafodd*. The English source text must therefore be altered in some way in Welsh translation. An impersonal verb would be grammatically possible (*Gyrrwyd ysgub i Peter*), although not very appropriate for the informal register of the dialogue. So the only remaining solution is to eliminate the English passive and translate as an active sentence (literally 'Someone has sent a broom to Potter'):

'Potter's been sent a broomstick, Professor,' said Malfoy quickly. [STONE 105]	'Mae rhywun wedi gyrru ysgub i Potter, Athro,' meddai Mallwyd yn gyflym. [MAEN 130]

The same solution was adopted in the following group of examples, all of which present the same kind of problem: the grammatical subject of these

English passives is either an indirect object (*offer something to someone*) or the object of a preposition (*make a cup of tea for someone*). English freely allows such objects to be promoted to subject of a passive sentence, but Welsh, like many other languages, does not:

... she told me her brother would be angry **if I wasn't offered a drink.** [TIME 81]	... dywedodd hi y byddai'i brawd yn flin **pe na bai hi'n cynnig diod i mi.** [AMSER 129]
He was being made a cup of strong tea back in Hagrid's hut ... [STONE 237–8]	**Roedd o'n cael paned o de cryf** yng nghaban Hagrid ... [MAEN 151]
... whenever **she was told to shut up**, she had to shut up. [MAT 49]	... a phryd bynnag y **byddai rhywun yn dweud wrthi am gau ei cheg**, roedd rhaid iddi gau ei cheg. [MAT 43]

Sometimes a difference in transitivity between the two languages requires a grammatical transposition. The English verb *to rob* is a transitive verb (*to rob someone*), but the Welsh *dwyn* is not (*dwyn oddi ar rywun*). This entails the elimination of the English passive in the Welsh translation:

I don't know why, but villains take a special dislike **to being robbed** themselves. [TIME 24]	Wn i ddim pam chwaith, ond mae lladron wastad yn gwrthwynebu'n chwyrn **pan fydd pobl eraill yn dwyn** oddi arnyn nhw. [AMSER 37]

The Welsh impersonal verbs do not have the same limitations as the Welsh passive, so when the register of the text is sufficiently formal or literary in style, an impersonal verb can readily be found as the equivalent of such a passive in English:

Wedyn, aeth hi'n ffrae a **gofynnwyd i'r pendefigion** adael. [HUNAN 133]	An argument ensued and **the aristocrats were asked** to leave. [SOLVA 134]
Nos trannoeth yr oedd yn salach, ac **aed i nôl** ei fam. [TRAED 29]	The next night he was worse, and **they sent for** his mother. [FEET 25]
Ron couldn't see what was exciting about a game with only one ball	Doedd Ron ddim yn deall beth oedd mor gyffrous ynghylch

where **no one was allowed** to fly.
[STONE 178]

gêm a chwareid ag un bêl a lle
na chaniateid i neb hedfan.
[MAEN 114]

This is another important way in which Welsh impersonals differ from the *cael* passive; the impersonal is grammatically a bit more flexible.

We end this section with an example of the impersonal form ending in *-er*, which is used as an impersonal imperative:

Cofier nad rhyw socs byrion a
wisgid yr oes honno, 'sanau yn
cyrraedd dros y pen glin, yn mesur
o flaen y troed i'r top yn agos i dair
troedfedd. [CWM 12]

It should be remembered that
it was not short socks that were
worn at that time but stockings
that came over the knee, measuring
nearly three feet from top to toe.
[GORSE 15]

The possible translations here include the command 'Remember' or a formula such as 'Let it be remembered'. The translator opted to introduce an English modal, *should*, a fitting choice here and one which brings us to our next topic.

5.5 Mood and modality

Modality refers to any and all of the linguistic devices that allow a speaker to talk about situations other than those of the real world as it currently exists: in other words, hypothetical, potential and imagined situations of various kinds. The linguistic tools of modality include inflectional categories of the verb such as conditionals and imperatives, as well as modal verbs like the English *will / would, can / could, may / might, shall / should, must / ought to / have to*, and adverbs like *perhaps, maybe*, as well as formulas like *It is necessary to*. To do justice to any of these topics – for instance, modal verbs – would require a book-length study of its own. Here, the task must be much more modest. We have selected a few important points to make by way of contrasting English and Welsh in translation which may usefully feed the reflections of a student of Welsh language, translation or style. This section is divided into the following four subsections, although it is important to note that there is a fair amount of overlap between these categories: (1) hypotheticality, (2) possibility, opportunity and permission, (3) necessity and obligation, and (4) supposition. These categories should be viewed as heuristic headings rather than hard and fast categories.

5.5.1 Hypotheticality

The prototypical expression of hypotheticality is the if-then sentence. There are three main levels of hypotheticality:

Open conditions	*If I **have** time, I **will** go to the beach.* *Os **bydd** amser gyda fi, fe **af** i i'r traeth.*
Closed conditions	*If I **had** time, I **would go** to the beach.* *Pe **bai** amser gyda fi, fe **awn** i i'r traeth.*
Counterfactual conditions	*If I **had had** time, I **would have gone** to the beach.* ***Petai** amser **wedi bod** gyda fi, **byddwn i wedi mynd** i'r traeth.*

Conditional sentences consist of two clauses, the conditional clause or if-clause (preceded by *if* in English and *os* or *pe* in Welsh) and a result clause, which may occur in either order. English and Welsh conditional sentences differ in that, in Welsh, the same verb forms are used in both clauses: present or future in open conditions, present conditional in closed conditions, and past conditional in counterfactual conditions. There is a great deal of variation in the verb forms of Welsh conditional sentences; the reader is urged to consult grammars for details.

Open conditions enable a speaker to represent real possibilities that he or she believes are as likely to come to pass as not. The Welsh word *os* is used for 'if' in open conditions:

'If he **is** violent, we **shall take** you away to your aunt's at Harrow.' [BAND 225]	'Os **bydd** e'n dreisgar, yna fe **wnawn** ni eich symud i dŷ eich modryb yn Harrow.' [CYLCH 38]
Mi **gaf** wylio drwy'r ffenestr os **na allaf** i gysgu, ac wedyn mi anghofiaf yr oriau. [MONICA 7]	**I'll be able** to look out of the window if I **can't** [lit. won't be able to] sleep, and then I shan't notice the hours passing. [MONICA 6]

In closed conditions (which use the Welsh *pe* for 'if'), a speaker represents hypothetical situations whose chances of coming to pass are regarded as possible but not necessarily likely:

'...if the Queen **was** to find it out, we **should** all **have** our heads cut off, you know.' [ALICE 78]	'...a phe **bai**'r Frenhines yn cael gwybod fe **dorrai** ein pennau ni i ffwrdd, wyddoch chi.' [ALYS II 77]

'You **would be** a lot better off, Miss Honey,' she said, 'if you **gave** up your job and drew unemployment money.' [MAT 204]

'Fe **fyddech** chi'n llawer gwell eich byd, Miss Honey,' meddai, '**petaech** chi'n **rhoi**'r gorau i'ch swydd ac yn codi arian diweithdra.' [MAT 198]

Counterfactual conditions (also using *pe* for 'if') are those which are regarded as contrary to fact; they represent speculation about possible worlds that could have been if things had gone differently:

He suspected he **wouldn't have lost** so badly if Percy **hadn't tried** to help him so much. [STONE 253]

Amheuai'n gryf na **fyddai ddim** **wedi colli** mor ddychrynllyd **pe na bai** Percy **wedi ceisio** helpu cymaint arno. [MAEN 161][25]

Had she lived – had you decided to make a go of things together – I **would have been** happy about it. [VICT 45]

[P]etai hi **wedi byw**, a **phetaech chi** **wedi penderfynu** rhoi cynnig arni efo'ch gilydd, mi **fyddwn i wedi bod** yn ddigon bodlon. [LLINYN 51]

The fact that Welsh uses *os* in open conditions and *pe* in closed and counter-factual conditions means that Welsh if-then sentences may eliminate an ambiguity present in English. Consider the English if-then sentence in the example below and its Welsh translation:

The wind had sprung up. Mike's window rattled in the wind. **If it woke him he'd go into Sue's bed**. [VICT 27]

Roedd hi wedi codi'n wynt. Bydd ffenest llofft Dylan yn rhincian yn y gwynt. **Os byddai'n deffro, fe âi at Nia i'w gwely hi.** [LLINYN 29]

Out of context, the English sentence would read like a closed condition. But in context, we understand that this is an open condition which happens to be set in a past habitual context: the meaning is basically the same as 'Whenever it woke him, he would go into Sue's bed.' While the English conditional sentence is formally ambiguous, the Welsh translation is not: *pe byddai'n deffro* 'if he woke' would mark a closed condition, whereas *os byddai'n deffro* marks an open condition which happens to be set in a past context.

---

[25] *Oni bai* sometimes occurs where *pe na bai* might have been expected:

'Mi **faswn i wedi angori** ar y lan ddwsina o weithia' **oni bai** am yr hen goesa' y felltith 'ma [. . .]' [CHWAL 110]

'I **would have anchored** on shore dozens of times **if it wasn't** for these cursed old legs of mine [. . .]' [OUT 116]

There are also hypothetical sentences that do not necessarily take the form of the biclausal if-then statement. The first two examples below were translated as if-then statements even though the original did not have this form:

'Wel,' ebe fi, 'er eich bod chi'n edrach yn ifanc, Miss Hughes, synnwn i ddim nad ydach chi'n ddeugen.' [RHYS 231] [lit. 'I wouldn't be surprised that you are forty.']	'Well,' replied I, 'though you look young, Miss Hughes, I shouldn't wonder if you were somewhere about forty.' [RHYS 221]
And here I wish I could tell you half the things Alice used to say [THRO 130]	Ac yma fe hoffwn pe gallwn ddweud wrthoch chi hanner y pethau y byddai Alys yn eu dweud . . . [TRWY 16] [lit. I would like [it] if I could tell you . . .]
'She **could have been born** fifty years ago and fitted in.' [VICT 38]	'Mi **allasa hi fod wedi cael 'i geni** hanner can mlynedd yn ôl ac mi fasa wedi ffitio'n iawn.' [LLINYN 42]

The modals *will* and *would* have numerous other uses beyond the expression of hypotheticality; we mention four such uses briefly below.

First, we saw earlier that *would* can be used in past habitual contexts, roughly as a synonym of *used to*; in such cases the Welsh equivalent is either the synthetic or the periphrastic imperfect:

Megid yno rai ugeiniau o betris a ffesants, bob haf [. . .] O'u tarfu **codai'**r rhain yn dwr chwyrn gyda'i gilydd, a thrwst eu hadenydd fel taran. [HDF 123]	Scores of partridges and pheasants were reared there every summer [. . .] When startled they **would rise** suddenly together with the sound of their wings like thunder. [OFH 152]

Secondly, English *would* and the Welsh conditional/imperfect (both the synthetic and the periphrastic version using *bod*) are used for the future-in-the-past. The future-in-the-past generally results from principles of sequence of tense after verbs of discourse or thought when these are set in a past context. For example, a sentence like *I know you will be happy*, when transposed into the past, normally becomes *I knew you would be happy*, in which the future tense (*you will be*) of the original thought has become a future-in-the-past, expressed morphologically as a conditional (*you would be*):

Dywedodd na chadwai mohonof fwy na phum munud. [MONICA 33]	He said he wouldn't keep me more than five minutes. [MONICA 31]
Really, she was hoping he would open up a little more . . . [KNOTS 166]	Mewn gwirionedd, roedd hi'n gobeithio y byddai'n agor allan ychydig mwy . . . [CHWERW 142]
Edrychai ymlaen at ei swper. Gwyddai y câi gig oer a thatws wedi eu twymo. [TRAED 168]	He looked forward to his supper for he knew there would be cold meat and warmed-up potatoes. [FEET 140]

It is not always necessary for the verb of thought or discourse to be explicit in order to get a future-in-the-past reading. The following passage contains a sequence of three such verbs which clearly imply that we are seeing the character's thoughts even though no cognitive verb is overtly present; that is, the text implies something like '*she knew* the milk-boy would be calling in half an hour':

Cymerth sigarét a'i thanio ac eisteddodd ar y gwely plu i'w hysmygu. Deg o'r gloch ydoedd. Mewn hanner awr **galwai'r** bachgen llefrith. Wedyn **deuai'r** car llysiau heibio iddi a'r car pysgod ar ei ôl. **Câi** ddefnyddiau felly i wneud pryd bwyd iddi ei hun ganol dydd. [TRAED 37]	She took out a cigarette, lit it and sat down on the feather bed to smoke. It was ten o'clock. In half an hour the milk-boy **would be calling**. Then the grocer's cart **would come** round and the fishmonger's after that. Thus she **would get** the provisions necessary to make herself a meal at mid-day. [FEET 36]

The future-in-the-past can also be handled with an imperfect in Welsh and a past progressive in English instead of a conditional:

Y noson honno gofynnodd i'w fam a **oedd hi am ddyfod** i'r cyfarfod. [TRAED 69]	That night he asked his mother if **she was coming** to the ceremony. [FEET 61]

Thirdly, the use of English modals, particularly *would* and *could*, is common as a way to make an utterance more polite. A question like 'Could you help me?' is rarely a real question about a person's ability to help (although in can be); it is more often simply an indirect way of saying 'Please help me.' Adding a modal, and using the conditional instead of the present tense, are common strategies of indirectness (and thus politeness) which Welsh shares with English:

Could you try to explain that a little bit. [MAT 73]	**Allet ti geisio** egluro ryw ychydig ar hynny? [MAT 67]
'Oh sir, do you not think **you could help me** too, and at least throw a little light through the dense darkness which surrounds me?' [BAND 210]	'O, syr, ydych chi'n tybio y **gallech chi fy helpu** innau hefyd, ac o leiaf daflu ychydig o oleuni trwy'r tywyllwch dudew sy'n fy amgylchynu?' [CYLCH 15]
'Perhaps **you'd have** him in here and we'll –', Lingard stopped short as the door opened. [TIME 76]	'Ella y **basach chi gystal â'i alw** o i fewn yma ac fe . . .' stopiodd Lingard wrth i'r drws agor. [AMSER 120]
He said that he was at the club with a problem or two [. . .] so **would Rogers care to look in** before seven-thirty for whatever it was that worried him. [TIME 100]	Dywedodd ei fod yn y clwb a bod ganddo broblem neu ddwy [. . .] felly **a fyddai Rogers gystal â tharo heibio** cyn hanner awr wedi saith i drafod ei broblem. [AMSER 159]
'You can't possibly do that,' said the Rose. '*I* **should advise** you to walk the other way.' [THRO 143]	'Dim posibl ichi wneud hyn'na,' ebe'r Rhosyn. '**Fe'ch cynghorwn** *i* chi i gerdded y ffordd arall.' [TRWY 29]

Fourthly, *will* and *would* can still occur in their historically oldest use as verbs of volition ('be willing to'). In such cases translating them with a conditional is inadequate; a Welsh verb of volition such as *mynnu* or *bod eisiau* must be inserted, or, when negative, a verb of negative volition such as *gwrthod* or *nacáu* (both meaning 'to refuse'):

She **would never let them** copy ('How will you learn?'), but by asking her to read it through, they got the right answers anyway. [STONE 225]	**Gwrthodai adael iddyn nhw** gopïo ('Ddysgech chi byth'), ond drwy ofyn iddi hi ddarllen drwyddo, roedden nhw'n cael yr atebion yn gywir beth bynnag. [MAEN 143]
'Ffŵl oedd Bob,' ebe fe. 'Ddaru dy dad a fine ddim rhoi *chance* iddo redeg i ffwrdd y noswaith y cafodd o ei gymeryd i'r *jail*? Ond **fyne fo ddim rhedeg**, ac fel nerco aeth i'r *jail*.' [RHYS 279]	'Bob was a fool,' he observed. 'Didn't your father and I give him a chance of bolting on the night of his arrest? But **he wouldn't**, and so, like a ninny, he was taken to gaol.' [RHYS 275]

5.5.2 Possibility, opportunity and permission

One of the main kinds of modality routinely expressed in English with modals (especially *can / could* but also *may / might*) is possibility. This category spills over into the neighboring areas of *opportunity* and *permission*. The equivalent Welsh strategies are somewhat more varied than the English ones, as we will see.

The prototypical use of *can / could* is as an expression of physical or mental capability. This is most often conveyed with *gallu* or *medru* in Welsh. Somewhat more loosely, these verbs can also refer to enablement because of circumstances, as in the last example below:

'A **fedar** hitha ddim gair o Saesneg,' meddai'r tad. [TRAED 69]

'And she **can't speak** a word of English, either,' said the father. [FEET 61]

. . . he whispered into my ear so gently that **it was all I could do to distinguish** the words: [BAND 235]

. . . sibrydodd yn fy nghlust unwaith eto, a'i lais mor ysgafn mai **prin y gallwn ddeall** ei union eiriau: [CYLCH 52]

'Mi wela' siâp y pentra' a Choed-y-Brain uwch 'i ben o, ond **'fedra' i wneud dim allan** yn fanwl.' [CYCHWYN 33]

'I can see the shape of the village and Coed-y-Brain above it, but I **can't make anything out** exactly.' [BEGIN 32]

Bydden ni'n edrych mlaen at yr adeg pan **allen ni fwrw heibio**'r bŵts hoelion trwm hynny roedd yn rhaid i ni'u gwisgo am y rhan fywa o'r flwyddyn. [HUNAN 33]

We all looked forward to the time when **we could discard** those heavy hobnailed boots that we had to wear for most of the year. [SOLVA 33]

Can / could are often not strictly about physical capability but are rather about having the opportunity or the permission to do something. For instance, when a child asks if his friend 'can come out to play', this is unlikely to be about physical ability and is more often about having the parents' permission. *Cael* is usually chosen for the permission sense in Welsh. (See Chapter 7 for a fuller treatment of the many uses of *cael*).

. . . **mi geiff hi aros yn 'i gwely** nes daw'r hen Fargiad Williams yma i gynna' mymryn o dân a gwneud 'panad iddi. [CHWAL 205]

. . . she **can stay in her bed** till old Margaret Williams comes here to light a bit of fire and make a cup of tea for her. [OUT 216]

Mi a i ofyn i Fam Huw **gaiff o ddwad allan** i chwara. [NOS 7]

I'll go and ask Huw's Mam if **he can come out** to play. [NIGHT 1]

Bwytâi'r bechgyn ar eu traed heb dynnu eu cotiau er mwyn **cael brysio allan drachefn.** [TRAED 31]

The boys would eat standing up without taking their coats off so that **they could hurry out again.** [FEET 28]

Can / could sometimes, and *may / might* frequently have the meaning 'it is (was) possible that'. Fittingly, the Welsh equivalents often deploy an adverb meaning 'possibly' (*efallai* or *hwyrach*) or a phrase meaning 'it is possible that' (*mae hi'n bosib*) and a verb in the future or future-in-the-past (though a *bod*-clause is also possible):

He **could** be mistaken, but he was thinking that she was halfway to being sloshed already, notwithstanding what she had said about not drinking on her own. [TIME 103]

Efallai ei fod yn camgymryd, ond credai ei bod hi bron yn feddw rhacs yn barod, beth bynnag a ddywedai am beidio ag yfed ar ei phen ei hun. [AMSER 164]

Fe ddôi Owen adre, ac **efallai y deuai** Elin i fyny brynhawn dydd Nadolig. **Efallai y deuai** Sioned a'r gŵr a'r babi, ond ni faliai Jane Gruffydd am hynny. [TRAED 134]

Owen would be coming home, and Elin **might come** up on Christmas afternoon. **Perhaps** Sioned and her husband and the baby **would come**, but Jane did not look forward to that. [FEET 119]

'Paid â siarad fel yna, Wmffre, mae o wedi'i drenio i ymladd, a finne ddim, a **hwyrach y lladdiff o fi**,' ebe Harri. [GWEN 89]

'Don't talk rubbish, Humphrey. He's had training and I've had none. He **may kill me.**' [GWEN 78]

'**You may** advise me how to walk amid the dangers which encompass me.' [BAND 211]

'**Hwyrach y medrwch chi** gynnig cyngor sut y gallaf droedio'n ddiogel drwy'r peryglon sydd o 'nghwmpas.' [CYLCH 16–17]

And remember, our missing Debbie Studley **may yet return** from a quite uneventful evening out with a couple of friends. [TIME 25]

A chofia, **mae hi'n bosib o hyd y daw** Debbie Studley yn ei hôl wedi noson dawel efo ffrindiau. [AMSER 38]

'Do you think we **might** have been lovers in a different life?' She was quite serious. [TIME 110]

'Ydach chi'n meddwl ei bod hi'n **bosib ein bod ni wedi bod** yn gariadon mewn bywyd arall?' Ac roedd hi'n hollol o ddifri ynglŷn â'r peth. [AMSER 176]

Gallu, medru, and also the impersonal expression *bod modd* are also found in the possibility reading:

'No, he had an appointment last Wednesday, but I **thought they might have asked** him to come back.' [UNSUIT 23]

'Nac oedd. Fe aeth o yno ddydd Mercher d'wetha ond ro'n i'n rhyw feddwl y **gallen nhw fod wedi gofyn** iddo ddychwelyd.' [GORTYN 13]

She **could be** anywhere and until we get useful information naming her friends and associates [. . .] there isn't anywhere we can usefully look. [TIME 90]

Mi **fedrai hi fod** yn rhywle, a than i ni gael gwybodaeth ynglŷn â'i ffrindiau a'i chydnabod [. . .] does gennym ddim syniad ble i chwilio. [AMSER 143–4]

Lingard **could** have caught him up with ease, but was curious to discover where he intended to go. [TIME 77]

Roedd modd i Lingard ei oddiweddyd yn hawdd, ond roedd yn chwilfrydig i gael gwybod i ble'r oedd o'n mynd. [AMSER 122]

. . . mae'n debyg **fod modd** i lanc gael syrffed ar addysg. [CRYMAN 248]

I suppose a lad **can** have too much education. [SICKLE 205]

The translation corpus reveals that there are numerous occurrences of English modals, particularly *could*, which are simply not present in the equivalent Welsh text. First, with verbs of perception (*hear, see, feel* etc.) the modals *can* and *could* are routinely included in English but their equivalents are often absent in Welsh:

Heno, **clywai** anadlu Paul yn llond yr ystafell. [LLEIFIOR 34]

Tonight she **could hear** Paul's breathing filling the room. [RETURN 27]

Clywid sŵn cerrig yn disgyn o domen y chwarel, ac yn y pellter eithaf clywid saethu Llanberis fel terfysg o bell. [TRAED 18]

They **could hear** the sound of slates sliding down from the quarry tip, and far away the sound of firing at the Llanberis quarry. [FEET 16]

Gwelai hogiau'r sied, eu capiau
i lawr yn isel am eu pennau . . .
[TRAED 124]

He **could see** the men in the shed,
their caps pulled down over their
eyes . . . [FEET 110]

. . . all she **could see**, when she
looked down, was an immense
length of neck . . . [ALICE 55]

. . . y cwbl a **welai** wrth edrych i
lawr oedd clamp o wddf hir . . .
[ALYS II 51]

Clywodd Harri'i wddw'n llenwi.
[LLEIFIOR 16]

Harri **could feel** his throat
tightening. [RETURN 11]

Similarly with certain verbs of cognition like *remember*, *understand*:

Cofiaf fy mam yn dod i mewn i'r
gegin yn sydyn . . . [O LAW 106]

I can remember my mother coming
suddenly into the kitchen . . .
[FROM 81]

'I wish **I could remember**.'
[KNOTS 87]

'Fasa'n dda gen i **taswn i'n cofio**.'
[CHWERW 74]

Roedd llyfr dysgu wedi dod 'da'r
gitâr: *First Steps: Play Guitar in a
week!* **Do'n i'n deall dim** arno fe –
dwli oedd e i fi . . . [HUNAN 61]

A tutor book had come with the
guitar, *First Steps: Play Guitar in
a Day.* **I couldn't understand**
any of it. It was nonsense to me;
[SOLVA 61]

Thus, while the preterites *gwelodd* and *clywodd* have 'saw' and 'heard' as
their usual translation equivalents, the imperfect forms *gwelai* and *clywai* are
equivalent to 'could see' and 'could hear'. Why should this be? The purpose
of the English modal verbs in these cases has less to do with expressing capability than with marking durative or continuative aspect. For instance, in
the example above from *Yn ôl i Leifior*, to translate the Welsh *clywai anadlu
Paul* as 'she heard Paul's breathing', which is a perfectly possible translation,
would imply most readily that the hearing was punctual rather than durative;
it would fail to convey the prolonged nature of the event that Welsh marks
morphologically by selecting the imperfect (*gwelai*). By ostensibly referring
to a capability – which is an inherently stative or durative feature – rather
than to an event per se, the modal *could* achieves a similar effect in English.
Thus, whenever durativity is desired rather than punctuality, it is customary
in English to use the modal verb *can/could* with verbs of perception and
cognition.

It is, of course, not impossible to use *gallu* or *medru* with verbs of perception in Welsh, as seen in the following:

Gallwn eu clywed nhw lawr llawr yn chwerthin ac yn tynnu coes, yn bur feddw . . . [HUNAN 186]	I **could hear them** below, laughing and joking and pretty drunk. [SOLVA 186]
. . . and **we could see** that she was indeed in a pitiable state of agitation . . . [BAND 209]	. . . a **gallem weld** ei bod hi'n wir mewn stad alaethus o ofid . . . [CYLCH 14]

An instance like the example from the Welsh translation of *The Speckled Band* might have been considered an overtranslation until it is observed that even a text originally composed in Welsh like Meic Stevens's autobiography can use *gallu* with a verb of perception. The usage is therefore not (or not any longer) foreign to Welsh style.

It is also common to find *can / could* present in clauses in English headed by conjunctions of time (*before, until*) or purpose (*in order that, so that*), where the Welsh equivalents often lack the modal. This pattern is attested in both directions (adding the English modal when translating from Welsh, and leaving it out when translating into Welsh):

Ond **cyn iddo orffen** ei frawddeg yr oedd tad Begw wedi torri ar ei draws. [TE 69]	But **before he could finish** his sentence Begw's father cut across him. [TE 64]
Rhedodd **o flaen ei thad** i'r stafell ymolchi, troes y tap a glanhaodd y basn. [MONICA 29]	She ran into the bathroom **before her father could get there**, turned on the tap and wiped the basin. [MONICA 27]
Doedd neb yn y Cwrdd wedi dechrau siarad eto, pawb yn aros i ymdawelu **cyn toddi i mewn i'r ysbryd iawn.** [RHANDIR 159]	No one in the Meeting had spoken yet, everyone waited for the stillness that must come **before they could centre down.** [FAIR 155]
Dyma fo'n gwyro i lawr a deud yn fy nghlust i . . . Rwan, medda fo yn ei lais ei hun, ar ôl sythu i fyny, a finna'n gorfod plygu ngwegil yn ôl **i sbio arno fo.** [NOS 69]	Then he bent down and whispered in my ear . . . Now, he said in his normal voice, after he'd straightened up and I had my neck bent back **so I could look at him.** [NIGHT 56]

The use of a modal in these contexts is a stylistic preference of English that doesn't significantly change the meaning; 'before he could finish his sentence' and 'before he [had] finished his sentence' are compatible with the same state of affairs. This is not to say, of course, that a modal is always superfluous in these contexts. The use of *cael* followed by a verb-noun in the following example refers to capacity in the sense of having an opportunity to do something, which is generally rendered with *can / could* in English:

Bwytâi'r bechgyn ar eu traed heb dynnu eu cotiau **er mwyn cael brysio allan** drachefn. [TRAED 31]	The boys would eat standing up without taking their coats off **so that they could hurry out** again. [FEET 28]

Particularly when translating from English into Welsh, though, rendering the modal in the cases examined so far may constitute an overtranslation.

Related to possibility, of course, is probability, expressing a higher level of certainty. The category of probability has a number of different linguistic exponents in both languages. In Welsh, the term *tebyg* appears in many guises, many of which are equivalent to 'probably' in English:

Duw a ŵyr lle'r o'n nhw i gyd yn cysgu, **debyg gen i nad oedden nhw**, roedd y gerddoriaeth yn dal i fynd yn ddi-dor. [CRWYD 52]	*God only knows where they all slept. I think they probably didn't, as the music was going on incessantly.*
Beth a wnâi ei mam a'i thad rŵan, tybed? Ar eu te, **mae'n debyg**. [TRAED 18]	What were her father and mother doing now, she wondered. Having tea, **probably**. [FEET 16]
Heddiw, mae deunod balch corn gwddwg yr estron lliwgar hwn, y ceiliog ffesant, mor fud yn y parthau yma â'r estron lliwgar arall hwnnw, y Barwn Normanaidd a'i dug yma gyntaf, **yn ddigon tebyg**, ac a fu gynt, fel yntau, yn uchel ei gloch yn y Cantref Mawr. [HDF 124]	To-day the proud, throaty two-noted cry of this colourful foreigner, the cock pheasant, is as silent in these parts as that other alien, the Norman baron, who **probably** brought him here and whose own voice also was once loud in the Cantref Mawr. [OFH 154]
Yn f'ymdrechion, **tebyg i mi dynnu sylw** gŵr ieuanc a safai yn f'ymyl . . . [CYMER 54]	In my efforts, **I must have drawn the attention** of a young man standing beside me . . .
'Why, the Lion and the Unicorn, **of course**,' said the King. [THRO 198]	'Wel, y Llew a'r Ungorn, **debyg iawn**,' ebe'r Brenin. [TRWY 90]
He told her that he'd heard somebody messing about with his	Mi ddeudodd wrthi'i fod o'n clywed rhywun yn 'mela â'i gar, ei fod o ar

car, **probably** about to steal it again. [TIME 40]

fin cael ei ddwyn eto, **fwy na thebyg.** [AMSER 63]

You said yourself that they **probably** hadn't intended killing him. [TIME 43]

Ddaru ti ddeud dy hun nad oedden nhw, **yn ôl pob tebyg**, yn bwriadu'i ladd o. [AMSER 67]

The following set of examples illustrates the English 'I suppose', another discourse device used for expressing a moderately high level of expectation akin to 'probably', and some equivalent Welsh expressions.

She was one of the reasons I left him and **I suppose** I should be grateful for that. [TIME 106]

Hi oedd un o'r rhesymau dros i mi'i adael o, ac **am wn i** y dylwn i fod yn ddiolchgar iddi am hynny. [AMSER 169]

'Your sister asked for it, **I suppose?**' [BAND 228]

'Eich chwaer ofynnodd amdani, **siŵr o fod?**' [CYLCH 41]

Well, *this* turn goes to the hill, **I suppose.** [THRO 139]

Wel, mae'r drofa hon yn arwain i'r bryn, **dybia' i.** [TRWY 25]

'You'll be looking for a new job, **I suppose?**' [UNSUIT 10]

'Rwyt ti allan o waith nawr, **sbo.**' [GORTYN 15]

. . . **siawns fawr** na ddôi enw John Gwarco'd i mewn, rywle. [HDF 170]

. . . **in all probability** John Gwarcoed's name would come into it. [OFH 213]

5.5.3 Necessity and obligation

Deontic modality is the area of obligation and necessity. The primary English modals here come in two sets, *must / have to* and *should / ought to*. The forms *must / have to* are roughly synonymous and are used for expressing fairly strong obligation or expressing commands. The most common Welsh equivalent for both is *(mae) rhaid i rywun wneud rhywbeth*, though the verb *gorfod* also occurs here:

Yn awr, Alis, **rhaid iti orwedd yn ôl** a cheisio cysgu. [MONICA 7]

Now Alice, **you must lie down** and try to sleep. [MONICA 6]

'He was a shit,' he spat out. 'An arsehole, if **you have to know.**' [TIME 31]

'Hen gythraul oedd o,' poerodd. 'Cachwr, os **oes rhaid i chi gael gwybod.**' [AMSER 47]

Gan mai dim ond chwech a gâi ysgoloriaeth y pryd hynny, a chan ei fod yn cystadlu yn erbyn plant y dref, ac yn **gorfod ysgrifennu** yn Saesneg, yr oedd hyn yn gryn gamp. [NOS 41]

This was quite an achievement for only six scholarships were awarded in those days, and he had to compete against the town children, and **had to write** in English. [NIGHT 37]

The pair of modals *should / ought to* are weaker and are often used for giving advice. The Welsh usually involves the modal *dylai*:

He should have got himself a Browning and blown the lot of them away. [KNOTS 189]

Fe ddylai fod wedi cael gafael ar wn, a'u saethu nhw'n siwtrws. [CHWERW 161]

'Blimmin' deserter too.' She said. 'Got his call-up papers September, I was told. **Should've reported** last month.' [CIDER 42]

'Llwfrgi cythraul ydy o,' meddai hithau. 'Mi glywais i ei fod o wedi cael ei alw i'r fyddin ers mis Medi, ac y **dylai o fod wedi mynd** ers wythnosa.' [SEIDR 61]

She was one of the reasons I left him and I suppose **I should be grateful** for that. [TIME 106]

Hi oedd un o'r rhesymau dros i mi'i adael o, ac am wn i y **dylwn i fod yn ddiolchgar** iddi am hynny. [AMSER 169]

. . . y **dylai Preis godi dwbl** neu drebl ar ŵr a adawsai i'w farf dyfu am wythnos gyfan. [O LAW 80]

. . . that Price **ought to double** or triple his charges for shaving a man who let his beard grow for a whole week. [FROM 58]

The line between the stronger expression *must* and the weaker *should* is not always rigid:

Follow me, please! **We really mustn't** keep stopping like this. [CHARLIE 104]

Dilynwch fi, os gwelwch yn dda! **Ddylen ni ddim aros** fel hyn o hyd. [SIOCLED 137]

In negative formulations, the Welsh expression *nid (yw) gwiw i rywun wneud rhywbeth* has a number of English translation equivalents, including '(one) must not / dare not / would hate to', or, expressed impersonally, 'it is useless to / there's no point in / woe betide anyone who. . .':

Does wiw i Gruffydd Davies besychu ne' dishan pan fydd hi'n cysgu: mae'r dyn yn cerddad o gwmpas fel byrglar yn 'i dŷ 'i hun. [CHWAL 226]

Griffith Davies **dare not** cough or sneeze when she is sleeping; the man is walking about like a burglar in his own house. [OUT 238]

Yr oedd ei fargen ef a'i bartneriaid yn sâl. **Nid oedd wiw ymliw** am un well, nac ymbilio am well pris. [TRAED 87–8]

The bargain he and his partners were forced to make was a poor one, but **it was useless to show disgust** or to beg for a better price. [FEET 73–4]

Dysgodd hefyd fod amser i gael anwes ac amser i fodloni hebddo, ac **nad oedd wiw** troi at Dadi os oedd Mam wedi dwrdio, na throi at Mam os oedd Dadi. [LLEIFIOR 204]

He also learned that there was a time for cuddling and a time to do without it, and that **there was no point in** turning to his father if his mother had scolded him, or the other way around. [RETURN 177]

. . . **I'd hate to think** I'd overlooked the possibility that you're in the habit of providing a bolt-hole for any woman tasteless enough to have been to bed with you. [TIME 126]

. . . **does wiw i mi** anwybyddu'r posibilrwydd y gallsech chi guddio yn fan'no unrhyw ddynes sy'n ddigon di-chwaeth i fynd i'r gwely efo *chi*. [AMSER 201]

'Un o'r dynion nobla' oedd disgrifiad cyson f'Ewythr Huw ohono, ac **nid gwiw i neb ddweud gair** yn ei erbyn yn ein tŷ ni. [O LAW 163]

'One of the noblest of men,' was Uncle Huw's unvarying description of him, and **woe-betide anyone who said a word** against him in our house. [FROM 131]

Dyheai hithau am gael bod yn ôl yno, a chael cwpanaid o de poeth, ffres, yn ei thŷ ei hun. Ond **nid oedd wiw** sôn am fyned yn ôl. [TRAED 165–6]

. . . and she longed to be back there having a hot fresh cup of tea under her own roof. But **she dared not** suggest going back. [FEET 137]

Ond **doedd fiw i chi** fynd yn rhy agos . . . dyna 'nghamgymeriad i mae arna i ofn. [PLA 132]

But **you couldn't risk** getting too close. That was the mistake I made. [PEST 92]

Can and *could* are not the only modals whose use in English is not always rendered directly in Welsh; this is also the case with *should*. A significant use of English *should* is to mark certain subordinate verbs that are not being asserted but rather are being named as an idea about which a comment is formulated, rather in the vein of the subjunctive in languages like Spanish or French. This usage is found, for instance, in subordinate clauses following matrix formulas like *to be anxious that, to be odd / surprising / just as well that, to insist that*, and conjunctions like *for fear that* or *lest*:

Yr unig beth ddaru diclo tipyn ar fy ffansi i oedd yr Hen Grafwr yn **insistio am** i ti bregethu o flaen y seiat . . . [RHYS 316]	The only thing that tickled my fancy a bit was Old Scraper **insisting that** you should be asked to preach before Communion . . . [RHYS 316]
. . . ac ofnai ei berchennog ei throi allan **rhag** dyfod dan ei melltith. [GWEN 35]	. . . and the owner **was afraid of** evicting her lest he should come under her spell. [GWEN 40]
Yr oedd Twm yn dra **awyddus am** inni fod yn y plygain mewn pryd . . . [GWEN 21]	Twm **was very anxious that** we should arrive at the carol service early . . . [GWEN 28]
Cymer lenyddiaeth Gymraeg. Y darlithoedd yn Saesneg a finna', hogyn o Lechfaen, yn ofni ateb cwestiwn **rhag** ofni faglu tros eiria' yn yr iaith fain. [CHWAL 170]	Take Welsh literature. The lectures in English, and me, a boy from Llechfaen, afraid to answer a question **for fear** I should stumble over words in the thin language. [OUT 178–9]
Yr hyn sydd yn fy synnu fwyaf ydyw, fod pawb wedi cymryd i fyny gyda mi . . . [RHYS 7]	**What surprises me most is that** everyone should have been so taken with me . . . [RHYS 13]
How odd that a moment of time so important to him should pass without his knowledge. [UNSUIT 18]	**Dyna od** fod eiliad mor bwysig o'i fywyd wedi mynd heibio'n ddiarwybod iddo. [GORTYN 9]
It is perhaps as well that the facts should now come to light [BAND 207]	**Efallai ei bod yn llawn cystal** i'r ffeithiau hynny weld golau dydd nawr . . . [CYLCH 12]

What the use of *should* after these phrases accomplishes is that the event in question is not being asserted. The reader does not actually know, at least without looking at the larger context, whether the event in question ever happened or not. We do not know whether the owner referred to in *Gwen Tomos* ever did come under a spell or whether the 'we' in question did in fact arrive at the carol service early. This is because the *should*-clauses refer to these events only as ideas about which a subjective attitude is expressed, not (yet) as actual episodes in a story. This function of *should* is not a function of *dylai* or any of the other Welsh modals, meaning that no use of a Welsh modal would be appropriate here. In fact, the Welsh versions of these utterances typically end up as *bod*-clauses, with no inflected verb.

Some specific uses of modal verbs are part of a construction—a conventionalised pairing of form and meaning – for which an equivalent construction often exists in the other language, but which does not necessarily consist of the same component parts. This is the case, for instance, with the formula *you should have seen / heard* . . . which speakers sometimes use when recounting an event that was surprising, impressive, or otherwise memorable (*You should have seen Fred dancing at the party*). This is an idiomatic use of the modal *should have* which departs from its canonical use as a formula of reproach (*You should have studied harder for that test!*) Welsh has an equivalent formula (*byddai'n werth i rywun wneud rhywbeth*) which does not use the modal *dylai*:

Dew, roedd gen Mam feddwl y byd ohono fe hefyd. **Mi fyddai'n werth ichi ei gweld hi**'m smwddio'i wenwisg a'i stôl o ar y bwrdd yn tŷ ni. [NOS 21]

Dew, Mam thought the world of him as well. **You should have seen her** ironing his surplice and stole on the table at home. [NIGHT 14]

Ond **mi fasan' werth ichi weld** Gres Elin. [NOS 77]

But **you should have seen** Grace Ellen. [NIGHT 64]

Similarly, the construction illustrated by *Who should come in but* . . . which is similarly used to express surprise is an idiom in which the Welsh equivalent does not use a modal verb:

Pan oeddan ni'n dwad at ymyl tŷ pen Rhesi Gwynion, lle mae Mam Now Bach Glo'n byw, **pwy oedd yn sefyll** yn y drws a hancaits bocad fawr yn i llaw hi a hitha'n sychu'i thrwyn, ond Mam Now Bach Glo. [NOS 13]

As we were coming up to the house at the end of White Houses, where Little Owen the Coal's Mam lives, **who should be standing** in the doorway with a great big hankie in her hand wiping her nose, but Little Owen the Coal's Mam. [NIGHT 7]

Ryw fore tuag amser brecwast, ynte, **pwy ddaeth** i mewn i'r gegin ond yr hen gymydog pwyllog, hirben . . . [HDF 112]

One morning about breakfast-time **who should come** into our kitchen but our canny old neighbor . . . [OFH 138]

5.5.4 Supposition

A last use of *must* and *should* that will be mentioned here involves the expression of a supposition or an inference:

Rhaid ei bod ymhell ar y nos . . . [TE 11]	It **must have been** late . . . [TEA 14]
He **must have** left the house very late last night of before I woke up early this morning. I didn't hear him. [UNSUIT 23]	**Mae'n rhaid ei fod** o wedi gadael yn hwyr neithiwr neu'n gynnar y bore 'ma. Chlywais i mono fo. [GORTYN 13]
She thought **he must be** joking and then saw that he wasn't. [VICT 127]	Tynnu arni roedd o, **mae'n rhaid**. Ond pan welodd ei wyneb gwelodd ei fod yn hollol o ddifri. [LLINYN 142]
Bydd e 'di dychwelyd erbyn hyn a dw i 'di dod â llond bag o goodies i godi'i gallon . . . [FFYDD 205]	Paddy **should be back** by now, so I've bought him a bag of goodies which may help lift his spirits. [FAITH 143]

Here, *(mae) rhaid* is followed by a bod-clause, whereas it is followed by an *i*-clause when the intended meaning is obligation. Compare the following:

Mae rhaid iddo adael.	'He must / has to leave.' (obligation)
Mae rhaid ei fod yn gadael.	'He must be leaving.' (inference, supposition)

The last example above shows the Welsh future perfect (literally 'he will have returned') as another way of expressing a supposition.

5.6 Subject-verb agreement issues

In most familiar western European languages, conjoined singular subjects (two subjects joined by a conjunction like *and*) take a verb with plural agreement morphology. For instance, 'Gwen and I' would be understood to equate to 'we', so the verb would customarily be in the first person plural; 'Gwen and you [singular]' is equivalent to a second person plural, 'Gwen and Sara' is equal to 'they'. Traditionally, in Welsh, on the other hand, the verb agrees only with the first member of the conjunct, not the two together.

'**Roeddat ti a Gwen** yn canmol fy
marddoniaeth i y noson o'r blaen.'
[CHWAL 169]

'You and Gwen were praising my
poetry the other night.' [OUT 178]

'Na, mi **ofalwn i ac Ella** na châi o
ddim piltran yn y tŷ . . .' [O LAW 58]

'No, Ella and me saw to it that
he didn't have to pilter about the
house . . .' [FROM 40]

Gwyddwn i a'm mam . . .
[O LAW 198]

Both my mother and I knew . . .
[FROM 163]

'Roedd Iorwerth yn proffwydo
y bydde fe a finne farw o newyn
cyn pen wythnos.
[LLEIFIOR 57]

Iorwerth was predicting that he and
I would be dying of hunger within
the week. [RETURN 47]

'Ia, **mi'r wyt ti a minna** wedi
mwynhau clywed y bennod yna
lawer gwaith, pan nad oedd dim yn
ein poeni ni.' [BYW 41]

'Yes, you and I have both enjoyed
hearing that chapter many times
when there was nothing troubling
us.' [AWAKE 41]

''Ron i'n meddwl **'i fod o a
Wil ei frawd** efo'r soldiwrs.'
[CYCHWYN 60]

'I was thinking he and Will his
brother were with the soldiers.'
[BEGIN 60]

Erbyn **ei ddyfod ef a minnau** i
gysylltiad agos â'n gilydd, yr oedd
tymor rhyw gastiau bachgennaidd
drosodd . . . [CYMER 54]

*By the time we had come into close
association with one another, the
period of boyish pranks was over . . .*

This is reminiscent of agreement patterns after a preposition, where agreement
is with the first member of the conjunct (when that member is a pronoun),
rather than with the sum of both of them together.

You and Elly fell out? [CIDER 19]

Mi aeth pethau o chwith **rhyngot ti
a dy fam**. [SEIDR 26]

Yr oedd fel crempog fawr a lot o
dyllau ynddi a chyllell ddur las
rhyngddi a Sir Fôn. [TE 10]

Her eyes ranged over the snow,
far over the snow that lay like a
crumpet, pitted with holes, and
between her and Anglesey, the
steel-blue knife-blade of the Straits.
[TEA 14]

His animosity towards George – he was more tolerant of Sue – was almost palpable. [VICT 25]

Doedd pethau ddim yn rhy ddrwg **rhyngddo fo a Nia**, ond bron na ellid teimlo ei atgasedd tuag at Alun. [LLINYN 27]

Similarly, when numbers are joined by *neu* 'or' to give an approximate enumeration of a noun, the noun often occurs after the first number rather than the second, in Welsh (that is, 'two or three pounds' is expressed literally as 'two pounds or three'):

Dim ond imi ddeud wrtho fo fy mod i am fynd i'r Sowth i helpu Kate, mi ga 'i fenthyg **dwybunt neu dair** gynno fo ar unwaith. [CHWAL 145]

I have only to tell him I want to go to the South to help Kate and I shall have a loan of two or three pounds from him at once. [OUT 153]

. . . am **ddeuddydd neu dri** [CRYMAN 96]

. . . for two or three days [SICKLE 78]

Y ffaith oedd, pan fyddai yn y cyfryw amgylchiadau ei hun, y gwelid hi ymhen **tridiau neu bedwar** yn cerdded o gwmpas y gymdogaeth. [GWEN 11]

The truth is that when she herself was in that condition she would be seen walking about the village two or three days after her confinement. [GWEN 18]

Ac wedi hwylio am **dridiau neu bedwar** . . . [PLA 63]

. . . after three or four days . . . [PEST 47]

Yr oedd Twm wedi dyfod â baich ei gefn o goed tân i'm mam **ddwywaith neu dair** . . . [GWEN 20]

He had brought two or three loads of firewood for my mother . . . [GWEN 27]

. . . ac arferai aros yn hwy yn yr un plas, o wythnos i bythefnos – hen dŷ gwag neu feudy allan, rhyw led **dau gae neu dri** oddi wrth y ffermydd. [CWM 54–5]

. . . *and he would stay longer on the same farm, from a week to a fortnight – and old empty house or an outbuilding, some **two or three fields' width** away from the farms.*

This is not exceptionless, however:

Here Alice wound **two or three turns** of the worsted round the kitten's neck, just to see how it would look . . . [THRO 128]

Yna lapiodd Alys **ddau neu dri tro** o'r gwlân am wddf y gath fach i weld sut yr edrychai . . . [TRWY 14]

Bu Wil yn yr hen dŷ am **o chwech** | There was a great snowstorm,
i wyth wythnos yn methu symud | with a fierce blizzard, and Wil had
ei luest, ac yn gorfod byw ar **ddwy** | perforce to remain in the old house
neu dair o ffermydd am hir o amser | for some six weeks or two months.
pan na allai fyned i le'n y byd arall. | He could not move away and he had
[CWM 55] | to depend upon two or three of the
 | neighbouring farms for his food.
 | [GORSE 59]

5.7 Summary

In this chapter, the contrastive study of Welsh and English in the translation corpus has revealed a number of places where the two languages do not always match up exactly. Rather, there are several possible solutions to many of the translation issues examined, meaning that the Welsh writer or translator often has a variety of options from which to choose. Below, we briefly recap some of the major findings for the six areas treated in depth in this chapter.

(1) **The Present Tense.** English makes an obligatory distinction between progressive (*she is singing*) and habitual (*she sings*) which Welsh does not (*mae hi'n canu* corresponds to both of the English forms). Welsh can make the same distinctions optionally in a variety of ways. The present habitual can be rendered with the verb-noun *arfer* or with the *byddaf* paradigm of *bod* (*mae hi'n arfer canu, bydd hi'n canu*), and the short or synthetic present in Welsh is available in literary styles for stative verbs (*meddyliaf* 'I think') or as a 'dramatic' or narrative present (*cerddaf* 'I walk').

(2) **The Preterite and the Imperfect.** Here it is Welsh which makes an obligatory distinction that is left as an option in English. Welsh divides the realm of the past tense into preterite (*canodd hi*) and imperfect, the latter taking either the form *canai* (in literary style) or *roedd hi'n canu* (in more colloquial styles), where English often uses *she sang* for all of these. The imperfect is ambiguous between past progressive and past habitual interpretations, and these can be disambiguated periphrastically to insist on a progressive reading, using *wrthi* (*roedd hi wrthi'n canu*) or a habitual reading, using *arfer* (*roedd hi'n arfer canu*). Welsh also has stylistic variants of the preterite, using one of several helping verbs (*gwnaeth hi ganu, ddaru hi ganu, bu iddi hi ganu*) and a form combining the preterite of *bod* with a verb-noun, to give an expression whose nuances are not directly translatable into English (*buodd hi'n canu*).

(3) **The use of perfect tenses.** Perfect tenses (e.g. *she has sung / mae hi wedi canu*), which express anteriority, taking a verb out of the strict chronological sequence of events to situate it in an earlier time, generally serve to background the event so marked. While English and Welsh have a similar range of perfect tenses, English is more concerned to mark anteriority than is Welsh, which often prefers a preterite where English uses a present perfect or pluperfect.

(4) **The impersonal forms.** The Welsh impersonal forms (*canwyd, cenid, cenir*) do not have an exact equivalent in English, though their most usual translation equivalents are English passives (*canwyd y gân* 'the song was sung'). However, they are in fact a bit more flexible than the Welsh *cael* passive, since an English passive in which an indirect object or object of a preposition has become the subject (such as *I was sung to*) can be rendered quite readily as *canwyd i fi*, whereas no exact equivalent of this sentence is possible with *cael*. The impersonal forms are also useful as a fairly rapid way to index formal register in Welsh.

(5) **Mood and modality.** Modality was discussed under the following four headings: (1) hypotheticality, (2) possibility, opportunity and permission, (3) necessity and obligation, and (4) supposition. One of the main lessons of this section was that a given English modal does not necessarily have a single Welsh equivalent across the board. We saw, for instance, that in a past descriptive context, *could* combined with a verb of perception is typically rendered in Welsh using the imperfect of the verb of perception rather than with a modal, e.g. *she could hear → clywai hi*. The English modal *should* is another clear example of a routine mismatch between the two languages, taking forms of *dylwn* when the linguistic function is to give advice (*you should leave / dylet ti adael*) but not when the function is simply to move a subordinate verb out of the realm of things being asserted and into the realm of ideas being commented on (*He insisted that we should leave*).

(6) **Issues of subject-verb agreement.** When two noun phrases or pronouns are conjoined in English, the effect is to treat the combination as a single whole with the value of the two together (*John and she were leaving*, where the verb form *were* reflects the fact that together *John and she* form a third person plural subject). Traditionally in Welsh, when one of the conjuncts is a pronoun, agreement is with the pronoun closest to the verb, e.g. *roeddet ti a Siôn yn canu* 'Siôn and you were singing'.[26]

---

[26] It is more difficult to illustrate this in English than in Welsh, since English has very little agreement morphology on verbs, distinguishing in most cases only between third person singular (*sings*) and everything else (*sing*).

6

Phrasal Verbs

6.0 Introduction

Phrasal verbs have been called 'one of the most characteristic traits of the English language' (Jespersen 1961: 323). Also known by other names, including verb-particle constructions and two-word verbs, phrasal verbs generally consist of a verb of movement (*go, come, run, fly*) or action (*break, work, cut, hold, bring*) plus a directional particle (*in, out, up, down, on, off, away, back*). There are hundreds of combinations which vary greatly in their degree of compositionality, making them notoriously difficult for learners of English. This complexity has spawned a huge literature, including dictionaries of phrasal verbs and a variety of pedagogical guides intended to help the foreign learner acquire and use them.[1] Phrasal verbs are also an inevitable part of any discussion of translating between English and other languages because of their great frequency in English and the idiomatic nature of many of the combinations. Indeed, as we will see in this chapter, they are a particularly important consideration when translating English into Welsh, since Welsh can often mirror English quite closely in certain styles and registers. The task for the Welsh writer and translator is often to strike a balance between hewing close to an English-inspired thought, or striving for a traditional Welsh idiomatic formulation.

Grammarians and linguists have proposed various typologies of English phrasal verbs. Many of these (such as MacArthur 1992) are syntactically based, dividing phrasal verbs into categories according to whether the directional particle functions as a preposition, an adverb, or both, while others are more semantically based, assigning phrasal verbs to categories depending on how literal or idiomatic they are. We will touch on syntactic issues briefly in section 6.2, but for the most part such matters involve grammatical constraints

---

[1] Among the dictionaries are those published by Longman (Courtney 1983) and Cambridge (*Cambridge Phrasal Verbs Dictionary*, 2006). Other pedagogical material includes Hart (2009).

rather than stylistic options. Since our concern is to explore options available to the translator or the writer of Welsh, a semantically-based typology is more applicable here. We will use a fairly simple but workable tripartite categorisation: LITERAL PHRASAL VERBS, SEMI-IDIOMATIC PHRASAL VERBS, and IDIOMATIC PHRASAL VERBS.[2]

The category of LITERAL PHRASAL VERBS involves combinations of motion verb + directional particle which are readily interpretable as long as one understands the meaning of the verb and the meaning of the particle, such as:

a.   The boy *ran up* the hill.
b.   The bird *flew away*.
c.   The flowerpot *fell out* of the window.

In examples (a) through (c), the verbs *run, fly* and *fall* have their most usual, literal meanings as verbs denoting particular kinds of movement. Similarly, the particles *up, away* and *out* identify the literal direction of the movement. Thus, the meaning of *run up, fly away*, or *fall out* is fully compositional.

Many verb-particle combinations depart from this transparency to varying degrees. This leads to the second category, SEMI-IDIOMATIC PHRASAL VERBS, in which the verb has more or less its literal meaning but the particle does not. This is often the case with verbs that do not express manner of motion and with which the particle is therefore unlikely to express a literal direction. Many of the English particles have come to be used in figurative ways. For instance:

d.   The cat *drank up* the milk. [= drank all of it]
e.   The old friends *chatted away* into the wee hours. [= kept chatting]
f.   The children *dress down* to go outside and play. [= wear casual clothing]

The expressions *drink up, chat away* and *dress down* involve straightforward meanings of the verbs *drink, chat* and *dress*, but the semantic contribution of the particles *up, away* and *down* in these cases is non-literal, as no actual directionality is involved. As a result, such phrasal verbs are partially idiomatic, or less than fully interpretable just from a knowledge of their component parts.

---

[2] A number of researchers have used a similar three-way typology when working on English phrasal verbs. Thim (2012: 13–14) discusses literal, aspectual, and non-compositional (or idiomatic) uses and provides references to other writers using more or less this typology, including Bolinger (1971).

Idiomatic uses of the particles are of two kinds. First, they can be *aspectual*, serving to mark verbal aspect as in (d) and (e). The particle *up* in (d) serves to turn the verb *drink*, a verb describing a process or activity that has no inherent end point, into one that has a clear endpoint (a *telic* verb, in linguistic terminology).[3] The particle *away* in (e) emphasises the continuing (or *durative*) nature of the chatting. Secondly, the particle can be used *metaphorically*; the particle *down* in (f) situates the type of *dressing* involved on a metaphorical scale – in this case, one in which *dress down* refers to wearing more casual clothing as opposed to *dress up*, which is to wear more elegant attire.

The most extreme cases make up our third category, IDIOMATIC PHRASAL VERBS, where neither the verb nor the particle can be taken in its literal sense. These combinations can be thought of as non-compositional and are generally learned as idioms. Examples (g) through (i) show a few such cases:

g.   I can't *make out* the address. [= distinguish clearly]
h.   John *puts* people *off* with his racy humour. [= irritates, alienates]
i.   My keys still haven't *turned up*. [= come to light, been located]

In examples (g) through (i), there is no literal *making*, *putting* or *turning* involved, nor is there any literal directionality corresponding to *out*, *off* or *up*. It follows that knowing what these words mean when used in isolation will not be of much help in understanding these idioms, which must simply be learned as such.

There is clearly a continuum between fully transparent phrasal verbs like *fly away* and totally idiomatic ones like *make out* 'distinguish'. The three-way typology sketched above will, however, serve our purposes well enough for the discussion which follows in which we examine translation equivalences between English and Welsh.

Translating English phrasal verbs into Welsh raises numerous questions. Welsh traditionally works very much like English where literal phrasal verbs are concerned. Thus, meanings like 'come in', 'go out', 'ride away', 'fly off' are typically expressed in both languages with a verb of manner of motion

---

[3]   If John *drinks up his beer*, we know when the event comes to an end, namely when the glass is empty. This is a *telic* verb. But if John is simply *drinking beer*, this is presented as an open-ended activity which could go on indefinitely. This, then, is an *atelic* verb. A good way to distinguish the two is that atelic verbs can occur with *for* phrases (*John drank beer for an hour*) and telic verbs with *in* phrases (*John drank up his beer in ten minutes*), whereas the reversed combinations are odd or downright ungrammatical: *?John drank beer in an hour; *John drank up his beer for an hour.*

followed by a directional particle.[4] Sentences (a) through (c) above may thus be translated straightforwardly into Welsh as follows:

a. *Rhedodd* y bachgen *i fyny*'r bryn. 'The boy *ran up* the hill.'
b. *Hedfanodd* yr aderyn *i ffwrdd.* 'The bird *flew away.*'
c. *Syrthiodd* y pot blodau *allan* o'r ffenestr. 'The flowerpot *fell out* of the window.'

With the semi-idiomatic and idiomatic categories, however, word-for-word translations into Welsh are more problematic and have been criticised in reference works, pedagogical works and sometimes dictionaries, at least when the desire is to produce a more careful or formal Welsh style. Hincks (n.d.) expresses this point of view quite succinctly:[5]

> Mae llawer iawn o briod-ddulliau Saesneg sy'n defnyddio un o'r adferfau out, in, off, on, up, down ac around, a'r perygl yw trosi'r rhain yn gaeth ac yn ddi-ddychymyg, yn enwedig wrth sgwrsio. Prin yw'r bobl nad ydynt yn 'gwneud eu meddwl i fyny/lan' erbyn hyn, er enghraifft, er na fyddai'r Cymry llengar sy'n arfer yr ymadrodd hwnnw wrth ymddiddan yn ei ddefnyddio wrth ysgrifennu'n safonol. Dichon fod y priod-ddull hwnnw a rhai o'r lleill a nodwyd yma yn ddigon derbyniol wrth siarad, ond dylid bob amser arfer y

---

[4] At least since Talmy (1991), linguistic typologists divide languages into two large categories with respect to how they encode manner of motion and direction in a verb phrase: (a) *satellite-framed languages,* in which the manner of motion is typically expressed in a verb (such as *run, fly, skip, float, saunter*) whereas the path (or direction) is indicated by one or another kind of satellite, including particles such as *in, out, away, off*; (b) *verb-framed languages,* in which the path is marked in the verb (with meanings like *enter, exit, ascend, descend*) whereas the manner of motion is expressed in an optional complement (which is quite often a participle). The Romance languages, such as French, are typical examples of verb-framed languages. The French equivalent of the English sentence *He danced into the room* would be *Il est entré dans la pièce en dansant,* literally 'He entered the room by dancing.' In Talmy's typology, Welsh and English are both satellite-framed.

[5] 'There are very many English idioms which use one of the adverbs out, in, off, on, up, down and around, and the danger lies in translating these slavishly and unimaginatively, especially when talking. Rare are the people who do not "make their minds up" these days, for example, although the learned Welsh speaker who uses this expression in conversation would not use it when writing standard Welsh. It may be that that idiom and some of the others noted here are fairly acceptable in speech, but the Welsh idiom should always be used when writing, unless there is a need to create a special mood.' (translation ours)

priod-ddull Cymraeg wrth ysgrifennu, oni bai fod angen creu naws arbennig. (Hincks n.d.)

A similar point of view is expressed by Cownie (2001: viii):

> The phrases <u>gwneud eich ffwrdd i</u> (<u>to make your way to</u>), and <u>gwneud i ffwrdd â</u> (<u>to do away with</u>) are just two examples of many English idiomatic phrases expressed with Welsh words that, while not importing an alien construction into Welsh, are at present on the vague border between acceptable and unacceptable Welsh.

Indeed, as we will see, traditional Welsh style offers a wealth of idiomatic ways to convey many of the same notions as English phrasal verbs, without resorting to simple and direct word-for-word translation from English.

In the next section we will briefly discuss a few issues of translating phrasal verbs which are largely matters of grammatical constraints rather than stylistic options. Then in the remainder of the chapter we will explore phrasal verbs through the lens of the stylistic option.

6.1 The directional particle: Constraints and options

Welsh and English both have a battery of directional particles[6] which are more or less direct equivalents. The table below shows the different particles in combination with *to come* in English and their usual translation equivalents in Welsh:

to come in	dod i mewn
to come out	dod allan (S: mas)[7]
to come up	dod i fyny (S: lan)
to come down	dod i lawr
to come back	dod yn ôl

---

[6] A note about the term *particle*. In the sentence 'The man came down the stairs' or its Welsh equivalent *Daeth y dyn i lawr y grisiau*, in traditional terms one would say that *down* and *i lawr* are prepositions that take complements or objects (*the stairs / y grisiau* respectively). It is also possible to leave out the complements (*The man came down, Daeth y dyn i lawr*), and in this case, *down / i lawr* would traditionally be seen as adverbs. The label *particle* is a useful cover term that includes both kinds of uses.

[7] In south Walian, three of the particles are different from those used in the standard language and in the North; these are marked 'S' in the table. Literary Welsh (Lit) also offers a few additional choices of particle.

to come along / forward / on	dod ymlaen
to come off / away	dod i ffwrdd (Lit: ymaith; S: bant)
to come by / past	dod heibio
to come across	dod ar draws
to come round (around) / about	dod o gwmpas (Lit: o amgylch)
to come over	dod draw; dod drosodd

The fact that the particles can be presented as equivalent in a table like the above does not mean that they are all perfect matches, however. For instance, the Welsh particle *i ffwrdd* corresponds to both the English particles *off* and *away*, and *ymlaen* functions variously as the equivalent of *along, forward, forth*, and sometimes *on*. In other cases the syntactic behaviors are not identical. For instance, the particles *up* and *i fyny* behave quite similarly. This can be illustrated with the common phrasal verbs *come up / dod i fyny*, both of which can appear in three different complementation patterns. First, they can take a complement (e.g. 'come up the street' / 'dod i fyny'r stryd'):

Ond dacw Mrs North yn **dyfod i fyny'r stryd** fel sgwner dan ei hwyliau. [MONICA 43]	Mrs North now **came up the street** like a schooner at full sail. [MONICA 42]

Secondly, they can be used intransitively (e.g. *to come up / dod i fyny*):

Fe ddôi Owen adre, ac efallai y **deuai Elin i fyny** brynhawn dydd Nadolig. [TRAED 134][8]	Owen would be coming home, and Elin might **come up** on Christmas afternoon. [FEET 119]

Thirdly, they can be used with a following prepositional phrase, shown here with a double underline:

Ymhen rhyw bythefnos **daeth Sioned a Bertie i fyny** o'r dref ar brynhawn Sul. Cafwyd te yn y gegin orau, ac yr oedd y llestri gorau allan. [TRAED 111]	After about a fortnight Sioned and Bertie **came up** from town on a Sunday afternoon. They had tea in the best kitchen, and the best crockery was on the table. [FEET 99]

---

[8] Note that in this example, '(on) Christmas afternoon' / 'brynhawn dydd Nadolig' is a non-essential adverbial adjunct and is therefore not part of the complement structure of this verb.

But if *up* and *i fyny* display the same syntactic possibilities, this is not always the case with other particles. For instance, the Welsh *i ffwrdd* works like *off* when the latter has no complement:

I'm surprised it didn't **take** the whole of the top of your head **off!** [MAT 64]	Dw i'n synnu na **thynnodd** e gorun dy ben di **i ffwrdd!** [MAT 58]
One of the police panda cars **drove off** first and the Mini followed. [UNSUIT 155]	**Gyrrodd** un o geir panda'r heddlu **i ffwrdd** yn gyntaf, a'r Mini'n ei ddilyn. [GORTYN 199]

However, the English particle *off* can also be used with a complement (i.e. as a preposition) whereas *i ffwrdd* cannot; the latter is generally replaced by *oddi ar* when there is a complement:

She'd **driven off a straight stretch of highway** into a tree. [CIDER 19]	Roedd hi wedi **gyrru oddi ar y ffordd** a mynd ar ei phen i goeden. [SEIDR 27]
'Count Basie, Alan,' mae'n ailadrodd, wrth wthio'i hun i eistedd, gafael yn y gwydryn dŵr **oddi ar y bwrdd** ger ei wely a gosod y dannedd oedd yn socian yn yr hylif yn ôl yn ei geg. [FFYDD 100]	'Count Basie, Alan,' he repeats, sitting up slowly. He grabs the glass of water **off the bedside table** and puts his false teeth back in. [FAITH 73]

This kind of difference is a matter of language-specific facts about the particles involved. Such differences represent constraints rather than options. It is the grammatical conventions of Welsh that specify that *i fyny* may function as a preposition, whereas *i ffwrdd* may not.

   An additional type of language-specific constraint concerns word order facts. Thus in English, there are well-known differences in word orders depending on how literal or idiomatic a given verb + particle combination is. The two sentences *She ran up a hill* and *She ran up a bill* look structurally identical. But permutations of these sentences reveal important differences. It is possible to separate *run* from *up* when the combination has its literal meaning and *up* is simply a preposition (e.g. *Up which hill she did run?*), just as one can regularly separate a verb from a locative preposition in formal English (*To which store did she go? Along which canal did she walk?* etc.) But when the combination is idiomatic, this is generally impossible (thus **Up which bill did she run?*) Similarly, the placement of direct object pronouns is different in the two cases. When the particle is a real locative preposition we get the usual order preposition + pronoun, thus *She ran up the hill* becomes *She ran up it*. But when the combination is idiomatic we generally get a different order, thus *She ran up the bill* becomes *She ran it up*. These kinds of word-order facts are unlikely to have any direct incidence on translation, because they belong to the domain of language-specific constraints rather than options.

The kinds of issues which are most relevant for our purposes concern the question of whether to select a phrasal verb at all in Welsh. The following sections focus on these issues.

6.2 Category 1: Literal Phrasal Verbs in Welsh and English

The meaning of a literal phrasal combination such as with *come / dod* is compositional; it suffices to know the meaning of the verb and the meaning of the particle to understand the meaning of the combination. Thus, translating literal phrasal verbs between Welsh and English is often straightforward. The following examples of *cerdded* 'to walk' illustrate this:

Does wiw i Gruffydd Davies besychu ne' dishan pan fydd hi'n cysgu: mae'r dyn yn **cerddad o gwmpas** fel byrglar yn 'i dŷ 'i hun. [CHWAL 226]

Griffith Davies dare not cough or sneeze when she is sleeping; the man is **walking about** like a burglar in his own house. [OUT 238]

Cerddes i lawr y pafin ar ochor dde Bute Street am ryw hanner milltir . . . [HUNAN 80]

. . . **walking down** the pavement on the right-hand side of Bute Street, then onwards for about half a mile. [SOLVA 80]

Taflodd ei sialc ar y ddesg, gwisgodd ei gôt a **cherddodd allan** o'r ysgol heb roi gwers ynddi'r bore hwnnw. [TRAED 162]

He threw his chalk on the desk, put on his coat, and **walked out** of the school without having given a single lesson. [FEET 134]

Am bump, ar y dot, ma Floyd yn **cerdded i mewn** ac yn fy nal wrth i mi adael am y dydd. [FFYDD 296]

At five o'clock, **in walks** Floyd, catching me as I prepare to leave for the day. [FAITH 203]

You could have just packed up and **walked away**. [MAT 200]

Fe allech chi fod wedi codi pac a **cherdded i ffwrdd**. [MAT 194]

[S]he quickly pushed open the gate and **walked up the path**. [MAT 186]

[G]wthiodd y glwyd ar agor yn gyflym a **cherdded i fyny'r llwybr**. [MAT 180]

... he decided to work off his remaining stiffness by **walking back to his office** ... [TIME 85]

Penderfynodd hefyd gael gwared ar y stiffrwydd a oedd yn dal i'w blagio trwy **gerdded yn ôl i'w swyddfa** ... [AMSER 135]

'Now put your hands out in front of you. And as I **walk past** I want you to turn them over so I can see if they are clean on both sides.' [MAT 142]

'Nawr rhowch eich dwylo allan o'ch blaenau. Ac wrth i mi **gerdded heibio** dw i eisiau i chi eu troi nhw drosodd er mwyn i mi weld a ydyn nhw'n lân ar y ddwy ochr.' [MAT 136]

Literal combinations like the above occur freely with any number of intransitive verbs of motion in addition to *walk / cerdded*. The following examples illustrate combinations with an assortment of other verbs (*dod* 'to come', *mynd* 'to go', *dringo* 'to climb', *gyrru* 'to drive', *neidio* 'to jump', *troi* 'to turn', *rhedeg* 'to run'):

Cyn hir ysgydwai'r ci Tos ei gynffon arnynt, gan **droi ymaith** wedyn i gyfarth am ei feistr. [CHWAL 17]

Before long the dog Toss was wagging his tail at them, before **turning away** to bark for his master. [OUT 17]

'Mi **redais i lawr** rhag ofn bod Mam wedi bod yn gas wrthoch chi.' 'Mae arna i ofn mai fi fuo'n gas wrth 'ych mam,' meddai Jane. [TRAED 16]

'I **ran down** in case Mother had been nasty to you.' 'I'm afraid I was the one to be nasty,' said Jane. [FEET 14]

... the mother **came in** carrying a large tray [MAT 55]

... **daeth** y fam **i mewn** yn cario hambwrdd mawr [MAT 49]

Alice got behind a tree, for fear of being run over, and watched them **go by**. [THRO 195]

Aeth Alys y tu ôl i goeden rhag ofn cael ei sathru, a'u gwylio'n **mynd heibio**. [TRWY 86]

Reaching the iron bridge crossing the canal, Sleath hesitated only momentarily before **climbing down** the slope of the grass bank to the towpath ... [TIME 77]

Wrth iddo gyrraedd y bont haearn a groesai'r gamlas, oedodd Saunders am ennyd cyn **dringo i lawr** y llethr glaswelltog tua'r llwybr ... [AMSER 122]

One of the police panda cars **drove off** first and the Mini followed. [UNSUIT 155]

Gyrrodd un o geir panda'r heddlu **i ffwrdd** yn gyntaf, a'r Mini'n ei ddilyn. [GORTYN 199]

'Do you call *that* a whisper?' cried
the poor King, **jumping up** and
shaking himself. [THRO 198]

'Dyna 'dych chi'n ei alw'n sibrwd?'
gwaeddodd y Brenin druan gan
neidio i fyny a'i ysgwyd ei hun.
[TRWY, 89]

Verbs expressing manner of motion (like *run, jump, fly, drive, float*) are intransitive verbs. There is a similar pattern of transitive verbs describing different ways of causing motion (*to float the logs down the river, to drive the car into the garage*). This pattern also includes verbs of putting (*put, pull, push, throw, toss, drag*), verbs of leading or sending (*lead, escort, take, follow, send*) and verbs of cutting or breaking (*cut, tear, rip, break*):

Agorodd y drws, **llusgodd Trev
fi i mewn** gerfydd fy mraich . . .
[HUNAN 92]

With that, the door opened and
Trev dragged me IN by the arm . . .
[SOLVA 92]

Dyma fi'n **taflyd dillad gwely i
ffwrdd** a codi i sbio trwy ffenast.
[NOS 160]

I **threw the bedclothes OFF** and
got up to look through the window.
[NIGHT 134]

Following Stuchley OUT through
the partly-filled waiting room, he
remembered that the asked-for
coffee had never arrived. [TIME 57]

Wrth **ddilyn Stuchley allan** drwy'r
ystafell aros hanner-llawn, cofiodd
na chyrhaeddodd y coffi wedi'r cwbl.
[AMSER 90]

. . . to keep his head from being **cut
OFF**. [THRO 170]

. . . rhag i'w ben gael ei **dorri i
ffwrdd**. [TRWY 58]

She was suddenly overcome with
tiredness. She longed for nothing
but **to put down her head** on the
hall table and sleep. [UNSUIT 153]

Roedd hi bron marw eisiau **rhoi'i
phen i lawr** ar fwrdd y cyntedd a
mynd i gysgu. [GORTYN 196]

These literal verb-particle combinations are a completely usual way of expressing motion and direction in Welsh as well as in English. The particle in these cases makes a concrete and easily identifiable semantic contribution to the sentence.

However, even with literal phrasal verbs like these, including the particle is not automatic in Welsh. Studying the two languages through a comparative lens shows that the particles are traditionally more common in English than in Welsh, even in such literal uses. In addition to fairly exact equivalence as in the examples above, there are several other patterns of correspondence to which we now turn.

First, it is not unusual for English to have an overt particle which is absent from the Welsh text. When translating from Welsh into English, particles may be added that were not present in the Welsh original. The added particles are shown in small caps below:

Gan amlaf y mae'n helpu yn y siop, ond bydd yn **teithio** weithiau. [MONICA 10]

Usually he helps in the shop, but sometimes he **travels AROUND**. [MONICA 9]

Yr oedd blwyddyn wedi **hedfan** . . . [CRYMAN 263]

A year had **flown BY** . . . [SICKLE 227]

Plygodd wrth fyned dan y simnai fawr gan ei fod mor dal. [TE 28]

He was so tall that when he came to the chimney beam above the open fireplace he had to **bend DOWN**. [TEA 29]

Aeth Mr Jones i'w gyfarfod cyn i'r Yswain gael cyrraedd y drws a churo . . . [GWEN 103]

Before he had time to knock on the door Mr Jones **went OUT** to greet him . . . [GWEN 89]

Ond i chwilio am dorchan **aeth** Moi. [NOS 132]

But Moi **went OFF** to look for a clump of turf. [NIGHT 112]

. . . dim ond gwrando ar sŵn y dail yn y coed [. . .] a llais Defi Difas yn cael ei **gario** hefo'r gwynt. [NOS 144]

I just listened to the sound of the wind in the leaves [. . .] and David Evans's voice being **carried AWAY** on the wind. [NIGHT 120–1]

Fel yna y rhedai meddyliau Wiliam, a'r trên yn **symud** yn araf, gan chwythu fel dyn yn mynd i fyny gallt. [TRAED 124]

Those were Wiliam's thoughts as the train **moved** slowly **ALONG**, puffing like a man going up a steep hill. [FEET 103]

A ddaru o ddim gweiddi na dim byd, dim ond gweddïo, pan oeddan nhw wrthi'n **cnocio'r hoelion**. [NOS, 61]

And he didn't scream or anything, he just prayed, while they were busy **knocking the nails IN**. [NIGHT, 49]

Going in the other direction, a particle present in the English original may be omitted in the Welsh translation:

. . . she **ran OFF** as hard as she could, and soon found herself safe in a thick wood. [ALICE 46]

. . . **rhedodd** nerth ei choesau ac yn fuan iawn roedd hi'n ddiogel mewn coedwig fawr. [ALYS 40]

As they **walked OFF** together, Alice heard the King say in a low voice . . . [ALICE 89–90]	Tra oedden nhw'n **cerdded** gyda'i gilydd, clywodd Alis y Brenin yn dweud mewn llais isel . . . [ALYS 91]
'Rendcome's **sent OFF** a telegram.' [VICT 14]	'Mae Japheth wedi **anfon** telegram.' [LLINYN 13]
'You don't look well, you know [. . .] You'd better sit before you **fall OVER.**' [TIME 78]	'Dwyt ti ddim yn edrych yn rhyw iach iawn, wyddost ti [. . .] Well iti eistedd cyn iti **syrthio.**' [AMSER 124]
'You should **come ALONG** some time.' [VICT 9]	'Mi ddylet titha **ddŵad** rywdro.' [LLINYN 7]
Harry **turned AROUND** – and saw, quite clearly, what. [STONE 199]	**Trodd** Harri – a gweld, yn hollol glir, *beth.* [MAEN 127]

Clearly the overt marking of trajectories and spatial relations is an important emphasis in English, whereas Welsh is more comfortable leaving these implicit.

Additionally, English frequently combines a particle with a prepositional phrase, thus doubly marking the path, where Welsh may have a prepositional phrase but no particle. In the following examples, the prepositional phrases present in both languages are marked with a double underline. Going from Welsh to English, the translator has thus added a particle (shown in all caps) not present in the Welsh original:

Cerddodd <u>tua'i lety</u> yn nannedd gwynt oer ac yr oedd yn dda ganddo gyrraedd ei ystafell. [CHWAL 170]	He **walked BACK** <u>to his lodgings</u> in the teeth of a biting wind and was glad to get to his room. [OUT 179]
Cochodd Sioned a **cherddodd** yn benuchel <u>drwy'r siop</u> . . . [TRAED 96]	Sioned flushed and **walked OFF** haughtily <u>through the shop</u> . . . [FEET 81]
. . . **aeth** <u>ar ei gliniau</u> i dynnu'r llwch oddi ar y llawr. [CYCHWYN 38]	. . . she **went DOWN** <u>on her knees</u> to sweep up the dust on the floor. [BEGIN 37]
'Wir,' meddai Mrs Huws, ''d wn i ddim ydy hi'n dryst gadael i ddwy hogan wyth oed **fynd** 'u hunain <u>i'r mynydd.</u>' [TE 37]	'Don't you think it's a bit risky to let two girls, only eight years old, **go UP** alone <u>on the mountain</u>?' Mrs Huws asked. [TEA 37]

Eisteddodd yntau <u>yn y gadair freichiau</u>, ac estyn ei bibell i gymryd smôc... [TRAED 194]

He **sat DOWN** <u>in the armchair</u> and reached for his pipe to have a smoke... [FEET 160]

Fel arfer, daeth Owen â'r cerdyn gwahoddiad ymyl aur adref i'w dad a'i fam, ac fel arfer **taflodd** Jane Gruffydd ef <u>ar y bwrdd</u>. [TRAED 77]

As usual, Owen brought the gilt-edged invitation card home to his father and mother, and as usual, Jane Gruyffydd **threw it DOWN** <u>on the table</u>. [FEET 63]

... edrychodd yn siomedig pan **roddais** y botel <u>yn fy mhoced</u>... [GWEN 207]

...but was very disappointed when he saw me **putting** the bottle **BACK** <u>into my pocket</u>... [GWEN 162]

Rhoes y cwpan <u>ar y bwrdd</u> wrth y gwely... [CYCHWYN 32]

He **put** the cup **DOWN** <u>on the bedside table</u>... [BEGIN 31]

And in the opposite direction (English to Welsh), translators may opt to leave the particle out and translate only the prepositional phrase:

When Rogers **stepped OUT** <u>into the dark and mist-bound street</u>... [TIME 18]

Camodd Rogers <u>i'r stryd dywyll, niwlog</u>... [AMSER 27]

'... and afterwards I shall **walk DOWN** <u>to Doctors' Commons</u>, where I hope to get some data which may help us in this matter.' [BAND 223]

'... ac wedyn fe **gerddaf** <u>i Lys y Meddygon</u>, lle rwy'n gobeithio cael gafael ar ddata a all ein cynorthwyo ni'n y mater sydd ger ein bron.' [CYLCH 34]

He **pushed** himself **UP** <u>from his chair</u>. [TIME 57]

Gwthiodd ei hun <u>o'i gadair</u>. [AMSER 90]

At twenty minutes to two George Webber went into his wife's bedroom and gently **turned her OVER** <u>on her side</u>. [VICT 8]

Am ugain munud i ddau aeth Alun Hardwick i lofft ei wraig **a'i throi**'n dyner <u>ar ei hochr</u>. [LLINYN 60]

Tessa picked it up and **put it AWAY** tidily <u>on the bookshelf</u>. [VICT 129]

Cododd Tess y gyfrol a'i **gosod** yn daclus <u>ar y silff</u>. [LLINYN 144]

It was a big red ball – very soft, very bouncy. He **threw it UP** <u>into an apple tree</u>. My wife, Sue, who

Pêl fawr goch oedd hi, un feddal, fownsiog. **Taflodd** Dylan **hi** <u>i'r pren afal</u>. **Dringodd** Nia oedd yn heini

was very agile, very quick, **climbed
UP** into the tree after the ball.
[VICT 142]

iawn i ben y goeden i'w nôl . . .
[LLINYN 161]

The presence of a prepositional phrase of direction or location seems to make the inclusion of a particle less likely (though not impossible) in Welsh style.

In some cases English uses only a particle where Welsh has a full prepositional phrase which can be seen as its functional equivalent, serving to explain or 'unpack' its meaning. Thus, in the context of gifts hidden under a shawl, *out* and *o dan y siôl* ('from under the shawl') amount to two ways of saying the same thing, as do *i'r tŷ* ('into the house') and *in*:

Gwyddai Begw fod ganddi lot o bethau o dan ei siôl [. . .] yr un pethau bob blwyddyn. Na, wir, dyma rywbeth arall yn **dyfod** o dan y siôl mewn papur sidan, crafat i Begw. [TE 28]

Begw knew that she had lots of things under her shawl [. . .] The same things, every year. But no . . . something else **came OUT**, wrapped in tissue paper, a scarf for Begw. [TEA 29]

'**Dowch** i'r tŷ er mwyn inni gael ych gweld chi'n iawn, Tomos,' ebe'r fam. [TE 69]

'**Come IN** so that we can see you properly, Twm,' said Begw's mother. [TEA 64]

In the examples below, the Welsh translator has rendered the English particle by a more explicit prepositional phrase which serves to 'unpack' or explain its meaning. Thus, *away* has become *o 'na* 'from there', *out* has become *o'i boced* 'from his pocket', and so on:

'She's not there. She's been **taken AWAY** and I saw it happen.'
[TIME 14]

'Dydi hi ddim yna. Cafodd hi ei **chymryd** o 'na; mi'i gwelais i hi'n mynd.' [AMSER 21]

He **took OUT** his tiny ivory box . . .
[TIME 65]

Tynnodd ei flwch ifori bychan o'i boced . . . [AMSER 102]

That, and his appearance from the house, his early warning system well in evidence, **hurrying OUT** to meet him. [TIME 38]

Hynny, a'r ffaith iddo **frysio** o'r tŷ i'w gyfarfod. [AMSER 59]

. . . he was looking through the window at a view of sunlit slate roofs and wondering morosely

. . . roedd yn edrych drwy'r ffenest ar doi llechi'n sgleinio yn yr haul ac yn ceisio dyfalu pam gythraul

why it wasn't, congruous with his mood, **pouring DOWN** grey rain. [TIME 60]

nad oedd hi'n **tywallt** y glaw <u>o awyr oedd mor lwyd ac mor ddiflas</u> ag y teimlai yntau. [AMSER 94–5]

She wished Tessa would leave the cake and **go AWAY**. [VICT 129]

Byddai'n dda ganddi pe bai Tess yn gadael y gacen ac yn **mynd <u>adre</u>**. [LLINYN 144]

It'd be nice to think we had another fractured skull **staggering AROUND** waiting to be handcuffed, wouldn't it? [TIME 86]

Basa'n braf meddwl fod gynnon ni ddyn arall â phenglog friw yn **crwydro <u>hyd y lle 'ma</u>**'n disgwyl cyffion? [TIME 137]

English may have two particles at the same time, showing again a high level of attention to path. Welsh typically includes only one particle:

[C]lywodd y peiriant yn cychwyn a'r car yn **symud i lawr yr heol** . . . [MONICA 74]

[S]he heard the engine start and the car **moving OFF DOWN the road** . . . [MONICA 75]

So, resolutely turning her back upon the house, she **set OUT** once more **DOWN** the path, determined to keep straight on till she got to the hill. [THRO 139]

Felly, gan droi ei chefn yn ddybryd ar y tŷ **cychwynnodd** unwaith eto **i lawr** y llwybr yn benderfynol o ddal yn syth ymlaen nes deuai at y bryn. [TRWY 25]

The giant **sat BACK DOWN** on the sofa, which sagged under his weight . . . [STONE 50]

Eisteddodd y cawr yn ôl gan sigo'r soffa a gwneud iddi bantio dan ei bwysau. [MAEN 37]

Outside and **walking BACK UP** the slope to collect their cars . . . [TIME 49]

Wrth **gerdded i fyny**'r allt i nôl eu ceir . . . [AMSER 77]

Nonetheless, it is not impossible to have two particles in Welsh,[9] but such cases are less typical of Welsh than of English.

The various patterns shown above reveal a markedly greater preference for explicitly marking the path of motion and direction in English than in Welsh. One does occasionally find apparent counterexamples like the following:

---

[9] In most of the examples we have collected in which there are two particles simultaneously in Welsh, one of them is usually the particle *yn ôl* 'back'.

| Erbyn **cyrraedd yn ôl** yn yr Arches mae 'nghalon, o'r diwedd, wedi ailddarganfod ei churiad arferol. [FFYDD 253] | By the time I **reach** the Arches, my heart has regained its natural rhythm. [FAITH 175] |

Here, Welsh has the particle *yn ôl* which is not rendered in the English translation, but it is fairly easy to see why this is so. The verb *reach* in the sense of 'arrive' is incompatible with directional particles; one can *reach a place again* but not **reach back a place*. The translator could have selected *get back to the Arches* or *arrive back at the Arches*, but neither of these conveys the physical effort involved to the same degree that *reach* does. The character narrating this scene is getting around by bicycle, so the implication of effort is clearly intentional in the choice of verb.

Occasionally both languages have a particle, but not the same one; the translator may choose to focus on a different aspect of the movement. In the next example, the English *bobbing away* marks the movement away from an observer, whereas the Welsh *sboncio i fyny ac i lawr* highlights the repeated vertical movement of the lamp, leaving the departing implicit:

| . . . and he turned and started back toward the castle, his lamp **bobbing AWAY** in the darkness. [STONE 310] | Trodd, gan gychwyn yn ôl tua'r castell, a'i lamp yn **sboncio i fyny ac i lawr** yn y tywyllwch. [MAEN 198] |

The last frequent correspondence to be noted concerns those cases in which a phrasal verb alternates with a simplex verb (i.e. single word). This kind of alternation can be found internally to both English and Welsh as well as in translations between them. For instance, English has alternations like the following:

go in ~ enter
go out ~ exit; leave
go on ~ continue; happen
go down ~ descend; set (of the sun)
go up ~ ascend; climb
go back ~ return

Similar alternations are found in Welsh, though not always for the same verbs (for instance, there is no non-phrasal equivalent of *mynd i mewn* 'go in' in Welsh):

mynd i fyny ~ esgyn; dringo
mynd i lawr ~ disgyn; machlud (of the sun)

mynd ymlaen ~ parhau; digwydd
mynd i ffwrdd ~ gadael, ymadael
mynd yn ôl ~ dychwelyd

In both languages, it is often claimed that use of a phrasal verb is characteristic of informal language, whereas use of a simplex word is more appropriate in formal styles. This distribution represents a tendency or a preference rather than an absolute rule, and thus, a phrasal verb in one language is not always translated by a phrasal verb in the other, even when one would have been possible. In the following example, the Welsh phrasal verb *tynnu (rhywbeth) i lawr* alternates with *gostwng*, both verbs occurring within a few sentences of each other:

Yna cododd a mynd at y ffenestr	. . . then got up and went over to
i **dynnu'r bleind i lawr** [. . .]	the window **to pull down the blind**
Wedi iddo **ostwng y bleind**	[. . .] Then, **pulling down the blind**,
dychwelodd yn araf i'w gadair . . .	he went slowly back to his chair . . .
[CYCHWYN 119][10]	[BEGIN 118]

The published English translation in this case used *pull down* twice in this passage, but the translator could have chosen the verb *to lower* for one or the other occurrence. In the same example, *dychwelodd* could have been translated as 'returned' or as 'went back' / 'came back'. So we see that there is not a one-to-one relation between phrasal verbs or simplex verbs in English and Welsh. A phrasal verb in one language may be translated by a phrasal verb or a simplex verb in the other. These appear to be more or less in free variation with each other in both languages, with a noticeable preference for simplex verbs in more formal styles.

In summary, in this section we have discussed five frequent patterns of translation equivalence where literal phrasal verbs are concerned:

a)   Both languages deploy a literal phrasal verb;
b)   For a literal phrasal verb in English, the Welsh text deploys an equivalent verb of motion without a particle;

---

[10] It is worth noting that precisely the same Welsh expression is also attested with the verb *tynnu* but no particle: *Dw i'n **tynnu** bleinds y sied ac yn cloi'r drws drachefn* . . . [FFYDD 239]. This reveals that the relationship between the use (or non-use) of phrasal verbs and the degree of formality of the text is not as direct as is sometimes claimed. The Welsh of the novel *Y Cychwyn* quoted in the text is considerably less colloquial overall than that of *Ffydd, Gobaith, Cariad* quoted here, and yet it is the former which has the phrasal verb in this case and the latter a simplex verb.

c)   English has a directional particle while Welsh has a functionally equivalent prepositional phrase that explains or 'unpacks' the meaning of the particle in a more explicit way;

d)   English has two particles simultaneously while Welsh has one;

e)   One language has a phrasal verb while the other uses a simplex verb conveying the same sense.

In all of these cases the particle has more or less its literal sense, marking trajectory or location. This is not the case with our second category, that of the semi-idiomatic phrasal verbs, as we will see in the next section.

6.3 Category 2: semi-idiomatic Phrasal verbs

We have seen that the phrasal verbs discussed in the previous section (CATEGORY 1) involve verbs identifying a manner of motion and particles identifying a literal direction or location of the movement. Particles are found as well with verbs describing kinds of action other than manner of motion. In such cases the particle usually does not refer to a literal place, but rather takes on various aspectual or metaphorical meanings. We group these phrasal verbs together as *semi-idiomatic phrasal verbs* (CATEGORY 2). In these cases the particle makes an identifiable semantic contribution, albeit of a non-literal nature, making the resulting phrasal verbs more or less analysable once these metaphors are perceived.[11]

The notion of verbal aspect refers to 'the pattern of distribution through time of an action or state' (Talmy 1985: 132). This can include information about whether the event is *punctual* (happening in a very short time so that it is conceived of as a point in time), *durative* (being prolonged so that it is thought of as continuing), *iterative* (happening more than once), *habitual* (happening repeatedly, on a regular basis), etc. The following English examples illustrate aspectual uses of particles:

> For some minutes it **puffed away** without speaking; but at last it unfolded its arms, took the hookah out of its mouth again, and said . . . [ALICE 50]

---

[11]   The Cognitive Linguistic literature has examined the extensive role of metaphor in language, and the use of directional particles and prepositions in English has figured significantly in this work. See for example Lakoff and Johnson (1980).

Snape put them all into pairs and set them to **mixing up** a simple
potion to cure boils. [STONE 172]

Harry **counted out** five little bronze coins . . . [STONE 77]

In the first example, the particle *away* serves to mark durativity, suggesting
that the smoking goes on for some time. *Out* and *up* also serve aspectual functions, here serving to make the events *telic* (i.e. implying a definite endpoint).
The difference between *mixing a potion* and *mixing up a potion* is that the
former focuses on the activity of mixing but not on the endpoint. One might
infer that a target is reached (that of having made a potion), but this fact is
not encoded explicitly, whereas *to mix up a potion* emphasises that the event
heads towards an identifiable endpoint. The same is true for *out* in *counted
out five coins.*

Other uses of the particles are metaphorical,[12] as in the following three
literary citations:

She was up on the chimney-piece while she said this, though she
hardly knew how she had got there. And certainly the glass *was*
beginning **to melt away**, just like a bright silvery mist. [THRO, 131]

'Or, perhaps, he left his car, **crept up** behind him wearing trainers
and did it at close range.' [TIME 13]

'Girls of that age have lovers. If the parents are uncaring they **sleep
around**.' [VICT 15]

The literal use of the particle *away* (e.g. *The car drove away, The ship sailed
away*) denotes departure from a reference point or observer, with gradually
increasing distance such that the person or thing departing gets smaller and
harder to see. In the example of *melt away*, we have a metaphorical extension
from this literal sense. The 'departure' here does not involve literal movement,
but rather a change of physical state; both 'departure' and 'melting' entail an
object's becoming ever smaller until it is no longer visible. In *creep up*, we see
one of the common figurative extensions of the particle *up*, from the literal
sense 'motion to a higher point on a vertical plane' to 'motion towards some
reference point'. In this extended meaning no verticality need be involved.

---

[12] Some of the uses are based on metonymies rather than metaphors, but this distinction will generally not be important here. *Metaphor* will be used as a cover term for all
figurative extensions of meaning.

And in our third example, *to sleep around* 'sleep in different places' has come by metonymy to mean 'sleep with different people'.

It is not always possible or desirable to assign just one non-literal meaning to a particle. The different semantic nuances they reveal partially overlap with each other. For instance, in the case of *melt away*, although we focused on a metaphorical interpretation of *away*, it is not difficult to hear resonances of the *away* that marks durativity, as in *puffed away*. It seems quite likely that both an aspectual and a metaphorical nuance are present simultaneously in *melt away*.[13]

Non-literal meanings of the particles are an idiosyncratic development in English. There is no reason to expect that another language should share precisely the same metaphorical extensions or even be concerned to mark the same nuances that English does. Indeed, when translating from English into other languages, the nuances of these particles are often ignored, or the information they convey may be rendered in a different way, one appropriate to the mechanics of the target language. But it happens that in the case of Welsh, things have played out differently. Given that English and Welsh have been in intimate contact over many centuries, many non-literal uses of the particles have been taken over into Welsh. It is thus often possible to translate an English particle directly into Welsh even when its use is aspectual or metaphorical.

However, an examination of Welsh stylistic resources shows that translating these English idioms directly is not the only solution. The Welsh language has characteristic idioms of its own which can be drawn on in writing and translating. In the category of semi-idiomatic phrasal verbs, the verb can generally be translated literally from English into Welsh. The translator's task is to decide whether to render the aspectual or metaphorical sense of the English particle, and if so, how. There are three primary translation strategies found for this category:

a) The Welsh text may simply ignore the particle.
b) The Welsh text may render the sense of the particle in a semantically more explicit way, sometimes one that focuses on a different aspect of the event.
c) The particle may be translated literally into Welsh.

Solution (c) can work when the polysemies and metaphorical extensions of the English particles are possible in Welsh as well. Relying on this kind of

---

[13] Some scholars have focused more on aspectual uses of English particles (e.g. Brinton 1988) while others have been more interested in metaphoric or metonymic uses (e.g. Lindner 1983).

convergence of the two languages is of course an easy solution, and it is not uncommon in informal texts or speech, but solutions (a) and (b) are often preferred in more careful style.

Solution (a), simply ignoring the particle in Welsh translation, is a common solution. In many instances the semantic contribution of the English particle is slight and subtle, having more to do with stylistic preferences of English than with the real semantic content of the sentence. It is the translator's task to decide what the essential elements are that must be represented overtly and what elements can be inferred from context, or left unmentioned, without doing violence to the text. The inclusion of a particle in Welsh in some cases has the result not of enriching the meaning, but simply of making Welsh correspond more closely to English. A writer or translator may thus prefer to leave the particle out in Welsh. This was the case with the examples discussed above, whose published translations are shown below:

For some minutes it **puffed AWAY** without speaking; [ALICE 50]	Am rai munudau **smociodd** y Lindysyn heb ddweud yr un gair . . . [ALYS 45]
Snape put them all into pairs and set them to **mixing UP** a simple potion to cure boils. [STONE 172]	Gwnaeth Sneip iddyn nhw weithio fesul pâr i **gymysgu** dracht syml i wella cornwydydd. [MAEN 109]
Harry **counted OUT** five little bronze coins . . . [STONE 77]	**Cyfrodd** Harri bump o'r darnau bach efydd . . . [MAEN 49]
And certainly the glass *was* beginning **to melt AWAY**, just like a bright silvery mist. [THRO 131]	. . . ac yn wir ichi roedd y gwydr *yn* dechrau **toddi**, yn union fel rhyw darth arianaid disglair. [TRWY 18]

These examples show several different English particles being left out of the Welsh translation. The most common such particle is *up*. The following three examples further illustrate translations into Welsh where *up* was simply left out:

Hagrid **rolled UP** the note . . . [STONE 55]	Wedi **rowlio**'r memrwn . . . [MAEN 40]
George was **washing UP the accumulated dishes** of the day. [VICT 126]	Wrthi'n **golchi'r llestri** oedd wedi hel yn ystod y dydd yr oedd Alun . . . [LLINYN 143]
She could feel the anger **boiling UP** inside her. [MAT 28]	Gallai deimlo'r dicter yn **berwi** ynddi. [MAT 22]

Indeed, *up* is the most polysemous and idiomatic English particle, a point to which we will return.

The next group of examples shows the other direction, in which a non-literal particle has been *added* in English when translating from Welsh. Here too, a variety of particles are involved, but again, *up* is involved more frequently than any of the others:

'Nid fy siop fy hunan sy gen' i, wyddost ti, ac ni allwn wrthod **aros** i orffen y gwaith.' [MONICA 67]

'The shop isn't mine, you know, and I couldn't refuse **to stay ON** to finish a job.' [MONICA 69]

Ond mi'r oeddwn i wedi cael **i dalu fo** yn i goin. [TE 41]

But I'd **paid him BACK** in his own coin. [TEA 40]

Fesul tipyn medrai ddechrau **talu** tipyn mwy o'i biliau yn y siopau. [TRAED 144]

Gradually, she would be able **to pay OFF** more of the bills in the shops. [FEET 119]

Gwenodd yn ddiflas gan ystyried mai tra **sgubai** hi lofftydd y ffurfiwyd pob penderfyniad o dipyn bwys yn ei hanes. [MONICA 49]

She smiled wryly as the thought occurred to her that it was while **sweeping OUT** bedrooms she had made every decision of any consequence in her life. [MONICA 49]

... **caeodd** holl chwareli bychain y cylch. [TRAED 159]

... the smaller quarries in the area **shut DOWN**. [FEET 132]

Yn awr deuai llythyrau oddi wrth y bechgyn bob wythnos. Ni fyddai gan yr un ohonynt byth newydd, a byddai dweud hynny yn y llythyrau yn **llenwi** tipyn ar y papur. [TRAED 145]

Letters came from the boys every week. Not one of them would have any news to tell, but even saying that **filled UP** some part of the paper. [FEET 120]

... mi **wna** i wely ar y soffa i chi. [TE 70]

I'll **make UP** a bed for you on the sofa. [TEA 65]

... fe **oleuai** llygaid y claf. [MONICA 13]

... the sick woman's eyes would **light UP**. [MONICA 11]

A phob un o'r bechgyn hyn [...] **tyfasant** i gyd yn ddynion cyfrifol, goleuedig, glân eu bywydau ... [HDF 131]

All these boys [...] **grew UP** to be responsible, enlightened, and clean-living men ... [OFH 164]

The second pattern of translation equivalence found for verbs in Category 2 involves transforming the particle into some semantically more explicit element in Welsh. In the following example, *to sleep around* has become *cysgu efo hwn a'r llall* 'to sleep with this one and the other':

'Girls of that age have lovers. If the parents are uncaring they **sleep AROUND**.' [VICT 15]	'Mae gan genod ei hoed hi gariadon. Os ydi rhieni'n ddifalio mi wnân nhw **gysgu efo hwn a'r llall.**' [LLINYN 15]

In the next example the translator chose to focus on another aspect of the situation (a kind of *modulation*); the particle *around* in the English *wait around* suggests waiting 'in the area', thus referring to place, whereas in the translation, *loetran am dipyn* 'wait for a bit' refers to time:

She **waited AROUND**, went home late. Walked – unfortunately. [VICT 55]	Hi'n **loetran am dipyn** ac yna'n mynd adre am ei phen ei hun. Yn cerdded – yn anffodus. [LLINYN 62]

Indeed, a common solution when the English phrasal verb is about space is for the Welsh translation to be an adverbial expression. In the following, *to fit in* becomes 'to fit well' (*ffitio'n iawn*), *to push (something) away* becomes 'to push it out of sight' (*gwthio o'r golwg*), etc.:

'She could have been born fifty years ago and **fitted IN**.' [VICT 38]	'Mi allasa hi fod wedi cael 'i geni hanner can mlynedd yn ôl ac mi fasa wedi **ffitio'n iawn.**' [LLINYN 42]
'Get on with your own job. **Keep OUT** of mine.' [VICT 115]	'Caria di 'mlaen efo dy waith a **cad yn glir** o'n libart i.' [LLINYN 128]
Samantha's room, she noted, was still locked. More memories **pushed safely AWAY**. [KNOTS 144]	Sylwodd fod stafell Samantha yn dal dan glo. Mwy o atgofion wedi'u **gwthio'n ddiogel o'r golwg**. [CHWERW 122]
When I told her that Miss Stuchley had been missing from her apartment since last evening she immediately **jumped IN** and said that she'd known she'd come to a bad end. [TIME 65]	Pan ddaru mi ddeud wrthi fod Miss Stuchley 'di bod ar goll o'i fflat ers neithiwr, **neidiodd i'r fei** ar unwaith a deud 'i bod hi'n gwybod na ddôi unrhyw dda iddi hi yn y diwedd. [AMSER 102]

But I **pulled AWAY** from his weak grip and left the cell. [KNOTS 193]	Ond **tynnais fy hun yn rhydd** o'i afael a mynd allan o'r gell. [CHWERW 16]
He got up and pulled out a chair. If the bastard didn't sit down he'd **fall DOWN**.[14] [VICT 16]	Cododd ac estyn cadair. Os na fyddai'r llymbar yma'n eistedd fe **ddisgynnai'n glewt**. [LLINYN 17]

In each of these cases, the Welsh rendering is more explicit than the English original, with an adverbial phrase explaining or interpreting the English particle.

Given the frequency of *up* (whose metaphorical extensions will be explored more fully below), numerous examples show it transformed into something semantically more explicit:

What's so bloody secret about being married and separated that you've got to **lock the evidence of it UP** and keep it under your bed? [TIME 72]	Be sy mor blydi dirgel ynglyn â bod yn briod a gwahanu wedyn fel bod rhaid i chi **gloi'r dystiolaeth mewn cês** a'i gadw o dan y gwely? [AMSER 115]
'I borrowed [the bike] without asking and wrapped it around a lamp-post [. . .] She didn't even bawl me out, just **cleaned me UP** . . .' [VICT 38]	'Mi gymeres i'i fenthyg o heb ofyn a reidio ar 'y mhen i bolyn lamp [. . .] Wnaeth hi ddim gwylltio na gweiddi, dim ond **llnau'r gwaed oddi ar 'y mhenglinia** . . . [LLINYN 42]
He should have got himself a Browning and **blown the lot of them AWAY**. [KNOTS 189]	Fe ddylai fod wedi cael gafael ar wn, a'**u saethu nhw'n siwtrws**. [CHWERW 161]
Paul, **collecting UP his papers**, looked at him thoughtfully. [VICT 75]	Edrychodd Owen yn feddylgar ar Ian wrth **gasglu'i bapurau ynghyd**. [LLINYN 85]
. . . they were running hand in hand, and the Queen went so fast that it was all she could do **to keep UP with her**. [THRO 145–6]	Y cwbl a gofia hi yw eu bod yn rhedeg law yn llaw, a'r Frenhines yn mynd mor gyflym roedd hi'n gymaint ag a allai hi ei wneud i **aros wrth ei hochr** . . . [TRWY 32]

---

[14] The meaning of *down* in *fall down* is of course directional, but arguably the main function of the particle is not to indicate the direction of falling, which is obvious, but to emphasise telicity.

The caging and the breaking and then the **patching UP**. [KNOTS 216]

Y carcharu a'r rhwygo ac yna'r ymgais i **wnïo'r darnau ynghyd** wedyn. [CHWERW 183]

. . . whenever she was told **to shut UP**, she had **to shut UP**. [MAT 49]

. . . a phryd bynnag y byddai rhywun yn dweud wrthi am **gau ei cheg**, roedd rhaid iddi **gau ei cheg**. [MAT 43]

The third solution is to translate the particle literally into Welsh. This can be illustrated with one of the most straightforward particles, *back*, which has several metaphorical meanings: (a) backwards, in the direction of the back (*to lean back in one's chair*); (b) return to a place where one had been earlier (*to walk back to one's office*); (c) return to a previous time (*travel back in time, think back to yesterday*); (d) return to a prior state or condition (*change her hair colour back to red*); (e) do something again (*sit back down*); (f) do something in return (*smile back at someone, repeat the phone number back*).

All six of these senses of *back* are also found with the Welsh particle *yn ôl*. These are shown below with one relevant example per sense:

(a) Backwards / in the direction of the back (as opposed to forward)[15]

Yna **camodd yn ôl** i wylio Vera'n feirniadol. [LLEIFIOR 56]

Then he **stepped BACK** to look at Vera more critically. [RETURN 46]

(b) Return to an earlier place

. . . he decided to work off his remaining stiffness by **walking BACK to his office** . . . [TIME 85]

Penderfynodd hefyd gael gwared ar y stiffrwydd a oedd yn dal i'w blagio trwy **gerdded yn ôl i'w swyddfa** . . . [AMSER 135]

(c) Return to an earlier time

'but it's no use **going BACK to yesterday**, because I was a different person then.' [ALICE 99]

'[O]nd dim iws **mynd yn ôl at ddoe** oherwydd roeddwn i'n rhywun gwahanol bryd hynny. [ALYS II 102–3]

---

[15] The sense 'backward' can sometimes be translated with the expression *wysg ei gefn*: 'He stumbled **backward** and knocked over his lamp . . .' [STONE 256], 'Baglodd **wysg ei gefn** a tharo'i lamp drosodd' [MAEN 162].

(d) Return to an earlier state or condition

'Will that **change the colour BACK?**'   'Fydd hynny'n **newid y lliw 'nôl?**'
the father asked anxiously.   gofynnodd y tad yn bryderus.
'Of course it won't, you twit,' the   'Wrth gwrs na fydd e, yr iolyn,'
mother said. [MAT 64]   meddai'r fam. [MAT 58]

(e) To do something again[16]

... a **rhoid ei sbectol yn ôl** ac   ... and **put his glasses BACK on** and
eistadd i lawr. [NOS 58]   sat down. [NIGHT 59]

(f) To do something in return

One of the girls, rather formidable-   Daeth un o'r merched, a godai
looking in her dark suit, came to the   fraw braidd ar Lingard, yn ei siwt
counter and smiled an unlipsticked   dywyll, ar y cowntar gan wenu gwên
smile at him. Lingard **returned the**   ddifinlliw. **Gwenodd Lingard yn**
smile ... [TIME 75]   **ôl** ... [AMSER 119]

Even though the semantics of *back* and *yn ôl* correspond rather closely, this
does not mean that the use of one automatically entails use of the other in
translation. Indeed, *back* is more common in English than *yn ôl* is in Welsh.
There are both examples where *back* is added in an English translation, and
examples where it is omitted in a Welsh one:

Aethant i'w llety'**n chwil** ...   They then **staggered BACK** to their
[TRAED 162]   lodgings ... [FEET 134]

... ac weithiau medrent **dalu**   Sometimes they managed **to pay**
ychydig o'r hawl o'r cyflog. Rhyw   **BACK some of the capital** from the
ddiwrnod caent orffen talu hwnnw,   wages. One day they would repay it
a byddai'r tyddyn yn eiddo iddynt.   all and the property would be theirs.
[TRAED 24]   [FEET 21]

Ond mi'r oeddwn i wedi cael **i dalu**   But I'd **paid him BACK** in his own
fo yn i goin. [TE 41]   coin. [TEA 40]

---

[16] 'Again' seems to be the usual meaning whenever *back* is used simultaneously with
another particle, but not when it is used alone; compare *He sat back*, and *He sat back
down*. The latter sentence seems to mean the same as *He sat down again*. It is of course
possible to translate this sense as *unwaith eto* or *drachefn*, e.g. He **leaned BACK IN**
before shutting the door. [KNOTS 168] **Plygodd i mewn unwaith eto** cyn cau'r drws.
[CHWERW 144]

Outside and in his car, Rogers **crawled BACK** to his office in second gear on dipped headlights . . . [TIME 33]	Unwaith yr oedd yn ei gar, **symudodd Rogers fel malwoden** mewn ail gêr a'i oleuadau wedi'u dipio . . . [AMSER 52]
Gill was pacing to and fro, **sniffing BACK tears**. [KNOTS 199]	. . . a Gill yn camu yn ôl ac ymlaen gan **snwffian crio**. [CHWERW 168]

The particle *back* is a good example of one which has a single usual translation equivalent in Welsh. But some of the other particles have less isomorphic equivalents. We examine a few such cases below. Subtopics will be divided into two sections, those dealing with uses of the particles which are primarily aspectual, and those where it is primarily metaphorical.

6.3.1 Issues in the translation of aspectual particles

Partially or fully aspectual readings exist for a number of English particles, including *up, down, out, off, through, over*, and *away* (Talmy 1985: 114–15, Brinton 1988: 169). The verbal aspect most commonly marked with particles is telicity (Brinton 1988: 167). In other words, the particle can introduce 'the concept of a goal or an endpoint to durative situations which otherwise have no necessary terminus' (Brinton 1988:168).[17] This use of *up* is common, often with the additional nuance of completion, suggesting that the verb's complement is not partially but totally affected by the action (*drink up the milk, eat up the pizza, cut up the newspaper*).

Both telicity and atelicity can be marked in Welsh using directional particles in ways which mirror the English models. The use of *up* to emphasise telicity is reflected in Welsh *i fyny*:

. . . allai Didi feddwl am ddim arall ond neidio i'r gwely efo Matt a'i **fwyta fo i fyny**, roedd o'n edrych mor dda. [LLADD 284]	. . . *Didi could think of nothing but jumping into bed with Matt and **eating him UP**, he looked so good.*

However, this use of *i fyny* is fairly limited in Welsh and seems to occur only in heavily anglicised styles and in very informal speech. In more careful and idiomatic Welsh style, *i fyny* is not customarily used this way. In some cases there are existing idiomatic Welsh equivalents that serve the purpose without

---

[17] As Thim notes, *up* is not the only particle which can be used to mark telicity, though it is by far the most frequent. The particles *down, out, over* and *through* can also have a telic function.

relying on English idiom. These include the correspondences illustrated in the following examples:

Dechreues i feddwl am Tessa a bys Solfach, ac ro'n i wrthi'n **rhoi clec i 'mheint** yn barod i fynd pan gerddodd hi drwy'r drws . . . [HUNAN 184] [lit. give a bang to my pint]	I was thinking about Tessa and the Solva bus and was **drinking UP** to go when she walked through the door . . . [SOLVA 184]
Yfodd Ned y llaeth **ar ei dalcen** . . . [HENAT 125] [lit. drank . . . on his forehead]	Ned **drank UP** the milk **in one draught** . . . [LOCUST 108]
He took the letter and **tore it UP**. [VICT 149]	Gafaelodd yn y llythyr a'i **dorri'n ddarnau mân**. [LLINYN 168] [lit. and tore it to small pieces.]
Wilfred Twite, graduate in morbid pathology, slapdash rather than professionally deft in his **cutting UP** of the dead . . . [TIME 18]	Tueddai Gwilym Trefor, myfyriwr graddedig mewn patholeg forbid, i fod braidd yn ddi-hid yn hytrach na phroffesiynol fedrus wrth **dorri'r meirw yn ddarnau mân**; [AMSER 27] [lit. and cut the dead in small pieces]

In other cases, the telic use of *up* simply does not have any Welsh exponent in the translation. This *up* may be added when translating from Welsh into English:

Rhoesai hwnnw'i lif heibio ac aethai ati i **hollti** dau neu dri o flociau yn goed tân [. . .] [CHWAL 202]	The latter had laid aside his saw and was busily **splitting UP** logs into firewood [. . .] [OUT 214]
Yr oedd y frwydr honno mor araf, mor ddidosturi, mor annheg, rhyw fud dân yn **deifio** llawenydd pawb o'i gwmpas, rhyw ormes cudd, annhyblyg, anghymodlawn. [CHWAL 147]	That battle was so slow, so merciless, so unfair, a smouldering fire **burning UP** the happiness of everybody around; a hidden, inflexible, implacable tyranny. [OUT 155]

It may also be omitted when translating from English into Welsh:

I limped around the kitchen, **tidying up** ... [CIDER 62]	Herciais o gwmpas y gegin i **dacluso ychydig ar y lle**. [SEIDR 89]
She had been **cleaned up** with her own handkerchief ... [VICT 12]	Roedd y llofrudd wedi'i **glanhau** hi â'i hances hi'i hun ... [LLINYN 11]
... imagination gets **wrapped up** in a sort of blanket ... [VICT 40]	... mae'r dychymyg yn cael'i **lapio** mewn rhyw fath o blanced ... [LLINYN 45]
Already Lavender's scheming mind was going over the possibilities that this water-jug job had **opened up** for her. [MAT 136]	Roedd meddwl cyfwrys Lavender eisoes yn mynd dros y posibiliadau roedd y gwaith o nôl y jwg ddŵr wedi'u **hagor** iddi. [MAT 130]

Atelicity, or continuative aspect, marking the prolonging or continuing of an activity that does not have a necessary endpoint, can be marked in English using the particles *away*, *on* or *along*, for example *to chatter away*, *to drive along*, *to talk on*.[18] In Welsh, this can be accomplished with the particle *ymlaen* and, in literary style, the inflected preposition *rhagddo* (which is inflected to agree with the subject):

'Y stori yma,' meddai. 'Mae hi'n ddigri' dros ben.' Sychodd ei sbectol a **darllen ymlaen**. [HENLLYS]	*'This story,' he said. 'It's extremely funny.' He wiped his eyeglasses and* **read on**.
Sgrifennodd rhagddo am rai munudau, ac eisteddodd Ceridwen a chodi'r Post i'w ddarllen. [FFENEST 39]	*He* **wrote on** *for several minutes, and Ceridwen sat and picked up the mail to read through it.*
Yr oedd hi'n **mynd rhagddi** â'i chynlluniau yn agored ac yn wargaled, er gwaethaf Harri a Marged ... [CRYMAN 262]	She was **going on** with her plans, despite Harri and Marged ... [SICKLE 227]
She was **rambling on** in this way when she reached the wood: it looked very cool and shady. [THRO 156]	Roedd hi'n **baldorddi ymlaen** fel hyn pan gyrhaeddodd y goedwig: ymddangosai'n oeraidd braf a chysgodol. [TRWY 44]

[18] Talmy (1985: 115) makes a subtle distinction between these particles, glossing *away* as 'continue Ving with dedication/abandon', *on* as 'continue Ving without stopping', and *along* as 'proceed in the process of Ving'.

The sleepers did not mind these stares, and they **dreamed ON**, though nobody bothered to inquire what it was they dreamed of, and no one thought them important. [KNOTS 117]	Doedd waeth gan y cysgwyr am y bobl hunangyfiawn hyn, a **breuddwydient ymlaen**, er na thrafferthai neb ofyn am beth y breuddwydient; doedd neb yn eu hystyried yn bwysig. [CHWERW 98]

Marking atelicity with a particle is not the only solution. Idiomatic Welsh style can mark this with *dal i* plus a verb-noun, literally 'to keep doing (something)':

Dal i redeg a chael ei bod yn mynd ar i lawr. [TE 44]	. . . **running ON** until she found herself going downhill . . . [TEA 42]

Eisteddai'r torrwr cerrig ar ei bentwr yn ei London Iorcs a sbectol weiran am ei lygaid, yn **dal i gnocio** fel pe tai heb glywed sŵn troed neb a heb droi ei ben. [TE 17]	The roadmender sat on his heap in his striped trousers, with his wire spectacles, **tap-tapping AWAY** as if he hadn't heard their footsteps, without turning his head towards them. [TEA 19]

Dal i bwffian run fath ag injian trên bach Chwaral ddaru Wmffra am dipyn. [NOS 69]	And Humphrey **puffed AWAY** for a while just like the little train in the quarry. [NOS 56]

Another equivalent structure is repetition of a verb or an adverb using *a(c)* 'and':

Yna dechreuodd dynnu ym mhlanhigion y corn carw a dyfai gan ymgordeddu'n dynn am fonion y grug. **Tynnai a thynnai** yn amyneddgar â'i llaw wydn, ac yna wedi cael digon, rhoes ef o gwmpas ei phen fel torch. [TE 42]	She began plucking the staghorn moss that clung round the heather stalks, **plucking AWAY** with her strong hands and then, when there was enough of it, putting it round her head like a tiara. [TEA 41]

R'wyt ti heb sylwi o gwbl. Wyddost ti ddim am y dyhead yma sy'n **fy nghnoi o hyd ac o hyd**? [RHANDIR 92]	Thou hast not noticed anything at all, not noticed this desire **gnawing AWAY at me all the time**? [FAIR 92]

Atelicity may be sufficiently encoded already in an adverb or a verb, making a particle unnecessary. Sometimes an adverbial implies the durative nature of the activity already (*yn yr oes hon* literally 'in this age', *am rai munudau* 'for some minutes'):

Ond yn yr oes hon, John bach – **hala** yn 'u cyfer **yw hi**. [HDF 88]	To-day, John bach, **it's** nothing but spending, **spending AWAY**. [OFH 108]
For some minutes it **puffed AWAY** without speaking; but at last it unfolded its arms, took the hookah out of its mouth again, and said . . . [ALICE 50]	Am rai munudau **smociodd** y Lindysyn heb ddweud yr un gair, ond o'r diwedd dadblethodd ei freichiau, cymerodd yr hwca o'i geg unwaith eto, a dywedodd . . . [ALYS 45]

In other cases, the choice of verb tense already encodes durativity (the imperfect in *tipiai* 'was ticking', the periphrastic imperfect in *(roedd) yn canu grwndi* 'it was purring', the periphrastic present in *(mae) yn gweithio* 'is working'):

Tipiai'r cloc. [TRAED 29]	The clock **ticked AWAY**. [FEET 26]
. . . a'r gath yn eistadd wrth y ffendar o flaen tân **yn canu grwndi** . . . [NOS 179]	. . . and the cat sitting by the fender in front of the fire **purring AWAY** . . . [NIGHT 152]
. . . that jungle the tourists never saw, being too busy **snapping AWAY** at the ancient golden temples . . . [KNOTS 220]	. . . y jyngl na châi'r ymwelwyr byth gip arno, gan eu bod nhw'n rhy brysur yn **clician eu camerâu** o flaen rhyw demlau hynafol [CHWERW 187]
Someone **working AWAY** quietly at a computer terminal somewhere? [KNOTS 164]	Rhywun yn **gweithio**'n ddistaw wrth derfynell cyfrifiadur yn rhywle? [CHWERW 140]

In such cases, durativity is unambiguously marked already in Welsh without a particle.

6.3.2 Issues in the translation of metaphorical particles

Below we offer a case study of a few of the most frequent semantic extensions of the particle *up*:[19] The intense and prolonged contact between English and

---

[19] The literature on the semantic analysis of the particles in English phrasal verbs is huge, and different typologies have been proposed which overlap but are not identical. The analysis of *up* followed here is based on Lindner (1983), with heavy modification. There is no attempt to be exhaustive here.

Welsh has led to a state of affairs in which these metaphorical extensions have entered Welsh usage to one degree or another. That is, given the equation *up* = *i fyny* found in the expression of literal phrasal verbs, speakers have extended the semantic space of *i fyny* so that it matches the range of meanings of *up* even in its highly metaphorical uses. This result, though significant in the impact it has had on the Welsh language, is not a particularly surprising outcome of prolonged and extensive bilingualism.

All the same, it is useful to be aware that traditional Welsh style makes available some other ways of representing the ideas that can be conveyed by 'up'. Some of these possibilities are explored in the following paragraphs.

6.3.2.1 Positions of the human body

Using directional particles such as *i fyny* 'up' and *i lawr* 'down' with verbs describing positions of the body is well attested in Welsh with a variety of verbs such as *sefyll* 'stand', *neidio* 'jump', *eistedd* 'sit', *gorwedd* 'lie' and *troi* 'turn'. The use of particles competes here with a different pattern of Welsh idiom which in most cases does not have an exact English equivalent, namely verbal expressions that include a possessive idiom (see also Chapter 4).[20] These include *ar (ei) draed* 'on (his) feet', *ar (ei) eistedd* 'on (his) sitting', *ar (ei) hyd* 'on his length', *yn (ei) unfan* 'in (his) spot', *i('w) sefyll* 'to his standing', and *ar (ei) orwedd* 'on (his) lying'. Some examples of these equivalents are indicated in the following table:

English phrasal verb	English-style Welsh phrasal verb	Traditional Welsh possessive idiom
stand up	sefyll i fyny	sefyll ar ei draed codi ar ei draed codi i'w sefyll
jump up	neidio i fyny	neidio ar ei draed
sit up	eistedd i fyny	codi ar ei eistedd bod ar ei eistedd
stay up (at night)	aros i fyny	aros ar ei draed

---

[20] The antiquity of the possessive patterns is clear not only from an examination of older Welsh texts, but also from patterns in Breton, Welsh's sister language, where very close equivalents of the possessive pattern can be found: *Sevel **war e goazez** a reas ar Gripi* 'The Gryphon sat up' (lit. 'rise **on its sitting** did the Gryphon'); *lammas **en he sav*** 'she jumped up' (lit. '[she] jumped **in her standing**') (Carrol / Kerrain 1995 p. 153); *Mont a reas **en e c'hourvez** war e wele* 'He lay back on his bunk' (lit. 'he went **in his lying** on his bed') (Steinbeck/Braz 69/49).

ENGLISH PHRASAL VERB	ENGLISH-STYLE WELSH PHRASAL VERB	TRADITIONAL WELSH POSSESSIVE IDIOM
be up (before going to bed, or after getting out of bed)	bod i fyny	bod ar ei draed
lie down (to stretch out)	gorwedd i lawr	gorwedd ar ei hyd gorwedd ar ei gefn
fall down	syrthio / cwympo / disgyn i lawr	syrthio ar ei hyd
turn around	troi rownd	troi yn ei unfan

Thus, 'to stand up' can be found as *sefyll i fyny* using a particle, but also as *sefyll ar ei draed* or *codi ar ei draed* which deploy the possessive idiom *ar ei draed* 'on his feet', and *codi i'w sefyll*, literally 'rise to his standing':

A doedd Titsh, pan oedd o'n **sefyll i fyny**, ddim yn cyrraedd dim ond at bennagliniau Wil Robaits . . . [NOS 128]

And when Titch was **standing UP**, he barely came up to the knees of Will Roberts . . . [NIGHT 109]

Na, paid â rhedag, medda Huw, wnaiff o ddim byd iti. Fedar o ddim **codi ar i draed**. [NOS 12]

No, don't run, Huw said, he won't do anything to you. He can't **stand UP**. [NIGHT 5]

Cododd Karl i'w sefyll ac edrych arni. [LLEIFIOR 33]

Karl got UP and looked at her. [RETURN 26]

He **stood UP** as George Webber was shown in and indicated a chair. [VICT 79]

Safodd ar ei draed pan ddaeth Alun Hardwick i mewn a gofyn iddo eistedd. [LLINYN 89]

Similarly, *neidio i fyny* 'to jump up' competes with *neidio ar ei draed*:

'Do you call *that* a whisper?' cried the poor King, **jumping UP** and shaking himself. [THRO 198]

'Dyna 'dych chi'n ei alw'n sibrwd?' gwaeddodd y Brenin druan gan **neidio i fyny** a'i ysgwyd ei hun. [TRWY 89]

Everyone fell over laughing except Hermione, who **leapt UP** and performed the countercurse. [STONE 270]

Dechreuodd pawb ond Hermione rowlio chwerthin. **Neidiodd hi ar ei thraed** ar unwaith a gwneud gwrthfelltith. [MAEN 171]

As for the verb *eistedd*, it can, like the English verb *sit*, denote either an action (*he sat up*), or simply describe a person's posture (*he was sitting up in bed*). Both notions can be rendered as *eistedd i fyny* ('sit up'), but they can also use the possessive construction *ar ei eistedd* 'on his sitting': the action is *codi ar ei eistedd* (lit. 'to rise on one's sitting') and the static description of posture is *bod ar ei eistedd* (lit. 'to be on one's sitting'):

'Oh gosh,' Matilda said, **sitting up** and looking around. [MAT 214]

'O'r annwyl,' meddai Matilda, gan **eistedd i fyny** ac edrych o gwmpas. [MAT 208]

Erbyn hynny **eisteddai i fyny** yn ei wely, a thynasid ymaith y rhwymau oddi am ei ben, gan adael y plaster yn unig. [CYCHWYN 32]

He was by now **sitting UP** in bed, the head-bandages had been taken off and only the plaster remained. [BEGIN 31]

Cododd Alis ar ei heistedd eilwaith gan syllu ar y cwmni dros y ffordd. [MONICA 7]

Alice sat UP again and peered out at the people across the road. [MONICA 6]

Yr oedd Gwyn ar ei eistedd erbyn hyn. [CHWAL 59]

Gwyn was sitting UP in bed now. [OUT 61]

A related metaphorical extension of *up* describes the condition of one who is awake and has not gone to bed, as in the phrases 'to be up' or 'to stay up'. In Welsh, *bod i fyny / aros i fyny* compete with *bod ar ei draed / aros ar ei draed*:

. . . yr oedd Twm yn brysur anghyffredin, ac wedi sôn wrthyf fwy nag unwaith, tybed a gaffai ef ddyfod i'n tŷ ni i 'joinio' gwneud cyflaith, ac i **aros i fyny** hyd adeg y plygain yn yr Eglwys. [GWEN 20]

. . . Twm was doing his best to get an invitation to our house to join us in the making of treacle toffee, and **to sit UP** until it was time to go to the carol service in the church. [GWEN 26]

Yr oedd yr hen Nansi ar ei thraed yn blygeiniol drannoeth . . . [GWEN 124]

Old Nansi **was up and about** at dawn next morning . . . [GWEN 106]

A'i Fam o'n cadw gola lamp ac **aros ar ei thraed** trwy'r nos yn disgwyl amdano fo. [NOS 42]

And his Mam keeping the lamp lit and **staying UP** all night waiting for him. [NIGHT, 33]

Codai'n foreach, **eisteddai**'n hwyr **ar ei draed** yn darllen. [CRYMAN 98]	He got up earlier, and **sat UP** late reading. [SICKLE 81]

Given that 'up' (and *i fyny*) can refer to the vertical positions of the human body associated with wakefulness and daytime activity, 'down' (and *i lawr*) can refer to the non-vertical positions of kneeling, sitting, crouching, falling, and lying down:

. . . ond cyn iddo gyrraedd y drws baglodd ar draws plyg yng ngharped y gegin a thrawodd ei ben ar ochr y drws wrth **ddisgyn yn glep i lawr.** [AC YNA 28]	*But before he reached the door he tripped on a fold in the kitchen carpet and struck his head on the side of the door as he **fell DOWN with a thud.***
Yna **eisteddodd** y dyrnwyr **i lawr** ynghanol y gwellt a'r sgubau i wylio a gwrando ar Dai'n mynd rhagddo . . . [HDF 92]	Then the threshers **sat DOWN** on the straw and the sheaves to watch Dai and listen to him proceeding . . . [OFH 113]
'You need *rest.*' 'I am resting, look, **lying DOWN** and everything.' [STONE 374]	'Rwyt ti angen *gorffwys.*' 'Dwi *yn* gorffwyso, wir, dwi'n **gorwedd i lawr** a phopeth.' [MAEN 239]

They can appear with no directional particle, presumably because the semantics of the verb make the direction sufficiently obvious:[21]

Canmolodd ei doethineb hi yn ymwrthod â chaledwaith, yn **gorwedd** ac yn segura. [MONICA 56]	He had praised her good sense in refusing to do any hard work, in **lying DOWN** and taking things easy. [MONICA 56]
'You don't look well, you know [. . .] You'd better **sit** before you **fall OVER.**' [TIME 78]	'Dwyt ti ddim yn edrych yn rhyw iach iawn, wyddost ti [. . .] Well iti **eistedd** cyn iti **syrthio.**' [AMSER 124]
He sat **DOWN** in an armchair . . . [MAT 50]	**Eisteddodd** mewn cadair freichiau . . . [MAT 44]

---

[21] The particle is optional with some verbs in English as well. The inclusion of 'down' in 'He sat (down) at the table' or 'He stumbled and fell (down)' does not obviously change the meaning of the sentence.

And in some of these cases (as for 'to lie down', 'to fall down'), traditional Welsh style can use the possessive idiom *ar (ei) hyd* 'on (his) length' or *ar ei gefn* 'on (his) back':

Gorweddodd ar ei hyd ar y ddaear gynnes, ac edrych ar yr awyr las a oedd fel parasôl mawr uwch ei phen. [TE 44]	She **lay DOWN** on the warm earth, looking up at the blue sky like a parasol above her. [TEA 42-43]
... **gorweddai Gordon Reeve ar ei gefn** ac edrych i fyny arna i efo llygaid fel lleuad lawn. [CHWERW 161]	... Gordon Reeve **lay DOWN** and stared up at me with eyes like the full moons of winter. [KNOTS 189]
... a bu ond y dim iddo **ddisgyn ar ei hyd** i'r bedd. [PLA 118]	'... and had almost swayed into the open grave.' [PEST 61] [lit. '... and he nearly **fell on his length** / **full length** into the grave.']
A oedd Ned Tŷ Crwn gyda hwy y noson honno pan **aeth** y cipar o Sais hwnnw **ar ei hyd** i'r afon? [CYCHWYN 37]	Was Ned Tŷ Crwn with them that night when that English water-bailiff **went full-length** into the river? [BEGIN 37]

A different possessive idiom is found in equivalents of 'turn around'. In addition to *troi rownd* (where the particle is not simply in imitation of English but is in fact borrowed from it), one finds the Welsh possessive idiom *yn ei unfan* literally 'in his spot'. Occasionally other equivalents are found such as *troi ei ben* 'to turn his head':

Mae hyn yn gwneud iddo **droi rownd** unwaith eto. [FFYDD 250]	This makes him **turn around** once more. [FAITH 153]
Cododd fy ngolygon ato, ac roeddwn ar fin agor fy ngheg pan **drodd yntau yn ei unfan** a dechrau craffu o gwmpas yr ystafell. [CAER 224]	'*I looked up at him, and I was about to open my mouth when he turned around and began staring around the room.*'
Roedden nhw mewn hwylie da, yn chwerthin trwy'r trwch ac yn amlwg am gael noson i'r brenin. Roedd pobol yn **troi'u penne** ac yn	They were in high spirits, laughing a lot and obviously out for a good time. People were **turning round** and shushing them up, as they did

eu hishtio nhw fel y bydden nhw yn
y dyddie hynny cyn meicroffone.
[HUNAN 184]

in those days before
microphones . . . [SOLVA 184]

Some verbs of bodily position may lack a possessive idiom but have an
ym-prefixed variant (for which see also Chapter 9). 'To straighten up' occurs
as *ymsythu, sythu*, and *sythu i fyny*:

Dyma fo'n gwyro i lawr a deud yn
fy nghlust i . . . Rwan, medda fo yn
ei lais ei hun, ar ôl **sythu i fyny**, a
finna'n gorfod plygu ngwegil yn ôl i
sbio arno fo. [NOS 69]

Then he bent down and whispered
in my ear . . . Now, he said in his
normal voice, after he'd **straightened
up** and I had my neck bent back so I
could look at him. [NIGHT 56]

Yr oedd Owen o'i ben a'i
ysgwyddau'n dalach nag ef, ac
ymsythodd i'w wneud ei hun yn
dalach fyth. [CYCHWYN 15]

Owen, a head and shoulders taller
than he, **straightened up** to make
himself taller yet. [BEGIN 13]

Sythodd hi unwaith eto.
[CHWERW 97]

She **straightened up** again.
[KNOTS 114]

Aspectual meanings and metaphorical meanings of the particles are
not always easy to separate. The verbs *to grow* and *tyfu* are atelic, having
no inherent endpoint. Letting one's beard grow could in principle go on
and on:

. . . y dylai Preis godi dwbl neu drebl
ar ŵr a adawsai i'w farf **dyfu** am
wythnos gyfan. [O LAW 80]

. . . that Price ought to double or
triple his charges for shaving a man
who let his beard **grow** for a whole
week. [FROM 58]

The addition of the particle in *grow up* (and Welsh *tyfu i fyny*) is not only a
figurative extension based on the prototypical upward pattern of growth, but
it also makes the verb telic. The following example would be decidedly odd
without the particle or some other strategy for making the verb telic, since
the desired reading is something like 'grow to full maturity', that is, grow until
the normal biological endpoint is reached:

Efallai fod dynion yn aeddfedu,
ond so nhw byth yn **tyfu i fyny**.
[FFYDD 261]

Maybe men do mature, but they
never really **grow up**. [FAITH 180]

Other ways are attested of making *tyfu* telic besides using the particle *i fyny*, notably the addition of a complement specifying the endpoint of the growth. In the following we see *(tyfu) yn ddynion cyfrifol* '(grow) into responsible men' and *(tyfu) i dipyn o faint* '(grow) to a bit of size' serving the same function as *i fyny* in the preceding examples:[22]

A phob un o'r bechgyn hyn [. . .] **tyfasant** i gyd yn ddynion cyfrifol, goleuedig, glân eu bywydau, yn asgwrn cefn i'r gymdeithas y troent ynddi . . . [HDF 131]	All these boys [. . .] **grew UP** to be responsible, enlightened, and clean-living men, the backbone of their society . . . [OFH 164]
Pan **dyfodd** y bachgen i dipyn o faint aeth yn bla ar y gymdogaeth [GWEN 12]	As soon as the boy **grew UP** he became a nuisance in the neighborhood . . . [GWEN 19]

Related to the use of particles to describe positions of the body, the particles can also designate the direction of one's gaze or attention, as with verbs of looking, staring or smiling in a particular direction. It is not impossible to render these in Welsh just as in English:

. . . all she could see, when she **looked DOWN**, was an immense length of neck . . . [ALICE 55]	. . . y cwbl a welai wrth **edrych i lawr** oedd clamp o wddf hir . . . [ALYS II 51]
'Oh gosh,' Matilda said, sitting up and **looking around**. [MAT 214]	'O'r annwyl,' meddai Matilda, gan eistedd i fyny ac **edrych o gwmpas**. [MAT 208]
. . . and neither of the others took the least notice of her going, though she **looked BACK** once or twice, half hoping that they would call after her: [ALICE 75]	. . . a 'chymerodd yr un o'r lleill ddim sylw o gwbl o'i hymaddawiad, er iddi **edrych yn ôl** unwaith neu ddwy gan hanner gobeithio y buasen nhw'n galw ar ei hôl. [ALIS II 74–5]

---

[22] In English too, it is possible to leave out the telic particle *up* if the relevant endpoint is named. The following example is interesting in that the Welsh original has both the particle and the specification of an endpoint: *Ond fel y dywedwyd eisoes, **tyfodd Twm i fyny** yn hogyn cryf, caled, a drwg.* [GWEN 17]. The English translation omits the particle: *As has already been said **Twm grew** to be a big, tough, wicked boy* [GWEN 24]. The inclusion of *up* in English would be odd here, because it would imply that the process was complete, whereas growing into any kind of boy is still not completing the process of growth.

But Welsh style often renders these expressions differently. Typical expressions are shown in the right-hand column below.

look up	edrych i fyny	codi ei olwg (ei olygon)
		codi ei lygaid
		codi ei ben
look back	edrych yn ôl	troi ei olygon yn ôl
		edrych dros ei
		ysgwyddai
look around	edrych o gwmpas	troi ei olygon
look away	edrych i ffwrdd	troi ei ben draw

Thus, for 'to look up', Welsh has not only *edrych i fyny*, but also *codi ei olwg* (or plural *ei olygon*) / *ei lygaid* / *ei ben* 'raise one's gaze / one's eyes / one's head', where the directionality is indicated not by a particle, but by the verb itself. These are examples of the equivalence pattern known as *chassé-croisé*, as the English verb 'look' corresponds semantically to the Welsh complement *ei olwg* (or by metonymy, *ei lygaid, ei ben*), and the English particle 'up' corresponds to the Welsh verb *codi*:

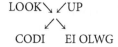

The following examples illustrate these alternate formulations, using the verbs *codi* or *troi*:

Pan **gododd ei olwg**, gwyrodd ei ben yn gyflym drachefn i guddio gwên. [CYCHWYN 123]

Looking UP, he hurriedly bent his head to hide a smile. [BEGIN 123]

... a phan **gododd ei llygaid** yr oeddent fel dwy seren. [CRYMAN 97]

... and when she **looked UP** her eyes were starry. [SICKLE 79]

Canlynodd ei briod ar ei gweu heb **godi'i phen**. [CRYMAN 10]

His wife went on knitting and didn't **look UP**. [SICKLE 6]

Troai Jane **ei golygon yn ôl** o hyd i gyfeiriad yr Eifl, a deuai pang o hiraeth iddi wrth feddwl am ei chartref y tu hwnt iddynt. [TRAED 18]

Janed frequently **looked BACK** in the direction of the Eifl, and felt *hiraeth* as she thought of her home beyond those mountains. [FEET 16]

Paul **looked AWAY from him.**   **Trodd** Owen **ei ben draw.**
[VICT 76]   [LLINYN 86]

These examples show the strong tendency of English to mark directionality using a particle, whereas it is not always necessary or desirable in Welsh
style to focus on directionality, or this may be done differently in traditional
Welsh style.

6.3.2.2 Location on a metaphorical scale

The second big group of figurative uses of *up* involves an implicit metaphor of
a scale which is thought of as vertical and where 'up' values are more positive
or more intense than 'down' values. The conceptual scales, present in both
English and Welsh, can measure many different things, such as temperature,
volume, or speed. People speak readily of *warming something up* or *turning
up the heat*, metaphorical references to a scale of temperatures thought of
vertically like a thermometer, where 'high' on the scale is hot and 'low' on
the scale is cold (cf. *cool down*). Similarly for sound, we refer to *turning the
volume up or down*:

"Na fe, 'na fe, ma 'bach o siâp 'ma   *'That's it, that's it, it's looking good*
nawr, a dalwch hi ar y top fynna am   *now, and keep it on top there for a*
ryw ddwy funud inni ga'l **cynhesu**   *couple minutes so we can **warm UP***
lan 'm bach.' [DAL 35]   *a bit.'*

Trodd Cledwyn y sŵn i fyny ar y   *Cledwyn **turned UP** the volume on*
chwaraewr CDs . . . [CRAWIA 281]   *the CD player . . .*

Wrth fyned i bregethu yma ac acw   *When going to preach here and there*
y naill Sabboth ar ol y llall, oni   *one Sabbath after another, was he not*
frawychodd fwy nag unwaith wrth   *alarmed more than once to discover*
ganfod ei fod wedi **oeri i lawr** i allu *that he had **cooled down** to the point*
gwneyd hyny ymron yn *mechanical*?   *of being able to do so mechanically?*
[RHYS 325]

When prices *go up* or someone *runs up a bill*, the metaphor implies a scale
in which the 'higher' the figure, the larger the amount of money involved:

Ac os ydy pris menyn a moch wedi   And if the price of butter and pigs
codi, mae'u bwydydd nhw wedi codi   has **gone UP**, so too have feeding
hefyd, ac mae llog arian wedi **mynd**   costs, and the rate of interest on
i fyny. [TRAED 187]   the money we've had to borrow has
                                          gone UP as well. [FEET 154]

Even human expectations can be thought of on a vertical scale. Thus, *live / come / measure up to (someone's) expectations* implies that positions higher on the scale (or 'up') correspond to greater success or approval, and positions lower on the scale represent disapproval or less stringent expectations:

... disgwylid i ni'r plant ddysgu'n gyson y testun bore Sul a'i adrodd yn y seiet y nos Wener dilynol. Ni **ddown i fyny â'r disgwyliad**, bob amser, mae'n wir; a digon tolciog yr awn trwyddi'n fynych. [HDF 101]

... we children were expected to learn the Sunday morning text always and to recite it in society on Friday evening. I did not always **come UP to expectation**, it is true; I often went through it haltingly. [OFH 123]

Gallai ymlacio'n braf efo Cit heb orfod malio sut roedd o'n edrych na phoeni os oedd ei berfformiad **i fyny â'r gofynion**. [MIS O FEHEFIN 147]

He could relax with Cit without caring how he looked or worrying whether his performance was UP to the demands.

It is worth noting that the metaphorical scale can be seen in other ways beyond the use of directional particles, including lexical choices such as *codi* 'to rise' and *codiad* 'raise, rise (noun)':

Peth hap a siawns oedd **codiad** yng nghyflogau athrawon y pryd hwnnw. [TRAED 143]

A **rise in salary** was a matter of luck or chance in those days. [FEET 118]

'Mi **goda** i dipyn ar dy rent di fel na chaiff dy ddegwm di ddim bod yn uwch na'th rent.' [CWM 22]

We'll **put** the rent UP just a little higher than the tithe. [GORSE 22]

But there is also evidence of different ways of talking about such measurements in Welsh, sometimes using different metaphors. Amounts of money can be discussed in terms of metaphors of size (e.g. *lleihau* 'to get smaller', *cynyddu* 'to increase', *mynd yn fwy* 'to get bigger'):[23]

... ac wrth weld ei gyflog yn **lleihau** yn lle **mynd yn fwy** ... [TRAED 90]

... and as Wiliam saw his wages **going DOWN instead of UP** ... [FEET 76]

[23] Speaking of money in terms of size is possible in English too ('My bank account is getting smaller by the day'), though it is worth noting that the quoted English translations opted for the more customary English metaphor of vertical scale.

Cofiai o hyd am gyflog **bychan** ei dad, ac am filiau'r siop yn **cynyddu** . . . [TRAED 143]	He always remembered his father's **low** wages, and the **mounting** bills in the shops . . . [FEET 118]

Similarly, if one can 'warm up' (*twymo i fyny* or *twymo lan*), one can also *magu gwres* (lit. 'nurture heat'), and if one can 'come up to' (*dod i fyny â*) expectations, one can also 'satisfy' (*bodloni*) them:

Cerddai Edward yn ôl a blaen i geisio **magu gwres**. [RHANNU 215]	*Edward walked back and forth, trying to **warm UP**.*
'I'm the sixth one in our family to go to Hogwarts. You could say I've got a lot **to live UP to**.' [STONE 124]	'Fi ydi'r chweched yn ein teulu ni i fynd i Hogwarts, ac fel y gelli di ddychmygu, mae gen i dipyn i'w neud i **fodloni eu disgwyliadau**.' [MAEN 78]

Of course, as is often the case, the metaphorical particle is not necessarily present in Welsh at all:

. . . the Boss screaming at him **to speed UP** . . . [KNOTS 80]	. . . y Bòs yn sgrechian arno i **gyflymu** . . . [CHWERW 69]
Nid **arafodd** y *Gloria* wrth ei basio . . . [CRYMAN 42]	The car didn't **slow DOWN** as it passed . . . [SICKLE 33]
Edrychai ymlaen at ei swper. Gwyddai y câi gig oer a thatws wedi eu **twymo**. [TRAED 168]	He looked forward to his supper for he knew there would be cold meat and **warmed-up** potatoes. [FEET 140]

6.3.2.3 Feelings and emotions

The metaphor HAPPY IS UP; SAD IS DOWN (Lakoff and Johnson 1980) is found in e.g. *cheer up, brighten up, perk up* (cf. *down* which can refer to negative emotions such as depression). The semantic development seems to be that positive human emotions are associated with wakefulness and activity (thus, UP), while negative emotions are associated with inertia or sickness (thus, DOWN).[24] This metaphor is certainly present in the Welsh lexicon, even apart

---

[24] Lakoff and Johnson (1980 Chapter 4) introduce the concept of orientational metaphors, of which a key one is HAPPY IS UP; SAD IS DOWN, which has numerous lexicalised exponents in English (I'm feeling *up*. That *boosted* my spirits. My spirits *rose*. You're in *high* spirits, etc.)

from phrasal verbs. For instance, 'to cheer someone up' is expressed quite idiomatically in Welsh as *codi calon rhywun*, literally 'to raise someone's heart':

[T]ybiwn iddo ddyfod atom ni er mwyn gwneud ymdrech i **godi calon fy nhad**. [O LAW 209]	I imagined that he came over to try **to cheer my father UP**. [FROM 173]

While English routinely uses UP in phrasal verbs dealing with stimulating positive human emotions, the metaphor is not often marked with particles in Welsh literature and translation. The following examples are typical:

Wel, mae digon o le iddi hi, Martha bach, gwaetha'r modd, ac mi fasa' hi'n **llonni tipyn ar yr aelwyd**, on' fasa'? [CHWAL 226]	Well, there's plenty of place for her, Martha bach, more's the pity, and she would **cheer UP the home a bit**, wouldn't she? [OUT 239]
Siriolodd eiliad a dechrau chwerthin. [TE 75]	She **cheered UP** for a second and began to laugh. [TEA 76]
Er ei bod hi'n wyn ei chroen, mae ganddi wallt mor gyrliog â Gladys Knight a gwên a all **oleuo**'r ffurfafen. [FFYDD 206]	Although her skin is pretty pale, her hair's as curly as an afro, and her toothy smile could **light up** the heavens. [FAITH 143]
On the walk back across the field Harry tried to **liven things up** by unfastening Barbara's headscarf and passing it to Duke. [CIDER 43]	Wrth i ni gerdded yn ôl ar draws y cae, ceisiodd Harry **sirioli tipyn ar bethau** drwy gipio sgarff Barbara oddi ar ei phen a'i roi i Duke. [SEIDR 62]
The old man perked UP and said his was a pint of Usher's . . . [CIDER 88]	**Siriolodd yr hen ŵr drwyddo** a dweud mai peint arall o seidr gymerai o. [SEIDR 120]

Nonetheless, inclusion of the particle *i fyny* in such cases can be found, though it is probably safely considered an anglicism, at least in origin:

Diflannodd y llinella i fyny trwyna'r hogia mewn eiliad, a **sbriwsiodd pawb i fyny**'n syth. [CRAWIA 76]	*The lines [of cocaine] disappeared up the boys' noses in an instant, and everyone **perked UP** straight away.*
Ond prysurais yn fy mlaen, gan geisio **cadw fy ysbryd i fyny**. [RHYS 90]	*But I hurried along, trying to **keep my spirits UP**.*

6.3.2.4 Assembling, building, creating

The use of the 'up' metaphor in talking about assembling or building some-thing (e.g. *put up the Christmas tree, set up equipment*) is based on the prototypical situation in which building involves creating vertical elevation. And probably by extension from this sense, *up* is used in a number of phrasal verbs having to do with creating, making, preparing or bringing something into existence, even when the thing being created is an abstraction and does not involve any literal vertical elevation (e.g. *think up, dream up, whip up, mix up, draw up*).

The 'up' and 'down' metaphor is attested here, though probably more in speech or casual style than in more careful writing.

O'r dechrau cyntaf wedi i 'nhadcu symud i Benrhiw ymddengys iddo fwrw iddi'n ddyfal ac egniol 'yn cloddio a bwrw tail,' yn diwreiddio ac yn plannu, yn **tynnu i lawr ac yn adeiladu**. [HDF 75]	When my grandfather came to Penrhiw he threw himself into it from the start, energetically and persistently 'digging and dunging,' uprooting and planting, **taking DOWN and putting UP**. [OFH 90]
Bydd dilyniant yn y cyrsiau yn ystod y gaeaf pan fydd hyfforddiant ar gael i ofalu am y peiriannau, pa beiriannau i'w cael a sut i'w **gosod i fyny** . . . [*Y Cymro*, 5 Mehefin 2000: 21]	*There will be progression in the courses during the winter when training is available about the machines, how to take care of the machines, what machines to get and how to set them UP.*

More often, the particle is simply left out of such expressions in Welsh ('think up' > *meddwl*; 'dream up' > *breuddwydio am*, literally 'dream about'):

She didn't want to lunch with Rachel but wasn't quick enough to **think UP** a plausible excuse. [VICT 36]	Doedd arni ddim eisio cael cinio efo Carol ond methodd **feddwl** am esgus credadwy'n ddigon sydyn. [LLINYN 40]
You've **dreamed him UP**. [TIME 97]	Wedi **breuddwydio amdano** fo wyt ti. [AMSER 153]

Otherwise, the meaning may be unpacked, or a single-word equivalent may be given instead:

to rustle up	>	gwneud yn weddol sydyn (lit. 'to make fairly quickly')

to make something up	>	cyfansoddi (lit. 'to compose')
to think up	>	dyfeisio (lit. 'to invent')
to come up with	>	meddwl am

He had **rustled UP** a round of tuna fish and tomato sandwiches . . . [KNOTS 77]

Roedd wedi llwyddo i **wneud** brechdanau tiwna a thomato **yn weddol sydyn** . . . [CHWERW 65]

I **made bits UP**, invented whole dialogues and characters. [KNOTS 189]

Cyfansoddwn ddarnau fy hun, a dyfeisio deialogau cyfain a chymeriadau newydd. [CHWERW 160–1]

I played games in my head, **thought UP** crossword puzzle clues and little linguistic tricks. [KNOTS 181]

Chwaraewn gêmau yn fy mhen, **dyfeisiwn** gliwiau ar gyfer croeseiriau, a thriciau geriol. [CHWERW 153]

It was *her* turn now to become a heroine if only she could **come UP with** a brilliant plot. [MAT 136]

Ei thro *hi* oedd hi bellach i fod yn arwres, petai hi ond yn gallu **meddwl am** gynllwyn gwych. [MAT 130]

6.3.2.5 Making something available for consideration or accessible to perception

The image here is that of bringing an object closer to the participants who serve as point of reference, or raising something closer to the eyes to increase visibility. This metaphor is certainly present in Welsh as well as in English:

Ond er noson y ddamwain, yr oedd yr olwynion nid yn unig wedi troi ond wedi chwyrnellu. **Corddent i fyny** bob hen grach o waelodion ei hymwybod, o'i hisymwybod weithiau. [LLEIFIOR 114–15]

But since that night, the wheels hadn't just turned – they'd spun, **churning UP** every old grievance from the depths of her conscious and sometimes her unconscious mind. [RETURN 98]

'I'm sorry **to bring this up**, but does any of this stem from Deborah's running off to Thurnholme Bay when she was a schoolgirl?' [TIME 54]

'Mae hi'n flin gen i,' meddai, 'am **godi'r mater**, ond a ydi hyn yn deillio'n rhannol o'r adeg ddaru Deborah ddengid i Aberdewin pan oedd hi'n ferch ysgol?' [AMSER 85]

He was supposed to be working here this afternoon, but didn't **turn UP**. [TIME 123–4]

Roedd o i fod i weithio yma p'nawn 'ma, ond ddaru o ddim **troi fyny**. [AMSER 197]

However, it is not necessarily rendered literally every time it is present in an English text. Indeed, the use of *turn* in the expression *to turn up* is quite idiomatic, since there is no literal turning involved. Although *troi i fyny* can be found in Welsh as above, other Welsh formulations may be preferred as below:

The next morning she did not **turn UP** at school. [MAT 227]	Y bore canlynol **ddaeth** hi ddim i'r ysgol. [MAT 221]
'I've lost him! He keeps getting away from me!' 'He'll **turn UP**,' said Harry. [STONE 130]	'Dwi wedi'i golli o! Mae o'n dianc o hyd!' 'Fe **ddaw o i'r fei**,' meddai Harri. [MAEN 81]
If they **turned up** on Saturday, it would be up to me to do the explaining. [CIDER 32]	... ac os bydde nhw'n **ymddangos** ddydd Sadwrn, fy ngwaith i fyddai egluro iddo. [SEIDR 45]

6.3.2.6 Moving closer to a goal or reference point
This metaphor is found in expressions like *He ran up to me, We went up to the ticket window, The cat crept up to the house*. This use of *up* need not imply any movement from a lower to a higher elevation; it can describe an entirely horizontal trajectory with the interpretation 'all the way to' or 'as far as'. The Welsh preposition *at* 'towards, to, up' is traditionally used with precisely the desired meaning:

Daeth Dickie **at y bar** i godi diodydd, a phan welodd fi'n iste yno yn y cysgodion dan fy hat ddu, roedd e wedi'i synnu ar ei draws. [HUNAN 184]	Dickie **came UP TO the bar** to order drinks, and when he saw me sitting in the shadows underneath my black hat his jaw dropped. [SOLVA 184]
Ond heddiw fe **nesaodd at y drws** i glywed Iolyn Offeiriad yn mynd trwy 'i bethau: [PLA 134]	Today, the leper **crept UP TO the entrance** to hear Iolyn the Priest's prayer. [PEST 94]
Mi gymerais fy hances a **mynd ato** a sychu ei dalcen. [MONICA 34]	I took my handkerchief and **went UP TO him** to wipe his brows. [MONICA 33]
... meddai Edward Vaughan, gan **glosio at y tân** melyn llydan er ei waethaf. [CRYMAN 10]	... said Edward Vaughan, **drawing a chair UP TO the fire** despite himself. [SICKLE 6]
Un ganol dydd, pan oedd Owen yn sefyllian ar y cae chwarae ar ôl	One mid-day when Owen was loitering on the playing field after

cinio, **daeth ato** a gofyn iddo . . .
[TRAED 67]

dinner, she **came UP TO him** and
said . . . [FEET 56]

Wedyn dyma Guto'n **nofio ataf fi** a
lluchio dŵr ataf fi. [NOS 153]

Then Guto **swam UP TO me**
and splashed water over me.
[NIGHT 129]

Dw i'n **camu at** y drws ffrynt ac yn
cnoc-cnocio'n ysgafn. [FFYDD 284]

I **go UP TO** the front door and knock
quietly. [FAITH 195]

You could see he was now beginning
to wonder **what** all this was **leading
UP TO**. [MAT 123]

Gallech chi weld ei fod nawr yn
dechrau meddwl tybed **at beth**
roedd hyn i gyd yn **arwain**.
[MAT 117]

As usual, though, English usage can be found reflected in Welsh, at least in
informal styles:

Aeth Les **lan at y corff** ar y llawr.
[DAL 83]

Les went UP to the body on the floor.

Ond pwy gododd o'i sêt yn sydyn
yng ngwaelod Llawr wrth y drws, a
cherddad i fyny yn steil i gyd, hefo
fêl a sboia gwynion arni hi dros ei
gwynab ond Gres Elin Siop Sgidia.
[NOS 76]

But who suddenly got up from her
pew at the back of the Floor by the
door, and **walked UP** dressed to the
nines with a white-spotted veil over
her face but Grace Ellen Shoe Shop.
[NIGHT 63]

Erbyn hyn oedd pobol Llawr yn
llifo i fyny'n un rhes hir at yr Allor.
[NOS 75]

By this time, the people from the
Floor were **streaming UP** in a long
line to the Altar. [NIGHT 62]

'Or, perhaps, he left his car, **crept UP**
behind him wearing trainers and did
it at close range.' [TIME 13]

Neu ella 'i fod o 'di gadael ei gar,
cripian i fyny y tu ôl iddo'n gwisgo
sgidiau rhedeg a'i wneud o fel yna,
yn agos reit. [AMSER 17]

We now leave behind the particle UP in order to say a few words briefly
about two frequent uses of ON and OFF.

6.3.3 Metaphoric uses of *on* and *off*

To close this section on the metaphorical uses of directional particles, we
briefly examine two different extended uses of the English particles *on* and
off. The first use has to do with *putting* or *turning on* or *off* a light or electrical

appliance.[25] It happens that *ymlaen* and *i ffwrdd* can be used like the English particles, although they are not obligatory in Welsh. For 'turn on (the light, etc.)' one has a choice between *cynnau'r golau, rhoi'r golau* and (less frequently) *tanio*, with no particle, as well as *rhoi'r golau ymlaen* and *troi'r golau ymlaen*:

Es i lan i ben yr ail stâr lle roedd stafell y myfyriwr, agor y drws a **chynne'r gole**. [HUNAN 265]

I [. . .] crept to the top of the second flight of stairs where the student's room was, opened the door and **turned on the light**. [SOLVA 265]

Yr oedd yn rhaid iddi ffonio. Ffonio'r plismyn. Ffonio am help. Ond ni feiddiai **roi golau**. [AC YNA 160]

*She had to phone. Phone the policeman. Phone for help. But she didn't dare **turn on a light**.*

Taniodd ei theledu lliw newydd, anrheg iddi hi ei hun o arian yswiriant bywyd Wil druan, ac eisteddodd ar flaen ei chadair i rythu'n ddisgwylgar ar y sgrîn. [AC YNA 27]

*She **turned on her new color television**, a gift to herself from poor Wil's life insurance money, and she sat on the edge of her chair to stare expectantly at the screen.*

A doedd y *night watchman* ddim yn mynd i wneud mwy na **rhoi golau'r sied ymlaen** a gyrru ei gŵn o gwmpas unwaith neu ddwy. [LLADD 236]

*And the night watchman was going to do no more than to **turn on the light in the shed** and send his dogs around once or twice.*

Tessa took her into a cubicle at the end of the room and **turned on the lamp**. [VICT 84]

Aeth Tess â hi i stafell driniaeth fach a **throi'r lamp ymlaen**. [LLINYN 95]

Turn the telly on and let's not have any more talk. [MAT 55]

Tro'r teledu ymlaen a dim rhagor o siarad. [MAT 49]

For 'turn off (the light, etc.)' the usual choices are either *diffodd* (with no particle) or *troi i ffwrdd*:

---

[25] The metaphorical senses of *on* and *off* are interesting cases in that a garment or an appliance can be described as *on* or *off* even in the absence of any particular verb. This is not generally the case with other phrasal verbs. A potion that is *mixed up* cannot be described as *up*.

Daeth Dat i mewn i **droi'r lamp i ffwrdd** a thynnu carthen dros Mam a fi cyn mynd allan gan fwmblian, 'Nos da, ferched bach.' [DAL 133]	*Dat came in to turn the lamp off and pull the sheet over Mam and me before going out mumbling 'Good night, sweet ladies.'*
After **turning off the gas fire** . . . [TIME 22]	Ar ôl **diffodd y tân nwy** . . . [AMSER 34]

The second use of ON and OFF involves *putting on* or *taking off* garments or accessories, and here Welsh patterns do not mirror English so exactly. In Welsh, 'to take off (a garment)' can be expressed either as *tynnu* by itself, or as *tynnu i ffwrdd* (the particle is not strictly necessary):

Bwytâi'r bechgyn ar eu traed heb **dynnu eu cotiau** er mwyn cael brysio allan drachefn. [TRAED 31]	The boys would eat standing up without **taking their coats off** so that they could hurry out again. [FEET 28]
Clywodd Nedw'n cyrraedd i gyfeiliant cŵn Johnny, ac agorodd ddrws y garafán i weld yr hogyn yn **tynnu'i helmed i ffwrdd**. [LLADD 272]	*He heard Nedw arriving to the accompaniment of Johnny's dogs, and he opened the door of the caravan to see the boy **taking his helmet off**.*

On the other hand, 'to put on a garment' is generally not done as a phrasal verb at all in Welsh. The usual pattern here is to use *rhoi* 'to put, place' or *gwisgo* 'to put on, wear' plus the garment as direct object:

Rhoesai ei mam sbectol i archwilio ei gwaith smwddio . . . [TE 15]	Her mother **put ON** her glasses to examine her work . . . [TEA 17]
Taflodd ei sialc ar y ddesg, **gwisgodd ei gôt** a cherddodd allan o'r ysgol heb roi gwers ynddi'r bore hwnnw. [TRAED 162]	He threw his chalk on the desk, **put ON his coat**, and walked out of the school without having given a single lesson. [FEET 134]

Quite commonly, the part of the body concerned by the garment is specified in Welsh by a prepositional phrase. Note that, though possible in English ('to put his cap on his head'), the particle 'on' more often occurs in English without naming the body part ('to put his cap on'):

. . . dyma fi'n ôl i'r siambar a dechra gwisgo amdanaf a **rhoid fy sgidia am fy nhraed**. [NOS 33]	I went straight back to the bedroom and started getting dressed and **putting my shoes ON**. [NIGHT 25]

Bore Iau, pan **rôi Eric ei gap am ei ben** cyn cychwyn i'r ysgol . . . [TRAED 163]	Thursday morning, as Eric was **putting ON his cap** before going to school . . . [FEET 145]
Os **rhôi ei sbectol ar ei thrwyn** i ddarllen llyfr gyda'r nos, syrthiai i gysgu. [TRAED 89]	If she **put ON her spectacles** to read in the evening, without fail she would fall asleep. [FEET 75]

In all three instances, the Welsh prepositional phrase specifying the body part is simply translated as 'on' in English.

Having examined a fair number of phrasal verbs involving more or less literal uses of the verb but figurative extensions of the particle, we turn now to the last category, in which the verb + particle combination has generally been regarded as non-compositional.

6.4 Category 3: Idiomatic phrasal verbs

Our third and final category of phrasal verbs includes the non-transparent uses in which neither the verb nor the particle could be said to be used in its literal sense. Consider for instance the English phrasal verbs *own up*, *knock off*, and *chip in*. These idioms do not have anything to do with owning, knocking, or chipping: *own up* means 'confess', *knock off* means 'kill', and *chip in* means 'contribute' (usually with reference to money).

In many ways, this is the easiest of the three categories to deal with, because, as with idioms in general, the solution is generally to find an equivalent Welsh formulation rather than to translate literally from English. The most natural Welsh translation may be a simplex verb (*cyfaddef* 'confess', *lladd* 'kill'), or it may be a phrase (*talu ei siâr* 'to pay his share'):

Os sefwch chi, mi ro'i ddecpunt at eich coste chi fy hun. Ac mi ga' i'r ffermwyr eraill bob un i **dalu'i siâr**. Mi ofala'i na fyddwch chi ddim yn eich colled o ddime. [CRYMAN 221]	If you put up, I'll give you ten pounds towards your expenses, and all the other farmers will **chip IN**. I'll make sure you won't be a ha'penny out of pocket. [SICKLE 183]
On the other hand, she was certainly not about **to own UP**. [MAT 162]	Ar y llaw arall, doedd hi'n sicr ddim ar fin **cyfaddef**. [MAT 156]
I'd say she's either heavily tied up in **the knocking OFF** of Stephanakis,	Yn fy marn i, naill ai mae hi'n gysylltiedig go iawn efo **lladd**

or she knew enough about it not to have waited around when the balloon went up. [TIME 96]

Stephanakis, neu mae hi'n gwybod digon amdano fo i beidio ag aros yno ar ôl i bethau fynd yn draed moch. [AMSER 152]

Sometimes a literal calque of an English phrasal idiom is well attested in Welsh, and in informal style this may be exactly the right choice. In other cases it is not always desirable to settle for a straightforward phrasal verb calqued on English. Thus, for the idiomatic sense 'to run out of (a commodity)', the calque *rhedeg allan o* is attested. But so are a number of Welsh translations such as *gorffen*, *dod i ben*, and *darfod*:

Dydan ni ddim wedi **rhedeg allan o amser** fel mae'r pundits yn ei honni. [ROBHUNAN 32]

We haven't **run OUT of time** like the pundits claim.

Ymhen tipyn dechreuodd ei fenyn, ei fara, ei gig moch a'i wyau **orffen** cyn diwedd yr wythnos [. . .] Un wythnos **darfuasai** ei fara, ei wyau a'i gig moch erbyn bore Iau . . . [TRAED 130]

After a while he began **to run OUT** of bread, butter, bacon and eggs before the end of the week [. . .] One week he **had run out of** bread, eggs and bacon by Thursday morning . . . [FEET 116]

Roedd f'arian i'n **dod i ben** . . . [HUNAN 118]

My money was **running OUT**; [SOLVA 118]

. . . ac yng ngolau cannwyll gan fod **yr olew wedi gorffen** yn siopau'r pentref . . . [CYCHWYN 188]

. . . and reading by candlelight because the village shops had **run OUT of paraffin** . . . [BEGIN 190]

They lay together afterwards, he guiltily, and cursing the facts of his confusion and the fact that he had **run OUT of cigarettes** . . . [KNOTS 80]

Buont yn gorwedd ochr yn ochr wedyn, fo'n euog, ac yn ei regi'i hun am fod mor gymysglyd, ac **am beidio â gofalu fod ganddo gyflenwad o sigarennau** . . . [CHWERW 69]

Other English phrasal verbs which are quite often calqued directly into Welsh are *give up* (rendered as *rhoi i fyny*) and *find out* (rendered as *ffeindio allan*). In both of these cases as well, translators and writers often opt for native Welsh idioms instead of using the English-inspired idiom. For *give up*, in addition to *rhoi i fyny*, we see *rhoi heibio* and *rhoi'r gorau i*, as well as other context-specific equivalents like *taflu* and *torri*:

Mi welais na fedrwn i mo'th adael di'n llonydd na'th **roi di i fyny**. [MONICA 72]

I could see that I could neither leave you alone nor **give you UP**. [MONICA 73]

Rai blynyddoedd cyn diwedd ei oes, **wedi iddo roi heibio ffarmio**, aeth Nwncwl Josi i fyw at Jane ei ferch i'r Felin, Rhydcymerau, wrth ymyl y capel. [HDF 73]

Some years before the end of his life, **when he had given UP farming**, Uncle Josi went to live with his daughter Jane in Y Felin, beside the chapel. [OFH 88]

Erbyn cyrraedd Bangor y noson honno, cafodd fod Arthur, ei hen gyfaill yn yr ysgol, wedi **taflu** ei waith ymchwil ac wedi ymuno. [TRAED 161]

When he arrived in Bangor that night, he learned that Arthur, his old school friend, had **given UP** his research to join the forces. [FEET 143]

Gwell na gweld ei gafael ar ŵr ifancach lawer na hi yn darfod o ddydd i ddydd ydoedd **torri'r frwydr** yn awr. [MONICA 50]

Rather than see her hold on a much younger man grow weaker from one day to the next, it was better **to give UP the struggle** now. [MONICA 49–50]

'You would be a lot better off, Miss Honey [...] if you **gave UP** your job and drew unemployment money.' [MAT 204]

'Fe fyddech chi'n llawer gwell eich byd, Miss honey [...] petaech chi'n **rhoi'r gorau** i'ch swydd ac yn codi arian diweithdra.' [MAT 198]

And for *to find out*, the translation equivalents are numerous. In addition to *cael gwybod*, which is by far the most common in our corpus, *darganfod, dod i wybod*, and *cael allan* are also used where English has *to find out*:

Cododd Abel ar ei draed; ac er nad oeddwn ond hogyn, gwyddwn os gallai rhywun **gael allan** a oedd marworyn o'r tân Dwyfol wedi disgyn i enaid Thomas a Barbara mai Abel oedd yr un hwnnw ... [RHYS 174]

Abel got upon his feet. Although but a lad, I knew that if anyone could **find OUT** whether a spark of the divine fire had descended upon the souls of Thomas and Barbara, it was Abel. [RHYS 167]

'Especially not when you know I'd **find OUT** anyway.' [...] 'As I expect you'll also **be finding out**.' [TIME 30]

'Yn arbennig gan eich bod yn gwybod y bydda i'n **ffeindio allan** beth bynnag.' [...] 'A dw i 'di bod yn y fan 'ma, ar y *premises*, ers chwech heno. Fel y **cewch wybod**, mae'n debyg.' [AMSER 47]

There was a mystery here in this house, a great mystery, there was no doubt about that, and Matilda was longing to **find out** what it was. [MAT 191]

Roedd dirgelwch yma yn y tŷ hwn, dirgelwch mawr, doedd dim dwywaith am hynny, ac roedd Matilda'n ysu am **gael gwybod** beth oedd e. [MAT 185]

I **found out** something about him. [STONE 238]

Dwi wedi **darganfod** rhywbeth yn ei gylch o. [MAEN 151]

I **found out** who owned it. [MAT 202]

Fe **ddes i wybod** pwy oedd yn berchen arno. [MAT 196]

A last example of this kind involves *to put up with (someone or something)*, often rendered literally as *rhoi i fyny gyda* (or *efo*), but other formulations are found such as *dygymod â* and *dioddef*:

A bu'n rhaid iddi **roi i fyny efo** lot fawr o dynnu coes hefyd – yn enwedig gan Sam Bach, yr ienga ohonyn nhw. [LLADD 143]

*And he had to **put UP WITH** a lot of leg-pulling also – especially from Little Sam, the youngest of them.*

Bydd yn rhaid imi **ddygymod â** lliain arall yn fy llety, y mae'n debyg, a gwaith go anodd fydd hynny. [O LAW 106]

I suppose I shall have to **put UP WITH** another tablecloth at my lodgings, and I shall not find it easy to do that. [FROM 80]

Matilda longed for her parents to be good and loving and understanding and honourable and intelligent. The fact that they were none of these things was something she had **to put UP WITH**. [MAT 49]

Roedd Matilda yn dyheu am i'w rhieni fod yn dda ac yn gariadus ac yn llawn dealltwriaeth ac yn anrhydeddus ac yn ddeallus. Roedd yn rhaid iddi **ddioddef** y ffaith nad oedden nhw'n unrhyw un o'r pethau hyn. [MAT 43]

Before closing this chapter we will mention that a heavily anglicised style can often be achieved by treating the English verb as a borrowing, attaching a verb-noun ending to it (usually *-io*), and translating the particle into Welsh:

Craciodd pawb **i fyny** eto. [CRAWIA 78]

*Everyone **cracked UP** again.*

'Everybody says "come on!" here,' thought Alice, as she went slowly after it: 'I never was so **ordered ABOUT** before in all my life, never!' [ALICE 90]

'Mae pawb yn dweud "dowch!" yn y lle'ma,' meddyliodd Alys gan ei ddilyn yn araf. 'Chefais i 'rioed fy **ordro o gwmpas** fel hyn yn fy mywyd, naddo 'rioed!' [ALYS 92]

... yn sydyn, penderfynais fynd i lawr i gapel Siloam. Gyfeillion – rhyw **snecio i mewn** i'r sedd wrth y drws a wneuthum. [EI FFANFFER EI HUN 27]

*Suddenly, I decided to come down to Siloam Chapel. Friends, what I did was **sneak IN** to the seat.*

This would, of course, be unexpected in formal or literary style, but is unsurprising in informal dialogue.

6.5 Conclusions

The phrasal verb pattern has lent itself in English to extremely productive metaphorical and even idiomatic uses, in which the meaning of the verb-particle combination is not readily inferrable, or even not inferrable at all, from the meanings of the elements that make it up. In the context of intense contact with English, such metaphorical and idiomatic combinations have entered the Welsh language as well, and in Welsh writing of the twentieth and twenty-first century it is not uncommon to find even the most idiomatic English phrasal verb translated directly into Welsh. This is undoubtedly possible because it happened that Welsh was, like English, a satellite-framed language with an extensive system of directional particle that quite easily came to be identified in a one-to-one way with English particles.

The key for the Welsh stylist is to be aware that there are options. It can be helpful to observe that the options are, in fact, widely selected by other writers and translators instead of, or in addition to, literal translations of English idioms.

7

Cael and Get

7.0 Introduction

In contemporary spoken Welsh, at least as used by some speakers, the Welsh verb *cael* and the English verb *get* are not infrequently treated as translation equivalents of each other in an increasing number of contexts. It is certainly the case that there are uses in which this equation holds true, but in more standard varieties of Welsh it is by no means true in all uses. The purpose of this chapter is therefore to lay out the patterns found in the parallel corpus contrasting the major uses of *cael* and *get*.

Cael has numerous uses: first, it occurs as a full lexical verb generally meaning 'to acquire, receive, obtain', and in these uses Welsh *cael* and English *get* generally work as translation equivalents of each other. But lexical *cael* has several additional uses such as 'have, partake of (a meal, an item of food or drink)' where 'get' works less well in English or does not have quite the same meaning: *to have coffee (in the morning)* and *to get coffee* do not describe the same state of affairs, the former meaning 'I partake of coffee (i.e. I drink it)' and the latter meaning 'I fetch coffee (i.e. I go and get it, whether for my own consumption or for someone else's)'. These and other senses of lexical *cael* are covered in section 1.

Secondly, *cael* is used as a helping verb in two grammatical constructions: the colloquial passive, and the causative. Since English can construct both passives and causatives with *get*, it is quite likely that these uses may also have contributed to the perception that *cael* = *get*. These patterns are described briefly in section 2.

Thirdly, *cael* functions as a kind of modal verb to refer to having ability, opportunity, or permission, and it can also have a general future sense. Of these four, only the opportunity sense is conveyed with *get* in English, as we will see in section 3.

The English verb *get* has several intransitive uses not traditionally shared by Welsh *cael*. These include the meaning 'to become', e.g. *to get cold* (see section 4), and the use of *get* plus a directional particle to express a general verb of motion, e.g. *to get out of the house, to get into the car* (section 5). Finally in section 6, we briefly review some idiomatic expressions formulated using the verb *to get* in English.

7.1 The lexical verb 'cael'

The primary meaning of *cael* as a lexical verb is 'to get, receive, obtain (e.g. a material object)', that is, to come to have an object in one's possession. The English verb *get* is often found in this same group of uses, and indeed, it is probably because of this equivalence that speakers have sometimes equated *cael* and *get* in an ever-increasing number of contexts. The following examples illustrate this central use:

'**Un llythyr gefais i** oddi wrth ei dad o.' [CRYMAN 233]

'I did **receive a letter** from his father.' [SICKLE 202]

Mawn a losgai y mwyafrif y dyddiau hynny, a **chael bwyd** oedd y pwnc mawr. [CWM 10]

In those days the majority burnt peat, and the great problem was not fuel but how **to obtain food**. [GORSE 10]

Fel yr adroddwyd yn nechrau yr hanes hwn, byd mawr fu hi ar Nansi i **gael caban i drigo ynddo**, ac wedi ei gael, ni thalodd hi byth ffyrling o rent amdano . . . [GWEN 35]

As I have already said, Nansi found great difficulty in **getting another cottage**, but having secured one, she never paid a farthing's rent for it . . . [GWEN 40]

Cafodd dyn y *mail* bach **gôt goch**, a bu'r gôt goch yn yr ardal yn hir ar ôl i ddyn y *mail* bach ei throi heibio, yn cael ei phrynu a'i gwerthu gan y naill hogyn i'r llall. [CWM 193]

The driver of the little mail coach **got a new red coat** in celebration of the event, a coat that seemed to be everlasting for it changed hands from one lad to the other for years after the driver of the little mail car had done with it. [GORSE 187]

Roedd ganddyn nhw biano fawr yno nes i Dic fethu talu'r rhent a gorfod 'i gwerthu hi. Mi glywis i **na chafodd o fawr** amdani hi, chwaith. [OLAW 23]

They had a big piano there till Dick failed to pay the rent, and had to sell it. I heard that **he didn't get much** for it, either. [FROM HAND 8]

The thing that one 'gets' or 'obtains' with *cael* need not be a material object. It may be something more abstract such as a reaction, a word from someone, a lesson, a birthday, a day of pure triumph or a first view of something, as in the examples below. The English renderings generally involve either *have* or *get*; quite often, either one would be possible:

'Gwraig Madog Morris ddaru'i bedyddio hi, a **'chafodd llong erioed y fath 'Hwrê!'** ag a gafodd y *Maid.*' [CHWAL 118]	The wife of Madoc Morris christened her, and no ship ever **got such a big 'Hooray!'** as the Maid did. [OUT 124]
Ni châi neb air ganddo, ers oriau – a finnau'n synnu beth oedd yn bod arno, mor wahanol i arfer. [HDF 188]	**No one had got a word from him** for hours, and I wondered what on earth was the matter with him, he was so different from his usual self. [OFH 236]
. . . ryw fis cyn i mi **gael fy mhen blwydd cyntaf.** [HDF 64]	. . . a month or so before my first birthday. [OFH 77] [lit. before **I had my first birthday**]
. . . **yr unig ddydd o orfoledd digymysg a gefais** yn fy mywyd. [MONICA 35]	. . . **the only day of pure triumph I've had** in my whole life. [MONICA 33]
Yr olwg gyntaf a gafodd yr ymfudwyr o Ddolgellau ar eu cartref newydd oedd tir gwastad Philadelphia [RHANDIR 98]	**The first view the Dolgellau settlers had** of their new home was the rain pouring down on the lowlands of Philadelphia [FAIR 97]

An extension from the central sense of receiving or obtaining, where *cael* and *get* are both quite usual, adds a result, e.g. 'to get a ring off a finger', 'to get the answers right', where 'off a finger' and 'right' describe the desired state of the object as a result of 'getting' it:

Wedi i'r ddau y tu allan hen gyrraedd pen eu tennyn ac yn awyddus i'w heglu hi (ac wedi i Ibn **gael y fodrwy werthfawr yn rhydd**) penderfynodd ei bod hi'n bryd manteisio ar y syniad a gafodd. [PLA 88]	The other two were frantic with impatience, longing to get out. And at last Salah **wrenched the ring from the dead prelate's finger**, and embarked on stage two of his private plan. [PEST 69] [lit . . . **got the expensive ring free**]
She would never let them copy ('How will you learn?'), but by	Gwrthodai adael iddyn nhw gopïo ('Ddysgech chi byth'), ond drwy

asking her to read it through, they **got the right answers** anyway. [STONE 225]	ofyn iddi hi ddarllen drwyddo, roedden nhw'n **cael yr atebion yn gywir** beth bynnag. [MAEN 143] [lit. . . . **got the answers right**]

In a few uses of lexical *cael* we see that English *get* is not generally possible. This is true, for instance, when the complement refers to a meal or an item of food or drink. In this sense, English normally uses *to have (a meal, a beverage, a dish)*:[1]

Arhosodd Greta yn ei gwely nes bod y lleill wedi **cael eu brecwast**. [CRYMAN 236]	Greta had stayed in bed until the others **had their breakfast**. [SICKLE 205]
I'd earlier **had a curry**. It made me thirsty. [VICT 52]	Ro'n i wedi **cael cyri i swper** ac roedd hwnnw wedi codi syched arno i. [LLINYN 60]

The use of *get* with such complements generally means 'obtain or prepare (food or drink)', either for oneself or someone else, rather than 'partake of' it. The Welsh original in such cases is not *cael* but *gwneud* 'make' or *paratoi* 'prepare':

. . . brysiwn yn ôl i'r tŷ i gynorthwyo fy nhad i glirio'r bwrdd a **pharatoi cwpanaid o de** a thamaid o swper i'm mam. [OLAW 118]	. . . to help my father clear the table and **get a cup of tea** and a bit of supper for my mother. [FROM HAND 91]

Richard Ruck's translation of the dialogues in the novel *Chwalfa* hews very close to Welsh word choice and sentence structure as a way of reminding the reader that the characters were speaking Welsh. In the following example we see both the use of 'get' where 'have' would be more usual in English, and a fronting construction (for the discussion of which see Chapter 11):

'Te go sâl gewch chi, mae arna' i ofn,' ymddiheurodd i'r dieithryn . . . [CHWAL 29]	'A **very poor tea you'll get**,' I'm afraid,' she told the stranger apologetically . . . [OUT 29]

[1] Note however that certain command forms common in English such as *Have a good meal*, as also with other expression such as *Have a good time*, do not use *cael* in Welsh. Rather, one would get *Mwynhewch y pryd o fwyd*.

The final two examples in this section differ significantly in that, whereas in all of the preceding cases the grammatical subject is the 'receiver' or 'obtainer', in the following examples of 'to have an influence' / 'to have an effect', the grammatical subject is not the recipient but rather the source of the effect or influence.

Digwyddodd dau beth mawr iddo yn yr ysgol, pethau a **gafodd fwy o ddylanwad arno** na'r addysg a gafodd yno – ei garwriaeth â Gwen, merch Doli Rhyd Garreg, a'i gyfeillgarwch â Thwm ei frawd. [TRAED 67]

Two great things happened to him at the school, things that **influenced him more** than the formal education he received there – falling in love with Gwen, Doli Rhyd Garreg's daughter, and the close bond which developed between him and his brother Twm. [FEET 60]

Manylais ar hyn oblegid **yr effaith ryfedd a gafodd ei agwedd** ar y bechgyn; [WILLAT 34]

*I have gone into detail about this because of the strange **effect that his attitude had** on the boys;*

In this use, *get* is not a possible choice.

7.2 *Cael* in the passive and the causative

The verb *cael* in used in constructing the informal passive (see also Chapter 5):

Cafodd cannoedd ar filoedd o bobol **eu gadael** yn sownd ar yr ynys drwy'r nos. [HUNAN 194]

Hundreds of thousands **were left** stranded on the island all night. [SOLVA 194]

I can't think there could be any doubt about his identity when **he was found dead** by a neighbour who knew him by sight. [TIME 104–5]

Fedra i ddim meddwl fod 'na unrhyw amheuaeth ac yntau **wedi cael 'i ddarganfod yn farw** gan gymydog oedd yn 'i nabod o'n iawn o ran ei weld. [AMSER 167]

One of the relevant points here is that, as we see in the English versions of the two examples, the English passive can use *to be* or *to get* as an auxiliary; the *get*-passive contributes overall to the interlingual identification *cael* = *get*.

The causative is the construction in which one *makes, gets, or has someone do something*, and in English all three of the above verbs are commonly found in this construction. In Welsh, *cael*, *gwneud* and occasionally *peri* 'to cause' are used to construct the causative, so this is another usage in which *cael* and *get* are both possible.

There are two slightly different patterns for using *cael* as a causative verb. The first takes the shape *cael rhywun i wneud rhywbeth*, where the person being made to do something is the direct object of *cael*, and the thing he or she is made to do appears as a verb-noun after the preposition *i*:

Fe fynnai fynd i chwilio am Winni **a chael ei mam i ofyn iddi ddŵad i de** efo digon o jeli, er mwyn ei chlywed yn siarad. [TE 46]	She would go and find Winni. Then **she'd ask her mother to ask Winni to tea**, and plenty of jelly, just to hear her talk. [TEA 44]
Gwichymbil pwyllgorddyn a oedd wedi hen arfer ennill dadl <u>a chael pobol i ochri ag o</u>. [PLA 159]	*The wheezing entreaty of a councilman who was quite used to winning arguments and **getting people to side with him**.*

The second construction found more often in more formal styles follows the pattern *cael gan rywun (i) wneud rhywbeth*, where the person being made to do something is the object of the preposition *gan*, and the verb-noun is variably preceded or not by the preposition *i*:

... a chanddo'r ddawn i **gael gan eraill i gydweithio**'n ewyllysgar ag ef ... [HDF 75]	... with a gift for **getting others to cooperate** willingly ... [OFH 90]
Medrodd **gael gan Owen ddyfod** unwaith neu ddwy ... [TRAED 85]	He managed **to persuade Owen to go with him** once or twice [FEET 70]

There are also reduced causatives, in which one can *get something done* or *have something done* without naming the agent. Here too, two patterns are attested: *cael* + VERB-NOUN + DIRECT OBJECT, and *cael rhywbeth wedi ei* + VERB-NOUN:

'Do I look very pale?' said Tweedledum, coming up **to have his helmet tied on.** [THRO 170]	'Ydw i'n edrych yn welw?' gofynnodd Twidl-dwm, yn dod ati i **gael clymu ei helm ar ei ben.** [TRWY 58]
You'll have to **have it dyed** black. [MAT 65]	Fe fydd rhaid i ti **ei gael e wedi'i liwio**'n ddu. [MAT 58]

The second of the two patterns, though widely used, might be criticised as an Anglicism.

The last three examples in this section show the causative with verbs other than *cael*, namely *peri* (*peri i rywun wneud rhywbeth*) and *gwneud* (*gwneud i rywun wneud rhywbeth*):

Ond yr oedd swyn yn y geiriau, ac yn sŵn eu treigl, a **barodd i mi'n gynnar garu'r iaith**, a dechrau ymglywed â rhin ei chyfoeth dihenydd. [HDF 101]	But the words and the sound of them as they ran along had a charm for me that **led me early to love the language** and to begin to listen to the magic of its ageless wealth. [OFH 124]
Dechreuodd y Gannwyll guro ei gefn yn galed ond **gwnaeth hyn iddo besychu**'n ffyrnig. [PLA 175]	*The Candle began to strike his back hard but **this made him cough** fiercely.*
How are your ears, Eric, after your last encounter with Miss Trunchbull?' **'She stretched them,'** Eric said. 'My mother says she's positive they're bigger than they were.' [MAT 215]	'Sut mae dy glustiau di, Eric, ar ôl i ti gyfarfod â Miss Trunchbull y tro diwethaf?' **'Fe wnaeth hi iddyn nhw ymestyn,'** meddai Eric. 'Mae fy mam yn dweud ei bod hi'n bendant eu bod nhw'n fwy nag oedden nhw.' [MAT 209]

7.3 *Cael* as a modal verb

Cael often takes a verb-noun complement, in which case it can be considered a modal verb. Modal functions of *cael* are of at least four types: the expression of ability, permission, opportunity, or futurity. These four categories are not rigidly distinct and two or more uses may be present in a single occurrence, but it is still useful to illustrate them separately. We will see that a final group of modal uses of *cael* is generally not even translated into English at all.

To begin, then, *cael* may express ability; in this use it is roughly synonymous with *gallu*. The following examples are about ability to see (by leaving the curtains open, or by holding something up close because the light is poor), and inability to work because of sickness:

'Paid â thynnu'r llenni ynteu [. . .] Mi **gaf wylio** drwy'r ffenestr os na	'Don't close the curtains, will you? [. . .] **I'll be able** to look out of the

allaf i gysgu, ac wedyn mi anghofiaf yr oriau.' [MONICA 7]

window if I can't sleep, and then I shan't notice the hours passing.' [MONICA 6]

Cododd un darn o bapur **er mwyn cael ei weld yn well** yn yr hanner tywyllwch. [RHANDIR 29]

She lifted up one sheet of paper **in order to see it better** in the semi-darkness. [FAIR 28]

Ni **châi** ei gŵr **weithio** am wythnosau, dôi arian ei glwb i lawr, ac ar ôl hynny ni allai weithio'n galed. [TRAED 30]

Her husband **would not be able** to work for weeks, the money from the club would be cut, and after that he would not be able to work at full pace. [FEET 26]

Closely related to having the ability to do something is having the opportunity to do it, that is, 'getting' to do it. For this reading, the verb *get* is quite usual in English, whereas it is impossible for the ability reading. (If *get* were used in any of the above, the example would cease to be about ability and would be understood, rather anomalously, to be about opportunity).

Weles i mohonyn nhw ym Manceinion a **ches i ddim recordio** dim mwy ar gyfer *Y Dydd*. [HUNAN 154]

I didn't get to see them in Manchester and **I didn't get to record** any more for the programme. [SOLVA 154]

A dyna sut ro'n i am **gael gweld** y plant. [HUNAN 279]

This was how I **got to see** the children. [SOLVA 279]

Os nad oedd arian i'w cael am weinyddu'r ddwy swydd cawn fraint a werthfawrogwn yn fwy hyd yn oed nag arian – **cael defnyddio'r meicroscop** bryd y mynnwn heb neb i aflonyddu arnaf. [WILLAT 33]

If there was no money to be had for these these two jobs I got a privilege which I valued even more than money – **getting to use the microscope** *when I wanted without anyone bothering me.*

The following example makes the opportunity reading unusually explicit in translation:

Yr oedd y lobi'n dywyll, ac yr oedd y plant mwyaf wrth eu bodd yn **cael pinsio'i gilydd** a sticio pinnau yn ei gilydd, a phan ddaeth dyn yno i'w gwylio fe sticiwyd pin yn hwnnw hefyd. [TRAED 34]

The porch was dark and the older children welcomed **the opportunity to pinch** and stick pins into each other, and when a man came to look after them they stuck a pin in him too. [FEET 31]

But quite often the translations are similar to those for the ability reading in using *can* or *could*, and only the context reveals that we are dealing here more with opportunity than ability:

Ei bwriad cyntaf oedd mynd yn ôl i'w gwely er mwyn **cael crio'n iawn** a rhoi ei phen o dan y dillad. [TE 9]	Her first thought was to go back to bed, where she **could cry her heart out**, with her head under the bedclothes. [TEA 13]
Bwytâi'r bechgyn ar eu traed heb dynnu eu cotiau er mwyn **cael brysio allan** drachefn. [TRAED 31]	The boys would eat standing up without taking their coats off so that they **could hurry out** again. [FEET 28]
Eisio i chi fynnu cael golchi 'i ddillad o a'ch dillad ych hun, Winni, dim ods beth ddyfyd ych mam, er mwyn i chi **gael mynd** o gwmpas yn o ddel. [TE 58]	You ought to insist on washing his clothes, and your own too, never mind what she says, so that you **can go about** looking tidy. [TEA 54]

More often than not, the *cael* of opportunity is simply not represented at all in the English text. Adding a form of *get to* would sometimes be possible without doing violence to the meaning; for instance, the first example below could easily have been translated as *getting to come home*. But in most cases, adding *get* to these examples would feel superfluous:

Er difyrred oedd Bangor, ac er bod y tymhorau cyflym yn feddwol gan firi, yr oedd **cael dod adref** i Leifior bob tro yn hyfrydwch ar wahân. [CRYMAN 165]	However pleasant life was in Bangor, and though the terms slipped by with fun and high jinks, **coming home** to Lleifior was always a special delight. [SICKLE 136]
. . . teimlwn ar yr un pryd mor hyfryd fuasai gennyf **gael darllen hanes** dyn cyffredin . . . [RHYS 4]	I, at the same time, felt how delightful it would be **to read the history** of a commonplace man . . . [RHYS 9]
Bywyd caled oedd bywyd y gwŷr hyn, ar y cyfan. Eu tâl pennaf ydoedd **cael gweld y byd**. [HDF 147]	These men had a hard life, on the whole. Their principal remuneration was **seeing the world**. [OFH 184]
Ond wedi cyrraedd y tŷ **a chael eistedd yn y gadair**, dechreuodd meddwl Begw weithio ar yr hyn a	But when she got into the house **and sat down**, Begw's mind began to dwell on what she had heard her

glywsai ei mam yn ei ddweud am fam Winni. [TE 46]

mother say about Winni's mother. [TEA 44]

Os oedd Ifan yn mynd i farw, ei dymuniad oedd **cael bod yno** 'i hunan efo fo. [TRAED 28]

If Ifan was going to die, her one wish was **to be** alone with him. [FEET 25]

An element present in almost all of the above examples, and which is suggested by the term 'opportunity', is that the activity in question is something that the grammatical subject wants to do or finds desirable. Put differently, all of the examples so far involve intentionality. But this may not be a necessary component, as the following example suggests:

Buasai wrth ei bodd yn ei gweld yn fflamio – **y ddol yn cael mynd i'r 'tân mawr'** ac nid Begw – y hi a'i hen wyneb paent, hyll. [TE 9–10]

She'd like to see it burning, **the doll in hell-fire** instead of Begw, the doll with her ugly painted face. [TEA 13]

It seems quite unlikely that the doll, if it were capable of wanting anything, would want to be in hell-fire in Begw's place; rather, it is Begw that wants this to happen.

Thirdly, *cael* is the modal used for requesting, granting, or talking about permission. Sometimes this comes out clearly in the English as well, by using the modal *may* or the expression *be allowed to*:

Un prynhawn Sul yn yr haf yr oeddwn yn **cael aros adref** i fendio'r annwyd; [HENAT 113]

One Sunday afternoon in summer **I had been allowed to stay at home** to cure a cold; [LOCUST 98]

Cofiai am fore Llun yn niwedd Gorffennaf a'r ysgol newydd dorri ac yntau'n fawr ei siom **am na châi fynd** i'r chwarel. [CYCHWYN 11]

He remembered a Monday morning at the end of July when the school had just broken up, and his bitter disappointment at **not being allowed to start work** in the quarry. [BEGIN 9]

May I ask something of you that is perhaps not asked by a woman? [TIME 36]

Ga i ofyn rhywbeth iti . . . rhywbeth nad ydi dynes yn arfer 'i ofyn? [AMSER 56]

I wish to heavens **I was still allowed to use** the birch and belt as **I did** in the good old days! [MAT 89]

Trueni mawr nad ydw i'n **cael defnyddio'r gansen a'r gwregys** fel roeddwn i'n **cael gwneud** yn yr hen ddyddiau da! [MAT 83]

In other cases, *can* and *could* are used, not to talk about ability or opportunity in this case, but about permission, a common (albeit prescriptively criticised) usage:

"'R ydw i'n dŵad efo chi i'r mynydd,' meddai.   'I'm coming with you up the mountain,' she said.

'Pwy ddeudodd y **caech chi ddŵad**?' meddai Mair. [TE 38]   'Who said you **could**?' asked Mair. [TEA 38]

'Neville, you **can look**!' Ron said. [STONE 237]   'Nefydd, **gei di edrych** rŵan!' meddai Ron. [MAEN 150]

The denial of permission may also be conveyed with an implicit order, phrased as though it were a declarative ('no one leaves the table' clearly has the intended meaning 'no one may leave the table'). The Welsh translator of *Matilda* made this more explicit by inserting *cael*:

'Supper is a family gathering and no one **leaves** the table till it's over!' [MAT 28]   'Rhywbeth i'r teulu yw swper a does neb yn **cael gadael y bwrdd** nes ein bod ni wedi gorffen!' [MAT 22]

Fourthly, there are numerous examples of *cael* as a modal where the English parallel text focuses not on ability, opportunity or permission, but simply futurity, thus using *shall* or *will* (*'ll*):

Mi fydd hi'n goblyn o ffrae yma mewn munud, **gei di weld** . . . [NOS 12]   There'll be a hell of a row here in a minute, **you'll see**. . . [NIGHT 5]

'Be wyddost ti am Gymreigio geiriau?' meddai Wiliam. "Rwyt ti'n rhy fechan.' '**Mi gei weld** toc,' meddai Owen. [TRAED 34]   'What do you know about it?' said William. 'You're far too young.' '**You'll soon see**,' said Owen. [FEET 31]

'Wel,' meddai ei wraig, 'mi **gaiff Owen fynd** i'r Ysgol Ganolraddol, petai ddim ond i bryfocio Doli Rhyd Garreg.' [TRAED 50]   'Well,' said his wife, '**Owen shall go** to the County School, if it's only to spite Doli Rhyd Garreg.' [FEET 44]

Estyn y *draughts* 'na imi **gael rhoi** cweir i'th dad a thitha hefo'ch gilydd. [O LAW 71]   Fetch that draughts board there, and **I'll lick** you and your father together. [FROM 49]

. . . so either way **I'll get into the garden**, and I don't care which happens! [ALICE 25]	Felly, sut bynnag y bydd hi, **mi gaf fynd i mewn i'r ardd**, a dydi o ddim o bwys gen i p'run a ddigwydd! [ALYS II 14]

A rather striking feature of Welsh writing, particularly when compared with English via a parallel corpus, is the large number of instances in which modal *cael* is not only left untranslated, but no possible translation even suggests itself.

Yn y fan yna y **cafodd Ifan egluro** i'w wraig mai hon oedd Doli Rhyd Garreg, y bu'n ei chanlyn ac yn meddwl ei phriodi rywdro. [TRAED 11]	**Ifan explained** that this was Doli Rhyd Garreg, whom he once went out with and was going to marry. [FEET 10]
Pan oedd Begw yn meddwl pa bryd y **caent ddechrau** ar eu te, dyma Winni yn dechrau arni wedyn. [TE 41]	Just as Begw was thinking of **starting** with her tea, Winni began talking again. [TEA 40]
Eisio i chi fynnu **cael golchi 'i ddillad** o a'ch dillad ych hun, Winni, dim ods beth ddyfyd ych mam, er mwyn i chi gael mynd o gwmpas yn o ddel. [TE 58]	You ought to insist on **washing** his clothes, and your own too, never mind what she says, so that you can go about looking tidy. [TEA 54]
. . . teimlwn ar yr un pryd mor hyfryd fuasai gennyf **gael darllen** hanes dyn cyffredin . . . [RHYS 4]	I, at the same time, felt how delightful it would be **to read** the history of a commonplace man . . . [RHYS 9]
'Nid o *gariad* yr anfones i'r arian, ond er mwyn **cael teimlo**'n gleniach.' [CRYMAN 233]	'I didn't send the money out of love, but in order **to feel** kinder in myself.' [SICKLE 203]
Deuai arian y moch i dalu'r dreth a llog yr arian a fenthyciwyd i brynu eu tyddyn, ac weithiau medrent dalu ychydig o'r hawl o'r cyflog. Rhyw ddiwrnod **caent orffen talu hwnnw**, a byddai'r tyddyn yn eiddo iddynt. [TRAED 24]	The money from the pigs came to pay the rates and the interest on the money they borrowed to buy the smallholding. Sometimes they managed to pay back some of the capital from the wages. One day they **would repay it all** and the property would be theirs. [FEET 21]

Fydda i ddim byw'n hir, a **waeth iti gael peidio â thalu'r rheina**, mwy nag inni adael yr arian iti ar ein holau. [TRAED 159]	I shan't live long, and **you might as well not repay the debt** as for us to leave the money to you when we're gone. [FEET 141]

It is difficult to say exactly what purpose *cael* serves in these cases, but they are not obviously about waiting for or seizing an opportunity. For instance, in *Te yn y Grug*, Begw can start on her tea whenever she wants—she is not waiting for circumstances to create the right opportunity. And in the two examples from *Traed mewn Cyffion*, 'getting' to repay the debts would not serve the purpose at all; the point involves actually repaying them.

The use of *cael* seen here is, however, part of the general tendency in Modern Welsh to prefer periphrastic (or analytic) verb forms over synthetic ones, which is the same tendency seen, for instance, in rendering the preterite with an auxiliary plus verb-noun (e.g. *ddaru mi fynd* or *wnes i fynd* in place of *es i*. These patterns were discussed in Chapter 5). The occurrence of *cael* as a modal with a minimal semantic contribution must be seen, at least in part, in connection with this larger tendency of present-day Welsh.

We turn our attention now to particular uses of English *get* which are not traditionally rendered with *cael* in Welsh. What the criticised uses have in common is largely a problem of transitivity; English *get* has both transitive and intransitive uses, whereas *cael* is historically a transitive verb only.

7.4 *To get* meaning 'to become'

The first intransitive use of *get* not traditionally shared by *cael* is the sense 'to become', for which the use of *cael* is occasionally heard today, though it is absent in careful styles and written Welsh. The most common way to render 'become' in Welsh is *mynd yn* + adjective:

Ro'n i'n bedair ar ddeg oed ac roedd bywyd yn dechre **mynd yn ddifrifol**. [HUNAN 57]	I was fourteen years old and life was beginning to **get serious**. [SOLVA 57]
The confusion **got worse** every moment . . . [THRO 195–6]	**Aeth** y dryswch **yn waeth** bob munud . . . [TRWY 86]
However, the egg only **got larger and larger** [THRO 183]	Sut bynnag, y cwbl a wnaeth yr wy oedd **mynd yn fwy ac yn fwy** . . . [TRWY 72]

In other cases, a context-specific alternative is found such as *troi yn oer* 'to get cold / turn cold (of the weather)':

'Only it **got so cold**, and it snowed so, they had to leave off.' [THRO 128]	'Ond **fe drodd mor oer**, a bwrw eira gymaint fel y bu rhaid iddyn nhw roi'r gorau iddi.' [TRWY 14]

Frequently, though, Welsh can convey the meaning 'become' using a simplex verb derived from an adjective, such as *meddwi* 'get drunk' (from *meddw* 'drunk'), *teneuo* 'to grow thinner' (from *tenau* 'thin') or *cochi* 'to redden, turn red, become red' (from *coch* ' red'):

... ac yn trial gwneud iawn am yr amser oedd wedi'i fradu yn **meddwi** hyd a lled De Cymru ... [HUNAN 112]	... and trying to make up for time wasted **getting drunk** around south Wales ... [SOLVA 112]
In the weeks that followed he did seem to be **getting paler and thinner**, but it didn't look as though he'd cracked yet. [STONE 282]	Yn yr wythnosau dilynol ymddangosai fel petai'n **gwelwi ac yn teneuo** o ddydd i ddydd, ond doedd dim golwg ildio arno. [MAEN 181]
I'm sure the woods look sleepy in the autumn, when the leaves **are getting brown**. [THRO 130]	Rwy'n siwr fod y goedwig yn **edrych yn gysglyd** yn yr hydref pan yw'r dail yn **cochi**. [TRWY 16]

Unlike the intransitive use of *get* meaning 'become', the related transitive use *get someone or something* (*prepared, ready, undressed, made up*, etc.) can accommodate *cael* in Welsh:

Diolchodd fy mam yn gynnes iawn iddo, ac addawodd y cawn fyned cyn gynted ag y gallai hi **fy nghael yn barod**. [CWM 191]	My mother was grateful and promised that I should go as soon as I could be got ready, and off she went **to see to my clothes**. [GORSE 183] [lit. ... **to get me ready**]

7.5 *To get* as a motion verb

A second group of uses of *get* that sometimes cause problems in Welsh translation is its use coupled with a directional particle or phrase which together function as a kind of motion verb. Here too, it is important to distinguish between transitive uses (*get the child into the car, get the box down the stairs*) and intransitive uses (*get into the car, get down the stairs, get in, get down*). For the transitive uses, it is often possible to use *cael*, though the parallel corpus reveals a mixture of occurrences of *cael* and other semantically richer verbs. The following table lists some of the major transitive combinations, followed by examples from the parallel corpus, some of which use *cael*, and others a semantically richer verb such as *cludo* 'transport' or *tynnu* 'pull, draw':

get sth. through	Cyrhaeddodd y lan yn hwylus ac fe **gludwyd y casgenni**'n llafurus trwy'r wig hyd nes y daeth pentref di-nod – rhyw lond dwrn o hofeldai ac eglwys – i'r golwg. [PLA 62]	They reached the shore and after beaching the boats, laboriously **got the casks through the woods**. The village, when it came into sight, looked unremarkable, a mere handful of hovels clustered round the church. [PEST 47]
get sth. out	Haigha took a large cake out of the bag, and gave it to Alice to hold, while **he got out a dish** and carving-knife. [THRO 202]	Cymerodd Dahur deisen fawr allan o'r bag a'i rhoi i Alys i'w dal tra **tynnodd** yntau **allan** ddysgl a chyllell gig. [TRWY 94]
	She opened the bag and **got out a powder compact** that had a small round mirror on the inside of the lid. [MAT 62]	Agorodd y bag a **thynnu** blwch powdr oedd â drych y tu mewn i'r clawr. [MAT 56]
	Bu deirgwaith o dan gwymp. Mae'n debyg, a thunelli o gerrig ar ei ben – a'i gydweithwyr **yn ei gael allan yn fyw** bob tro, rywsut, a hynny heb iddo dorri'r un asgwrn . . . [CHWECH 100]	*Three times he had been under a fall of rubble. With a ton of stones on his head, and his co-workers **getting him out alive** each time, somehow, without his breaking a single bone . . .*
	'Mae o'n cachu ar 'y mhen i, siŵr! **Cael fi allan o'r ffordd**, a gwneud enw iddo fo'i hun . .' [CRAWIA 231]	*He's shitting on me, sure! **Getting me out of the way**, and making a name for himself. . .*

get sth. out (contd.)	Holmes turned to his desk, and unlocking it, **drew out a small case-book** which he consulted. [BAND 210]	Trodd Holmes tuag at ei ddesg, ac ar ôl datgloi'r clawr **estynnodd lyfryn bychan ohoni** a gynhwysai fanylion achosion blaenorol a phori ynddo. [CYLCH 16]
get sth. in	It took some little time **to fit the key into the lock**, but that was the last problem. [UNSUIT 156]	Ei thasg olaf oedd **cael yr allwedd i mewn i'r clo**. [GORTYN 200]
get sth. back	Oni ddylwn inne **gael yn ôl yr arian** a wariwyd gennyf fi? [RHANDIR 51]	Should not I too **get back the money** spent by me? [FAIR 51]
get sth. off	At breakfast Matilda said to him, 'You *must* try **to get those bits off your forehead**, daddy. It looks as though you've got little brown insects crawling about all over you. People will think you've got lice.' [MAT 37]	Amser brecwast meddai Matilda wrtho, 'Rhaid i ti geisio **cael gwared ar y darnau oddi ar dy dalcen**, Dad. Mae'n edrych fel tasai pryfed bach brown yn cropian drosot ti i gyd. Fe fydd pobl yn meddwl bod gyda ti lau pen.' [MAT 31]
	Ond roedd rhaid iddo'i **gael o ffwrdd o'i feddwl**. [CRAWIA 208]	*But he had **to get it off his mind**.*

The next groups of examples illustrate the intransitive use. Indeed, *cael* is occasionally attested here:

Wedi inni ein dau **gael i mewn i gegin y Tŷ Cerrig**, 'Dowch ymlaen eich dau' gwaeddodd yr hen ŵr a'i lygaid yn pefrio gan ddiddordeb. [WILLAT 107]	*After the two of us **got into the kitchen** of the Stone House, the old man shouted, 'Come along, you two,' his eyes sparkling with interest.*

But it is highly unusual to find *cael* in intransitive uses in careful Welsh style (as reflected in its virtual absence from the literary corpus – the example above is an isolated case). Instead, one typically finds *mynd* or *dod*, as well as semantically richer verbs like *crwydro* 'to wander', *cychwyn* 'to set out', *dringo* 'to climb', *diengyd/dianc* 'to escape', etc.

get about	Daeth i gael blas ar **grwydro**, drwy fod breciau'n rhedeg i'r dref, ac âi'r trên o'r fan honno i'r fan a fynnid. [TRAED 91]	He developed a taste for **getting about**; there was a brake service to the town, and a train would take him anywhere from there. [FEET 82]
get around = **circulate, travel**	... the news did **get around**. [UNSUIT 162]	... aeth y newyddion **o gwmpas** fel tân gwyllt. [GORTYN 208]
get back = **return**	... pan **ddes i'n ôl** o'r gwaith neithiwr ... [FFYDD 205]	... when I got back from work yesterday ... [FAITH 143]
get beyond	'It would never do to say "How d'ye do?" *now*' she said to herself. 'We seem **to have got beyond that**, somehow.' [THRO 161]	'Wnâi hi byth mo'r tro i ddweud "Sut rydych chi?" *yn awr*', ebe hi wrthi'i hun. 'Rydyn ni **wedi mynd tu hwnt i hynny**, rywsut.' [TRWY 49]
get in(to) = **enter**	Please understand once and for all that I only saw them for a short while when they were **getting into the car**. [TIME 15]	Mae'n rhaid i chi ddeall ar unwaith ac am byth mai dim ond ychydig, tra'u bod nhw'n **mynd i fewn i'r car** y gwelais i nhw. [AMSER 23]
get off, get away (to)	If you're not hurt at all, you'd better **get off** to Gryffindor tower. [STONE 221]	Os nad ydych chi wedi brifo o gwbl, well i chi **ei throi hi** am Dŵr Llereurol. [MAEN 141]
	Mi gwelodd Mistar Huws o'n **cychwyn** ffordd arall, a fedra fo ddim ond ei gneud hi am y Weun neu Braich y ffordd honno. [NOS 35]	Mister Hughes saw him **getting off** in the opposite direction, and he could only be making for the Waun or the Braich that way. [NIGHT 27]

get on (a team, a horse, etc.)

This time it was a White Knight. He drew up at Alice's side, and tumbled off his horse just as the Red Knight had done; then he **got on again**, and the two Knights sat and looked at each other for some time without speaking. [THRO 205]

Y tro hwn y Marchog Gwyn ydoedd. Arafodd a sefyll wrth ochr Alys a chwympo oddi ar ei farch yn union fel y gwnaeth y Marchog Coch. Yna **dringodd yn ôl** ac eisteddodd y ddau Farchog yn llygadu ei gilydd heb ddweud dim. [TRWY 98]

get out

Sut **cest ti ddwad allan**, Moi? Meddwn i. [NIGHT 34]

How did **you get out**, Moi? I said. [NIGHT 26]

He **got out of the car** to consult the other driver. [UNSUIT 156]

Aeth allan o'r car i ymgynhori â'r gyrrwr arall . . . [GORTYN 200]

Peth cynta welais i pan agorais i fy llgada a deffro bora wedyn oedd pry cop ar ffenast to yn treio **diengyd allan** trwy ffenast, a honno wedi cau. [NOS 181]

The first thing I saw when I woke up and opened my eyes next morning was a spider on the skylight trying **to get out** through the window, but it was closed. [NIGHT 154]

Wedi i'r ddau y tu allan hen gyrraedd pen eu tennyn ac yn awyddus **i'w heglu hi** . . . [PLA 88]

The other two were frantic with impatience, longing **to get out**. [PEST 69]

Roedd yn rhaid iddo'**i baglu hi** odd'ma cyn iddo dorri i grio o flaen y bastad esgeulus a eisteddai wrth y ddesg. [LLINYN 93]

He had **to get out** before he broke down in front of the incompetent bastard behind the desk. [VICT 82]

get to a place = arrive, reach

Ond **wedi cyrraedd y tŷ** a chael eistedd yn y gadair, dechreuodd meddwl Begw weithio ar yr hyn a glywsai ei mam yn ei ddweud am fam Winni. [TE 46]

But when **she got into the house** and sat down, Begw's mind began to dwell on what she had heard her mother say about Winni's mother. [TEA 44]

get there = **arrive**	For a heavyweight he'd moved fast **to get there** before me. [CIDER 126]	O ddyn o'i faint, mae'n rhaid ei fod wedi symud yn eithriadol o gyflym i **gyrraedd yno** o fy mlaen. [SEIDR 168]
get up (on his feet, out of bed, etc.)	**Codai**'n foreach, eisteddai'n hwyr ar ei draed yn darllen. [CRYMAN 98]	He **got up** earlier, and sat up late reading. [SICKLE 81]

7.6 Idioms involving *to get*

We close this chapter with a brief discussion of some idioms making use of *get* in English. As is always the case with idioms, the Welsh writer or translator must seek a stylistically and semantically appropriate equivalent idiom in such cases, rather than simply calquing the English idea.

*get away with = escape without punishment

[Y]m myd teledu, mae'na gwt hir o bobol wastad yn aros eu cyfle i gamu i le rhywun arall os ydyn nhw'n credu **na fydd hi ddim gwaeth arnyn nhw**! [HUNAN 264]

[I]n television there is always a long queue of people waiting to jump into the front man's shoes, if they think they can **get away with it**. [SOLVA 264]

. . . roedd o'n mynd i wneud yn siŵr nad oeddan nhw'n **cael getawê efo hi**. [CRAWIA 130]²

'*He was going to make sure they didn't get away with it.*'

'Since then, apart from **getting away with the charge** and the assault on me, he gives me the old two-fingered "up yours" when we see each other.' [TIME 99]

'Ers hynny, ar wahân i **gael ei draed yn rhydd** o'r cyhuddiad o ymosod arna i, mae o'n codi dau fys "ffwcio chdi'r cont" arna i pan 'dan ni'n gweld ein gilydd.' [AMSER 157]

'How can she **get *away* with it**?'
[. . .] 'Never do anything by halves if you want **to get away with it**.'
[MAT 117]

'Sut nad yw hi'n **cael ei chosbi** am hyn?' [. . .] 'Paid byth â hanner gwneud rhywbeth os wyt ti eisiau **osgoi cael dy gosbi**.' [MAT 111]

---

² This remarkable north Walian idiom (*cael getawê efo*) apparently seeks to have the best of both worlds, using both *cael* and English *get*.

*get back at – get s.o. = take revenge on

All they really wanted now was a way of **getting back at Malfoy** . . . [STONE 203]

Y cyfan roedden nhw am ei wneud yn awr oedd dod o hyd i ddull o **dalu'n ôl i Mallwyd** . . . [MAEN 129]

*get on – get along = manage

Rhedai Dafydd i lawr i Bonc Britannia bron bob awr ginio i weld sut y **deuai'i frawd ymlaen** ac i'w hyfforddi yn ei grefft, gan ddysgu iddo bopeth a wyddai ef. [CYCHWYN 71]

Dafydd would run down to Britannia Gallery almost every dinner-hour to see how **his brother was getting on** and to coach him in his work teaching him everything he himself knew. [BEGIN 71]

Meddyliai **sut hwyl a gâi**, tybed, ar dywydd mwll fel hyn. [TRAED 146]

She wondered **how he was getting on** in such sultry weather as this. [FEET 129]

'Mi ddaeth adra' o'r chwaral ganol dydd fel 'tai *o*, ac nid chi, oedd yn ista'r arholiad. "Sut mae o'n **bwrw drwyddi**, tybad?" medda' fo dro ar ôl tro amsar cinio, ar biga'r drain.' [CYCHWYN 200]

'He came home from the quarry midday as though he, and not you, was sitting the examination. He was like a cat on hot bricks at dinnertime and saying "How is he **getting on**, I wonder?" over and over again. [BEGIN 201]

*get on with = get along with

Roedden ni'n **cyd-daro** i'r dim ac yn cael blas mawr ar gwmni ein gilydd, a chyn bo hir ro'n i mewn cariad eto! [HUNAN 281]

We got on like a house on fire and enjoyed each other's company tremendously. [SOLVA 281]

Roedd hyn yn dân ar groen ei dad; roedd 'da fe wenwyn at ei fab, a dyna pam nad o'n nhw'n **cyd-dynnu**. [HUNAN 129]

This annoyed his father, who was jealous of his son, and that is why they did not **get on**. [SOLVA 128]

Roedd e ar ei flwyddyn derfynol yn stiwdio beintio Malthouse, ond heb fod yn **tynnu mlaen 'da'r tiwtoried** o gwbwl. [HUNAN 110]

He was in his final year at Malthouse's painting studio, and he was not **getting on with the tutors** at all. [SOLVA 110]

*to get over sth. = to recover

'Fedra 'i ddim **dŵad dros 'Nhad,**' meddai Nel. 'Fuo 'neb mwy *strict* na fo 'rioed. 'Roeddwn i ofn edrach ar hogyn pan fyddai o gwmpas, a dyna fo yn rhoi gwahoddiad i chi adra y tro cynta' iddo fo'ch cwarfod chi!' [O LAW 149]

'I can't **get over Dad,**' said Nell. 'There was never a more strict one than he is. I was frightened to look at a boy when he was about, and here he is, inviting you to come over to our home the first time he meets you!' [FROM 118–19]

Bydd yn rhaid iddi wahodd Archesgob Cymru ei hun i de er mwyn **gwella o'r sioc.** [MONICA 44]

She'll have to invite the Archbishop of Wales, no less, to tea, **to get over the shock.** [MONICA 43]

He breathed hard, thinking back to his days on the rock-strewn beach, **recovering** from his breakdown. [KNOTS 124]

Anadlodd yn galed, gan ei atgoffa'i hun am ei ddyddiau ar y traeth caregog, yn **dod ato'i hun** ar ôl ei salwch nerfol. [CHWERW 104]

*to get (someone) into trouble

... achos leiciwn i ddim **dŵad â neb i drwbwl.** [GWEN 24]

... because I don't like **to get people into trouble.** [GWEN 30]

... mae'n syndod na chafon ni unrhyw ddamweinie na **mynd i helynt** 'da'r gyfraith. [HUNAN 126]

... it was a miracle that we had neither accidents nor brushes with the law. [SOLVA 126]

Diflannais gyntaf y medrwn rhag ofn **dwyn Henry i drafferth.** [RHWNG 74]

I disappeared as quickly as I could lest I got Henry into trouble.

I'm not trying **to get you into trouble** [. . .] I don't want **to get Albert in trouble.** [TIME 134–5]

... dydw i ddim **isio'ch cael chi i drafferth** [. . .] Dydw i ddim isio **cael Albert i drafferth.** [AMSER 213]

I didn't **get into any kind of trouble.** [CIDER 19]

... wnes i ddim **mynd i drwbwl** na dim byd felly. [SEIDR 27]

Like English *get*, Welsh *cael* occurs in numerous collocations and idioms. Some of these are illustrated in Chapter 9, as part of a larger discussion of collocations.

7.7 Conclusions

In this chapter we have explored the Welsh verb *cael* and its most frequent English equivalent *get* with a view to sorting out in what uses they are true translation equivalents of one another, and in what uses other kinds of solutions are generally sought. Generally speaking, it emerges that transitive uses of *get* can, with only a few exceptions, be rendered using *cael*, although there are often other solutions as well; but intransitive uses of *get* cannot traditionally take *cael*, the latter being historically a transitive verb. We stress, as always, that it is up to the individual writer / translator / speaker of Welsh to decide what kind of Welsh to use; our purpose is primarily to draw attention to some of the issues and make the user of Welsh aware of some options.

The following table summarises the different uses of Welsh *cael* and indicates for each one whether *get* is a possible translation equivalent:

Lexical verb	1. To acquire, receive, obtain	*Get* is a common equivalent.
	2. To partake of a meal, food or drink	Generally *have*.
	3. Resultative cael	Generally *get*
Auxiliary	Passive	The English passive can use *to be* or *to get (bitten by a dog)*.
	Causative	The English causative uses *have*, *make* or *get (someone to do something)*.
Modal	1. Ability	Generally *can/could*.
	2. Opportunity	*Get* is possible and common; often, this modal use is not rendered in English.
	3. Permission	*May* or *can/could* are usual.
	4. Futurity	*Shall* or *will*.

Finally, in the last table, we indicate a few additional uses of English *get* and summarise whether Welsh *cael* is generally used this way or not.

Lexical verb	1. 'to become'	*Cael* is not traditionally possible here; instead, *mynd yn* + ADJ, or single-word equivalents e.g. *meddwi* 'to get drunk', *teneuo* 'to get thin'

Lexical verb (contd.)	2. (transitive verb of motion: e.g. *get the child into the car*)	*Cael* is attested in this use and is not infrequent; semantically richer verbs of motion are sometimes preferred solutions.
	3. (intransitive verb of motion: e.g. *get into the car*)	*Cael* is traditionally impossible since it is not an intransitive verb

8

Adjectives and Adverbs

8.1 Adjectives – Introduction

Adjectives in Welsh and English in general perform similar roles. They may have different forms based on gender and number in Welsh (although this is far from constant and should in general be viewed as an aspect which is not as productive as it once was in the language). The Welsh adjective usually follows whatever it is describing but may also occur prenominally which we discuss in 8.1.2. It is also possible for verb-nouns or nouns to be used as modifiers in Welsh e.g. *ystafell fyw* >>> *living* room and *ystafell wely* >>> *bedroom*. However our main concern in this chapter is the ways in which their use, for example as modifiers or intensifiers, differs between one language and the other. This will be discussed in particular through the lens of the translator. A particularly useful example of this is section 8.1.6 which deals with participial verb forms used as modifiers. These can often present the translator with a considerable challenge in Welsh. For example, the following line includes the two participial forms '*well-worn, patterned carpet*':

A couple of shabby mismatched easy chairs and the **well-worn patterned** carpet were manifestly the legal requirements of an apartment rented as fully furnished. [Time 22]	Prin ddigon oedd yr ychydig gadeiriau esmywth di-raen, nad oeddynt yn perthyn i set, a'r carped **patrymog treuliedig**, i gyfiawnhau rhentu'r fflat fel un oedd wedi ei ddodrefnu. [Amser 33]

The translator has opted here to go for (i) an adjective formed from the noun '*patrwm*' (*pattern*) by adding the adjectival suffix *-og* and (ii) an adjective formed by adding the *-edig* suffix to the verb-noun '*treulio*' (*to spend, to wear out*). However, it is not possible to use either of these strategies as universal ones. It is not possible to say **patrymedig* or **treuliog* even though *patrwm* can become the verb-noun *patrymu* and the noun *traul* gives the morphological base for *treulio*. The translator into Welsh does not, therefore, possess a blanket equivalent of the participial verb forms so frequently encountered in English.

The ways in which adjectives in Welsh can operate as modifiers merit specific attention as they can also present challenges when dealing with – especially long – strings of adverbial modifiers in English. Again, Welsh employs different strategies for dealing with these e.g. adjective + preposition 'o' + adjective >> *rhyfeddol o dda = amazingly good* or postposition >> *da ryfeddol*. However, none of these, again, can be applied to all possible circumstances. The principle linguistic strategies for these are outlined in 8.1.5 as well as giving attention to some of the more common preadjectival degree modifiers.

8.1.1 Agreements

Although many adjectives possess traditional feminine and/or plural forms,

gwyn   >>>   fem. *gwen*   >>>   plural *gwynion*

their use in contemporary Welsh is in decline.[1] Nevertheless, examples of them can be found as either predicate adjectives or topicalised adjectives agreeing with the gender and/or number of the noun which they describe. This occurs principally in very formal registers. Again, this predicative adjectival gender/number agreement is very infrequently attested in modern writing or translation.

Yr oedd y cyflogau'**n fychain**. [TRAED 56]

*The wages were **small**.* Bychan = small >>> plural: bychain.

... ac ar y parcdir goed derw preiffion â'u dail **yn drymion** drostynt. [CRYMAN 14]

... and some fine oak trees in full leaf. [SICKLE 9] Trwm = heavy >>> plural: trymion.

Nid oedd yr ymgom ond **ber**, sef fel y canlyn: [ENOC 218]

*The conversation was only **brief**, as follows:* Byr = short >>> feminine singular: ber

Bechan oedd yr ardd oedd tu cefn i'r tŷ ... [GWEN 2–3]

The garden at the back of the house was **small** ... [GWEN 10] Bychan = small >>> fem. singular: bechan

---

[1] See, for example, PWT 4.68.

Notwithstanding the above, it is still very much the case that adjectives following singular feminine nouns will take the soft mutation:

merch + bach	>>>	*merch fach*
tref + mawr	>>>	*tref fawr*
cadair + cyfforddus	>>>	*cadair gyfforddus*

In cases of multiple attributive adjectives, this soft mutation continues across all the adjectives as illustrated in the following examples from translations into Welsh:

... a **dullish black** crow. [TIME 39]

... fel brân **ddu ddiflas** yr olwg. [AMSER 60]

... the **large blue porcelain** water-jug. [MAT 160]

... y jwg ddŵr **las borslen**. [MAT 154]

... a **small country** station. [CIDER 26]

... gorsaf **fechan wledig** ... [SEIDR 36]

There is – in principle – no limit to the number of times this may occur:

Dynes **fawr, lawen, ffraeth, dreiddgar**, oedd fy modryb Marged ... [HENAT 34]

Auntie Margaret was **large of body, happy, ready of speech** and **keen of perception** ... [LOCUST 35]

However, the addition of a conjunction such as '*a*' [= *and*] will break the necessity to employ the soft mutation:

... ar ffarm **fras a gwastad**. [CHWECH 19]

... *on an **abundant and flat** farm*.

... hen wreigan **fechan, fain a dreng** oedd Siân Roberts. [WILLAT 130]

... *Siân Roberts was a **small, thin and morose** old little woman*.

The next example may appear contradictory but it should be remembered here that '*llachar*' actually describes the adjective '*glas* >> *las*' here not the noun '*côt*' and therefore, does not need to undergo a soft mutation.

Managing, as he usually did, to look like the owner of a with-it

Gyda'i siwt **las-lwyd**, ei grys pinc a'i dei fflamgoch o dan gôt **fawr**

boutique, he wore a **silver-grey** suit,
a pink shirt and a flaring red tie
beneath a **kingfisher-blue** overcoat.
[TIME 18]

las llachar, edrychai'n debyg
i berchennog bwtîc ffasiynol.
[AMSER 28]

8.1.2 Modifier word orders

The normal order in Welsh is Noun + Adjective. There are some adjectives
which usually occur prenominally (for example, *holl*, *prif*, *hen* etc.) but these
are very much the exception rather than the rule. As we have seen, in more
formal registers, some adjectives may have particular feminine and/or plural
forms although any adjective following a singular feminine noun will undergo
a soft mutation in all registers of Welsh.

8.1.2.i Prenominal adjectives

When any adjective is placed prenominally, the noun following it – irrespec-
tive of gender or number – will take a soft mutation:

dyn	>>>	*hen ddyn*
prif	>>>	*prif reswm*
holl	>>>	*holl blant*

In formal and literary registers, there is a certain amount of freedom as to
whether adjectives precede or follow the noun. This can occur where there
is an accepted collocation between a prenominal adjective and a noun in
expressions such as:

dyledus + parch	>>>	*dyledus barch* [= *due respect*]
mân + newidiadau	>>>	*mân newidiadau* [= *insignificant, little changes*]
brith + cof	>>>	*brith gof* [= *speckled > vague memory*]

In each of the above, the normal order is Adjective plus Noun. It would be
inappropriate to say '*parch dyledus*' or '*cof brith*'. '*Newidiadau mân*' could
be possible but carries with it a semantic change suggesting changes which
are small, of not a very large degree rather than of insignificance.

Knowing that prenominal adjectives are indicative of a literary style can
be of assistance to the translator who wishes to convey that style from one
language to the other.

Am ennyd byr yr oedd y cymylau
duon wedi gwasgaru, a mawrhydi

For a moment the black clouds had
dispersed, and the vast majority of

aruthr clogwyni Eryri yn ysgythru
dan yr **afrifed sêr**. [HENAT 8]

the Snowdon crags shimmered
beneath the **unnumbered stars**.
[LOCUST 14]

'Holmes,' I cried, 'I seem to **see
dimly** what you are hitting at.'
[BAND 233]

'Holmes,' llefais, 'mae gen i ryw
fras syniad [lit. a vague idea] o'r
hyn rydych chi'n ei awgrymu.'
[CYLCH 50]

Yr oedd y frwydr honno mor araf,
mor ddidosturi, mor annheg, rhyw
fud dân yn deifio llawenydd pawb
o'i gwmpas . . . [CHWAL 147]

That battle was so slow, so merciless,
so unfair, a **smouldering fire**
burning up the happiness of
everybody around . . . [OUT 155]

8.1.2.ii Preposed comparative or superlative

It is also usual for the comparative and superlative forms of adjectives to
follow the noun. Once again, however, in more formal and literary registers,
they may precede the noun (especially the comparative 'gwell' = better which
itself may connect with a further comparative as seen below and occur in
all registers). In contrast to the prenominal adjectives discussed above, the
noun following the comparative or superlative forms does not need a soft
mutation.

Mi fasa lobscows yn **well pryd** i'r
hogan yna . . . [TE 53]

Lobscouse would make a **better
meal** for that girl . . . [TEA 50]

Yr oedd Gwen a'm mam yn
gyfeillgar iawn, a thybiwn innau
nad oedd **gwell na phrydferthach
geneth** yn y byd crwn na Gwen . . .
[GWEN 37]

Gwen and my mother were great
friends and I believed that there
was no **prettier or better girl** in the
whole wide world. [GWEN 42]

Yr oedd yn ddeuddeg oed – wel, o
fewn mis i hynny, beth bynnag – ac
yn **dalach a chryfach hogyn** na
Huw Rôb a Wil Cochyn, ei gyfeillion
yn yr ysgol. [CYCHWYN 11]

He was within a month of his
twelfth birthday and **taller and
stronger** than his school friends
Huw Rob and Will-Ginger.
[BEGIN 9]

Fel hen athro, hefyd, fe wn am
lawer llanc a llances a aeth yn
ddisglair fuddugoliaethus drwy
Ysgol a Choleg ar gof da eu **pennaf
cynhysgaeth**. [HDF 101]

As a teacher I know many young
people who went triumphantly
through school and college on the
strength of their **principal dower**, a
good memory. [OFH 124]

8.1.3 Adjective comparative / equative / superlative morphology

The equative in Welsh may be used as a predicate with certain prepositions – some of which (*gan*) are more restricted to literary and formal registers while others (*er*) are more widespread. It is normal in these instances for the adjective to occur with the appropriate ending *-ed* although it is possible also for the modifier *mor* to be used.

Eto, **gan luosoced** y storïau a glywais, gallwn feddwl fod rhyw hwyl a sbort ddiniwed, yn feunyddiol ar waith yno; [HDF 94]	Yet the stories I heard about it **are so many** that I should think there was some bit of innocent fun on the go every day amid the high spirits . . . [OFH 115]
Er difyrred oedd Bangor, ac er bod y tymhorau cyflym yn feddwol gan firi, yr oedd cael dod adref i Leifior bob tro yn hyfrydwch ar wahân. [CRYMAN 165]	**However pleasant life was in Bangor**, and though the terms slipped by with fun and high jinks, coming home to Lleifior was always a special delight. [SICKLE 136]
Treuliodd Dan awr arall tros yr ysgrif, **er byrred oedd hi**, ond ni fedrai yn ei fyw ddilyn awgrym y Golygydd. [CHWAL 96]	Dan spent another hour over the article, **short though it was,** but could not for the life of him carry out the Editor's suggestion. [OUT 100]
Er mor fras ydoedd llawer o'r canu, ac **er lluosoced** oedd y seiniau anghywir [. . .] caem lawer o hwyl yn y cyfarfodydd . . . [WILLAT 142]	*How ever rough much of the singing was and **however frequent** the wrong sounds [. . .] we had a lot of fun in the meetings . . .*

The superlative with '*gan*' in the expression '*gan amlaf* [= *mostly, most frequently*] should also be noted.

The equative used with a possessive may take on the sense of a participle or a noun in English – again, in more formal contexts:

Gallai glywed aroglau'r coed fel y byddent yn awyr glir dechreunos Medi, a gweld eu pocedi'n bochio gan **eu llawned o gnau**. [TRAED 185]	[H]e could now almost recapture the scent of trees in the clear light of a September evening, and they with their pockets **bulging with nuts**. [FEET 153]

Yn lle hynny, syllodd ar hyd y llawr teiliau du a gwyn, a dotio at **eu glaned**, a chael gorffwys yn eu patrwm. [LLEIFIOR 107]

Rather, he gazed at the black-and-white tiles, much taken with **their cleanliness** and finding relief in their design. [RETURN 91]

It is also possible to see the comparative employed with a possessive to convey a sense of none/nothing + comparative adjective (e.g. *none better / braver* etc) in English in a similar way:

'R oedd ef a'i bartner, Benni Bwlch y Mynydd, **gŵr nad oedd ei wreiddiolach yn y wlad**, un tro wedi cymryd contract gan ryw ffarmwr digon tyn am y geiniog, i godi clawdd. [HDF 145]

He and his partner, Benni Bwlch y Mynydd, **than whom there was no one more original to be found in the country**, had once taken a contract of some farmer who was tight enough in money matters, to make him a hedge-bank. [OFH 181]

. . . 'darn o fywyd gwerth ei bortreadu', meddai Dyfnallt yn *Y Tyst*; a 'nid wyf yn meddwl fod **ei doniolach** yn yr iaith', meddai Llew Owain yn *Y Genedl*. [TROW 87]

. . . *'a piece of life worth portraying',* *said Dyfnallt in Y Tyst; and 'I* *don't think there's **anything more*** ***humorous to be had** in the language',* *said Llew Owain in Y Genedl.*

Comparatives, equatives and superlatives in Welsh can be formed syntheti-cally (by the addition of an ending) or analytically (by using *mor / mwy / mwyaf* plus the adjective). The synthetic forms of some adjectives are some-times only found in more formal registers of the language, as evidenced by our examples below, and again suggest a more literary style.

Dyma fanc **cyfoethocaf** bywyd. [HDF 101]

This is life's **richest** bank. [OFH 124]

Abram oedd y mwyaf golygus ohonom **a'r llithricaf ei dafod**. [CHWECH 132]

Abram was the most handsome of us *all **and the most slippery of tongue**.*

Gosodai'r mân-goed a'r bras-goed yn garnau bonfon, **cyhyd**, ar wahân, yn hwylus at law'r stocer ar yr aelwyd. [HDF 108]

She put the small wood and the thick wood in two heaps with the thicker ends of the pieces towards each other, **and all of equal length**, ready for the stoker's hand at the fireside. [OFH 132]

Yr oedd yma alaru, mae'n wir, ond **ddistawed** oedd y galaru hwn, **gyniled**! [LLEIFIOR 106]	There was mourning here, to be sure, but it was **so calm, so restrained**! [RETURN 90]

The superlative can be modified by the noun *oll – yr olaf >>> yr olaf oll* [= *the last >>> the very last*]. It is also possible, more informally, for '*un*' or '*dim*' to fulfill a similar modifying role with the superlative.

[Y]sgrifennodd fath o Hunan Gofiant dan y teitl 'Trem yn ôl', **y llyfr salaf oll** yn yr iaith Gymraeg, yn ôl barn ostyngedig ei annwyl nai amdano. [HDF 174]	He wrote a sort of autobiography entitled *A Look Back (Trem yn ôl)*, **the worst book** in the language in his humble nephew's opinion. [OFH 219]
. . . fel yr ystyriaf y ddau hyn, hyd heddiw, ymhlith **fy nghyfeillion agosaf oll**. [CHWECH 38]	*. . . so that I consider both of them, even today, to be amongst **my closest friends (of all)**.*
. . . holodd Ibn yn bwyllog gan gredu ei fod wedi cael **yr anffawd fwyaf un** o bosib: gorfod dal pen rheswm â gwallgofddyn. [PLA 105]	Salah decided that he had been overtaken by yet another misfortune [lit. the greatest misfortune ever possibly] that of attempting to reason with a madman. [PEST 79]
Yr hyn a'm synnodd i **yn bennaf dim** ar y daith gyntaf honno bant i'r gweithfeydd . . . [CHWECH 94]	*What surprised me **more than anything** on that first trip away to the works. . .*

8.1.4 How + adjective

When this occurs as an exclamation, the adjective follows the demonstrative '*dyna*' = '*there is/are*':

How odd that a moment of time so important to him should pass without his knowledge. [UNSUIT 18]	**Dyna od** fod eiliad mor bwysig o'i fywyd wedi mynd heibio'n ddiarwybod iddo. [GORTYN 9]
How fast those Queens *can* run! [THRO 201]	**Dyna gyflym** mae'r Breninesau 'na'n medru rhedeg! [TRWY 92]

Although this is possible with the equative '*mor*' in more formal registers[2]:

---

[2] One example of this is the well known hymn '*Mor fawr wyt ti* / *How great thou art*'.

Pan dynnai fy mam y llwch oddi ar ddodrefn y parlwr, **mor dyner** yr âi'r cadach dros gadair f' ewythr! [O LAW 99]	When my mother dusted the parlour furniture, **how lightly and caressingly** she drew the duster over the chair! [FROM 73]

However, when English uses 'how' + adjective to introduce a direct or indirect question with an element of degree, Welsh employs [pa] mor + adjective. It should also be remembered that English 'how + long' can also be rendered by 'faint' in Welsh as in our second example below.

I don't know **how deep** this thing goes. [STONE 343]	Wn i ddim **pa mor ddwfn** ydi'r lle yma. [MAEN 219]
If you're going to ask me **how long** it took him to die, I'm saying it depends. [TIME 19]	Os wyt ti ar fin gofyn i mi[3] **faint o amser** gymerodd hi iddo fo farw, wel mi ddeudwn i fod hynny'n dibynnu. [AMSER 29]

More generally, with a comparative sense of the degree to which, i.e. *how X [= adjective]* someone or something is something, the equative modifier 'mor' can be used.

. . . troes Ifan olwg hanner ymbilgar, hanner ymddiheurol ar ei wraig. Meddyliai hithau **mor dda** yr edrychai yn ei siwt briodas. [TRAED 10]	. . . he gave his wife a half-pleading, half-apologetic look. She thought **how handsome** he was in his wedding suit. [FEET 9]
Ac fel y sylwai Owen ar fechgyn eraill o 'rybelwyr', sylweddolai **mor hynod ffodus** ydoedd. [CYCHWYN 71]	And Owen, observing the other boys, rubble-shifters like himself, realised **how remarkably fortunate** he was. [BEGIN 71]
. . . teimlwn ar yr un pryd **mor hyfryd** fuasai gennyf gael darllen hanes dyn cyffredin . . . [RHYS 4]	I, at the same time, felt **how delightful** it would be to read the history of a commonplace man . . . [RHYS 9]

Occasionally, this may be expanded to include the interrogative 'pa' too even though there is no indirect question.

---

[3] It would also be possible to use 'pa mor' here with the adjective 'hir' (= *long*) >>> **pa mor hir** gymerodd hi iddo fo farw . . . .

'I had . . . come to an entirely erroneous conclusion, which shows, my dear Watson, **how dangerous** it always is to reason from insufficient data.' [BAND 238]

'. . . roeddwn i wedi dod i gasgliad anghywir – sy'n dangos, f'annwyl Watson, **pa mor beryglus** bob amser yw ceisio rhesymu heb ddigon o fanylion.' [CYLCH 57]

8.1.5 Intensifiers and degree modifiers

There are a number of ways of using intensifiers and degree modifiers in Welsh. We list these below under headings which describe the particular construction employed.

8.1.5.i The preposition 'o' following the intensifier and followed by the adjective

In Chapter 2 we saw that it is possible to use the preposition 'o' to modify two nouns e.g. *cawr o ddyn* >>> *a giant of a man*. The element being modified or intensified always follows the preposition. Similarly, this is also possible with either adjective (modifier) + o + noun >>> *da o beth* >>> *a good thing* as well as adjective (modifier) + o + adjective. Typical examples of these intensifier adjectives (which in English often appear as adverbs) are:

anarferol	=	unusual	>>>	anarferol o boeth	=	unusually hot
dychrynllyd/				dychrynllyd o anodd		
ofnadwy	=	awful, terrible	>>>	ofnadwy o anodd	=	awfully difficult
eithriadol	=	exceptional	>>>	eithriadol o hardd	=	exceptionally beautiful
hynod	=	remarkable	>>>	hynod o garedig	=	remarkably kind
rhyfeddol	=	amazing	>>>	rhyfeddol o hael	=	amazingly generous
uffernol	=	hellish	>>>	uffernol o ddrud	=	hellish expensive

The list is not limited to the intensifiers noted above. The following examples give further evidence of these being used in context:

Ysywaeth yr oedd lleisiau'r ddau ar dorri, ac amryw frawddegau yn **anobeithiol o uchel** iddynt. [WILLAT 148]

*However both their voices were about to break and some of the sentences were **hopelessly high** for them.*

Roedd y dŵr yn **ddychrynllyd o oer** . . . [PLA 169]

*The water was **awfully cold** . . .*

Gwisgai blazer ddu neu lasddu tywyll iawn, crys a choler gwyn a thei clwb **hynod o liwgar** . . . [SELYF 51]

*[He] wore a black or very dark navy blazer, a white shirt and collar and a **really colourful** club tie . . .*

A dyna'r byd **rhyfeddol o gyfoethog** y'm ganed iddo . . . [HDF 118]

Such was the **wonderfully rich** world into which I was born . . . [OFH 145]

'Wn i ddim pryd medra' i alw eto,' meddai. 'Mi dan ni'n **sobor o brysur** . . . lot o bobol ddiarth yn aros yn y Castall.' [RHANNU 179]

*'I don't know when I'll be able to call again,' he said. 'We are[4] **really busy** . . . there are a lot of strange people staying at the Castle.'*

Eisteddodd Owen ar y drafael, ac o dan gyfarwyddyd Huw Jones llwyddodd i naddu pen ac ochr i'r grawen, er mai **yn boenus o araf** y gwnâi hynny. [CYCHWYN 23]

Owen seated himself at the block, and under Huw Jones's guidance succeeded in whittling one end and side of a 'rough', although his progress was **painfully slow**. [BEGIN 21]

8.1.5.ii Adjective + adjective

It is also possible for two adjectives to co-occur with one modifying the other. The modifying adjective usually comes first but this is not always the case. The second adjective always undergoes a soft mutation whether it is the modifier or not.

Gwrandawodd Ned yn **amyneddgar fonheddig** hyd y diwedd. [HENAT 124–5]

Ned listened **with gentlemanly patience**. [LOCUST 108]

. . . a gofynnodd yn **fwriadol dawel a chadarn**. [PLA 101]

He put his question **with deliberation** [*Lit: intentionally calmly and robustly*] [PEST 83]

---

[4] Welsh here has the intensifier '*sobor*' [= *sober*]. This is probably best rendered in English as '*really / extremely*'.

Yr oedd y gegin yn **hyfryd oer** wedi'r gwres y tu allan. [CRYMAN 10]	The kitchen was **pleasantly cool** after the heat of the day. [SICKLE 6]
[D]ywedaf eto mai **gwael ddifrifol** oedd y Gyfundrefn Addysg y pryd hwnnw. [WILLAT 41]	*Once again I say that the Education System was **extremely poor** at that time.*
Bu'n **ddifrifol wael** am fisoedd cyn marw yn 1941 yn 38 mlwydd oed. [TROW 118]	*[He] had been **extremely ill** for months before [he] died in 1941 at 38 years of age.*

8.1.5.iii Intensifier + adjective

The intensifiers here precede the adjective which then undergoes soft muta-tion. Some of the more common intensifiers are listed here:

cymharol	-	comparatively
[g]wir	-	really, truly
gwirioneddol	-	really
hollol	-	completely
hynod	-	remarkably, very
lled	-	rather

Examples of these (and others) in context are given here:

Yr oeddwn wedi synnu, oblegid tybiwn fod wyau ieir yn **anhraethol fwy gwerthfawr** . . . [GWEN 28]	I was amazed at this because I believed that hens' eggs . . . were **far more valuable**. [GWEN 34]
Yr oedd bron bob un ohonom yn dyfod o gartrefi **cymharol dlawd**, a heb fod yn gyfarwydd ag arferion y Dosbarth Canol. [WILLAT 90]	*Nearly every one of us came from **comparatively poor** households and weren't familiar with the customs of the Middle Class.*
Byr a fu ei dymor yntau, ac y mae'n **wir flin** gennyf orfod nodi'r rheswm diflas am hynny. [CHWECH 135]	*His term was also short and I am **really sorry** to have to note the miserable reason for that.*
It was **quite clear** to them that they were at this moment standing in the presence of a master. [MAT 108]	Roedd hi'n **hollol amlwg** iddyn nhw eu bod nhw'n sefyll yng ngŵydd meistr yr eiliad honno. [MAT 102]

'Ia', meddai Owen gan roi tro ar ei ben a gwenu'n **hynod gyfeillgar** ar bartner ei dad. [CYCHWYN 19]

'Yes', replied Owen, turning his head with a **most friendly** smile at his dad's partner. [BEGIN 17]

Gŵr **lled fyr** oedd Nwncwl Jâms, na thrwm nac ysgafn o gorff, ac o flewyn tywyll. [HDF 157]

Uncle Jâms was **rather a short man**, neither heavy nor light in build, dark-haired. [OFH 196]

It is possible for the intensifier to be postposed – adjective + intensifier – however it should be noted that this usually happens for stylistic reasons and, given that this order runs contrary to the norm, can have the effect of intensifying the intensifier.

... gŵr **doniol anghyffredin** ... [CHWECH 149]

... an unusually funny man ...

Ac yn **sydyn hollol** dyna Wini yn gwneud peth a brofai mai pobl yr ardal a oedd yn iawn. [TE 44]

And then, **all of a sudden**, Winni does something that shows that people were right after all. [TEA 42]

Am ryw reswm rhy ddyrys i geisio'i 'sbonio saif y trwmpedwr hwn yn **fyw ryfeddol** yn fy nghof hyd heddiw ... [HDF 95]

For some inexplicable reason the trumpeter stands in my memory till this day, **extraordinarily vividly** ... [OFH 116]

'Mi fydd hwn yn lle **drud ofnadwy**, Owen', meddai Mary'n nerfus. [CYCHWYN 199]

'This will be a **terribly expensive** place, Owen', said Mary nervously. [BEGIN 200]

This section concludes with various other preadjectival degree modifiers which are commonly encountered and therefore merit particular mention.

cwbl

totally, completely

... teimlai John Williams na fu'r bore yn **gwbl ofer** wedi'r cyfan. [RHANNU 107]

*... John Williams felt that the morning hadn't been **totally in vain** / a total waste after all.*

digon

enough, sufficiently

It should be noted that adjectives following '*digon*' do not undergo a soft mutation.

... hyd y deallais, 'r oedd 'nhadcu
yn ddyn **digon caredig** a hawddgar i
weithio gydag e. [HDF 67]

I understand that my grandfather
was **kind** [*Lit: kind enough*] and
pleasant to work with. [OFH 80]

'*Digon*' may also be postposed (and will then take a soft mutation itself as for
any other adjective in this position).

Gweithiai Jac a fi yn **ddigon**
caled yno, Duw a'i gŵyr, ond
bychan ddigon oedd ein harian.
[CHWECH 182]

*Jac and I worked **hard enough** there,*
*God knows, but our money was **little***
***enough**.*

go

rather, quite

'Te **go sâl** gewch chi, mae arna' i
ofn,' ymddiheurodd i'r dieithryn ...
[CHWAL 29]

'A **very poor** tea you'll get, I'm
afraid,' she told the stranger
apologetically ... [OUT 29]

Common collocations with '*go*' include:

go dda	-	*very, rather good*
go iawn	-	*real*
go lew	=	*go dda*

gweddol

fairly, rather

Heblaw hynny yr oedd yno
ysgolfeistr o Gymro twymgalon a
llenor **gweddol wych**. [CWM 193]

Still more important was the fact
that the schoolmaster was a warm-
hearted Welshman and a **pretty**
good writer. [GORSE 186]

llawn

just as ..., enough

'*Llawn*' will always be followed by the equative degree of the adjective apart
from in combinations such as '*llawn digon / gormod*'.

Yr olaf oll oedd yr hen Ifan Pant
y Crwys, a'i blant ieuengaf yn yr
ysgol yr un pryd â mi – a Ianto, hir
ei ên, brychlyd ei wyneb, a'i gap a
chlustiau yr un ffunud â'i dad, ac

The last was old Ifan Pant y Crwys,
whose youngest children were in
school with me, and Ianto was in my
class, long-chinned and freckled and
wearing a cap with ear-flaps to it,

yn **llawn mor ddoniol**, yn yr un dosbarth â mi. [HDF 146]

the image of his father and equally humorous. [OFH 182]

Gallai ddala pen rheswm gyda'r hen yn **llawn cystal â** chyda'r ifanc; ac yr oedd ei storiau a'i ddywediadau doniol yn destun siarad y fro. [CHWECH 79]

*He could chat along with the old **just as well as** with the young; and his stories and his funny sayings were the talk of the area.*

'R oedd rhyw ugain i bum mlynedd ar hugain o'r gorchwyl hwn yn **llawn digon** i'r cryfaf ohonynt. [CHWECH 100]

*Some twenty to twenty five years of this task were **more than enough** for the strongest of them.*

pur

quite

Gallwn eu clywed nhw lawr llawr yn chwerthin ac yn tynnu coes, yn **bur feddw**, ac yn rhaid 'mod i wedi syrthio i gysgu ar fy mhen. [HUNAN 186]

I could hear them below, laughing and joking and **pretty drunk**. I must have fallen asleep instantly. [SOLVA 186]

reit

'right', very

The use of '*reit*' in (mainly NW) Welsh mirrors its use as a modifier in (mainly Northern varieties of) English. It is a marker of more informal or NW registers but operates as a normal Welsh modifier, including the soft mutation of the adjective which follows it.

"Dydi Kate Idris ddim yma," meddai Gwyn.
'A hitha'n mynd i gâl babi yn **reit fuan**? . . .' [CHWAL 60]

'Kate Idris isn't here,' Gwyn remarked.
'And her going to have a baby **very soon**? . . .' [OUT 62]

tra

extremely, very

This modifier is more associated with formal registers and causes any adjectives following to undergo an aspirate mutation.

Yr oedd Twm yn **dra awyddus** am inni fod yn y plygain mewn pryd . . . [GWEN 21]

Twm was **very anxious** that we should arrive at the carol service early . . . [GWEN 28]

. . . darn o ddyn tywyll ei groen a du ei flewyn, gan ddwyn ar gof i mi heddiw, rywsut, y llun o Joseph Stalin a fu'n **dra phoblogaidd** ar un adeg. [CHWECH 165]	*. . . a hunk of a man with dark skin and black hair, which brings to mind today, somehow, the picture of Joseph Stalin which was **extremely popular** at one time.*

8.1.6 Participial verb forms used as modifiers

These participial verb forms (past or present) can present considerable challenges to translators from both languages. We look at this initially from the standpoint of Welsh to English equivalence.

8.1.6.i -edig

Morphologically, the adjectival suffix *-edig* is only added to verb-nouns and is mainly associated with the English past participle. The first set of examples show, however, that it can sometimes be better rendered in English as a present participle equivalent:

. . . i anadlu'r ager a godai o'r jwg o ddŵr **berwedig**[5]. [CHWAL 147]	. . . to inhale the steam from a jug of **boiling** water [OUT 156]
. . . **rotting** lock gates, long fallen into disuse . . . [TIME 77	. . . gatiau loc **pydredig** a fu'n segur ers talwm . . . [AMSER 122]
Ni ddywedwyd ychwaneg am y peth, a chredodd fy mam a minnau mai rhyw ysfa sydyn a **diflanedig** a ddaethai trosto ef. [O LAW 200]	Nothing more was said on the subject, and my mother and I thought that it was just a sudden, **passing** impulse that had come over him. [FROM 165]
. . . pointing a **quivering** finger at her husband. [MAT 61]	. . . gan bwyntio bys **sigledig** tuag at ei gŵr. [MAT 55]

Otherwise, the *-edig* suffix will normally convey a past participle. However, as can be seen in the example below, it should not be taken for granted that a verb-noun modified by the adjectival suffix *-edig* can always be an acceptable equivalent for an English past participle:

---

[5] PWT I.91a notes that '*berwedig*' is a rare example of the *-edig* suffix where the meaning is past or present > *boiling* or *boiled*.

Taking from it the **folded** sheet of plain paper, he read its **pencilled** message in an **educated** and quite **shaky** italic . . . [TIME 88]	Cymerodd y darn papur gwyn **a oedd wedi ei blygu** a darllen y neges **a ysgrifennwyd â phensel** mewn ysgrifen italig **addysgiedig**, digon **crynedig** . . . [AMSER 139]

Here, at least in the first two cases, the translator has opted for relative clauses rather than adding -*edig*. Morphologically, *plygu* > *plygedig* and *ysgrifennu â phensel* > *ysgrifenedig â phensel* are both possible but stylistically they would not be appropriate. However, *ysgrifen italig **a oedd wedi'i haddysgu*** would not make much sense given that there is already an adjective (*italig*) following the noun (*ysgrifen*) and in particular when the -*edig* adjective in Welsh is a modified past participle in English – ***digon** crynedig* – it is not possible to replace it with a relative clause. -*Edig* is also preferred when the past participle is used with an adverbial sense, as in the first example here.

. . . her voice was **educated** . . . [TIME 101]	. . . roedd ei llais yn swnio'n **addysgedig**[6] . . . [AMSER 161]
The lady coloured deeply, and covered over her **injured** wrist. [BAND 219]	Gwridodd y foneddiges, a gorchuddio'i harddwrn **briwedig**. [CYLCH 29]
Ro'n i bron yn sicr bod Tess'n achos **colledig**, a'i bod hi'n anochel y bydde rhaid i ni wahanu. [HUNAN 278]	I had almost convinced myself that Tess was a **lost** cause and that we'd have to go our separate ways. [SOLVA 278]
. . . y fath ydoedd y 'pietas' **cysegredig** a gylchynai y rhain i gyd iddi hi fel nad oedd na bai na ffaeledd yn bod yn neb na dim yno. [HDF 175]	. . . such was the **sacred** pietas that surrounded them to her that there could be no fault or failing among them all. [OFH 220]
The only book in the whole of this **enlightened** household was something called *Easy Cooking*. [MAT 11]	Yr unig lyfr yn y cartref **goleuedig** hwn i gyd oedd rhywbeth o'r enw *Coginio Syml* . . . [MAT 5]
. . . let me deal with my sick and **maimed**. [TIME 57]	. . . gadael i mi drin y sâl a'r **methedig**. [AMSER 90]

[6] Literally here, the Welsh has '*her voice sounded educated*'.

She didn't believe any of it. It was a horror story that had sprung out of his **twisted** imagination. [VICT 127]

Doedd hi'n credu'r un gair. Stori arswyd roedd ei hen ddychymyg **gwyrdroëdig** o wedi'i chreu oedd hon. [LLINYN 142]

. . . fel y disgynnodd ei phen ar fraich **estynedig** Elwyn. [SELYF 161]

. . . *as her head descended onto Elwyn's **extended** arm.*

8.1.6.ii -[i]og

Unlike *-edig*, this suffix is not confined to verb-nouns. In fact, it is more commonly found with nouns than with other parts of speech. It offers another (if more limited) option for conveying the English past participle in Welsh in particular when the participle is more applicable to a noun related verb. The first example here is an example of this but also illustrates how actual nouns may also be used in Welsh when this may be better rendered in English with a past participle.

Mewn lle **coediog** fel Penrhiw 'r oedd yno **gludwair fawr o goed tân**, wrth dalcen y tŷ, gerllaw'r cartws **to gwellt** a'i chwe philer crwn o gerrig **gwyngalch**. [HDF 107]

In a **wooded** place like Penrhiw there was always a **well-stocked** woodyard, at the end of the house near the **straw-thatched** carthouse on its six round pillars of **whitewashed** stone. [OFH 131]

A couple of shabby mismatched easy chairs and the well-worn **patterned** carpet were manifestly the legal requirements of an apartment rented as fully furnished. [TIME 22]

Prin ddigon oedd yr ychydig gadeiriau esmwyth di-raen, nad oeddynt yn perthyn i set, a'r carped **patrymog** treuliedig, i gyfiawnhau rhentu'r fflat fel un oedd wedi ei dodrefnu. [AMSER 33]

Trawsai hen gôt **glytiog** amdano, ac am ei ben gwisgai het galed felynwen a'i hymyl yn dechrau ffarwelio â'r gweddill ohoni. [CYCHWYN 21]

He had donned an old, **patched** coat and was wearing a whitish-yellow bowler, its brim beginning to part company with the rest of it. [BEGIN 20]

[N]id yn fynych y gwelid y llofft hon heb ryw helwriaeth neu'i gilydd, **clustiog** neu **bluog**, yn hongian wrthi. [HDF 108]

[N]ot often was this ceiling seen without some game, **long-eared** or **feathered**, hanging from it. [OFH 132]

It is also possible (but not usual) for the English present participle to be an equivalent here too:

Araf fu'r daith i waelod y chwarel, a daeth ofn i'm calon wrth imi sylwi ar lwybr **troellog** y Neidr yn hongian ar serthni'r mynydd o'n blaen. [O LAW 201]	Our journey to the bottom of the quarry was slow indeed, and my heart sank as I looked at the 'Snake', the **winding** path that clung to the steep mountain-slope in front of us. [FROM 165]

8.1.6.iii English past participle > *wedi*

Although adjectives created by adding the suffixes *-edig / -[i]og* may be a possible way of rendering the English past participle, our discussion has already indicated that they are not possible in every situation e.g. when the participle is modified or when such an adjective is not available or stylistically appropriate. Another alternative is to use the preposition *wedi* with a verb-noun (sometimes with a dependent pronoun referring back to the object being described).

– neu bennog hallt **wedi'i ferwi** ar ben tatws trwy'u crwyn, neu ledan hallt **wedi'i ffrio**. [TRAED 21]	– or a salted[7] herring **boiled** with potatoes in their jackets, or a salted flatfish, **fried**. [FEET 19]
Mae hi'n ddel, ond bod ganddi wyneb fel plentyn **wedi'i sbwylio**, a phwt o drwyn. [MONICA 7]	She's pretty, but she has the face of a **spoilt** child, and a snub nose. [MONICA 5]
. . . and both footmen, Alice noticed, had **powdered** hair that curled all over their heads. [ALICE 58]	. . . a sylwodd Alys fod gan y ddau fwtler wallt **wedi'i bowdro**, yn gyrliau i gyd. [ALYS II 54]
. . . dyma ddyn tal, tene 'da locsyn yn cerdded i mewn, yn gwisgo siwt Levi las **wedi colli'i lliw**. [HUNAN 140]	.. came a tall thin bearded guy dressed in a **faded** blue Levi suit. [SOLVA 140]

8.1.6.iv English participle (past/present) > other

The last example in 8.1.6.iii includes the English past participles '*bearded*' and '*dressed*'. These – unlike '*faded*' – do not correspond to the '*wedi + VN*' construction. They correspond, respectively, to (i) a noun > *locsyn [= beard >>*

---

[7] Here is a good example of why *wedi* is not always suitable or possible. Welsh possesses an adjective '*hallt*' which has a direct translation '*salty/salted*'. There is therefore no need to construct a participle which combines *wedi* with the verb-noun *halltu [=to salt]*.

with a beard] and (ii) a verb-noun after the predicate > *yn cerdded*. This final section concentrates on other options for giving the English past participle in Welsh other than those already discussed.

a) With a noun/ preposition '*yn*' + noun

Buasai wrth ei bodd yn ei gweld yn fflamio – y ddol yn cael mynd i'r 'tân mawr' ac nid Begw – y hi a'i hen wyneb **paent**, hyll. [TE 9–10]

She'd like to see it burning, the doll in hell-fire instead of Begw, the doll with her ugly **painted** face. [TEA 13]

... a chadwch eich bysedd **ynghroes** ... [SELYF 245]

*... and keep your fingers **crossed** ...*

A few underclothes, clean but not ironed, were **folded** on the ledge above. [UNSUIT 45]

Roedd ei ddillad isa' glân **yn eu plyg** ar y silff uwchben. [GORTYN 57]

Edrychodd Jojo ar y ffag rhwng ei fysedd. Roedd hi'n dal **ynghynn**. [LLADD 253]

*Jojo looked at the fag between his fingers. It was still **alight**.*

b) With a literary passive (to render a passive past participle)

These examples could be viewed (stylistically) as more literary equivalents to 8.1.6.iii and they are also used to convey passive past participles, again in a more formal register[8].

Left on his desk blotting pad for his information was a copy of a message **sent** by records to Hagbourne. [TIME 25–6]

Gadawyd copi o neges a **anfonwyd** gan yr Adran Gofnodion at Howells ar ei ddesg, er gwybodaeth. [AMSER 39]

... the papers **found** in Stephanakis's briefcase ... [TIME 92]

... y papurau **a ganfuwyd** yng nghês Stephanakis ... [AMSER 147]

c) Verb-noun clause or finite verb as English present participle

The clause will be introduced by the predicate '*yn*' with the verb-noun. It can be viewed as the present participle equivalent of the use of '*wedi*' in 8.1.6 iii.

---

[8] For a fuller discussion of these see section 5.4 'The Impersonal Forms' in Chapter 5.

Soon the hut was full of the sound and smell of **sizzling** sausage. [STONE 60]	Yn fuan roedd y cwt yn llawn sŵn ac arogl sosejys **yn ffrio**[9]. [MAEN 37–8]
As a doorkeeper, or whatever he was supposed to be, he made a sham of the enamelled security badge pinned to his **straining** dinner jacket. [TIME 28]	Fel porthor, neu beth bynnag ydoedd, dygai anghlod ar y bathodyn diogelwch enamel a biniwyd ar ei siaced ddu, **a oedd yn rhy fach iddo**. [AMSER 43]

d) With an adjective

We have already seen an example of this with '*hallt* > *salty/salted*' in 8.1.6.iii. This use is restricted to those adjectives where this is possible and which may be used in this way e.g. *crwydro [= to wander] >>> crwydrol [= wandering]* in the first example below:

He had no friends at all save the **wandering** gipsies . . . [BAND 213]	Does ganddo'r un cyfaill ar wahân i'r sipsiwn **crwydrol** . . . [CYLCH 19]
. . . troes Ifan olwg hanner **ymbilgar**, hanner **ymddiheurol** ar ei wraig. [TRAED 10]	. . . he gave his wife a half-**pleading**, half-**apologetic** look. [FEET 9]

8.1.7 Verb-noun as adjective

The verb-noun in Welsh may also operate in a descriptive way, as an adjective. An obvious example here would be the use of the verb-noun '*bwyta*' [= *to eat*] with the noun '*ystafell*' [= *room*] to give '*dining room* = *ystafell fwyta*'. Often these verb-nouns used adjectivally will be rendered by a present participle in English (although not always). As they operate like adjectives, they will in turn take a soft mutation when they describe a singular feminine noun.

One pair of **protective** gloves. [STONE 82]	Un pâr o fenig **amddiffyn**. [MAEN 52]

[9] Literally here the meaning is '*sausages frying*'. If we were to change '*yn*' to '*wedi*' the meaning would become '*fried sausages*' with the action complete. It would also be possible to extend this to a full clause '*sosejys a oedd yn ffrio*' > '*sausages which were frying*' although this is not necessary here. Note that this is used in example 3 here to give the idea of a dinner jacket which is '*straining*'. The modifier '*rhy*' here means that '*yn + VN*' is not an option.

Un o ferched Prance, Iris, a ddaeth yn Mrs Beer yn ddiweddarach ac a oedd yn dal i fyw yn Anchor House, oedd fy athrawes **ganu**. [CRWYD 110]

*One of the Prance girls, Iris, who later became Mrs Beer and who still lived in Anchor House, was my **singing** teacher.*

Bellach, roedd yr ymweliadau â Llwybrmain wedi peidio'n llwyr, a dim ond sgwrs **crafu'r wyneb** a gaent pan alwai Elen yn y siop. [RHANNU 180]

*Now, the visits to Llwybrmain had ceased completely, and they would only have a **superficial** [Lit: scratching the surface] chat when Elen called by in the shop.*

8.1.8 Numbers as modifiers (giving a time)

The usual position of an adjective in Welsh is after the noun and similarly, numbers which are used as modifiers with a sense of time, will also follow the noun to which the time element refers. Therefore, in example one below, '*trên saith y bore*' is literally '*train seven of the morning*' but corresponds to '*the seven o'clock [am] train*'.

Cerddem, bob un ohonom, bump, chwech, neu saith milltir, dros y mynydd i ddal y **trên saith y bore** yn Llanybydder . . . [CHWECH 87]

*We would walk, all of us, five, six or seven miles, over the mountain to catch the **seven o'clock [in the morning] train** in Llanybydder . . .*

. . . it was the **nine o'clock news** on the wireless. [CIDER 28]

. . . ond sylweddolais mai'r **newyddion naw** ar y radio roeddwn i'n ei glywed. [SEIDR 40]

. . . ac yr oedd yn falch o weld Huw Jones yn codi ac o'i glywed yn awgrymu '**panad ddeg**'. [CYCHWYN 168]

. . . and he was not sorry to see Huw Jones get up and hear him suggest a '**ten o'clock cup of tea**'. [BEGIN 168]

Pan ganodd corn **un ar ddeg** . . . [O LAW 206]

When the **eleven o'clock** hooter sounded . . . [FROM 170]

8.1.9 *So adjective/adverb (that) / *Nes

The equative in Welsh can be formed by using the modifier '*mor*' plus an adjective followed by '*â*', for example:

mor las â'r môr   -   as blue as the sea

The equative with '*mor*' may also be followed by an adverbial sub-clause introduced by '*nes*' [= *until*] to translate the English '*so + adjective/adverb + (that) sub-clause*'. An alternative to '*nes*' is '*fel*' [= *like*].

Yr oedd ei gyraeddiadau **mor fychain** fel stiward hyd yn oed, **nes oedd arno ofn colli ei swydd** . . . [TRAED 55]	Even his abilities as a Steward **were so limited that he was afraid of losing his job** . . . [FEET 45]
Her body was **so slim and fragile one got the feeling** that if she fell over she would smash into a thousand pieces, like a porcelain figure. [MAT 66]	Roedd ei chorff **mor denau a bregus nes bod rhywun yn cael y teimlad**, petai hi'n cwympo, y byddai hi'n chwalu'n fil o ddarnau, fel ffigwr porslen. [MAT 60]
. . . and soon Amanda Thripp was travelling **so fast she became a blur.** [MAT 115]	. . . a chyn hir roedd Amanda Thripp yn teithio **mor gyflym fel ei bod hi'n anodd ei gweld hi'n iawn.** [MAT 109]

8.1.10 "*The more . . . the more . . .*"

Standard, literary Welsh uses the superlative form of the adjective in this construction which compares to what degree a quality has increased or lessened. The adjective referring to this degree of change is introduced by '*po*' and not the definite article:

> *Gorau po gyntaf* - *The sooner/quicker the better*

Here, the degree of change is expressed by '*cyntaf / quickest > quicker*' and it is preceded by '*po*'. '*Gorau / best > better*' does not need an article.

Yn wir, **gorau po leiaf o bobl** a wyddai lle'r oedd lleidr banc yn cuddio. [SELYF 168]	Indeed, **the less people** who knew where a bank robber was hiding **the better**.
A **pho gryfaf, arbenicaf, neu hynotaf**, os mynner, y bo'r ddau, wrth natur, **anhawsaf** oll yw'r broblem. [HDF 180]	And **the stronger, more particular or more peculiar**, if you will, the two of them are, **the more difficult** the problem is.
. . . ond **gore po fwya meddw** fyddwch chi . . . [CRWYD 16]	. . . but **the drunker** you are **the better** . . .

However, this more formal expression of the construction is often avoided by different strategies. For example, by adding '*yn y byd*' to the superlative forms and dropping the '*po*'. The first of our examples below shows how the '*gorau po gyntaf* expression may be reconfigured in this way:

The quicker he leaves this forest, **the better**. [STONE 320]	**Cyntaf yn y byd** y bydd yn gadael y Goedwig, **gorau'n y byd**. [MAEN 204]
... **mwya'n y byd** oeddan ni'n gerddad, **pella'n y byd** oedd y niwl yna'n mynd, a **mwya'n y byd** o ochr y Foel oedd yn dwad i'r golwg. [NOS 46]	... **the further** we walked, **the further** the mist went, and **the more** mountainside was coming into view. [NIGHT 37]
Cerddes i lawr y pafin ar ochor dde Bute Street am ryw hanner milltir, a **phella** o'n i'n mynd, **mwya'n y byd** oedd y stryd yn prysuro ... [HUNAN 80]	... walking down the pavement on the right-hand side of Bute Street, then onwards for about half a mile. **The further** I went, **the busier** the street became ... [SOLVA 80]

8.2 Adverbs – Introduction

Adverbs consisting of adjectival phrases in Welsh are formed by the adjective following the predicate '*yn*' and undergoing a soft mutation, in exactly the same way as an adjective behaves with the copula:

*Mae'r car **yn gyflym**.*   -   *The car is **fast**.*   >>>
*Daeth y car i lawr y stryd **yn gyflym**.*   -   *The car came down the street **quickly**.*

Ffurfiai ei barn **yn bwyllog a rhesymol**; [HDF 115]	She formed her opinions **slowly and rationally**. [OFH 142]

These may be modified and the modifier will then itself take a soft mutation as it follows the predicate and may cause the adverb it modifies to take one too:

Ac yno y buont wrthi'n dyrnu, yn dyrnu, ac yn dyrnu, 'Clap! Clap! Clap! Clap!' **yn gwbwl undonog** am oriau ... [HDF 92]	And they kept at it *clap clap clap clap* **resolutely and monotonously** for hours and hours ... [OFH 112]

Occasionally, the modifier may come after the adverb:

Am ryw reswm rhy ddyrys i geisio'i 'sbonio saif y trwmpedwr hwn **yn fyw ryfeddol**[10] yn fy nghof hyd heddiw... [HDF 95]

For some inexplicable reason the trumpeter stands in my memory till this day, **extraordinarily vividly**... [OFH 116]

Adverbial phrases will take a soft mutation on the initial element (apart from '*byth*'):

Ond yr enw a roddai'r bechgyn ar yr Athro oedd 'Stupright', oddi wrth ei arfer o gerdded o un pen yr ystafell i'r llall, a dweud **ddwsinau o weithiau**, '*Sit upright boys!*' [WILLAT 73]

*But the name the boys gave the Teacher was 'Stupright' from his custom of walking from one end of the room to the other saying **dozens of times**, 'Sit upright boys!'*

Malfoy's eagle owl was **always** bringing him packages of sweets from home... [STONE 179]

Roedd tylluan eryr Mallwyd **byth a hefyd** yn dod â phecynnau o fferins iddo o'i gartre... [MAEN 114]

Some adverbial phrases correspond to particular idioms in both languages, for example, where a pronoun might be used in Welsh to personalise them[11]:

dan ei sang	-	*packed out, full to the brim*
nerth ei lais	-	*at the top of his voice*
nerth ei thraed	-	*as fast as her feet could carry her*

... ac roedd yr olwg ar ei hwyneb yn debyg i'r un fyddai ar wyneb person sy'n sownd mewn cae bach gyda tharw cynddeiriog yn rhuthro **nerth ei garnau** tuag ato. [MAT 107–8]

... and the look on her face was similar to the one which would be on the face of a person who was stuck in a small field with a frenzied bull running towards him as fast as its hooves could carry it.

The position of an adverbial phrase in Welsh may be dictated by the need to follow it with an appropriate sub-clause. An example of this would be '*ychydig*'

[10] It is worth also noting the alternative to '*rhyfeddol*' >> '*i'w ryfeddu*' [= *to be marvelled, amazed (at)*]:

A chafodd y ddau y peth **yn ddigrif i'w ryfeddu**. [CYCHWYN 199]

And both found that **wonderfully amusing**. [BEGIN 201]

[11] See Chapter 4 for a fuller treatment.

[= *little*] which follows the verb in English but would precede the verb in Welsh and change it to a sub-clause:

Yr oedd yn hapus iawn yn nhŷ William Jenkins, ond **ychydig a welai** ar ei hen bartner Bob Twm yn awr. [CHWAL 129]	He was happy enough in William Jenkins's house, but **saw very little** of his old partner Bob Tom now. [OUT 136]

8.2.1 Adverb placement

A variation on where the adverb may be located in Welsh is found in the pattern *yn [predicate]* + *adjective* + *verb-noun*. We begin by looking at '*half*' as in '*to half do something*' as the English here more closely mirrors the Welsh. As will be seen, when the *yn* + *adjective* + *verb-noun* placement is used, the verb-noun undergoes a soft mutation (as one might expect when an adjective precedes a noun or verb). There is no mutation in the case of '*hanner*' [= *half*].

Ac yn sicr ni hoffai'r syniad o gael ei ddal gyda dwy ferch **ar hanner gwisgo**, neu **hanner diosg**, yn ei ystafell wely. [SELYF 201]	*And he definitely didn't like the idea of being caught with two girls **half-dressed** or **half-undressed** in his bedroom.*
One of his eyes was bloodshot and **partially closed**. [CIDER 29]	Roedd un o'i lygaid yn waedgoch ac **yn hanner cau**. [SEIDR 41]
Grandpa Joe and Charlie were **half running** and **half walking** to keep up with Mr Wonka . . . [CHARLIE 100]	Roedd Tad-cu Joe a Charlie'n **hanner rhedeg** a **hanner cerdded** er mwyn cadw i fyny â Mr Wonka . . . [SIOCLED 132]

Adverb placement is sometimes a stylistic preference. Let us consider the following example:

. . . a'r poen **yn graddol gilio** . . . [CHWECH 65]	*. . . and the pain **gradually receding** . . .*

In both languages, it would be possible to place the adverb as above or after the verb:

   a'r poen yn cilio'n raddol   -   and the pain receding gradually

This is a mainly stylistic decision reflecting, on the whole, a more literary register than when the adverb follows the verb. The adverb itself is treated in Welsh as the first element of a verb-noun following the predicate '*yn*' and therefore does not mutate. The verb following the adverb, however, will invariably take a soft mutation[12].

Roedd gwawn lwyd **yn araf gripian** trwy frig y nos . . . [PLA 64]	Around them, gossamer-grey, the dusk **was softly gathering**. [PEST 48-9]
. . . daeth myfyriwr ro'n i'**n ei fras nabod** i mewn i ffreutur yr Undeb . . . [HUNAN 150]	. . . a student I **vaguely knew** came into the Union refectory . . . [SOLVA 150]
A thros y gefnen yr oedd cromen borffor Moel yr Afr **yn cyflym doddi** i'r gwyll. [CRYMAN 14]	. . . and over the ridge the purple dome of Moel yr Afr **was fast melting** into the twilight. [SICKLE 9]

The possibility of dual placement is not always available as shown by this final set of examples. '*Cwbl*', '*gwir*', '*prysur*' and '*hen*' here can only precede the verb-noun.

Credai yn yr egwyddor, ond nid oedd hyd yn oed Esperanto **yn ei gwbl fodloni**. [CYMER 124]	*He believed in the principle, but not even Esperanto* **completely satisfied him**.
. . . ac yna nid oedd ond un **yn gwir deimlo** fod pob man yn wag heb Mrs Trefor. [ENOC 312]	*. . . and then only one* **truly / really feeling** *that everywhere was empty without Mrs Trefor.*
Roedd y goeden dderw wedi **ei hen lorio** erbyn hyn ac yn gorwedd ar draws y ffordd. [PLA 157]	*The oak tree had* **well floored him** *by now and was lying across the road.*
'She was but thirty at the time of her death, and yet her hair had already begun to whiten, even as mine has.' [BAND 213]	'Dim ond deg ar hugain oed oedd hi pan fu hi farw, ond roedd ei gwallt eisoes wedi dechrau gwynnu, yn yr un modd ag y mae fy ngwallt innau **yn prysur golli** ei liw.' [*Lit: . . .in the*

---

[12] Of course, if the phrase occurs with a conjugated verb and in a position where that verb would need to be mutated, then a soft mutation does obtain, e.g.:

Ond yr hyn **a fawr ofnaf** a ddaeth arnaf;   *But that which* **I greatly feared** *came* [CHWECH 141]   *upon me.*

> *same way as my own hair is swiftly*
> *losing its colour*] [CYLCH 20]

8.2.2 Adjective (modifier) + preposition 'o' + adjective (used adverbially)

This is also discussed in 8.1.5i above. However, this construction can also be used adverbially with an adjective modifier or intensifier connected to the adjective by the preposition '*o*':

Eisteddodd Owen ar y drafael, ac o dan gyfarwyddyd Huw Jones llwyddodd i naddu pen ac ochr i'r grawen, er mai **yn boenus o araf** y gwnâi hynny. [CYCHWYN 23]	Owen seated himself at the block, and under Huw Jones's guidance succeeded in whittling one end and side of a 'rough', although his progress was **painfully slow**. [BEGIN 21]
A thrawodd Huw Jones ei het ar yr heol **mor ffyrnig o ddiofal** nes i'w hymyl, mewn dychryn, ffarwelio â'r gweddill ohoni. [CYCHWYN 124]	And Huw Jones had clapped his hat onto its nail **so recklessly** that its brim, panic-stricken, had parted company with the rest of it. [BEGIN 123–4]
Mae'r glaw yn disgyn **yn drofannol o drwm** . . . [FFYDD 60]	The rain's bucketing down [*Lit: The rain is falling tropically heavy*] [FAITH 47]

8.2.3 Specific adverbs

Certain adverbs present challenges to the translators working with English and Welsh. A glance at a dictionary will list two or three possibilities at least for the first item here '*almost*'. The discussion that follows deals with some of the more common of these and the different strategies available to convey them in the other language.

8.2.3.a Almost/Nearly

- *agos i*

'*Agos*' is more closely associated with the meaning '*near*' and is followed by the prepositions '*i*' or '*at*'. The predicative '*yn*' may precede '*agos*' but it does not have to. In the example below, the alternative '*bron*' could also have been used. However, '*agos*' is a useful option especially with quantifiable amounts or time.

Roedd 'na gonscripsiwn ar y pryd ac roedd gan **agos i** bob teulu feibion yn y lluoedd arfog. [HUNAN 131]	There was conscription, and **almost** every family had sons in the military. [SOLVA 131–2]

- *braidd [na]*

'*Braidd*' is more commonly associated with the English modifiers '*rather, somewhat*' and will be followed by the predicative '*yn*'.

Mae <u>braidd yn</u> dwym heddiw.	It's <u>rather</u> warm today.

However, when it is followed by a relative clause (usually a negative clause) its meaning is much closer to '*almost*'. It should be noted that this same construction can also be used with both '*bron*' and '*prin*' below to similar effect.

Braidd nad anghofiodd am Alis . . . [MONICA 12]	She **almost** forgot about Alice . . . [MONICA 10]

The negative element in the Welsh cannot be transferred to the English here as that would alter the meaning of the original >>> **she almost didn't forget about Alice.*

- *bron*

In the same way as '*braidd*' above, '*bron*' can be followed by a relative clause (again, often with the negative) to connect the meaning of '*almost*' with a verb:

Bron na loywai derw'r hen dresal Gymreig lawn cymaint â'r jygiau copr a hongiai tros ei silffoedd a thros y rhesi heirdd o blatiau gleision. [O LAW 153]	The oak of the old Welsh dresser **shone almost** as brightly as the burnished copper jugs hanging down from its shelves and over the rows of handsome blue dishes. [FROM 122]
. . . a **bron na ddisgwyliai** Owen glywed Robin Ifans yn taflu 'Amen' i ganol y tawelwch. [CYCHWYN 125–6]	. . . and Owen **almost expected** to hear Robin Evans interpolate an "Amen" when there was a pause. [BEGIN 125–6]

To include the negative element in the English here would, again, be erroneous – **Owen didn't expect to hear Robin Evans . . .* is the exact opposite of the original.

'*Bron*' is the most common Welsh equivalent to '*almost*' and may occur in the same position as any other adverb (after a verbal phrase although it does not always correspond exactly to the position of '*almost*' in English):

Syfrdanwyd Jane Gruffudd ormod i siarad **bron**. [TRAED 48]	Jane Gruffydd was **almost** too shocked to speak. [FEET 43]
Roedd 'na rwydwaith o gêbls trydan uwchben yn rhannu'r ddinas, a gallech chi fynd i unman **bron** ar drolibws. [HUNAN 77]	Overhead a network of electric cables dissected the city like a horizontal spider's web. You could go **almost** anywhere on a trolley bus. [SOLVA 78]
Ond yn hollol ddisymwth, cyn iddo gael cyfle i hel ei feddyliau at ei gilydd **bron**, roedd hi wedi troi ar ei sawdl ac yn disgwyl amdano wrth y drws. [PLA 73]	Then suddenly, [*almost*] before he could gather his wits, she turned, waiting for him at the door. [PEST 55-6]

The expression '*bron â bod*' [literally '*almost being*'] is another less formal possibility here too:

Ro'n i wedi cefnu ar fy ngradd yn y Saesneg **bron â bod**, er mawr siom a gofid i mi. [CRWYD 101-2]	*I had **almost** turned my back on my degree in English, to my great disappointment and regret.*

Combined with the preposition '*â*' (already referred to above in the expression '*bron â bod*[13]'), this is an alternative way of expressing '*almost*' with a verb.

... when she came up close **you could almost feel** the dangerous heat radiating from her. [MAT 67]	... a phan oedd hi'n dod yn agos **gallet ti bron â theimlo'r gwres peryglus** yn pelydru ohoni. [MAT 61]

[13] '*Bron â bod*' may even be modified as in this example where '*iawn*' comes directly after '*bron*':
Leaving his car in the **almost deserted** Lysle Street ... [TIME 27]   Gan adael ei gar yn Stryd Gefn, **a oedd erbyn hyn bron iawn â bod yn wag** ... [AMSER 42]

[B]ûm bron â throi adre'n ôl a chario allan fy hen fwriad – mynd efo 'Nhad i weithio yn y chwarel. [WILLAT 11]	*I almost turned back and carried out my original intention – going with Dad to work in the quarry.*

The informal '*jest/jyst/dest*' is an alternative to '*bron*' in the examples above.

Her nose was **almost** as prominent as his own, though femininely shapely and less thrusting. [TIME 102]	Roedd ei thrwyn **jyst iawn** mor amlwg â'i un ef, er yn fenywaidd siapus ac yn llai ymwthgar. [AMSER 162]
Mae'ch recordiadau chi i gyd gen i, dwi **jyst â marw** isio'ch cyfarfod chi ers amser. [CRWYD 111]	*I've got all your recordings, I've been almost/just dying to meet you for ages.*

It is possible for a comparative to follow '*bron*' and when an adjective or a numeral (or a noun) follows it, then the predicative '*yn*' is used too >> *almost ready* >> *bron yn barod* [never: *bron parod].

Hermione Granger was **almost as nervous** about flying **as** Neville was. [STONE 261]	Roedd Hermione Granger **bron mor nerfus** â Nefydd ynghylch hedfan. [MAEN 114]
He could be mistaken, but he was thinking that she was **halfway to being sloshed** already . . . [TIME 103]	Efallai ei fod yn camgymryd, ond credai ei bod **bron yn feddw rhacs** yn barod . . . [AMSER 164]
'R oedd y tŷ **bron yn wag**, y celfi, gan mwyaf, wedi eu symud y dyddiau cynt; [HDF 188]	The house was **almost** empty as the furniture for the most part had been removed the previous day. [OFH 236]
. . . yr wyf **bron yn hanner cant oed** a'r rhan fwyaf o'm hoes wedi myned gyda'r gwynt. [HENAT 7]	I am **approaching fifty** [*Lit: I am almost fifty*] and most of my life has gone with the wind. [LOCUST 13]

'*Almost*' is an adverb of degree and when it modifies a verb in English, the construction [*bod* >> *bu/roedd etc*] + *bron* + *i* + *subject* is used in Welsh. Our examples illustrate that a form of the verb '*bod*' is not always needed but when it is, it will be in the third person singular of the appropriate tense.

An owl hooted loudly, and
Harry nearly fell out of the tree.
[STONE 281]

Hwtiodd gwdihŵ yn uchel a **bu
bron i Harry syrthio** o'r goeden.
[MAEN 179]

'A the, mae'n debyg?' gofynnodd
y forwyn. 'O, ia, te. **Bron imi
anghofio'r te.**'
[CYCHWYN 199]

'Oh, yes, tea. **I nearly forgot the tea.**'
[BEGIN 201]

'*Agos*' can occasionally occur in this adverbial clause position too as well as
'*ond y dim i*':

Bu agos i Owen dagu gan
chwerthin. [TRAED 79]

Owen nearly choked with laughter.
[FEET 70]

. . . a **bu ond y dim iddo ddisgyn** ar
ei hyd i'r bedd [PLA 118]

. . . and **had almost swayed** into the
open grave [PEST 61]

- other

We note these further two examples where Welsh has a verb-noun which corresponds to the English '*almost*' or has replaced it. The literal translations of
'*bygwth > threaten*' and '*gyrru > drive*' respectively would hold little meaning
if carried over into the English.

'Sorry,' he grunted, as the tiny old
man stumbled and **almost fell**.
[STONE 6]

'Drwg gen i,' chwyrnodd, wrth
i'r hen ŵr bychan faglu a **bygwth
syrthio**. [MAEN 4]

Yr oedd Sioned yn **gyrru ar ei
dwy-ar-bymtheg oed**, ac mewn
ysgol wnïo ym Mhont Garrog.
[TRAED 47]

Sioned was **almost seventeen** and
in a sewing school in Pont Garrog.
[FEET 42]

8.2.3.b Any

i) In interrogatives

The indefinite adjective '*unrhyw*' plus a noun is usually used for '*any*'. However,
in compounds such as '*anyone / anything*' etc., Welsh has the option of either
'*unrhyw un / unrhyw beth*' or the equivalent compounds '*rhywun / rhywbeth*'
(= *someone / something*).

'Did you find **anything bent** at his place?' [TIME 121]

'Ddaru chi ddod ar draws **unrhyw beth amheus** yn 'i le fo?' [AMSER 193]

Knowing your daughter – as I do not – have you **any idea** of why she should go away like this? [TIME 90]

O 'nabod eich merch – a thydw *i* ddim – oes gynnoch chi **unrhyw syniadau** pam y byddai hi'n mynd i ffwrdd fel hyn? [AMSER 142]

Ddaru mi ladd **rhwfun**[14]? *no danger.* Ddaru mi neyd cam a **rhwfun**? Dydw i ddim yn gwbod. [RHYS 331–2]

Have I killed **anybody**? No danger. Have I wronged **anybody**? I don't know that I have. [RHYS 316]

ii) Neither negative nor interrogative

Again, it is possible to use either '*unrhyw*' with a noun/pronoun or the compounds '*rhywun / rhywbeth / rhywle*' etc. Our first example includes both in the same quotation.

'Wn i ddim a oedd **unrhyw sail** i'r dannod hwn ai peidio, ynteu rheitheg dyn ym mhoethder ei dymer ydoedd, yn barod i gydio mewn **rhywbeth** a allai ddolurio rhagor . . . [HDF 185]

I don't know whether there was **any substance** in this taunt or whether it was the rhetoric of a man in the hotness of his temper ready to catch hold of **anything** that would hurt ever more . . . [OFH 232]

'R own i'n rhy ifanc i gymryd **unrhyw ran** yn y gweithrediadau; [HDF 122]

I was too young to take **any part** in the proceedings. [OFH 150–1]

Gwrando, Marged, mi wna'i **rywbeth** 'rwyt ti'n ofyn. [LLEIFIOR 36]

Listen, Marged, I'll do **anything** you want. [RETURN 29]

Cododd Abel ar ei draed; ac er nad oeddwn ond hogyn, gwyddwn os gallai **rhywun** gael allan a oedd marworyn o'r tân Dwyfol wedi disgyn i enaid Thomas a Barbara mai Abel oedd yr un hwnnw . . . [RHYS 174]

Abel got upon his feet. Although but a lad, I knew that if **anyone** could find out whether a spark of the divine fire had descended upon the souls of Thomas and Barbara, it was Abel. [RHYS 167]

---

[14] '*Rhwfun*' is a dialect form of '*rhywun*'.

An alternative for 'unrhyw un / rhywun' [= anyone / someone] is 'neb' [= no-one / nobody] which unusually here does not require a negative verb. Note that our two examples here include implicit comparisons – nobody in the world / nobody in the country:

Ar un wedd yr oedd yn well ganddo Geini na **neb yn y byd**, ond ei wraig a'i blant . . . [TRAED 62]	There was a sense in which he preferred Geini to **anybody** except his wife and children. [FEET 55]
Ac eto, anodd gennyf gredu fod **neb yn y wlad**, y gellid, yn rhesymol, ei alw'n llengar a ŵyr lai o farddoniaeth ar ei gof na mi . . . [HDF 100]	Yet I find it difficult to believe that there is **anyone** in the land who can reasonably be called a devotee of literature who knows less poetry by heart than I . . . [OFH 122–3]

Clearly, literal translations here would again alter the meaning substantially:

There was a sense in which he preferred Geini to **nobody**. . .

Yet I find it difficult to believe that there is **nobody** in the land who can reasonably be called a devotee of literature who knows less poetry by heart than I

Another option for 'unrhyw le / rhywle' [= anywhere / somewhere] is 'unman' (sometimes seen as '[n]unlle' in informal registers) which like 'neb' carries a negative connotation [= nowhere].

'But murder,' he said, shaking his head, 'for a wheel you can buy **anywhere**.' [TIME 42]	'Ond llofruddio,' mwmialodd, gan ysgwyd ei ben, 'am olwyn y medrech ei phrynu yn **rhywle**?' [AMSER 66]
Yr oedd yn anodd cael **yn unman** fwy o amrywiaeth creigiau, a'r rheini wedi eu cerfio'n rhamantus gan lifogydd o ddyfroedd, a lafa eiriasboeth, a rhew. [WILLAT 39]	It was difficult to find **anywhere** a greater variety of rocks. They had been romantically carved by floods of water, and red hot lava, and ice.

'Unrhyw' may be replaced by 'yr un' plus the noun being modified or 'dim' as a non-modifier. Once again, there are negative associations here similar to those noted above.

... byd, hefyd, hyd y gwelaf i, lle'r oedd pawb, yn ôl ei oed a'i brofiad, mor gyfatebol gydradd ag y gellir disgwyl i**'r un gymdeithas ddynol** fod. [HDF 118]

... and a world too, as far as I am able to judge, where all, in proportion to their age and experience, were as equal as **any human community** can be expected to be. [OFH 145]

Y pwnc a'm diddorai fwyaf y pryd hwnnw oedd Human Physiology, a llyfr rhagorol Huxley yn fwy blasus i mi na**'r un nofel** a ddarllenais erioed. [WILLAT 37]

*The subject that interested me most at that time was Human Physiology, and Huxley's outstanding book was more appealing to me than **any novel** I have ever read.*

Fel y dywedais eisoes yr oedd eu hamrywiaeth galluoedd a'u nodweddion yn llawer mwy na **dim** a geir heddiw. [WILLAT 227]

*As I have already mentioned, the variation in their abilities and their characteristics were far greater than **anything** one might have today.*

iii) After the negative

The alternatives discussed in (ii) above all hold here, namely:

unrhyw + noun / pronoun	>>>	yr un
unrhyw beth	>>>	dim [byd]
unrhyw un	>>>	neb
unrhyw le	>>>	unman

The final example in this set introduces 'mwyach' for 'any more'. An alternative (possibly more SW orientated) is 'rhagor'.

At the moment, other than her, Rogers couldn't think of **anybody** or **anything** he wished to be saved from. [TIME 17]

A'r funud honno ni fedrai Rogers feddwl am **unrhyw beth** nac **unrhyw un** y dymunai gael ei arbed rhagddo, ond y hi. [AMSER 26][15]

I would never have believed it of **any of you**. [STONE 302]

Chredwn i byth y gallai**'r un ohonoch chi'ch tri** fod wedi gwneud y fath beth. [MAEN 192]

[15] The translator here could just as equally have used: 'A'r funud honno ni fedrai Rogers feddwl am **ddim** na **neb** y dymunai gael ei arbed rhagddo, ond y hi'.

Ni wnaf i **ddim** iti, y ffolog benwan. [MONICA 18]	I won't do **anything** to you, you silly girl. [MONICA 170]
'You sure tha's all right? I ain't sure he is, and I ain't supposed to let **anyone** in who ain't a member.' [TIME 28]	'Ti'n siwr fod hynny'n ol-reit? Tydw i ddim, a dw i ddim i fod i adael **neb** i mewn sy ddim yn *member.* [AMSER 43]
Turn the telly on and let's **not** have **any more talk**. [MAT 55]	Tro'r teledu ymlaen a **dim rhagor o siarad**. [MAT 49]
It didn't seem very important **anymore**. [STONE 260]	Doedd o ddim fel petai'n bwysig **mwyach**. [MAEN 165]

8.2.3.c Negative 'fawr'

The negative '*fawr*' (the adjective '*mawr* = big, large*' which in the negative is always mutated) can be considered as a modifying adverb with the meaning '*not . . . much/greatly*' or '*hardly*'. Informally, '*fawr*' may be followed by a second dependent negative such as '*dim*' and sometimes connected by the preposition '*o*' >> '*fawr ddim / fawr o ddim*' >> '*hardly anything*'.

Doedd o fawr o le er fod lliwiau ei wrychoedd a'i goedydd yn rhai na welai o'r blaen . . . [PLA 63]	**This looked a poor enough place** [*Lit: It wasn't much of a place*], though there were more trees about it than there would have been at home. [PEST 48]
Does gan y dyfodol **fawr** i'w gynnig i'r rhan fwya ohonon ni, ond mae ganddoch chi'r gallu i neud rwbath ohono fo a'r cyfla i ddianc o'r uffarn yma. [RHANNU 195]	*The future doesn't have **much** to offer most of us, but you have the ability to make something of it and escape from this hell.*
Fydden ni'n gwneud **fawr ddim o** Shakespeare, oedd yn fy siwtio i i'r dim. [CRWYD 102]	*We wouldn't do **hardly any** Shakespeare, which suited me to a T.*

8.2.3.d Prin / O'r braidd

These correspond to the English '*hardly / scarcely*'. '*Prin*' is followed by a relative clause and connects in that way with the verb it is modifying. It may also be followed by a noun where it (as an adjective) comes first and causes a soft mutation. '*O'r braidd*' behaves like an adverb and will stand independently.

There was something very queer
about the water, she thought, as
every now and then the oars got fast
in it, and would **hardly come out**
again. [THRO 179]

Roedd rhywbeth yn ddieithr iawn
ynghylch y dŵr, meddyliodd,
oherwydd bob yn awr ac eilwaith
âi'r rhwyfau'n sownd ynddo, a **phrin
y deuent allan**. [TRWY 67]

Prin ro'n i'n gallu credu 'i bod hi'n
dod ar ôl yr holl gyfnod cythryblus.
[HUNAN 233]

I could hardly believe that she was
arriving after all these troubled
times. [SOLVA 233]

Aeth i'w fedd yn ei hen ddyddiau,
heb ddant yn eisiau, na **phrin
flewyn brith** yn y trwch o wallt
gwineuddu ar ei ben. [OFH 168]

He died in old age without a tooth
missing from his mouth, and with
hardly a grey hair in all that thick
growth of dark brown. [HDF 210]

O'r braidd roedd hi i'w gweld yn fy
nabod i. [HUNAN 233]

She **barely** seemed to recognise me.
[SOLVA 233]

8.2.3.e *Rhyw*

There is an indefinite sense with *'rhyw'* usually corresponding to English
'some / some [kind of]'. This can be a useful device, therefore, when there is
a need to convey an indefinite article in English which does not exist *per se*
in Welsh.

And certainly the glass *was*
beginning to melt away, just like **a**
bright silvery mist. [THRO 131]

. . . ac yn wir ichi, roedd y gwydr *yn*
dechrau toddi, yn union fel **rhyw**
darth arianaid disglair. [TRWY 18]

'Wel, y diawl bach,' meddai **rhyw**
fachgen o'r tu ôl, 'Y nhwrn i oedd
hwnna.' [TRAED 35]

'Well, the little devil,' said **a** boy
from behind, 'that was my turn.'
[FEET 31–2]

Our set of examples illustrate that it is possible to render *'rhyw'* in a variety of
ways in English, all including the indefinite element which is inherent in it.

Cof gennyf fy mod yn cysylltu **rhyw**
ddirgelwch mawr ynglŷn â'r cwd
gwyrdd yn yr hwn y cariai y bechgyn
eu llyfrau i ysgol Mr Smith. [RHYS 34]

I remember associating **some** great
mystery with the green bags in
which his scholars used to carry
their books. [RHYS 37]

'Ac mi gaiff pob un ohonom ni **ryw**
chwephunt yr un,' meddai Betsan.
[TRAED 102]

'And everyone will get **a paltry**
six pounds each,' said Betsan.
[FEET 92]

In a similar way, 'rhyw' is equally useful when giving a sense of approximation or denoting an unspecific amount / characteristic from English into Welsh.

... it had, in fact, **a sort of** mixed flavour of cherry-tart, custard, pine-apple, roast turkey, toffy, and hot buttered toast ... [ALICE 24]	... mewn gwirionedd, **rhyw** gymysgedd o flas teisen geirios, a chwstard, ac afal-pin, a thwrci wedi ei rostio, a thaffi, a thôst poeth yn nofio o ymenyn ... [ALYS I 16]
She's at the hospital with Sargeant Jarvis, incidentally, who being a widow herself should be **something of** a comfort. [TIME 40]	Mae hi yn y 'sbyty efo Sarjant Jarvis, gyda llaw. Gan mai gweddw ydi hithau hefyd, dylai hi fod o **ryw** gysur iddi. [AMSER 63]
... when I was perhaps four years old **or so**. [OFH 151]	... a minnau'n **rhyw** bedair oed, efallai. [HDF 122]
... a phob **rhyw** gerdd ... [HDF 156]	... and all **kinds** of music ... [OFH 195]

'Rhyw' may be used to modify a verb-noun making its meaning less definite – an equivalent to English 'sort of / just doing something'. It can convey an approximate way of doing something e.g. 'meddwl >> rhyw feddwl' >> 'thinking >> kind of / sort of thinking'

Lingard was **dismissive**.[16] [TIME 66]	**Rhyw wffltio'r** syniad wnaeth Lingard. [AMSER 104]
... ac 'roeddwn i'n **rhyw feddwl** y licet ti ddod i'r dre y pnawn 'ma am sgawt. [CRYMAN 47]	I was **sort of wondering** whether you'd like to go into town this afternoon for a look-around. [SICKLE 37]
Bwytaodd y ddau ohonyn nhw ond **rhyw bigo fel iâr** a wnaeth yr arglwyddes. [PLA 194]	*Both of them ate but the Lady was* ***just kind of picking at it like a*** ***chicken.***
Dyna beth oedd addysg, nid **rhyw bori fel gafr** wrth gadwyn. [CHWAL 172]	That was what education was, not **just grazing like a goat** on a chain. [OUT 173]

---

[16] 'Dismissive' is given by the Welsh translator as 'Lingard sort of / kind of dismissed the idea'.

It is worth noting the use of '*rhyw*' with expressions of time to indicate, once again, an approximation rather than a definite, specified occasion.

Ella bydd yn dda iti wrth y bwyd yma **ryw ddiwrnod**. [TRAED 48]	Perhaps you'll be glad to eat at this table **one day**. [FEET 43]
There was comparative calm in the Wormwood household **for about a week** after the Superglue episode. [MAT 38]	Fe fu hi'n gymharol dawel yng nghartref y teulu Wormwood **am ryw wythnos** ar ôl y digwyddiad gyda'r glud cryf. [MAT 32]
. . . **ryw fis** cyn i mi gael fy mhen blwydd cyntaf. [HDF 64]	. . . **a month or so** before my first birthday. [OFH 77]
Dyma fel y dechreuai'r hen ŵr arni, **ryw dro**, meddai nhad . . . [HDF 88]	'This is how the old man opened out **once**,' said my father . . . [OFH 107]

8.3 Conclusions

Dealing with past and present participles in English can be problematic for translators and as we have shown, it is not possible to give a 'one size fits all' solution here. Morphologically it is possible to use suffixes such as *-edig* or *-iog* to convey a sense of the participle but this is not always an option which is sensible to use either semantically or stylistically. We have seen, therefore, that a decision has to made as to whether one should then use a sub-clause, a *wedi* construction or another device. It should also be remembered that the solution might be found in converting the participle to another part of speech, for example a noun:

I have read all the collected works of Saunders Lewis
Rwyf wedi darllen y casgliad cyflawn o waith Saunders Lewis

Here, '*all the collected works of* is rendered by '*the complete collection of work*'. The question is how to decide which of the ways we have discussed would best convey the meaning of the original in Welsh and will strike the reader as natural as well as being stylistically appropriate. In a similar manner, the juxtaposition of the adverb with an adjective in English requires thought as to which option is likely to be the most successful when translating into Welsh as a direct equivalent does not exist.

In the opposite direction, the option of using a participle when translating from a Welsh source into English could be considered as well as the possibility of rendering a relative sub-clause by an *adverb + adjective/participle* construction, rather than a more literal translation:

Symudais i dŷ newydd ar stad a adeiladwyd yn ddiweddar.

Two options are available here:

(i)   I moved to a new house on an estate which had been recently built.
(ii) I moved to a new house on a recently built estate.

It is likely that (i) would be preferable if the emphasis is on the fact that the house itself had been recently built but (ii) might be better if we wish to emphasise the fact that the whole estate was of a recent construction.

9

Lexical Issues:
Word formation and collocations

9.0 Introduction

Word formation and the way in which words or lexical items work together (*collocations* – see section 3) can present major challenges to students, writers and language users. Often there can be fairly minor differences, for example in English we *sit an exam* but in Welsh we *sefyll arholiad* 'stand an exam'. Sometimes, there are direct equivalents as in, for example, *talu pris / pay a price* but it is not always possible to extend these further: *talu teyrnged* 'to pay tribute' is fine but *talu'n hallt (= to pay dearly)* does not find an equivalent in **to pay saltily*. Similarly, *to pay a visit* is better rendered in Welsh as *ymweld â* rather than *talu ymweliad*[1].

In the first two sections of this chapter, we consider some specific lexical items and how their different semantic fields can be rendered in translation. They are representative of some of the more common items in both languages but should not be considered as an exhaustive list.

9.1.a Fields of meaning: English items

BAD [*see* POOR]
TO BORE [BORING]

'*To get bored/fed up of* ' has an equivalent in '*diflasu/alaru ar*' (see Chapter 3.2ii). Combinations with the adjective '*diflas*' are often used otherwise for the condition of '*being bored*' or to describe something as '*boring*'.

---

[1] Although GPC (3426) includes '*talu ymweliad*' dated 1868, this is generally viewed as an anglicisation and the verb-noun '*ymweld â*' is preferred.

I hope you won't be **bored**. [VICT 95]	Gobeithio na fyddwch chi ddim yn meddwl **'i fod o'n ddiflas**. [LLINYN 108]
Tref fach **ddiflas** oedd Amwythig, heb fod hanner mor fywiog â Henffordd dafliad carreg lawr yr hewl. [HUNAN 128]	Shrewsbury was a **boring** little border town, not half as lively as Hereford. [SOLVA 128]
Mae barddoniaeth a rhyddiaith dda yn wledd wastadol i mi; ac nid oes dim yn **ddiflasach** gennyf na gwaith troetrwm, di-awen. [HDF 100]	Good poetry and prose are a perpetual feast to me, and I find nothing more **boring** than flat-footed and uninspired writing. [OFH 122–3]

TO EMBARRASS [EMBARRASSED/-ING]

There is no direct Welsh equivalent for the English verb 'to embarrass'. This is also true of the adjectives 'embarrassed' and 'embarrassing'. There is evidence that the borrowed noun 'embaras' is well established in Welsh writing and is usually combined with a verb-noun e.g. 'creu/teimlo/achosi/codi' etc. or an appropriate modifier. Its use can be eschewed by some writers, however, particularly in more formal registers where approximate synonyms may be preferred.

. . . she was taking great care not to say anything **to embarrass** her companion. [MAT 189]	. . . roedd hi'n ofalus iawn i beidio â dweud dim a fyddai'n **codi embaras ar** ei chydymaith. [MAT 183]
And then, as though **embarrassed** at having revealed such a secret part of herself, she quickly pushed open the gate and walked up the path. [MAT 186]	Ac yna, fel petai'n **teimlo embaras** oherwydd iddi ddatgelu rhan mor gyfrinachol o'i hunan, gwthiodd y glwyd ar agor yn gyflym a cherdded i fyny'r llwybr. [MAT 180]
He felt nothing more than a frozen **embarrassment**. [VICT 118]	**Teimlai embaras**, yn fwy na dim arall. [LLINYN 132]
. . . rhywbeth oedd yn **destun embaras** iddo fe; [HUNAN 122]	This was something he found profoundly **embarrassing**. [SOLVA 122]
Dw i'n rhyw amau fod y sefyllfa wedi **achosi cryn embaras** i Kiddle druan. [AMSER 73]	*I kind of suspect that the situation has considerably **embarrassed** poor Kiddle.*

There followed a rather long and **embarrassing** silence. [MAT 194]	Bu tawelwch eithaf hir a **llawn embaras**. [MAT 188]
Ro'n i'n teimlo'n **annifyr**. [HUNAN 275]	I felt **embarrassed**
... hen ganeuon pop Americanaidd wedi'u cyfieithu'n anghelfydd i'r iaith Gymraeg a'u canu gan gantorese digon i **godi gwrid arnoch chi** ... [HUNAN 161]	... old American pop songs crudely translated into the Welsh language, and sung by **embarrassing** lady singers ... [SOLVA 161]

EVENING / NIGHT

The options available in Welsh mean that it is not always possible to select a direct equivalent without considering the exact period of time in question. '*Nos*' is the antonym of '*dydd*' (i.e. the period of time when there is darkness) and can be combined with individual days of the week to give a specific night (but changes to '*nosweithiau*' in plural combinations). '*Noson*' which originally arose from a contraction of '*nos*' with the demonstrative '*hon*' refers more to a period of time or the events of the night or evening. '*Noswaith*' refers more specifically to the time period between day and night and both '*noswaith*' and '*nos*' (but not '*noson*') are collocated with '*da*' as a time specific greeting e.g. '*Noswaith dda*' for 'good evening' and '*Nos da*' for 'good night' with the implication in the latter of a final taking of leave at the end of the day.

Literary registers of Welsh offer the option of '*hwyrnos*' or '*hwyrddydd*' as alternatives for the evening period. '*Gyda'r nos*', '*gyda'r hwyr*' and '*min nos*' are additional possibilities which are also possible in less formal registers. Although these are adverbial expressions of time they can also be used as nouns.

The combinations '*this evening*', '*tonight*' and '*on this night*' find expression in '*heno*' (compare also: '*heddiw*' = today, this day, on this day) and '*neithiwr*' is used for '*last night*'. '*Noswyl*' is a combination of '*nos*' and '*gŵyl*' used to refer to the vigil before a religious feast e.g. '*Noswyl y Nadolig*' for 'Christmas Eve' (note that New Year's Eve is '*Nos Galan*').

Bydde John hefyd yn mynd i Gapel Baptist Ararat bob **nos Sul** a byddwn i'n mynd gyda fe jyst i gael morio canu. [HUNAN 83]	John also went to Ararat Baptist Chapel on **Sunday evenings** and I used to go with him just for a good sing. [SOLVA 84]

Ddwyweth yr wythnos – **ar nosweithie Mercher a Sadwrn** – bydde clwb jazz 'da Mike Harries mewn seler yn High Street. The Mavis June School of Ballroom Dancing oedd e bob **noson** arall. [HUNAN 90]

Mike Harries had a jazz club in a cellar on **Wednesdays and Saturdays** [*evenings*] – the rest of the week [*every other **night***] it was the Mavis June School of Ballroom Dancing. [SOLVA 90]

And remember, our missing Debbie Studley may yet return from a quite uneventful **evening** out with a couple of friends. [TIME 25]

A chofia, mae hi'n bosib o hyd y daw Debbie Studley yn ei hôl wedi **noson** dawel efo ffrindiau. [AMSER 38]

Un **noson**, ym mis Ionawr 1893, yr oedd cyfarfod y plant yn y capel, a'r pedwar plentyn yno. [TRAED 31]

One **evening** in January 1893 there was a children's meeting at the chapel and the four children were there. [FEET 28]

Aberthodd swper er mwyn hynny, ac yn ei gwely bu'n troi a throsi ac yn ail-fyw'r **noson** hyd oriau mân y bore. [TRAED 50]

She has sacrificed supper for that, and in bed she turned and tossed until the small hours of the morning as she re-lived the events of the **evening**. [FEET 45]

Hwyrddydd o haf, neu, efallai, o hydref cynnar, oedd hi'r tro hwn, a'r coed yn nhalcen y berllan, fel 'r wy'n cofio'n dda, yn eu llawn dail. [HDF 159]

It was a summer **evening**, or perhaps an early autumn evening, with the trees at the end of the orchard in full leaf, I remember well. [OFH 199]

Bore Sul y doed o hyd i'r corff, hithau wedi ei lladd yr **hwyrnos** gynt. [CHWECH 33]

*The body was found on the Sunday morning and she had been killed the previous **night**.*

Ar ôl diwrnod mwll, tywyll, daeth yr haul allan **gyda'r nos** ac aeth i lawr dros fôr Iwerydd fel pêl o dân . . . [TRAED 153]

After a dark, sultry day, the sun came out **in the late evening** and went down into the Irish Sea like a ball of fire . . . [FEET 127]

Bob **gyda'r nos** a phrynhawn Sadwrn clywid eco ei gŷn a'i forthwyl dros yr ardal . . . [TRAED 27]

Every **evening** and Saturday afternoon the sound of his hammer and chisel was heard throughout the district . . . [FEET 24]

He asked them if they had seen the **evening** papers. [VICT 21]

Holodd a oedden nhw wedi gweld y papurau **min nos**. [LLINYN 23]

'Dr Roylott has gone to town, and it is unlikely that he will be back before **evening**.' [BAND 225]

'Mae Dr Roylott wedi mynd i Lundain, ac yn annhebygol o ddychwelyd cyn **min nos**.' [CYLCH 37]

[B]yddai hi'n anfon y gaethferch i'w gyrchu i'r tŷ **gyda'r hwyr**. [PLA 72]

... but promised to send a servant to guide him to their house that **evening**. [PEST 54]

Yr oedd yr **hwyr** yn dawel iawn ... [CHWAL 25]

It was a very still **evening** ... [OUT 25]

When I told her that Miss Stuchley had been missing from her apartment since **last evening** she immediately jumped in ... [TIME 65]

Pan ddaru mi ddeud wrthi fod Miss Stuchley 'di bod ar goll o'i fflat ers **neithiwr**, neidiodd i'r fei ar unwaith ... [AMSER 102]

A **heno**, yr oedd y plasty bach hynafol yn dangnefedd i gyd, a choch y gorllewin yn ei res ffenestri Sioraidd. [CRYMAN 12]

This evening, the ancient little grange looked so peaceful, with the red glow from the western sky reflected in its row of Georgian windows. [SICKLE 8]

TO FIND

Although the informal *'ffeindio'* can cover many of the same semantic fields as 'FIND' in English, it is often (and best) avoided in all other registers. When the meaning is either *'see'*, *'look for'* or *'discover'* then the corresponding verbs *'gweld'*, *'chwilio/edrych am'* or *'darganfod/canfod'* are appropriate.

Fe fynnai fynd i **chwilio am** Winni a chael ei mam i ofyn iddi ddŵad i de efo digon o jeli, er mwyn ei chlywed yn siarad. [TE 46]

She would go and **find** Winni. Then she'd ask her mother to ask Winni to tea, and plenty of jelly, just to hear her talk. [TEA 44]

It was early in April, in the year '83, that I woke one morning **to find** Sherlock Holmes standing, fully dressed, by the side of my bed. [BAND 207]

Dechrau mis Ebrill oedd hi, yn y flwyddyn '83, pan ddeffrois un bore **a gweld** Sherlock Holmes, yn ei ddillad gwaith, yn sefyll wrth erchwyn fy ngwely. [CYLCH 12]

He had already told Magnus of the **finding** of cocaine on Stephanakis's body. [TIME 71]

Roedd eisoes wedi sôn wrth Magnus iddo **ganfod** cocên ar gorff Stephanakis. [AMSER 113]

... the papers **found** in Stephanakis's briefcase... [TIME 92]

... y papurau a **ganfuwyd** yng nghês Stephanakis ... [AMSER 147]

I can't think there could be any doubt about his identity when he was **found** dead by a neighbour who knew him by sight. [TIME 104–5]

Fedra i ddim meddwl fod 'na unrhyw amheuaeth ac yntau wedi cael 'i **ddarganfod** yn farw gan gymydog oedd yn 'i nabod o'n iawn o ran ei weld. [AMSER 167]

... a hithau mor ddiofn, mor ddi-feddwl-ddrwg, yn rhedeg yn ysgafndroed i lawr y grisiau, ac yna, drwy golyn y drws, cyn dyfod hyd yn oed un amheuaeth drugarog i dorri'r garw, yn **darganfod** Bob a'r forwyn ynghyd ar y soffa. [MONICA 46]

So fearless, so trusting, so light of foot, she ran down the stairs, and through the half-open door, without even one merciful twinge of suspicion which would have prepared her for the worst, there **to find** Bob and the maid together on the sofa. [MONICA 45]

If a directly corresponding verb is difficult, for most other meanings of English 'FIND' either '*cael*' or '*dod*' may be combined with '*(o) hyd i*' as in the following examples. An additional possibility for the meaning of '*to come across something*' is shown here with '*dod ar draws*':

[W]hen Alice first **found** her in the ashes, she had been only three inches high – and here she was, half a head taller than Alice herself! [THRO 143]

[P]an **gafodd** Alys **hyd iddi** yn y lludw 'doedd hi'n ddim mwy na thair modfedd o uchder, a dyma hi'n awr, drwyn a thalcen yn dalach nag Alys ei hun! [TRWY 29]

There were five photographs in the envelope he had **found** in the sideboard drawer. [TIME 27]

Roedd pum llun yn yr amserlen y **daeth o hyd iddi** yn nrôr y seidbord. [AMSER 41]

The confusion got worse every moment, and Alice was very glad to get out of the wood into an open place, where she **found** the White King seated on the ground... [THRO 195–6]

Aeth y dryswch yn waeth bob munud, ac yr oedd Alys yn falch o fynd i le agored, lle **daeth o hyd i'r** Brenin Gwyn yn eistedd ar lawr... [TRWY 86]

Felly, dyma ni, yn ddau drempyn cysglyd, yn **cael hyd i'**r man croeso a'r dollborth, nad oedd yn bod –

*So, here we were, two sleepy tramps, having **found** the reception area and customs, which didn't exist – nobody*

neb i fwrw golwg ar ein pasbortiau Prydeinig newydd glân – a dyma **ddod o hyd i** far eto. [CRWYD 28]

*to take a look at our brand new British passports – and **finding** a bar once again.*

Magnus's **finding** it had answered his earlier question as to whether Deborah Stuchley had been an addict. [TIME 71]

Roedd y ffaith fod Magnus wedi **dod ar ei draws** yn ateb ei gwestiwn cynharach ynglŷn â ph'run ai oedd Deborah Stuchley yn gaeth i'r cyffur ai peidio. [AMSER 113]

'*Cael*' with the dependent personal pronoun '*ei*' (third person singular – feminine but used impersonally) coupled with an adjective can be used with the particular meaning of '*to experience/feel*'[2]:

To me, it's completely explicable that if she had heard of it – and there's no reason why she shouldn't have if she's still somewhere locally – then she **would find it difficult** to refer to a man she had been living with and about whom she must presume I knew nothing. [TIME 90]

Os oedd hi wedi clywed amdano – a does dim rheswm pam na ddylai hi fod wedi gwneud os ydi hi'n dal i fod yn rhywle lleol – yna mi fyddai hi'n **ei chael hi'n anodd** cyfeirio at ddyn yr oedd hi wedi bod yn byw efo fo, a hithau'n cymryd yn ganiataol na wyddwn i ddim am y peth. [AMSER 143]

She said that **they found it difficult** to understand with the proprietor interpreting . . . [TIME 46]

Dywedodd hithau **eu bod nhw'n ei chael hi'n anodd** deall gan fod y perchennog yn cyfieithu . . . [AMSER 72–3]

TO HELP

'*Helpu*' is the verb in Welsh which corresponds in general to the English '*to help*'. Note the occasional (but not obligatory) use of the preposition '*ar*' after '*helpu*'. '*Cynorthwyo*' conveys a similar meaning but tends to be used as a direct translation of '*to assist*' and in more formal registers.

'*Mae* hi'n braf arnoch chi, Gwen, yn cael hogiau ifanc i'ch **helpu** a rhoi fferis i chi.' Ac ni chylwsai Gwen yn eu cywiro chwaith. [TRAED 69]

'You are lucky, Gwen, to have boys **to help you** and give you sweets.' And he would not have heard Gwen offer any correction. [FEET 61]

---

[2] See Chapter 7 for a more detailed discussion of '*cael*'.

Gan amlaf y **mae'n helpu yn y siop**, ond bydd yn teithio weithiau. [MONICA 10]	Usually **he helps in the shop**, but sometimes he travels around. [MONICA 9]
He suspected he wouldn't have lost so badly if Percy hadn't tried to **help him so much.** [STONE 253]	Amheuai'n gryf na fyddai ddim wedi colli mor ddychrynllyd pe na bai Percy wedi ceisio **helpu cymaint arno.** [MAEN 161]

Welsh often prefers the use of the nouns '*help*' or '*cymorth*' where English maintains a verb. The collocation '*help + llaw*' is frequently encountered in Welsh too (it would not be possible to use '*cymorth*' as an alternative in this collocation in a similar way to English '*a helping hand*' but not '*an assisting hand*'). Our final example is one where English '*help*' in the negating expression '*couldn't help but doing something*' finds no direct equivalent in Welsh.

Mae ei wallt tywyll yn glynu wrth ei ben **gyda help llaw** gan y styling gel. [FFYDD 44]	His dark hair sticks to his head **with serious assistance** from his styling gel. [FAITH 35]
His being out in the cold **doesn't help**. [TIME 19]	**Dydi o ddim help** ei fod o allan yn yr oerfel. [AMSER 29]
The frustrated warrior in you, Wilfred, and **it's going to help.** [TIME 20]	Mae 'na filwr rhwystredig ynot ti yn rhywle, Gwilym, ac **mi fydd hynny'n help** i ni. [AMSER 31]
Yr oedd gweinidogion yn rhy gyfrwys garedig, yn rhy dwyllodrus gysurlon, i fod yn **gymorth** iachus i'w pobl. [LLEIFIOR 110]	Ministers were too crafty in their kindness, too deceitful in their attempts to console, to be of practical **help** to their people. [RETURN 94]
Rhoesai'r gwrid poeth yn ei hwyneb le i welwder melyn erbyn hyn, ac **ni fedrai Sioned lai na sylwi** ar hynny. [TRAED 116]	Her flushed face turned into a yellow pallor, and **Sioned could not help noticing** this. [FEET 103]

TO KEEP [CONTINUE] DOING SOMETHING

Although it is possible to use '*cadw*' plus the preposition '*i*' to render this, another verb '*dal*' with the conjugated preposition (with an impersonal meaning) '*ati*' is often preferred. Another option is to use the verb relating to the action to be continued with appropriate adverbial support (often '*o hyd*').

Cadwodd hi i wisgo du am flwyddyn yn hwy na'i chwaer. [MONICA 22]

She had **continued to** wear black for a year longer than her sister. [MONICA 20]

'The daisies are worst of all. When one speaks, they all begin together, and it's enough to make one wither to hear the way **they go on**.' [THRO 141]

'Y Llygad y Dydd yw'r gwaethaf. Pan fydd un yn siarad maen nhw i gyd yn dechrau gyda'i gilydd, ac mae'n ddigon i wneud i rywun wywo y ffordd y **maen nhw'n dal ati**.' [TRWY 27]

Keep playing. [STONE 343]

Dal ati i chwarae. [MAEN 219]

She **kept staring** at me . . . [TIME 82]

Roedd hi'n **syllu** arna i **drwy'r amser**. [AMSER 130]

The only thing that he knew for certain was that the law forbade the Trunchball to hit him with the riding-crop that she **kept smacking** against her thigh. [MAT 123]

Yr unig beth a wyddai i sicrwydd oedd fod y gyfraith yn gwahardd y Trunchball rhag ei daro â'r chwip roedd hi'n **bwrw** yn erbyn ei chlun **o hyd ac o hyd**.

Follow me, please! We really mustn't **keep stopping** like this. [CHARLIE 104]

Dilynwch fi, os gwelwch yn dda! Ddylen ni ddim **aros** fel hyn **o hyd**. [SIOCLED 137]

TO LOOK [see also 'TO SEEM/APPEAR']

When '*look*' refers to having sight of someone or something it is most often rendered by the verb '*edrych*' in Welsh. If it is semantically closer to having or giving the appearance of someone or something, '*edrych*' (often followed by '*fel*' or '*yn debyg i*') is still possible (as is the more literal '*ymddangos*') but an expression using the noun '*golwg*' + either an adjective or a noun connected by *fel* + the preposition *ar* is also commonly employed. When the semantic field equates to '*seem*' this idiomatic expression is preferred.[3]

---

[3] GyrA [832] refers to the use of '*edrych*' with this meaning as an 'anglicism' (albeit in common use).

'What's happened to me! **I look** terrible! **I look just like *you*** gone wrong!' [MAT 63]

'Beth sydd wedi digwydd i mi? **Dw i'n edrych** yn ofnadwy! Dw i'n **edrych un union fel *ti*** wedi mynd o chwith!' [MAT 57]

Edrychai'r bryniau a'r chwareli'n dywyll a digalon. Yr oedd naws gaeaf yn y gwynt. [TRAED 81]

The hills and quarries **looked** dark and depressing, and there was a wintry nip in the wind. [FEET 71]

Here Alice wound two or three turns of the worsted round the kitten's neck, just to see **how it would look**... [THRO 128]

Yna lapiodd Alys ddau neu tri [*sic*] tro o'r gwlân am wddf y gath fach i weld **sut yr edrychai**... [TRWY 14]

Stuchley shook his head helplessly. It could have been Rogers's imagination, but **he looked** deflated in spirit. [TIME 90]

Ysgydwodd Stuchley ei ben mewn anobaith. Efallai mai dychymyg Rogers oedd ar fai, ond **edrychai** fel dyn a roes ei adenydd i lawr. [AMSER 142]

Managing, as he usually did, **to look like** the owner of a with-it boutique. He wore a silver-grey suit, a pink shirt and a flaring red tie beneath a kingfisher-blue overcoat. [TIME 18]

Gyda'i siwt las-lwyd, ei grys pinc a'i dei fflamgoch o dan gôt fawr las llachar, **edrychai'n debyg** i berchennog bwtîc ffasiynol. [AMSER 28]

She was rambling on in this way when she reached the wood: **it looked** very cool and shady. [THRO 156]

Roedd hi'n baldorddi ymlaen fel hyn pan gyrhaeddodd y goedwig: **ymddangosai**'n oeraidd braf a chysgodol. [TRWY 44]

'Beth ddaeth drosot ti,' ebe Mr Sheriff wrthi un bore tua diwedd Tachwedd, '**mae golwg fel llances arnat ti** eto.' [MONICA 26]

'Whatever's come over you?' Mr Sheriff asked her one morning towards the end of November. '**You look like a young girl** again.' [MONICA 24]

Roedd **golwg bryderus ar Trevor**... [HUNAN 92]

Trev put on **a worried look**... [SOLVA 92]

Er mor wahanol yw **golwg y lle** heddiw, heb neb yn byw yn y tŷ, ers blynyddoedd... [HDF 99]

In spite of the difference in **the look of the place** to-day, the house being uninhabited for many years... [OFH 121]

'Mae golwg wedi blino arnoch chi, Grace,' meddai'n bryderus. 'Synnwn i damad nad ydach chi'n hel am y ffliw . . .' [RHANNU 181]

'*You look tired, Grace,*' she said with concern. '*I wouldn't be at all surprised if you weren't coming down with 'flu . . .'*

The impersonal '*i'w weld*' with '*bod*' can be used even when the context in English is not an impersonal one. The expression '*yr un ffunud â*' can stand in for look when the implication is of a '*very similar/same appearance*' and would correspond to the English expression '*a spitting image*'. Our final example here illustrates the further possibility of using the expression '*o ran pryd a gwedd*':

'Mi fasa'n dda gin i petaswn i'n medru dallt y dyn yna oedd yn rhannu'r gwobrwyon,' meddai Jane Gruffydd, 'on'd **oedd o i'w weld yn ddyn clên**? Oedd o'n siarad yn dda, Owen?' [TRAED 80]

'I wish I could have understood that man who was giving out the prizes,' said Jane Gruffydd. '**Didn't he look a proper man!** Did he make a good speech Owen?' [FEET 70]

Roedd y Coleg Brenhinol yn ddewis arall, ond roedd hwnnw **i'w weld** yn obaith rhy wan . . . [HUNAN 66–7]

The Royal College of Art was another possibility, but I didn't think that I'd have much of a chance. (*that **looked/was to be seen** as*) [SOLVA 66]

He saw the night street as a Lowry landscape in which everyone **looked the same**. [VICT 23]

Yn ei feddwl roedd y stryd gefn nos fel darlun gan Lowry, a phawb **yr un ffunud â'i gilydd**. [LLINYN 24–5]

It was only recently that Ian had discovered **what Webber looked like**. [VICT 135]

Yn ddiweddar iawn y daethai Ian i wybod **sut un oedd Webber o ran pryd a gwedd**. [LLINYN 152]

TO MISS

In general, when the verb carries the meaning of *feeling an absence of someone or something*, Welsh prefers the expression '*gweld eisiau X*'. However, the following examples illustrate a variety of less common ways of rendering this either with combinations of '*gweld*' + '*colli*'/'*colled*' or more infrequently with the adjective '*chwith*' + '*ar ôl*':

I **missed** my mother terribly. [MAT 196]

Roeddwn i'n **gweld eisiau** fy mam yn ofnadwy. [MAT 190]

Yn ystod cyfnod cynllunie'r sioe, ro'n i'n **gweld isie** fy mhlant fwyfwy. [HUNAN 247]

During the planning stages of the show, I found myself **missing** the children more and more. [SOLVA 247]

O, do, a bu ond y dim iddo roi ei droed ynddi drwy gyfaddef ar funud gwan ei fod yn **gweld ei cholli.** [RHANNU 102]

*Oh yes, and he nearly put his foot in it by confessing that he **missed her.***

Golygfa hyfryd a heddychlon dwi wastad yn **gweld colled fawr ar ei hôl.** [HUNAN 74]

A lovely and peaceful scene, which **I miss as much now as I did then.** [SOLVA 74]

Yr oedd wedi **teimlo colli** Mrs Vaughan oddi wrth y bwrdd ac oddi ar yr aelwyd gymaint ag un ohonynt. [CRYMAN 99]

He'd **missed** Mrs Vaughan from table and hearth as much as any of them. [SICKLE 81]

Dinah'**ll miss me very much** tonight, I should think [ALICE 21]

Mae'n siŵr y **bydd yn chwith gan Deina ar f'ôl heno.** [ALYS II 10][4]

In the majority of its other fields of meaning, Welsh uses the verbs '*Colli*' or '*Methu*':

'My dear fellow, I would not **miss it** for anything.' [BAND 208]

'Fy nghyfaill annwyl . . . fyddwn i ddim **am golli'r cyfle** am bris yn y byd.' [CYLCH 13]

When I told her that Miss Stuchley had been **missing** from her apartment since last evening she immediately jumped in and said that she'd known she'd come to a bad end. [TIME 65]

Pan ddaru mi ddeud wrthi fod Miss Stuchley 'di bod **ar goll** o'i fflat ers neithiwr, neidiodd i'r fei ar unwaith a deud 'i bod hi'n gwybod na ddôi unrhyw dda iddi hi yn y diwedd. [AMSER 102]

---

[4] There is often an added sense of strangeness or singularity associated with the use of *chwith gan* . . . e.g.

'Mi **gwêl** 'i dad o hi'n **chwith** ar 'i ôl o yn y chwarel' [TRAED 126]

'His father **will see it strange** in the quarry without him' [FEET 112]

'Pryd mae Owen yn dechrau yn y Coleg?' meddai un. 'Ymhen tair wsnos.' '**Mi gwelwch hi'n chwith iawn.**' [TRAED 118]

'When is Owen starting at the college?' asked one. 'In three weeks.' '**You'll find it odd without him.**' [FEET 104]

POOR [*also* 'BAD' >> 'DRWG' in section 9.1.b]

The adjective '*tlawd*' conveys '*poor*' as an antonym to '*rich*' with the meaning of not having enough money or other means. However, '*tlawd*' does not extend to all other uses of the English '*poor*'. The noun '*truan*' may also be used as an adjective when there is an implication of wretchedness or misfortune which is deserving of pity[5]. The expression '*truan o* (or) *â*' with a person's name or occupation conveys sympathy for that person in their state of misfortune. The plural of the adjective '*truain*' can occasionally be seen in very formal registers but is best avoided (although the noun plural '*trueiniaid*' referring to the '*poor/pitiful ones*' again with an element of sympathy is more frequently observed). '*Creadur*' (fem. '*creadures*') is another option in informal registers associated mainly with NW.

. . . ar y llaw arall, y mae'n llawer iawn **tlotach** arnaf i. Collais hi pan oedd arnaf fwyaf o'i heisiau. [HENAT 61]	On the other hand my life is far **poorer** without her. I lost her when I had most need of her. [LOCUST 57]
'Do you call *that* a whisper?' cried the **poor** King, jumping up and shaking himself. [THRO 198]	'Dyna 'dych chi'n ei alw'n sibrwd?' gwaeddodd y Brenin **druan** gan neidio i fyny a'i ysgwyd ei hun. [TRWY 89]
But alas for **poor** Alice! When she got to the door, she found she had forgotten the little golden key . . . [ALICE 24]	Ond **druan** o Alys! Pan gyrhaeddodd y drws gwelodd ei bod wedi anghofio'r allwedd fach aur . . . [ALYS II 14]
Druan o'r wraig; ni allai wneuthur dim ond rhoddi'r gadair i'r capel lleol. [RHWNG 98]	*The **poor woman**; there was nothing she could do but to give the chair to the local chapel.*
[S]ynnwn i fawr nad y fi, o bawb o'n cyd-athrawon, a bwysai drymaf ar y disgyblion **druain** i ddysgu'n helaeth ar eu cof . . . [HDF 101]	And I should not be surprised if it were I, above all my colleagues, who most strongly urged the **poor** pupils to learn by heart extensively . . . [OFH 123]
Mi'r oedd yn dda i'r **gryduras** gael mynd i'w bedd. [TE 40]	She's better off in her grave, **poor thing**. [TEA 39]

[5] As can be seen in the examples, '*truan*' may take a soft mutation when this would not normally be expected. PWT [II.22] discusses this further.

In English, '*poor*' also has the meaning of '*deficient, bad, of an inferior quality*' for which neither '*truan*' or '*tlawd*' are appropriate in Welsh. '*Poor*' (= *bad*) as an antonym to '*good*' can generally be given by '*gwael*' although '*sâl*' with its association with '*illness*' can be seen in particular in the context of '*inferior quality*'. Both '*gwael*' and '*sâl*' have an association with '*bad health*'. However, when '*bad*' is semantically more connected with '*wickedness*' then often '*drwg*' is preferred [see also 'DRWG'].

Teimlwn yn sicr fy mod wedi gwneud mor **wael** yn y pwnc hwn (a minnau'n arfer cael fy ystyried yn dda ynddo) fel y byddwn yn debyg o suddo i'r Ail Ddosbarth. [WILLAT 89]

*I felt sure that I had done so **poorly/badly** in this subject (and me usually having been regarded as being good in it) that I would be likely to drop into Form Two.*

Yr oedd i fod i fyned i dorri 'gwellt Medi' i'r gwartheg, ond gadawodd iddynt ar eu cythlwng ar y borfa **wael** hyd drannoeth. [TRAED 152–3]

He had planned to cut some June hay for the cattle but he let them manage the best they could on the **poor** pasture until the next day. [FEET 135]

Yr oedd yn **wael** ei iechyd ar y pryd. [CWM 183]

He was in **poor** health . . . [GORSE 176]

Yr oedd fy chwaer Edith, a oedd tua dwy ar bymtheg oed, yn **wael** a'r meddyg newydd ddywedyd wrth fy mam nad oedd obaith iddi wella o'i chlefyd. [HENAT 54]

My seventeen-year old sister Edith, was desperately **ill** and the doctor had just told my mother there was no hope of recovery. [LOCUST 51]

'It's a **poor** sort of memory that only works backwards,' the Queen remarked. [THRO 172]

'Hen gof digon **sâl** sy'n gweithio'n ôl yn unig,' meddai'r Frenhines. [TRWY 62]

Yr oedd ei fargen ef a'i bartneriaid yn **sâl**. Nid oedd wiw ymliw am un well, nac ymbilio am well pris. [TRAED 87–8]

The bargain he and his partners were forced to make was a **poor** one, but it was useless to show disgust or to beg for a better price. [FEET 73–4]

[Y]sgrifennodd fath o Hunan Gofiant dan y teitl 'Trem yn ôl', y llyfr **salaf** oll yn yr iaith Gymraeg, yn ôl barn ostyngedig ei annwyl

He wrote a sort of autobiography entitled *A Look Back (Trem yn ôl)*, the **worst** book in the language in his humble nephew's opinion. It is

nai amdano. Y mae mor **sâl** fel y byddai'n werth ei ail argraffu a'i astudio'n fanwl, o glawr i glawr, fel Gwerslyfr ar 'Sut i Beidio â Sgrifennu.' [HDF 174]

so **bad** that it would be worthwhile issuing another edition of it to be studied from cover to cover as a textbook on How Not To Write. [OFH 219]

'Te go **sâl** gewch chi, mae arna' i ofn,' ymddiheurodd i'r dieithryn . . . [CHWAL 29]

'A very **poor** tea you'll get, I'm afraid,' she told the stranger apologetically . . . [OUT 29]

Ond rhedwr **sâl** oedd Huw, a chlywai Llew draed a lleisiau'r dilynwyr yn ennill arnynt. [CHWAL 112]

But Huw was no sprinter [*Huw was a **poor/bad** runner*] and the sound of voices and running feet told Llew that their pursuers were gaining on them. [OUT 118]

'Wel i ti,' ebe fe, 'seiat ydi lot o bobol dda yn meddwl 'u bod nhw'n **ddrwg**, ac yn cyfarfod 'u gilydd bob nos Fawrth i feio ac i redeg 'u hunain i lawr.' [RHYS 68]

'Do you see, Jack,' said he, 'Communion means a lot of good folk who think themselves **bad**, coming together every Tuesday night, to find fault with themselves, and run each other down.' [RHYS 65]

TO SEEM/APPEAR [see also 'TO LOOK']

The most obvious equivalent for this in Welsh is '*ymddangos*'. Given the close relationship to the semantic field for '*to look*', there is an inevitable overlap at times between the two and '*edrych*' or '*edrych yn debyg*' can also be closer to '*seem/appear*' than '*look*'. Welsh sometimes prefers an impersonal '*ymddengys/ mae'n ymddangos*' followed by a personalised clause where English only has a personalised form of the verb.

Another option – in particular where a direct correlation between *seem/ appear = ymddangos* is less appropriate or is possible, but requires a degree of modification – is the use of the conjunction *fel + pe + imperfect subjunctive* or *pluperfect* of the verb '*bod*' [THO 312, 416 and PWT 2.27]. This construction or the use of '*gweld*' as a transitive verb is particularly useful to convey '*seeming*', '*like*' or '*apparent*'.

The shop **seemed** to be full of all manner of curious things. [THRO 178]

Ymddangosai fod y siop yn llawn o bob math ar bethau od. [TRWY 66]

'You **seem** very clever at explaining words, Sir,' said Alice. [THRO 189]

'**Mae'n ymddangos** eich bod yn fedrus iawn yn egluro geiriau, Syr,' meddai Alys. [TRWY 79]

. . . she **seems** to have been here. [TIME 31]

. . . **mae'n edrych yn debyg** ei bod hi 'di bod yma. [AMSER 49]

Hagbourne **appeared** not to be thinking much of any of it. [TIME 23]

Nid oedd Howells **fel petai'n** meddwl rhyw lawer ohono. [AMSER 36]

The egg **seems** to get further away the more I walk towards it. [THRO 182]

Mae'r wy **fel pe bai'n** mynd ymhellach wrth imi gerdded tuag ato. [TRWY 71]

. . . he **appeared not to be looking** where he was going and occasionally bumped into people. [TIME 77]

Doedd o ddim fel pe bai'n edrych i ble'r oedd o'n mynd ac o bryd i'w gilydd byddai'n cerdded i mewn i rywun. [AMSER 121]

From outside came the occasional cry of a nightbird, and once at our very window a long drawn, cat-**like** whine, which told us that the cheetah was indeed at liberty. [BAND 236]

O'r tu allan, o bryd i'w gilydd, fe dreiddiai cri ddolefus un o adar cyffredin y nos; ac unwaith o leiaf fe glywsom nadu hir **fel pe bai** o enau cath, a oedd yn arwydd diamau i ni fod y llewpart yn rhydd. [CYLCH 53]

Ond heddiw **roedd fel pe wedi colli** arno'i hun . . . [PLA 25]

But now **he seemed** utterly beside himself . . . [PEST 18]

Quirrell **seemed** to have given in at last. [STONE 306]

Edrychai fel petai Quirrél wedi ildio o'r diwedd. [MAEN 196]

Gwelai Dan y peint yn fawr iawn ac ni wyddai yn y byd sut y medrai ei ddihysbyddu. [CHWAL 175]

To Dan the pint **seemed enormous**, and he wondered, in dismay, how he could finish it. [OUT 185]

Chwarddodd Geini, ac edrychodd y ddau arall arni'n hurt **wrth ei gweled** mor ddifater. [TRAED 60]

Geini laughed, and the others stared in amazement at her **seeming** lack of concern. [FEET 52]

Roedd Caerdydd **i'w weld** yn anferth. [HUNAN 77]

Cardiff **seemed** huge to me. [SOLVA 77]

'Y fi?' ebe Marged. 'O . . . 'roeddwn i'n **ei gweld hi'n** lodes ffein iawn.' [LLEIFIOR 57]

'Me?' replied Marged. 'O . . . I **thought she was** a very nice girl. [RETURN 47]

The following are examples of either using an auxiliary verb with a conditional meaning, an adverbial expression or omission of 'seem/appear' altogether, relying on the rest of the sentence to convey apparency.

To go with it, he could fairly be described as being unbeautiful, his features **seeming to be modelled** from grainy putty by inexpert thumbs, a choirboy's pink-lipped mouth stuck on them as an afterthought. [TIME 28]	Ar yr un pryd, medrid ei ddisgrifio'n ddigon teg fel person diolwg; **gallai ei wyneb fod wedi ei fodelu** o bwti gan ddwylo amatur ac yna ceg fach binc geriwbaidd wedi ei glynu wrtho. [AMSER 43]
'I've heard from Deborah! **It seems** she's alright after all.' [TIME 87]	'Dw i 'di clywed gan Deborah! Mae hi'n iawn wedi'r cyfan, **yn ôl pob golwg**.' [AMSER 137]
. . . a foul stench reached his nostrils, a mixture of old socks and the kind of public toilet no one **seems** to clean. [STONE 216]	. . . daeth drewdod dychrynllyd i'w ffroenau; cymysgedd o hen sanau a'r math o doiled cyhoeddus sydd byth yn cael ei lanhau. [MAEN 137]

TO STOP

The borrowing from English 'stopio' covers many of the same meanings of the original and is not semantically restricted in its use. The sense of coming to a halt, cessation can be covered by the verbs 'aros', 'sefyll' and 'peidio' (the latter in particular with negative imperative forms together with 'taw â'). Welsh possesses a particular idiomatic expression which equates to English 'give up, quit' namely 'rhoi'r gorau [i]' (occasionally also 'rhoi heibio' which is not followed by a preposition and can be used intransitively). A common collocate with 'aros' and 'sefyll' is 'yn stond' which strengthens the meaning of stopping or standing still. The verb 'rhoi' collocates with 'stop' and 'taw' and the preposition 'ar' to offer an alternative, more idiomatic way of rendering 'to stop'. 'Rhwystro' or 'atal' give the meaning of 'prevention'.

'Perhaps you'd have him in here and we'll –', Lingard **stopped** short as the door opened. [TIME 76]	'Ella y basech chi gystal â'i alw o i fewn yma ac fe . . .' **stopiodd** Lingard wrth i'r drws agor. [AMSER 120]
Stopiais y car ac euthum allan ohono . . . [HENAT 8]	I **stopped** the car and got out. [LOCUST 14]

Rogers **stopped** [talking] and leaned forward, peering as if anxious at Lingard's face. [TIME 70]

Safodd Rogers a phwyso ymlaen, â thipyn o ymdrech, yn ôl synau ei feingefn. Syllodd ar wyneb Lingard fel pe bai rhywbeth yn ei boeni. [AMSER 111]

Matilda stood up and began to recite the two-times table. When she got to twice twelve is twenty-four she **didn't stop**. [MAT 70]

Cododd Matilda a dechrau adrodd tabl dau. Pan ddaeth hi at un deg dau dau yw dau ddeg pedwar, **arhosodd hi ddim**. [MAT 64]

Pan gododd y dynion oddi wrth de yr oedd y glaw wedi **peidio**. [CRYMAN 31]

By the time the men had finished their tea the rain had **stopped**. [SICKLE 23]

'**Stop** picking your nose.' [MAT 34]

'**Paid â** phigo dy drwyn.' [MAT 28]

'**Taw â** chlegar,' oddi wrth ei thad. Clegar – clegar – hen air hyll. Ei thad yn defnyddio hen air fel yna a Sgiatan wedi – wedi – marw! [TE 9]

'**Stop** that yowling!' cried her father. Yowling . . . an ugly word . . . fancy her father using an ugly word like that, and Sgiatan, well, Sgiatan dead. [TEA 13]

'Don't you *ever* **stop** reading?' he snapped at her. [MAT 39]

'Wyt ti *byth* yn **rhoi'r gorau i** ddarllen?' meddai'n swta wrthi. [MAT 33]

[M]ae'n rhaid i chi **roi heibio** siarad fel yna efo fi . . . [GWEN 133]

You must **stop** talking to me like this. [GWEN 114]

The others followed her, waving their weapons. Then they **stopped**. They stared around the room. [MAT 46-7]

Dilynodd y lleill hi, gan chwifio eu harfau. Wedyn **arhoson nhw'n stond**. Syllon nhw o gwmpas yr ystafell. [MAT 41]

Ac ar ôl i mi **stopio'n stond**, hwya'n y byd oeddwn i'n sefyll mwya'n y byd oeddwn i'n meddwl am gnocio hoelion . . . [NOS 62]

And when I **stood still**, the longer I stood the more I thought about people hammering nails . . . [NIGHT 50]

She had wanted to go and sit at his table [. . .] He had **stopped** her. [VICT 135]

Roedd hi ar dân i fynd i eistedd wrth yr un bwrdd ag o [. . .] Fe **roddodd stop arni**, wrth gwrs. [LLINYN 152]

He began telling her, but she **stopped** him impatiently. [VICT 153]	Dechreuodd ddweud hynny wrthi ond **rhoddodd daw arno**'n ddiamynedd. [LLINYN 173]
'We are only just in time to **prevent** some subtle and horrible crime.' [BAND 233]	'... Ac os felly, cael a chael fydd hi arnom i **rwystro** trosedd gyfrwys ac ofnadwy.' [CYLCH 50]
... er fy mod ... yn edrych arno fel peth hynod Ragluniaethol i mi ddyfod yma i'ch **atal** rhag priodi eich chwaer. [ENOC 376]	... although ... I see it as an extremely providential thing that I came here to **stop** you from marrying you sister.

TO UPSET [UPSET]

This is another example of an English verb which lacks a direct Welsh equivalent. Near synonyms such as '*cynhyrfu/cyffroi*' or expressions such as '*achosi poen/gofid*' can be employed. GPC attests to the English borrowing '*ypsetio*'[6] but this is normally confined to dialogue or informal registers.

She's pretty **upset** herself ... [CIDER 106]	Roedd hithau wedi **cynhyrfu drwyddi** ... [SEIDR 143]
It's true that she was pretty **upset** and so were the Lockwoods. [CIDER 117]	Mae'n wir ei bod hi wedi **cyffroi** tipyn, a'i rhieni hefyd ... [SEIDR 156]
Yr oedd Twm yn llon iawn, a daeth ar ei union i ddiolch i'm mam, ond ni wnaeth hi lawer o siapri ohono, oblegid yr oedd wedi **achosi llawer o boen diachos iddi** ... [GWEN 28]	Twm was delighted, and he immediately came to thank my mother, but she did not make him very welcome because her appearance in court had **upset** her ... [GWEN 34]
Roedd yr heddlu wrthi'n rhoi tâp glas o amgylch y darn hwnnw o'r fynwent, ac roedd y bobol yn sefyll o gwmpas ymysg y beddi – rhai yn crafu'u pennau ac un neu ddau yn amlwg wedi **ypsetio**. [LLADD 183]	*The police were busy placing blue tape around that section of the graveyard, and the people were standing around among the graves – some scratching their heads and one of two obviously upset.*

---

[6] The GPC examples (p. 3820) are both twentieth-century and taken from spoken Welsh.

TO WISH

Although the verbs '*dymuno*' and (less frequently) '*hoffi*' can be used with this meaning, there is a *chassé croisé* pattern (a double grammatical transposition – see Chapter 1) '*bod yn dda gan*' which can also be employed, in particular when there is a sense of aspiration, longing or desire. The examples below illustrate that this is often preferred to the direct equivalent '*dymuno*' especially in a conditional tense construction in Welsh which can correspond to the present in English:

Ni bu gair croes rhyngom erioed ac yn wir ni ellid **dymuno** am well na ffyddlonach cyfaill. [RHWNG 84]

*There was never a cross word between us and indeed, one couldn't **wish** for a more faithful friend.*

Ond dydw i ddim yn bwriadu rhoi clust iddyn nhw, nac yn **dymuno** aros yng nghwmni bradwr. [RHANNU 270]

*But I don't intend listening to them, neither do I **wish** to remain in the company of a traitor.*

And here **I wish** I could tell you half the things Alice used to say. [THRO 130]

Ac yma **fe hoffwn** pe gallwn ddweud wrthoch chi hanner y pethau y byddai Alys yn eu dweud . . . [TRWY 16]

'**Mi fasa'n dda gin i** petaswn i'n medru dallt y dyn yna oedd yn rhannu'r gwobrwyon,' meddai Jane Gruffydd . . . [TRAED 79]

'**I wish** I could have understood that man who was giving out the prizes,' said Jane Gruffydd . . . [FEET 70]

Harriet wished she could find the right words that would make him feel better again. [VICT 99]

Byddai'n dda calon gan Enid pe bai hi'n gallu dod o hyd i'r geiriau a fyddai'n gwneud iddo deimlo'n well eto. [LLINYN 112]

'Rough night last night was it, Jimmy?'
'**I wish** I could remember.' [KNOTS 87]

'Noson fawr neithiwr, ia, Jimmy?'
'**Fasa'n dda gen i** taswn i'n cofio.' [CHWERW 74]

TO WONDER

The nearest direct equivalent to this verb in Welsh is '*tybio*' and its derivative '*tybed*' both of which are discussed below. There are many examples of the English 'WONDER' being rendered by a verb with a direct closer field of meaning, for example:

Wonder > doubt	=	*amau*
Wonder > guess	=	*dyfalu*
Wonder > think, ponder	=	*meddwl* or *ystyried*
Wonder > be amazed at	=	*rhyfeddu at*
Wonder > be surprised at	=	*synnu at*

Ei adwaith cyntaf oedd **amau na busai'n well iddo** pe cymerai'r modur y foment honno a dianc. [SELYF 101]

*His first reaction was **wondering whether he wouldn't be better off** taking the car at that moment and fleeing.*

It left him **wondering** what the hell she had meant by referring to the late Mrs Stephanakis [TIME 94]

Doedd dim i'w wneud ond **dyfalu** beth ar y ddaear a olygai wrth gyfeirio at y diweddar Mrs Stephanakis [AMSER 149]

Tra oedd Ibn yn syllu ar yr haul yn codi, **meddyliodd a oedd** yr awdur ifanc yn ddigon treiddgar i ama fod tinc eironig yng ngoslef ei lais? [PLA 98]

As Salah watched the sun rise, he **wondered whether** the poet had detected the irony in his little speech. [PEST 75]

Harry, Ron and Hermione looked at one another, **wondering** what to tell him. [STONE 238]

Edrychodd Harry, Ron a Hermione ar ei gilydd, gan **ystyried** beth i'w ddweud wrtho. [MAEN 151]

Specifically, he **wondered** again at the excess of friendliness where there might have been wariness and even dislike. [TIME 107]

Rhyfeddodd eto **at** ei gorgyfeillgarwch lle'r oedd hi cynt yn ochelgar ... [AMSER 171]

Alice **wondered** a little at this, but she was too much in awe of the Queen to disbelieve it. [THRO 144]

Synnodd Alys **at** hyn, ond roedd arni ormod o ofn y Frenhines i beidio â'i goelio. [TRWY 30]

'*Tybio*' is the verb with the closest semantic relationship to '*wonder*' in English as a purely transitive verb. It is however often encountered as '*tybed*'[7]

[7] PWT (6.73b) notes that it is most often used in an interrogative context together with its close dialectal cognate *ys gwn i/'sgwn i*. Both can be used as independent expressions of wonder but usually are followed by the interrogative particle '*a*' [not '*os*'] plus a soft mutation.

frequently (but not exclusively) with a personalised meaning e.g. *I wonder* which is loosely semantically connected to the first person singular present *tybiaf = I wonder, suppose* although generally with a suggestion of increased doubt. In addition, '*tybed*' readily follows other verbs e.g. *amau, dyfalu, ceisio dyfalu, meddwl* to reinforce and underline the '*wonder*' element of their meaning (it is not possible for *tybiaf* to fulfill this role).

He was cautious, **wondering** what she was getting at . . . [TIME 36]

Yr oedd yn wyliadwrus, ac yn **tybio** beth oedd ganddi mewn golwg. [AMSER 56]

Beth a wnâi ei mam a'i thad rŵan, **tybed**? Ar eu te, mae'n debyg. [TRAED 18]

What were her father and mother doing now, **she wondered**. Having tea, probably. [FEET 16]

I wonder if I shall fall right *through* the earth! [ALICE 21]

Tybed a wnaf syrthio *drwy'r* ddaear! [ALICE 13]

'The Lord forgive me for saying it about a dead man,' Hagbourne said mock piously, 'but **what about** Stephanakis having done some pimping?' [TIME 24]

'Duw faddeuo imi am ddeud y fath beth am ddyn marw,' dywedodd Howells yn goeg-dduwiol, 'ond **tybed** a fu Stephanakis yn pimpio ryw ychydig?' [AMSER 37]

She wondered about his position in Sir Ronald Callender's household. [UNSUIT 18]

Beth, **tybed**, oedd safle Lunn yng nghartref Syr Ronald Callender? [GORTYN 25–6]

And now, which of these finger-posts ought I to follow, **I wonder**? [THRO 157]

Ac yn awr, prun o'r mynegbyst hyn ddylwn i ei ddilyn, **ysgwn i**? [TRWY 45]

I wonder if a gambler's blood runs hot enough in his veins for him to be jealous? [TIME 66]

Ys gwn i a ydi gwaed gamblwr yn berwi digon yn ei wythiennau i'w 'neud o'n foi cenfigennus. [AMSER 104]

Daeth cnoc eiddil ar y drws. Yr oedd wedi ymgolli gymaint yn ei feddyliau nes iddo ddechrau **amau tybed** nad yr ail gnoc oedd hwn. [SELYF 117]

There was a weak knock on the door. He had lost himself so much in his thoughts that he began to **wonder** *whether this was the second knock.*

He had seen against the light from a street lamp the unmistakable

Roedd yn siŵr iddo weld amlinell dywyll dynes yn y sedd arall a

silhouette of a woman in the passenger seat, and he **wondered** whose wife it was that Twite had kept him from recognising. [TIME 21]

cheisiodd ddyfalu gwraig pwy, **tybed**, yr oedd Trefor yn ei chuddio oddi wrtho. [AMSER 32]

Meddyliai sut hwyl a gâi, **tybed**, ar dywydd mwll fel hyn. [TRAED 146]

She wondered how he was getting on in such sultry weather as this. [FEET 129]

The final set of examples include the very informal borrowing form 'wondro' (best avoided and confined here to dialogue only) together with various other strategies for conveying 'wonder' indirectly:

'Sylwis i ddim byd – er, o'n i'n **wondro** lle oedda chdi weithia, pan o'n i'n methu ffeindio chdi.' [LLADD 45]

'*I didn't notice anything – though I was **wondering** where you were sometimes when I couldn't find you.*'

'There's one other flower in the garden that can move about like you,' said the Rose. '**I wonder** how you do it –' [THRO 142]

'Mae yna un blodeuyn arall yn yr ardd a fedr symud fel chi,' ebe'r Rhosyn. '**Mae'n ddirgelwch i mi** sut y medrwch chi –' [TRWY 28]

She **wondered** whether Bernie had decided to kill himself in his office so that the little house would be uncontaminated and undisturbed. [UNSUIT 23]

Ai dyna paham y lladdodd Bernie ei hun yn y swyddfa? Er mwyn cadw'r tŷ yn lân ac yn ddilychwin? [GORTYN 14]

Gofyn iddo'i hun yr oedd pa beth oedd neges y ffarmwr corffol hwn . . . [CRYMAN 217]

He was wondering what this stout farmer wanted . . . [SICKLE 180]

WRONG

The adjective '*wrong*' can be considered from its general meaning of '*incorrect*' or '*erroneous*' to correspond mainly to the Welsh adjective '*anghywir*'. Two common Welsh idioms can be employed to give the other sense of something being '*amiss*' or '*awry*' namely '*mae rhywbeth o'i le [ar]*' or '*mae rhywbeth yn bod [ar]*'. By extension, the '*yn bod*' is occasionally omitted as shown in the third example below. '*Mynd o'i le*' is one possible translation of the English collocation '*go wrong*' although '*mynd o chwith*' is particularly useful for emphasising that something has gone awry. The final example illustrates the use of the English adjective in a very informal register.

Amlwg fod rhywbeth **o'i le** ar y trwmped neu'r trwmpedwr, canys fe'i gwyliai'n sarrug. [HDF 95]	It was obvious that there was something **wrong** with the trumpet or the trumpeter, for he was watching him and giving him such surly looks. [OFH 116]
Wonder **what's wrong** with his leg? [STONE 225]	'Sgwn i **be sy'n bod ar** ei goes? [MAEN 143]
'Be' oedd ar dy ben di, hogyn, yn gadal iddo fo drampio mor bell? Lle'r oedd dy synnwyr di?' [CHWAL 28]	**'What was wrong with your head**, boy, letting him tramp so far? Where was your sense? [OUT 29]
'What's happened to me! I look terrible! I look just like *you* **gone wrong**!' [MAT 63]	'Beth sydd wedi digwydd i mi? Dw i'n edrych yn ofnadwy! Dw i'n edrych yn union fel *ti* wedi **mynd o chwith**!' [MAT 57]
Pan **âi pethau o chwith** yn y tŷ neu pan groesid hi mewn rhyw ffordd . . . [CHWAL 98–9]	When **things went wrong** in the house, or if she were thwarted in any way . . . [OUT 102–3]
Ond fe **aeth pethau o chwith**. [CRYMAN 56]	But **things had gone terribly wrong**. [SICKLE 69]
"Sa i'n gwybod ble **aeth popeth mor wrong**.' [FFYDD 182]	'I don't know where **it all went wrong**.' [FAITH 127]

Further examples show '*wrong*' as a verb in the sense of '*doing wrong to some-one*' – '*gwneud cam â rhywun*' and being '*proved wrong*' here conveyed by '*gwrthbrofi*' which often corresponds to '*disprove/refute*'. Finally, there is an example of the noun '*pengamrwydd*' as '*wrongheadedness*' although this is best considered as mainly literary usage.

Ddaru mi ladd rhwfun? *no danger.* Ddaru mi **neyd cam** â rhwfun? Dydw i ddim yn gwbod. Ddaru mi feddwi? *never.* Does dim isio i *chap* neyd y pethe ene i gael ei adel. Beth ydw i wedi neyd? [RHYS 331–2]	Have I killed anybody? No danger. Have I **wronged** anybody? I don't know that I have. Have I got drunk? Never. But a chap needn't do any of those things to be left behind. What have I done? [RHYS 316]

... he was always ready to be **proved wrong**. [TIME 25]	... roedd o wastad yn barod i gael ei **wrthbrofi**. [AMSER 38]
Ond yn gymysg â hyn oll yr oedd rhyw **bengamrwydd** pinwyngar a'i gwnâi hi'n fynych yn anodd iawn byw gydag ef. [HDF 143]	But mixed with this there was that opinionated **wrongheadedness** that sometimes made it a very hard thing to live with him. [OFH 179]

9.1.b Fields of meaning: Welsh items

BWRW

On its own, '*bwrw*' generally equates to the idea of '*hitting*', '*striking*' or '*throwing*'. There is also the meaning of '*to cast*' when it forms a collocation with specific nouns e.g. *bwrw cysgod, bwrw pleidlais, bwrw swyn* (*to cast a shadow, to cast a vote, to cast a spell*). However, it is most frequently encountered as the base of a collocation followed either by a preposition (sometimes conjugated) or a noun:

(a)
Bwrw allan	-	To throw out
Bwrw ati	-	To keep at it
Bwrw drwyddi	-	To get through something (i.e. an experience)
Bwrw heibio	-	To discard
Bwrw iddi	-	To throw (oneself) into something
Bwrw i lawr	-	To knock down
Bwrw ymlaen	-	To carry on

(b) Bwrw + weather element
Bwrw eira	-	To snow
Bwrw glaw	-	To rain

Bwrw = to spend time
Bwrw'r diwrnod	-	To spend the day
Bwrw'r nos	-	To spend the night
Bwrw'r Sul	-	To spend the weekend
Bwrw blinder	-	To get over tiredness
Bwrw dirmyg (ar)	-	To throw/pour contempt (at)
Bwrw golwg (ar/dros)	-	To take a look, glance (at/over)
Bwrw hiraeth	-	To stop missing someone/something

The particular example of '*A bwrw bod*...' introducing a condition '*Assuming that/Granted that*...' is worth noting.

The only thing that he knew for certain was that the law forbode the Trunchbull to hit him with the riding-crop that she kept **smacking against her thigh**. [MAT 123]

Yr unig beth a wyddai i sicrwydd oedd fod y gyfraith yn gwahardd y Trunchbull rhag ei daro[8] â'r chwip roedd hi'n **ei bwrw yn erbyn ei chlun** o hyd ac o hyd. [MAT 117]

Yr oedd y capel yn **bwrw ei gysgod** dros holl egnïon fy mywyd i a'm teulu. [HENAT 111]

Chapel **threw its shadow** on all the activities of my life and that of my family. [LOCUST 96]

Daliai'r ystorm i lacio, fel petai'r lleuad ifanc [. . .] yn **bwrw swyn** ar y gwynt a thros gynddaredd y môr. [CHWAL 109]

The storm continued to abate, as though the young moon [. . .] were **casting its spell** on the gale and over the raging waters. [OUT 115]

. . . ni fu dewis gan y fainc namyn **bwrw allan** yr achos. [HDF 138]

. . .the Bench had no option but to **throw out** the case. [OFH 172]

Yr oedd Ifan yn falch bod ei wraig yn **bwrw drwyddi** mor huawdl, ac yn dangos y fath synnwyr wrth fynegi'r drwg a achosodd Sioned i'w modryb Geini. [TRAED 63]

Ifan was pleased that his wife was **dealing with the situation** so capably and showing such good sense by pointing out to Sioned the harm she had done to her Aunt Geini. [FEET 55]

Bydden ni'n edrych mlaen at yr adeg pan allen ni **fwrw heibio'r bŵts** hoelion trwm hynny roedd yn rhaid i ni'u gwisgo am y rhan fwya o'r flwyddyn. [HUNAN 33]

We all looked forward to the time when we could **discard those** heavy hobnailed **boots** that we had to wear for most of the year. [SOLVA 33]

O'r dechrau cyntaf wedi i 'nhadcu symud i Benrhiw ymddengys iddo **fwrw iddi**'n ddyfal ac egniol 'yn cloddio a bwrw tail,' yn diwreiddio ac yn plannu, yn tynnu i lawr ac yn adeiladu. [HDF 75]

When my grandfather came to Penrhiw he **threw himself into it** from the start, energetically and persistently 'digging and dunging', uprooting and planting, taking down and putting up. [OFH 90]

. . . that had to be harvested by hand, rather than **shaken down** by the polers. [CIDER 33]

. . . roedd yn rhaid eu tynnu â llaw yn hytrach na'u **bwrw i lawr** â pholion fel yr afalau eraill. [SEIDR 46]

---

[8] This example contrasts the use of 'taro' which also mean 'to hit' and 'bwrw' used here with a similar meaning as the riding-crop is being 'struck' by Trunchbull against her thigh.

She **picked up the thread**.
[CIDER 19]

Bwriodd ymlaen â'i stori.
[SEIDR 26]

'Only it got so cold, and it
snowed so, they had to leave off.'
[THRO 128]

'Ond fe drodd mor oer, a **bwrw eira**
gymaint fel y bu rhaid iddyn nhw
roi'r gorau iddi.' [TRWY 14]

Brysiodd i fyny i'w hystafell a
bwrw'r diwrnod nad oedd eto ond
ar ei draean heibio i ganlyn ei dillad
gwaith. [RHANNU 246]

*She rushed to her room and spent
the day which was only a third of the
way through in pursuit of her work
clothes.*

Er ei bod yn ysu am gael cyrraedd
ei haelwyd ei hun, bu'n rhaid iddi
oedi fwy nag unwaith i geisio **bwrw
'i blinder**, ond i ddim pwrpas.
[RHANNU 136]

*Although she was longing to reach
her own home, she had to pull up
more than once to try and refresh
herself, but to no avail.*

Ond roedd hi wedi bod mor
hawdd **bwrw'i dirmyg** ar Tom.
[RHANNU 234]

*But it has been so easy to pour her
contempt at Tom.*

In **glancing over** my notes of the
seventy odd cases in which I have
during the last eight years studied
the methods of my friend Sherlock
Holmes . . . [BAND 207]

O **fwrw golwg dros** fy nodiadau ar
y deg a thrigain o achosion dros yr
wyth mlynedd diwethaf sy'n cofnodi
dulliau gwaith fy nghyfaill Sherlock
Holmes . . . [CYLCH 11]

Piti oedd i 'Mam farw mor ifanc
– dim ond 47. Ni **fwriodd 'Nhad
ei hiraeth amdani** tra fu fyw.
[WILLAT 250]

*It was a pity that my mother died so
young – only 47. My father didn't
stop missing her for the rest of his
life.*

CERDDED

'*Cerdded*' is included here to bring attention to its occasional use as a transitive verb where a sensation is felt – in a figurative sense – moving through a person. Our examples illustrate a strong connection with '*ias*' (= *chill, fear*) in this context although other nouns of sensation are included. The first example in particular couples the use of '*cerdded*' in this way with the verb-noun '*clywed*' [*see* CLYWED] in its wider sense of '*to feel*'.

Pan ddarllenodd y canon y
gollyngdod, **clywodd Harri wefr yn**

As the canon read the committal,
Harri **felt a sensation running**

ei gerdded a oedd yn debyg i wefr grefyddol. [LLEIFIOR 107]

through him which was akin to something religious. [RETURN 91]

Teimlodd Daniel **ias oer yn ei gerdded**. [RHANNU 212]

*Daniel felt a **cold chill creep** over him.*

Teimlodd **ias yn ei cherdded**. [CRYMAN 145]

She felt **fear stalking her**. [SICKLE 120]

Mi fydd ias oer yn 'y ngherdded i weithie wrth gofio fel yr amheues i ddoethineb Henri'n ei phriodi hi. [LLEIFIOR 103]

I shudder to think how I doubted Henry's judgment in marrying her. [RETURN 87]

Ni theimlasai mor unig erioed ag y gwnaethai drwy'r dydd heddiw. Bu'r felan **yn ei gerdded** o'r munud y'i deffrowyd ar doriad gwawr gan y poenau'n ei ben a'i ochr . . . [AC YNA 69]

*He had never felt as lonely as he had done all day today. **He had been depressed** [lit. the blues had been walking through him] from the minute he was awoken at the break of dawn by the pains in his head and in his side . . .*

CLYWED

We note the verb '*clywed*' here as, apart from its usual meaning of '*to hear*', it can also be used (in both informal and formal registers although usually when these relate to NW examples) to translate '*to smell*' (often collocated with '*ogla(u)*' = '*smell/s*') or '*to feel*' (in particular sensations in the body such as pain).

Can you **smell** something? [STONE 216]

Glywi di ogla rhywbeth? [MAEN 216]

Clywodd Monica boen sydyn . . . [MONICA 46]

Monica **felt** a sudden stab of pain . . . [MONICA 46]

Clywodd Harri'i wddw'n llenwi. [LLEIFIOR 16]

Harry could **feel** his throat tightening. [RETURN 11]

DRWG [*also* 'POOR/BAD' in section 9.1.a]

'*Drwg*' operates as either an adjective or a noun conveying the sense of '*bad/evil* > *the bad/trouble/problem/harm*' or '*naughty*' as an antonym of '*da*' (*good*). Similarly, it can be used with the verb '*bod*' and the preposition '*gan*' to express regret:

mae'n <u>dda</u> gen i glywed hynny   -   *I am <u>pleased</u> to hear that*
mae'n <u>ddrwg</u> gen i glywed hynny   -   *I am <u>sorry</u> to hear that*

The formula '*y drwg yw/ydy . . .*' is a useful way of translating the equivalent English forumla '*the trouble is . . .*'.

Teimlai'n bur heini, a thybiai mai'r amnesia ydoedd yr unig **ddrwg** arno o ganlyniad i'r ddamwain. [SELYF 72]	*He felt quite fit and supposed that the amnesia was the only **thing wrong** with him as result of the accident.*
'We've heard,' said Hagrid **grumpily**. [STONE 316]	'Glywson ni,' meddai Hagrid **yn ddrwg ei hwyl**. [MAEN 201]
Yr oedd Ifan yn falch bod ei wraig yn bwrw drwyddi mor huawdl, ac yn dangos y fath synnwyr wrth fynegi'r **drwg** a achosodd Sioned i'w modryb Geini. [TRAED 63]	Ifan was pleased that his wife was dealing with the situation so capably and showing such good sense by pointing out to Sioned the **harm** she had done to her aunt Geini. [FEET 55]
Ei nodwedd fwyaf arbennig oedd balchder – **drwg** gennyf nad oes gennyf well enw arno . . . [HENAT 13]	Her most striking characteristic was pride – I **regret** I have no better word for it . . . [LOCUST 17]
'Ffordd yma,' meddai Gwen o hyd tan ei arwain, ac o'r diwedd gafaelodd yn ei fraich. Nid oedd yn **ddrwg** ganddo am hynny. [TRAED 73]	'This way,' Gwen would frequently say, trying to guide him, and at last she had to take hold of his arm. He **did not mind** that at all. [FEET 64]
Trouble is, they mustn't be seen carrying an illegal dragon. [STONE 295]	**Y drwg ydi**, na fiw iddyn nhw gael eu gweld yn cario draig anghyfreithlon. [MAEN 188]

GORAU [RHOI'R GORAU I]

The equivalent Welsh idiom for the English '*give up/leave off/quit*' is normally '*rhoi'r gorau i*' with '*gorau*' being the superlative (relative) of the adjective '*da*' (*good*). It can be followed by a noun, a verb-noun or nothing in which case the preposition '*i*' remains and is conjugated in the third person singular (feminine).

'You would be a lot better off, Miss Honey,' she said, 'if you **gave up your job** and drew unemployment money.' [MAT 204]

'Fe fyddech chi'n llawer gwell eich byd, Miss Honey,' meddai, 'petaech chi'n **rhoi'r gorau i'ch swydd** ac yn codi arian diweithdra.' [MAT 198]

He had **ceased to strike**, and was gazing up at the ventilator . . . [BAND 236–7]

Erbyn hyn roedd Holmes wedi **rhoi'r gorau i'r fflangellu** ac yn rhythu ar agoriad yr awyrydd . . . [CYLCH 55]

'Only it got so cold, and it snowed so, they had to **leave it off**.' [THRO 128]

'Ond fe drodd mor oer, a bwrw eira gymaint fel y bu rhaid iddyn nhw **roi'r gorau iddi**.' [TRWY 14]

GWAITH

Attention is drawn to the use of '*gwaith*' (here corresponding to the English noun '*work*') because it can be used in Welsh together with a verb-noun to emphasise the work or labour element of a task (even non-physical tasks such as thinking) without an equivalent in English. Its use with temporal phrases to illustrate how long a task may last should also be noted.

He had been almost obsessively neat and tidy. His garden tools were wiped after use and carefully put away [. . .] Yet he had abandoned his **digging** less than two feet from the end of a row . . . [UNSUIT 46]

Hogyn taclus oedd Mark. Byddai'n glanhau'i offer garddio ar ôl eu defnyddio a'u rhoi i gadw'n drefnus ar wal y sied [. . .] Eto i gyd, roedd wedi rhoi'r gorau i'w **waith palu** ryw ddwy droedfedd o ben y rhes . . . [GORTYN 59]

'Mi ddois â mymryn o fwyd efo mi. Mi wna i ginio ac mi gei di fynd i siopa yn syth wedyn. Mae gen ti dipyn o **waith prynu**.' [Ac yna 32]

'I brought a bit of food with me. I'll make dinner and you can go shopping straight afterwards. You've got quite a bit of **buying** to do.'

He had insisted on the domestic rôle, unwisely she believed, but she had tactfully not interfered. [VICT 163]

Doedd hi ddim yn siŵr a oedd o wedi gwneud peth call yn mynnu gwneud yr holl **waith coginio**[9] ac ati . . . ond roedd hi'n ddigon doeth i beidio â busnesu. [LLINYN 185]

---

[9] The translator here has paraphrased 'the domestic rôle' with 'doing all the cooking' using 'gwaith' to emphasise the work element.

He had some **thinking** to do, thinking about how in the world he could find Reeve. [KNOTS 217]

Roedd ganddo **waith meddwl** a **phendroni**, pendroni ymhle yn y byd y gallai ddod o hyd i Gordon Reeve. [CHWERW 184]

Mynnais i Glyn droi adref yn gynnar, tuag wyth, gan fod ganddo **waith awr o gerdded** i'r llechwedd yr ochr arall i'r llyn, a bwriadwn innau droi i'm gwely yn bur fuan wedyn. [O LAW 15]

I had insisted on Glyn's going off home early, round about eight o'clock, as he had **an hour's walk** [*literally: an hour's work of walking*] to the slope on the far side of the lake; and I myself had meant to turn in very soon afterwards. [FROM 2]

Faint o **waith cerddad** sy gynnon ni eto? Medda Huw wrth Meri Eirin. Dim ond **gwaith hannar awr**. [NOS 47]

How much more **walking** have we got? Huw asked Mary Plums. Only **half an hour**. [NIGHT 38]

GWELD [*also* 'TO SEEM/APPEAR' in section 9.1.a]

By way of extension to its usual meaning of '*to see*', '*gweld/gweled*'[10] (as noted in section 9.1.a above) can also be used to give an idea of how something or someone '*seems*' or '*appears*'. Further along the semantic continuum, there is a connection with '*to envisage*' and '*to think/opine*' (i.e. '*to view something as . . .*'). The idiom '*gweld bai ar*' is an alternative way of expressing '*to blame*' (literally '*to see blame on*').

Chwarddodd Geini, ac edrychodd y ddau arall arni'n hurt wrth ei **gweled** mor ddifater. [TRAED 60]

Geini laughed, and the others stared in amazement at her **seeming** lack of concern. [FEET 52]

'Mi fasa'n dda gin i petaswn i'n medru dallt y dyn yna oedd yn rhannu'r gwobrwyon,' meddai Jane Gruffydd, 'on'd oedd o **i'w weld** yn ddyn clên? Oedd o'n siarad yn dda, Owen?' [TRAED 80]

'I wish I could have understood that man who was giving out the prizes,' said Jane Gruffydd. 'Didn't he **look** a proper man! Did he make a good speech Owen?' [FEET 70]

Dydach chi ddim yn fy **ngweld** i wedi aros ddigon hir? [TRAED 59]

Don't you **think** I have waited long enough? [FEET 52]

---

[10] *Gweled* is a rather archaic and formal form of *gweld*. However it can be seen in derivatives of '*gweld/gweled*' such as '*gweledigaeth*' (vision) or '*gweledig*' (visible).

368 Comparative Stylistics of Welsh and English

Mitsio fyddwn i, a dweud y gwir, achos mod i'n **gweld celf mor hawdd** ... [HUNAN 69]

If the truth be known I was skiving – art **came so easily to me** ... [SOLVA 69]

Ond er y boen a'r ymdrech, cliriodd ei phlatiau'n o dda, **er gweld** y grefi'n rhy denau a'r pwdin reis yn rhy dew. [CHWAL 104]

But in spite of her discomfort and the effort to bring herself to eat, she made a fairly clean sweep of what was put before her, **although in her view**, the gravy was too thin and the rice pudding too thick. [OUT 109]

I **don't blame you.** [CIDER 117]

Wela i ddim bai arnat ti. [SEIDR 157]

Ofnai y byddai'r ffyddloniaid, yn eu hanwybodaeth o'r amgylchiadau, yn **gweld bai arno.** [RHANNU 113]

*He feared that the faithful, in their ignorance of the circumstances, would **blame him**.*

HANES

The noun *'hanes'* is primarily associated in modern Welsh with *'history'* or *'story'*. A particular expression *'yn ôl yr hanes'* is useful for translating *'it is said that/so it is said'*. However, *'hanes'* by itself can also convey a sense of *'what happened to someone/what became of someone/news of someone'*. In a similar way, it may refer to there being *'evidence'* or a *'sign'* of someone or something. The expression *'yn ôl pob hanes'* corresponds to the English *'by all accounts'*.

Magwyd yno deuluoedd graenus; ac **yn ôl yr hanes** nid aeth neb o Benrhiw erioed heb fod yn well ei fyd ... [HDF 64]

Families were brought up there obviously well, and **the story is** that no one ever left Penrhiw but in improved circumstances ... [OFH 76]

Gwenodd yn ddiflas gan ystyried mai tra sgubai hi lofftydd y ffurfiwyd pob penderfyniad o dipyn bwys **yn ei hanes.** [MONICA 49]

She smiled wryly as the thought occurred to her that it was while sweeping out bedrooms she had made every decision of any consequence **in her life**. [MONICA 49]

Byw yno fu hanes Pat Newman a'i phlant – a Tessa a 'mhlant inne'n gwmni iddyn nhw. [HUNAN 279]

Pat Newman and her children, accompanied by Tessa and my children, **ended up living there**. [*i.e. that's what became of them*]. [SOLVA 279]

Yn ddiweddarach, fe syrthies i mewn cariad â merch o *au-pair* o Odense yn Nenmarc [...] Ymhen hir a hwyr, **cysgu 'da hi fu'n hanes i.** [HUNAN 117]

I fell in love with a Danish *au-pair* from Odense [...] Finally, **I ended up sleeping with her.** [SOLVA 117]

*What **had become of her**, by now?*

Beth **oedd ei hanes hi**, erbyn hyn, tybed? [LLINYN 156]

No sign of her anywhere. [VICT 170]

Dim hanes ohoni yn unman. [LLINYN 193]

... roedd o wedi cael y frech wen erstalwm a honno wedi gadael craith ar ochor ei geg o [...] Ond pan roedd o'n rowlio chwerthin run fath a ddaru o am fy mhen i'r adag honno, toedd na **ddim hanas** o'r graith. [NOS 20]

... cos he'd had smallpox a long time ago and that had left a scar on the side of his mouth [...] But when he was laughing his head off at something, like he was at me that time, there was **no sign** of the scar. [NIGHT 13]

... fel Homer gynt yn canu am ei swper, siaradai Ned am ei gwrw, ac **yn ôl pob hanes** yr oedd ei athrylith yn llawn haeddu ei gwobr. [HENAT 123]

Homer sang for his supper, and likewise Ned sang for his beer, and **by all accounts** his talents fully deserved their reward. [LOCUST 107]

HEL

Etymologically, '*hel*' and '*hela*' ('*to hunt*') are related. In Modern Welsh '*hel*' tends to convey '*gathering, collecting*' with '*hela*' mainly reserved for '*to hunt*'. It is often combined with '*at ei gilydd*' corresponding to the English '(*gather*) *together*'. '*Hel*' (also '*hala*' in SW varieties) can also be an alternative for '*anfon*' ('*to send*') although this is usually associated with less formal registers. By extension, '*hel*' has come to be associated with the idea of '*going around, frequenting*'. Compare the following two examples:

'Fiw imi,' meddai Winni, 'ne' mi ga' i gweir gan Lisi Jên am fynd i **hel tai**.' [TE 58]

'I daren't,' said Winni. 'If I did, Liza Jane would give me a beating for **going to other people's houses**.' [TEA 54]

'Mi fasa'n well i Lisi Mos forol am fwyd i'w theulu na **cherdded tai**.' [RHANNU 116]

'It would be better for Lisi Mos to take care of food for her family rather than going around other people's houses.'

The following examples illustrate the different uses of 'hel':

Yr oedd hanner dwsin o bregethwyr wedi **hel at ei gilydd** a chael compartment iddynt eu hunain, a dyna lle'r oedd 'Seiat Brofiad' bur felys yn mynd ymlaen. [WILLAT 159]	*Half a dozen preachers had **gathered together** and got a compartment for themselves and that was where a very agreeable 'Seiat Brofiad' [religious meeting] was taking place.*
Amser pryderus oedd hwn arnom, ond **heliodd Twm ni i'w rwyd** yn lled ddidrafferth. [GWEN 42]	We went through an agonising time, but **Twm got us safely into his net** without much trouble. [GWEN 45]
Hel dy betha at 'i gilydd! [PLA 25]	Now, just **get your belongings together**. [PEST 17]
. . . aethon nhw â fi i **hel tafarne**'r noson honno. [HUNAN 126]	. . . and they **took me on a pub crawl**. [SOLVA 125]
Doedd y ffaith ei bod hi wedi cael blaen esgid o'i swydd yn newid dim ar ffordd Tessa o fyw. Roedd hi'n dal i yfed a **hel clybie** 'da bois y byd adloniant. [HUNAN 264]	The fact that she'd been sacked from her job didn't alter her lifestyle; she still hung around with the TV crowd and went drinking and **clubbing** with the showbiz set. [SOLVA 264]

There are a number of productive collocations associated with 'hel' some of which are noted here:

Hel annwyd	-	To develop a cold
Hel cardod	-	To beg / go begging
Hel esgus	-	To make an excuse
Hel meddyliau	-	To think / gather ones thoughts
Hel straeon	-	To gossip / make up stories
Hel traed	-	To run around / be off / 'leg it'

She thought he looked ill and wondered if **he had a cold coming on**. [VICT 125]	Edrychai'i gŵr yn ddigon gwachul a meddyliodd hi tybed a **oedd o'n hel annwyd**. [LLINYN 140]
'Nid ar y mynydd y bydd trampars yn **hel cardod**, Mrs Huws.' [TE 37]	'Tramps don't **go begging** on the mountain.' [TEA 37]
'Don't **make excuses**,' said the Guard. [THRO 150]	'Peidiwch â **hel esgusion**,' meddai'r Gard. [TRWY 37]

Câi amser i **hel meddyliau** yn awr, wedi i'r holl brysurdeb beidio. [CHWAL 149]

Now that all the stir and bustle was over she would have time to **collect her thoughts**. [OUT 157]

Ond doedd y Rhaglaw ddim yn mynd i **hel meddyliau** drwg wrth iddo frasgamu ar hyd y llwybr a phastwn yn ei law. [PLA 61]

The Steward tried not to **think of this** as he hurried along the path, staff in hand. [PEST 46]

Ond yn hollol ddisymwth, cyn iddo gael cyfle i **hel ei feddyliau at ei gilydd** bron, roedd hi wedi troi ar ei sawdl ac yn disgwyl amdano wrth y drws. [PLA 73]

Then suddenly, before he could **gather his wits**, she turned, waiting for him at the door. [PEST 55-6]

Eich gwraig chi ddaru achwyn bod Mam yn **hel streuon** arni hi . . . [NOS 69]

. . . it was your wife saying that Mom was **gossiping** about her . . . [NIGHT 56]

Doedd y bywyd strêt roedd hi a'i gŵr yn ei fyw ddim yn ddigon da ganddi, ac roedd hi'n trial cael ysgariad trwy **hel ei thraed** mewn tafarne, clybie a llefydd eraill 'da phobol 'diddorol' gyda'i giang o ynfytion anwes. [HUNAN 278]

The straight life that she and her husband led was not good enough for her, and she was trying to organise a divorce by **running around** the pubs, clubs and other 'more interesting' places with her gang of pet loonies. [SOLVA 278-9]

. . . **I'm off**. [TIME 19]

. . . dw i am **hel fy nhraed** o 'ma. [AMSER 19]

HEN

We include 'hen' (= old) here to note its frequent use as an appreciative or depreciative qualifier of nouns [see PWT 4.92c]. Our first example is depreciative:

'Taw â chlegar,' oddi wrth ei thad. Clegar - clegar - **hen air hyll**. Ei thad yn defnyddio **hen air** fel yna a Sgiatan wedi - wedi - marw! [TE 9]

'Stop that yowling!' cried her father. Yowling . . . **an ugly word** . . . fancy her father using an **ugly word** like that, and Sgiatan, well, Sgiatan dead. [TEA 13]

'Hen' here is not carried over into the English translation but it would have been equally possible to insert 'old' here > '. . . **an ugly (old) word** . . .'

This is the case with some of the following examples although it would not be possible in each one especially when used to emphasise the element being deprecated. Note the addition of the definite article when used to address an object directly as in the first example.

'Oh, **you wicked, wicked little thing!**' cried Alice, catching up the kitten, and giving it a little kiss to make it understand that it was in disgrace. [THRO 128]

'O, **yr hen gath fach ddrwg!**' gwaeddodd Alys gan godi'r gath fach a rhoi cusan iddi ddeall ei bod dan gerydd. [TRWY 13]

'He was a **shit**,' he spat out. 'An arsehole, if you have to know.' [TIME 31]

'**Hen gythraul** oedd o,' poerodd. 'Cachwr, os oes rhaid i chi gael gwybod.' [AMSER 47]

Mae honno'n **hen gân** gan Winni, mae hi bownd o gyrraedd adra cyn nos iti. [TE 45]

That's an **old story** of hers, she's bound to go home before dark. [TEA 43]

'It's a **poor sort of memory** that only works backwards,' the Queen remarked. [THRO 172]

'**Hen gof digon sâl** sy'n gweithio'n ôl yn unig,' meddai'r Frenhines. [TRWY 62]

. . . ending up as I am now with a dislike for all you untrustworthy bastards. I've rarely met one anyway who wasn't a **sex-mad pig** at heart. [TIME 105]

A rŵan rydw i'n casáu pob bastard twyllodrus o ddyn. Ddois i 'rioed ar draws 'run nad oedd, yn y bôn, yn **rêl hen fochyn**, yn meddwl am ddim ond am ryw. [AMSER 168]

Duw a ŵyr 'dan ni wedi mynd trwy **hen ddigon** fel y mae hi. [PLA 159]

God knows we've gone through **enough** *as it is.*

LLOND / -AID

In this section, we have combined discussion of the noun 'llond' together with the (measure) suffix '-aid' both used generally to convey a 'noun + ful' of something. 'Llond' is in fact a contraction of the adjective 'llawn (= full)' with the suffix '-aid' > llond + -aid > llondaid > llond. Our initial example gives both employed within the same section of work:

'. . . dos i'r tŷ i nôl **powlaid o laeth** i mi.' [. . .] a daeth â **llond powlen** iddo. [HENAT 125]

'. . . go to the house and get me a **bowl**[*ful*] **of milk.**' [. . .] and brought him a **full bowl.** [LOCUST 108]

'*Llond*' may be followed by a noun (as in '*llond powlen*' above) or in the combination *llond* + possessive pronoun + noun (often a part of the body). Some of these have an extended meaning, for example *llond* + *bol(a)* is a '*stomach/belly full*' but may also convey a feeling of being '*fed up*' or having '*had enough*' of something. Final examples here give '*llond*' preceded by a possessive pronoun which is an idiomatic alternative to translate '*full of*'.

Yno digwyddai fod **llond hewl o blant** allan yn chwarae hanner dydd. [CHWECH 74]	*There happened, then, to be a* ***streetful of children*** *out playing at mid-day.*
I am **fed up with** you useless bunch of midgets. [MAT 169]	Dw i wedi cael **llond bol arnoch** chi'r criw corachod di-werth! [MAT 163]
Ac yn hollol ddirybudd fe luchiodd **lond dwrn o ludw** dros ymyl y pulpud. Cymerodd pawb eu gwynt atynt. [PLA 135]	Without warning, the friar threw a **fistful of ash** over the edge of the pulpit. There was an audible gasp from the congregation. [PEST 95]
Pistyllodd un taeog **lond ceg** o fedd am ben y tafarnwr. [PLA 147]	One of the serfs sprayed the innkeeper with a **mouthful** of mead. [PEST 102]
She looked at Nigel, **her eyes wide with distress**. [VICT 116]	Edrychodd hithau ar Iorwerth **a gofid lond ei llygaid**. [LLINYN 129]
Ond wedi'r misoedd o ymlafnio diarbed ym mwrllwch afiach y tanddaearolion leoedd fe garent drachefn anadlu **llond eu hysgyfaint** o awyr iach y bryniau. [CHWECH 97]	*But after months of unremitting slog in the unhealthy smog of these underground places they would love once again to breathe **their lungs full** of the fresh air of the hills.*
Ac am y tro cynta er dyddiau lawer fe agorodd y chwaer Clara ei llygaid, ond er hyn roedd hi'n dal yn wan iawn a gwres afiach **lond ei chorff**. [PLA 155]	*And for the first time in many days sister Clara opened her eyes, however inspite of this, she was still very weak and her **body full** of an unhealthy fever.*
Cyn i Ruffydd Davies gychwyn i'r gegin fach hefo **llond ei ddwylo o lestri**, oedodd Ifor ennyd wrth danio'i sigaret i ddweud yn fawreddog . . . [CHWAL 105]	Before Griffith Davies left for the back-kitchen with **a load** [lit. hands full] **of dishes** Ivor, pausing to light a cigarette, said importantly . . . [OUT 109]

374 Comparative Stylistics of Welsh and English

... plygai'r cwc dros y tân gan droi **llond crochan mawr o gawl.** [ALYS 57]

*... the cook bent over the fire stirring a **huge cauldron full of cawl.***

Gofalodd am gario **llond ei ffedog** o feini mawr i wneud sarn i groesi ar hyd-ddi. [WILLAT 64]

*... took charge of carrying an **apronful** of large stones to make a causeway to cross over.*

... ac roedd **llond y lle o** stondinau a gwerthwyr stryd. [CRWYD 33]

*... and the **place was full of** stalls and street vendors.*

This comes with all the **love in the world and kisses** for you both. [CIDER 21]

Rwy'n anfon pob tamaid o'm cariad a **llond gwlad o gusanau** i chi'ch dwy. [SEIDR 30]

Parhaodd pawb i fwyta a **llond eu cegau** o fara. [PLA 190]

*Everybody carried on eating with **mouthfuls** of bread.*

... dwy flynedd **a'u llond o ddelfrydau uchel** ... [WILLAT 92]

*... two years **full of high ideals** ... [lit: two year and their full of high ideals . . .]*

... crochan haearn **a'i llond hi** o flawd pys. [PLA 181]

*... an iron cauldron **full of** [lit: and its full of. . .] peasemeal.*

Ofynnon ni am *crêpes complets* – crempog **â'u llond o gig moch,** wyau, menyn a chaws. [CRWYD 29]

*We asked for crêpes complets – pancakes **full of** [lit. with their full of] bacon, eggs, butter and cheese.*

Aeth anobaith Owen yn wrthryfel sydyn ynddo, yn chwerwder, yn elyniaeth. Fo **a'i lond mur o lyfrau!**

Owen's inward despair suddenly changed to a feeling of rebellion, bitterness, hostility. He and **his wall lined with books!** [BEGIN 181]

The alternative to the '*llond*' construction if to add the suffix '*-aid*' (sometimes reduced to its spoken equivalent *-ed* in SW or *-ad* in NW). This suffix is connected with the idea of *measure/amount* and although commonly seen after nouns such as '*cwpan/dishgl*' >>> '*cwpanaid/panad/dishgled*' to specifiy a '*cup (full) of*', our examples show that it's very productive in its possible applications.

... was paying for **a bottle** [*i.e. a full bottle*] **of Tizer.** [CIDER 31]

... yn talu am **botelaid o bop.** [SEIDR 43]

Glasaid o win gwyn ydoedd hi'r tro hwn ... [HDF 169]

This time it was **a glass of white wine** ... [OFH 212]

Dychwelodd y wraig ymhen ennyd, gan ddwyn i mewn dorth a chaws a **jygaid o lefrith**. [CHWAL 19]

A moment later she came back, bearing a loaf, cheese and **a jug** [*full*] **of milk**. [OUT 19]

. . . **a row** [*full*] **of** six small stucco houses. [UNSUIT 107]

. . . **rhesaid o** dai bychain – chwech ohonynt i gyd. [GORTYN 135]

At four the following afternoon Mrs Lockwood took a **large basket** containing [*full of*] freshly baked scones and a **bowl** [*full of*] cream to the field where the harvesters were at work, and I was given the **jug** of cider to top up their bottles. [CIDER 28–9]

Am bedwar o'r gloch y prynhawn, aeth Mrs Lockwood â **basgedaid** fawr o sgons newydd eu crasu a **bowlenaid** o hufen i'r cae lle roedd y gweithwyr yn brysur yn cynaeafu'r ŷd. Cefais innau'r cyfrifoldeb o'i dilyn gan gario **jwg** anferth o seidr. [SEIDR 40]

. . . a chymerodd y tri ohonynt **gegaid** o ddŵr o'r nant. . . [CHWAL 17]

. . . all three gulped down a **mouthful** of water from the stream. . . [OUT 17]

Tynnodd Harri **ffroenaid** o awyr y Foel i'w ysgyfaint. Nid oedd arno flas mwg na blas heli, dim ond blas awyr. [CRYMAN 12]

Harri took a **draught** [*lit: a nostril full*] of the mountain air into his lungs. It didn't have the taste of smoke or the sea, only that of pure air . . . [SICKLE 8]

PETHAU > EI BETHAU/EI PHETHAU

'*Peth*' is a versatile noun in Welsh – as is its equivalent in English '*thing*'. When used in its plural form '*pethau*' (or more informally SW '*pethe*' or NW '*petha*') it can be used idiomatically to refer to '*things*' in an area or field which appeal or are of a particular interest to someone, something one is '*into*' (see our first example below). One particular phrase is '*mynd trwy* (or: *o gwmpas*) *ei bethau/ei phethau*' which equates to '*going about one's business or "stuff"*'. The possessive is usually in the third person but can be used in conjunction with the first or second too. '*Bod o gwmpas eich pethau*' conveys a sense of '*being alert/aware*' of what is happening around the speaker.

– jazz oedd **ei bethe fe** . . . [HUNAN 85]

Clive was **into** jazz . . . [SOLVA 85]

Paffio **oedd pethe Dada**, fel y bydden ni'n ei alw, ac roedd ring

Dada was a keen boxing **fan** and he had a boxing ring in one of his

baffio 'da fe yn un o'i weithdai yn Solfach Isaf lle bydde'n hyfforddi'i feibion a rhai o'r bechgyn eraill yn y gamp. [HUNAN 13]

workshops in Lower Solva where he'd train his sons and some of the other boys to box. [SOLVA 13]

Ond heddiw fe nesaodd at y drws i glywed Iolyn Offeiriad yn **mynd trwy 'i bethau** [PLA 134]

Today, the leper crept up to the entrance to hear Iolyn the Priest's **prayer** (*i.e. the activity he was carrying out and going through at that moment*). [PEST 94]

Roedd 'da M Tomas allweddi i'r system nerfol, heb os nac oni bai! Gobeithio o'n i 'i fod e'n **deall ei bethe**. [CRWYD 20]

*There was no doubt that M Tomas had keys to the nervous system! I just hoped that **he knew his stuff**.*

Lle garw yw e. Well i ti **fod o gwmpas dy bethe'** os ei di lawr 'na. [HUNAN 78]

It's a very rough place. You'd better **be on the alert** if you go down there. [SOLVA 79]

PIAU

As a verb form, '*piau*' is only found in the third person singular. Its main semantic function is to note a sense of ownership, belonging yet given that it retains a sense of a relative clause, the order is normally: subject + [bod] +[11]*p/biau* + object. Therefore, '*fi sydd biau'r car*' is '*me [I] + it is who + belongs + to the car*' >>> '*The car belongs to me*' or '*I own the car*'. The examples given below demonstrate how this versatile construction can be used idiomatically to convey different shades of meaning in English. In particular, expressions such as '*taw b/piau hi*' ('*silence it is that belongs to it*' >>> '*best keep quiet*') suggest that a particular course of action is advised or best followed.

'I am **all attention**, madam.' [BAND 211]

'Y chi **biau** fy holl sylw, madam.' [CYLCH 17] [lit. 'You belong to all my attention, madam']

In the end he had to conclude that **it was Paul's privilege** to do what he liked with his money. [VICT 136]

Roedd wedi ildio yn y diwedd a chyfadde mai **Owen oedd pia dweud** beth roedd o am ei wneud efo'i bres. [LLINYN 153]

---

[11] Note that both mutated and non-mutated versions of '*p/biau*' are arbitrarily found.

Hi piau nhw, yn siŵr iti.
[MONICA 7]

They're hers, I'd wager.
[MONICA 6]

'Gan bwyll. **Castie llwynog piau hi**,
Meic.' [HUNAN 278]

'Cool down, and **box clever**, Meic.'
[SOLVA 278] (*Lit: Fox tricks belong
to it >>> Best use the tricks of a fox
>>> Box clever!*)

Barnodd Edward unwaith yn
rhagor mai **taw oedd piau hi** . . .
[RHANNU 191]

Edward judged once again that it **was
better to be silent** . . .

Digonedd o ganu, dawnso a
phrancio **oedd piau hi** y noson
honno ac fe feddwon ni'n chwil ulw
gaib. [HUNAN 280]

A lot of singing, dancing and
cavorting **was the order of the
night** and we got very pissed.
[SOLVA 281]

TIPYN

'*Tipyn*' corresponds to the English '*a little, a bit*' and is often followed by the
preposition '*o*'. By extension, it can also be useful for saying '*a bit of a . . .*',
'*quite a . . .*' or '*a real . . .*'. The final examples illustrate more idiomatic use of
'*tipyn*' for example, to modify '*tyfu (= to grow)*' or followed by another noun
with a disparaging meaning.

He was **one for the ladies**, then?
[CIDER 18]

Roedd o'n **dipyn o un am y
merched**, felly? [SEIDR 25]
(*Lit: He was a bit of a one for the
ladies . . .*)

That was **a summer** for parties.
[CIDER 88]

Roedd honno'n **dipyn o flwyddyn**
am bartïon. [SEIDR 120] (*Implicit
in the English is that this was
quite a summer for parties. The
translator has sustituted 'summer'
for 'year'.*)

It's true that she was **pretty** upset
and so were the Lockwoods.
[CIDER 117]

Mae'n wir ei bod hi wedi cyffroi
tipyn, a'i rhieni hefyd. [SEIDR 156]

This took a long time to manage,
though Alice held the bag open very
carefully, because the Knight was so

Cymerodd amser maith i wneud
hyn er i Alys ddal y bag yn agored
yn ofalus iawn, oherwydd roedd y

very awkward in putting in the dish; the first two or three times that he tried he fell in himself instead. 'It's **rather a tight fit**, you see,' he said, as they got it in at last . . . [THRO 208]

Marchog mor ofnadwy o ddrwsgl yn rhoi'r ddysgl i mewn. Y ddau neu'r tri tro cyntaf, cwympodd i mewn ei hun. 'Mae hi'n **dipyn o wasgfa**, welwch chi,' meddai wrth ei chael i mewn o'r diwedd . . . [TRWY 1010]

Pan **dyfodd** y bachgen **i dipyn o faint** aeth yn bla ar y gymdogaeth . . . [GWEN 12]

As soon as the boy **grew up** he became a nuisance in the neighbourhood . . . [GWEN 19]

I've written the story. It's the lead on Sunday. So you can stuff **your exclusive**. [CIDER 164].

Rydw i wedi ysgrifennu'r stori ac mi fydd hi ar y dudalen flaen ddydd Sul. Felly, mi gei di stwffio **dy dipyn stori**. [SEIDR 216]

[A] WNELO

The expression '*bod a wnelo â*' is an interesting fossilisation of the future subjunctive of the verb '*gwneud*' retained in this context to correspond to the English '*to do with / to be concerned with*'. The tense used in this expression is modified by the appropriate tense of the verb '*bod*' with our final example showing a conditional use in a more informal register.

One thing was certain, that the *white* kitten **had had nothing to do with it** – it was the black kitten's fault entirely. [THRO 127]

Roedd un peth yn sicr, **nad oedd** y gath fach wen **a wnelo ddim ag ef**: bai'r gath fach ddu ydoedd yn gyfangwbl. [TRWY 13]

'I recall the case; **it was concerned with** an opal tiara.' [BAND 210]

'Rwy'n cofio'r wraig y gwnaethoch chi sôn amdani gynnau fach. **Roedd a wnelo'r** achos hwnnw â thiara opal.' [CYLCH 16]

This relates to something you asked me earlier, doesn't it? [CIDER 115]

Mae a wnelo hyn â rhywbeth ofynnaist ti i mi'r prynhawn 'ma, on'd oes? [SEIDR 155]

How would she cope with it? **If her mother had anything to do with it,** she would cope admirably . . . [KNOTS 82]

Sut y gallai ddelio â'r cyfan? **Os byddai a wnelo'i mam rywbeth â hynny,** fe ddeuai drwyddi'n iawn . . . [CHWERW 70]

9.2 Other lexical matters

9.2.a. Lexical Gaps

We have grouped together in this section examples of where it is difficult or impossible to render exactly a word or phrase from one language into the other. As a result, it could be stated that '*lexical gaps*' exist between Welsh and English for which different strategies have to be employed by the translator in order to *fill* the gap.

9.2.a.i Simplex word in one language, no exact equivalent in the other

The examples all include simplex (non-compounded) words in one language which have no direct equivalent in the other:

'*lend*', '*inform*', '*blink*', '*offend*', '*accompany*', '*addict*', '*suspect*'
'*nosi*', '*gwrthbrofi*'

The strategy (similar to iii below) is to use a defining phrase or clause (as in the example of '*suspect*') in the target language to convey the same meaning. One particularly good instance of this is the English verb '*to blink*'. Although GM gives '*amrantu*' or '*taro llygad*' for this, the only two examples in GPC relate to the seventeenth century and the '*taro llygad*' collocation is recorded with the meaning of '*to have a look at, glance*'. The examples given below illustrate how contemporary translators have tackled this challenge by expanding it to '*agor a chau llygaid*' [lit: *opening and closing eyes*] modified by an appropriate adverb. The example of '*unblinkingly*' (which will not be found in any dictionary) is another good example of this strategy in operation.

I **lent** him to Dumbledore [STONE 151]	. . . **rois i ei fenthyg** i Dumbledore [MAEN 151]
McNeill had . . . **informed** the PC . . . [TIME 45]	Roedd McNeill wedi **rhoi gwybod i'r** plismon [AMSER 70]
I **blinked** up at him in some surprise, and perhaps just a little resentment, for I was myself regular in my habits. [BAND 208]	. . . **agorais a chau fy llygaid** yn syn a braidd yn ddig, efallai, o gofio fy mod innau'n greadur defodol iawn. [CYLCH 12]
Rogers **blinked** several times, feeling mist collecting on his eyelashes and eyebrows. [TIME 19]	**Agorodd** Roger **ei lygaid a'u cau eto'n gyflym**, sawl gwaith, gan deimlo niwl yn cronni ar ei aeliau a'i amrannau. [AMSER 30]

Being informed that **addicts** usually possessed an inborn psychopathic tendency and, later, a psychical degeneration leading to insanity was something he had to accept . . . [TIME 64]

Dysgodd fod y **rhai sy'n gaeth i'r cyffur** fel arfer yn amlygu tueddiadau seicopathig cynhenid, ac, yn ddiweddarach, ddirywiad seicolegol sy'n arwain yn aml at wallgofrwydd . . . [AMSER 100]

Lingard was no man to put helpful words in a **suspect**'s mouth. [TIME 82]

Nid oedd Lingard yn ddyn i roi geiriau o gymorth yng ngenau **dyn yr oedd yn ei amau**. [AMSER 128]

. . . gofynnodd yn ffurfiol iawn, a hynny yng nghlyw ei thad, a fyddai'n fodlon ystyried **mynd yn gwmni iddo** i Fangor brynhawn Sadwrn. [RHANNU 240]

*He asked very formally, and this in her father's hearing, whether she would be willing to consider **accompanying** him to Bangor on Saturday afternoon.*

A chyn bo hir byddai wedi nosi a **doedd wybod** lle'r oedd Angharad Ferch Madog wedi mynd . . . [PLA 162]

The light was fading and there was no sign of Angharad daughter of Madog. [PEST 107]

He was always ready to be **proved wrong**. [TIME 25]

Roedd o wastad yn barod i gael ei **wrthbrofi**. [AMSER 38]

9.2.a.ii Cultural words without exact equivalents

Our examples below relate to a particular novel by Kate Roberts (*Traed mewn cyffion*) written in a specific area of Wales and including terminology specific to the north Wales quarrying industry. They have no direct equivalents and the translator has expanded their definition to make their meanings clear to the English reader. This is a useful strategy to employ when there is a lexical gap caused by a cultural or domain-based mismatch.

Petai'r **fargen** a'r cerrig yn dda, pris isel oedd i'w ddisgwyl, ond gan eu bod fel arall, gallent ddisgwyl pris gwell ar ddechrau mis. [TRAED 88]

If **the place allotted to them to work** was a good one and the rock easy to handle they could expect a low price, but since it was otherwise they could expect a much better price at the beginning of the month. [FEET 79]

Rybela y bu William hyd yn hyn, gwaith hap a siawns, ac nid oedd

Until now William had had **to depend on others for getting stones**

ganddo obaith am ddim byd arall, ond cael ei gymryd yn 'jermon' at griw. [TRAED 88]	to work with, and he had no hope of anything better unless he could persuade some crew to take him on as a day labourer. [FEET 79]

9.2.a.iii Compound in one language = phrase or clause in translation

This is an aspect of English which can create challenges for the translator into Welsh. Such compounds in English do not always lend themselves to similar compounds in Welsh (however see 9.2.a.v and vi below) and therefore need to be reworked as either phrases or clauses. The final example demonstrates how the reverse is also possible whereby a Welsh clause is condensed into an English compound.

Hermione was now refusing to speak to Harry and Ron, but she was such a **bossy know-it-all** that they saw this as an added bonus. [STONE 203]	Gwrthodai Hermione siarad â Harri a Ron, ond gan ei bod hi'n gymaint o **fadam a dybiai ei bod yn gwybod pob dim**, ystyriai'r ddau hynny yn fantais fawr. [MAEN 129]
Stubby, **nicotine-stained** fingers [CIDER 87]	Bysedd byrion **ac ôl smocio trwm arnyn nhw.** [SEIDR 118]
. . . ending up as I am now with a dislike for all you untrustworthy bastards. I've rarely met one anyway who wasn't a **sex-mad** pig at heart. [TIME 105]	A rŵan rydw i'n casáu pob bastard twyllodrus o ddyn. Ddois i 'rioed ar draws 'run nad oedd, yn y bôn, yn rêl hen fochyn, **yn meddwl am ddim ond am ryw.** [AMSER 168]
O'r 'llonyddwch' i'r 'Doldrums' a'u cymysgedd o heulwen a storm, o awyr las a tharanau, o dywyllwch dudew a mellt **a rwygai'r llygaid bron** . . . [CHWAL 122]	Out of the calm into the Doldrums, with their mixture of sunshine and squalls, blue skies and thunder, the darkness of Erebus and **eye-searing** lightning . . . [OUT 128]

9.2.a.iv Derivation in one language with no single-word derived equivalent in the other

Prefixes and suffixes can be added in both languages to change the semantic function of a lexical item. No dictionary can be expected to include all of these especially as individual authors may 'create' their own derivations. The obvious strategy to deal with this is to expand the translation into either an appropriate descriptive clause or multi-word definition equivalent.

A thu ôl i'r **academeiddiwch** gwyntog ugeinoed yr oedd yr **academeiddiwch** arall. [CRYMAN 231]

Behind the windy, **pseudo-academic talk** of the twenty-year-olds there was another kind ... [SICKLE 191]

Gosodai'r mân-goed a'r bras-goed yn garnau bonfon, **cyhyd**, ar wahân, yn hwylus at law'r stocer ar yr aelwyd. [HDF 108]

She put the small wood and the thick wood in two heaps with the thicker ends of the pieces towards each other, **and all of equal length**, ready for the stoker's hand at the fireside. [OFH 132]

... hen biano **canhwyllog**. [CRYMAN 78]

... an ancient piano **with candlesticks on it.** [SICKLE 63]

... nid hiraeth brwnt fel hwnnw yn yr eglwys **ganhwyllog arogldarthus** ar fore Sul [LLEIFIOR 28]

... [a pleasant kind of longing], not the sort she felt in church, **with its candles and incense**, on Sunday mornings. [RETURN 22]

Ystafell gyffredin oedd hi (ond gweddol gysurus) â llaweroedd o **ddilladach** trymion yn hongian ar y waliau ... [PLA 78]

The room, though not particularly big, was comfortable, with **woven hangings** and a low door ... [PEST 59]

They're like a machine churning away with their endless files and **bits of paper** and producing nothing at all. [VICT 40]

Maen nhw fel rhyw beiriant anferth efo miloedd o ffeilia a'r holl **dameidiach papur** 'ma ... [LLINYN 45]

He said that he was at the club with a problem or two, that he couldn't leave it to visit Roger's office because he had an **unmissable** appointment later, so would Rogers care to look in before seven-thirty for whatever it was that worried him. [TIME 100]

Dywedodd ei fod yn y clwb a bod ganddo broblem neu ddwy. Ni fedrai ddod i swyddfa Rogers oherwydd fod ganddo drefniant **yr oedd yn rhaid iddo'i gadw** yn ddiweddarach, felly a fyddai Rogers gystal â tharo heibio cyn hanner awr wedi saith i drafod ei broblem. [AMSER 159]

A couple of shabby **mismatched** easy chairs and the well-worn patterned carpet were manifestly the legal requirements of an apartment rented as fully furnished. [TIME 22]

Prin ddigon oedd yr ychydig gadeiriau esmwyth di-raen, **nad oeddynt yn perthyn i set**, a'r carped patrymog treuliedig, i gyfiawnhau rhentu'r fflat fel un oedd wedi ei ddodrefnu. [AMSER 33]

9.2.a.v English compounding 'unpacked' in Welsh

The first example here includes an instance of Welsh equivalent compounding ('*dirgel-ddwfn*') as well as an 'unpacking' or re-rendering of the English compound when (as is more often the case) no equivalent exists or could be reasonably created. Our other examples illustrate the ways in which translators have successfully 'unpacked' English compounds.

. . . while his **deep-set, bile-shot** eyes and the **high thin fleshless** nose, gave him somewhat the resemblance to a fierce old bird of prey. [BAND 221]	. . . ac roedd ei lygaid **dirgel-ddwfn, gwaetgoch a llawn bustl**, a'r drwyn **main â'i bont uchel, esgyrnog**, yn gwneud iddo edrych yn debyg iawn i hen fwltur ysglyfaethus a ffyrnig. [CYLCH 32]
When his telephone bell rang again, he was looking through the window at a view of **sunlit** slate roofs and wondering morosely why it wasn't, congruous with his mood, pouring down grey rain. [TIME 60]	Pan ganodd ei deliffon drachefn, roedd yn edrych drwy'r ffenest ar doi llechi'**n sgleinio yn yr haul** ac yn ceisio dyfalu pam gythraul nad oedd hi'n tywallt y glaw o awyr oedd mor llwyd ac mor ddiflas ag y teimlai yntau. [AMSER 94–5]
Already Lavender's scheming mind was going over the possibilities that this **water-jug job** had opened up for her. [MAT 136]	Roedd meddwl cyfrwys Lavender eisoes yn mynd dros y posibiliadau roedd y **gwaith o nôl y jwg ddŵr** wedi'u hagor iddi. [MAT 130]
A phob un o'r bechgyn hyn, ynteu, o hen wehelyth y fro, ac yn ddyledus iddi am bron bopeth a feddent, tyfasant i gyd yn ddynion cyfrifol, gleuedig, **glân eu bywydau** . . . [HDF 131]	All these boys, coming from the old families of the neighbourhood and indebted to it for everything they possessed, grew up to be responsible, enlightened, and **clean-living** men . . . [OFH 164]

9.2.a.vi Compounding in English = derivation in Welsh

Translators should not fear pairing a compound in English with a simple derivation in Welsh if this means that the meaning from the original is not altered significantly. In the example below, '*mist-bound*' is translated by the simple adjective '*niwlog*' (= *misty*) with no loss of meaning.

When Rogers stepped out into the dark and **mist-bound** room . . . [TIME 18]	Camodd Rogers i'r stryd dywyll, **niwlog** . . . [AMSER 27]

9.2.a.vii Verbs of manner of motion (see also Chapter 10 on Verbless Clauses)

Many English verbs of motion do not find exact equivalents in Welsh. In cases such as these, it is common for Welsh to use a verb which has a looser semantic relationship and then qualifying it with an adverb or phrase which gives the reader information about the exact manner of motion. For example, the English verb '*to tiptoe*' in the example below is conveyed using the verb '*cerdded*' (= *to walk*) plus the phrase '*ar flaenau ei thraed*' equating with '*on tiptoes*'.

It was after midnight when she **tiptoed** past the open door of my room. [CIDER 39]	Roedd wedi troi hanner nos pan glywais hi'n **cerdded ar flaenau ei thraed** heibio i ddrws cilagored fy stafell. [SEIDR 56]

Further examples of this are given in the table below together with a list of others noted in English-Welsh/Welsh-English translations. Translators need to bear this useful strategy in mind when dictionaries may offer Welsh equivalents which do not correspond with all the semantic possiblities of a verb of motion. '*To march*' is one example. A dictionary may list it with its military meaning as '*ymdeithio*' or '*gorymdeithio*' but in the context of our first example below, this clearly would not be appropriate and the translator has used '*cerdded*' and described the manner of motion with the adverb '*yn bwrpasol*' (= *purposefully*). It should also be noted that this is often a more natural sounding and idiomatic solution even when a direct Welsh equivalent is listed.

She wrenched open doors and **marched** along corridors . . . [STONE 186]	Lluchiodd ddrysau ar agor a **cherddd yn bwrpasol** ar hyd coridorau . . . [MAEN 118]
She dropped her thick black veil over her face and **glided from the room.** [BAND 220]	Ailorchuddiodd ei hwyneb gyda'r rhwyden ddu drwchus a **llithrodd allan** o'r ystafell **yn dawel ac yn ddigyffro.** [CYLCH 30]
Daeth hen gerbyd bregus **ar wib** i lawr y ffordd, yn tynnu olgert yn llawn o gelfi gwersyll. [CRYMAN 74]	An old, ramshackle van **came racing** down the road, towing a trailer full of camping equipment. [SICKLE 60]
Wrth **hwylio'n droedrydd** i lawr Allensbank Road . . . [FFYDD 60]	As I **freewheel** down Allensbank Road . . . [FAITH 150]

Daeth rhyw fyddigions drwy'r drws **dan hanner baglu,** a'u dillad nhw'n edrych fel rhywbeth ar gyfer yr opera neu'r Savoy Hotel. [HUNAN 133]

Some society toffs **staggered** through the door, dressed for the opera or the Savoy Hotel. [SOLVA 133]

They **inched** closer. [STONE 318]

Fesul modfedd, aethant yn nes. [MAEN 202]

Ymwthiodd trwy'r dorf gan **fynd igam ogam** ar draws y sgwâr hyd nes y cyrhaeddodd risiau'r eglwys anferth ar yr ochr bellaf. [PLA 72]

He hurried through the crowds, **zigzagging** across the square until he reached the steps of the church on the other side. [PEST 54]

Bwrais y mwg yn glep 'nôl ar y ford. [DAL 87]

I slammed the mug down on the table.

Ac **aeth** y ferch tua'r hofeldy **ar ysgafndroed** tra **cherddodd y taeog yn sionc** ar ôl ei yrr i lawr tua'r buarth. [PLA 121]

So she **hops off** to his hut and he **skips off** to his milking. [PEST 63]

Other possibilities noted include:

[in his car, he] Crawled back to his office ...	>	Symudodd fel malwoden ...
Creeping up to me ...	>	Dod ataf ar flaenau ei draed ...
[she] Dawdled ...	>	Aeth o lech i lwyn ...
Flitted across her face ...	>	Daeth i'w hwyneb am eiliad ...
[he] Lumbered over to us ...	>	Roedd yn camu'n drwsgl tuag atom ...
Lurching to left and right ...	>	Crwydro'n ddiamcan i'r chwith ac i'r dde ...
[she] Sauntered away ...	>	[dyma hi'n] Cerdded i ffwrdd ling-di-long ...
[the four of them] Sprinted ...	>	Gwibiodd [y pedwar] nerth eu traed ...
Stomp ...	>	Camu'n drwm ...
Trotted slowly back again ...	>	Dod yn ôl ar drot araf ...

| Whooshing away . . . | > | Yn rhuthro i ffwrdd ar ffrwst . . . |
| Wobble . . . | > | Camu'n sigledig . . . |

9.2.b. Lexical Compounding
9.2.b.i Compounds in Welsh

Lexical compounding is frequently used by writers in Welsh as a means of giving expression to a specific descriptive element or idea for which no exact equivalent exists. The process of forming a compound in Welsh is relatively simple and in general, the meaning of the compound is sufficiently clear to the reader for it to be a useful creative, stylistic device in writing. Compounds in Welsh are formed by the combination of more than one stem and can be used to form:

Nouns – e.g. *anwar (uncivilised)* + *dyn (man)* > *anwarddyn*

Yr oedd yn amlwg fod cabledd a chelwyddau'r **anwarddyn** cegrwth yn ei boeni. [WILLAT 20]	*It was obvious that the gaping,* ***boorish man's*** *blasphemy and lies were worrying him.*

Verb-nouns – e.g. *chwerw (bitter)* + *mwynhau (to enjoy)* > *chwerw-fwynhau*

Bu'n rhaid iddi hi a'i phriod **chwerw-fwynhau** gwaith ei llaw. [MONICA 42]	She and her husband had **had the bitter pleasure** of having to eat her handiwork. [MONICA 41]

Adjectives – e.g. *tal (tall)* + *syth (straight, upright)* > *talsyth*

Cerddodd yn **dalsyth** tua'r tŷ, yn cario'i bum mlwydd a thrigain yn ysgafn iawn. [CRYMAN 10]	**Tall and upright**, he walked towards the house, carrying his sixty-five years very lightly. [SICKLE 6]

It is usual to classify compounds as being either '*proper compounds*' (i.e. a modifier and the head) or '*improper compounds*' (the head is the first element followed by a modifier). The second element of a proper compound always takes a soft mutation whereas in an improper compound, any mutation will depend on whether this is necessary or not in line with the headword. For example, both '*pentref*' and '*mam-gu*' are improper compounds but only '*-cu*' in the second case has a soft mutation as here it is an adjective describing a singular, feminine noun.

Of particular interest is how translators have dealt with compounds in their work. The following examples illustrate possible approaches:

Y dyddiau cyntaf hynny ni **ddrwgdybiodd** ef ymddygiad Monica. Canmolodd ei doethineb hi yn ymwrthod â **chaledwaith**, yn gorwedd ac yn segura. [MONICA 56]

In those early days **he had no misgivings** about Monica's behaviour. He had praised her good sense in refusing to do any **hard work**, in lying down and taking things easy. [MONICA 56]

Ac aeth Paul yn **wenfflam**. [LLEIFIOR 31]

Paul was **very angry**. [RETURN 24]

... yr oedd coed a physt telegraff a gwartheg yn pori'n ddu ac yn wyn **yn yr hafddydd**. [CRYMAN 41]

... there were now trees and telegraph poles and black-and-white cattle grazing **in the heat of the summer's day**. [SICKLE 32]

Yr oedd ystryd **hirgul** Bryn Llwyd yn un berw o sŵn, yn ystorm o fwyniant ... [CYCHWYN 101]

Bryn Llwyd's **long, narrow** thoroughfare was a boiling sea of uproar and merriment ... [BEGIN 102]

Fe fu droeon yn ceisio ysgwyd y syniad o'i groen; ceisio'i ddarbwyllo'i hun mai wedi'i **lygad-dynnu**'r oedd gan ei harddwch hi [...] Ac yr oedd ei newydd-deb wedi'i **lygad-dynnu** ac wedi cyflymu'i galon. [CRYMAN 43]

He had several times tried to rid himself of this notion; he had tried to convince himself that **his head had been turned** merely by her beauty [...] Her novelty had **captivated** him and made his heart race. [SICKLE 33]

Bob hydref dôi'r eogiaid i fyny i afonydd y blaenau 'i gladdu' neu i fwrw eu hwyau yn 'y cladd' a wnâi eu torrau drwy **sigl-rwbio** yn y graean ar waelod y pwll. [HDF 121]

Every autumn the salmon came up to the upper reaches of the rivers to bury – that is, to shed their eggs in the hollows they made with their bellies by **rubbing to and fro** in the gravel on the bottom of the pool. [OFH 150]

'Oh sir, do you not think you could help me too, and at least throw a little light through the **dense** darkness which surrounds me?' [BAND 210]

'O, syr, ydych chi'n tybio y gallech chi fy helpu innau hefyd, ac o leiaf daflu ychydig o oleuni trwy'r tywyllwch **dudew** sy'n fy amgylchynu?' [CYLCH 15]

With a **grave** face he lit the lamp, and led the way down the corridor. [BAND 237]	Ag wyneb **difrifddwys**, goleuodd Holmes y lamp olew ac arwain y ffordd ar hyd y coridor. [CYLCH 55]

Many of the compounds in our examples cannot be found in standard Welsh dictionaries and the translator will often need to convey their exact meaning through a more literal rendering[12]. Expressions, idioms and even conjugated forms of verbs may form compounds in Welsh too and act as adjectives.

. . . bu'r edrychiad **faswn-i-ddim-yn-gneud-hynna-taswn-i-chi** a gafodd gan ei wraig a safai wrth y cownter yn ddigon i'w rhewi'n ei hunfan. [RHANNU 136]	. . . the **I wouldn't do that if I were you** look that she got from his wife who was standing by the counter was enough to freeze her on the spot.
Roedd y Moulders yn dafarn **ffwrdd-â-hi**, ddiddorol. [HUNAN 103]	The Moulders was a **rough and ready** but interesting hostelry. [SOLVA 103]
Gwnaeth Mrs Vaughan ystumiau **tewch-â-sôn** ar ran Harri a gwenodd Edward Vaughan ar gadwyn aur ei wasgod, ond roedd Mrs Pugh yn bendant. [CRYMAN 52]	Mrs Vaughan made a gesture as if to say on Harri's behalf, **'Go on with you,'** and Edward Vaughan smiled down at the gold chain on his waistcoat. But Mrs Pugh was adamant. [SICKLE 41]
He was instantly reminded of Rendcome's speech. It was **circumlocutory**, but the point, when he came to it, had been valid. [VICT 77]	Atgoffodd ei dull **rownd-sir-Fôn-o-fynd-i-Fangor** hi o'r sgwrs a gawsai efo Japheth ynghynt. Roedd gan hwnnw rywbeth gwerth ei ddweud yn y diwedd. [LLINYN 87–8]
He told her **coolly** that nothing was the matter. [VICT 162]	Dywedodd wrthi'n ddigon **ffwrdd-â-hi** nad oedd dim byd yn bod. [LLINYN 184]
[V]ery likely she was one of the new intakes who wasn't yet into more **casual** clothes. [CIDER 2]	Un o'r glasfyfyrwyr nad oedd hyd yma wedi mabwysiadu'r dull **ffwrdd-â-hi** o wisgo. [SEIDR 7]

---

[12] This can at times be quite challenging. How, for example, could 'celf-a-chrefftus' in the following example from [CRWYD 135] be best translated into English? 'Daeth cantores pync o America heibio, Patty Paladin, 'run peth â The Ramones ond yn fwy dwys a **chelf-a-chrefftus**, fel Lou Reed.'

He told her about the interview, but tried to **make light of it**. [VICT 131]	Soniodd Alun am y cyfweliad, mor **ffwrdd-â-hi** ag y gallai. [LLINYN 147]

9.2.b.ii Compounds with numbers

Compounds formed with mainly cardinal numbers (although there are examples with ordinals too) are fairly common in Welsh. Numbers with an /a/ in them experience affection when they form the first element of a compound, e.g.

dau	>>	deu
tair	>>	teir
ail	>>	eil
ugain	>>	ugein

The dual combination with a body part can be a stylistic alternative to using the established plural form (although in the case of '*dwylo*' (*hands*) this is the only plural form possible).

. . . mwy na hynny, deellais yn llygaid y gynulleidfa fy mod innau dan amheuaeth bellach yn gymaint â'm bod yn eistedd nesaf ato a phawb yn **unfryd unfarn** mai 'drygioni' oedd y cwlwm rhyngom. [DYDD 94]	*More than that, I understood from the eyes of the congregation that I too had come under suspicion insofar as I sat next to him, and everyone **was convinced** [lit. of one unanimous opinion] that mischiefmaking was the bond between us.*
. . . ond niwlen denau o law mynydd y gallech weld drwyddo amlinell bryncyn a choeden a thŷ, y cwbwl yn **unlliw** ac yn anhyfryd laith. [CRYMAN 69]	. . . but a thin veil of mountain rain through which could be seen the occasional hill and tree and house, all in **monochrome** and unpleasantly damp. [SICKLE 56]
Ni chododd hi o'i gwely ers **deufis**. [MONICA 54]	She hasn't got out of bed these last **two months**. [MONICA 55]
A hithau mewn ysbyty, yn anadlu awyr **deufyd**. [CRYMAN 226]	. . . while she lay in hospital, hovering between **life and death** [lit. breathing the air of two worlds]. [SICKLE 187]
'Two days ago some repairs were started in the west wing of the building . . .' [BAND 218]	'**Ddeuddydd** yn ôl dechreuwyd ar waith atgyweirio yn adain orllewinol y plasty . . .' [CYLCH 27]

Nid arafodd y *Gloria* wrth ei basio, ond yr oedd Paul Rushmere yn ddigon cyflym i ddarllen arno'r **ddeuair** freision: CYMRU WALES. [CRYMAN 42]

The car didn't slow down as it passed, but Paul Rushmere was quick enough to read the **two boldly** painted **words**: CYMRU WALES. [SICKLE 33]

Ond yr oedd y glas yn dal dan ei lygaid, a'r gwyn ar ei ruddiau. Ni allai dim amrywio'r **ddeuliw** hynny ond newydd da. [CRYMAN 36]

But the shadows remained under his eyes and the pallor on his cheeks. Only good news would shift **them** [lit. those two colours]. [SICKLE 28]

Gwledd i'm **dwyglust** oedd clywed hwyl y pregethwr; a chaffai fy llygaid gymaint a hynny o fwynhad o weld ei **ddwyfraich** yn chwifio . . . [WILLAT 26]

*Hearing the 'hwyl' of the preacher was a feast for my **ears**; and my eyes had just as much enjoyment seeing his **arms** waving about . . .*

. . . ar y stôl **drithroed**. [CYCHWYN 86]

. . . the **three-legged** stool. [BEGIN 86]

. . . bob rhyw **deirllath**. [CHWAL 33]

. . . **three yards** apart. [OUT 33]

Prin **deirblwydd** oed, a'i fochau'n gymysgedd amryliw o laid a jam. [CRYMAN 33]

He was scarcely **three years old**, his cheeks smeared with dirt and jam. [SICKLE 25]

. . . ryw **bumswllt**. [O LAW 211]

. . . about **five shillings**. [FROM 173]

. . . bref baban **wythmis** . . . [CRYMAN 32]

. . . the bawling of an **eight-month-old** baby . . . [SICKLE 24]

A thu ôl i'r acadameiddiwch gwyntog **ugeinoed** yr oedd yr acadameiddiwch arall. [CRYMAN 231]

Behind the windy, pseudo-academic talk of **twenty-year-olds** there was another kind. [SICKLE 191]

9.2.b.iii Compounds with body parts

One productive source of compounds in Welsh are combinations with parts of the body. These often provide more meaningful, effective means of description than simple stand alone adjectives. In the example below, the compound adjective '*blewgoch*' (*blew + coch/ fur + red*) describes the orang-utan in a concise and clear way whereas an adjective and a noun are needed in English:

... orang-utan **blewgoch** yn eistedd â'i goesau ar led yng nghanol y sedd gefn; gorila **arianwallt** yn nodio'i ben i rythm ei stereo personol. [FFYDD 61]

An open-legged orangutan sits in the middle of the back row, picking fleas from his **ginger thatch**, while a **silver-backed** gorilla nods his head to the beat of his personal stereo. [FAITH 48]

Below we have listed examples of compounds with particular parts of the body to illustrate how this process can be useful in refining and defining descriptive elements. Note that many of these are examples of translators into Welsh adapting compounds to corresponding non-compound words or phrases in the English original.

Boch (*cheek*)

Hogyn tew, **bochgoch**, oedd Huw, yn gryf fel tarw ond mor ddiniwed ag oen. [CYCHWYN 86]

Huw, though a **rubicund**, burly lad and as strong as a bull, was nevertheless as artless as a baby. [BEGIN 86]

Bol (*belly*)

... rhyw glorwth o Sgotyn **bolfras** ... [CHWECH 40]

*... some great hulky **fat-bellied** Scots fellow ...*

Bron (*breast*)

Ond fel eu brodyr, y morwyr ar y don fradwrus, yr oedd y glowyr hyn yn bobl lawen, **ysgafnfron**. [CHWECH 127]

*But like their brothers, the sailors on the treacherous sea, these miners were happy, **light of heart**.*

Calon (*heart*)

Heblaw hynny yr oedd yno ysgolfeistr o Gymro **twymgalon** a llenor gweddol wych. [CWM 193]

Still more important was the fact that the schoolmaster was a **warm-hearted** Welshman and a pretty good writer. [GORSE 186]

Ceg (*mouth*)

... he was trying to get everyone laughing at how a **wide-mouthed** tree frog would be replacing Harry as seeker next. [STONE 241]

... roedd wedi ceisio cael pawb i chwerthin drwy ddweud y byddai llyffant coeden **cegrwth** yn cymryd lle Harri fel Chwiliwr y tro nesaf. [MAEN 153]

Cefn (*back*)

... ac felly aethant i'r arferiad o wrando yn eu crwmach, ac aeth rhai ohonynt yn naturiol **gefngrwn**. [GWEN 60–1]

To over-come this they slouched in their seats, and as a result became permanently **round shouldered**. [GWEN 58]

Cesail (*armpit*)

[M]ae e'n rhoi ei fraich rownd fy ysgwydd ac yn fy nghofleidio heb dynnu **'ngheseilwallt** na dyrnu fy aren na dim. [FFYDD 179]

Will actually puts his arm around me and gives me a hug without pulling my **underarm hair** or pinching my flesh. [FAITH 125]

Coes (*leg*)

Yr oedd bachgen bach **melyngoes** yn croesi'r cae ... [CRYMAN 40]

A small boy **in short trousers** was coming across the field ... [SICKLE 31]

Croen (*skin*)

Yn ddiweddarach, rhwng y Rhyfel Byd Cynta a'r Ail, roedd jazz yn cael ei chwarae'n aml gan gerddorion **croendywyll** o Tiger Bay ... [HUNAN 99]

Later, between the wars, jazz was often played by **coloured** musicians from Tiger Bay ... [SOLVA 99]

Corff (*body*)

... her **slim-bodied** elegance [TIME 37]

... ei cheinder **meingorff** [AMSER 57]

Gwaed (*blood*)

One of his eyes was **bloodshot** and partially closed. [CIDER 29]

Roedd un o'i lygaid yn **waedgoch** ac yn hanner cau. [SEIDR 41]

Gwallt (*hair*)

To the waist, a man **with red hair** and a beard . . . [STONE 312]

Uwchben y gwasg, dyn barfog, **gwalltgoch** ydoedd . . . [MAEN 200]

Llaw (*hand*)

'so possibly I've been a little **hard** on him.' [TIME 97]

'mae'n bosib 'mod i 'di bod braidd yn **llawdrwm** arno fe.' [AMSER 154]

Llygad (*eye*)

It would be a **sharp-eyed** coroner indeed who could distinguish the two little dark punctures which would show where the poison fangs had done their work. [BAND 239]

Fe fyddai angen crwner eithriadol o **lygatgraff** i sylwi ar y ddau smotyn tywyll a fyddai'n dangos lle y bu i'r ddau ddant gwenwynig chwistrellu angau. [CYLCH 59]

Min (*lip*)

. . . y merched **mingoch** brwd, wedi'u gollwng o gaethiwed ysgol . . . [CRYMAN 230]

. . . the keen girls, recently out of school, **plastered with make-up** . . . [SICKLE 191]

Pen (*head*)

Her hostility had been directed against **red-haired** customers at the shop where she worked. [VICT 157]

Rhoesai ei chas ar bob cwsmer **pengoch** a ddeuai i'r siop lle gweithiai . . . [LLINYN 177]

Tafod (*tongue*)

Yr oedd wedi dioddef dan ddiffygion y letenant ers rhai misoedd, ac yn tueddu i fod yn rhy **dafotrydd** wrth sôn amdanynt o flaen y morwyr. [HENAT 96]

He had suffered from the incompetence of the lieutenant for some months, and was inclined to be too **free with his tongue** about it in front of the seamen. [LOCUST 85]

Troed (*foot*)

Ac ar y ffordd mi welodd y ferch'ma
yn cerddad yn **droednoeth** o'i flaen
o'n y gwlith. [PLA 119]

... when he saw the most beautiful
girl you could ever imagine,
barefoot in the dew ... [PEST 62]

Trwyn (*nose*)

... i'r ferch **drwynfain**,
sbectolaidd ... [CHWAL 160]

... the bespectacled, **razor-nosed**
female receptionist. [OUT 170]

Wyneb (*face*)

A 'Mari Ffidl-Ffadl' oedd yr enw
ar groten o ail forwyn yno, rhyw
dwlpen fach, dew, **wynepgoch** a
fyddai'n rhedeg drot-drot trwy'r
dydd gwyn, heb fod fawr yn nes o'i
dal hi, erbyn nos. [HDF 153]

... and Mari Fiddle-Faddle was
his name for our second maid, a
plump, **redfaced** bundle of a girl
who ran trot-trot the livelong day
without being by the evening much
nearer catching what she was after.
[OFH 191]

9.2.c. Prefix CYD* + Verb-noun

The prefix CYD- may be combined with a verb-noun to give the meaning of
an activity which is happening jointly or together, accompanied by someone
or something or to engage in an activity with someone or something else. This
prefix causes the accompanying verb-noun to undergo a soft mutation and is
frequently followed by the preposition 'â/ag'.

Yr oedd drws y parlwr cefn yn gil-
agored ac yno ar y soffa gwelodd
ei gŵr a'r forwyn yn **cydorwedd**.
[MONICA 44]

The door of the back parlour was
ajar and there on the sofa her
husband and the maid were **lying
together**. [MONICA 43]

Mae'r trawsdoriad rhyfeddol o bobl
yn cymharu mewn ffordd i garchar
gan fod pobl o bob cefndir a chred
yn cael eu taflu i'r crochan ac yn
gorfod **cydferwi**. [FFYDD 45]

The amazing variety of people is
comparable in a way to the prison
population I've recently left behind.
People from all walks of life –
different religions, backgrounds
and so on – are thrown into the
same cauldron to **simmer together**.
[FAITH 37]

... y dyn tawel, caredig y bu'n **cydgerdded ag ef** i'r chwarel ... [TRAED 104]

... that quiet, kind man who had **walked with him** to the quarry ... [FEET 92]

... but a civilised excuse for not **drinking with** a character he expected one day to put handcuffs on ... [TIME 32]

Roedd o'n esgus dros beidio â **chydyfed â** dyn y rhoddai gyffion amdano ryw ddydd. [AMSER 49]

'R oedd gwaith yn beth rhwydd a didrafferth iddo, a'i natur dda yn gwneud ei egni'n heintus i'r sawl a **gydweithiai ag** ef. [HDF 96]

Work was no trouble to him, and his good nature made his energy contagious to those who **were working by his side**. [OFH 118]

Roedd hyn yn dân ar groen ei dad; roedd 'da fe wenwyn at ei fab, a dyna pam nad o'n nhw'n **cyd-dynnu**. [HUNAN 129]

This annoyed his father, who was jealous of his son, and that is why they did not **get on** [lit. pull together]. [SOLVA 128]

Roedd Tessa mewn ffrog hir osgeiddig iawn o satin llwydfelyn ac arian 'da sgidie'n **cyd-fynd**. [HUNAN 249]

Tessa was dressed in a long and elegant dress of beige and silver satin with shoes to **match** [lit. 'to go together'] [SOLVA 249]

Roedden ni'n **cyd-daro** i'r dim ac yn cael blas mawr ar gwmni ein gilydd ... [HUNAN 281]

We **got on** like a house on fire and enjoyed each other's company tremendously ... [SOLVA 281]

'Amen,' **cydfurmurodd** pawb. [PLA 134]

'Amen,' **said** the congregation **as one**. [PEST 94]

9.2.d PREFIX HUNAN-

The prefix '*hunan-*' corresponds to the English '*self-*' and produces a soft mutation at the beginning of the word to which it is affixed. All our examples illustrate this use of the prefix, however it should be remembered that '*hunan-*' combinations can sometimes be translated into English by equivalents which do not include '*self* – for example, '*hunanladdiad*' (lit. '*self-killing*') corresponds to English '*suicide*' and '*hunanreolaeth*' (lit. '*self-control*') to '*autonomy*'.

Gwawriodd peth o'i meddwl ar Ifan, ac wrth weled yr olwg **hunan-gyfiawn**, glwyfedig oedd ar fwyafrif ei deulu, cronnodd holl

Some idea of what she was thinking dawned on Ifan, and seeing the **self-righteous**, wounded looks on the faces of most of his family, all

anghyfiawnder oes yn ei fynwes, a byrlymodd allan. [TRAED 101]

the injustices of a lifetime that had gathered in his breast broke loose. [FEET 90]

[13]The call had left him vaguely irritated with what had sounded to be a bossy and hard-nosed female – though one with a sense of humour – and, not least, because she must have in her turn thought him a **pompous** and uptight bugger. [TIME 94]

Roedd ei llais caled wedi ei adael yn flin braidd er fod ganddi ddogn go dda o hiwmor a hwyrach ei bod hithau, yn ei thro, wedi meddwl ei fod yntau hefyd yn hen ddiawl **hunangyfiawn**, sychlyd. [AMSER 149]

Mewn **hunan-ymholiad** mor onest ag y meiddiaf ei gynnal arnaf fy hun teimlaf fy mod i'n ddiffygiol ddigon yn y tri. [HDF 100]

In as honest a **self-examination** as I am able to hold, I find myself only too deficient in the three. [OFH 122]

Roedd ei rêfio hi'n beth **hunan-ddyrchafedig, hunanganiataëdig**, ansanteiddiedig, aflanwaith, anhrugarog, ac roedd hi ar ben ei digon yn ei hedoniaeth! [HUNAN 87]

Her **self-made, self-sanctioned**, unsanctified, unhygienic, unmerciful rave that was a blissful hedonistic blitz! [SOLVA 87]

9.2.e. Colours: Compound

Compounds formed with colours in Welsh merit specific mention as they enable writers to convey extra nuances in their descriptions which can some-times be difficult to capture fully in the English translation. For example, in [HDF 103] we have:

Dafydd Trefenty a'i farf **frithlwyd**, hir . . .

The Welsh compound '*brithlwyd*' suggests not only that his beard is grey but that the grey in the beard is not uniform but '*speckled*'. This element within the compound is missing from the English [OFH 126]:

Dafydd Trefenty, with his long **grey** beard . . .

Names of colours in English have developed and expanded through the evolu-tion of the language and its contact with other languages so that we not only

---

[13] The translator here chooses to convey the English 'pompous' with **hunangyfiawn** which in the context works better than other dictionary possibilities such as 'rhwysg-fawr' or 'balch'.

have *'brown'* but also *'beige'*, *'maroon'*, *'chestnut'* etc. Colour compounds in Welsh provide an effective strategy for conveying these nuances so that *'gwyrddlas'* (*green* + *blue*) might correspond to *'ultramarine'* or *'cringoch'* (*withered* + *red*) to *'russet'*. These are almost always proper compounds.

Arian (*silver*)

The trees were black against a **silver grey** sky. A waning moon. Milk-white stars. [VICT 100]	Edrychai'r coed yn ddu a'r awyr tu cefn yn **arianllwyd**. Gewin o leuad. Sêr lliw llefrith. [LLINYN 113]

Brith (*speckled*)

... a barf **frithgoch** ar ei wyneb tenau ... [CYCHWYN 66]	... with his **ruddy** beard **flecked with grey** ... [BEGIN 66]

Brown (*brown*)

Yr oedd ei gwallt **brownddu** yn llaes at ei sgwyddau. [LLEIFIOR 49]	Her sleek, **dark-brown** hair fell to her shoulders. [RETURN 40]

Coch (*red*)

... a phelydrau llesg o'r haul gaerau dros Fôn yn dangos twr eglwys Llangaffo ac ystum **cochddu** eglwys Brynsiencyn. [HENAT 64]	... and the wan rays of the sun over Anglesey, picking out the tower of Llangaffo and the **red-brown** shape of Brynsiencyn church. [LOCUST 60]

Du (*black*)

Five little **livid** spots, the marks of four fingers and a thumb, were printed upon the white wrist. [BAND 219]	Daeth pum smotyn **dulas** i'r golwg, marciau pedwar bys a bawd, a'r rheiny i'w gweld yn glir ar yr arddwrn gwyn. [CYLCH 28]

Glas (*blue*)

Wrth edrych drwy'r ffenestr, yr hyn a wnâi Owen yn aml, gwelai domen y chwarel, a edrychai'n **lasgoch** yn ei ymyl. [TRAED 71]	Gazing through the window, Owen could see the **purple** face of the quarry. [FEET 59]

Gwyn (*white*)

* In this example, the compound consists of a colour '*gwyn*' plus a non-colour adjective '*gwlanog*' (*woolly*):

It was a perfect day, with a bright sun and a few **fleecy** clouds in the heavens. [BAND 224]

Roedd hi'n ddiwrnod bendigedig o braf, yr haul yn disgleirio a llond llaw o gymylau **gwyn-wlanog** yn y ffurfafen. [CYLCH 35]

Gwyrdd (*green*)

Gorweddai cwrlid sidanblu yn donnau **gwyrddlas** ar y blancedi . . . [MONICA 57]

An eiderdown made **blue-green** waves over the blankets . . . [MONICA 58]

Lliw (*colour*)

* Using '*lliw*' with a noun is an alternative when a two colour compound might not be sufficient.

. . . her **ash-coloured** hair worn straight and short-cropped. [TIME 81]

. . . gwisgai ei gwallt **lliw arian golau** yn syth ac wedi'i dorri'n fyr. [AMSER 80]

He remembered Sally Gray quite clearly. **Mouse-brown** hair – good hands. [VICT 106]

Cofiai Llinos Rees yn dda. Gwallt **brown lliw llygoden** a dwylo medrus. [LLINYN 117]

. . . on the **birch-grey** emulsioned wall area around him . . . [TIME 95]

. . . ar y waliau emylsion **lliw ffawydd** o'i amgylch . . . [AMSER 151]

Llwyd (*grey*)

Bydde'r prifathro [. . .] yn gwisgo côt law **lwydfelen** â belt oedd wedi gweld dyddie gwell, trowser brown, clipie beic a chap stabal brethyn. [HUNAN 83]

The principal [. . .] dressed in a **beige**, belted mackintosh that had seen better days, brown trousers, bicycle clips and a flat tweed cap. [SOLVA 83]

I'r dde, roedd stafell fyw eang **lwydwyrdd** 'da *chaise longue* o'i gyfnod, cadeirie 'da choese o gyfnod y Frenhines Anne a soffa anferth. [HUNAN 174]

[T]o the right was a spacious and opulent sitting-room furnished in **sage green** with a period chaise longue, Queen Anne chairs and a huge sofa. [SOLVA 175–6]

Melyn (*yellow*)

Short – say five-five – thickset with **sandy-coloured**, crinkly hair? [CIDER 87]

Un eitha byr oedd o, tua phum troedfedd pum modfedd efallai, ond roedd o'n bur lydan gyda gwallt crychiog, **melyngoch**. [SEIDR 118]

... the **lemonish-green** dusk ... [TIME 92]

... y gwyll **melynwyrdd** ... [AMSER 147]

Merch fechan eiddil yr olwg ond prydferth fel dol oedd hi, a'i llygaid glas, breuddwydiol, a'i chroen glân a chlir a'i gwallt **melynwyn** yn gwneud i rywun feddwl am un o'r Tylwyth Teg. [CHWAL 74]

Small and frail-looking, she was a girl with a doll like beauty, her dreamy blue eyes, fair clear skin and **pale golden** hair reminding one of a fairy. [OUT 77]

Piws (*purple, puce*)

... drove his car along the narrow road that twisted between the massive earthen breasts of the moor, washed now in the **purple and brown** of dying heather and dead bracken. [TIME 50]

Ymlwybrai'r ffordd yn gul a throellog rhwng bronnau haul y rhos a orchuddiwyd gan rug **piwsgoch a brown** oedd ar fin gwywo. [AMSER 79]

Rhudd (*crimson*)

... yng ngwyll **rhuddgoch** y gegin ... [CRYMAN 165]

... in the **ruddy** half-light of the kitchen ... [SICKLE 136]

Others

... caeodd drysau'r moduron ar y galarwyr a llithrasant yn rhes ddistaw **loywddu** drwy'r ddinas ... [LLEIFIOR 106]

... the mourners got into their cars, which made their way in a **sleek black** procession through the city streets ... [RETURN 90]

Yr oedd wyneb yr hen Elias Thomas
yn **welwlas** pan ddychwelodd
yn nannedd y rhewynt . . .
[CYCHWYN 167]

Old Elias Thomas's face was **blue
with cold** when he battled his
way through the icy blizzard . . .
[BEGIN 168]

Pan gaeodd Robert Pugh y drws ar
ei ôl, boliodd cwmwl ar gwmwl o
fwg allan o'r grât fach **bygddu** yn y
gornel . . . [CRYMAN 218]

When Robert Pugh closed the
door behind him, clouds of smoke
billowed out from the **pitch-black**
grate in the corner . . . [SICKLE 180]

9.2.f. Colours: Simplex but different from English usage

Some simplex colours in Welsh may be used to correspond to more than one
colour in English. One obvious example of this is '*glas*' which in contemporary
usage normally conveys the colour '*blue*'. However, there is also a longstanding
connection to the colour '*green*' e.g. '*porfeydd gleision*' is the Biblical '*green
pastures*' as well as '*grey/silver*' e.g. '*ceffyl glas*' would be a '*silver/grey horse*'
and not a '*blue horse*' and '*arian gleision*' is used for '*silver coins*' rather than
'*arian cochion/copper coins*'. Below are further examples:

Sypyn ydoedd mewn **papur llwyd**,
ac wedi'i lapio'n daclus. [RHYS 152]

It was a small **brown-paper** bundle,
neatly packaged. [RHYS 148]

. . . gwrandewais yn amyneddgar ar
Ned yn adrodd ei epig am gampau
rhyw **gi coch** a oedd ganddo ar y
pryd . . . [HENAT 128]

I listened patiently to Ned
relating his epic on the feats of a
brown dog he had at the time . . .
[LOCUST 110]

Heddiw, yr oedd Edward Vaughan
wedi lladd ei wair. Yr oedd chwech
o dri chan cyfer Lleifior yn
gorwedd yn ystod ar ystod **las** dan y
machlud . . . [CRYMAN 9]

Today, Edward Vaughan had begun
cutting his hay. Six of Lleifior's three
hundred acres, swathe after **green**
swathe, lay in the setting sun . . .
[SICKLE 5]

9.2.g. Colours: Simplex – Other possibilities

Notwithstanding the sections above, there are other possibilities in Welsh to
express the extent or quality of particular colours. An increasing comparative degree may find an equivalence in a simple verb-noun as shown in our
first example:

Harry watched Hagrid **getting redder
and redder** in the face as he called for
more wine . . . [STONE 252]

Gwyliodd Harri wyneb Hagrid **yn
cochi mwy** bob munud wrth iddo
alw am fwy o win . . . [MAEN 160]

Verb-nouns such as 'cochi' above or 'duo' (from du = black) are preferred when there is an idea of someone or something becoming or turning into the respective colour.

I'm sure the woods look sleepy in the autumn, when the leaves **are getting brown.** [THRO 130]

Rwy'n siŵr fod y goedwig yn edrych yn gysglyd yn yr hydref pan **yw'r** dail **yn cochi.** [TRWY 16]

In 9.2.e. 'others' there was an example of 'pitch-black' as a compound 'pygddu'. It is also possible to substitute this for a comparison:

The library was **pitch-black** and very eerie. [STONE 255]

Y tu mewn i'r llyfrgell roedd yn **ddu fel bol buwch,** ac yn iasol tu hwnt. [MAEN 162]

The English adjective 'blond' finds no direct equivalent in Welsh. Its meaning is usually carried over by either 'melyn' (= yellow) or 'golau' (= light) either on their own when the meaning is obvious or as modifiers of descriptive nouns (e.g. 'gwallt' – hair). This adjective can also be used as a noun in English which requires an appropriate corresponding noun in Welsh plus 'melyn' or 'golau'.

Mrs Dursley was thin and **blond.** [STONE 1]

Dynes denau **â gwallt melyn** oedd Mrs Dursley. [MAEN 1]

Honno â'r **gwallt golau cyrliog** wedi'i shinglo yw hi? [MONICA 7]

Is that her with the **curly blonde** shingled hair? [MONICA 5]

Oedd, yr oedd Greta'n ei ddisgwyl, a'i **phen golau cyrliog** yn destun llygadrythu i'r ddau borter llipa wrth y llidiart. [CRYMAN 11]

Yes, Greta had come to meet him, and her **blonde good looks** were receiving the attention of two idle porters at the gate. [SICKLE 7]

Nid oedd y **dwylath penfelyn** hwnnw'n cael dim diddanwch mewn arian pêl-droed . . . [CRYMAN 38]

The **blond six-footer** took no pleasure in football pools . . . [SICKLE 30]

A blondie with blue eyes like lit-up glowworms she said who she thought was a wee softie, probably because he was polite with her. [TIME 66]

Un golau, efo llygaid gleision fel magïod yn llosgi, meddai hi, ac roedd hi'n meddwl 'i fod o'n annwyl, am 'i fod o'n glên iawn efo hi mwy na thebyg. [AMSER 104]

. . . Rogers was generally mistrustful of men he thought of as **Nordic blonds** . . . [TIME 68]	. . . roedd Rogers yn tueddu i amau **dynion pryd golau Norwyaidd yr olwg** . . . [AMSER 106–7]

9.2.h. Reduplication

Reduplication involves a particular group of compounds (mostly adjectives or verb-nouns) where the headword is either repeated or undergoes vowel/consonant change in the second element. Below, we consider in our examples how reduplication (i) can be a useful tool to the translator and (ii) how it can be handled when translating from Welsh into English.

9.2.h.i Reduplication translated with an adjective and an intensifier ('very' or other)

Adjectival reduplication in Welsh can occur in order to signify an intensification of meaning. *'Gwyn'* may mean *'white'* but *'gwyn gwyn'* signifies *'very white'* as an alternative to *'gwyn iawn'*. The translators in the examples below have acknowledged this by using appropriate intensifiers in their work.

Dy weld di'n sâl yn dy wely a'th wynab a'th ddwylo di mor wyn â'r gobennydd a'th lygaid di'n **ddisglair, ddisglair.** [CYCHWYN 236]	Seeing you ill in bed and your face and hands as white as the pillow and your eyes shining **so very brightly.** [BEGIN 238]
Fel rheol, gwnâi'r llun hwnnw o'r ddynes **fer fer** a'r dyn **tal tal** iddo chwerthin wrtho'i hun, ond heno ni ddôi gwên i'w wyneb. [CHWAL 172]	Ordinarily, the picture of the **strikingly short** woman and **remarkably tall** man made him laugh inwardly, but tonight he did not smile. [OUT 181]
His **very blue** eyes . . . [TIME 40]	Ei lygaid **glas, glas.** [AMSER 63]

9.2.h.ii Reduplication translated with two different but semantically similar adjectives in English

Rather than viewing the reduplication as an intensifier, the translators in our examples have followed the headword adjective with a different one which is semantically similar to it.

Onid oeddwn innau, bellach, yn un o'r fyddin a droediai'r ffordd i'r chwarel? Yr hoelion yn **galed, galed,** ar y lôn . . . [O LAW 92]	Was not I, now, one of the army that foot-slogged it to the quarry? The nails striking **crisp and hard** on the road . . . [FROM 67]

Dyn **bychan, bychan** oedd 'Y Manawyd', fel y gelwid ef yn aml, un o'r dynion lleiaf a welsoch chwi erioed ... [O LAW 72]

'The Awl', as he was generally called, was a **tiny, little** man, one of the smallest you ever saw ... [FROM 51]

Fel petai'n codi o'r môr, dringodd Neifion, duw y dyfnder, dros y bow, a'i farf yn **llaes llaes** a rhaffau o wymon yn hongian ar bob rhan o'i gorff. [CHWAL 122]

Neptune, with a **long flowing** beard and festooned in seaweed, climbed over the bows as though he had risen from the depths. [OUT 128]

9.2.h.iii Reduplication translated with just one (usually intense) English adjective

Oedd y llawr yn **las, las** a'r haul yn sgleinio arno fo, ac yn mynd draw allan yn bell a mynd yn un hefo wal arian y Nefoedd yn y pen draw. [NOS 164]

The floor was **the bluest of blues**, and the sun was shining on it, and it stretched far far away and then joined the silver wall of Heaven in the far distance. [NIGHT 138]

Roedd yn union fel codi spîd yn **gyflym gyflym** wrth adael y goleuadau – y wefr fwya gorfoleddus bosib. [Rankin 58]

It was the **fastest** piece of acceleration from traffic lights that you could experience – ever. [Rankin 69]

'R oedd yna draddodiad **distaw, distaw**, yn nheulu fy nhad ... [HDF 59]

There was a **quiet** tradition in my father's family ... [OFH 70]

Our next example illustrates the same process in reverse with the Welsh translator using reduplication for English adjectives when there is a sense of intensification.

It had not been unlike looking into a **dazzling** light. [TIME 24]

Roedd e fel edrych ar olau **llachar, llachar**. [AMSER 37]

His very blue eyes [TIME 40]

Ei lygaid glas, glas [AMSER 63]

9.2.h.iv Reduplicated comparative translated as comparative
Although the direct English equivalent (as in our last example) can be connected and repeated with '*and*', the reduplicated Welsh comparative usually translates into a single comparative in English.

Fel y treiai golau'r dydd o'r ystafell, âi golau'r lamp ddarllen dal yn eu hymyl **yn felynach, felynach**, gan euro gwallt y naill a chochi gwallt y llall. [CRYMAN 49–50]

As daylight retreated from the room, the gleam from the tall standard-lamp at their side grew **brighter**, casting a golden glow on the hair of one and reddening the other's. [SICKLE 39]

. . . âi'r Neuadd yn **wacach, wacach** o noson i noson . . . [FROM 108]

. . . the Village Hall got **emptier** every night . . . [FROM 82]

. . . distawodd Paul o dipyn i beth, ac fel y gwanhaodd effaith y ddiod arno suddodd ei ên yn **ddyfnach, ddyfnach** i'w wasgod, a gyrrodd weddill y ffordd â'i lygaid yn rhowlio'n drymion yn ei ben. [LLEIFIOR 20]

Paul fell quiet, and as the effect of the drink began to wear off he sank his chin **lower and lower** into his waistcoat, and drove the rest of the way with his eyes rolling heavily in his head. [RETURN 15]

9.2.h.v Reduplicated verb

We have so far concentrated on reduplicated adjectives, however the reduplication of verbs in Welsh also occurs. The following three examples show how the English translators deal with this either by intensifying the verb or by adding an adverb.

Yr oedd y trwch cymylau'n symud yn wastad i'r gorllewin, a'r glas uwchben yn **lledu, lledu**, nes dod o'r diwedd ar warthaf yr haul yn ei guddfan. [CRYMAN 31]

The bank of clouds was moving steadily westwards, the blue sky **spreading ever wider**, and soon the sun came out from behind a cloud, bathing the countryside in its golden rays. [SICKLE 23]

Llawer prynhawn a dreuliais ar ymylon yr hen afon yn edrych ar ei dwfr yn **mynd, mynd**, ac y mae yn dal i fynd heddiw yr un fath. [GWEN 41]

Many were the afternoons that I spent on the banks of the old river looking at its water **flowing incessantly**, as it still does today in the same old way. [GWEN 44]

Yna dechreuodd dynnu ym mhlanhigion y corn carw a dyfai gan ymgordeddu'n dynn am fonion y grug. **Tynnai a thynnai** yn amyneddgar â'i llaw wedyn, ac yna wedi cael digon, rhoes ef o gwmpas ei phen fel torch. [TE 42]

She began plucking the staghorn moss that clung round the heather stalks, **plucking away** with her strong hands and then, when there was enough of it, putting it round her head like a tiara. [TEA 41]

9.2.h.vi Reduplications of indefinites

The final group concentrates on indefinites and how translators have dealt with these in English using similar intensifying strategies to those noted above.

Nid fel **rhywun-rywun** y bydda' i'n labro ar y ffordd, ond fel mab Lleifior 'o bawb', yn syth o'r coleg. [CRYMAN 249]	It won't just be **any old navvy**, but the son of Lleifior, 'of all people', straight out of college. [SICKLE 206]
Paid ti â meddwl mai **rhwbath rhwbath** ydw i, dw i'n uchelwr, mi fydd gin i fy arfbais fy hun pan a'i adra. [PLA 107]	I'm not **just anyone** [lit. **rhwbath** > **rhywbeth** = *something*] you know. I'll get my own coat of arms when I get home. [PEST 80]

Our last examples demonstrate that the reduplication of indefinites is also a device used by translators into Welsh – in the instances given below, to convey adverbs and as an intensifier.

Sue's front bedroom curtains were **clumsily** drawn. [VICT 12]	Roedd llenni llofft Nia wedi'u cau **rywsut rywsut**. [LLINYN 11]
After that he would take a walk. **Anywhere**. On his own. [VICT 177]	Fe âi am dro wedyn, meddai. **I rywle rywle**. Ar ei ben ei hun. [LLINYN 201]

9.3 Collocations

Collocations in Welsh are a neglected area of study possibly due to the lack of a comprehensive, contemporary corpus in the language. Our intention here is to draw attention to some of the more common verb collocations in Welsh and the list should not be viewed as an exhaustive one.

Collocations are two (or more) words which have a lexical connection to each other i.e. they frequently occur together (Reppen and Simpson-Vlach in Schmitt, 2002: 98 describe collocates as '. . . *words that commonly occur with or in the vicinity of a target word (that is, with greater probability than random chance) . . . and the resulting sequences or sets of words are called 'collocations'*). For example, *'tynnu'* (*to pull*) and *'llun'* (*picture*) have a connection with each other in the collocation *'tynnu llun'* (*to draw a picture* or *to take a picture – with a camera*). We would refer to *'tynnu'* as the 'base' here and *'llun'* as the collocate. Close synonyms, however, do not create similar collocations: *'llusgo (= to drag) llun'* would not work and neither would *'tynnu lluniad (= a drawing)'*. Although some collocations may be mirrored in the other language (the final section here), many are unique to only one of the languages and in order to create a natural sounding translation, it is of great importance to be familiar with them and how they work together to make meaningful lexical clusters.

9.3.a. Cadw

Cadw barf — To wear/have a beard

Cadwai farf, peth tra eithriadol ymhlith gweithwyr tanddaear. [CHWECH 99]

He sported a beard, a very unusual thing amongst workers underground.

Cadw golwg ar — To keep a watch on / observe

I am probably being **observed**. [VICT 118]

Mae'n debyg fod 'na rywun yn **cadw golwg arna i**. [LLINYN 132]

Cadw gwely — To keep/take to one's bed

Bu'n **cadw gwely** ran helaeth o'i flwyddyn olaf. [HDF 64]

He had **kept to his bed** for a great part of his last year. [OFH 77]

Cadw oed — To keep an appointment

Then she'd at least have had an incentive [**to keep the appointment**]. [CIDER 140]

Mae'n sicr y byddai rhywbeth cryfach na mi wedi ei denu i **gadw'r oed** yno. [SEIDR 186]

Cadw sŵn — To make a lot of noise

'Mi edrychodd arno fo ac wedyn mi wylltiodd yn gacwn am fod Myrddin yn **cadw sŵn**.' [CYCHWYN 42]

'He looked at it and then was furious because Myrddin was **making a noise**.' [BEGIN 41]

Cadw trefn ar — To keep [someone/something] in order

Be 'di enw'r coesa main'na sy'n **cadw trefn arnoch chi**? [PLA 232]

*What is the name of that thin-legged man who **keeps you in order**?*

9.3.b. Cael

| Cael a chael | - | Touch and go / just in time |

'We are **only just in time** to prevent some subtle and horrible crime.' [BAND 233]

'Ac os felly, **cael a chael** fydd arnom i rwystro trosedd gyfrwys ac ofnadwy.' [CYLCH 50]

| Cael blaen esgid | - | To be sacked |

Doedd y ffaith ei bod hi wedi **cael blaen esgid** o'i swydd yn newid dim ar ffordd Tessa o fyw. Roedd hi'n dal i yfed a hel clybie 'da bois y byd adloniant. [HUNAN 264]

The fact that she's **been sacked** from her job didn't alter her lifestyle; she still hung around with the TV crowd and went drinking and clubbing with the showbiz set. [SOLVA 264]

| Cael y blaen ar | - | To arrive / do something first |

Someone else had **got here first**. [UNSUIT 122]

Roedd rhywun wedi **cael y blaen arnon ni**. [CORTYN 154]

| Cael blas ar | - | To get a taste for / enjoy |

Daeth i **gael blas ar grwydro**, drwy fod breciau'n rhedeg i'r dref, ac âi'r trên o'r fan honno i'r fan a fynnid. [TRAED 91]

He **developed a taste for getting about**; there was even a brake service to the town, and a train would take him anywhere from there. [FEET 82]

| Cael caniatâd (i) | - | To be allowed (to) |

'. . . and we were occasionally **allowed** to pay short visits at this lady's house.' [BAND 213]

'. . . a phob hyn a hyn roeddem yn **cael caniatâd** i ymweld â hi am gyfnodau byr yn ei chartref.' [CYLCH 20–1]

| Cael eich gwynt atoch | - | To recover one's breath |

Safodd y cwmni ar ei hysgwydd ac yr oedd Elias Thomas, yn amlwg, yn falch o'r seibiant ac o gyfle i **gael ei wynt ato**. [CYCHWYN 19]

The little group of men halted on the shoulder of the mound and Elias Thomas was evidently glad to pause and **recover his breath**. [BEGIN 18]

Cael gafael ar — To get (a hold of)

'. . . and afterwards I shall walk down to Doctors' Commons, where I hope **to get** some data which may help us in this matter.' [BAND 223]

'. . . ac wedyn fe gerddaf i Lys y Meddygon, lle rwy'n gobeithio **cael gafael ar** ddata a all ein cynorthwyo ni'n y mater sydd ger ein bron.' [CYLCH 34]

Cael gwaith gwneud [*something*] — To have trouble doing [*something*]

Ychydig o gof sydd gennyf am fy nhad yn y gaeaf, dim ond bod ei ddwylo'n torri'n arw ac yn ddarnau o blaster i gyd, a bod fy mam yn **cael tipyn o waith sychu** ei ddillad yn aml. [TROW 168]

*I don't remember much about my father in the winter, only that his hands were all cut and covered in pieces of plaster, and that my mother **often had trouble drying** his clothes.*

Cael gwared ar/o — To get rid of

At breakfast Matilda said to him, 'You *must* try **to get those bits off your forehead**, daddy. It looks as though you've got little brown insects crawling about all over you.' [MAT 37]

Amser brecwast meddai Matilda wrtho, 'Rhaid i ti geisio **cael gwared ar y darnau oddi ar dy dalcen**, Dad. Mae'n edrych fel tasai pryfed bach brown yn cropian drosot ti i gyd.' [MAT 31]

Cael y gorau ar — To get the best of / outsmart

The words I'd used on Digby were almost out of my mouth again before I thought better of it. She'd **outsmarted me.** [CIDER 68]

Roeddwn i ar fin ei diawlio hithau, ond sylweddolais ei bod hi wedi **cael y gorau arnaf.** [SEIDR 95]

Cael hen ddigon ar — To have enough of

She'd **had enough.** [CIDER 43]

Roedd hi wedi **cael hen ddigon** ar bawb. [SEIDR 62]

Cael hwyl ar — To do well in / get on with (lit. to have fun at)

He had been assigned the job of tailing her and **wasn't very good at it.** [VICT 70]

Fo a gawsai'r job o'i dilyn hi ond doedd o ddim yn **cael hwyl arbennig ar y gwaith** [LLINYN 78–9]

Cael llond bol / syrffed ar — To be fed up with

I am **fed up** with you useless bunch of midgets. [MAT 169]

Dw i wedi **cael llond bol ar**noch chi'r criw corachod di-werth! [MAT 163]

. . . mae'n debyg fod modd i lanc **gael syrffed ar addysg.** [CRYMAN 248]

I suppose a lad can **have too much education.** [SICKLE 205]

Cael trafferth i — To have trouble in

Ar ôl iddynt fynd i'w gwely dôi eu mam â joi o gyfleth a'i roi yn eu cegau [. . .] Os byddai'r joi'n fawr byddai hyn yn waith anodd, a **cheid trafferth i'w throi** yn eu genau. [TRAED 134]

. . . their mother would come and place a lump of toffee in their mouths [. . .] If it was a big lump, that was very difficult; **they had trouble turning it** in their mouths . . . [FEET 119]

9.3.c. Codi

Codi ar ei eistedd — To sit up (see Chapter 6, Phrasal Verbs)

Cododd yntau ar ei eistedd. Yr oedd y wlad yn braf o'i gwmpas. [TRAED 44]

He sat up. The countryside was lovely around him. [FEET 36]

Codi arian (ar) / siec / tâl — To charge money / pick up a cheque / charge a payment

. . . but **she wouldn't charge him.** [UNSUIT 110]

. . . ond **chodai hi ddim ar** Syr Ronald Callender amdano. [GORTYN 138]

Drannoeth, es i swyddfa Warners i **godi siec** am £50,000 . . . [HUNAN 195]

The following day I went to Warners to **pick up a cheque** for £50,000. [SOLVA 196]

Oh, we're getting popular, we are! Any more of you and I'll have to **charge for the show.** [UNSUIT 110]

O, rydyn ni'n boblogaidd iawn y dyddie hyn! Fe fydd raid i mi ddechrau **codi tâl am y sioe.** [GORTYN 138

Codi bwganod	-	To bring up a bugbear, possible undesired consequence

'Mae hi a'r hogyn wedi ffraeo, mae arna' i ofn. Deud 'i fod wedi dechra' yfad.'
'Dan?'
'Ia. Ond efalla' mai **codi bwganod** mae Kate.' [CHWAL 131]

'She and the boy have quarreled, I am afraid. Says he has started drinking.'
'Dan?'
'Yes. But perhaps it's **raising bogeys** Kate is.' [OUT 138] (*An idiomatic translation here however the main thrust is that Kate is raising bugbears which may not necessarily have the expected consequences.*)

Codi calon	-	To encourage, cheer up

Bydd e 'di dychwelyd erbyn hyn a dw i 'di dod â llond bag o goodies i **godi'i galon** . . . [FFYDD 205]

Paddy should be back by now, so I've bought him a bag of goodies which may help **lift his spirits**. [FAITH 143]

Codi canu	-	To get people on their feet to sing

Ef, yn aml, fyddai ysgrifennydd neu drysorydd neu **godwr canu** ei eglwys ac efallai'n arweinydd côr cystadleuol y cylch. [CHWECH 50]

*Often, he would be the secretary or treasurer or **the one to rouse people to their feet to sing** (NB although 'codwr' here is a noun, this collocation is usually seen in a verbal context) in his church and perhaps the leader of the area's competitive choir.*

Codi dadl(au) / twrw / ffrae	-	To cause/start an argument

Comiwnydd oedd Trev, a bydde fe'n **codi llawer o ddadle** lle bynnag bydde fe'n mynd . . . [HUNAN 90]

Trev was a communist, and used to **cause a lot of arguments** wherever he went . . . [SOLVA 89–90]

Mae 'na lond Llechfaen o blismyn, ac yn y Rhinws y byddi di os **codi di dwrw**. [CHWAL 23]

Llechfaen is full of p'licemen, and it's in the lock-up you'll be if **you make a row**. [OUT 23]

Codi embaras / ofn / ias / cywilydd /amheuon / awydd

- To cause embarrasment / frighten / fill with fear / cause shame / cast doubt / provoke a desire or wish

. . . she was taking great care not to say anything to **embarrass her companion.** [MAT 189]

. . . roedd hi'n ofalus iawn i beidio â dweud dim a fyddai'n **codi embaras ar ei chydymaith.** [MAT 183]

I mustn't **frighten you** before you've been here a week. [MAT 108]

Rhaid i mi beidio â **chodi ofn arnoch chi** cyn i chi fod yma am wythnos. [MAT 103]

Mae gweld fy mrawd yn **codi ias arna i.** [FFYDD 55]

Seeing my brother **fills me with dread.** [FAITH 43]

'And all about a rattle!' said Alice, still hoping **to make them a *little* ashamed** of fighting for such a trifle. [THRO 171]

'A'r cwbl o achos rhyw degan', meddai Alys, yn dal i obeithio **codi cywilydd arnynt** am ymladd dros beth mor ddibwys. [TRWY 59]

Codi llaw

- To wave (goodbye)

He forgot **to wave,** he was too taken up with that awful dangling monkey hanging from the car window. [VICT 119]

Roedd mei-nabs yn rhy brysur yn chwarae efo'r hen fwnci ffwr 'na oedd yn crogi ar ffenest ôl y car i gofio **codi llaw.** [LLINYN 132]

Codi peint / diod

- To buy a pint / a drink (a round)

Cynigiodd Dickie **godi diod i fi** a chynnig pàs gartre i fi. [HUNAN 184]

Dickie offered **to buy me a drink** and give me a lift home. [SOLVA 186]

Codi pendro / syched / pwys / cyfog

- To make giddy / make one thirsty / make one feel sick

. . . you **make one quite giddy.** [ALICE 66]

. . . rydych chi'n **codi pendro arna' i.** [ALYS 64]

I'd earlier had a curry. It **made me thirsty.** [VICT 52]

Ro'n i wedi cael cyri i swper ac roedd hwnnw wedi **codi syched arno i.** [LLINYN 60]

Roedd golwg y fall arni! Dwi'n credu bod anhwylder Ashcroft yn **codi pwys ar** fechgyn yr Ysgol Gelf . . . [HUNAN 87]

She looked dreadful and I think that any of the art school boys were more than a little **revolted** by Ashcroft's complaint . . . [SOLVA 87]

Codi sgwrs / pwnc / cwestiwn/ mater

- To engage in conversation / to bring a subject up / raise an issue

A merched – peidiwich â sôn – yn bolaheulo mewn bicinis ar y gwellt! I lawr â ni ling-di-long yn ysgyfala a **chodi sgwrs â nhw.** [HUNAN 119]

And there were girls alright, sunbathing in bathing costumes on the grass! Nonchalantly, we strolled down and **engaged them in conversation.** [SOLVA 119]

Alice did not at all like the tone of this remark, and thought it would be as well **to introduce some other subject of conversation.** [ALICE 61]

Doedd Alys ddim yn hoffi tôn y sylw yna, a meddyliodd y byddai'n well **codi rhyw bwnc arall** i sgwrsio amdano. [ALYS II 58]

'I'm sorry **to bring this up**, but does any of this stem from Deborah's running off to Thurnholme Bay when she was a schoolgirl?' [TIME 54]

'Mae hi'n flin gen i,' meddai, 'am **godi'r mater**, ond a ydi hyn yn deillio'n rhannol o'r adeg ddaru Deborah ddengid i Aberddewin pan oedd hi'n ferch ysgol?' [AMSER 85]

Codi tocyn

- To buy a ticket

Cododd docynnau. Dilynodd hithau lamp drydan y porthor hyd onid ymsuddodd hi yn un o seti plwsh y sinema. [Lewis 1930: 16]

'**He bought tickets.** She followed the usher's torch until she was settled into one of the cinema's plush seats.' [Stephens 1997: 15]

Codi + others

When you begin **to point the finger**, you point it with some certainty. [VICT 117]

Mae'n rhaid i rywun fod yn weddol sicr cyn **codi bys ar neb.** [LLINYN 130]

. . . and we heard the hoarse roar of the Doctor's voice, and saw the fury with which **he shook his clenched fists** at him. [BAND 232]

Yna clywsom ru cryg y meddyg a gwelsom ei gynddaredd wrth iddo **godi ei ddwrn ar** y llanc. [CYLCH 48]

Miss Jennifer Honey was a mild and quiet person who never **raised her voice** and was seldom seen to smile . . . [MAT 66–7]	Person hynaws a thawel oedd Miss Jennifer Honey; ni fyddai byth yn **codi ei llais** ac yn anaml y byddai'n gwenu . . . [MAT 60]
. . . **dusting** and clearing. [VICT 163]	. . . i glirio a **chodi llwch**. [LLINYN 184]
You could have just **packed up** and walked away. [MAT 200]	Fe allech chi fod wedi **codi pac** a cherdded i ffwrdd. [MAT 194]

9.3.d. Dwyn

Dwyn [*something*] ar gof [*someone*] -	To remind [*someone*] of [*something*]
. . . darn o ddyn tywyll ei groen a du ei flewyn, gan **ddwyn ar gof** i mi heddiw, rywsut, y llun o Joseph Stalin a fu'n dra phoblogaidd ar un adeg. [CHWECH 165]	. . . *a bit of a dark-skinned, black-haired man, **reminding** me today, somehow, of the picture of Joseph Stalin that used to be really popular at one time.*
Dwyn cyrch	- To make an assault
Felly, un bore braf, fe **ddygon ni gyrch** ar riw Solfach ar ein beics . . . [HUNAN 31]	So one fine morning we **made an assault** on Solva hill by bicycle. [SOLVA 31]
Dwyn elw	- To make / be a source of profit
Yr hyn sydd yn fy synnu fwyaf ydyw, fod pawb wedi cymryd i fyny gyda mi, ac ymddwyn tuag ataf fel pe buaswn yn **dwyn llawer o elw** iddynt . . . [RHYS 7]	What surprises me most is that everyone should have been so taken with me, and behave towards me as if I had been **a source of profit** to everybody . . . [RHYS 13]
Dwyn i fyny	- To bring up (e.g. a family)
Ond yr oeddynt yn onest ac yn unplyg, ac yn barod eu cymwynas i bawb, ac ni wn i am neb a ymegnïodd fwy i **ddwyn i fyny ei thyaid mawr o blant** na 'modryb Marged . . . [HENAT 34]	But they were honest and sincere, and always ready to do a good turn, and I know of no-one who put so much energy into **bringing up a large family** as Auntie Margaret . . . [LOCUST 35]

Dwyn perswâd ar	- To persuade
Dyma nhw'n **dwyn perswâd ar** blentyn iau i dynnu coes Aneurin . . . [HUNAN 70]	They **persuaded** some juniors to wind up Aneurin . . . [SOLVA 70]

Dwyn y teitl	- To hold the title
Yn un o lyfrau'r ysgol nad oedd yn werslyfr cyffredin gennym cofiaf ddarllen stori yn **dwyn y teitl** 'Owen Glendower's Oak . . . [CHWECH 67]	*In one of the schoolbooks which wasn't one of our ordinary textbooks, I remember reading a story **called (which had the title)** 'Owen Glendower's Oak . . .*

9.3.e. Rhoi

Rhoi [*something*] ar dân	- To set fire to [*something*]
Lladdwyd Chang ganddynt, ond **rhoes Koong-Se ei chartref ar dân**, gan ei llosgi ei hun i farwolaeth yn y fflamau. [O LAW 222]	Chang was slain, but Koong-Se **set fire to her house** and perished in the flames. [FROM 185]

Rhoi ei bryd ar [*something*]	- To set one's heart on [*something*]
'Mi fydda Gwen yn torri'i chalon. Roedd hi wedi **rhoi'i bryd ar** ei weld o'n mynd i'r Weinidogaeth.' [RHANNU 115]	*'Gwen would break her heart. She had **set her heart on** seeing him going in to the Ministry.'*

Rhoi cam	- To take a step
A hithau'n mynd drwy'r drws **rhoes** Wil **gam** tuag ati a dweud . . . [CRYMAN 98]	As she went through the door, Will **took a step** towards her and said . . . [SICKLE 80]

Rhoi clep ar	- To slam
. . . mi aeth hi i mewn i tŷ a **rhoid clep ar y drws** yn fy ngwynab i. [NOS 185]	. . . she went into the house and **slammed the door** in my face. [NIGHT 158]

Rhoi clust i [*something/someone*] - To give [*something/someone*] an ear

Ond dydw i ddim yn bwriadu **rhoi clust iddyn nhw,** nac yn dymuno aros yng nghwmni bradwr. [RHANNU 270]	*But I don't intend **listening to them,** nor do I wish to remain in the company of a traitor.*

Rhoi coel/cred ar - To believe in

''Mam bach, 'ydach chi ddim yn **rhoi coel ar** betha' fel'na, 'does bosib'?' [CYCHWYN 236]	'Mam bach, you surely don't **believe in** such things?' [BEGIN 238]

Rhoi cwlwm ar - To tie a knot in

'[M]ae'n ddrwg gin' i, 'r hen ddyn . . . [n]a faswn i wedi **rhoi cwlwm ar** y tafod 'ma sy gin' i.' [CHWAL 139]	'I *am* sorry, old man [. . .] [t]hat i didn't **tie a knot in** this tongue of mine.' [OUT 147]

Rhoi cweir/coten i - To give a thrashing to

Estyn y *draughts* 'na imi gael **rhoi cweir** i'th dad a thitha hefo'ch gilydd. [O LAW 71]	Fetch that draughts board there, and I'll **lick** (= *give you a thrashing*) you and your father together. [FROM 49]

Rhoi cychwyn ar - To start something off

She'd definitely said she was going to **start the milking.** [CIDER 45]	Roedd hi'n bendant wedi dweud ei bod hi'n mynd i **roi cychwyn ar y godro.** [SEIDR 64]

Rhoi cynnig ar - To have a go at / try

Had she lived – had you decided **to make a go of things** together – I would have been happy about it. [VICT 45]	[P]etai hi wedi byw, a phetaech chi wedi penderfynu **rhoi cynnig arni** efo'ch gilydd. Mi fyddwn i wedi bod yn ddigon bodlon. [LLINYN 51]

Rhoi diwedd / stop /taw/ terfyn ar - To put an end to

'Wel, fel y gwyddost ti, mae'na ddigon o bobol yn beio'r Pwyllgor am beidio â symud i **roi diwadd ar** yr helynt.' [CHWAL 132]

'Well, as you know, there are plenty of people blaming the Committee for not moving to **put an end to** the affair.' [OUT 139]

Now I'm still angry, and I'm afraid too. But that won't **stop me**. [VICT 108]

Dwi'n dal yn gynddeiriog, ond mae arna i ofn erbyn hyn hefyd. Nid y **rhoith hynny stop arna i**. [LLINYN 120]

He began telling her, but she **stopped him** impatiently. [VICT 153]

Dechreuodd ddweud hynny wrthi ond **rhoddodd daw arno**'n ddiamynedd. [LLINYN 173]

... the main reason she **took her life**. [CIDER 50]

... oedd wedi ei harwain i **roi terfyn ar ei bywyd**. [SEIDR 73]

Rhoi [*someone*] i eistedd - To sit [*someone*] up

... and **she sat me** on the sofa while she got me the drink. [TIME 82]

... a **rhoddodd hi fi i eistedd** ar y soffa tra 'i bod hi'n nôl diod i mi. [AMSER 129–30]

Rhoi ffrwyn ar - To curb, rein in

Dwedodd y llythyr nesa o Amwythig y bydde'n rhaid i fi **roi ffrwyn ar fy mrwdfrydedd** a chelco 'mhum syllte nes oedd pymtheg punt 'da fi. [HUNAN 59]

The next letter from Shrewsbury said that I'd have to **curb my enthusiasm** and save up my five bobs until I'd got the magical sum of fifteen quid ... [SOLVA 59]

Rhoi llonydd i - To leave alone / in peace

Wel, **mi rown i lonydd i chi** feddwl am yr ysgrifa' na. [CYCHWYN 9]

Well, **we'll leave you alone** to think about those articles. [BEGIN 7]

Rhoi pen ar - To do away with (i.e. bring to an end)

Mae arna i ofn wir y **rhydd y dyn yna ben ar i fywyd** ryw ddiwrnod. [TE 23]

I'm afraid he'll **do away with himself** some day. [TE 24]

Rhoi prawf ar	-	To test

'It's only a hypothesis.' 'Is there any way I could **test it**?' [CIDER 135]

'Dim ond damcaniaethu rydw i.' 'Oes 'na unrhyw ffordd y gallwn i **roi prawf ar** y ddamcaniaeth?' [SEIDR 180

Rhoi trefn ar	-	To put in order / set right

'**We shall** soon **set matters right**, I have no doubt.' [BAND 209]

'Fe **rown ni drefn ar bethau** mewn dim, rwy'n siŵr.' [CYLCH 14]

Rhoi tro ar	-	To turn

Dyma Owen yn gafael yn Eric ac yn **rhoi tro arno** â'i wyneb i'r cyfeiriad arall. [TRAED 183]

Owen grabbed hold of Eric and **swung him round** to face the other way. [FEET 151]

9.3.f. Torri

Torri enw	-	To sign one's name / a contract

Y fargen oedd y byddwn i'n **torri f'enw ar gytundeb** 'da'i gwmni e. [HUNAN 150]

The deal was that I'd **sign a contract** with his company . . . [SOLVA 150

Torri gair â	-	To utter a word to / talk to

Doedden nhw ddim wedi **torri gair â'i gilydd** ers o leia ddeuddydd. [PLA 230]

*They hadn't **spoken/uttered a word** to each other for at least two days.*

Torri syched	-	To quench a thirst

Galwodd yn yr 'Harp' ar ei ffordd adref, a llonnodd Wil Llongwr drwyddo wrth ei weld. Buasai Wil yn segura am fisoedd lawer, a dibynnai yn awr ar haelioni rhai fel yr Ap er mwyn **torri'i syched**. [CHWAL 195]

He looked in at the Harp on his way home, much to Bill Sailor's delight. Bill had been out of work for many months and was dependent on the bounty of Ap, and others like him, **to quench his thirst**. [OUT 206]

9.3.g. Tynnu

Tynnu ar ôl — To take after (someone)

Tynnu ar ôl eu mam yr oeddynt
hwy, yn dal a chringoch a siaradus
fel hithau. [CHWAL 81]

They **took after their mother**,
both being, like her, tall, reddish-
haired, and talkative.
[OUT 84]

Tynnu at [number] — To approach, be close to [number]

Ac yntau'n **tynnu at ei ugain oed**
ac Owen yn ddim ond deuddeg . . .
[CYCHWYN 72]

Dafydd, **nearing twenty** [. . .] Owen,
who was only twelve years old.
[BEGIN 73]

Tynnu coes — To pull a leg / wind up

. . . y giwed o ddisgyblion dosbarth
pump a dosbarth chwech oedd yn
hala hydoedd yn **tynnu coes** y staff
academaidd ac yn eu dychryn nhw.
[HUNAN 69]

. . . a group of fifth and sixth
formers, including prefects, who
spent a lot of time **winding up**
and terrorising the academic staff.
[SOLVA 69]

Tynnu dillad / esgidiau — To take off clothes / shoes

. . . a chyn pen dim roedden ni
wedi **tynnu'n dillad** a'u rhoi
nhw ar y gwresogydd . . .
[HUNAN 115]

Soon **our clothes were off** . . .
[SOLVA 115]

Tynnu sgwrs â — To have a chat to

Roedd y gyrwyr yn falch o gael
rhywun i **dynnu sgwrs â nhw** . . .
[HUNAN 109]

Often, the drivers were pleased
to have somebody **to talk to** . . .
[SOLVA 128]

Tynnu sylw — To catch / draw attention

The object which had **caught
his eye** was a small dog lash
hung on one corner of the bed.
[BAND 230]

Y gwrthrych oedd wedi **tynnu ei
sylw** oedd tennyn ci bychan oedd yn
hongian dros gornel troed y gwely.
[CYLCH 44]

Tynnu wyneb	- To make a face
Fel y proffwydasai Ap Menai, **tynnodd wyneb** – ond wyneb o fwynhad digymysg. [CHWAL 94]	As Ap Menai had prophesised, **he made a face**, but it was one of sheer enjoyment. [OUT 97]
Tynnu ymlaen	- To get on
Roedd e ar ei flwyddyn derfynol yn stiwdio beintio Malthouse, ond heb fod yn **tynnu mlaen** 'da'r tiwtoried o gwbwl. [HUNAN 110]	He was in his final year at Malthouse's painting studio, and he was not **getting on** with the tutors at all. [SOLVA 110]

9.3.h. Examples of other verbal collocations

Dod atoch (eich hun)	- To come to, recover
However, she could find nothing but a bottle of ink, and when she got back with it she found **he had recovered**, and he and the Queen were talking together in a frightened whisper . . . [THRO 135]	Sut bynnag, ni allai weld dim ond potel o inc, ac erbyn iddi ddychwelyd ag ef gwelodd ei fod wedi **dod ato'i hun** a'i fod ef a'r Frenhines yn sisial sgwrsio yn ofnus . . . [TRWY 21]
Ennill eich tamaid	- To earn one's living
Chwarelwr oedd Em, ond **enillai Harri ei damaid** drwy gasglu carpiau a hen haearn a'u gwerthu ar ddiwedd pob pythefnos i ddyn a ddeuai i fyny o'r dref i'w nôl. [CHWAL 151]	Em was a quarryman, but Harri **earned a living** by collecting rags and old iron which he sold fortnightly to a junk dealer who used to come up from town to fetch the stuff. [OUT 160]
Lladd gwair	- To cut grass / hay
Heddiw, yr oedd Edward Vaughan wedi **lladd ei wair**. [CRYMAN 9]	Today, Edward Vaughan had begun **cutting his hay**. [SICKLE 5]
Magu gwres	- To heat / warm up
Cerddai Edward yn ôl a blaen i geisio **magu gwres**. [RHANNU 215]	*Edward walked back and forth, trying to **warm up**.*

Palu / rhaffu celwyddau	- To tell / string lies
Harry? He was **lying through his teeth**. [CIDER 116]	Harry? **Palu celwyddau** roedd hwnnw. [SEIDR 155]

The following collocations are either based on English models or have much in common with them. Nevertheless, they (in addition to many others) can be considered to be productive and accepted in Welsh as these examples illustrate:

Dal dŵr	- To hold water
Roedd e'n hollol agored ei gasineb tuag at y Cymry ond chlywes i rioed mono fe'n cynnig unrhyw reswm oedd yn **dal dŵr** dros fod â'i lach ar 'bobol gwlad y gân'. [HUNAN 222]	He was quite open about his dislike of the Welsh, but I never heard him come across with any **coherent reason** [lit. any reason which **held water**] for his dislike of *pobl gwlad y gân*. [SOLVA 221–2]

Ennill arian (da)	- Earn (good) money
Roedd y rhan fwya ohonon ni'n **ennill arian da** ac yn <u>chwarae'n galed</u>[14] hefyd. [HUNAN 220]	Most of us **earned good money** and could play hard too. [SOLVA 220]

Golchi dwylo (o)	- To wash one's hands (of)
Roedd mam Tessa [. . .] **wedi golchi'i dwylo o** helyntion ei merch ers blynydde i bob pwrpas . . . [HUNAN 238]	Tess's mother had all but **washed her hands of** her daughter years ago . . . [SOLVA 238]

Taro bargen	- To strike a bargain
Can we **do a deal on this?** [CIDER 68]	Efallai y gallwn ni **daro rhyw fath o fargen**. [SEIDR 95]

[14] 'Chwarae'n galed' (play hard) can also be considered in this category of collocations.

Torri tir newydd	- To break new ground

Roedd Wilbert ar ben ei ddigon
o weld llwyddiant ei fenter gyntaf
ym myd roc a rôl, ac roedd y
perfformwyr i gyd yn gwbod eu bod
nhw'n rhan o gynhyrchiad oedd yn
torri tir newydd. [HUNAN 248]

Wilbert was overjoyed at his first
foray into the world of rock-'n'-roll,
and all of the performers knew
that they were part of a **ground-
breaking** production. [SOLVA 248]

9.4 Borrowing

In the bilingual context of contemporary Wales in which users of Welsh are
in constant contact with English as well, it is inevitable that there will be
an element of borrowing – predominantly (although not exclusively) from
English into Welsh. This is generally more of a feature in more informal registers of Welsh and indeed, may be used by some translators to signify use of
an informal register. The two examples below include the use of borrowings
(sometimes evidenced by the use of italics) when direct Welsh equivalents
are not possible in order to give a precise semantic rendition and other strategies may not work either (although stylistically, this is avoided as much as
possible):

Yn anffodus, mae Kenco'n
technophobe . . . [FFAWD 14]

Unfortunately, Kenco is a
technophobe.

If anyone were a psychosexual
pervert it was Louis himself.
[VICT 127]

Os oedd rhywun yn **pervert**
seicorywiol, yna Celt ei hun oedd
hwnnw. [LLINYN 142]

An exact definition of what exactly constitutes a 'borrowing' can be
difficult and controversial. The next set of examples all include lexical items
which have undoubtedly been 'borrowed' from English. Nevertheless, in
most cases, these 'borrowings' both 'sound' natural to most users of Welsh
and more importantly, they behave like native Welsh words – undergoing
mutation for example (even the /t/ element of the /tʃ/ in our third example
of 'chocolates'):

Wrth ffarwelio â mi cyn esgyn y
goach, torrodd Wmffre i wylo . . .
[GWEN 189]

Before parting from me and
boarding the **coach**, he broke down
and wept bitterly. [GWEN 149]

Roedd 'na **fêc-yp** ar ei gruddiau, a dilynais ei llygaid tuag at y botel wag o'dd ar y ford. [DAL 85]	*There was **make-up** on her cheeks, and I followed her eyes towards the empty bottle on the table.*
. . . cyn estyn bocs o **joclets** o dan ei gôt. [CRAWIA 182]	*. . . before passing a box of **chocolates** under his coat.*
'Sut gwyddost ti y basat ti'n licio mynd yn **brintar**?' [TRAED 185]	'How do you know you'd like to be a **printer**?' [FEET 152]
'Be' mae Dan yn wneud?' 'Mae o yn y Coleg, yn mynd yn *deacher*.' [CHWAL 26]	'What is Dan doing?' 'In College, going for a **Teacher**.' [OUT 27]

These examples cover a time span of over a century and represent an on-going process. The inclusion of the English '*teacher*' in the last example from T. Rowland Hughes's 1946 novel *Chwalfa* may appear at odds with the regular use of '*athro*' or '*athrawes*' in contemporary Welsh, however it must be viewed as being representative of the typical informal register usage of its time when this was normal. To use '*athro/athrawes*' for '*teacher*' in informal speech from this period of time could be considered anachronistic.

Borrowings from languages other than English are sometimes kept in the language of origin or translated into Welsh. The last example below is a rare one where a Welsh lexical item is maintained in the English translation.

'It's always one too many for me, George, and all I can hope for now is that he'll resist being arrested. He really does owe me that.' 'You think you owe it to your **amour propre**, David,' Rogers corrected him. [TIME 99]	'Mae o'n troi arna i, George; dw i ond yn gobeithio rŵan y bydd o'n osgoi cael ei arestio; mae arno fo hynny o leia i mi.' 'Rwyt tithau'n meddwl fod arnat ti rywbeth i dy **amour propre**, Dafydd,' cywirodd Rogers ef. [AMSER 157]
The note could have been written in an attempt to pull the plug on the nasty suspicions of the police; to perhaps suggest **sotto voce** that we might chuck in our hand at trying to find her. [TIME 96]	Ella fod y nodyn wedi'i sgwennu mewn ymgais i ddileu amheuon yr heddlu; i awgrymu ella **yn ddistaw bach**, y gallan ni roi'r gorau i geisio dod o hyd iddi. [AMSER 153]
Troai Jane ei golygon yn ôl o hyd i gyfeiriad yr Eifl, a deuai pang o	Jane frequently looked back in the direction of the Eifl, and felt *hiraeth*

hiraeth iddi wrth feddwl am ei chartref y tu hwnt iddynt. [TRAED 18]	as she thought of her home beyond those mountains. [FEET 16]

9.5 Two Verb-nouns in a row

Welsh has a particular strategy for modifying a verb-noun without necessarily using an adjective or an adverb. This is accomplished by placing two verb-nouns together with the first one acting as a modifier of the second and giving information as to the way in which an activity is performed. We have divided our examples of this into a number of descriptive categories:

9.5.i Ways of crying

He could hear her **muffled sobs** and closed the door so that he couldn't hear them. [VICT 148]	Gallai ei chlywed yn **igian crio** [lit. hiccup cry] a chaeodd y drws rhag ei fod yn ei chlywed. [LLINYN 167]
Gill was pacing to and fro, **sniffing back tears**. [KNOTS 199]	. . . a Gill yn camu yn ôl ac ymlaen gan **snwffian crio**. [lit. sniffle cry] [CHWERW 168]
Dechreuodd Robin **feichio crio**, ac yna o'r tu ôl iddo, o enau Wil Cochyn, daeth cri plentyn yn torri'i galon yn lân. [CYCHWYN 224]	Robin **sobbed** [lit. encumber cry[15]], and from behind him Will-Ginger imitated a child crying his heart out. [BEGIN 226]
A thorrodd hi ac Owen i **weiddi crio**. [TRAED 188]	Both she and Owen broke down and **wept**. [lit. shout cry]. [FEET 155]

9.5.ii Ways of going

Daeth y bys Western Welsh coch rownd y gornel dan **sgerbydu mynd** a dyma fi arno fe gan godi llaw i ganu'n iach ar fy nghyfnither Jean y jeifr . . . [HUNAN 74]	The red Western Welsh bus came **rattling round** [lit. skeletonise go] the corner and I climbed aboard with a goodbye wave to cousin Jean the jiver . . . [SOLVA 74]
Peiriannau'n refio, rhegfeydd, olwynion certi'n **clecian mynd** a	Engines revved, curses flowed, cartwheels **rattled** [lit. click go] and

---

[15] *'Beichio crio/wylo'* can be considered a collocation in Welsh too with the sense of *'crying uncontrollably'* or *'burst out crying'*.

thyrfe a dyrnodie llwythi trymion yn cael eu lluchio o gwmpas fel sachedie o blu. [HUNAN 133]	heavy loads crashed and thudded as they were thrown around like sacks of feathers. [SOLVA 133]
Syllodd Ibn ar rywbeth yn **diflannu mynd** ... [PLA 126]	*Ibn noticed something **disappearing off** ...* [lit. disappear go].
They had been on the motorway for some time now, **grinding along** like the high whine of a dentist's drill. [VICT 181]	Roedden nhw ar y ffordd ddeuol ers tipyn rŵan, a'r Metro'n **dyrnu mynd** [lit. thrash go] fel dril deintydd henffasiwn. [LLINYN 206]

9.5.iii Ways of laughing

... a Canon yn **rowlio chwerthin** [...] Ond dal i **rowlio chwerthin** ddaru Canon. [NOS 20]	... and Canon **roared with laughter** [lit. roll laugh] [...] But Canon was still **laughing his head off.** [NIGHT 13]
Mike, **screaming with laughter,** came and sat down on her stomach. [VICT 64]	Eisteddodd Dylan ar ei bol gan **floeddio chwerthin.** [lit. shout laugh] [LLINYN 73]
... whispering and **sniggering.** [Rankin 98]	... ac yn sibrwd a **phiffian chwerthin.** [lit. titter laugh] [Rankin 84]
Shrieks of laughter and snatches of singing could be heard coming through the closed door. [CHARLIE 104]	Roedd **sgrechian chwerthin** [lit. screech laugh] ac ychydig o ganu i'w glywed yn dod drwy'r drws caeedig. [SIOCLED 137]
Chwarddodd ei gyfeillion yn groch gan bwnio'i gilydd yn eu hafiaith, a daliasant i **ruo chwerthin** tra galwai'r Cadeirydd yn ofer am osteg. [CYCHWYN 224]	His companions laughed uproariously, nudging each other delightedly, and **their guffaws persisted** [lit. roar laugh] while the Chairman called vainly for order. [BEGIN 226]

9.5.iv Ways of raining

Bu'n **pistyllio bwrw** ac roedd y glaw yn llifo i mewn i'r ystafell trwy nifer o fân dyllau yn y to ... [PLA 346]	It was **raining hard** [lit. downpour rain], and water dripped from the holes in the roof ... [PEST 206]

... a hitha'n **pigo bwrw** erbyn hyn. [PLA 351]

*... and by now it was **starting to rain*** [lit. pick rain[16]]

It had been **pissing down** for a week. [KNOTS 186]

... ar ôl iddi fod yn **piso bwrw** [lit. piss rain] am wythnos. [CHWERW 158]

9.5.v Ways of singing

Roedd y sgwâr yn wag ar wahân i hen foi oedd yn cerdded yn igam ogam i fyny'r ochr draw, gan **floeddio canu** 'Delilah'. [GWRACH 214–15]

*The square was empty apart from an old boy staggering up the other side **screeching** 'Delilah' **at the top of his voice.*** [lit. shout sing]

Bydde John hefyd yn mynd i Gapel Baptist Ararat bob nos Sul a byddwn i'n mynd gyda fe jyst i gael **morio canu**. [HUNAN 83]

John also went to Ararat Baptist Chapel on Sunday evenings, and I used to go with him just for **a good sing**. [lit. sail sing] [SOLVA 84]

From behind the partition, **humming**, brushing invisible dust from his hands, came an older, chubbier, smiling Gordon Reeve. [KNOTS 241]

O'r tu ôl i'r pared, daeth Gordon Reeve i'r golwg dan **fwmian canu** [lit. mutter sing] – yn hŷn, yn fwy crwn, ac yn gwenu, gan frwsio llwch anweledig oddi ar ei ddwylo. [CHWERW 207]

9.5.vi Ways of sleeping

Roedd ei fam a'i ferch yn **chwyrnu cysgu'**n y gwellt ... [PLA 125]

Chwilen Bwm's mother and daughter were **fast asleep** ... [lit. snore sleep] [PEST 64]

Pendwmpian a hanner **hepian cysgu** ar ei draed roedd Dafydd Offeiriad pan glywodd sŵn. [PLA 328]

Brother Dafydd was **dozing fitfully** [lit. doze sleep] on his feet when he heard a noise. [PEST 192]

Roedd Edward yn **pendwmpian cysgu** ... [Roberts 70]

*Edward was **snoozing*** ... [lit. snooze sleep]

---

[16] *'Picking to rain'* can be heard as an expression in the English spoken in parts of south Wales with the meaning that it has started to rain but it is not, as yet, raining heavily.

9.5.vii Ways of talking

However, she could find nothing but a bottle of ink, and when she got back with it she found he had recovered, and he and the Queen were **talking together in a frighted whisper** . . . [THRO 135]

Sut bynnag, ni allai weld dim ond potel o inc, ac erbyn iddi ddychwelyd ag ef gwelodd ei fod wedi dod ato'i hun a'i fod ef a'r Frenhines yn **sisial sgwrsio** [lit. whisper converse] yn ofnus . . . [TRWY 21]

Mi'r oedd Mistar Huws i lawr wrth yr afon, yn cerddad yn ôl a blaen ac yn **mwngial siarad** efo fo'i hun. [TE 23]

Mr Huws was down by the river, walking about and **muttering** [lit. mutter talk] to himself. [TEA 24]

Rebus knew from her voice, **from its slurred growliness**, that she would be fast asleep by the time he reached the kitchen. [KNOTS 81]

Gwyddai oddi wrth ei llais, oddi wrth y ffordd roedd hi'n **llusgo siarad** [lit. drag talk], y byddai'n cysgu fel twrch erbyn iddo gyrraedd y gegin. [CHWERW 70]

9.5.viii Ways of walking

Cyflymodd y tri eu camau'n reddfol, Wil gan **swagro cerdded** a phoeri i'r grug a chwifio'i wialen. [CYCHWYN 101]

They quickened their pace instinctively and Will **swaggered along** [lit. swagger walk] flourishing his switch. [BEGIN 102]

. . . roedd hi wedi bod fel merch yn ei harddegau unwaith eto, yn **dawnsio cerdded** o gwmpas y tŷ tra'n hymian rhyw hen alawon nad oedd wedi eu clywed ers achau. [LLADD 327]

. . . *she had been like a girl in her teens once again, **prancing** [lit. dance walk] around the house whilst humming some old tunes she hadn't heard for ages.*

9.5.ix Other

The last squire **dragged out his existence** there . . . [BAND 211]

Yno bu'r sgweier olaf yn **llusgo byw** [lit. drag live] hyd at ei ddiwedd . . . [CYLCH 15]

The clock was **ticking very loudly**, throbbing into the silence like a heart beat. [VICT 189]

Roedd y cloc yn **bloeddio tician** [lit. shout tick], fel calon yn curo yn y tywyllwch. [LLINYN 216]

Alle Tessa ddim yfed alcohol, medde hi, oherwydd y moddion, felly fe ofynnodd hi am sudd ffrwythe a **phigo bwyta**'i homled a'i llysie, tato wedi'i berwi a salad. [HUNAN 235]

Tess said that she couldn't drink alcohol because of her medication, so she ordered fruit juice, before **picking at** [lit. pick eat] her omelette, vegetables, boiled spuds and salad. [SOLVA 235]

'Ac eto rydach chi'n awgrymu gofyn i'r ffyddloniaid, nad ydyn nhw ond prin yn gallu **crafu byw**'u hunain, gyfrannu at gynnal dyn ofer sydd wedi gwastraffu 'i arian ar y ddiod feddwol . . .' [RHANNU 111]

*'And yet you are suggesting asking the faithful who can scarcely **eke out a living** [lit. scratch live] themsleves, to contribute to the maintenance of a profligate man who has wasted his money on alcoholic drink . . .'*

As she turned over, she turned into the woman with the **choking cries** of his climax. [KNOTS 138]

Hithau'n troi'n ddynes wrth iddo fo **dagu gweiddi** [lit. choke shout] ar anterth eu caru. [CHWERW 117]

9.6 Swearing / Profanity and Interjections

Ensuring that any swearing or profanity is successfully transferred from one language to another is a considerable challenge. It is vital that not only is an appropriate register used but also that the impact of the word or phrase is kept in the target language. We could conceptualise swearing on a 'mild to strong' spectrum or continuum and locating a corresponding item at a similar position on both continua can be difficult. The first example below from an original English text [CIDER 42] has been rendered into Welsh [SEIDR 61] and includes swearing which ranges from a milder '*blimmin*'' to a stronger '*buggered*' and a '*soddin*' *bastard*'.

Mr Lockwood spat copiously into the straw. 'If that **soddin' bastard** –'
His wife cut in, and I thought she was taking exception to his language, but no.
'**Blimmin'** deserter too.' She said. 'Got his call-up papers September, I was told. Should've reported last month.'

Poerodd Mr Lockwood yn ffyrnig i ganol y gwellt. 'Os ydy'r **bastard diawl** yna . . .'
Torrodd ei wraig ar ei draws, disgwyliwn glywed y ffermwr yn cael cerydd am ddefnyddio'r fath iaith. 'Llwfrgi **cythraul** ydy o,' meddai hithau. 'Mi glywais i ei fod o wedi cael ei alw i'r fyddin ers mis Medi, ac y dylai o fod wedi mynd ers wythnosa.'

'**Buggered** if he's holin' up 'ere,'   'Mi wna i'n siwr nad ydy'r **cachgi**
Mr Lockwood decided, on his feet.   **budr** yn mynd i guddio o gwmpas y
                                                            fferm yma, beth bynnag.'

Much of the English terminology towards the stronger end of the spectrum
has also been borrowed into Welsh – to a greater extent than terminology
towards the milder end. GPC confirms that *bastard* (also *bastad, bastart*)
– albeit in its original English sense of *illigitimate child* – has been used in
Welsh since the fourteeth century. Other 'borrowings' either conform to
Welsh orthographic conventions e.g. *blydi* (bloody), *ffycin* (fucking) or show
evidence of similar morphological changes to native Welsh words e.g. *ffwc/
ffyc* > *ffwcedig* and *bygro* (to bugger). In the case of '*ffycin*' (although interestingly not so much in the case of '*blydi*'[17]), the element being modified by it
frequently also undergoes mutation as evidenced below:

'Wel, dwi'n falch o **ffycin g**lywed,   '*Well, bloody hell, I'm **fucking** glad to
myn uffarn i!' [LLADD 276]   hear that*'

'Na i gyd ma nhw'n wbod yw sut ma   *All they know about is how to put on
neud sioe **ffycin g**erdd. [DAL 34]   a **fucking** musical.*

'Gwna rwbath ynglŷn â dy **ffwcin**   '*Do something about your **fucking**
wraig y pidlan sgwarnog uffar!'   wife, you stupid prick!*'
(Roberts 213)

More 'native' Welsh expletives, interjections and profanities tend to have a
semantic connection with religious domains, for example:

Diawl > diawledig > diawl(i)o	=	Devil
Cythraul > cythreulig	=	Devil
Uffern/uffar > uffernol	=	Hell
Dam(i)o	=	Damn
'Su / 'Asu / Iesu	=	Jesus
Esgob	=	Bishop

Our examples group together usage (from 'mild' to 'stronger') as (i) adjectives
or adverbs or (ii) nouns.

---

[17] Indeed, PWT (4.102) notes that '*blydi*' does not cause a soft mutation whereas other
modifiers of adjectives do.

9.6.i Adjectives or adverbs

I like you, she thought. But you're as **wary as hell** of me, and I wish you weren't. [VICT 86]

Dwi'n dy licio di, meddyliodd Caryl, ond mi rwyt ti'n **uffernol o amheus**[18] ohona i ac mi fydda'n dda calon gen i petait ti ddim. [LLINYN 98]

I was tired and it was **bloody late** for a bedtime story . . . [CIDER 24]

Roeddwn i'n flinedig, ac roedd hi'n **uffernol o hwyr** i gychwyn ar stori amser gwely . . . [SEIDR 34]

'Mi fasat isio staen tywyll **ar y diawl** i gael y ddau i flendio.' [CAER 210]

*'You would need a **helluva** dark stain to get the two to blend.'*

Roedd **cryts y diawl** ar yr hewl pryd 'ny . . . [HUNAN 110]

There were a **hell of a lot** of kids on the road at that time . . . [SOLVA 110]

Roedd cyrch awyr wedi bod yn ystod y nos ac roedd **lle ar y diawl** yno. [HUNAN 8]

There had been an air raid during the night and there was a **hell of a mess**. [SOLVA 8]

'**Bloody** lunatic!' [CIDER 81]

'**Y diawl** lloerig!' [SEIDR 111]

'Dwi'n dallt dim ar 'i **ffwc** iaith o; pam ddylswn i?' [Paradwys 79]

*'I don't understand any of his **fucking** language; why should I?'*

'Mae o'n dal ei **ffycin** afael, mae hynny'n saff, Did! Ond mi **ffycin** gawn ni o i ti! Mae rhaid i ni!' [LLADD 52]

*'He's keeping his **fucking** grip, Did, that's for certain! But we'll **fucking** get him for you! We've got to!'*

9.6.ii Expletive + preposition 'o' + noun

Mi fydd hi'n **goblyn o ffrae** yma mewn munud, gei di weld . . . [NOS 12]

There'll be a **hell of a row** here in a minute, you'll see . . . [NIGHT 5]

'Mae Dan bach 'di ca'l **cythral o gollad**. Ond dyn iawn mae Laura angan, nid rhyw gadach llawr fel hwnna.' [RHANNU 214]

*'Good old Dan had a **helluva loss**. But Laura needs a real man, not a floormop like him.'*

---

[18] Note that it is possible for the modifying swear word to either follow the adjective '*amheus uffernol*' or precede it linked with the preposition '*o*' > '*uffernol o amheus*'

'Dyna i chdi **uffar o beth** i'w ddeud wrth ddynas o gig a gwaed.' [CAER 215]	'That's a **helluva thing** to say to a woman of flesh and blood.'
I'r clwb gwerin fyddwn ni'n mynd fel arfer – **sdim diawl o ddim** yn digwydd yn Solfach y dyddie 'ma. [HUNAN 186]	We usually go to the folk club – there's **bugger all** happening in Solva these days. [SOLVA 187]
'Oes 'na rywbeth i'w yfed yma? Gin i **ffwc o sychad.**' [Paradwys 79]	'Is there anything to drink here? I'm really **fucking** thirsty'.
'Dwi'n **ffycin** marw, Tracy!' 'Stop swearing. You'll wake the kids.' '**Ffwc o bwys** gen i! Gwna rwbath!' [GWRACH 27]	'I'm **fucking** dying, Tracy!' 'Stop swearing. You'll wake the kids.' 'I couldn't give a **fuck!** Do something!'

In a similar way to swearing, interjections can be considered to move from 'mild' to 'strong' along a continuum. The first table of examples includes Welsh interjections from the milder spectrum and would be appropriate in most informal settings. Again, there is often a religious connection (e.g. *Nefoedd wen!* – lit. *Blessed heaven!* and *Iesu/Arglwydd mawr!* – *Great Jesus/ Lord!*) although others are borrowed or adapted from English (e.g. *Diar annwyl!* – lit. *Dear* in Welsh plus 'dear' directly from English which would correspond to *Goodness me/Dear me*).

'**Alas!**' replied our visitor. [BAND 210]	'**Och, gwae fi!**'[19] atebodd ein hymwelydd. [CYLCH 16]
'**Oh, my God!** Helen! It was the band! The speckled band!' [BAND 216]	'O, [20]**Dduw mawr!** Helen! Y cylch oedd o! Y cylch brith!' [CYLCH 24]
'**Good heavens!**' she cried, 'he has followed me, then.' [BAND 225]	'**Nefoedd wen!**' ebychodd. 'Roedd o wedi fy nilyn felly.' [CYLCH 37]
'**Bloody hell,**' he breathed, his jaw dropping. 'It can't be true.' [TIME 24]	'**Iesgob**'[21] anadlodd, a'i ên yn disgyn, 'mae hyn yn amhosib!' [AMSER 36]

---

[19] Stylistically, this might be considered slightly old-fashioned now corresponding to something near to 'Alas, woe betide me' although it is suitable in the context of the work translated in our example here.

[20] Initial mutation of interjections is common.

[21] 'Iesgob' is a variation of 'Esgob' (= bishop) which is probably a further variation on 'Esgyrn >> Esgyrn Dafydd' (= bones > the bones of David) an interjection referring to

'**Y nefoedd fawr!** Huw Deg Ugian!'
[CHWAL 127]

'**Good heavens!**[22] Huw Ten-Score!'
[OUT 133]

'**Yr argian Dafydd**, 'ydi hwn yn
dallt Cymraeg?' gofynnodd i Huw.
[CHWAL 127]

'**Lord of David!** Does he understand
Welsh?' Simon asked Huw.
[OUT 126]

Jesus, one minute I found a new
daddy and the next he was on a
murder rap. [CIDER 20]

Uffern, roeddwn i newydd
ddarganfod tad newydd a'r eiliad
nesa roedd o'n cael ei gyhuddo o
lofruddiaeth! [SEIDR 28]

Tad annwyl, mae yna ddigon o
ddewis o waith yn yr oes yma.
[CRYMAN 79]

Good heavens, there's plenty of
choice these days. [SICKLE 64]

Nefi blw[23] [CRYMAN 78]

Good heavens. [SICKLE 64]

'**Jiw, jiw**[24] Gwynfor.' [CADW 58]

'*Good God Gwynfor.*'

''Le chi di bod, Gwynfor? **Er mwyn
dyn**.[25] Ma'r te yn y pot ers dros
ugen munud. Ma' fe'n o'r nawr.'
[CADW 57]

'*Where have you been, Gwynfor?* ***For
heaven's sake.*** *The tea's been in the
pot for over twenty minutes. It's cold
now.*'

Esgob, rydw i eisio bwyd, Mam.
[NOS 17]

Lor, I'm hungry, Mam. [NIGHT 11]

'Yndi **tad**!'[26] [GWRACH 196]

'Ia **tad**.' [GWRACH 197]

---

a relic and an echo from the Catholic Wales of the past. It can also be considered a
deformed version of '*Iesu*' (= *Jesus*) as a way of softening.

[22] The translator kept the original '*Nefoedd fawr*' – we have changed this to '*Good heavens*' to illustrate how these interjections would more usually correspond to each other.

[23] Originally from the English '*Navy blue*'

[24] A common interjection especially in SW. It is a reduplication of '*Duw*' (= *God*) and
has no direct equivalent in English.

[25] '*Duw*' and '*dyn*' (= *man*) can be interchangeable in Welsh probably to avoid blas-
phemy e.g. '*er mwyn Duw/dyn*' (= *for God's sake/* lit. *for man's sake*) as well as '*Duw/
dyn a ŵyr*' (= *God knows/* lit. *man knows*). The nearest equivalent in English would be
to use '*Heaven*' in the place of '*God*'.

[26] We have included these examples of '*tad*' (= *father*) which are typical of the informal
NW spoken register. This can be used even when speaking to someone who isn't one's
father (or even a family relative). There is no direct translation possible in English and
the choice of a corresponding interjection would depend on the context of the dialogue.

Bobol annwyl, beth pe bai rhywun wedi gofyn iddo neithiwr am gael gweld cynnwys y bag? [SELYF 64]

Good grief, what if someone had asked him last night to see the contents of the bag?

The following three examples are from the stronger end of the interjection continuum and again are clearly heavily influenced by the corresponding terminology on the English continuum and being used in very informal contexts. The use of italics in the first example highlights the fact that these are borrowings, although – again in the context of the work (and in very informal speech) – this would sound familiar to the contemporary reader of Welsh.

'**Shit**', meddai'r gyrrwr yn uchel, ac rwy'n teimlo unwaith eto mai er fy mwyn i y mae hyn. '**Bollocks**,' ac mae'n amlwg na alla i gadw'n dawel yma.
'Newyddion drwg?' rwy'n gofyn, a dwy' ddim yn llwyddo i guddio fy niffyg diddordeb.
'O **God** ydi. Ti ddim yn dilyn pêl-droed?' [CADW 27]

'**Shit**', *said the driver out aloud, and once again I feel like he's doing this for my sake.*
'**Bollocks**,' *and it's obvious that I can't keep quiet here.*
'Bad news?' *I enquire, and I don't manage to hide my lack of interest.*
'Oh **God** yes. You don't follow football?'*

'**Ffacin hel**, OK! **Jîsys**! 'Dan ni'm yn ffrindia 'fo nhw, siŵr!! Jysd nabod 'i gariad o, efo'i gwaith, mae Elin.' [CRAWIA 74]

'**Fucking hell**, OK! **Jesus**! Of course we're not friends with them!! Elin just knows his girlfriend, through work.'*

'**Ffycin hel**, Dat! Be sy arno ti'n hela ofan arna i felna?' [DAL 85]

'**Fucking hell**, Dad! What's wrong with you making me scared like that?'*

A particular Welsh construction typically used in forming oaths is the use of the non-pronominal preposition 'myn' (only ever used in this context) followed by whatever the oath is taken by. In this position, 'myn' corresponds to 'by' in an English oath although the use of these in contemporary Welsh (as shown in our examples) is as an interjection. The first person affixed pronoun 'i' sometimes follows the 'myn' oath. It is usually impossible to translate these oaths literally and an equivalent English formula needs to be sought.

'Pentra' o blismyn, **myn coblyn i!'** sylwodd Dic. [CHWAL 27]

'A villageful of p'licemen, ***myn coblyn i***[27]!' remarked Dic. [OUT 27]

'Gweithio i fi fy hun dwi isio'i neud. Dechra busnas. Cyfrifiaduron. Mi nesh i gwrs web design pan o'n i . . . i ffwr.'
'Pa! Cyfrifiaduron o ddiawl. Gweithio i chdi dy hun, **myn coblyn i.'** [CAER 188]

'What I want to do is work for me myself. Start a business. Computers. I did a web design course when I was a . . . away.'
*'Bah! Bloody computers. Working for yourself, **for God's sake.'***

Gwdig, **myn brain!** [CRYMAN 73]

Goodwick, **for heaven's sake**[28]! [SICKLE 59]

Myn uffarn i, allen ni ddim fod wedi gwneud mwy na beth naethon ni. [DAL 79]

***Hells bells**, we couldn't have done more than what we did.*

Our final set of examples in this section relate to swear words used after an interrogative. As the last example demonstrates, it is still possible to use English borrowings in this position especially when a strong meaning is desired. However, the use of native Welsh lexical items is more common – in particular, *'uffern/uffarn/uffach'* (= *hell*), *'diawl'* (= *devil*), *'cythraul'* (= *devil*), *'coblyn'* (= *goblin, sprite*) and *'aflwydd'* (= *misfortune*).

'Pwy **uffach** yw Boner a sut fath o enw yw hwnna?' [FFYDD 208]

'Who **the hell** is Boner and what sort of a name is that supposed to be?' [FAITH 145]

Pwy **uffarn** wyt ti'n meddwl wyt ti? [DAL 87]

*Who **the hell** do you think you are?*

Be **ddiawl** maen nhw wedi'i neud iddi? Wnaiff hyn fyth mo'r tro! [HUNAN 237]

What **the hell**[29] have they done to her? This will never do! [SOLVA 237]

---

[27] Literally, *'by a goblin/sprite'*. Here, the translator has chosen to keep the Welsh oath-interjection in the English version. A comparable formula in English, expressing surprise, might be *'my word / good gracious'*.

[28] In this example, the literal translation would be *'by the crows'*. This is sometimes translated into the English *'stone the crows'*.

[29] *'What the devil . . .'* would also have been possible in English, being a more literal translation. Nevertheless, that might convey a certain type or 'class' of English speaker not necessarily compatible with the original character in Welsh.

Pwy **gythraul** sydd yna rwan? Medda llais Now Bach Glo. [NOS 33]	Who **the devil** is it now? came Little Owen the Coal's voice. [NIGHT 26]
'Os nad hynny oedd dy fwriad di, pam **gythraul** y daethost ti'r ffordd yma?' [MONICA 18]	'If that wasn't what you had in mind, why **the hell** did you come this way with me?' [MONICA 17]
'Sut **goblyn** yr awn ni adra', dywad?' [CHWAL 114]	'How **the deuce** will we go home, say?' [OUT 120]
'Sut **aflwydd** y gwyddoch chi gymaint? Beth **aflwydd** ydi'ch enw chi?' [CRYMAN 85]	'How **the heck** do you know so much about me? What's *your* name?' [SICKLE 69]
'Pwy **ffwc** ti'n siarad efo, ffatso?!' medda Ceri. [LLADD 147]	*'Who **the fuck** are you talking to, fatso?!' said Ceri.*

9.7 YM- Prefixation

The prefix *ym-* in Welsh is historically associated with a reflexive meaning but also expresses reciprocity.[30] The verb-noun to which it is prefixed always undergoes an initial soft mutation e.g. *gadael >> ymadael* (= *leave >> depart*). An example of a creative use of the *ym-* prefix is the way in which the translator in [CYLCH 11] has rendered the English original's '... *acquirement of wealth ...*' as an *ym-* prefixed verb >>> '... *ymgyfoethogi ...*' (*ym-* with the verb-noun *cyfoethogi* = *to enrich*). Further examples (which note the original verb-noun in parenthesis) follow:

... in an instant his strange headgear began to move, and there **reared itself** from among his hair the squat, diamond-shaped head and puffed neck of a loathsome serpent. [BAND 238]	Yn sydyn, dechreuodd y penwisg rhyfedd symud yn llithrig, ac yn raddol o ganol gwallt y meddyg **ymgododd** [*ym-* + *codi* = *to get up, raise up*] pen byrdew siâp diemwnt a gwddf chwyddedig sarff atgas ei golwg. [CYLCH 56]

---

[30] See Rottet, Kevin J. 2010. 'Language contact in Welsh and Breton: The case of reflexive and reciprocal verbs.' *IULC Working Papers 9: New Perspectives on Language Contact and Contact-Induced Language Change.* Bloomington, IN: Indiana University Linguistics Club, edited by Clements, J. Clancy, Solon, Megan Elizabeth, Siegel, Jason F. and Steiner, B. Devan, pp. 61–82.

Rhan o swyn y caru hwn ydoedd ei ddirgelwch honedig i'r cariadon. Ni wyddai neb amdano ond hwy eu hunain, esgus – fel crwt a chroten, weithiau, yn **ymhoffi yn ei gilydd**, yn ddistaw bach, mewn dosbarth ysgol. [HDF 110]

A part of the charm of this courting was its pretence of being a secret between the two lovers. No one knew about it but themselves, as it were, just as a boy and girl sometimes **are in love with each other** [ym- + hoffi = to like] on the quiet in a class in school. [OFH 135]

Rhoes y cwpan ar y bwrdd wrth y gwely, ac yna **ymsythodd ar ei eistedd** a gwyro ymlaen i syllu drwy'r ffenestr. [CYCHWYN 32]

He put the cup down on the bedside table and then, **sitting bold upright** [ym- + sythu = to straighten] leaned forward to gaze through the window. [BEGIN 31]

He needed time to get himself together again. **To become** a sane, well-coordinated individual, not an emotional mess. [VICT 43]

Roedd angen amser arno i roi trefn arno'i hun – i **ymffurfio** [ym- + ffurfio = to form]'n berson call, rhesymol unwaith eto yn hytrach na sbradach o emosiynau rhacs. [LLINYN 49]

Cododd docynnau. Dilynodd hithau lamp drydan y porthor onid **ymsuddodd** hi yn un o seti plwsh y cinema. [MONICA 16]

He bought tickets. She followed the usher's torch until she **was settled** [ym- + suddo = to sink] into one of the cinema's plush seats. [MONICA 15]

Ond yr oedd swyn yn y geiriau, ac yn sŵn eu treigl, a barodd i mi'n gynnar garu'r iaith, a dechrau **ymglywed â** rhin ei chyfoeth dihenydd. [HDF 101]

But the words and the sound of them as they ran along had a charm for me that led me early to love the language and to begin to **listen to** [ym- + clywed = to hear] the magic of its ageless wealth. [OFH 124]

Bu'n cadw gwely ran helaeth o'i flwyddyn olaf – y corff gwydn, cymharol ysgafn, wedi **ymdreulio** i'r pen gan oes o waith caled. [HDF 64]

He had kept to his bed for a great part of his last year. His tough, comparatively light frame **was worn out** [ym- + treulio = to digest, wear] by a lifetime of hard work. [OFH 77]

9.8 Conclusions

The way in which fields of meaning operate between languages is a major consideration for the translator. It is beyond the scope of this book to look at every aspect of this in the context of the Welsh and English languages, however we have endeavoured to deal with some of the principal items which may be of concern to translators and writers. Moreover, developing a critical approach to fields of meaning will enable the translator to avoid some of the more obvious pitfalls that can occur when transferring information from one language to another. Lexical compounding is another aspect which requires clear translation strategies. It is often impossible to render a compound in one language with a similarly constructed compound in another – alternatives can include (i) phrases (ii) clauses (iii) unpacking of the compound. Let us consider, for example, the recent compound 'trydarfyd[31]'. This consists of 'trydar' (= to tweet) + 'byd' (= world). It describes the community or 'world' of people who engage with each other through the Twitter application. We could convey this in English in a number of ways (i) the 'Twitterati' (ii) those (= the community) who engage frequently with Twitter or (iii) the world of Twitter. We have seen that Welsh forms compounds in particular ways which (as shown by the very contemporary Trydarfyd) are still very productive both in the formal written register and the more informal spoken register.

Collocations have been given particular attention in this chapter considering how they may operate differently between languages e.g. tynnu llun >>> to take (or draw) a picture. Knowledge of which collocations are possible is a significant element of the translator's toolkit and is a lexical issue which merits more attention in Welsh. Finally, ensuring that expletives, profanities and interjections correspond at similar points along their respective continua is again an important consideration in making sure that the impact of the original is conveyed sufficiently powerfully in the other language. Sensitivity and awareness of how the lexicon operates in both languages and where/how a lexical item in one language corresponds to whatever its equivalent may be in the other's is a fundamental component of any translator's skillset.

---

[31] Attested in Welsh language blogs, tweets and online discussion groups e.g. https://haciaith.com/2014/01/05/mapior-trydarfyd-celtaidd/ (last accessed 13 June 2017).

Welsh Verbless Clauses and Verb-noun Clauses

10.0 Introduction

This chapter brings together a number of patterns in which Welsh style deploys considerably fewer finite (inflected) verbs than English does. This preference can take two forms: (1) Constructions in which both Welsh and English have a verb, but the Welsh pattern makes use of a *less actualised* verb form than English does; (2) Constructions in which Welsh uses no verb at all, while English deploys some verb form, whether fully inflected or participial.

The concept of *actualisation*[1] was developed by Jacqueline Guillemin-Flescher (1981[2]) in her comparison of English and French in translation as an important way in which those two languages differ in their stylistic preferences. It turns out that the same comparison is valid for English and Welsh, as we will show in this chapter. Actualisation refers to the anchoring of an event in a specific moment of place and time:

- An inflected verb in the preterite (*he left*) referring to a single, concrete occurrence represents maximal actualisation, since the event is represented as having occurred and achieved completion in a specific place and time. It is thus represented as being a fixed reference point in the discourse.
- An action in a progressive tense (*he was leaving*) represents a lesser degree of actualisation. Since the temporal bounds of the event are left fluid, it is less anchored in space and time; we know only that the action was in progress relative to some other event. Actions in perfect tenses (*he had left, he has left*) represent a similar level of actualisation – they

---

[1] This is our translation from Guillemin-Flescher's French term *actualisation*.
[2] Guillemin-Flescher, Jacqueline. 1981. *Syntaxe comparée du français et de l'anglais: Problèmes de traduction*. Éditions Ophrys.

portray an event with respect to its result, so we know only that the event happened at some previous time (that is, it is *anterior*). Put differently, both progressive and perfect tenses are relative tenses which are not independently anchored: their anchoring depends on some other event, generally one in the preterite.

- Non-assertive verb forms such as subjunctives (*[I insist] that he leave*) or hypothetical conditionals (*[if he wanted to,] he would leave*) are even less actualised because in these cases the action is being presented not as occurring at all, but only as a potential occurrence.
- Next on the cline of actualisation is the infinitive (*to leave*), since it simply refers to the *idea* of an event as an abstraction, with no temporal or spatial anchoring. It also lacks the personal inflections that characterise all of the previous forms in many languages.
- The least actualised way to refer to an event is with a nominalisation (*his departure*), which names the event in an abstract and non-verbal way.

We see, then, that actualisation is not a binary matter but a question of degree, with at least five levels, from most to least actualised as we move from left to right along the following scale:

he left	*he was leaving*	*(I insist) that he leave*	*(he wants)*	*his*
	he had left	*(if he wanted to) he would leave*	*to leave*	*departure*

English style is located rather far towards the left on this scale, with a very high density of maximally actualised events. The stylistic preferences of Welsh (and for French, in Guillemin-Flescher's development of these ideas) are located much further to the right, with a lower density of actualised events.[3] The five levels can be illustrated for Welsh as follows:

gadawodd	*gadawai*	*byddai fe'n gadael*	*(mae e*	*ei*
	roedd e'n gadael	*basai fe'n gadael*	*eisiau)*	*ymadawiad*
	roedd e wedi gadael		*gadael*	

It is possible to vary the degree of actualisation within a language, for stylistic effect or to change register. For instance, in English one can say *before he left* or *before his departure*. The former is maximally actualised, the latter

---

[3] This does not mean that French and Welsh make use of the *same* patterns; the specific patterns are generally quite different. But they have in common a significantly lesser degree of actualisation vis-à-vis English.

deactualised. Similarly, one can choose between *the building of the canal* and *the construction of the canal*. Although these two formulations denote the same state of affairs, the gerund form *building* is more actualised than the nominalisation *construction*, since the gerund represents the activity in its unfolding, with overt morphology homophonous with the progressive *-ing*, whereas the nominalisation simply names the activity as an abstraction. In English, deactualised forms like *before his departure* or *the construction of the canal* typically reflect a higher, often formal register, whereas actualised forms represent everyday language. Most English writing contains a high density of highly actualised forms.

As we will see in this chapter, the facts are quite different in Welsh, and this has numerous implications for the Welsh translator or stylist. There are many instances in which a translation will involve an English expression that is located further to the left on the above scales than the Welsh version of the same event. Many such cases represent grammatical constraints of the two languages, while others represent options and preferences rather than absolutes.

This chapter is organised as follows. In the first section we will discuss cases in which both Welsh and English deploy a verb form, but the Welsh pattern is deactualised by comparison with the English. In the second section of the chapter we will lay out patterns in which the Welsh construction uses no verb at all. Finally, in the third section, we will discuss absolute clauses, which can be of either type (having a verb-noun, or having no verb at all). Section four will summarise the findings of the chapter.

10.1 English actualised verb forms corresponding to Welsh verb-nouns

There are a number of patterns in which English uses one or another level of actualised verb form whereas Welsh uses the highly deactualised verb-noun. Probably the most common English equivalent of a Welsh verb-noun is a gerund in *-ing*, as seen in the following:[4]

Trigo yr ydwyf yma – **cysgu, gweithio, a bwyta** – ac nid byw. [HENAT 8]	Here I simply reside – **sleeping, working and eating**. I do not *live* here. [LOCUST 14]

---

[4] Despite their functional equivalence in many constructions, the Welsh verb-noun is a less actualised form than the English gerund. The verb-noun has more or less the same level of actualisation as the English infinitive.

Bywyd caled oedd bywyd y gwŷr hyn, ar y cyfan. Eu tâl pennaf ydoedd **cael gweld y byd**. [HDF 147]

These men had a hard life, on the whole. Their principal remuneration was **seeing the world**. [OFH 184]

Credwn mai wâst ar amser gwerthfawr oedd **canu**. [WILLAT 48]

*I believed that **singing** [in schools] was a waste of valuable time.*

He didn't feel much like **singing**. [STONE 338]

Doedd fawr o awydd **canu** arno. [MAEN 215]

The usage is even lexicalised in some expressions such as *ac / o ystyried* 'considering' and *a barnu* 'judging':

Hen foneddwr hynaws, a disgyblaeth yr ysgol yn lled dda **ac ystyried** yr amseroedd. [WILLAT 72–3]

*[He was] a kindly old gentleman, and the discipline in the school was fairly good **considering** the times.*

Ni chofiaf ei destun (fwy nag yntau, **a barnu** fel yr oedd wedi crwydro oddi wrtho), ond gwn mai stori'r Berth yn Llosgi oedd ei faes. [DYDD 93]

*I don't remember his text (any more than he did, **judging** from the way he had wandered from it) but I know that his subject was the Burning Bush.*

But in other constructions, the English translation of a verb-noun is a more actualised form – often, in fact, the preterite. An important constraint of Welsh grammar that contributes to the effect of decreased actualisation by comparison with English is the fact that numerous constructions involve a complement clause in which the verb is reduced to a verb-noun, even when it is interpreted in context as an actualised verb form. We turn to these patterns now.

The Welsh language has a battery of constructions in which a complement takes the form *i* + SUBJECT + VERB-NOUN, which regularly corresponds to a clause with an inflected verb in English, typically a preterite or a pluperfect. A number of prepositions and conjunctions take complements using this pattern, including *cyn* 'before', *am / oherwydd* 'because', *ar ôl / wedi* 'after', *wrth* 'as', *nes* 'until', *erbyn* 'by the time that', and *er* 'although':[5]

---

[5] The preposition is usually followed directly by the verb-noun, without the prepositional element, when the subject of the two clauses is the same. Compare the following:
Ar ôl dod allan o'r car, cwympodd Alun. 'After getting out of the car, Alun fell.'
Ar ôl iddyn nhw ddod allan o'r car, cwympodd Alun. 'After they got out of the car, Alun fell.'

Cyn iddi gael diffiniad i'w phlesio dyma gwestiwn arall fel bollt. [TE 48]

But **before she found** a satisfactory answer, another question was shot at her. [TEA 45]

Yr oedd yn siomedig am na ddangosodd neb lawer o lawenydd **am iddo ennill** ysgoloriaeth. [TRAED 43]

He was bitterly disappointed that nobody seemed very glad **that he had won** the scholarship. [FEET 36]

Ar ôl iddynt fynd i'w gwely dôi eu mam â joi o gyfleth a'i roi yn eu cegau . . . [TRAED 134]

After they had gone to bed, their mother would come and place a lump of toffee in their mouths . . . [FEET 111]

. . . **wedi i iechyd fy nhad dorri** lawr. [HDF 116]

. . . **when my father's health had broken** down. [OFH 143]

Araf fu'r daith i waelod y chwarel, a daeth ofn i'm calon **wrth imi sylwi** ar lwybr troellog y Neidr yn hongian ar serthni'r mynydd o'n blaen. [O LAW 201]

Our journey to the bottom of the quarry was slow indeed, and my heart sank **as I looked** at the 'Snake', the winding path that clung to the steep mountain-slope in front of us. [FROM 165]

Bennodd Tess lan – fel y rhan fwya o bobl oedd yn wael eu meddwl y dyddie hynny – wedi'i chlymu i fainc a darn o rwber wedi'i saco rhwng ei dannedd hi a cherrynt trydanol foltedd uchel yn rhedeg trwy'i hymennydd hi **nes iddi gael confylsiwn** a llewygu! [HUNAN 217]

She ended up like most mentally ill people in those days, strapped to a bench with a piece of rubber stuffed between her teeth and high voltage electrical current passing through her brain **until she convulsed** and passed out. [SOLVA 217]

Erbyn iddynt gyrraedd y ffair, yr oedd y goleuadau *naphtha* wedi'u cynnau ac yn poeri'n swnllyd uwch rhuthr o wynebau llwydfelyn. [CYCHWYN 101]

By the time they reached the fair the naphtha lamps had been lit and were hissing and spluttering noisily above the surge of faces, livid-hued in the glare. [BEGIN 102]

'R oedd erbyn hyn dipyn dros ei ddeugain oed; ac **er iddo gamdrin llawer ar ei gorff** drwy ddiota ac ymladd a phethau tebyg yn ei ddyddiau cynharach yr oedd o hyd yn rhyfeddol o gryf. [CHWECH 120]

*By this time he was a bit over forty; and **although he had greatly mistreated his body** by drinking and fighting and such in his early days, he was still amazingly strong.*

Welsh *i*-clauses are formally ambiguous as to their temporal interpretation; *cyn iddo adael* could mean 'before he leaves', 'before he had left' or 'before he left'. The appropriate temporal interpretation is determined of course by context. English can handle these clauses in a less actualised way as well, by using a participle instead of a preterite:

Before leaving his office he had telephoned Dr Stuchley . . . [TIME 50]	Roedd wedi ffonio Dr Stuchley **cyn iddo adael** ei swyddfa . . .[AMSER 79]

The English phrase 'before leaving' is less actualised than 'before he left', but it is still a more actualised form than the Welsh verb-noun (as discussed above).

The *i*-complement pattern is also used following a variety of verbs of cognition, of emotion or mental state, and of discourse. In this construction the subordinate verb generally has a preterite or a perfect interpretation For instance, this includes verbs of cognition like *gwybod* 'to know', *meddwl* 'to think', *tybio* 'to imagine, think', *credu* 'to believe', *cofio* 'to remember', *casglu* 'to gather / draw the conclusion', etc.:

Ond **gwn, yn hytrach, yn gwbl sicr, iddynt fod** i mi yn gynhaliaeth amhrisiadwy, yn ddiwylliannol, moesol, ac ysbrydol, weddill fy oes. [HDF 102]	But rather **I know for certain that they have been** invaluable sustenance culturally, morally, and spiritually during the rest of my life hitherto. [OFH 124]
[T]**ybiwn iddo ddyfod** atom ni er mwyn gwneud ymdrech i godi calon fy nhad. [O LAW 209]	**I imagined that he came** over to try to cheer my father up. [FROM 173]
Ac **nid wyf yn credu i neb fod** ar ei golled o estyn y rhyddid hwn iddynt. [HDF 128]	**I don't think anyone was** the worse off for extending him this privilege. [OFH 160]
'**Alla'i ddim cofio iddi ddweud dim** yn angharedig amdano fo mwy nag a ddwedodd hi amdani'i hun.' [LLEIFIOR 91]	'I can't recall her saying anything more unkind about him than she did about herself.' [RETURN 77]
Casglwn iddo bendrymu a gofidio tros gyflwr ei iechyd ers dyddiau, ac mai mawr eu rhyddhad o'i weld yn llonni fel hyn. [O LAW 154]	**I gathered that he had been moping and grieving** over his ill-health for many a day and that they were immensely relieved at seeing him so unusually cheerful. [FROM 123]

'You think he was killed because they were?' [TIME 53]

'Ydych chi'n meddwl iddo gael ei **ladd** oherwydd eu bod nhw'n cyd-fyw?' [AMSER 83–4]

It could have been his imagination, but **he thought he read** in the eyes studying him an almost predatory interest . . . [TIME 102]

Efallai mai ef oedd yn dychmygu, ond **credai iddo ddarllen** yn y llygaid ryw olwg sglyfaethus . . . [AMSER 162]

Or verbs of emotion or mental state:

Medrai ddarllen trwy ei hunanoldeb i gyd. **Yr oedd yn dda ganddo iddo ddeffro**'n awr, cyn i'r ffaith eu bod yn caru fynd i glustiau neb. Hyd y gwyddai, ni wyddai neb am eu carwriaeth. [TRAED 81]

He could see through her conceit, and **he was glad that he realised** this before anybody knew of their relationship. So far as he knew, nobody knew of their love affair. [FEET 72]

Pe rhoddid y cwbl at ei gilydd, **yr wyf yn sicr iddo fy nghario ar ei gefn** ugeiniau o filldiroedd, a hyny yn hollol ddirwgnach. [RHYS 89]

*All told, **I am sure that he carried me on his back** scores of times, entirely without grumbling.*

Or verbs of discourse (*dweud* 'to say', *datgan* 'to declare', etc.):

Dywedir iddo fod yn caru . . . [HDF 168]

He is said to have been courting . . . [OFH 211]

Clywais ddweud iddo ef fod yn dipyn o ebol ar un adeg, ac mai ei phwyll hi a'i mawrfrydedd hi a gadwodd y cartref wrth ei gilydd. [CHWECH 180]

I heard it said that he was a bit of a lad at the time, and that it was her prudence and her magnanimity that kept the home together.

And finally, various kinds of impersonal expressions can take an *i-clause* as their complement:

'Maen nhw'n deud mai bachgen direidus ydi Twm, ond er na dda gen i mo'i fam o, weles i ddim llawer o'i le ar y bachgen, a **mae'n arw o beth iddo syffro ar gam**.' [GWEN 28]

'They say that Twm is a mischievous boy, but I've never found much wrong with him, though I don't like his mother. **It would be a pity if he were to suffer any injustice**.' [GWEN 33]

Ymddangosai'i ben lawer yn rhy fawr i'w gorff, ac **nid rhyfedd iddo suddo i mewn** rhwng ysgwyddau'i berchennog, gan wneud i rywun feddwl am iâr yn ei phlu. [CYCHWYN 39]	His head looked far too big for his body and **it was not surprising that it had sunk** between its owner's shoulders, making one think of a hen with its head tucked into its feathers. [BEGIN 38]

In the above cases we saw that the *i*-complement clause generally has a preterite or a perfect interpretation. On the other hand, when the complement clause is interpreted as a present or imperfect tense (*yr amhenodol*), the complement clause takes a different form, that of the so-called *noun clause*, in which *bod* is not overtly inflected and just remains in the verb-noun form. There is thus a contrast between the following two patterns:

Yr wyf yn meddwl iddo adael. 'I think that he left (*or* has left).'
Yr wyf yn meddwl ei fod yn gadael. 'I think that he is (*or* was) leaving.'

A few examples of this second deactualised complementation pattern are shown below:

Edrychodd Gwdig i weld a oedd winc yn llygad Edward Vaughan. **Gwelodd fod**, ac yna dywedodd . . . [LLEIFIOR 55]	Goodwick looked to see whether there was a twinkle in Edward Vaughan's eye. He saw **there was** and said . . . [RETURN 45]
Cofiaf fod y gwrychoedd yn llawn blagur a'r llygaid-y-dydd yn garpedi gwynion ar rai o'r caeau. [O LAW 140]	**I remember that the hedges were** in full bud and that the daisies had spread white carpets over some of the fields. [FROM 111]
Roedd e i'w weld yn fachan iawn, a **dwedes i wrtho fy mod i'n aros** am Gary Farr oedd yn y swyddfa . . . [HUNAN 194]	He seemed a cool guy, and so **I told him I was waiting** for Gary Farr to complete his business in the office . . . [SOLVA 194]
Credaf fod rhyw ugain ohonynt yno . . . [O LAW 220]	**I imagine there must have been** about a score of them there . . . [FROM 183]
Wyt ti'n **gwybod dy fod ti'n mynd** i uffarn ar dy ben, i ganol tân a brwmstan ac i ddamnedigaeth am dragwyddoldeb a thragwyddoldeb? [NOS 43]	Do you **know you're going** to Hell, headfirst into the middle of the fire and brimstone, to damnation for all eternity? [NIGHT 34]

Hanging around like this, people will **think you're** up to something. [STONE 334]	Bydd pobl yn **meddwl eich bod** ar ryw berwyl drwg wrth eich gweld chi'n llercian o gwmpas fel hyn. [MAEN 213]

That noun clauses like the above are deactualised by comparison with English is clear in that they are formally ambiguous as to temporal interpretation. A sequence such as *fy mod i'n aros* could mean 'that I am waiting' or 'that I was waiting', with the appropriate interpretation inferrable only from context. The form itself is thus less anchored to time and place than the English translations, which are not ambiguous in this way.[6]

It is not only subordinate verbs in complement clauses like the above that can be reduced to the verb-noun in Welsh; main clause verbs can as well. It is a regular principle of Welsh style that when there is a series of three or more conjoined verbs in the same sentence, with identical subject and tense-mood-aspect (TMA) features, only the first verb is generally conjugated. The remaining ones are reduced to their verb-noun, with the understanding that they inherit subject and TMA features from the first verb in the series. In English the equivalents must be fully conjugated:

Aeth at y tân o lech i lwyn, **eistedd** ar y stôl a **beichio crio**. [TE 9]	She **dawdled** her way to the fire, **sat** on the stool and **burst** into tears. [TEA 13]
Gawn ni weld am hynny, **medda** finna, a **rhoid** fy nghap am fy mhen a **mynd** allan â chlep ar y drws. [NOS 195]	We'll see about that, I **said**, and I **put** my cap on and **went** out and slammed the door behind me. [NIGHT 166]
The next morning he **got up** early and **went** into the bathroom and **locked** the door. [MAT 56]	Y bore canlynol **cododd** yn gynnar a **mynd** i mewn i'r ystafell ymolchi a **chloi**'r drws. [MAT 50]

When the series consists of only two verbs, there is variation. It is not uncommon to follow the same pattern shown above, where only the first verb is inflected:

---

[6] Borsley, Tallerman and Willis (2007) analyse noun clauses as finite, despite their non-finite appearance. This may indeed be the case; however, they are certainly deactualised by comparison with inflected verbs that show tense-mood-aspect marking, and that is the relevant point here.

Ymfudodd Clive Williams i Seland Newydd a **chael** ei ladd, trista'r sôn, mewn damwain car rai blynyddoedd yn ddiweddarach. [HUNAN 120]

Clive Williams **emigrated** to New Zealand where, sadly, he **was** killed in a car accident some years later. [SOLVA 120]

But is not difficult to find cases where both verbs are inflected, revealing that when two verbs are involved we have an option rather than a constraint:

Gwasgodd hi tuag ato. **Troes** hithau ei hwyneb a **rhoddodd** un pigiad aderyn ar ei wefl laith. [MONICA 17]

He pressed her close. She **turned** her face to him and **gave** him one little peck on his moist lip. [MONICA 16]

Taflodd Owen yr arian ar y bwrdd mewn tymer, a **chafodd** glustan gan ei fam. [TRAED 37]

Owen **flung** the pennies on the table in a fit of temper, and his mother boxed his ears. [FEET 34] [lit. . . . and he **got** a box on the ears from his mother]

Madam Hooch then **showed** them how to mount their brooms without sliding off the end, and **walked** up and down the rows correcting their grips. [STONE 181]

Yna **dangosodd** Madam Heddwen iddyn nhw sut i fynd ar gefn yr ysgubau heb lithro oddi ar y pen, a **cherddodd** i fyny ac i lawr rhwng y rhesi gan gywiro'r ffordd roedden nhw'n cydio ynddynt. [MAEN 115]

In the three examples above, it would have been perfectly possible to reduce the second bolded verb to *rhoi*, *chael* and *cherdded* respectively, but the authors chose to use fully actualised forms in these cases.

Literary Welsh offers further possibilities of reducing verbs to their verb-noun that go beyond what is routinely found in the colloquial language. Sometimes a verb-noun is used instead of a finite verb after a conjunction such as *ond* 'but' or *cyn* 'before' or as the complement of a verb of cognition like *gwybod* 'to know'. In all these cases, English must translate using a finite verb:

Mae hi'n ddel, ond **bod** ganddi wyneb fel plentyn wedi'i sbwylio, a phwt o drwyn. [MONICA 7]

She's pretty, but **she has** the face of a spoilt child, and a snub nose. [MONICA 5]

. . . fe fydd y lleuad yn codi cyn **darfod** y machlud. [MONICA 7]

. . . the moon will be up before the sun **goes down**. [MONICA 6]

A gwyddai pawb **ddyfod** yr eiliad i
godi. [CRYMAN 23]

... and everyone knew the moment
had come to get to their feet.
[SICKLE 17]

A very literary pattern allows subjects to be presented as objects of the preposition *o* following their verb-noun:

Pan ganem y darn, âi popeth ymlaen
yn hollol hwylus, **nes cyrraedd
ohonom** y rhan fwyaf cynhyrfus;
[WILLAT 51]

*When we would sing the piece,
everything went along handily **until
we reached** the most exciting part;*

Ac yr oedd ei sylwadau craff a
buddiol wedi eu cyfleu mewn Saesneg
mor rhagorol, ac mewn brawddegau
mor ddewisol **nes teimlo ohonom**
eu bod yn werth eu cael, hyd yn oed
pan fyddai tipyn o watwareg y tu ôl
iddynt. [WILLAT 74]

*And his insightful and beneficial
observations were conveyed in such
exceptional English, and in such
choice sentences **that we felt** they
were worth having, even when there
was a bit of scorn behind them.*

Dywedodd rhyw Sais, '*Dates have
more stone in them than meat.*'
Ond yr oedd yn amlwg mai dyna
ddewisfwyd Arholydd y Bwrdd
Addysg; a rhoddodd farciau da
i fwyafrif y Dosbarth **am hoffi
ohonynt** y cyfryw ymborth caregog
a di-faeth. [WILLAT 88]

*Some Englishman said, '*Dates have
more stone in them than meat.*'
But it was obvious that that was
the Board of Education Examiner's
favourite food, and he gave good
marks to the majority of the class
because they liked such stony and
unnourishing food.*

In this section we have seen a number of patterns in which a Welsh verb-noun corresponds to a finite verb in English; thus, these are cases where English style is closer to the actualised end of the scale presented earlier in which events are represented as anchored to specific moments in space and time. In the next section we will examine patterns that are even more striking examples of this difference between the two languages, in that in these cases, the Welsh patterns have no overt verb at all.

10.2 Verbless Clauses in Welsh

Welsh has a number of constructions in which the verb can be omitted entirely. This is possible in part because Welsh has the particle *yn*, one of the functions of which is to mark the predicate. Predicates can therefore be clearly identified as such even in the absence of a verb. The types of predicate that can stand alone, without benefit of a verb, generally involve nouns and adjectives, as will be seen in the illustration of the following constructions:

10.2.1   Verbless predicate noun or predicate adjective constructions
10.2.2   Impersonal constructions
10.2.3   Dyma / dyna clauses
10.2.4   Fronting focus construction
10.2.5   Relative clauses

We will discuss and illustrate each of these patterns in turn.

10.2.1 Verbless predicate noun or predicate adjective constructions[7]
In some of the cases where nouns function alone as predicates (see also Chapter 2), the English translations involve inserting a semantically appropriate verb, which varies according to the specifics of the situation: for instance, in the first example below, *bysedd* and *bodiau* ('fingers' and 'thumbs') become the verb *poking*. When the inserted verb is not part of the main predication of the sentence, it is often rendered as a participle:

Ym mhen isa'r dyffryn, tua Henberth, yr oedd niwlen wen, a honno'n drifftio i fyny'r llechweddau coediog, **yn fysedd ac yn fodiau i gyd**. [CRYMAN 18]	At the lower end of the Vale, towards Henberth, a white mist drifted up the wooded slopes, **poking into every nook and cranny.** [SICKLE 13]
Merch mewn mantell werdd, ei gwallt gwinau**'n gwmwl** am ei phen ac yn cyrlio i'w llygaid ac yn sgleinio gan y glaw. [CRYMAN 70]	A girl in a green raincoat, her brown hair **framing** her head and curling into her eyes and shining in the rain. [SICKLE 57]
Yng ngwaelod y dresel, o dan y tair drôr, yr oedd powliau o bob lliw a llun a maint. Credaf fod rhyw ugain ohonynt yno, ond safai deg ar ei gilydd a'u pennau i lawr, **pedair yn sylfaen**, tair ar ben y rheini, dwy ar	At the bottom of the dresser, below the three drawers, were bowls of every colour, shape and size. I imagine there must have been about a score of them there, but there were certainly ten symmetrically

---

[7] See also Chapter 8 which deals at greater length with adjectival patterns.

eu pen hwythau, a'r olaf un o'r deg **yn dŵr ar y cwbl**. [O LAW 220]

arranged upside down, four of them **forming a base**, three placed on top of those, two more resting on these, with the tenth bowl **forming a pinnacle** above all. [FROM 183]

In other cases, the translation of a verbless predicate into English renders it as a full adverbial clause. These generally have a temporal interpretation, and consequently the English translator adds the conjunction 'while' or 'when' as well as a finite verb:

[C]âi'r plant ddifyrrwch mawr wrth fynd i gyfarfod y Bradwyr a'r plismyn **amser caniad** gan chwythu, mor ddirgelaidd ag y gallent, drwy'r cregyn. [CHWAL 11]

Needless to say, the children took huge delight in going to meet the Traitors and their escort of constables **when the hooter sounded for work to cease**, and in booing through these shells while keeping out of sight as far as possible. [OUT 117]

Yfa di hwn **yn boeth** rwan, yngwas i. [NOS 186]

Drink this **while it's hot** now, lad. [NIGHT 159]

'Mi gei fynd i'r chwaral pan fyddi di'n dair ar ddeg a dim cynt.' 'Ond mi gafodd Dafydd fynd **yn ddeuddag oed**. [CYCHWYN 11]

'You shall go to the quarry when you are thirteen, and not before.' 'But Dafydd was allowed to go **when he was twelve**. [BEGIN 9]

I fi'n grwt bach, roedd y blaen traeth yn lle grymus, ac mae'n chwith gen i weld y ceir drewllyd 'na wedi parcio ar ei ben e. [HUNAN 26]

When I was a small boy the foreshore was a powerful place, and it saddens me to see those stinking motorcars parked on it. [SOLVA 27]

10.2.2 Impersonal constructions

Impersonal expressions are a second group of constructions that can be verbless in Welsh. Impersonal expressions are those in which the subject is non-referential *it* in English and usually *hi* in Welsh. These pronouns are non-referential because they do not actually refer to anything and are simply present as dummy subjects. In such sentences it is often possible to delete both the pronoun and the verb (e.g. *Mae hi'n* or *Roedd hi'n*) in Welsh. Significantly, such deletions do not necessarily render the example informal in Welsh. The examples below are in fact rather literary.

Constructions in which deletion of verb and dummy subject are common include the following:

(Mae'n) gystal (i rywun wneud rhywbeth) '(Someone) might as well (do something)':[8]

Cystal dechrau gyda'r Dyn Hysbys canys fe fu ef gynt yn ŵr anhepgor yn y gymdeithas Gymreig . . . [PEATCYM 84]

I might as well begin with the village wise man, for he was formerly an inevitable figure in Welsh society . . .

Let's admit that I did feel a twinge of something – of guilt, remorse, I don't know precisely what – as I watched from the window. [CIDER 67]

Cystal imi fod yn onest, wrth edrych drwy'r ffenest arni'n gadael, teimlwn rywbeth yn cnoi – euogrwydd, cydwybod, edifeirwch – wn i ddim beth yn hollol. [SEIDR 94]

Expressions of surprise taking the form *(Mae'n) rhyfedd*:

O, mae'n ddrwg gennyf eich brifo, Mrs Maciwan, ond **rhyfedd** na ddeallwch chi fod yn amhosibl inni fod yn gyfeillion [MONICA 41]

Oh, I'm sorry if I offend you, Mrs MacEwan, but **I'm surprised** that you don't understand how out of the question it is for us to be friends. [MONICA 40–1]

Ymddangosai'i ben lawer yn rhy fawr i'w gorff, ac **nid rhyfedd** iddo suddo i mewn rhwng ysgwyddau'i berchennog, gan wneud i rywun feddwl am iâr yn ei phlu. [CYCHWYN 39]

His head looked far too big for his body and **it was not surprising** that it had sunk between its owner's shoulders, making one think of a hen with its head tucked into its feathers. [BEGIN 38]

Wrth gwrs, ceir cynrhychiolydd o ysgol Gruffydd Jones ym mhob ardal yng Nghymru, a **rhyfedd** mor debyg i'w gilydd yw nodweddion pob un ohonynt. [HENAT 128]

A 'bird' of the same feather can be found everywhere in Wales, and **it is remarkable** how alike they all are. [LOCUST 111]

---

[8] This expression also appears, especially in south Walian, as *Man a man i rywun wneud rhywbeth.*

The expression of need or obligation (*Mae*) *rhaid* (or *Mae'n*) *rhaid*:

Yn awr, Alis, **rhaid iti orwedd yn ôl** a cheisio cysgu. [MONICA 7]

Now Alice, **you must lie down** and try to sleep. [MONICA 6]

. . . mae o'r un fath â thorri ceffyl, **rhaid peidio â rhoi i mewn.** [TE 75]

Just as it is when you're breaking in a horse, **you mustn't yield.** [TEA 76]

Mae Trem-y-Gorwel 'ma'n ddigon taclus gennoch chi rwan. **Rhaid inni gofio** bod genno'ni le arall i edrych ar ei ôl hefyd, **yn rhaid?** [FFENEST 37][9]

'*You have Trem-y-Gorwel looking quite tidy now.* **We need to remember** *that we have another place to look after as well,* **don't we?**'

'There are a thousand details which I should desire to know before I decide upon our course of action. Yet **we have not a moment to lose.**' [BAND 219]

'Mae yna gant a mil o fanylion y dymunwn eu cael cyn i mi benderfynu ar y cam nesaf. Ond **rhaid gweithredu ar fyrder.**' [CYLCH 29]

The construction *Mae'n well (i rywun wneud rhywbeth)* '(Someone) had better (do something)'. Unlike *cystal* above, the soft mutation often remains (at least in speech) even after the deletion of subject and verb:

Lle garw yw e. **Well i ti fod** o gwmpas dy bethe' os ei di lawr 'na. [HUNAN 78]

It's a very rough place. **You'd better be** on the alert if you go down there. [SOLVA 79]

'**Well i chi fynd** yn ych ôl rŵan, rhag ofn i rywun yn gweld ni. Mi fedrwch fynd y ffordd yma. Daliwch ar ych union a throwch ar y chwith wedi i chi ddwad i'r mynydd.' [TRAED 73]

'**It would be better for you to go** back now, in case someone see us. You can go this way. Keep straight on, and turn left when you reach the mountain.' [FEET 65]

If you're not hurt at all, **you'd better get off** to Gryffindor tower. [STONE 221]

Os nad ydych chi wedi brifo o gwbl, **well i chi ei throi hi** am Dŵr Llereurol. [MAEN 141]

---

[9] Interestingly, some Welsh vernaculars almost treat *rhaid* as though it were a verb, in having it appear in tag questions as in this particular example.

The expression *(Bu) bron i (rywun wneud rhywbeth)* meaning '(Someone) nearly (did something)' which uses *bu*, the preterite of *bod*, is frequently relieved of this verb:

'A the, mae'n debyg?' gofynnodd y forwyn.
'O, ia, te. **Bron imi anghofio'r te.**' A chafodd y ddau y peth yn ddigrif i'w ryfeddu. [CYCHWYN 199]

'Oh, yes, tea. **I nearly forgot the tea.**' And both found that wonderfully amusing. [BEGIN 201]

He nearly had his leg ripped off once, he's not going to try it again in a hurry. [STONE 328–9]

Bron i'w goes o gael ei rhwygo i ffwrdd unwaith, a fydd o ddim am roi cynnig arni eto ar frys. [MAEN 209]

Other predicate adjectives (such as *gwir* 'true', *haws* 'easier', *ofer* 'in vain', in the following examples) may occur without the expected *Mae hi'n* (or *Roedd hi'n*, etc.)

Gwir bod yr ymarfer yn peri i mi weithio'n galetach; [WILLAT 205]

It is true that the exercise made me work harder.

Eto, **haws disgrifio** llawer cydnabyddiaeth ddigon damweiniol na rhoi syniad am gyfeillgarwch felly. [CYMER 106]

And yet, it is easier to describe many a rather accidental acquaintance than to give an idea of friendship in that way.

Mae'r ffyrdd o fagu plant yn eu perthynas â'u rhieni yn sicr mor amryfal a gwahanol i'w gilydd ag yw'r rhieni a'r plant eu hunain. **Ofer ceisio** gwag athronyddu ar y pwnc yn y fan hon. [CHWECH 89]

The ways of raising children in their relationship to their parents are certainly as varied and different from each other as the parents and children themselves. It is pointless to seek empty philosophising on this subject here.

10.2.3 Dyma / dyna clauses

Clauses headed by *dyma* or *dyna* (see also Chapter 11 on Information Structure) seem to serve several purposes, including adding a certain vividness to a narration; the event so described is as though being displayed for the viewing of the hearer or reader. Quite often there is also an element of suddenness about the event so marked, whence the frequent co-occurrence of adverbs like *yn sydyn* 'suddenly'. These clauses illustrate both of our patterns, as in some cases they have a verb-noun in lieu of a finite verb. The English translation is almost always a preterite:

Ac yn sydyn hollol **dyna Winni yn gwneud peth** a brofai mai pobl yr ardal a oedd yn iawn. [TE 44]

And then, all of a sudden, **Winni does something** that shows that people were right after all. [TEA 42]

Toc **dyma ddrws y capel yn agor**, a'r golau'n taro ar wynebau'r plant nesa at y drws. [TRAED 35]

Suddenly **the door opened** and the light fell on the faces of those children nearest to it. [FEET 31]

Then suddenly **he struck** again. [MAT 38]

Yna'n sydyn **dyma fe'n taro** eto. [MAT 32]

And in other cases a *dyma / dyna* phrase may contain no verb at all:

Yr oedd dau o aelodau'r dosbarth newydd yn gerddorion llawer gwell na chyffredin. **Un diwrnod dyma'r ddau ataf**. [WILLAT 29]

Two of the members of the new class were much better musicians than usual. One day the two came up to me.

Cyn iddi gael diffiniad i'w phlesio **dyma gwestiwn arall fel bollt**. [TE 48]

But before she found a satisfactory answer, **another question was shot at her**. [TEA 45]

In another moment **down went Alice after it**, never once considering how in the world she was to get out again. [ALICE, 20]

Mewn eiliad, **dyna Alys i lawr ar ei hôl**, heb feddwl o gwbl sut yn y byd y deuai allan eto. [ALYS I 12]

. . . and **the fall was over**. [ALICE, 21]

. . . a **dyna'r codwm ar ben**. [ALYS II 10]

What fun it'll be when they ask me how I liked my walk. [THRO 149]

A **dyna hwyl** pan ofynnan' nhw imi gartref sut y daru mi fwynhau fy nhro. [TRWY 36]

Whether there is a verb-noun in the Welsh phrase, or no verb at all, the English rendering always invariably involves a finite verb.

10.2.4 Fronting focus construction
Among the constructions in which the finite verb can be completely omitted in Welsh, one finds sentences in which an adjective or a predicate noun is fronted, or moved to the head of the clause, for the purpose of making it

a focus (see Chapter 11 for further discussion of information structure). In such cases, the adjective or noun suffices as a predicate in Welsh, and the expected verb can be omitted. This can be found in main clauses as well as in subordinate clauses. In the latter case, the particle *mai* is present to mark the clause as being a focused one:

Mor rhwydd a diymdrech ei eiriau! [CYCHWYN 222]	**How fluently and effortlessly** his words **came!** [BEGIN 224]
Dywedid **mai anodd cael ei ail** mewn cinio. [CWM 187]	He was a famous trencherman . . . [GORSE 179] [lit. It is said that **it is difficult** to find his peer at a lunch]
A gwyddai fel y darllenai ymlaen **mai gwir y gair**. [CHWAL 135]	And as he read on he knew **that this was true**. [OUT 142]
Casglwn iddo bendrymu a gofidio tros gyflwr ei iechyd ers dyddiau, ac **mai mawr eu rhyddhad** o'i weld yn llonni fel hyn. [O LAW 154]	I gathered that he had been moping and grieving over his ill-health for many a day and **that they were immensely relieved** at seeing him so unusually cheerful. [FROM 123]

It is perhaps most commonly found in negative sentences, after *nid* in main clauses or *nad* in subordinate clauses.

Fel y dywedais, prin iawn oedd ei eiriau, **ond nid segur ei feddwl o bell ffordd**. [DYDD 92]	*As I have said, his words were few but **his mind was by no means idle**.*
Oherwydd **nid hawdd** gwneuthur llawer o sŵn ar lawr pridd. [CWM 181]	. . . **it is not easy** to make much noise on an earthen floor. [GORSE 172]
Methodd â'm hadnabod; ac **nid syn hynny**, oherwydd y mae gwahaniaeth go fawr ar y gorau rhwng dyn yn un ar hugain oed ac o fewn dim i'w hanner cant. [CHWECH 187]	*He did not recognise me, and **that is not surprising**, for there is a rather big difference between a man who is twenty-one years old and one who is just a hair away from fifty.*

Predicate nouns can participate in the same construction:

Nid dynion gwellt mo bobl Cwm Eithin. [CWM 187]	The men of Cwm Eithin **were** no men of straw; [GORSE 178]

Ganwaith y dywedodd wrtho'i hun mai stynt oedd hyn gan Sali, a chanwaith y dywedodd rhywbeth wrtho **nad stynt mohono o gwbl**. [CRYMAN 98]

He told himself a hundred times that this was one of Sally's stunts, and each time something told him that **it wasn't a stunt at all**. [SICKLE 80]

... Dyffryn Ardudwy, Castell Harlech, Glas Ynys, Maen Orfferen, Penrhyn Deudraeth, a'u henwau i gyd yn farddoniaeth i mi, a llawer lle arall **nad gwiw dechrau eu nodi**. [CHWECH 223]

*... Dyffryn Ardudwy, Castell Harlech, Glas Ynys, Maen Orfferen, Penrhyn Deudraeth: all of their names were poetry to me, and many other places **that there is no point in mentioning**.*

Finally, a fronted element after *os* 'if' can suffice as a predicate with no overt verb:

'Hwda, tywallt hwn'na drwy'r ffenast' i'r ardd. **Os ffisig, ffisig amdani**, a hwnnw'n rhy chwerw i'w lyncu bron, nid rhyw lemonêd o ddiod fel'na.' [CYCHWYN 146]

'Here, take it and pour it out of the window into the garden. **If it's to be physic, then physic it must be**, and too bitter to swallow, almost; not some lemonade of a drink like that.' [BEGIN 147]

Ei dâl, **os tâl o gwbl**, fyddai ambell hanner cwarter o dybaco Ringers, gwerth saith ceiniog yr adeg honno. [CHWECH 39–40]

*His pay, **if there was any pay at all**, was a half quarter of Ringers tobacco, worth seven pence at that time.*

Yn rhyfedd, efallai, **os rhyfedd, hefyd**, o'i nabod yn dda, clywais ei gysylltu ef, yn aml, â'r hen Dom Cilwennau Isa, Jehu arall ymysg y calchwyr ... [HDF 171]

Strange to say, **if on better understanding it be strange at all**, I heard him being coupled with old Tom Cilwennau Isa, another Jehu among the lime-carrying men ... [OFH 215]

Ac mewn gwlad gomiwnyddol ei waith oedd pleser pob dyn, **os gwir y sôn**. [CRYMAN 101]

In a Communist society every man's work was his pleasure, **if what he'd heard was to be believed**. [SICKLE 83]

Ond **os dilewyrch fy maboed** yn yr ysgol, cefais fywyd brenhinaidd pan oeddwn yn rhydd oddi wrthi. [HENAT 105]

But **if my boyhood days were grey and drab** in school, I had a glorious time out of it. [LOCUST 92]

... **os da fy nghof** ... [CYMER 30]

*... **if memory serves** ...*

The above examples of *os* plus adjective reveal clearly how the English translators turned these clauses into complete finite clauses by adding an inflected verb and any other words necessary to form a complete and natural English sentence.

In the directional particle construction (PARTICLE â SUBJECT NP [ADV]), a directional particle (*i mewn* 'in', *allan* 'out', *yn ôl* 'back' etc.) is fronted, and the phrase is verbless in Welsh but must be translated into English with a verb, though there are two possible patterns for rendering it in English. The first has the particle preposed (PARTICLE + SUBJECT + VERB):

'I think I may as well go in at once.' And **in she went**. [ALICE 76]	'Waeth imi fynd i mewn ar unwaith.' **Ac i mewn â hi**. [ALYS II 75]
In another moment **down went Alice after it**, never once considering how in the the world she was to get out again. [ALICE 20]	Eiliad arall, ac **i lawr ag Alys ar ei hôl**, heb feddwl o gwbl sut yn y byd mawr y dôi hi allan eto. [ALYS II 8]

And the second English pattern maintains canonical word order (SUBJECT + VERB + PARTICLE):

A merched – peidiwch â sôn – yn bolaheulo mewn bicinis ar y gwellt! **I lawr** â **ni ling-di-long** yn ysgyfala a chodi sgwrs â nhw. [HUNAN 119]	And there were girls alright, sunbathing in bathing costumes on the grass! Nonchalantly, **we strolled down** and engaged them in conversation. [SOLVA 119]
Yna, **ymlaen ag ef** gyda hanes y teulu, eu hachau a'u cysylltiadau a phob rhyw gamp arnynt. [CYMER 110]	*Then **he went on** with the story of the family, their roots and connections and every one of their feats.*
They sped up a staircase to the third floor and tiptoed toward the trophy room. [STONE 192–3]	**I fyny grisiau** â nhw i'r trydydd llawr, ac yna ar flaenau'u traed i'r ystafell dlysau. [MAEN 124]
Immediately after lunch, **she dashed off** to the kitchen . . . [MAT 140]	Yn syth ar ôl cinio, **i ffwrdd â hi** ar wib i'r gegin . . . [MAT 134]

10.2.5 Nonfinite relative clauses and relative clause-like noun complements

An alternative way of handling negative relative clauses in Welsh uses the prepositional construction *heb fod*, literally 'without being', in place of the more usual finite relative clause pattern (e.g. *nad yw* 'that is not', *nad ydynt* 'that are not'). Thus, the first example below, *dyn heb fod yn rhy ifanc* 'one who's not too young' could also be expressed as *dyn nad yw'n rhy ifanc* (or, in the colloquial spoken language, *dyn sy ddim yn rhy ifanc*).

Mi fydd arnyn'hw eisie dyn **heb fod yn rhy ifanc** am na fydde gan un felly ddim profiad, a dyn **heb fod yn rhy hen** am na fydde gan un felly ddim egni. [LLEIFIOR 146-7]	They'll be wanting one **who's not too young** so that he'll have some experience and **not too old** so that he'll have plenty of energy left. [RETURN 125]
Roedd e ar ei flwyddyn derfynol yn stiwdio beintio Malthouse, ond **heb fod yn tynnu mlaen 'da'r tiwtoried o gwbwl.** [HUNAN 110]	He was in his final year at Malthouse's painting studio, **and he was not getting on with the tutors at all.** [SOLVA 110]
. . . a golwg **heb fod yn annhebyg i Albert Einstein** arno fe . . . [HUNAN 128]	. . . who, **looking rather like Albert Einstein** . . . [SOLVA 127]
Tref fach ddiflas oedd Amwythig, **heb fod hanner mor fywiog â Henffordd** dafliad carreg lawr yr hewl. [HUNAN 128]	Shrewsbury was a boring little border town, **not half as lively as Hereford** [SOLVA 128]
'Machgen i,' meddai, 'mae dau fath o gwrw – cwrw da a chwrw **heb fod cystal**, ond 'd oes dim cwrw sâl.' [HENAT 52]	'My lad,' said he, 'there are two kinds of beer – good beer, and beer **not quite so good**; but there is no such thing as bad beer.' [LOCUST 49]
She had a considerable sum of money, **not less than a thousand a year**, and this she bequeathed to Dr Roylott entirely . . . [BAND 212]	Roedd hi'n berchen ar swm sylweddol o arian – ei werth **heb' fod yn llai na mil o bunnau'r flwyddyn** – ac ewyllysiodd y swm hwnnw yn ei gyfanrwydd i Dr Roylott . . . [CYLCH 18]
He found a shirt and a pair of trousers **that didn't reek of tobacco** . . . [KNOTS 84]	Daeth o hyd i grys a throwsus **heb fod yn drewi o faco** . . . [CHWERW 72]

The collection of examples above reveals that the English translations are varied. Sometimes the construction is rendered as a complete relative clause in English (as in the first two examples), and sometimes as a conjoined main clause (cf. the third example 'and he was not getting on. . .') or yet as a reduced relative clause (cf. the fourth example: 'and beer not quite so good', compare the possible rendering 'and beer *which was* not quite so good', using a full relative clause).

Welsh has several additional kinds of prepositional phrase constructions that serve as noun complements, and in this way they are similar to relative clauses except that they lack any verb at all. The first pattern makes use of the preposition *gan*, but in the inflected literary forms which follow the conjunction *a* 'and': *a chanddo / a chanddi / a chanddynt*:

Aeth allan i'r storm drachefn **a chanddo bellach reswm newydd dros fyw**. [LLEIFIOR 48]	He now went out into the night. **He now had a new reason for living**. [RETURN 40] [lit. and with him now a new reason for living. . .]
Dynes fawr, lawen, ffraeth, dreiddgar, oedd fy modryb Marged, **a chanddi** ŵr bychan tanllyd a diddan. [HENAT 34]	Auntie Margaret was large of body, happy, ready of speech and keen of perception, **with a peppery and amusing little husband**. [LOCUST 35] [lit. and with her a short, fiery husband]
Before leaving his office he had telephoned Dr Stuchley. A man **with a pleasant and friendly voice**, there had been . . . [TIME 50]	Roedd wedi ffonio Dr Stuchley cyn iddo adael ei swyddfa, dyn **a chanddo** lais hawddgar, cyfeillgar . . . [AMSER 79] [lit. and with him an easygoing, friendly voice]

The second pattern uses the preposition *i* instead, i.e. *ac iddo / ac iddi / ac iddynt*:

Of all these varied cases, however, I cannot recall any **which presented more singular features** than that which was associated with the well-known Surrey family of the Roylotts of Stoke Moran. [BAND 207]	O'r holl achosion amrywiol hyn, fodd bynnag, fedra i ddim meddal am unrhyw un **ac iddo fwy o nodweddion unigryw** na hwnnw oedd yn gysylltiedig â theulu adnabyddus y Roylotts o Stoke Moran yn Swydd Surrey. [CYLCH 11]

It was a homely little room, **with a low ceiling** and a gaping fireplace, after the fashion of old country houses. [BAND 227]	Y stafell fechan ddigon cartrefol oedd honno, **ac iddi nenfwd isel** a lle tân agored fel a geid mewn hen dai gwledig. [CYLCH 40]
She made her way first to the east side of the cottage. Here, discreetly set back and almost smothered by the hedge, was a wooden privy **with its latched stable-like door.** [UNSUIT 42]	Cerddodd yn gyntaf i ochr ddwyreiniol y bwthyn ac yma, ynghudd ynghanol y drysi, darganfu dŷ bach **ac iddo ddrws stabl pren.** [GORTYN 54]
And into the clearing came – was it a man, or a horse? To the waist, a man, with red hair and a beard, but below that was a horse's gleaming chestnut body **with a long, reddish tail.** [STONE 312]	Ac i'r llannerch daeth – ai dyn oedd o, neu geffyl? Uwchben y gwasg, dyn barfog, gwalltgoch ydoedd, ond islaw roedd corff ceffyl lliw castan disglair, **ac iddo gynffon hir, gochlyd.** [MAEN 200]

The difference between the two prepositional patterns appears to be that the *gan* pattern is preferred when the referent is human, and the *i* pattern when it is inanimate (*achosion* 'cases', *ystafell fechan* 'a small room', *tŷ bach* 'a privy'), or at least non-human (*ceffyl* 'a horse').

10.3 Absolute Clauses

In the context of Welsh grammar, an absolute clause is a type of non-finite clause consisting of a noun or pronoun and one or more modifiers, which together have the function of modifying an independent clause. As a kind of modifier, the absolute clause is never obligatory – the independent clause being modified is always a complete utterance in and of itself, not needing the absolute clause to complete it. Absolute clauses are much more common in Welsh than in English. The typical Welsh absolute clause takes one of the following two forms:

a(c) + SUBJECT NOUN PHRASE / PRONOUN + yn + PREDICATE NOUN
OR ADJECTIVE

a(c) + SUBJECT NOUN PHRASE / PRONOUN + ASPECTUAL PARTICLE +
VERB-NOUN

Both patterns contain the following shared elements: the first word is 'and': *a* before a consonant (causing aspirate mutation) and *ac* before a vowel. The second word is the grammatical subject of the absolute clause, which can be either a full noun phrase or a pronoun. In the case of a pronoun, it is nearly always a conjunctive pronoun drawn from the set *minnau (finnau), tithau, yntau, hithau, ninnau, chithau, nhwthau.*[10] The remaining two elements distinguish the two absolute clause patterns. In the first, or verbless, pattern, the predicate is a noun or an adjective, preceded by the predicate marker *yn* and, crucially, no verb. In the second or verb-noun pattern, the predicate is a non-finite verb (i.e. a verb-noun), which is preceded by one of the aspectual particles (*yn, wedi, heb, ar fin, newydd. . .*) Crucially, one of the things that the two patterns have in common is that they do not contain any finite verb.

It is possible though fairly uncommon to translate a Welsh absolute clause by an equivalent absolute clause in English. Usually the English equivalent will contain a present participle or a past participle. We see these kinds of translation in the two examples below. First, the verbless example from *Cysgod y Cryman* shows that the English translator has added a semantically appropriate verb ('smeared'), since some verb is necessary in the English clause:

Prin deirblwydd oed, **a'i fochau'n gymysgedd amryliw o laid a jam.** [CRYMAN 33]

He was scarcely three years old, **his cheeks smeared with dirt and jam.** [SICKLE 25]

The next example shows a verb-noun absolute clause using the aspectual particle *wedi*. The appropriate English equivalent is then, naturally, a perfect participial form ('having put'):

Having put in an early bid for a computer crime check on car wheels reported stolen since the year's beginning, he had checked through the print-out flimsy delivered to him. [TIME 44]

Ac yntau **wedi gyrru archeb gynnar am archwiliad troseddau cyfrifiadurol i olwynion ceir gafodd eu dwyn ers dechrau'r flwyddyn,** cafodd gyfle i fynd drwy'r daflen brintiedig a ddanfonwyd ato. [AMSER 69]

---

[10] Very occasionally a simple pronoun can be found in an absolute clause:

Tua phum mlynedd ar hugain ar ôl hyn **a mi wedi ymddeol o fod yn Athro yn Aberystwyth,** safwn ar blatfform stesion Bangor yn disgwyl trên; [WILLAT 191]

About twenty-five years after this, **and I** *having retired from my professorship in* **Aberystwyth,** *I stood on the station platform in Bangor waiting for a train*

But this is much less frequent than using a conjunctive pronoun.

Another common way to translate Welsh absolute clauses makes use of the preposition 'with', and which may or may not contain a (participial) verb form; indeed, 'with'-clauses are considered a kind of absolute clause by some (Stump 1985). Semantically, we suggest that the function of 'with'-absolute clauses is to provide an accompanying circumstance:

Roedd yna tua dwsin o ddynion wedi dwad yno **a hitha'n ola leuad braf** . . . [NOS 34]	About a dozen men had turned up **with it being a fine moonlit night** . . . [NIGHT 26]
Wrth yrru tuag adref, **a'r haul diwedd blwyddyn eisoes yn isel uwchben y coed noethion i'r gorllewin**, meddyliodd Harri eto am y wefr a aeth drwyddo yn y gwasanaeth. [LLEIFIOR 109]	As they drove, **with the wintry sun already over the bare trees to the west**, Harri brought to mind the sensation he'd felt during the funeral service. [RETURN 92]
Fore'r Sul dilynol, aeth gyda Paul i'r eglwys yn ôl ei harfer. Ond gyda'r nos, **a Paul eto heb ddod yn ôl o chwarae golff**, cymerodd fws i'r ddinas ac aeth i'r capel. [LLEIFIOR 27]	The following Sunday morning, she went with Paul to church as usual. But in the evening, **with Paul not yet back from playing golf**, she took a bus into town and went to the chapel. [RETURN 21]
Pan ddôi yno ffarmwr i nôl rhywbeth o'r siop gwahoddid ef i'r gegin gefn, ac yno câi de o'r blasusaf, a wics cyrans Margiad Williams **a 'menyn tew arnynt**. [WILLAT 135]	*When a farmer would come to fetch something from the shop he would be invited into the back kitchen and served some of the tastiest tea, and Marged Williams's currant rolls* **with thick butter on them.**
Howling with pain, the troll twisted and flailed its club, **with Harry clinging on for dear life**. [STONE 218]	Gan udo mewn poen, trodd yr ellyll gan ffustio'i bastwn, **a Harri'n crafangio arno am ei fywyd**. [MAEN 139]

Much more commonly, Welsh absolute clauses are not translated as absolute clauses in English but by other kinds of construction. One common solution is to translate the absolute clause by a relative clause, which, by definition, involves adding a finite verb as well as a relative pronoun ('which', 'whom', 'that', 'whose', 'where', etc.):

... yn y chwarel, pan gâi gerrig da **a'r rhai hynny'n hollti fel aur,** ac yntau'n chwipio gwaith trwy ei ddwylo dan ganu ... [TRAED 90]

So it was in the quarry when he had good stones **which split cleanly and easily;** he would sing as the work skimmed through his hands ... [FEET 81]

... gŵr ifanc hynod dduwiolfrydig yn ôl y dystiolaeth amdano, **a'i feddwl ar bregethu'r efengyl.** [HDF 51]

... a godly young man, to go by everyone's testimony, **whose intention was to preach the Gospel.** [OFH 60]

Wedi dod i Abernant, **a'r hewl fawr yn mynd heibio i fwlch y clos,** 'r oedd yn rhaid bod yn fwy gofalus. [HDF 133]

After coming to Abernant, **where the main road went past the fold gate,** he had to be more careful. [OFH 166]

Yr olaf oll oedd yr hen Ifan Pant y Crwys, **a'i blant ieuengaf yn yr ysgol yr un pryd â mi** – a Ianto, hir ei ên, brychlyd ei wyneb, a'i gap a chlustiau yr un ffunud â'i dad, ac yn llawn mor ddoniol, yn yr un dosbarth â mi. [HDF 146]

The last was old Ifan Pant y Crwys, **whose youngest children were in school with me,** and Ianto was in my class, long-chinned and freckled and wearing a cap with ear-flaps to it, the image of his father and equally humorous. [OFH 182]

Dyn bychan, tew oedd y Doctor, a barf fel un bwch gafr ar ei ên, **a honno, fel ei wallt tenau, yn britho'n gyflym.** [CYCHWYN 39]

The doctor was a small, corpulent man with a goatee beard **which, like his scanty hair, was fast turning grey.** [BEGIN 38]

... she was hard at work on the white kitten, **which was lying quite still and trying to purr** [THRO 127]

... roedd hi'n brysur ar y gath fach wen, **a honno'n gorwedd yn berffaith llonydd gan geisio grwnan** [TRWY 13]

Malfoy's eagle owl was always bringing him packages of sweets from home, **which he opened gloatingly at the Slytherin table.** [STONE 179]

Roedd tylluan eryr Mallwyd byth a hefyd yn dod â phecynnau o fferins iddo o'i gartre, **ac yntau'n gwneud sioe o'u hagor wrth fwrdd Slafennog.** [MAEN 114]

To me, it's completely explicable that if she had heard of it – and there's no reason why she shouldn't have if she's still somewhere locally – then

Os oedd hi wedi clywed amdano – a does dim rheswm pam na ddylai hi fod wedi gwneud os ydi hi'n dal i fod yn rhywle lleol – yna mi fyddai

she would find it difficult to refer to a man she had been living with **and about whom she must presume I knew nothing.** [TIME 90]

hi'n ei chael hi'n anodd cyfeirio at ddyn yr oedd hi wedi bod yn byw efo fo, **a hithau'n cymryd yn ganiataol na wyddwn i ddim am y peth.** [AMSER 143]

Another common solution is to translate the Welsh absolute clause as a conjoined ('and') clause. Given the importance and frequency of this kind of translation, we give a number of examples below:

Cofiaf fod y gwrychoedd yn llawn blagur **a'r llygaid-y-dydd yn garpedi gwynion** ar rai o'r caeau. [O LAW 140]

I remember that the hedges were in full bud **and that the daisies had spread** white carpets over some of the fields. [FROM 111]

Yr oedd ei freuddwyd yn ffaith, **a'r ffaith yn talu.** [LLEIFIOR 35]

His dream had become fact, **and the fact was paying off.** [RETURN 28]

Roeddan ni'n gorffan u bwyta nhw dest cyn cyrraedd Rysgol **a'r cloc yn taro naw.** [NOS 7]

We were just finishing eating them as we got to School **and the clock was striking nine.** [NIGHT 1]

Un noson, ym mis Ionawr 1893, yr oedd cyfarfod y plant yn y capel, **a'r pedwar plentyn yno.** [TRAED 31]

One evening in January 1893 there was a children's meeting at the chapel **and the four children were there.** [FEET 28]

Yr oedd y noson hon yn noson loergan leuad, **a phopeth wedi rhewi dan draed.** [TRAED 31]

It was a clear moonlit night **and everything underfoot was frozen.** [FEET 28]

Yr oedd fy chwaer Edith, a oedd tua dwy ar bymtheg oed, yn wael, **a'r meddyg newydd ddywedyd wrth fy mam nad oedd obaith iddi wella o'i chlefyd.** [HENAT 54]

My seventeen-year old sister, Edith, was desperately ill, **and the doctor had just told my mother there was no hope of recovery.** [LOCUST 51]

Un noson yr oedd yn boeth annioddefol **a Ned yn sychedig iawn.** [HENAT 125]

One evening it was unbearably hot **and Ned was very thirsty.** [LOCUST 108]

Codai cyrn yr hen blasty bach rhyngddo a'r awyr, **a dwy o'i res ffenestri'n felyn olau.** [CRYMAN 226]

The chimneys of the old grange rose into the sky **and two of its rows of windows had lights in them.** [SICKLE 187]

Instead of a conjoined clause using 'and', the English equivalent may involve a juxtaposed clause, punctuated either as a brand new sentence, or as a complete sentence but set off with a semi-colon:

Doedd dim troi'n ôl i fod **ac yntau ar waith y Goron.** [PLA 311]

Nevertheless he must do his duty: **he was an agent of the Crown.** [PEST 185]

Disgynnodd din-ben-dros-ben ar lawr yr eglwys gadeiriol **a'i Arabeg clasurol yn diasbedain saethau bwaog hyd y nenfwd uchel.** [PLA 95]

Salah erupted from the tomb, and fell head over heels. **Classical Arabic rang from the corners of the church** . . . [PEST 73]

'Y *palio*?' Edrychodd yn hurt arni. 'Y rasus ceffyla. Un o uchafbwyntiau'r flwyddyn draw yn Siena. Dwi'n synnu nad ydach chi 'di clywad am y palio, **a channoedd o bobl Fflorens yn tyrru yno bob tymor.'** [PLA 71]

'The *palio*?' Salah was mystified. 'The horse race at Siena. I'm surprised you hadn't heard about it. **Lots of travellers go on there from Florence.'** [PEST 54]

Roedd hi run fath yn union â chodi o-farw-fyw pan ddeffrois i hefyd, **a finna'n methu dallt ble'r oeddwn i.** [NOS 63]

It was just like being raised from the dead when I woke up, too. **I didn't have a clue where I was.** [NIGHT 51]

. . . yn y chwarel, pan gâi gerrig da a'r rhai hynny'n hollti fel aur, **ac yntau'n chwipio gwaith trwy ei ddwylo dan ganu** . . . [TRAED 90]

So it was in the quarry when he had good stones which split cleanly and easily; **he would sing as the work skimmed through his hands** . . . [FEET 81]

Yn ddeuoedd y codwyd y tai newydd, **a phob dau yn dwt a chryno megis un tŷ o faint gweddol.** [MONICA 7]

The new houses were semi-detached; **each pair, neat and compact, would have made a fair-sized house.** [MONICA 5]

Yr oedd wrthi'n sgwrio'r trywsus melfaréd o'r dŵr cyntaf, **a'r dŵr yn sucio allan ohono o flaen y brws yn llwyd ac yn dew.** [TRAED 12]

She was scrubbing the corduroy trousers after the first washing; **the water squeezed out was thick and grey.** [FEET 11]

Sometimes the sense of the absolute clause is that it functions as a concessive clause. This is seen clearly in the English equivalents, which generally have an overt concessive conjunction ('though', 'although', 'even though', 'even when' or 'but'):

'Mi'r ydw i yn licio Winni.' 'A hitha wedi dy chwipio di a byta dy fwyd di?' [TE 49]

'I like her.' '**Although** she ate your food and struck you?' [TEA 47]

Mi fuo Ifan yn fab iddi ac yn dad i'r plant yna, a'r rhan fwya o'r rheini'n ddigon tebol i wneud llawn cimint ag yntau. [TRAED 21]

Ifan was a son to her and a father to the children, **even though** most of them were old enough to fend for themselves. [FEET 18]

Roedd blas bara sych Ficrej yn well na brechdan Nain a honno'n dew o fenyn. [NOS 23–4]

The taste of the Vicarage's dry bread was better than Gran's bread and butter, **even when** that was thick with butter. [NIGHT 16]

Peth cynta welais i pan agorais i fy llgada a deffro bora wedyn oedd pry cop ar ffenast to yn treio diengyd allan trwy ffenast, a honno wedi cau. [NOS 181]

The first thing I saw when I woke up and opened my eyes next morning was a spider on the skylight trying to get out through the window, **but** it was closed. [NIGHT 154]

Reminding him of Nanoushka, it seemed forthrightly aphrodisiacal, **though** that reaction need only be his admitted susceptibility to a perfume. [TIME 22]

Roedd yn ei atgoffa o Nanoushka, yn ei gynhyrfu ac yntau'n sglyfaeth barod i unrhyw bersawr ar y gorau. [AMSER 33]

Similarly, the Welsh absolute clause may have a temporal value; the English equivalent will generally include an appropriate adverb ('as', 'when', 'while') making this manifest:

Do wir, meddwn inna, **a'r lle'n fwg i gyd** o gwmpas gwynab Wmffra. [NOS 69]

Yes, really, I said **as the smoke swirled around Humphrey's face.** [NIGHT 56]

Bu Begw yn ddistaw am dipyn, yn synfyfyrio i'r grât **a'i mam yn trwsio ffustion**. [TE 47]

Begw kept quiet for a while, staring into the grate **while her mother mended a pair of corduroy trousers.** [TEA 45]

Cofiai am fore Llun yn niwedd Gorffennaf **a'r ysgol newydd dorri** ac yntau'n fawr ei siom am na châi fynd i'r chwarel. [CYCHWYN 11]

He remembered a Monday morning at the end of July **when the school had just broken up**, and his bitter disappointment at not being allowed to start work in the quarry. [BEGIN 9]

Ni fyddai'n golygu fawr iddo ystyried ei theimladau hi am ddim ond un noson, **a hithau yn ei gofid.** [LLEIFIOR 19]

It wouldn't have been too much to consider her feelings just for one night, **when she was still grieving.** [RETURN 14]

Ond yn fynych, fynych, **a hithau'n ddyfal wrth ei gwaith**, heb feddwl fod neb yn gwrando, fe'i clywn hi'n llafarganu ei gweddiau a'i myfyrdodau mewn ymson leddf . . . [HDF 115]

But very often **when she was busy at her work**, without dreaming that anyone was listening, I would hear her chanting her prayers and meditations in a plaintive and imploring monologue . . . [OFH 142]

. . . and she tried to curtsey as she spoke – fancy *curtseying* **as you're falling through the air!** [ALICE, 21]

A cheisiodd wneud cyrtsi wrth ofyn – meddyliwch am wneud *cyrtsi* **a chithau'n syrthio trwy'r awyr!** [ALYS II 10]

Looking at him **as he arranged himself in the visitor's chair** . . . [TIME 88]

Wrth edrych arno **ac yntau'n trefnu ei hun yn ei gadair** . . . [AMSER 139]

'Well, it's no use *your* talking about waking him,' said Tweedledum, **'when you're only one of the things in his dream**. You know very well you're not real.' [THRO 167]

'Wel, waeth i *chi* heb siarad ynghylch ei ddeffro,' ebe Twidl-dwm, **'â chithau'n ddim ond un o'r pethau yn ei freuddwyd**. Fe wyddoch yn dda nad ydych chi ddim yn real.' [TRWY 55][11]

Finally, the Welsh absolute clause may function as a kind of condition clause (see the inclusion of 'if' in the English translation of the first example below) or as a kind of reason clause ('since', 'for', 'because'):

---

[11] This example appears to show the preposition *â* instead of the conjunction *a*. It is probably best seen as a typo, but nonetheless one that is encountered fairly often.

Cyn dod i'r tŷ, **a'r hin yn fwyn**, tynnai fwgyn yn y fan honno yn ei chwrcwd myfyrgar uwchben ei deheuwaith. [HDF 108]	Before she returned to the house, **if the weather was mild**, she took a smoke of her pipe out there, squatting meditatively beside her handiwork. [OFH 132]
Ond 'does dim eisio arian, **a finna wedi ennill**. [TRAED 42]	But it will cost nothing **since I've won the scholarship**. [FEET 38]
Actually, he was surprised at his own inspired guess that Webber might be involved **for, so far as he remembered, he had never been suspected or convicted of breaking offences**. [TIME 94–5]	Fodd bynnag, roedd wedi'i synnu gan ei ysbrydoliaeth yn dyfalu bod gan Llywelyn ran yn yr achos, **a hwnnw heb ei amau na'i ddedfrydu erioed o droseddau'n ymwneud â thorri i mewn**. [AMSER 150]
Because he's visited Holland on several occasions it's possible he's involved in the smuggling end of it. [TIME 68]	Mae'n bosib fod gynno fo fys yn y smyglo **a fynta wedi ymweld â'r Iseldiroedd sawl tro**. [AMSER 108]

Absolute clauses are very frequent in Welsh style and also polyvalent in their uses, as seen in the above discussion. They contribute significantly to the overall impression that Welsh style is highly deactualised by comparison with English.

10.4 Summary and Conclusions

To recap some of the points raised in this chapter, let us consider two examples. First, the following passage from *Through the Looking Glass* and its translation:

So she brushed away her tears, and went on, as cheerfully as she could, 'At any rate I'd better be getting out of the wood, for really it's coming on very dark. Do you think it's going to rain?' [THRO 168]

Felly, ysgubodd ymaith ei dagrau, a mynd ymlaen mor llawen ag a allai, 'Sut bynnag, well imi fynd allan o'r goedwig oherwydd, yn wir, mae hi'n mynd yn dywyll iawn. Ydych chi'n meddwl ei bod hi am law?' [TRWY 56]

The English text contains nine verb forms. These are separated out in the lefthand column of the chart below, with the Welsh translations in the centre column. Finally, in the righthand column, the translation is commented on with respect to whether the Welsh translation maintains the same level of actualisation as the English original, or prefers a deactualised form. (In none of the nine instances does Welsh go in the opposite direction of preferring a higher level of actualisation than the English).

So **(1) she brushed** away her tears,	Felly, **(1)** **ysgubodd** ymaith ei dagrau,	Preterite in both languages: Equivalent level of actualisation
and **(2) went on**, as cheerfully	a **(2) mynd** **ymlaen** mor llawen	Deactualisation: the sequential use of inflected verbs in English turns all but the first into a verb-noun in Welsh
as **(3) she could**, 'At any rate	ag a **(3) allai**, 'Sut bynnag,	Inflected conditional in both languages: Equivalent level of actualisation
(4) I'd better	**(4) well** imi	Deactualisation: the Welsh verb *Mae'n* can be deleted in numerous impersonal expressions, as here.
(5) be getting out of the wood, for really	**(5) fynd allan** o'r goedwig oherwydd, yn wir,	Deactualisation: the English progressive infinitive *be getting* is reduced to a simple verb-noun, *mynd*
(6) it's coming on very dark	**(6) mae hi'n mynd** yn dywyll iawn.	Deactualisation: English progressive verb forms in *-ing* are more actualised than Welsh verb-nouns.
(7) Do you think	**(7) Ydych chi'n meddwl**	Equivalent level of actualisation
(8) it's going	**(8) ei bod hi**	Deactualisation: subordinate English present progressive becomes Welsh *bod* clause, in which marks of finiteness are suppressed.

(9) to rain?'	(9) am law?'	Deactualisation: the English infinitive *to rain* becomes the noun *rain*.

We see that of the nine verb forms in this passage, only three (instances [1], [3] and [7]) maintain the same level of actualisation as the English original. In the other six cases, the Welsh translation involves one or another level of deactualisation.

Let us take one more example, this time going from a Welsh original to an English translation:

Ymddangosai'i ben lawer yn rhy fawr i'w gorff, ac nid rhyfedd iddo suddo i mewn rhwng ysgwyddau'i berchennog, gan wneud i rywun feddwl am iâr yn ei phlu. [CYCHWYN 39]

His head looked far too big for his body and it was not surprising that it had sunk between its owner's shoulders, making one think of a hen with its head tucked into its feathers. [BEGIN 38]

Here there are four verb forms in the Welsh text and six in the English translation. These are presented separately, with a commentary, in the table below.

(1) **Ymddangosai**'i ben lawer yn rhy fawr i'w gorff,	His head (1) **looked** far too big for his body	Equivalent level of actualisation
ac (2) nid rhyfedd	and (2) **it was** not surprising	Increased actualisation: impersonal verbless expression in Welsh, to which a finite verb is added in English
(3) iddo **suddo** i mewn rhwng ysgwyddau'i berchennog,	that (3) it **had sunk** between its owner's shoulders,	Increased actualisation: a verb-noun is translated with a finite (pluperfect) form
gan (4) **wneud**	(4) **making**	Increased actualisation: a verb-noun becomes a present participle
(5) i rywun **feddwl**	(5) **one think**	Equivalent level of actualisation: verb-noun in Welsh and infinitive in English

| (6) am iâr yn ei phlu. | of a hen with (6) its head **tucked** into its feathers. | Increased actualisation: verbless phrase in Welsh becomes complete finite clause in English. |

Of the six verb forms in the English translation, two represent the addition of finite verbs that were not present in the Welsh original (instances [2] and [6]); two more represent increases in actualisation in that a Welsh verb-noun is rendered with a more actualised verb form in English (instances [3] and [4]). Only two of the six represent equivalent levels of actualisation in both languages ([1] and [5]).

Although of course not every passage would present a divergence between the two languages as striking as these two examples do, it is nonetheless clear that these passages are in no way unusual; the correspondences they illustrate are all abundantly documented in the translation corpus.

This does not mean that no counterexamples are ever encountered. One does indeed occasionally run across examples like the following, in which a Welsh passage has greater actualisation than the English translation:

Yr oedd tua phump a deugain, ond gwnâi ei wallt golau a'i lygaid gleision, direidus, iddo ymddangos lawer yn ieuangach. [CYCHWYN 19]	**About forty-five years of age**, his fair hair and mischievous blue eyes made him look far younger. [BEGIN 17]
Yr oedd y casglu drosodd, a rhoes emyn allan. [CYCHWYN 124]	**The collection over**, he gave out a hymn. [BEGIN 124]
'R oedd yno leisiau da, a **chafwyd hwyl anghyffredin** ar ganu'r pennill cyntaf a roddwyd ma's gan yr arweinydd . . . [HDF 92]	There were good voices there, and the first verse given out was sung **with great fervour**. [OFH 112]
'How are your ears, Eric, **after your last encounter** with Miss Trunchbull?' [MAT 215]	'Sut mae dy glustiau di, Eric, **ar ôl i ti gyfarfod** â Miss Trunchbull y tro diwethaf? [MAT 209]

In the first three examples above, a Welsh finite clause is translated verblessly into English, and in the fourth example, a Welsh prepositional clause deploying a verb-noun is translated by a nominalisation in English. However, such examples are striking for their infrequency. Whereas it is easy to find examples like the earlier passages from *Through the Looking Glass* and

The Beginning, one must search for some time to collect even a small number of examples like these four.

It is interesting to note finally that in a few cases, a translator has opted to maintain certain aspects of the Welsh style. In the examples below, Welsh absolute clauses were translated literally into English, thus with no finite verb:

Y Gwir amdani oedd nad trio neidio'r ceunant yr oedd, ond fe'i hyrddiwyd bron trosodd gan y twr bechgyn cryf a ddeuai ar ei ôl **ag yntau'n fychan**. [TRAED 33]	The fact was that he hadn't wished to jump the gully, but he had been almost flung over by the crowd of hefty lads coming behind him, **and he such a small boy**. [FEET 30]
'Peth rhyfedd iawn na fasa'r Scŵl wedi 'i goleuo hi ar y peth, **a fynta *yn* Scŵl**," meddai Edwart. [TRAED 102]	'It's a wonder that he didn't point that out to her, **and he a schoolmaster**,' said Edward. [FEET 91]
"Dydi Kate Idris ddim yma,' meddai Gwyn. **'A hitha'n mynd i gâl babi** yn reit fuan? Nac ydi, debyg iawn.' [CHWAL 60]	'Kate Idris isn't here,' Gwyn remarked. **'And her going to have a baby** very soon? No, of course she isn't.' [OUT 62]

Although the results are undoubtedly possible in certain kinds of English, they are much less typical of English than of Welsh, which is precisely why these translations are successful in conveying the impression that the characters are in fact speaking Welsh.

11

Information structure: Topic and focus

11.0 Introduction

Many of the linguistic choices speakers make while communicating reflect their beliefs about what their addressee already knows, and what he or she does not yet know. This, in itself, is not surprising. People rarely utter completely new pieces of information out of the blue in a way that is totally disconnected from things going on around them or matters of shared interest and attention. More often, the information a speaker delivers is intended to further an addressee's knowledge about someone or something that is of shared interest to both parties. Thus, most messages can be thought of as containing a TOPIC (the element of shared attention which the rest of the message is 'about') and a COMMENT (the informative part of the message that the speaker assumes the hearer does not yet know).

The field of INFORMATION STRUCTURE (henceforth IS) is the study of the kinds of strategies whose purpose is to enable speakers to package information according to their beliefs and expectations about what knowledge is shared with their addressees and what parts of the message represent new information. Different languages do not all use the same linguistic strategies to accomplish these goals. Some strategies are syntactic, involving word order choices, while others make use of particular intonation patterns, or even certain kinds of lexical choices. The skillful and appropriate use of such strategies facilitates successful communication, whereas inappropriate use of them can confuse listeners as to what the message is supposed to be.

We begin with a simple example. Imagine a situation in which the following sentence is overheard:

Prynodd rhyw wraig y crys glas ddoe.
'Some woman bought the blue shirt yesterday.'

We can safely conclude the following things: the speaker believes that the person he is addressing does not know which woman is being referred to;

she is almost certainly being mentioned in the conversation for the first time. Additionally, the hearer *is* believed to know which shirt was bought; we know that either the shirt was already referred to, or perhaps that it is present now in plain sight. These inferences can be made based on the choice of determiners in each case: *rhyw* *wraig* but *y crys glas*. *Rhyw* serves to introduce a new referent whose identity is not yet established in the discourse (as would the absence of an article, equivalent to an indefinite article in English), whereas the definite article in *y crys glas* serves to mark a noun whose referent is identifiable to both speaker and addressee. In other words, the blue shirt ('y crys glas') is represented as part of the COMMON GROUND shared by speaker and hearer. We can say that it is PRESUPPOSED.

This sentence can be compared to the following one:

Prynodd hi grys glas ddoe.
'She bought a blue shirt yesterday.'

Here we would draw exactly the opposite conclusions: the hearer *is* expected to know what woman is being referred to, but is *not* expected to know which shirt is being spoken about. The use of a pronoun like *hi* 'she' can only communicate successfully if one's addressees know to which entity in the discourse it refers. The identity of this woman is part of the common ground shared by both participants in the conversation.[1] Specifically, in our terms, she is the TOPIC of the above sentence, the purpose of which is, in large part, to tell us something about her: namely, what she did. The thing that she did (buy a shirt) is the 'new' information. It represents the informative part of the sentence which is generally called the FOCUS in the linguistic literature.

The kinds of linguistic choices illustrated so far are fairly basic examples of IS, involving the filling of a given slot in a sentence with one form instead of another (a definite article instead of an indefinite, or a pronoun instead of a noun phrase). There are more complex syntactic strategies that serve related functions which we will examine in this chapter.

Crucially for present purposes, the strategies deployed in two different languages may be quite similar, but they may also be very different. To illustrate this point, we reproduce below a group of examples from one of the

[1] Note that this does not mean that speaker or addressee necessarily know the woman personally; it means only that both participants understand the pronoun as a reference to a woman who has already been introduced into the discourse, and thus that both are able to connect the pronoun to the appropriate referent *in the discourse* - not necessarily in the real world.

classic works on IS, Lambrecht (1996), which discussed the following English examples:

a. (What did the children do next?) *The children / They* went to SCHOOL.
b. (Who went to school?) The CHILDREN went *to school.*
c. (What happened?) The CHILDREN went to SCHOOL.

The words in italics in these examples represent the old or presupposed information. Old information is backgrounded, made less prominent in the intonation, and often reduced in some way, as for instance reducing *the children* to the pronoun *they* in (a). On the other hand, the words in small caps contain what Lambrecht calls the FOCUS ACCENT, a particular intonation making those words stand out, marking them as the informative part of the sentence.

Let us compare these three English sentences to their Welsh equivalents below:

a. (Beth wnaeth y plant wedyn?) Aeth *y plant* / Aethon *nhw* i'r YSGOL.
b. (Pwy aeth i'r ysgol?) Y PLANT aeth *i'r ysgol.*
c. (Beth ddigwyddodd?) Aeth y PLANT i'r YSGOL.

In the English and Welsh (a) sentences, which function as the answer to the question 'What did the children do next? / Beth wnaeth y plant wedyn?', the noun phrase *the children / y plant* can readily be identified as the topic; the answer is 'about' the children, serving to add to the store of information that the addressee knows about them. What follows the topic (*went to school / aeth . . . i'r ysgol*) is the new information, the truly informative part of the answer which it can be assumed that the questioner did not already know (because if she had, she would not normally have asked this question). In this fairly straightforward and very common pattern, the topic coincides with the grammatical subject of the sentence, and the focus coincides with the predicate. In fact, Lambrecht (1996: 136) claims that such sentences represent the most common IS pattern in human language. The English and Welsh versions of (a) have essentially the same IS analysis (i.e. the order topic-comment), though expressed in conformity with each language's usual word order: subject-verb-object (SVO) in English, and verb-subject-object (VSO) in Welsh.[2]

---

[2] In Lambrecht's work, the location of the verb is not particularly relevant; it is the locations of the noun phrases serving as verbal arguments that determine the IS of the sentence.

In the (b) examples, the facts about which elements represent the pre-supposed information and which represent the new information are quite different. Here, the grammatical subject (*the children* / *y plant*) is now the informative or new part of the message, specifically answering the question *Who?* / *Pwy?*, whereas the predicate represents presupposed information: both participants in the exchange know that someone went to school: the purpose of the exchange is to establish who did so. English normally signals this pattern only by changing the intonation so that the subject now receives the focus accent. In Welsh, this strategy is sometimes used as well, as in the following:

(Pwy aeth i'r ysgol?) Aeth Y PLANT *i'r ysgol.*

However, a very different strategy is more usual in Welsh, namely moving the subject from post-verbal to preverbal position. Indeed, we will see that in Welsh the preverbal position is available as a site to move any sentence element that one wants to put in focus.

In the (c) examples, the answer to the question 'What happened?' does not have a topic (in the relevant sense) – the entire answer is new or informative.[3] Therefore, the focus accent is spread over both of the noun phrases (Y PLANT and I'R YSGOL).

In the space of one chapter we will not be able to offer an exhaustive analysis of Welsh IS.[4] What we wish to do is examine the main strategies that recur frequently enough to be of certain interest and relevance to the student of Welsh translation and stylistics.

By way of introduction, we propose the following model text from the Welsh novel *O Law i Law* by T. Rowland Hughes. This passage contains examples of several key phenomena that will be discussed in what follows. Each sentence (or, when relevant to the discussion, each clause) is numbered for easy reference in the discussion that follows.

[1]Galwodd Llew Hughes yn gynnar gyda'r nos ar ei ffordd adref o'r stesion.

[1-2]Llew Hughes called early on in the evening on his way home from the Railway Station, where he is employed as a clerk.

---

[3] In Lambrecht's theory of IS, every sentence must have a focus, but not every sentence has a topic. That is, not every sentence contains presupposed information. In the (c) examples it is entirely possible that neither the children nor the school were ever mentioned in the discourse preceding this exchange.

[4] For more information, see (among others): Morris Jones and Alan R. Thomas 1977. *The Welsh Language – studies in its syntax and semantics.* University of Wales Press for the Schools Council.

²Clerc yn yr orsaf yw Llew, ³ac ef sy'n canu'r organ yn y capel. ⁴Y mae'n fachgen byw ei feddwl ac yn ddarllenwr mawr. ⁵'Yr hen lyfra 'na,' medd ei fam, gweddw unig y bu Llew yn gefn iddi ers blynyddoedd bellach, a'i gorfu i wisgo sbectol ac a wnaeth ei wyneb mor llwyd a thenau. ⁶Llew yw ysgrifennydd dosbarth y WEA hefyd, ⁷a heb ei ynni ef prin y byddai dosbarth felly yn yr ardal. ⁸Ef, beth bynnag, a'm perswadiodd i ymuno ag ef ac i gymryd rhyw ddiddordeb mewn llenyddiaeth Gymraeg.

³⁻⁴Llew, our organist in the chapel, is a quick-witted lad and a voracious reader. ⁵According to his mother, a lonely widow whom he has supported for years, it is 'those old books' that are to blame for his having to wear glasses, and for his pallid, pinched face. ⁶He is also secretary of the local WEA Class, ⁷the very existence of which is in no small measure due to his energy and zeal. ⁸It was he, at any rate, who persuaded me to join the class and take an interest in Welsh literature.

⁹John Ellis, gweinidog yr Annibynnwyr yn Llaneithin, pentref ryw bum milltir i ffwrdd, yw'r athro, ¹⁰ac yn wir, y mae'n ŵr galluog a brwdfrydig iawn.¹¹Trueni na fuasai dosbarth fel hwn pan oedd f'Ewythr Huw yn fyw; ¹²gwn y mwynhâi ef bob eiliad ohono. ¹³Go lastwraidd ydym ni yn y dosbarth, y mae arnaf ofn; ¹⁴rhyw ddwsin sy'n mwynhau'r ddarlith a'r ymgom ar ei hôl ac yna'n troi adref i anghofio popeth a ddysgodd Mr Ellis inni. [O LAW 176]

⁹⁻¹⁰John Ellis, Congregational Minister at Llaneithin, a village some five miles distant, and a most able, enthusiastic man, is our teacher. ¹¹It's a pity that no class of this nature existed when Uncle Huw was alive; ¹²I know he would have fervently enjoyed every moment of it. ¹³⁻¹⁴As it is, I fear the dozen or so of us in the class are rather a tepid lot, who enjoy the lecture and the discussion that follows and then go home and promptly forget all Mr Ellis's teaching. [FROM 142]

The chapter will be organised around the discussion of three broad patterns: (1) the canonical topic-comment sentence (e.g. ¹*Galwodd Llew Hughes yn gynnar gyda'r nos* 'Llew Hughes called early on in the evening'); (2) the cleft sentence (e.g. ⁵*Yr hen lyfra 'na . . . a'i gorfu i wisgo sbectol* 'it is "those old books" that are to blame for his having to wear glasses'); (3) the identificational sentence (e.g. ²*Clerc yn yr orsaf yw Llew* 'Llew is a clerk at the station').

In the following section we will discuss each of these patterns in turn. The chapter will close with a discussion of intonation as a focusing strategy.

11.1 The three main patterns in Welsh information structure

11.1.1 The topic-comment sentence

We mentioned at the beginning of this chapter that, according to Lambrecht (1996), the IS pattern TOPIC-COMMENT, in which the topic coincides with the grammatical subject and the comment (or focus) coincides with the predicate, is the most common IS pattern in the languages of the world. Welsh is certainly no exception to this claim. There are, however, some language-specific facts to note, ways in which Welsh and English differ from each other even within this common pattern, as we will see in this section.

Let us look at the first few lines of our model text above. This portion is repeated below, with English translations that are somewhat more literal than those of the published translation given above:

¹GALWODD LLEW HUGHES YN GYNNAR GYDA'R NOS AR EI FFORDD ADREF O'R STESION.

¹Llew Hughes called early on in the evening on his way home from the Railway Station.

²Clerc yn yr orsaf yw Llew, ³ac ef sy'n canu'r organ yn y capel.

¹Llew is a clerk in the station, ³and he it is who plays the organ in the chapel.

⁴Y MAE'N FACHGEN BYW EI FEDDWL AC YN DDARLLENWR MAWR.

⁴He is a quick-witted lad and a voracious reader.

The first and fourth clauses (the ones in small caps) are topic-comment sentences. This text begins a new chapter in the novel. It is a common narrative technique in novels to bring the reader into a story that is already going on, as it were, and thus to present new discourse referents as though they were already familiar to the reader. The first sentence in this text works this way, using Llew Hughes as a topic as though readers already knew who he was.

The second and third sentences, which function almost like a parenthetical (*Clerc yn yr orsaf yw Llew, ac ef sy'n canu'r organ yn y capel.*), provide the missing information about who this character is; we will come back to this portion below, in the discussion of the identificational sentence. Then the fourth sentence picks up where the first one left off, using Llew as a canonical topic. In literary registers, as is the case in the narrated portions of *O Law i Law*, subject pronouns can be left out – so the topic in the sentence *Y mae'n fachgen byw ei feddwl* '[He] is a quick-witted lad' is the subject that is not overtly expressed (though it would be in English). In informal Welsh, on the other hand, the topic would normally be referenced with a pronoun, as in English.

Skipping for now over sentence 5 (a cleft sentence, to which we will return below), we come to the following lines:

[6]**Llew** yw ysgrifennydd dosbarth y WEA hefyd, [7]a heb ei ynni ef prin y byddai **dosbarth** felly yn yr ardal.	[6]He is also secretary of the local WEA Class, [7]the very existence of which is in no small measure due to his energy and zeal.

Here we have the introduction of a new referent, the *dosbarth* or class. As is commonly the case, it is brought in as part of the new information (the comment) in the sentence *Llew yw ysgrifennydd dosbarth y WEA* Once a referent has been introduced, it is available for use as a topic in what follows, and that is precisely what we find in the seventh sentence (*a heb ei ynni ef prin y byddai dosbarth felly yn yr ardal*), where *dosbarth* is now the grammatical subject and the IS topic.

The same pattern, namely introducing a new referent as part of the comment, only to pick up this referent as a topic for some part of the ensuing discourse, is found again just a couple sentences later:

[11]Trueni na fuasai dosbarth fel hwn pan oedd f'Ewythr Huw yn fyw; [12]gwn y mwynhâi ef bob eiliad ohono. [13]Go lastwraidd ydym ni yn y dosbarth, y mae arnaf ofn . . .	[11]It's a pity that no class of this nature existed when Uncle Huw was alive; [12]I know he would have fervently enjoyed every moment of it. [13]As it is, I fear the dozen or so of us in the class are rather a tepid lot . . .

Dosbarth is picked back up as the topic of sentence 11; the comment introduces a new referent, the narrator's Uncle Huw. Uncle Huw is now available to be used as a topic, and we see this happen in the following sentence, where this new topic takes its prototypical form as a pronoun ([12]*gwn y mwynhâi ef bob eiliad ohono*). After that, the topic shifts back to *dosbarth* – or more specifically, to the dozen or so students in the class, which is another way of referring to the class.

These examples have illustrated the way in which discourse referents generally are not used as topics upon their first mention. Rather, they are introduced as part of the new information, or as part of an adverbial clause of some kind. Once so introduced, they are thereafter available for use as a topic if a speaker wants to say something more about them.

It happens that Welsh has a specific strategy for shifting to a pronominal topic; in this case, English does not have a comparable strategy. Consider the following examples from a variety of texts:

Croesodd yn ei hôl ac aeth i siop y groser. Cyfarchodd **yntau** hi'n gynnes, gan ysgwyd llaw a rhoi cadair iddi eistedd. [BYW 46]

She crossed back and went to the grocer's. **He** greeted her warmly, shaking her hand. [AWAKENING 46]

Canodd gloch ar ei ddesg a daeth geneth ieuanc i mewn. Gofynnodd **yntau** iddi ddyfod â dwy gwpanaid o de i mewn heddiw yn lle un. [BYW 62]

He rang the bell on his desk and a young girl came in. **He** asked her to bring in two cups of tea that day, instead of one. Then he reached for a plate of cakes and put them on the table. [AWAKENING 62]

. . . troes Ifan olwg hanner ymbilgar, hanner ymddiheurol ar ei wraig. Meddyliai **hithau** mor dda yr edrychai yn ei siwt briodas. [TRAED 10]

. . . he gave his wife a half-pleading, half-apologetic look. **She** thought how handsome he was in his wedding suit. [FEET 9]

Cododd docynnau. Dilynodd **hithau** lamp drydan y porthor hyd onid ymsuddodd hi yn un o seti plwsh y cinema. [MONICA 16]

He bought tickets. **She** followed the usher's torch until she was settled into one of the cinema's plush seats. [MONICA 15]

She drank from her glass again and **he** looked at his wristwatch. [TIME 110]

Yfodd eto o'r gwydr ac edrychodd **yntau** ar ei wats. [AMSER 175]

Harry watched Hagrid getting redder and redder in the face as he called for more wine, finally kissing Professor McGonagall on the cheek, who, to Harry's amazement, giggled and blushed, her top hat lopsided. [STONE 252]

Gwyliodd Harri wyneb Hagrid yn cochi mwy bob munud wrth iddo alw am fwy o win, gan gusanu boch yr Athro McGonagal. Er mawr syndod i Harri, gwridodd **hithau** a dechrau piffian chwerthin, ei het silc wedi syrthio i un ochr. [MAEN 160]

In all of the above cases, there is a clause whose subject is a conjunctive pronoun (i.e. one drawn from the set *minnau/finnau, tithau, yntau, hithau, ninnau, chwithau, nhwthau*). Welsh grammars have routinely found it difficult to characterise the function of the conjunctive pronouns in uses like these. Grammars usually describe their function as being about 'emphasis' and 'contrast'. But clearly no particular emphasis is involved in any of the above cases. As for contrast, some of these uses might be described as contrastive, but only in the limited sense that in each case what we have is a switch to a new topic (which is, in all of these cases, also the grammatical subject of its clause, as is so often the case with topics). Some of these examples could (marginally) be read as contrastive topics: for instance, *Cododd docynnau. Dilynodd hithau lamp drydan y porthor* could be rendered 'He bought tickets. **As for her**, she followed the usher's torch . . .' But the most straightforward way to characterise the very frequent use of conjunctive pronouns seen in the above set of examples is to describe them in terms of topic shift.[5] In some cases the topic is a new one, picking up a referent previously introduced in a comment, as with *yntau* in the first example that refers back to *y groser*. In other cases the conjunctive pronoun shifts back to an earlier topic, as in the second example above: the businessman at his desk is the topic (and subject of *canodd gloch* '[he] rang a bell'), after which we have a temporary shift to a new topic (*daeth geneth ieuanc i mewn*), followed by a switch back to the businessman, marked clearly with *yntau*. In no sense is *yntau* emphatic here; its use is simply about topic shifting, as a way to signal to the reader that the referent functioning as topic and grammatical subject is different from the immediately preceding clause.[6]

11.1.2 The Cleft sentence

The English cleft sentence is a pattern in which what would normally be a single clause is turned into a biclausal sentence as a way of explicitly marking a portion of the sentence as a focus. The most common cleft pattern in English is the *It*-cleft:

It was in 1960 that he bought the big house.
It was his father who stopped him from studying law.

Neutral versions of these sentences would be monoclausal (*He bought the big house in 1960; His father stopped him from studying law*). The analogous Welsh pattern (variously called the 'mixed' sentence [THORNE §352], Fronting [PWT §6.125], the Emphatic Sentence/Brawddeg Bwyslais, or the Focus construction [Borsley, Tallerman and Willis 2007]) is no longer transparently biclausal in Modern Welsh; the verb form (or copula) which corresponded to the 'it is' or 'it was' of the English cleft formerly found in this construction has

---

[5] Rottet, Kevin J. 2011. 'Conjunctive pronouns in Modern Welsh: A preliminary corpus-based study.' In K. Jaskuła (ed.) *Formal and Historical Approaches to Celtic Languages*, special issue of *Lublin Studies in Celtic Languages* volume 7: 233–53. Lublin: Wydawnictwo KUL.
[6] Topic shifting is thus one of the two main uses of conjunctive pronouns, the other being their use in absolute clauses (for which, see Chapter 10). Other uses of these pronouns are described in Chapter 2.

ceased to be used.[7] What remains is a pattern in which some constituent of the sentence has been moved to the front of the sentence, or 'fronted', creating a sentence that departs from the usual VSO pattern.

Various kinds of constituents can be fronted in Welsh. Most commonly fronted are pronouns or full noun phrases, and our model passage has several examples of this:

... [3]ac **ef** sy'n canu'r organ yn y capel.	[3]Llew [*is*] our organist in the chapel ...
[5]'**Yr hen lyfra'na**,' medd ei fam, gweddw unig y bu Llew yn gefn iddi ers blynyddoedd bellach, **a'i gorfu i wisgo sbectol** ac a wnaeth ei wyneb mor llwyd a thenau.	[5]it is 'those old books' that are to blame for his having to wear glasses, and for his pallid, pinched face.
[8]**Ef, beth bynnag, a'm perswadiodd** i ymuno ag ef ac i gymryd rhyw ddiddordeb mewn llenyddiaeth Gymraeg.	[8]It was he, at any rate, who persuaded me to join the class and take an interest in Welsh literature.

When used for focus, the Welsh pattern is often equivalent to an English cleft sentence, as we see in model sentences five and eight above and their published translations.[8] Other examples of NP-fronting confirm this common equivalence. Note also that the particle *a* which occurs when the fronted constituent is the subject or the direct object (*a'i gorfu*, *a'm perswadiodd*) can be omitted, especially in speech or less formal writing:

Jane fach, yr iengaf o'r plant oedd yno, ac yn llefain 'i chalon hi. [HDF 92]	**It was little Jane, the youngest**, weeping her heart out. [OFH 112]

[7] The copula took the form *ys* in main clauses (e.g. *Ys mi a'r heirch* 'It's me who seeks her', example quoted from *The White Book Mabinogion* by Tallerman 1996: 102), and variously *mai* or *taw* in subordinate clauses. The main-clause copula *ys* fell out of use in the Middle Welsh period, whereas the subordinate forms *mai* [=*mae*] / *taw* are still generally used today, though they have been reanalysed as complementisers (conjunctions) and are no longer thought of as verb forms. This is seen as well in the respelling of *mae* in this use as *mai*.

[8] Tallerman (1996) notes that the construction has to some extent also taken over the topicalising functions of a Middle Welsh pattern called the abnormal sentence. This is arguably what we see in the first example (*ac ef sy'n canu'r organ yn y capel*).

My luck held, because **it was Barbara who** came out of the farmhouse, alerted by the noise. [CIDER 31]

Roedd lwc o'm plaid, **Barbara** ddaeth allan o'r ffermdy i'n cyfarfod. [SEIDR 44]

Meri a gwynai fwyaf am y ci. [WILLIAM 156]

It was Mary who complained most about the dog. [WILLIAM 124]

When the fronting takes place in an embedded clause, the particle takes the form *mai* (or *taw* in southern dialects):

'Mi redais i lawr rhag ofn bod Mam wedi bod yn gas wrthoch chi.' 'Mae arna i ofn **mai fi** fuo'n gas wrth 'ych mam,' meddai Jane. [TRAED 16]

'I ran down in case Mother had been nasty to you.' 'I'm afraid **I was the one** to be nasty,' said Jane. [FEET 14]

We note in passing a northern dialect version of these clefts, where the auxiliary *ddaru* may be used in this construction. *Ddaru* is not limited to cleft sentences, though it seems particularly likely in them (we return to *ddaru* later on):[9]

'**Gwraig Madog Morris** ddaru'i bedyddio hi, a 'chafodd llong erioed y fath "Hwrê!" ag a gafodd y *Maid*.' [CHWAL 118]

The wife of Madoc Morris christened her, and no ship ever got such a big "Hooray!" as the Maid did. [OUT 124]

'I couldn't help it,' said Five in a sulky tone. '**Seven** jogged my elbow.' [ALICE 77]

'Doedd gen i mo'r help,' ebe Pump yn bwdus. '**Saith** ddaru daro 'mhenelin i.' [ALYS II 76]

'You say **it was a woman** who called you?' [KNOTS 170]

'Ddwedaist ti **mai merch** ddaru dy ffônio di?' [CHWERW 145]

Occasionally a Welsh focus construction may have a contextual English equivalent that is not a cleft but rather some other construction, such as focus intonation. Focus intonation may not be indicated at all in writing (as in 'the wife of Madoc Morris' above), but it can also be suggested by the use of italics:

---

[9] See also Chapter 5 on the various periphrastic preterite constructions.

And I'd bet my broomstick *he* let that troll in, to make a diversion! [STONE 227]	A fetia i f'ysgub mai *fo* ollyngodd yr ellyll yna i mewn – er mwyn tynnu sylw pawb! [MAEN 144]

Fronted NPs or pronouns are most often grammatical subjects, as in all of the preceding examples, but a direct object may also be fronted:

Cofier **nad rhyw socs byrion** a wisgid yr oes honno, 'sanau yn cyrraedd dros y pen glin, yn mesur o flaen y troed i'r top yn agos i dair troedfedd. [CWM 12]	It should be remembered that **it was not short socks** that were worn at that time but stockings that came over the knee, measuring nearly three feet from top to toe. [GORSE 15]
Er **mai Saesneg y siaradai ef yn yr ysgol**, ni chlywais i sôn am y Welsh Not, sef y gosb am siarad Cymraeg. [CWM 193]	Although **he invariably spoke English in the school**, I never heard of the *Welsh Not*, the usual punishment for speaking Welsh, while in that school. [GORSE 186]

In addition to NPs and pronouns, the other constituents that can be fronted include adjectives and adverbs, prepositional phrases, verb phrases, and even entire clauses:

[13]**Go lastwraidd** ydym ni yn y dosbarth, y mae arnaf ofn . . .	[13]As it is, I fear the dozen or so of us in the class are **rather a tepid lot** . . .
Nid ar y mynydd y bydd trampars yn hel cardod, Mrs Huws. [TE 37]	Tramps don't go begging **up on the mountain**. [TEA 37]
'Fyddwn i byth wedi gadal o 'newis fy hun.' 'Cael eich gorfodi ddaru chi 'te.' [RHANNU 130]	*'I would never have left by choice.'* *'So you were compelled then.'*
Gwenodd yn ddiflas gan ystyried **mai tra sgubai hi lofftydd** y ffurfiwyd pob penderfyniad o dipyn bwys yn ei hanes. [MONICA 49]	She smiled wryly as the thought occurred to her that **it was while sweeping out bedrooms** she had made every decision of any consequence in her life. [MONICA 49]

The English equivalents are not necessarily clefts in these cases. It is not particularly common to cleft adjective phrases in English:

Bechan oedd yr ardd oedd tu cefn i'r tŷ... [GWEN 3]

The garden at the back of the house was **small**... [GWEN 10]

Cas gennyf, yn grwt, ydoedd dweud fy adnod ar goedd yn y capel... a **digon tolciog** yr awn trwyddi'n fynych. [HDF 101]

As a boy I hated saying my verse publicly in chapel... I often went through it **haltingly**. [OFH 123]

With prepositional phrases a cleft is possible in English, though less common than in Welsh. Thus, the example from *Hen Dŷ Ffarm* below is translated with an English cleft, but the example from *Te yn y Grug* is not:

Syn yw meddwl **mai i Benrhiw lethrog ei gaeau,** ar wahân i'r dolydd ar y gwaelod, y daeth y peiriant torri gwair cyntaf i'r cymdogaethau hyn, yr hen 'Bamford' drom ei chocasau. [HDF 82]

It seems strange that **it was to Penrhiw, whose fields had such steep slopes,** all except the meadows at the bottom, that the mowing machine first came to these parts, the old heavy-cogged Bamford. [OFH 99]

Cawsant ganiatâd i fynd yn bennoeth gan **mai i'r mynydd** yr aent, a'u rubanau gwallt fel ieir bach yr ha' ar ochr eu pennau. [TE 37]

They were allowed to go without hats, as they were only going **up the mountain,** and their hair ribbons were like little butterflies at the side of their heads. [TEA 37]

The fact that clefting of constituents such as prepositional phrases is so common and so typical of Welsh, and relatively unusual in English, means that this feature has sometimes been used in the English dialogue of published translations to convey the sense that the characters were speaking Welsh. Richard Ruck, the translator of T. Rowland Hughes's novels, often maintained such clefts and even other features to create a very Welsh-sounding English:

Mae'na lond Llechfaen o blismyn, ac **yn y Rhinws** y byddi di os codi di dwrw. [CHWAL 23]

Llechfaen is full of p'licemen, and **it's in the lock-up** you'll be if you make a row. [OUT 23]

Commonly fronted elements in Welsh include verbs, but inflected verbs are never fronted; this can only be done with verb-nouns. We note that when

a verb-noun is fronted, the predicate particle *yn* is deleted, and there must
be a finite verb in the base sentence (the non-fronted part) which bears the
necessary inflection:

Ond **sôn** a fynnwn i amdani fel un arall o'r gwehelyth a ddôi'n achlysurol i aeafu ym Mhenrhiw. [HDF 107]	... but I wanted **to speak** of her as one of the kindred coming occasionally to winter in Penrhiw. [OFH 131]
Trigo yr ydwyf yma – cysgu, gweithio, a bwyta – ac nid byw. [HENAT 8]	Here I simply **reside** – sleeping, working and eating. I do not *live* here. [LOCUST 14]
Cysgu oedd hi pan ddois i allan. [NOS 184]	She was **asleep** when I came out. [NIGHT 156] [lit. She was **sleeping**...]

If the verb is transitive, its complements must be fronted along with it, so that
the verb phrase remains together:

Gwyrodd uwchben y gwely a daliodd ei fys i fyny. 'Dilyn di 'mys i efo 'th lygaid, ond paid â symud dy ben ... Hm ... Hm ... 'Fedra' i ddim deud yn iawn tan 'fory, ond yr ydw' i'n meddwl **mai codi bwganod yr wyt ti.'** [CYCHWYN 40]	He bent over the bed and held up a finger. 'Follow my finger with your eyes, but don't move your head ... Hm... Hm... I can't say for certain until tomorrow, but **I think you're imagining things.'** [BEGIN 39]
Wedi bod yn gweld 'i ysgol newydd y mae o – mi fydd yn sgŵl-mastar yrŵan welwch chi. [WILLAT 85]	*He's been to see his new school – he'll schoolmaster now, you see.*
'Anyway, I know Malfoy's always going on about how good he is at Quidditch, but I bet **that's all talk.'** [STONE 177–8]	'Beth bynnag, wn i fod Dreigo'n brolio mor wych ydi o am chwarae Quidditch, ond fetia i **mai malu awyr mae o.'** [MAEN 113]

The final group of examples shows the result of fronting when the fronted verb
would otherwise have been inflected in the preterite. It can only be fronted
as a verb-noun, of course, but an auxiliary verb needs to step in to bear the
tense-mood-aspect and person features. In the Welsh preterite, this auxiliary
can variously be *gwneud*, or, in northern dialect, *ddaru*:

Mynd i'r gwely wnes i, ar ôl
ffaelu dod i gysylltiad â'r meddyg,
a dihuno i gael y tŷ ar dân.
[HUNAN 270]

After failing to get in touch with
the doctor I **just** went to bed.
[SOLVA 270]

Gwenu'n dywyll a wnaeth hi, a
dweud . . . [FFENEST 27]

She smiled darkly, and said . . .

'**Symud i borfa frasach** 'nath o, ia?'
[RHANNU 311]

*He moved to broader pastures, did
he?*

'**Cael ei ladd** ddaru o?' [CAER 82]

Did he get killed?

'**Bradychu'i Grist** ddaru Judas,
Grace.' [RHANNU 127]

Judas betrayed his Christ, Grace.

The last thing to note before closing this section on clefts is a variation on
the cleft sentence in which the presentative word *dyma* or *dyna* precedes the
clefted element. The semantics of this pattern can be quite varied, as revealed
in the different English translation equivalents in the small collection of
examples given below. The presentative word can precede a NP (causing soft
mutation of the first word of the latter):

'**What a bunch of nauseating little
warts** you are.' [MAT 141]

'**Dyna griw o benbyliaid bach
cyfoglyd** ydych chi.' [MAT 135]

Such a sweet soft voice it had!
[THRO 157]

Dyna lais tawel melys oedd ganddo!
[TRWY 45]

Dyma or *dyna* can itself function as a kind of demonstrative pronoun:

Mewn gwirionedd clywsai er y
bore, a **dyna** a ddaeth â hi i'r dref.
[TRAED 49]

In fact she had heard early that
morning, for **it was that** that had
brought her to town. [FEET 44]

'Do you call **that** a whisper?' cried
the poor King, jumping up and
shaking himself. [TRWY 198]

'**Dyna** 'dych chi'n ei alw'n sibrwd?'
gwaeddodd y Brenin druan gan
neidio i fyny a'i ysgwyd ei hun.
[TRWY 89]

Don't I tell you? [THRO 197] [lit.
That's what I'm telling you].

Dyna rwy'n ei ddweud wrthoch chi.
[TRWY 88]

Finally the presentative word may precede an adjective:

A **dyna braf** fasa hi wedyn cael codi o-farw-fyw Dy Sul Pasg run fath â Iesu Grist . . . [NOS 63]	And it would be **great** afterwards to be raised from the dead on Easter Sunday just like Jesus . . . [NIGHT 51]
How funny it'll seem to come out among the people that walk with their heads downwards! [ALICE, 21]	**Dyna od** fydd dyfod allan ymhlith pobl sy'n cerdded â'u pennau i lawr! [ALYS I 13]
The forest was **black and silent**. [STONE 312]	**Dyna ddu a thawel** oedd y Goedwig. [MAEN 199]

In several instances the construction is used as a kind of exclamation: *What a . . .!* or *Such a . . .!* before a noun, and *How . . .!* before an adjective. But glosses like these are not necessarily always used even when they would be possible. For instance, the quote from the Welsh novel *Un Nos Ola Leuad* above (*A dyna braf fasa hi wedyn . . .*) could have been rendered as the exclamative 'How great it would be then. . ', but the translator has opted for a simple declarative English equivalent: 'And it would be great afterwards. . ?[10]

In the next section we turn to the third major IS-related sentence pattern, the identificational sentence.

11.1.3 Identificational (equational) sentences

A copular or equational sentence is one in which a given entity is identified either as being a member of a category, e.g. *My brother is a doctor*, or as being referentially identical to another term, e.g. *Louis XIV was the King of France*. The two nouns phrases (NPs) in an equational sentence are joined using a copula (normally the verb *bod / to be*). In the former case, the most common pattern in English has a definite NP (marked as such with a proper name, a definite article, a demonstrative, or a possessive) on the left-hand side of the equation, and an indefinite NP on the right which names a category to which the definite NP belongs. Typical examples include the following:

Fido	is	a big dog.
Sarah and Molly	are	teachers.
The man next door	is	a doctor.
These books	are	Welsh novels.
That	is	a German car.
My brother	is	a socialist.

---

[10] Other uses of *dyma/dyna* are discussed in Chapter 10.

In terms of IS, such English sentences are fairly straightforward: the NP on the left, construed as the grammatical subject of the sentence, is the topic, while the NP to the right of the copula is the predicate, representing the new information or focus.

In the most common Welsh equivalent for such a sentence the order of the two NPs is reversed, so that the predicate comes first. Typical Welsh translations for the above sentences are as follows:

Ci mawr	yw	Fido.[11]
Athrawesau	yw	Sara a Molly.
Meddyg	yw	'r dyn drws nesa.
Nofelau Cymraeg	yw	'r llyfrau hyn.
Car Almaenig	yw	hwnna.
Sosialydd	yw	fy mrawd.

Mirroring the English order of the two NPs results in ungrammatical Welsh (*Fido yw ci mawr) and mirroring the Welsh order in English results at least in strangeness (??A big dog is Fido).

The following examples (the first from the model text, and the remainder from our parallel corpus) illustrate this very common pattern. The relevant copula is in SMALL CAPS in each example below:

²Clerc yn yr orsaf YW Llew.

²Llew IS a clerk in the Station.

Dyn bychan, tew OEDD y Doctor, a barf fel un bwch gafr ar ei ên, a honno, fel ei wallt tenau, yn brithro'n gyflym. [CYCHWYN 39]

The doctor WAS a small, corpulent man with a goatee beard which, like his scanty hair, was fast turning grey. [BEGIN 38]

Blynyddoedd go anodd i 'nhadcu yn Llywele FU 1835–8. [HDF 51]

1835–8 WERE difficult years for my grandfather in Llywele. [OFH 60]

Un o Fôn OEDD y gŵr . . . [WILLAT 213]

The husband was from Anglesey.

The village school for younger children WAS a bleak brick building called Crunchem Hall Primary School. [MAT 66]

Adeilad brics llwm o'r enw Ysgol Gynradd Crunchem Hall OEDD ysgol y pentref i blant iau. [MAT 60]

---

[11] The copula generally appears as ydy in north Wales.

An equational sentence is a common way of saying where a person is from in Welsh, as seen in the last example above (literally, '*The husband* WAS *one from Anglesey.*')

The definite NP may just be a pronoun, including a demonstrative such as *hon* (e.g. *Stori arswyd . . . oedd hon.* 'This was a horror story.') or *hwnnw* 'that (one)', or a subject pronoun (*nhw* 'they', etc.):

Merch fechan eiddil yr olwg ond prydferth fel dol OEDD hi . . . [CHWAL 74]	Small and frail-looking, she WAS a girl with a doll-like beauty . . . [OUT 77]
Ond i Margaret Vaughan yr oedd unpeth mwy na llwyddo. Iechyd OEDD hwnnw. [CRYMAN 36]	But for Margaret Vaughan there was one thing more important than success, and that WAS health. [SICKLE 28]
She didn't believe any of it. It WAS a horror story that had sprung out of his twisted imagination. [VICT 127]	Doedd hi'n credu'r un gair. Stori arswyd roedd ei hen ddychymyg gwyrdroëdig o wedi'i chreu OEDD hon. [LLINYN 142]
'Madam,' he growled, 'I'M a police officer needing an interview with Mrs Stephanakis . . .' [TIME 93]	'Madam,' ysgyrnygodd, 'un o swyddogion yr heddlu YDW i ac mae arna i eisio sirarad â Mrs Stephanakis . . .' [AMSER 148]
I saw marks on Barbara's throat that I now know to be love bites . . . [CIDER 36] [lit. . . . I have no doubt that they WERE love bites]	Sylwais ar farciau cochion ar wddf Barbara ac, erbyn heddiw, does gen i ddim amheuaeth nad olion cusanu OEDDEN nhw . . . [SEIDR 52]

Personal pronouns and demonstratives are inherently definite, and thus this pattern generally works the same way as the previous cases in which both parts of the equation are full NPs. However, a subject pronoun may be omitted in Welsh. When this happens, the result is an equational sentence in which the right-hand side of the equation is not expressed overtly (e.g. *Bob MacIwan* YDOEDD 'It WAS Bob MacIwan'):

Hanes YDOEDD am anturiaethau ym meddrodau Lwcsor ac o amgylch pyramidiau'r Aifft. [MONICA 45]	**It WAS an adventure story** set among the tombs of Luxor and the pyramids of Egypt. [MONICA 44]
. . . a gwelodd Monica mai **Bob MacIwan YDOEDD**. [MONICA 47]	. . . and Monica saw that it WAS **Bob MacEwan**. [MONICA 47]

Un o Lechfaen YDOEDD yn
wreiddiol, ond symudasai'i deulu
i fyw i Lerpwl pan oedd ef tua
deuddeg oed. [CHWAL 159]

Originally he hailed from Llechfaen,
but the family had moved to
Liverpool when he was about twelve
years old. [OUT 169] [lit. He WAS
one from Llechfaen . . .]

Gofynnid amynedd mawr i yrru
gwyddau gan mai **cerddwyr gwael
iawn YDYNT.** [CWM 3]

Geese WERE poor walkers and the
goose driver had to be a patient
man. [GORSE 4]

We mentioned that a second type of equational sentence expresses the
total identity of two noun phrases:

Louis XIV	was	the King of France.
My favourite colour	is	green.
The capital of Spain	is	Madrid.

The most salient difference between this type and the preceding one is that
here, the two NPs may sometimes occur in either order without a significant difference in meaning or acceptability: *Prifddinas Sbaen yw Madrid* and
Madrid yw prifddinas Sbaen are both totally ordinary sentences. But even so,
the preferred word order in each language reflects its IS preferences: Welsh
prefers to put the new information first (in equational sentences), whereas
English prefers to start with the topic. This is why translations from one language into the other routinely reverse the order of the two noun phrases:

Eich cadw chi cyn belled oddi wrth
y Blaid ag y medra'i YDI 'nyletswydd
i rwan. [LLEIFIOR 66]

My duty now IS to keep you as
far away as I can from the Party.
[RETURN 55]

'Hen waith trwm YDI golchi
ffustion,' meddai Sioned Gruffydd.
[TRAED 13]

'Washing working-clothes IS a tiring
old job,' said Sioned. [FEET 11]

Methai Owen ddeall paham y troes
Gwen ei phen i ffwrdd a pheidio
â dyfod â'i mam ato (mae'n debyg
mai ei mam OEDD y ddynes gôt sîl).
[TRAED 70]

Owen could not understand why
Gwen had averted her eyes, and had
not introduced her mother to him.
(The woman in the sealskin coat WAS
probably her mother). [FEET 62]

Fel y gwyddoch chi, gynaicoleg [*sic*]
YDI maes Paul . . .' [LLEIFIOR 61]

'As you know, Paul specialises in
gynaecology . . .' [RETURN 51] [lit.
Paul's field is gynaecology . . .]

Most of the men drank cool cider from the bowls and firkins they'd filled at the start of the day, but the girls preferred tea. [CIDER 34] [lit. . . . the girl's drink was tea]

Yfai'r rhan fwyaf o'r dynion seidr oer o'r poteli roeddynt wedi eu llenwi'n barod ben bore, ond te OEDD diod y merched. [SEIDR 48]

This is not, however, without exception; occasionally the translator may keep the order of elements the same:

⁹John Ellis [. . .] YW'r athro

⁹John Ellis [. . .] IS our teacher.

'Wel, ydach chi'n gweld, 'Nhad YDI'r stiward yn y chwarel.' [TRAED 68]

'Well, you see, my father IS the manager in the quarry.' [FEET 56]

Nid oedd segurdod yng nghroen Pegi. A'r gludwair, yn anad unman arall, OEDD ei theyrnas hi. [HDF 107]

There was no idleness inside Pegi's skin. And above all places the woodyard WAS her kindgom. [OFH 131]

Since the two word orders seen in *The woodyard was her kingdom* and *Her kingdom was the woodyard* manifestly describe the same state of affairs, either one would be an adequate rendering of the Welsh original.

Another solution encountered is to translate a Welsh equational sentence (*X yw Y*) into English using a cleft construction, such as the one seen below (*It's X to do Y*):

'Peth mawr YDI colli partnar bywyd, Mr Vaughan.' [LLEIFIOR 82]

'It's an awful thing to lose one's life-partner, Mr Vaughan.' [RETURN 69]

'Eich cenhadaeth chi mewn bywyd, fel y gwn i'n dda, YDI ennill aelodau i'r Blaid' [LLEIFIOR 92]

'It's your mission in life, as I very well know, to recruit members for Plaid Cymru' [RETURN 77]

Since the English cleft construction specifically serves to move the focused element to the beginning of the utterance, this ends up being a very successful solution for translating a Welsh equational sentence while keeping the order of elements the same as in Welsh.

Note that the two halves of the equation may be very different in length. In this case, it is generally the predicate or focus part (that is, the indefinite NP) which may be quite long, even including multiple clauses such as relative clauses:

Ond gadawsant [y Gwyddyl] eu hôl ar Gymru yn yr arysgrifau Ogham a gafwyd yn y parthau a oresgynnwyd. **Sistem ysgrifennu arbennig, a ddyfeisiwyd y mae'n debyg gan Geltiaid paganaidd de Iwerddon oddeutu'r bumed ganrif OC** OEDD Ogham. [PEATCYM 45]

*But the Irish left their mark on Wales on the Ogham inscriptions which are found in the conquered regions. Ogham IS **a special writing system, probably invented by the pagan Celts of southern Ireland around the fifth century BC***

Un o ferched Prance, Iris, a ddaeth yn Mrs Beer yn ddiweddarach ac a oedd yn dal i fyw yn Anchor House, OEDD fy athrawes ganu. [CRWYD 110]

*My singing teacher WAS **one of the Prance girls, Iris, who became Mrs Beer later, and who was still living in Anchor House.***

Thus, we have seen that the most common pattern for equational sentences takes the following forms:

English:	definite NP	copula	indefinite NP
Welsh:	indefinite NP	copula	definite NP

In Welsh it is possible, though somewhat less frequent, to recast these sentences with the usual VSO word order. In this case, the indefinite NP is preceded by the predicate marker YN, which causes soft mutation on the predicate noun:

Roedd Rhydwen Williams **yn un o'n hoff bobl ni**, bardd, un o'r beirdd byw mwyaf yng Nghymru, a hefyd **yn actor** ac **yn bregethwr** lleyg aruthrol. [CRWYD 118]

Rhydwen Williams was one of our favorite people, a poet, one of the greatest living poets in Wales, and also an actor and an eloquent lay preacher.

Y mae'n fachgen byw ei feddwl ac **yn ddarllenwr mawr**. [O LAW 176]

Llew, our organist in the chapel, is a quick-witted lad and a voracious reader. [FROM 142]

Yr oedd Ann Ifans yn ddynes hynaws, ddigrif, a thra bu'r plant yn y capel diddorwyd Jane ac Ifan gan ei harabedd. [TRAED 36]

Ann Ifans was an easy-going, humorous woman, and while the children had been at the chapel she had regaled Jane and Ifan with her witty stories. [FEET 33]

. . . yr oedd hwn yn ŵr syn a thawel a dwys . . . [CYCHWYN 59]	Here was a man dazed, taciturn, grave; [BEGIN 59] [lit. . . . this was a dazed, taciturn and grave man]
Lingard was no man to put helpful words in a suspect's mouth. [TIME 82]	**Nid oedd Lingard yn ddyn** i roi geiriau o gymorth yng ngenau dyn yr oedd yn ei amau. [AMSER 128]

In the majority of examples from the corpus, the predicate noun (often just a word like *bachgen, merch, dyn,* or *dynes*) in such cases is not the important part of the focus; the new information is really the modifiers that accompany the noun.

Of course, an equational sentence may also be negative, to say that one thing is NOT something else. Negative equational sentences are constructed rather differently in English and in Welsh. In English these generally involve negating the copula, as in the first two examples below, but occasionally the negation may bear on the predicate noun as in the third example:

My brother	**is not (isn't)**	a doctor.
These	**are not (aren't)**	Welsh novels.
He	**is**	**no** minister.

In the equivalent Welsh construction, the negation is not placed on the verb, but rather on the focused (i.e. left-hand) noun phrase, using the particle NID in a main clause or its variant NAD in a subordinate clause.[12] There are two ways to complete the sentence, the first standard:

Nid meddyg	yw	fy mrawd.
Nid gweinidog	yw	ef.

and the second informal:

Nid meddyg	mo[13]	fy mrawd.
Nid gweinidog	mohono	ef.

The more standard pattern is shown in the following examples, both with full NPs as topics (the first two examples), and with pronominal topics (the second two examples):

[12] In informal Welsh there are several other negative elements which can occur instead of NID in this construction, including DIM, NACI, and NAGE.

[13] *Mo* is a contraction of *ddim o.*

Nid rhai crintachlyd oedd ffermwyr Cwm Eithin. [CWM 23]	**The Cwm Eithin farmers were not mean.** [GORSE 24] [lit. . . . not mean ones]
Ac nid oedd y gwasanaeth wedi cerdded ymhell y bore hwnnw, cyn iddi wawrio ar y gweddill ohonom **nad 'gwnidog'**[14] **oedd y gŵr . . .** [DYDD 41]	*And the service had not gone on for long that morning before it dawned on the majority of us that the man was not a minister . . .*
Ydach chi ddim yn cael eich pen blwydd tan mis nesa, Nain, medda finna. Felly **nid presant pen blwydd ydy o**, beth bynnag. [NOS 115]	It's not your birthday till next month, Gran, I said. So **it's not a birthday present**, anyway. [NIGHT 196]
. . . ond nawr, fan hyn, ar 'y mhen 'yn hunan, dw i'n sylwi **nad mater o *eisiau* ffrindiau yw hi**, ond *angen*. [FFYDD 50]	But now, sitting here alone, it dawns on me that it's not a matter of *wanting* friends, but rather a *need* for friends. [FAITH 40]

The pattern using the informal negator MO is shown below, in the first example with a full NP topic, and in the second and third examples with inflected forms of MO caused by the pronominal topics:

Mae gan rai pobol y syniad **nad gwaith go iawn mo cerddoriaeth** felly does dim angen talu cerddorion. [CRWYD 88]	*Some people have the idea that **music is not real work**, so there's no need to pay musicians.*
Ganwaith y dywedodd wrtho'i hun mai stynt oedd hyn gan Sali, a chanwaith y dywedodd rhywbeth wrtho **nad stynt mohono o gwbl**. [CRYMAN 98]	He told himself a hundred times that this was one of Sally's stunts, and each time something told him that **it wasn't a stunt at all**. [SICKLE 80]
Y gerddoriaeth ddalen gyntaf a brynais i oedd cân Wyddelig o'r enw 'The Spinning Wheel'. **Nid cân werin moni o gwbl**, fel ro'n i'n tybio ar y pryd; yn y 1920au sgrifennwyd hi, gan awdur anhysbys. [CRWYD 81]	*The first sheet music I bought was an Irish song named 'The Spinning Wheel.' **It's not a folksong at all**, as I thought at the time; it was written in the 1920s, by an unknown author.*

[14] i.e. gweinidog.

In the final section of this chapter we talk briefly about the use of intonation as the sole mark of focusing or topicalisation.

11.3 Emphasis via Intonation

In English, the most frequent strategy for making particular constituents more salient is simply to use focus intonation for them in speech, often – but not always – indicated typographically by the use of italics. In the examples below, the italics are original (i.e. present in the published text); we add bolding as well to make the stressed elements stand out visually. This kind of intonation can bear on verbs:

'Diar, *mae* gynnoch chi le crand, bwr molchi a bwr glàs a phob dim.' [TRAED 10]

'Dear me, you **do** have a grand place – washstand, dressing-table and all.' [FEET 9]

'Mi awn i gam ymhellach,' ebe Harri, 'a dweud eich **bod** chi'n ddiwerth.' [CRYMAN 254]

'I'd go a step further,' said Harri, 'and say you *are* worthless.' [SICKLE 220]

He didn't *catch* it, he nearly *swallowed* it. [STONE 237]

Wnaeth o mo'i *ddal* o, bu bron iddo'i *lyncu*. [MAEN 150]

'A Nimbus Two Thousand!' Ron moaned enviously. 'I've never even *touched* one.' [STONE 204]

'Nimbws Dwy Fil!' griddfanodd Ron yn eiddigus. 'Dwi erioed wedi *cyffwrdd* ag un hyd yn oed.' [MAEN 130]

It can also concern pronouns:

'Sut aflwydd y gwyddoch chi gymaint? Beth aflwydd ydi'ch enw *chi*?' [CRYMAN 85]

'How the heck do you know so much about me? What's *your* name?' [SICKLE 69]

Send *him*, we can afford to lose *him*. [STONE 247]

Anfon *o*, fedrwn ni fforddio'i golli *o*. [MAEN 157]

Then came the horses. Having four feet, these managed rather better than the foot-soldiers; but even *they* stumbled now and then; [THRO 195–6]

Yna daeth y meirch. Gan fod ganddynt bedwar carn llwyddodd y rhain ychydig yn well na'r gwŷr troed, ond syrthient *hwy* hyd yn oed, yn awr ac eilwaith. [TRWY 86]

'What's happened to me! I look terrible! I look just like *you* gone wrong!' [MAT 63]

'Beth sydd wedi digwydd i mi? Dw i'n edrych yn ofnadwy! Dw i'n edrych yn union fel *ti* wedi mynd o chwith.' [MAT 57]

And, perhaps more surprisingly, it can apply to the particles YN, WEDI and other TMA elements:

Roedd hi *yn* bisin yr adeg honno, daria hi. [CRYMAN 103]

She *was* a smart piece in those days, damn 'er eyes. [SICKLE 84]

She was up on the chimney-piece while she said this, though she hardly knew how she had got there. And certainly the glass *was* beginning to melt away, just like a bright silvery mist. [THRO 131]

Roedd hi i fyny ar y silff ben tân tra siaradai er mai prin y gwyddai sut yr aeth yno, ac yn wir ichi roedd y gwydr *yn* dechrau toddi, yn union fel rhyw darth arianaid disglair. [TRWY 18]

'Well, of course, that was the headmaster, quite different. You need *rest*.'
'I *am* resting, look, lying down and everything.' [STONE 374]

'Wrth gwrs, fo ydi'r Prifathro, mae hynny'n wahanol. Rwyt ti angen *gorffwys*.'
'Dwi *yn* gorffwyso, wir, dwi'n gorwedd i lawr a phopeth.' [MAEN 239]

She stood silent for a minute, thinking: then she suddenly began again. 'Then it really *has* happened, after all! And now, who am I? I *will* remember, if I can! I'm determined to do it!' [THRO 157]

Safodd am funud heb ddweud dim, ond meddwl. Yna dechreuodd eto, 'Mae *wedi* digwydd mewn gwirionedd, felly, wedi'r cwbl! Ac yn awr, pwy wyf fi? Rwyf *am* gofio, os gallaf. Rwy'n benderfynol o wneud!' [TRWY 44]

The use of intonation alone is, at least traditionally, much more characteristic of English than Welsh. Welsh prefers the syntactic strategies explored earlier in the chapter.

11.4 Summary and conclusions

In this chapter we have examined the three main strategies necessary to characterise IS in Welsh: the topic-comment pattern, the mixed sentence or cleft, and the identificational sentence. To recap these, we offer the following brief text which contains a rather clear example of each of the three patterns:

Nis gwn beth a feddylid yn ein dyddiau ni pe gellid cael **GLO** am y pris uchod. Ond nid oedd *pris y glo* nac yma nac acw i **DRIGOLION CWM EITHIN**. **MAWN** a losgai *y mwyafrif* y dyddiau hynny, a chael **BWYD** oedd y pwnc mawr. [CWM 10]	I do not know what would be said today if coal could be bought for that price. But for the inhabitants of Cwm Eithin the price of coal was neither here nor there. In those days the majority burnt peat, and the great problem was not fuel but how to obtain food. [GORSE 10]

Taking each sentence of this text separately, we can observe the following facts.

> Nis gwn beth a feddylid yn ein dyddiau ni pe gellid cael **GLO** am y pris uchod.

Here, GLO 'coal' is being introduced into the discourse for the first time as part of the new information and thus receives the focus intonation. Having been introduced into the discourse, *pris y glo* is now available for use as a topic, and indeed, this it what happens in the next sentence:

> Ond nid oedd *pris y glo* nac yma nac acw i **DRIGOLION CWM EITHIN**.

Pris y glo is now the topic, and treated in the most usual way for handling topics that coincide with grammatical subjects in Welsh, namely immediately after the verb in a sentence that follows the most common and unmarked Welsh sentence structure, VSO or verb-subject-object.

On the other hand, the 'new' information here is DRIGOLION CWM EITHIN 'the inhabitants of Cwm Eithin'. As a first mention in this portion of the text, these residents are introduced in the focus, after which they in turn are available to be used as a topic, should the speaker wish to say something more about them. And indeed, this is what happens in the next sentence:

> **MAWN** a losgai *y mwyafrif* y dyddiau hynny, a chael **BWYD** oedd y pwnc mawr.

We see here that *y mwyafrif* 'the majority', which refers to a subset of the same people introduced by the earlier phrase *drigolion Cwm Eithin*, is now the topic: the purpose of this sentence is to add to the addressee's knowledge about the inhabitants of Cwm Eithin. The two new discourse referents introduced here are MAWN 'peat' and BWYD 'food', which both receive focus intonation in two successive clauses. Each is introduced using a focus construction in which the focus or new information is made more salient by putting it in clause-initial position (as opposed to the usual post-verbal position for NP arguments in Welsh). In the first case, *Mawn a losgai y mwyafrif* 'the majority burned peat', we have a mixed sentence (or cleft) version of the more neutral VSO sentence *Llosgai y mwyafrif fawn*. The latter would also be possible here, but it would not draw as much attention to *mawn* as the marked focus construction does.

The second clause, *a chael* BWYD *oedd y pwnc mawr* 'and the great problem was how to obtain food' represents a classic identificational sentence, in which the focus generally comes first in Welsh.

Bibliography

Abbreviations

DAT   David A. Thorne, *Comprehensive Welsh Grammar*
GM   *Y Geiriadur Mawr*
GPC   *Geiriadur Prifysgol Cymru*
GyrA *Geiriadur yr Academi*
NW   north Wales
PWT   Peter Wynn Thomas, *Gramadeg y Gymraeg*
SW   south Wales

General Bibliography

Ball, Martin J. 1988. *The Use of Welsh*. Clevedon and Philadelphia: Multilingual Matters.

Bolinger, Dwight. 1971. *The Phrasal Verb in English*. Cambridge: Harvard University Press.

Borsley, Robert, Maggie Tallerman and Davis Willis. 2007. *The Syntax of Welsh*. Cambridge: Cambridge University Press.

Braz, Kristian. 2013. *A-ziwar logod ha tud*. Mouladurioù hor Yezh (Breton translation of *Of Mice and Men* by John Steinbeck).

Brinton, Laurel J. 1988. *The Development of English Aspectual Systems*. Cambridge: Cambridge University Press.

Cambridge Phrasal Verbs Dictionary. 2006. Cambridge: Cambridge University Press.

Courtney, Rosemary. 1983. *Longman Dictionary of Phrasal Verbs*. Harlow, England: Longman.

Cownie, Alun Rhys. 2001. *A dictionary of Welsh and English idiomatic phrases*. Cardiff: University of Wales Press.

Davies, Peredur. 2016. 'Age variation and language change in Welsh: auxiliary deletion and possessive constructions', in M. Durham and J. Morris (eds), *Sociolinguistics in Wales*. London: Palgrave, pp. 31–59.

Fife, James. 1986. 'Literary vs. colloquial Welsh: problems of definition', *Word*, 37 (3), 141–51.

Guillemin-Flescher, Jacqueline. 1981. *Syntaxe comparée du français et de l'anglais; Problèmes de traduction*. Paris: Éditions Ophrys.

Hart, Carl W. 2009. *The Ultimate Phrasal Verb Book*. Hauppage, NY: Barron's Educational Series.

Ifans, Rh. 2006. *Y Golygiadur*. Aberystwyth: Cymdeithas Lyfrau Ceredigion Cyf.

Jespersen, Otto. 1961. *A Modern English grammar on historical principles*, vol. 2. London: George Allen E. Unwin, Ltd.

Jones, Morris and Alan R. Thomas. 1977. *The Welsh Language: Studies in its syntax and semantics*. Cardiff: University of Wales Press for the Schools Council.

Jones, Bob Morris. 1993. *Ar Lafar ac ar Bapur*. Aberystwyth: Canolfan Astudiaethau Addysg.

Kerrain, Herve. 1995. *Troioù-kaer Alis e bro ar marzhoù* (Breton translation of *Alice's Adventures in Wonderland* by Lewis Carrol). Quimper: An Here.

Lakoff, George and Mark Johnson. 1980. *Metaphors We Live By*. Chicago: University of Chicago Press.

Lambrecht, Knud. 1994. *Information Structure and Sentence Form. Topic, Focus and the Mental Representation of Discourse Referents*. Cambridge: Cambridge University Press.

Lindner, Susan Jean. 1983. *A Lexico-Semantic Analysis of English Verb Particle Constructions with OUT and UP*. PhD dissertation, University of California San Diego; repr. Bloomington: Indiana University Linguistics Club.

McArthur, Tom (ed.). 1992. *The Oxford Companion to the English Language*. New York: Oxford University Press.

Prys, D. (ed.). 2014. *Ysgrifau ar ieithyddiaeth a geiriaduraeth Gymraeg*. Caerfyrddin: Coleg Cymraeg Cenedlaethol.

Prys, Myfyr. 2016. *Style in the vernacular and on the radio: code-switching and mutation as stylistic and social markers in Welsh*. PhD dissertation, Prifysgol Bangor University.

Reppen, R. and Simpson-Vlach, R. 2002. 'Corpus linguistics', in Schmitt, N. (ed.), *An Introduction to Applied Linguistics*. London: Arnold.

Rottet, Kevin J. 2010. 'Language contact in Welsh and Breton: The case of reflexive and reciprocal verbs', *IULC Working Papers 9: New Perspectives on Language Contact and Contact-Induced Language Change*, edited by Clements, J. Clancy, Solon, Megan Elizabeth, Siegel, Jason F. and Steiner, B. Devan. Bloomington, IN: Indiana University Linguistics Club, 61–82.

Rottet, Kevin J. 2011. 'Conjunctive pronouns in Modern Welsh: A preliminary corpus-based study', in K. Jaskuła (ed.), *Formal and Historical Approaches to Celtic Languages*, special issue of *Lublin Studies in Celtic Languages*, vol. 7, 233–53. Lublin: Wydawnictwo KUL.

Schmitt, N. (ed.). 2002. *An Introduction to Applied Linguistics*. London: Arnold.

Stump, Gregory T. 1985. *The semantic variability of absolute constructions*. Dordrecht: D. Reidel Publishing Company.

Tallerman, Maggie. 1996. 'Fronting constructions in Welsh,' in Robert D. Borsley and Ian Roberts (eds), *The Syntax of the Celtic languages: A Comparative Perspective*. Cambridge University Press, pp. 97–124.

Talmy, Leonard. 1985. 'Lexicalization patterns: Semantic structure in lexical forms,' in Timothy Shopen (ed.), *Language Typology and Syntactic Description, Vol. 3: Grammatical Categories and the Lexicon*, pp. 57–149. Cambridge: Cambridge University Press.

Talmy, Leonard. 1991. 'Path to Realization: A Typology of Event Conflation,' *Proceedings of the Seventeenth Annual Meeting of the Berkeley Linguistics Society: General Session and Parasession on The Grammar of Event Structure*, 480–519.

Thim, Stefan. 2012. *Phrasal Verbs: The English Verb-Particle Construction and its History*. Berlin: Mouton de Gruyter.

Thomas, Peter Wynn. 1996. *Gramadeg y Gymraeg*. Cardiff: University of Wales Press.

Thorne, David A. 1993. *A Comprehensive Welsh Grammar*. Oxford: Blackwell.

Vinay, Jean-Paul and Jean Darbelnet. 1958. *Stylistique comparée du français et de l'anglais Méthode de traduction*. Paris: Marcel Didier.

Vinay, Jean-Paul and Jean Darbelnet. 1995. *Comparative Stylistics of French and English: A Methodology for Translation*, ed. and trans. Juan C. Sager and M.-J. Hamel. Amsterdam/Philadelphia: John Benjamins.

Willis, David. 2014. 'Newid ac amrywiaeth mewn Cymraeg cyfoes,' in Delyth Prys (ed.), *Ysgrifau ar ieithyddiaeth a geiriaduraeth Gymraeg*. Caerfyrddin: Coleg Cymraeg Cenedlaethol, 84–102.

Willis, David. 2016. 'Cyfieithu iaith y caethweision yn Uncle Tom's Cabin a darluniadau o siaradwyr ail iaith mewn llenyddiaeth Gymraeg,' *Llên Cymru*, 39 (1), 56–72. https://doi.org/10.16922/lc.39.5.

Zimmer, Stefan. 2000. *Studies in Welsh Word-formation*. Dublin: Dublin Institute for Advanced Studies.

List of works cited and their translations

English texts with Welsh translation

Carroll, Lewis. 1960 [1865]. *Alice's Adventures in Wonderland*. New York: Signet Classic [ALICE].

Welsh translations
Roberts, Selyf. 1953. *Anturiaethau Alys yng ngwlad hud*. Dinbych:
Gwasg Gee [ALYS I].
Roberts, Selyf. 2010. *Anturiaethau Alys yng ngwlad hud*. Dublin:
Evertype [ALYS II].
Carroll, Lewis. 1960 [1871]. *Through the Looking-Glass, and What Alice
Found There*. New York: Signet Classic [THRO].
Welsh translation
Roberts, Selyf. 1984. *Trwy'r drych a'r hyn a welodd Alys yno*. Llandysul:
Gwasg Gomer [TRWY].
Conan Doyle, Arthur. 2007. *The Speckled Band*, in *The Adventures of
Sherlock Holmes*. London: Penguin Books, 207–40 [BAND].
Welsh translation
Jones, Eurwyn Pierce. 2014. *Y Cylch Brith*. Talybont: Y Lolfa [CYLCH].
Dahl, Roald. 1988. *Matilda*. NY: Penguin Putnam [MAT].
Welsh translation
Meek, Elin. 2008. *Matilda*. Hengoed: Rily Publications [MAT].
Dahl, Roald. 1964. *Charlie and the Chocolate Factory*. NY: Penguin Putnam
[CHARLIE].
Welsh translation
Meek, Elin. 2002. *Charlie a'r Ffatri Siocled*. Hengoed: Rily Publications
[SIOCLED].
Gill, B. M. 1981. *Victims*. Hodder and Stoughton: Coronet Books [VICT].
Welsh translation
Jones, Meinir Pierce. 1981. *Llinyn Rhy Dynn*. Llandysul: Gomer Press
[LLINYN].
James, P. D. 1972. *An Unsuitable Job for a Woman* [UNSUIT].
Welsh translation
Lisa, Mari. 1990. *Ar Gortyn Brau*. Cymdeithas Lyfrau Ceredigion
[GORTYN].
Lovesey, Peter. 1986. *Rough Cider*. New York: The Mysterious Press [CIDER].
Welsh translation
Griffith, Ieuan. 1991. *Seidr chwerw*. Llanrwst: Gwasg Carreg Gwalch
[SEIDR].
Pratchett, Terry. 2001. *Thief of Time*. New York: HarperTorch [THIEF].
Welsh translation
Parri, Dyfrig. 2002. *Lleidr amser*. Hengoed: Rily [LLEIDR].
Rankin, Ian. 1987. *Knots and Crosses*. The Bodley Head [KNOTS].
Welsh translation
Rowlands, John. 1990. *Chwerw'n troi'n chwarae*. Llandysul: Gwasg
Gomer [CHWERW].

Ross, Jonathan. 1989. *A Time for Dying*. New York: St Martin's Press [TIME].
Welsh translation
ap Hywel, Elin. 1991. *Amser i farw*. Caerdydd: Hughes a'i Fab [AMSER].
Rowling, J. K. 1997. *Harry Potter and the Sorcerer's Stone*. New York:
Scholastic Inc. [STONE].
Welsh translation
Huws, Emily. 2000. *Harri Potter a Maen yr Athronydd*. London:
Bloomsbury [MAEN].
Underwood, Michael. 1989. *A Compelling Case*. New York: St Martin's Press
[CASE].
Welsh translation
Roberts, Wyn G. 1989. *Bai ar Gam*. Llanrwst: Gwasg Carreg Gwalch [BAI].

Welsh texts with English translation

Elis, Islwyn Ffowc. 1990 [1953]. *Cysgod y Cryman*. Llandysul: Gwasg
Gomer [CRYMAN].
English translation
Stephens, Meic. 1998. *Shadow of the Sickle*. Llandysul: Gomer Press
[SICKLE].
Elis, Islwyn Ffowc. 1956. *Yn ôl i Leifior*. Aberystwyth: Gwasg Aberystwyth
[LLEIFIOR]
English translation
Stephens, Meic. 1999. *Return to Lleifior*. Llandysul: Gomer Press
[RETURN].
Evans, Hugh. 1931. *Cwm Eithin*. Liverpool: Y Brython Press, Hugh Evans
and Sons [CWM].
English translation
Humphreys, E. Morgan. 1948. *The Gorse Glen*. Liverpool: The Brython
Press, Hugh Evans and Sons [GORSE].
Gruffydd, W. J. 1942. *Hen Atgofion*. Gwasg Aberystwyth [HENAT].
English translation
Lloyd, D. Myrddin. 1976. *The Years of the Locust*. Llandysul: Gomer
Press [LOCUST].
Hughes, T. Rowland. 1979 [1946]. *Chwalfa*. Llandysul: Gwasg Gomer
[CHWAL].
English translation
Ruck, Richard. 1954. *Out of their Night*. Llandysul: Gomer Press [OUT].
Hughes, T. Rowland. 1947. *Y Cychwyn*. Llandysul: Gwasg Gomer
[CYCHWYN].
English translation
Ruck, Richard. 1969. *The Beginning*. Llandysul: Gomer Press [BEGIN].

Hughes, T. Rowland. 1943. *O law i law*. Llandysul: Gwasg Gomer [O LAW].
English translation
Ruck, Richard. 1950. *From hand to hand*. London: Methuen & Co. [FROM].
Lewis, Saunders. 1930. *Monica*. Llandysul: Gwasg Gomer [MONICA].
English translation
Stephens, Meic. 1997. *Monica*. Bridgend: Seren [MONICA].
Owen, Daniel. 1865. *Hunangofiant Rhys Lewis, Gweinidog Bethel* [RHYS].
English translation
Harris, James. 1888. *Rhys Lewis, Minister of Bethel: An Autobiography*.
Wrexham: Hughes and Son [RHYS].
Owen, Daniel. 1991 [1894]. *Gwen Tomos: Merch y Wernddu*. Caerdydd:
Hughes a'i Fab. [GWEN].
English translation
Williams, T. Ceiriog and E. R. Harries. 1963. *Gwen Tomos*. Wrexham:
Hughes and Son [GWEN].
Owen, Llwyd. 2006. *Ffydd Gobaith Cariad*. Talybont: Y Lolfa [FFYDD].
English translation
Owen, Llwyd. 2010. *Faith, Hope and Love*. Talybont: Alcemi [FAITH].
Prichard, Caradog. 1961. *Un Nos Ola Leuad*. Caernarfon: Gwasg Gwalia
[NOS].
English translation
Mitchell, Philip. 1995. *One Moonlit Night*. Edinburgh: Canongate
[NIGHT].
Roberts, Kate. 2001 [1936]. *Traed mewn Cyffion*. Llandysul: Gwasg Gomer
[TRAED].
English translation
Jones, John Idris. 2002. *Feet in Chains*. Bridgend: Seren [FEET].
Roberts, Kate. 1959. *Te yn y Grug*. Dinbych: Gwasg Gee [TE].
English translation
Griffith, Wyn. 1997. *Tea in the Heather*. Ruthin: John Jones [TEA].
Roberts, Kate. 1956. *Y Byw sy'n cysgu*. Gwasg Gee [BYW].
English translation
(i) Griffiths, W. 1981. *The Living Sleep*. Corgi Children's; (ii) James,
Siân. 2006. *The Awakening*. Seren) [AWAKENING].
Roberts, Wiliam Owen. 1987. *Y Pla*. Llanrwst: Gwasg Carreg Gwalch [PLA].
English translation
Roberts, Elisabeth. 1991. *Pestilence*. Bridgend: Seren [PEST].
Stevens, Meic. 2003. *Hunangofiant y Brawd Houdini*. Talybont: Y Lolfa
[HUNAN].
English translation
Stevens, Meic. 2004. *Solva Blues*. Talybont: Y Lolfa [SOLVA].

Williams, D. J. 1953. *Hen Dŷ Ffarm*. Llandysul: Gwasg Gomer [HDF].
English translation
Williams, Waldo. 1961. *The Old Farmhouse*. London: George G.
Harrap & Co. [OFH].

Welsh texts without English translation

Elis, Islwyn Ffowc. 1955. *Ffenestri tua'r Gwyll*. Llandysul: Gwasg Gomer
[FFENEST].
Griffith, W. J. 1958. *Storïau'r Henllys Fawr*. Gwasg Aberystwyth
[HENLLYS].
Gwanas, Bethan. 2003. *Gwrach y Gwyllt*. Llandysul: Gwasg Gomer
[GWRACH].
Jones, T. Gwynn. 1933. *Cymeriadau*. Wrecsam: Hughes a'i Fab [CYMER].
Lewis, Caryl. 2003. *Dal hi!* Talybont: Y Lolfa [DAL].
Martell, Owen. 2000. *Cadw dy ffydd, brawd*. Llandysul: Gwasg Gomer
[CADW].
Owen, Daniel. 1939. *Profedigaethau Enoc Huws*. Wrecsam: Hughes a'i Fab
[ENOC].
Peate, Iorwerth. 1942. *Diwylliant Gwerin Cymru*. Liverpool: Hugh Evans a'i
Feibion [PEATCYM].
Peate, Iorwerth. 1976. *Rhwng Dau Fyd: Darn o Hunangofiant*. Dinbych:
Gwasg Gee [RHWNG].
Price, Angharad. 2010. *Caersaint*. Talybont: Y Lolfa [CAER].
Prysor, Dewi. 2012. *Lladd Duw*. Talybont: Y Lolfa [LLADD].
Prysor, Dewi. 2008. *Crawia*. Talybont: Y Lolfa [CRAWIA].
Rees, Edward. 1968. *T. Rowland Hughes*. Llandysul: Gwasg Gomer [TROW].
Roberts, Selyf. 1965. *Wythnos o Hydref*. Dinbych: Gwasg Gee [SELYF].
Roberts, Eigra Lewis. 2003. *Rhannu'r tŷ*. Llandysul: Gwasg Gomer
[RHANNU].
Roberts, Eigra Lewis. 1980. *Mis o Fehefin*. Llandysul: Gwasg Gomer [MIS O
FEHEFIN].
Roberts, Wiliam O. 1990. *Hunangofiant (1973–1987): Cyfrol I: Y
Blynyddoedd Glas*. Caernarfon: Annwn [ROBHUNAN].
Stevens, Meic. 2009. *Y Crwydryn a mi: Ail ran ei hunangofiant*. Talybont: Y
Lolfa [CRWYD].
Williams, D. J. 1959. *Yn chwech ar hugain oed*. Aberystwyth: Gwasg
Aberystwyth [CHWECH].
Williams, Dr J. Lloyd. 1945. *Atgofion Tri Chwarter Canrif, cyfrol IV*.
Llundain: Gwasg Gymraeg Foyle [WILLAT].
Williams, Rhydwen. 1973. *Dyddiau Dyn. (Cwm Hiraeth: Y Trydydd Rhan)*.
Llandybie: Christopher Davies [DYDD].

Index of Terms

A

Ability, linguistic expression of 162, 201–8, 273, 279–83

Absolute phrases (or clauses) 61, 439, 459–67, 471, 481

Absolute tenses 158, 439

Active voice 191–7

Actualisation 437–47, 466–70

Adaptation (as a translation strategy) 11, 26–8

Adjectives 3; transposition and 16–18, 22, 29, 30, 32, 33, 39, 40, 44–5, 51, 58, 74, 81, 104–18, 131, 141–6, 154, 285, 297–336, 337, 338, 343, 345, 347, 349, 359–60, 364–5, 372, 383, 386, 388, 390–1, 398, 401–4, 423, 428, 429, 448, 452–6, 459–60, 485, 487–8; prenominal adjectives 297, 300–1

Adverbs 16–17, 29, 32, 75 fn. 11, 176, 197, 204, 224, 241, 242, 248–9, 297, 306, 313, 318, 320–5, 345, 353, 379, 383, 404, 429, 449, 452, 465; adverbial clauses 98–101, 479; adverbial directional particles 122, 125, 141, 219, 222 fn. 5, 223–6; ~ used to mark telicity 249; negative adverbs (*byth*, *erioed*) 185 fn. 21; focused fronting of 484

Age, linguistic expression of 73–4, 121, 152, 154–6

Agreement, adjective-noun 123, 298

Agreement, subject-verb 159, 189, 214–17, 218

-aid suffixation 272–5

Am clauses 101–2

Ambiguity 41, 54, 64, 132, 160, 169, 174, 199, 217, 442, 445

Analytic forms: *see* Periphrasis

Anteriority 158, 174–89, 218, 438

Aspect 158, 159, 167 fn. 8, 183 fn. 19, 184, 187–9, 206, 220 fn. 2, 221, 236–8, 245, 445; definition of 159; *see also* Verbs, Tense-Mood-Aspect (TMA)

Aspectual particles 161 fn. 4, 245–9, 459–60, 486

Assertion (assertiveness) 159, 212, 218, 238

Auxiliaries (or helping verbs) 158, 166–7, 171, 186 fn. 22, 217, 273, 277, 285, 294, 353, 486

B

Backgrounding 178, 184–7, 218, 475

Bilingualism 1, 250, 421

Body, bodily posture, positions of the body 134–8, 145, 25–56, 267–8, 364, 373, 389

Body parts 23; definite article with 36; in compound nouns 390–4

Borrowing, lexical 11–14, 28, 254, 271, 338, 353, 354, 359, 421–3, 428, 430–3

C

Calques, calquing 11, 14–15, 28; of
    phrasal verbs 269; of 'get' 291
Causative 14, 273, 277–9, 298
Chassé-croisé or Double
    transposition: definition of 17–18,
    66, 103–4, 113, 257, 356; *see also*
    Transposition
Cleft sentences 477, 479, 481–7, 492,
    497, 499
Cognition, verbs of 206, 442, 445
Collocations 4, 5–7, 102, 293, 300,
    310, 337, 344, 360, 361, 370, 379,
    405–21, 436
Colloquial Welsh: *see* Register
Colours 396–404
Commands 193, 197, 209, 276 fn. 1;
    see also Imperative
Comparative 110, 301, 303
Complements, of prepositions 122,
    125, 223–5, 256–7; of verbs 143,
    171, 222 fn. 4, 276, 279, 446, 486;
    of nouns 446, 458; complement
    clauses with *bod* 121, 131–3,
    444; complement clauses with *i*
    440–4
Compositionality 7, 219, 220, 221
Compounds (and compounding),
    lexical: in indefinites and
    interrogatives 328–9; with no
    translation equivalent 381–5;
    processes of lexical compounding
    386ff.; with numbers 389; with
    body parts 390–4; with colours
    396–400; reduplication as
    compounding 402–5; summary
    436
Conative construction 90–6
Concessive clauses 465
Conditional mood: 55, 159, 175,
    197, 198–202, 353, 356, 378, 438,

468; *see also* Verbs, Tense-Mood-
    Aspect (TMA)
Conditional sentences: *see*
    Hypotheticality
Conjunctions 57, 96, 132, 166, 179,
    212, 214, 299, 351, 440, 446, 466
    fn. 11; concessive conjunctions
    465; temporal conjunctions 180,
    207, 449
Conjunctive pronouns: *see* Pronouns
Constraints (or servitudes) 2–4, 15,
    16, 86, 121, 127, 133–4, 156,
    168, 189, 195, 219, 223–6, 439,
    440, 446
Culture, cultural references 1, 26,
    380–1

D

Dan clauses 98–100
Dative shift 78–9
Demonstratives 10, 36, 38, 39, 40, 45,
    59, 304, 339, 448, 488, 490
Derivation 19, 286, 356, 367 fn. 10,
    381, 383
Description 39, 195, 390, 396; in the
    past 168; of a state of mind 170;
    of posture 252
Dialect 10–11, 25, 123 fn. 5, 329
    fn. 14, 357 fn. 7, 483, 486
Discourse, verbs of 131–3, 200–1,
    442–3
Double transposition: *see*
    Chassé-croisé
Dummy (or nonreferential) direct
    object 47, 50
Dummy (or nonreferential) subject
    449–50
Durative aspect 168, 170, 206, 236,
    245, 249; *see also* Verbs, Tense-
    Mood-Aspect (TMA)

E

Emphasis 37, 54, 55 fn. 10, 58, 80, 98,
    160, 185, 221, 237, 242 fn. 14, 245,
    336, 360, 366, 372, 480, 496–7
English influence 115 fn. 33, 134, 158
    fn. 2, 432
Epithets 29, 37
Equational sentences 488–96
Equivalence (as a translation strategy)
    25–6, 28
Existentials 17, 194–5

F

Fields of meaning: *see* Semantic fields
Figurative language 20–4, 220,
    237, 255, 258, 268, 363; *see also*
    Metaphor, Metonymy, Simile
Focus constructions 172–3, 448,
    453–8, 478–99; definition of 474;
    focus accent 475–6; *see also*
    Information structure
Foregrounding 178, 184–5
Formal Welsh: *see* Register
Formulaic language 4, 7, 25–6, 40,
    197, 210–13, 365, 433 fn. 27
Fronting 276, 448, 453–9, 481, 483–8;
    see also Focus constructions
Future tense 8, 55, 102, 133, 158, 160,
    162, 164–7, 177–8, 198, 200, 204,
    214, 273, 378
Future-in-the-past 200–4

G

Gan clauses 96–8
Gender in the noun phrase 29–31, 40,
    44, 46, 53, 62, 297, 298, 300
Generic subjects 62–4, 189, 195
Gerunds (in English) 45, 439
Grammatical gender 29–31, 40, 44,
    46, 53, 62, 297–300

H

Habitual aspect 157, 159, 160, 161,
    164, 166, 169, 176, 189, 199, 200,
    217; *see also* Verbs, Tense-Mood-
    Aspect (TMA)
Height, linguistic expression of 152,
    154–6
Helping verbs: *see* Auxiliaries
Homophony 19, 439
Hypotheticality 159, 165 fn. 7, 197,
    198–202, 218, 438; *see also* Mood,
    Modality

I

Identificational sentences 80 fn. 13,
    478, 488–96, 498–9
Idioms 6, 7, 19, 23, 25, 47, 134, 139
    fn. 8, 140, 274; semi-idiomatic
    phrasal verbs 220, 222, 236–68;
    idiomatic phrasal verbs 221,
    268–72; idioms involving 'to get'
    291–3; adverbial idioms 323
Imperative 49 fn. 8, 189, 197, 353; *see*
    also Commands
Imperfect (*amherffaith/amhenodol*)
    55, 132, 133, 159, 167–75, 177,
    185 fn. 21, 189, 206, 217, 218, 249,
    351, 444
Impersonal expressions 47, 63, 205,
    210, 352, 443, 448, 449–52, 469
Impersonal verb forms 9, 159,
    189–97, 218, 316 fn. 8
Indefinites 55, 333; for generic human
    reference 62; interrogatives
    328–9; reduplication of 405;
    equivalents of English indefinite
    article 474; indefinite noun
    phrases 488, 492–3
Informal or Colloquial Welsh: *see*
    Register

Information structure 452, 454, 473–99; *see also* Focus, Topic

Intonation 473–7; focus intonation 483–4; emphasis conveyed using intonation 496–7

Intransitivity 189, 193, 195, 224, 273, 353; intransitive uses of 'get' 285–95

Isomorphism 158, 187 fn. 23, 245

L

Lexical gap 18, 379–86

Lexicalisation 130, 146, 260 fn. 24, 440

Literal translation 15

Literary Welsh: *see* Register

M

Metaphor 20, 22–3, 221; of the particles in phrasal verbs 236–68, 272; orientational metaphors 260 fn. 24; *see also* Figurative language

Metonymy 22–4, 237–8, 257; *see also* Figurative language

Modality: definition of 159, 197, 203, 218; deontic modality 210; *see also* Verbs, Tense-Mood-Aspect (TMA)

Modifiers 15, 29, 39, 45, 56, 58, 90–2, 134, 141, 156, 297–336; 386, 401, 423, 428, 459, 494; *see also* Adjectives, Adverbs

Modulation (as a translation strategy) 11, 19–25, 28, 241

Mood, definition of 158, 157, 197–214, 218, 445, 486; *see also* Verbs, Tense-Mood-Aspect (TMA)

Movement (or motion), verbs of 24, 98, 99–100, 134, 219, 220–1, 227, 228, 234–7, 264, 274; 'to get' as a motion verb 287, 295, 384

Mutation ~ and register 9; ~ of proper names 31–2; ~ with negation 8–9, 113, 332; after interrogative *a* 115 fn. 33, 357 fn. 7; after possessives and object pronouns 13, 47, 127; of *ddaru* 171 fn. 11; with feminine singular 3, 30, 299–300, 317; after prenominal adjectives 300; with *digon* 309–10; after *reit* 311; after *tra* 311; after *yn* 320, 323, 493; of adverbial phrases 321–2; with *prin* 332; of *truan* 349 fn. 5; of *piau* 376 fn. 11; in compounds 386; after prefixed *cyd-* 394; after *hunan* 395; of English borrowings 13–14, 421; with expletives 428; of interjections 430 fn. 20; after the prefix *ym-* 434; after *a* 'and' 299, 460; after *dyna/dyma* 487

N

Names: of diseases 26; of languages 146–7; of people or places or organisations (proper names) 11, 27, 28, 31, 349, 488; mutation of proper names 31–2; of products (trade names) 34; epithets and surnames 37; of occupations 37, 349; of colours 396–404

Narrative style, narration: first person narration 163–4; use of tenses in narration 167, 168, 177–8, 185, 187, 217; *dyma* and *dyna* in narrative style 452; subject pronoun omission in narration 468

Narrator's voice 9

Necessity 114, 197, 209, 218, 299

Negation 8–9, 24, 46, 60, 109–13, 113, 130, 157, 202, 210, 260, 325, 328–32, 344, 353, 454, 456, 494–5

Nominalisation 438, 439, 470

Noun clauses 131–32, 177, 444–5

Number in the noun phrase 29–31, 297, 298, 300

Numbers 134; possessives with 152–4, 154 fn. 9; numbers and agreement patterns 216; numbers as modifiers (giving times) 318; compounds with 389–90; 418

O

O clauses 102–3

Obligation 197, 209–13, 214, 218, 451

Oblique object 86, 195

Onomatopoeia 19

Opportunity, linguistic expression of 197, 203–9, 218, 273, 279–85, 294

Options (stylistic ~), 2–4, 13–16, 33, 58, 62, 63, 85–6, 121, 123, 127, 133–4, 156, 168, 187, 189, 195, 217, 220, 222–6, 253 fn. 21, 272, 294, 314, 316–17, 324, 328–9, 335–6, 339, 345, 349, 351, 439, 446

Overtranslation 2, 8, 207–8

P

Particles: Directional particles 122, 125, 141, 219, 222 fn. 5, 223–6; predicate particle YN 32, 33, 35, 118, 316, 320, 322–7, 448, 460, 486; *see also* Phrasal verbs

Passive voice: with *cael* 121, 128–31, 273, 277, 294; as equivalent to impersonal verb forms 189, 193–7, 218, 316

Past perfect tense (Pluperfect) 55, 158, 177, 178, 181–7, 218, 351, 469

Perception, verbs of 131, 162, 205–7, 218

Perfect tenses 128, 159, 167 fn. 9, 174, 177–89, 218, 437, 438, 444; *see also* Tense

Periphrasis, periphrastic forms (analytic forms) 34, 44, 285, 483; definition 158; preterite 157–8, 171–5; present 159–61, 164, 249; future 166–7; imperfect 169, 175–6, 200, 217, 249; perfect tenses 178, 186

Permission, linguistic expression of 197, 203, 218, 273, 279, 282–3, 294

Phrasal verbs 3, 4, 125, 134, 219–72, 409

Pluperfect: *see* Past perfect

Politeness 159, 201–2

Polysemy 238–40

Possessives 4, 13, 36, 61–2, 121–56, 250–5, 274, 302, 303, 373, 375, 488

Possibility, linguistic expression of 197, 203–9, 218

Posteriority 158

Predicates: predicate adjectives 113, 298, 448–9, 452, 454, 459–60; predicate nouns 35, 448–9, 453, 454, 459–60, 494; predicate particle YN 32, 33, 35, 118, 316, 320, 322–7, 448, 460, 486; and information structure 476, 478, 489, 492, 493

Prenominal adjectives: *see* adjectives

Prepositions 65–120; with nonreferential object 47; with resumptive pronoun 55; compound prepositions 50, 121, 122–7; preposition stranding 66, 118–19, 122 fn. 4; preposition mismatch 66–78; *see also under specific prepositions*

Present participle 33, 66, 97–8, 119, 312, 315, 316–17, 335, 460, 469

Present perfect tense 177, 178, 181, 182,182

Present tense 132, 157, 159–77, 181, 201, 217; *see also* Tense

Preterite 158–9, 167 fn. 9, 168–77, 181–9; *see also* Tense

Probability, linguistic expression of 208

Productivity 39, 43, 145–6, 148, 272, 297, 370, 374, 390, 420, 436

Progressive aspect 157, 159–62, 167–9, 178, 185 fn. 21, 187–9, 201, 217, 437–9, 468; *see also* Verbs, Tense-Mood-Aspect (TMA)

Pronouns: conjunctive pronouns 29, 59–61, 64, 152–3, 460, 480–1; demonstrative pronouns: *see* Demonstratives; infixed pronouns 9, 74; object pronouns 53, 127–8, 131, 156, 225; possessive pronouns 61–2, 373; reduplicated pronouns 54–5; reduplicated indefinite pronouns 405; resumptive pronouns 55; subject pronouns 8, 53, 107, 478, 490

Proper names (or proper nouns): *see* Names

Proverbs 25, 162

R

Reduplication 402–6, 431 fn. 24

Regional variation 8, 10, 157; *see also* Dialect

Register 2, 4, 8–11, 55, 121, 157, 220, 341, 427, 438; Colloquial Welsh/ Informal Welsh 4, 31, 31 fn. 2, 36, 38, 39, 40, 54, 56, 72 fn. 8, 87 fn. 16, 100, 112, 113, 114, 119, 195, 330, 355, 360, 364, 378, 421, 422, 431 fn. 26, 436; Spoken Welsh 54, 58, 118, 127, 175, 273, 355 fn. 6, 374, 431 fn. 26, 436, 457; Formal Welsh 58, 105, 113, 114, 115, 119, 122, 175, 192, 196, 218, 298, 300, 301, 302, 303, 311, 316, 322, 338, 344, 349, 364, 369, 436, 439; Literary Welsh 74, 175, 192, 196, 301, 302, 339, 478

Relative clauses 35, 46, 55, 73 fn. 9, 179, 313, 325, 332, 336, 376, 448, 456–9; Welsh absolute clauses translated as English relative clauses 461–3

S

Satellite-framed languages 222 fn. 4, 272

Semantic fields 34, 337, 341, 345, 348, 351, 357, 361, 436

Sequence of tense 178, 187, 200

Servitudes: *see* Constraints

Simile 22–3; *see also* Figurative language

Simultaneity 158, 184; *see also* Verbs, Tense-Mood-Aspect (TMA)

Source language (SL) or Source text 2, 4, 10, 14, 21, 23, 26

States of mind 81, 141, 145, 170 fn. 10

Stative verbs 162, 170, 217

Subjunctive 212, 352, 378, 438

Subordination, subordinate clauses 9, 157, 177–9, 211, 212, 218, 442, 445, 454, 468, 482, 494

Superlative 301–4, 319, 365

Supposition 197, 214, 218

Surnames 37

Synthesis, synthetic forms: definition
    158, 160, 162, 164, 171, 175, 178,
    200, 217, 285, 303,

T

Target language (TL) or target text
    2–5, 9–10, 14–18, 21, 24–30, 188,
    238, 379, 427
Telicity 221, 237, 242 fn. 14, 245–9,
    255–6
Tense, definition of 8, 55, 81 fn. 14,
    108, 128, 132–3, 157–218, 249,
    258, 272, 327, 356, 378, 437–8,
    444–5, 486; see also Present tense,
    Preterite, Perfect tenses, Sequence
    of tense, Verbs, Tense-Mood-
    Aspect (TMA)
Terms of address 11–12
Topic 473–99; definition of 474; topic
    shifting 481 fn. 6; contrastive
    topic 60–1, 480–1; see also
    Information structure
Topicalisation 298, 482 fn. 8, 496
Topic-comment word order 478–81
Transitivity 90, 92 fn. 20, 189, 193–6,
    224, 228, 273, 286–8, 294–5, 351,
    353, 357, 486
Translation equivalent 23, 42, 134,
    135, 139, 141, 174, 175, 189, 206,
    210, 218, 223, 245, 270, 273, 294,
    487
Translation units (TU) 4–7
Transposition 15–19, 22, 28, 103–4,
    143, 196
Trwy/Drwy clauses 100–1

V

Verb + particle constructions: see
    Phrasal verbs

Verb-framed languages 222 fn. 4
Verb-nouns: translated as a noun 29,
    44–5; used in idioms with ar 69,
    84, 96, 98, 101, 103, 104, 112,
    113 fn. 30; direct objects of 127;
    in passive constructions 128–30;
    in equivalents of English
    participles 128 fn. 6; 140, 316–17;
    in periphrastic expressions
    158–9, 161, 167, 171, 175–8, 217,
    285; with cael to express
    opportunity 208; English-origin
    verb-nouns 271; in the causative
    278; as a complement of modal
    cael 279; as modifiers 297; wedi
    plus verb-noun 315; used as
    adjective 317–18; with rhyw 334;
    two verb-nouns used in a row
    423–7; in absolute clauses
    437–72
Verbs of motion: see Movement (or
    motion), verbs of
Verbs, Tense-Mood-Aspect (TMA):
    see Absolute tenses, Conditional
    mood, Future tense, Future-in-the-
    past, Imperfect tense (amherffaith/
    amhenodol), Past perfect tense
    (Pluperfect), Present perfect tense,
    Present tense, Preterite tense,
    Progressive aspect
Volition, verbs of 162, 202

W

Weight, linguistic expression of 152,
    154–6
Wrth clauses 101

Y

Ym- prefixation 255, 434–5

Index of Words and Expressions

Welsh

(listed according to the conventions of the Welsh alphabet)

A

A, ac (= and) 248, 299
A wnelo â 378
Â (preposition) 66, 72,
  326, 394
Absennol 146
Acen 147
Acw ('cw) 38
Achub 77
Achwyn 86
Adnabod 92, 170
Aflonyddu 86
Aflwydd 433
Agor 84, 92
Agos 324, 328
Angen 84, 113
Anghywir 359
Ail (> eil) 389
Alaru 86, 337
Allan 223, 361, 456
Am 66, 67, 73, 79, 101–2,
  173, 440
Amau 115, 357, 358
Amdani 47
  Y gwir amdani 48
Amharu 86
Amheuaeth 115
Amheus 429
Amhosib(l) 131
Anafu 121
Anarferol 306
Andros (o) 40
Anfon 369
Annwyd 370
Annwyl 430
Anodd 121, 131, 147

Ar 17, 18, 65, 67–8, 79–96,
  104, 105, 106, 117,
  134, 252, 343
Ar + verb-noun 84
Ar draws 224
Ar gyfer 122, 124
Ar hyd 134, 136, 254
Ar ôl 50, 68, 122, 440
Arfer 161, 176
Arglwydd 430
Arholiad 6
Arian 397, 400, 420
Arni 48
Aros 134, 252, 353
At 67, 69, 119, 324
  At ei gilydd 369
Atal 77
Ati 49, 361
Athrawes 422
Athro 422

B

Bai 367
Balch 74, 110
Bargen 420
Barnu 440
Berwedig 312
Beth (interrogative) 46
Biau (*see* Piau)
Blaen 122, 123
Blinder 361
Blino 87, 92
Bloeddio 89
Blydi 428
Boch 391

Bod 17, 134, 159, 160,
  166, 167, 170, 171,
  173, 175, 176, 177,
  178, 202, 205, 213,
  252, 378, 444, 452,
  488
  Yn bod 359
  Wrthi 52
Bodloni 87, 260
Bol 373, 391
Braidd 325
  O'r braidd 332
Brathu 121
Breuddwydio 262
Brith 117, 397
Bron (noun) 391
Bron (adverb) 122, 324,
  325, 326, 327, 452
  Bron â bod 326
Brown 397
Bwrw 49, 361
Byd 144
Bygro 428
Bygwth 328
Bynnag 56
  Beth bynnag 56
  [Pa] Bryd bynnag 57
  [Pa] le bynnag, ble/lle
    bynnag 57
  Pa fodd bynnag 58
  Pwy bynnag/pwy
    fynno 58
  Sut bynnag 58
Byth 55, 185, 321
Byw 146, 170
Bywyd 147

C

Cadw 77, 344
Cadw + collocations 406
Cael 51, 121, 194, 203, 208,
    270, 273–96, 343
Cael + collocations
    407–9
Cael (+ passive use)
    128–31, 197, 218
  Ar gael 84
  O hyd i 342
Calan 339
Calon 110, 261, 391
Cam 147, 360
Camdrin 92
Canmol 91
Cannoedd 154
Canu 82, 189
Cardod 370
Cas 109, 111
Casáu 110
Casglu 442
Casineb 147
Cau 84
Cawr 306
Cefn 135, 254, 392
Ceg 392
Celwydd 420
Cerdded 195, 226, 227,
    363, 384
Ceryddu 92
Cesail 392
Clir 146
Cludo 287
Clyw 146
Clywed 133, 162, 206, 363,
    364
Coblyn (o) 40, 433
Coch 286, 397, 400
Cochi 286, 401
Codi 4, 7, 19, 91, 103, 121,
    134, 252, 257, 259,
    261
Codi + collocations 409–13
Coes 392

Cof 84, 117
Cofio 116, 442
Coll
  [Ar] goll 84
Colli 347, 348
Condemnio 93
Corff 392
Craffu 87
Creadur 349
Credu 170, 442
Croen 392
Crwmach 135
Crwman 134, 135
Crwydro 289, 317
Crwydrol 317
Cuddio 77
Cwbl 309, 323
Cwestiwn 115
Cwmpas 122, 124
Cwpan 374
Cwrcwd 121, 134, 135
Cychwyn 52, 289
Cyfaddef 268
Cyfoethogi 434
Cyffroi 355
Cylch 122, 124
Cymharol 308
Cymorth 344
Cymryd 88
Cyn 174, 440, 442, 446
Cynhyrfu 93, 355
Cynhyrfus 146
Cynnau 266
Cynorthwyo 343
Cynyddu 259
Cysgod 361
Cysgu 241
Cystal 450
Cythraul 428, 433
Cythreulig 428, 433
Cywilydd 84, 106

Ch

Chwant 84

Chwibanu 87
Chwim 146
Chwith 347, 348, 350

D

Da (adjective) 109, 110,
    111, 112, 298, 306,
    356, 364
Dafydd 430
Dagrau 121
Dal 248, 344, 420
  Ati 49
Dam(i)o 428
(O) Dan 66, 69–70,
    98–100, 232
  Dan ei sang 321
Danto 87
Darfod 269
Darganfod 270, 341
Darllen 189
Datgan 443
Dau (> deu) 389
Deall 93
Dechrau 48
Dianc 77, 289
Diar 430
Diawl (o) 40, 428, 433
Diawledig 428
Diflasu 337
Diffodd 266
Dig 145
Digio 93
Digon 309, 310, 313
Digwydd 235
Dim 304
  Dim (byd) 331
Diod 121
Dioddef 271
Disgyblu 93
Disgyn 234
Dishgl 374
Diwrnod 361
Dod 50, 98, 223, 224, 226,
    227, 288, 419

(Dod) i ben 269
O hyd i 342
Draw 224
    Pen draw (see Pen)
Dringo 227, 234, 289
Dros (see Tros)
Drosodd 224
Drwg 112, 121, 350, 364, 365
Drwy (see Trwy)
    Drwyddi 361
Du 397
Duo 401
Duw 431
Dweud 133, 443
Dwfn 145
Dŵr 420
Dwylo 389, 420
Dwyn 196
Dwyn + collocations 413–14
Dwywaith 116
Dyblau 134, 136
Dychryn 103
Dychrynllyd 306
Dychwelyd 235
Dyfalu 357, 358
Dygymod 271
Dylai 210, 213
Dyled 84, 117
Dyletswydd 81, 117
Dyma 58, 59, 452, 453, 486
Dymuno 356
Dyn (= man) 306
Dyn (generic human referent) 62
Dyna 58, 59, 304, 452, 453, 486, 488
Dysgu 94

Dd
Ddaru 171, 172, 173, 483, 486

E
Edifarhau 104, 105
Edrych 82, 88, 102, 105, 126, 257, 341, 345, 351
    Edrych ymlaen at 170
Efallai 204
Efo 72
Effeithio 88
Egluro 94
Eiddo 61–2
Eil (see Ail)
Eira 361
Eisiau (see also Gweld) 84, 113, 202
Eistedd 3, 4, 99, 121, 134, 136, 250, 252
Eithriadol 306
Embaras 18, 338
Ennill 419, 420
Enw 88
Enwi 88
Er 71–2, 302, 440
    Er mwyn 122
Erbyn 180, 440
    (Yn) Erbyn 122
Erfyn 88
Erioed 55, 185
Ers 180
Esgob 428
Esgus 370
Esgyn 234
Esgyrn 430

F
Fawr (modifier) 90, 332
Fel 22, 33, 319, 345

Ff
Ffeindio 269, 341
Ffeuen 3
Ffitio 241
Ffordd 223

Ffunud 347
Ffwc 428
Ffwdan 147
Ffycin 428

G
Gadael 235, 434, 438, 442
Gafael 44
Galw 88
Gallu 162, 203, 205, 206, 279
Gan 66, 72, 79, 80, 96–8, 112, 114, 115, 116, 118, 190, 191, 278, 302, 458, 459
    Gan amlaf 302
Gerbron 122
Glas 397, 400
Glaw 361
Go 310
    Go dda 310
    Go iawn 310
    Go lew 310
Gofid 355
Golau 266, 401
Golchi 194, 420
Golwg 84, 148, 241, 257, 345, 361
Gorau (see also Rhoi) 319
Gorfod 209
Gorffen 269
Gorwedd 134, 136, 250
Gorymdeithio 384
Gostwng 235
Gresynu 170
Gwaed 393
Gwael 146, 350
Gwaeth 112, 121
Gwag 146
Gwahardd 77
Gwair 419
Gwaith 366
    Ar waith 84

Gwala 148
Gwallt 393, 401
Gweddol 310
Gweiddi 89
Gweld 94, 127, 162, 189,
      206, 341, 351, 367
   Gweld eisiau 347
Gwell 110, 111, 301, 451
Gwen 298
Gwenu 89
Gwerdd (*see* Gwyrdd)
Gwerth 131
[G]wir, yn wir 58, 308,
      323, 452
   Y gwir amdani 29
Gwirioneddol 308
Gwisgo 267
Gwiw 113, 210
Gwlanog 398
Gwneud 51, 167, 171, 172,
      223, 276, 277, 278,
      279, 486
Gwres 260, 419
Gwrthbrofi 360, 379
Gwrthod 202
Gwthio 241
Gwybod 170, 270, 442
Gẁyl 339
Gwylio 77
Gwyn (gwynion) 298, 398,
      402
Gwynt 146
Gwyrdd, gwerdd 3, 398
Gyda 72, 79, 80
Gyrru 227, 328

H
Hallt 317
Hanes 368
Hanner 136, 140, 322
Hawdd 131
Haws 452
Heb 112, 130, 456
Heddiw 339

Hefyd 60
Heibio 224, 361
Hel(a) 369, 370
Help 344
Helpu 94, 343
Hen 300, 323, 371
Heno 339
Hiraeth 17, 106, 361
Hoffi 109, 356
Holl 300
Hollol 308
Hunan 395
Hwyl 121, 146
   Cael hwyl (arni) 48
Hwyrach 204
Hwyrddydd 339
Hwyrnos 339
Hyd (at) 174
Hyn 40
   Ar hyn o bryd 40
   Yn hyn o beth 40
   Yr hyn 46
Hynny 40
Hynod 306, 308

I
I [preposition] 66, 79–96,
         112, 114, 119, 129,
         134, 177, 214, 278,
         232, 324, 327, 344,
         365, 442, 443, 444,
         458, 459
   I fyny 3, 223, 225, 234,
         245, 250, 252, 253,
         255, 256, 257, 260,
         261, 262, 263, 264,
         265, 269, 271
   I ffwrdd 223, 224, 225,
         235, 257, 266
   I gyd 32
   I lawr 223, 234, 235,
         250, 361
   I mewn 4, 223, 456
Iaith 147

Ias 363
Iawn 241
Iddi 49, 361
Iechyd 148
Iesu 428, 430, 431
Isel 145
Ill 153

J
Jest/Jyst 327

L
Lawrlwytho 14

Ll
Lladd 268, 419
Llais 145
Llaw 393
Llawn 310, 372
Lle 144
Lled (modifier) 308
Lleihau 94, 257
Lliw 398
Llond 372, 373, 374
Llonni 94
Llun 436
Llwyd 398
Llygad 257, 379, 393

M
Machlud 234
Magu 95, 260, 419
Mai (particle) 454, 483
Manteisio 89
Manylu 89
Medru 162, 203, 205, 206
Meddw 286
Meddwi 286
Meddwl 146, 170, 262,
         357, 358, 442
   Meddyliau 370

Meistroli 95
Melyn 399, 401
Mennu 89
Mentro (ar) 52
Methu 348
Miloedd 154
Min 393
Mo 494, 495
Modd 205
Mor (see also Pa) 302, 303,
    305, 318
Mwy 303
Mwyach 331
Mwyaf 303
Mymryn 90, 91
Myn 432
Mynd 98, 126, 134, 195,
    227, 234, 288
  Mynd o'i le 359
  Mynd yn 84, 259,
    285
Mynnu 162, 202

N
Nacáu 202
Nadolig 339
Neb 330, 331
Nefoedd 430, 431
Neidio 134, 227, 250,
    251
Nerth
  Nerth ei lais 321
  Nerth ei thraed 321
Nes 318, 319, 440
Neu 216
Newid 95
Newydd 421
Newydd (+ verb-noun)
    128-9
Nos 339, 361
Nosi 379
Noson 339
Noswaith 339
Noswyl 339

O
O (preposition) 66, 73-5,
    102-3, 130, 298,
    306, 324, 332
  O amgylch 122, 124,
    125, 126
  O flaen 122
  O gwmpas 122, 125,
    126, 224, 257
Ochr 137
Oddi 75-7
  Oddi amgylch 76
  Oddi ar 76, 225
  Oddi mewn 77
  Oddi wrth 75-7
Oer 286
Ofer 452
Ofn 18, 19, 84, 104-5
Ofnadwy 306
Ogla(u) 364
Oherwydd 440
Ôl 122, 123
Olaf 304
Oll 304
Ond 446
Oni bai 199
Os 198-200, 455, 456

P
Pa
  Pa mor 305
Palu 420
Pan 166
Paratoi 276
Parch 148
Parhau 235
Pe 198, 199
Pedwar 134, 137
Peidio 111, 353
Pen 123, 257, 393
  Pen draw 257
Peri 277, 279
Peth/Pethau 42, 46, 306,
    375

Piau, biau 376
Piws 399
Pleidlais 361
Plesio 121
Plyg 134, 137
Po 319, 320
Poen 355
Poeni 95
Posib(l) 204
Prif 300
Prin 332
Prysur 323
Pur 311
Pygddu 401

R
Reit 311

Rh
Rhaffu 420
Rhag 77
  Rhagddo 247
Rhagor 331
Rhagori 89
Rhaid 114, 209, 214,
    451
Rhan
  O ran 74-5, 347
Rhedeg 99, 227
Rhoi 267, 269, 271, 353
Rhoi + collocations
    414-17
  Rhoi'r gorau (iddi) 49,
    269, 353, 365
Rhudd 399
Rhwystro 353
Rhybuddio 77
Rhyfedd 107, 108, 450
Rhyfeddol 298, 306,
    321
Rhyfeddu 357
Rhyw (= some) 333-5
Rhywbeth 328, 329

Rhywle 329, 330
Rhywun 63, 328, 329

S
Sâl 350
Sawl 62
Sefyll 4, 6, 134, 137, 250, 353
Siâr 268
Sicr, yn sicr 58
Siôl 232
Siom 71, 148
Sirioli 95
Siŵr 58
Sobor 307
Stopio 353
Straeon 370
Sul 361
Swyn 361
Syched 84
Sydyn 452
Syllu 90
Sylwi 90
Symud 95
Syn 107
Syndod 71, 108
Synnu 107, 357
Sythu 255

T
Ta beth 56
Tacluso 95
Tad 431
Taflu 269
Tafod 148, 393
Tair (> teir) 389
Talu 268
Tamaid 419
Tarfu 90
Taro 362, 379, 420
Tawel 145, 146
Tawelu 96
Te parti 15

Tebyg 208
Temtio 96
Tenau 286
Teneuo 286
Tipyn 90, 377
Tir 421
Tlawd 349, 350
Torri 50, 90, 96, 269, 421
Torri + collocations 417
Tra 311
Traed/Troed 134, 137, 148, 370, 384, 394
Trefn 81
Trefnu 194
Troed (see Traed)
Troi 4, 90, 121, 134, 227, 250, 254, 264, 266, 286
Tros, dros 70, 121, 257
Truan 439, 350
Trwy, drwy 66, 70-1, 100-1, 104, 105
Trwyn 394
Trydarfyd 436
Twymo 260
Tŷ 232
Tybed 356, 357, 358
Tybio 170, 356, 357, 358, 442
Tyfu 255, 256, 377
Tylwyth teg 26
Tymer 148
Tynnu 235, 267, 287
Tynnu + collocations 405, 418-19, 436
Tywydd 85-6

U
Uchel 145
Uffach 433
Uffern (o) 40, 428, 429
Uffernol 428, 429, 306
Ugain (> ugein) 389

Un 304
Unfan 4, 134, 138, 250, 254
Unman 331
Unrhyw 328, 329, 330, 331
Unwaith 84
Uwchben 122, 123

W
Wedi (= after) 440
Wnelo (see A wnelo â)
Wondro 359
Wrth 66, 77, 79, 101, 440
Wrthi 161, 177
Wyneb 138, 394

Y
Ychydig 322
Ynghylch 122
Ymadael 235, 434
Ymdeithio 384
Ymddangos 345, 351
Ymlaen 122, 125, 126, 224, 235, 247, 265, 361
(Yn) Ymyl 122
Yn (preposition) 78, 134
Yn ôl (+ according to, by) 368
Yn ôl (+ back) 125, 223, 233, 234, 235, 243, 244, 257, 456
Ypsetio 355
Yr un 330, 331
Ysgafnhau 96
Ysgrifennu 119
Ysgwydd 257
Ystafell fwyta 317
Ystafell fyw 297
Ystafell wely 297
Ystwytho 96
Ystyried 357, 440

English

A

About 67, 102, 122, 224, 289
  About to + verb 84
Above 122, 123
Absent-minded 146
Accompany 379
Acquire 294
Across 224
Addict 379
Admonish 92
Advantage, take 89
Affect 88, 89
Afraid 84
After 440
Against 122
Agitated 146
Alas! 430
Alert 375
Allowed 282, 407
Almost 324–8
Alone 416
Along 224, 247
Although 71, 440, 465
Amazing(-ly) 298, 306
Amiss 359
And 214, 248, 463
Angry 145
Annoy 93
Anxious 212
Any 328–32
Anyone 328, 330
Anything 328
Anywhere 330
Appear 345, 351, 353, 367
Appointment 406
Approach 418
Argument 410
Armpit 392
Around (preposition) 67,
    76, 122, 125, 134,
    224, 238, 241, 251,
    257, 289

Arrangements 194
Arrive 290, 291, 407
As (= like preposition) 22,
    33, 101
As (= introducing clause)
    440, 465
  As a result of 68
As well, too, also 60
Ascend 234
Ashamed 106
Assault 413
Assist 343
Assuming (that) 361
At
    At once 77, 84
Attention 418
Authority 80, 81
Autonomy 395
Available 84
Aware 375
Away 223, 224, 232, 237,
    238, 241, 245, 247,
    257, 289, 291
Awful(-ly) 306

B

Back (part of body) 250,
    392
Back (adverb) 125, 233,
    234, 243, 244, 245,
    257, 288, 289, 292,
    456
Bad 337, 350, 364
Badly off 143
Bargain 420
Bastard 428
Be 277
  Be off 370
Bean 3
Beat it, to 50
Because 98, 179, 440, 466

Become 294
Bed 121, 406
Bedroom 297
Before 77, 122, 174, 207,
    440, 442, 446
Beg 370
Believe 170, 415, 442
Belly 391
Belong 376
Bent 134
Berate 92
Beside 122
Best 319, 408
Better 301, 319, 451
Better off 143
Between 155
Beyond 289
Bishop 428, 430
Bit (a bit) 377
Bite 121
Black 397, 401
Blame 367
Blessed 430
Blink 379
Blond 401
Blood 393
Bloody (swear word) 428
Blue 397, 400
Body 392
Boiled 312
Boiling 312
Bone 430
Bore 337
Boring 337
Both 153
Break 421
Breast 391
Breath 407
Bring up (= raise) 413
Brown 397
Bugbear 410
Bugger 428

Business 375
But 446, 465
Buy 411, 412
By 72, 77, 101, 180, 190,
    224
    By all accounts 368
    By the time (that ...) 440
    By way of 77
    By + oath 432

C
Call 88
Calm 146
Can (verb) 203, 204, 205,
    206, 207, 208, 211,
    281, 283, 294
Carry
    Carry on 361
Cast 361
Catch 418
Cause 411
Change 95
Charge 409
Chat 418
Cheek 391
Cheer 94, 95
    Cheer up 410
Chip in 268
Christmas 339
Clear 146
Climb 227, 234, 289
Closed 84
Coin(s) 400
Cold (adjective) 286
Cold (noun: illness) 370
Collect 369
Colour 398
Come 98, 223, 224, 226,
    227
    Come to 419
Comparatively 308
Complain 86
Completely 308, 309
Concerned (with) 378

Concerning (relating to)
    74, 122
Conclusion 442
Condemn 93
Confess 268
Considering 440
Contempt 361
Continue 234
Conversation 412
Crimson 399
Crouch 121, 134
Crows (Stone the) 433
Cry 423
Cup 374
Curb (verb) 416
Cut 96, 419

D
Damn 428
David 430
Day 361
Dear (me) 430
Debt 66, 84, 117–18
Declare 443
Decrease 94
Deep 145
Depart 434
Descend 234
Desire 84, 102, 411
Detail 89
Devil 428, 433
Difficult 121, 131
Direct 140
Discard 361
Discipline 93
Disease 79–80
Disgust 90
Dislike, disliking 66, 109,
    111–13
Disprove 360
Disturb 86, 90
Do
    To well in/at something
        408

To do away with 416
To do with 378
Doubled 134
Doubt 66, 115, 411
Down 134, 234, 235, 242,
    245, 250, 251, 253,
    254, 258, 260
Download 14
Draw 418
Dream 262
Drink (noun) 121, 294,
    411
Drive 227
Drunk 286
    Get drunk 286
Duty 117

E
Ear 415
Earn 419
Easier 452
Easy 131
Effect 277
Embarrass(-ed/-ing) 18,
    338, 411
Emotion 66, 79–80
Encourage 410
End (verb) 416
Enjoy 407
Enough 309, 310, 373, 408
Enter 234, 289
Envisage 367
Escape 77, 289, 291
Ethnicity 40–1
Even 465
Evening 339
Ever 55, 56
Evil 364
Exactly 139
Exam(ination) 6
Examine 87
Excel 89
Exceptional(-ly) 306
Excite 93

Excuse (noun) 370
Exit 234
Experience 343
Explain 94
Extremely 307, 311
Eye 257, 393

F
Face 394, 419
Fairly 310
Fall 242
Family relationships 36
Fast, as fast as your feet can
    carry you 321
Father 431
Fear 84, 104–5, 363, 411
    (For) fear that 212
Fed up 87, 373, 409
Feel 205, 363, 364
Find 51, 118, 269, 270,
    341–3
Fire 414
Fit (verb) 241
Flexible 96
Food 294
Foot 394
For 66, 69, 70, 71, 72, 73,
    122, 173, 180, 466
    For the sake of 122
Forbid 77
Forward 125, 224
Four, on all fours 134
Frequent (verb) 369
Frequent(-ly) 302
Frighten 103, 411
From 73, 75, 77
Fucking 428
Full 372, 373
Fun 408

G
Gather 369, 442
Gaze 257

Get 273–96
    Get a hold of 408
    Get bigger 259
    Get on 419
    Get on with 408
    Get rid of 408
    Get smaller 259
    Get through 361
    Get up 134
Giant 306
Giddy 411
Give 415
    Give up 269, 353, 365
Given (that) 102
Glad 110
Glance 361, 379
Go 98, 227, 234, 423–5
    Go around 369
    Have a go 415
Goblin 433
God (knows) 431
Good 298, 306, 310
Good gracious! 433
Goodness (me)! 430
Gossip 370
Granted (that) 361
Grass 419
Greatly 332
Green 3, 398, 400
Grey 398, 400
Ground 421
Grow 255, 256, 286, 377

H
Hair 393, 401
Half 140, 322
Hand 393
Hands 389, 420
Happen 234
Hardly 332
Harm 87
Hate 110
Have 276, 277
Head 123, 393

Headfirst 139
Health 79–80
Hear 133, 205, 364
Heart 391, 414
Heat (up) 261, 419
Heaven(s) 430, 431
Hell 428, 433
Hellish 306
Help 94, 343
Hide 77
High 145
History 368
Hit 361, 362
Hold 414, 420
Homesick 106
House 232
How 305
How ...! 488
    How long 305
However 58
Hundreds 154
Hunt 369

I
If 115, 165, 198–200, 455,
    466
Illness 350
Imagine 442
Immediately 84, 139
Implore 88
Impossible 131
In 4, 78, 232, 234, 241,
    288, 289, 456
    In case 77
    'In for it', to be 51
    In front of 122
    In order (to/for/that)
        207, 406
Incorrect 359
Increase 259
Influence 277
Inform 379
Injure 121
Insist 212

Instantly 139
Intention 102
Interfere 87
Interrupt 90
Into 295, 375
Issue (noun) 412

J
Jesus 428, 430, 431
Judging (from/by) 440
Jump 134, 227, 250
Just (adverb) 327
    Just as ... 310

K
Keep 77, 344, 361, 406
    Keep doing something
    248
Kill 268
Knock 361
    Knock off 268
Knot (noun) 415
Know 92, 170, 442

L
Lack 84
Last (adjective) 304
Learn 94
Leave, to 50, 234, 434, 438,
    442
    Leave alone 416
Leg (see also Pull) 392
Lend 379
Lessen 94
Lest 212
Lie (down/up) 134, 250, 254
Lie (= untruth) 420
Light 401
Lighten 96
Like (preposition) 22, 33
Like (verb), liking 66, 109–11
Lip 393

Little (a little) 322, 377
Live (verb) 170
Living (noun) 419
Look 77, 82, 84, 87, 88,
    102, 257, 345, 351,
    361, 379
    Look forward to 170
Lost 84
Low 145

M
Make 223, 277
Man 306
March (verb) 384
Master (verb) 95
Maybe 197
Meal 276, 294
Measure 374
Memorised 84
Memory 117
Mentally ill 146
Mind 146
Misfortune 433
Miss (verb) 347, 361
Missing 84
Mistreat 92
Misuse 92
Money 420
Mood 81–3
Mostly 302
Mouth 392
Move 95
Must 209, 210, 214
My word! 433

N
Near 77
Nearly 155, 324, 328
Necessary 197
Necessity 114
Need 66, 80, 84, 113–14,
    170, 451
Never 55

New Year 339
Next (to) 122
Night 339, 361
Nobody 330
Noise 406
No-one 330
Nose 394
Nothing 46
Notice 90

O
Obligation 451
Obtain 274, 294
Odd 212
Of 73
Off 76, 224, 225, 245, 265,
    267, 288, 289
Offend 379
Old 371
On 5, 67, 79, 125, 234,
    247, 265, 267, 268,
    290, 292
One (generic human
    referent) 62
Open 84, 92
Or 216
Out 232, 234, 237, 245,
    287, 288, 290, 291,
    361, 456
Outsmart 408
Over 70, 121, 122, 134,
    155, 224, 245
Owe 84
Own 170, 376
    Own up 268

P
Packed (full) 321
Past (adverb) 224
Pay 268
Perhaps 197, 204
Persuade 414
Picture 405, 436

Place 144
Plan 194
Please (verb) 121
Poor 349, 350
Possess 170
Possible(-ly) 204, 208
Praise 91
Precisely 139
Pretend 88
Prevent 77, 353
Probable(-ly) 209
Profit 413
Property, possession 61
Pull 235, 287
    Pull leg 418
Purple 399
Push 241
Put 267, 416, 417
    Put up with 271

Q

Quench 417
Question 115
Quick-witted 146
Quiet 145, 376
Quieten 96
Quit 353, 365
Quite 310, 311, 377

R

Rain (verb) 361
Raise (an issue) 412
Raise (bring up) 261, 413
Rather 308, 310
Reach 154, 234, 290
Real 310
Really 307, 308
Rear (verb) 95
Receive 274, 294
Recognise 92
Recover 419
Red 286, 397
Redden 286

Refuse 202
Refute 360
Regards/Regarding 74
Regret 104, 105, 170, 364
Rein (in) 416
Remarkable(-ly) 306, 308
Remember 66, 116–17,
    206, 442
Remind 413
Return 234, 289
Revenge 292
Right (= correct) 417
Right (= modifier) 311
Rise 4, 121, 259
Rob 196
Room 297, 317
    Dining room 317
    Living room 297
Run 99, 227
    Run around 370
    Run out of 269

S

Sack (to be sacked) 407
Said, it is (that) 368
Salted 317
Salty 317
Satisfied 87
Satisfy 260
Save 77
Say 133, 443
Scarcely 332
Scatterbrained 146
Scrutinise 87
Seated 134
See 94, 205, 367
Seem 345, 351, 353, 367
Self 395
Send 369
Set (verb) 234, 414, 417
    Set fire 414
    Set out (for) 289
Shadow 361
Shame 77, 84, 106, 411

Share (noun) 268
Shawl 232
Shout 89
Shut 84
Sick 411
Sign 417
Silence 376
Silver 397, 400
Since 71, 76, 98, 179, 180,
    181, 466
Sing 410, 425
Sit 3, 6, 99, 121, 134, 250,
    409, 416
Size 39
Skin 392
Slam 414
Sleep 241, 425
Smell 83, 364
Smile 89
Snow (verb) 361
So that 207
Sober 307
Someone 328, 330, 333
Something 46, 328
Somewhere 330
Sorrow 105
Sorry 104
Sort of 334
Speckled 397
Spell 361
Spend 361
Spirit 121
Spitting image 347
Stand 4, 134, 250
Stare 90
Start (off) 415
Stay 134
Step 414
Stomach 373
Stop 353, 361
Story 368
Straight 140
Straighten 255
Strike (verb) 361, 420
Sufficiently 309

Suicide 395
Suppose 209
Surprise 107–9, 450
Surprising 212
Suspect (noun) 379
Suspicion 115

T
Take 267
    Take after someone 418
    Take off 418
Talk 426
Taste 83
Tea Party 15
Teacher 422
Tears (plural of 'tear') 121
Tell 420
Tempt 96
Terrible(-ly) 306
Terrify 93
Test 417
There is/are 195, 304
Thin 286
    Grow thinner 286
Thing 306, 375
Think 170, 262, 367, 370, 442
Thirst 84, 417
Thirsty 411
Though 465
Thousands 154
Thrash 415
Through 70, 245, 287
Throw 361
Ticket 412
Tidy (verb) 95
Tie (verb) 415
Time 85
Tiptoe 384
Tire 87, 92
Tiredness 361
Title 414
To 66, 69, 73
Today 339
Tongue 393

Tonight 339
Top of one's voice 321
Totally 309
Touch and go 407
Transport (verb) 287
Travel 289
Trouble 293, 365, 408, 409
True 452
Truly 308
Try 415
Turn 4, 121, 134, 154, 227,
        250, 254, 264, 286,
        417
Tweet 436
Twitter 436

U
Under 155
Understand 93, 206
Until 174, 207, 440
Unusual(-ly) 306
Up 3, 76, 134, 224, 225, 226,
        234, 237, 239, 240,
        242, 245, 246, 249,
        250, 251, 253, 255,
        256, 257, 258, 259,
        260, 261, 262, 263, 291
Upset 355
Utter 417

V
Vague 117
[In] Vain 452
Very 304, 308, 310, 311, 402
Voice 145
Vote 361

W
Wait 241
Walk 226, 227, 426
Wander 289, 317
Wandering 317
Want 84, 102, 113, 170

Warm (up) 260, 419
Warn 77
Wash 194, 420
Washing 194
Watch (verb) 77, 406
Water 420
Wave (verb) 411
Way 223
Wealth 434
Wear 267, 406
Weather 85–96
Weekend 361
Well off 143, 144
What a ...! 488
Whatever 56
When 101, 166, 449, 465
Whenever 57
Wherever 57
Whether 115
While 101, 449, 465
Whistle 87
White 398, 402
Whoever 58
Willing 202
Wish 356
With 66
Within 77
Without 130
Woe (betide) 430
Wonder 115, 356, 357,
        358, 359
Woolly 398
Word 417
Work 366
Working 84
World 144, 436
Worry 95
Worse 121
Worse off 143
Worth 131
Write 119
Wrong 359, 360

Y
Yellow 399